Core JAVA

An Integrated Approach

Covers Concepts, Programs
and Interview Questions

Authored by:

Dr. R. Nageswara Rao

&

Kogent Learning Solutions Inc.

Published by:

ISBN: 978-81-7722-836-6

Edition: 2014

Printed at: Durga Printographics, Delhi

Dedicated affectionately to

Sri Posani Suresh Kumar who is the best teacher the world has and to my students whose admiration inspires me to teach forever.

Acknowledgements

I wish to acknowledge my deep gratitude to Arti Pandey, Publisher, Dreamtech Press and Rudraksh Batra for his cooperation. I am also thankful to his staff that provided staunch support throughout this project and helped me to complete this book successfully.

My sincere appreciation also goes to Mansoor Baig and Srinivas Goud who actually initiated this project.

My apologies are to my wife and my two kids whom I neglected for months during the course of developing the content of this book. My wife, Vijaya, has proved that she is more than half of my mind and soul.

Some errors may have inadvertently crept in this book despite my best efforts to keep them out. Readers are therefore encouraged to point out these errors so that they are not repeated in the next edition. Suggestions to improve the book are also welcome.

About the Author

Dr. R Nageswara Rao has been associated with teaching Computer Science since 1993. He has worked at various colleges as HOD (Dept. of Computers) and as a freelance developer for some time for a couple of organizations. He has been teaching Java since 2000, and is currently associated with DurgaSoft Solutions, Hyderabad, a prestigious training division, imparting specialized training in Java.

Dr. R Nageswara Rao is teaching and interacting with more than 1000 new students every month, including software developers and foreign students.

Since 1998, Dr. Rao is associated with 'Computer Vignanam', a widely circulated monthly magazine, published in Telugu. He has been on the editorial board of this magazine for the past six years. He published several articles, including articles on Virtual Reality, Mobile communications, Blue tooth technology and Global positioning systems. He also published hundreds of articles on C/C++ and Java.

Content at a Glance

Core Java – An Integrated Approach

Table of Contents

Preface

The importance of Java language cannot be denied as it has already started ruling over the entire Software Industry. Companies have started recruiting programmers but there is still a dearth of Java programmers. I set teaching as my profession in 1993, and have ever since engaged my time in teaching and training thousands of students in Computer Sciences. Since 2000, I started teaching Java to students. When my students asked me to prescribe a book for their reference, I naturally thought of writing an ideal book for them that would fulfill the following goals:

❑ The book should be written in such a way that learners without any background in programming should be able to follow it and understand it entirely. This meant that the book should discuss the *concepts* of Java in a simple and straightforward language with a clear-cut explanation, without beating about the bush.

❑ Once the students understood the book, they should be able to at least write simple programs on their own, as this is the first requirement to become a Java programmer. It meant the book should provide ample solved *programs,* which could be used by the students not only in their examinations but also to remove the fear of programming from their minds.

❑ After reading the book, the students should have the confidence to apply for a software development company, face the interview board and come out successful. It meant the book should also cover sample *interview questions,* which were asked in various interviews. This would help the students to prepare well for their future careers.

I searched the market for such a book and to my dismay, I could not found a single one. I found some books that provided the concepts, but were lacking in programming examples. A few books gave programs without any insight into the concepts. None of them was useful to learn Java. To address this need, I thought of writing a book on Java with a three-stage formula: concepts + programs + interview questions. The result of my endeavour is the book you have in your hands now!

Since many students are opting for Computers or IT as the subject of their study, there is a growing need for them to learn Java from the ground up as well as learn good programming skills, and finally pursue a career in software development as a Java professional. This book will help them achieve these goals by following a three-stage process focusing on understanding Java, writing programs, and facing interviews.

Many Indian students may wish to use this book to solve the programs generally asked in their exams, since this book covers programs such as generating the Fibonacci number series, finding prime, generating primes, finding the product of matrices, creating subclasses such as rectangle, circle, triangle from a super class, creating interfaces, and so on. Such programs are commonly asked in the exams of Indian universities, at B.C.A, B.Sc, M.Sc, M.C.A and Engineering levels.

The coverage of interview questions along with the subject matter will help students do well in interviews. The questions presented in this book have been collected from various interviews conducted by top companies while recruiting the candidates.

What this book contains

This book has 32 chapters in all, arranged in increasing order of complexity. Hence, it is advised that readers start reading this book from the beginning unless they have some previous knowledge of the subject. The first ten chapters will help bring readers from the novice stage to a stage where they will have gained a proper understanding the fundamentals. These chapters cover the concepts of Java and JVM along with the basic elements of writing a Java program.

Chapter 11 is on OOPS, and covers the concepts on which the Java language was built. The subsequent chapters explain these concepts (Classes, Objects and Methods) with programs.

Inheritance and Polymorphism, two powerful features of an OOP language, are covered in chapters 15 to 17. Abstract classes and interfaces are discussed in chapters 18 and 19.

Once the software is developed, packaging the classes and providing an API document are necessary. These issues are discussed in Chapter 20.

Handling errors and exceptions that occur in a Java program are discussed in Chapter 21, while Chapter 22 discusses how to convert fundamental data into object form.

Chapters 23 to 32 are devoted to advanced concepts. The process of arranging various objects in the memory comes under the collection framework, which has been described in Chapter 23; Chapter 24 tells you how to create files using streams; Chapter 25 shows you how to create client and server programs for a network; and, Chapter 26 covers Threads.

Chapters 27 to 30 discuss the GUI programs, which provide an enhanced user experience.

Chapter 31 is on Generics and Chapter 32, the last chapter of the book, deals with writing Java programs to communicate with any database.

Version used in this book

While this book is not a complete reference, it covers all core concepts in a methodical way. The focus is on the important concepts and not on version-specific issues. Hence, you can use this book to learn Java without worrying too much about the version.

ALL ABOUT NETWORKS

We shall begin this chapter with an understanding of networking concepts and proceed further to know why languages, like C/C++, are not opted for a network and why Java is a language suited for a network, especially Internet.

Interconnection of computers is called *network*. A network may contain two or more computers connected with or without a cable. For example, you can connect a computer in Delhi to one placed in Hyderabad with the help of a satellite and data can be sent or received via satellite in the form of electromagnetic waves. So, a network may or may not have a cable.

The primary purpose of a network is *resource sharing*, which means a computer can share its resources, like data, memory, software, hardware, CPU, etc. with other computers on the network. In the network, one computer may ask the other computer for some service. The computer, which requests for some service is called *client* and the other computer, which provides that service to the client is called *server*. A network can have several clients and servers and such a network architecture is also called a *client/server architecture*.

Figure 1.1 shows a client /server architecture. Here, you can see that the request goes from the client to the server and the server gives back the response.

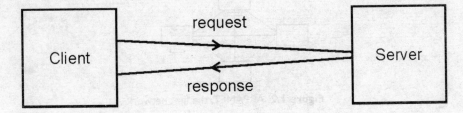

Client sends request for service.
Server sends response to client.

Figure 1.1 A network with two computers

What is the advantage of a network?

The main advantage of a network is that it makes resource sharing possible among the connected systems, thus helping in better utilization of resources.

Now, let us see how we can connect one computer to another. Following are the requirements for setting up a network of computers:

- **Hardware**: Computer systems, Network Interface Cards (NIC), cables, modems, hubs, satellites, etc.

- **Software**: Any software, which supports networking features, like Unix, Linux, Windows NT, etc. so that data can be sent or received.

- **Protocol**: *Protocol* could be defined as a standard procedure for regulating data transmission between computers. It specifies a way to identify the destination and source computers and establish a connection between them to receive or send data. For example, TCP/IP or UDP protocols help to divide data into small packets of several bytes, insert the packets into frames, and then send those frames to the destination computer over the network. Protocol is the underlying feature of the software used on the network.

What Comprises the Internet?

Internet could be defined as the network of all the computers existing on the earth. Not only individual computers but also a network of computers can be connected into the Internet. For example, a company may have 100 computers, all connected by the cable. Now, this local network can be directly connected to the Internet, so that it becomes a part of the Internet. So, Internet is also sometimes defined as a global network of all networks.

Going back to the history of Internet in 1969, DoD (Department of Defense), which is a US military defense department, got 4 computers which they connected with a cable. These 4 computers were connected by a cable and Unix was installed on them. This is the first network on the earth, which is also called ARPANET (Advanced Research Project Agency Network). Figure 1.2 shows how computers were connected in an ARPANET.

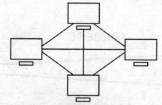

Figure 1.2 ARPANET, the first network

Later on, NSFNET (National Science Foundation (NSF)) encouraged individual users to get connected into this network. Any user can simply connect his computer into this network by using a cable. But the first problem faced by the users is purchasing and installing the cables. For example, imagine how much lengthy cable is needed if a person in India wants to connect his computer to this network. So they thought of an alternative. If already available cables are used, this problem will be resolved. By that time, telephone networks are widely available. Hence, telephone companies like AT&T, Hyundai, British Telecom, etc. came forward and offered their networks for use. Now, the problem of connecting personal computers with a network is solved. People who want to connect to the network can simply sit in their homes and connect their computers to the telephone jack. Thus, more and more computers have started becoming a part of this network and the network has grown rapidly. Today, this network has trillions of computers connected with each other. Thus, it became the biggest network on the earth. This network is called Internet.

A network of computers within an organization is called *Intranet*. An external network connecting an organization's network with that of another organization is called *Extranet*. In other words, we can take Extranet as a network outside an organization connecting it to other organizations' network. Similarly, an organization may use the services of a third party private network to communicate with outside networks. This third party private network is called *VAN* (Value Added Network). Now, let us try to understand the concept of Intranet and Extranet with the help of a figure. In Figure 1.3, you can notice that the network within an organization is called Intranet and that connecting the networks of two organizations is known as an Extranet.

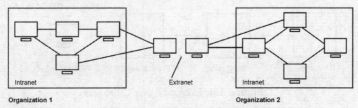

Figure 1.3 Intranet and Extranet

How does Internet Function?

Like any network, Internet also requires certain hardware, software, and protocols to perform its functions. For example, hardware like computer systems, cables, hubs, routers, satellites, etc. are needed to connect different computers with each other. The computer, which is connected to Internet Service Provider's (ISP) computer is called *client* and the ISP's computer is called *server*. Other than ISP servers, many other servers are maintained and used privately by some organizations. Currently, millions of servers are available on Internet. Some servers focus on a single area like maintaining employees' attendance in a company or scheduling the jobs for the employees of different branches. Such servers are called *Application servers*. Some servers provide services purely related to Internet, for example, maintaining the Websites and communicating with clients on Internet. Such servers are called *Web servers*.

A client machine and a server machine on Internet also need software. The software that is installed on an Internet client is called *Web browser*. Popular Web browsers are Internet Explorer, Netscape Navigator, Mozilla Firefox, Mosaic, etc. The software that is installed on an Internet server machine is called *Web server*. There are several Web servers, like IIS (Internet Information Server), Web logic, Web dynamics, Apache, JBoss, etc.

Apart from software, protocols are also used on Internet. The most widely used protocol on Internet is http, which stands for hypertext transfer protocol. http is responsible for displaying the html pages (or Web pages) on your client machine when you browse Internet. When you download a file from Internet to your client machine, you are using ftp (file transfer protocol). When you send mails, SMTP (Simple Mail Transfer Protocol) is used, and while receiving mails POP (Post Office Protocol) is used.

Important Interview Question

Which is the most widely used protocol on Internet?

Hypertext transfer protocol (http) is the most widely used protocol on Internet. The text on Internet is sent or received from one machine to another using this protocol only.

Software Development for Internet

Suppose we are writing a C program with the name x.c. This means x.c file contains source code. When we compile this program, we get x.obj file that contains machine language code, which is just equal to the source code in x.c file. For example, this x.obj file contains the first statement to include a header file, like <stdio.h>. When we run the program, C compiler goes to the C standard library (it is found generally in tc\lib) and searches for the header file <stdio.h> there. When the header file is found, C compiler copies the entire code (this code will be in machine language format) from the header file into the C program. So, if you write a C program of 10 lines and the <stdio.h> file contains 200 lines, then the total size of the file will be 210 lines. This file is also called x.exe file. This file is a full-fledged file that contains the entire program in machine language instructions. These instructions are understandable to the microprocessor. So it executes them and gives the results. Figure 1.4 shows how the source code in a C program is converted to machine language instructions before being executed by the compiler.

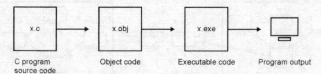

C program   Object code   Executable code   Program output
source code

Figure 1.4 Execution of a C program

There are several microprocessors developed by many companies, for example, Intel Corporation. Every microprocessor can recognize a group of instructions called the *Instruction set* of that microprocessor. So the instructions recognized by Pentium processor may not be understandable to the Celeron and similarly the instructions of Celeron may not be understandable by Spark processor.

If we generate x.exe file on a computer with Pentium processor, then that x.exe file contains machine language instructions understandable to Pentium only. If we try to execute this x.exe file on another computer with Spark processor, it may not be able to execute the instructions of x.exe file. The reason is Spark processor cannot understand the Pentium processor instructions, which are in x.exe.

Similarly, develop x.exe file using an operating system like DOS. Then copy this x.exe into other operating system like UNIX. Now, try to execute the x.exe file on UNIX. You will see that you cannot! The reason for this is that every operating system stores the data and instructions in different formats. For example, the instruction for addition of two values may be stored by DOS as: add a,b; whereas the same instruction may be stored by UNIX as: a add b. So, if we try to execute add a, b instruction in UNIX, it cannot understand it since its format is different from what it is expecting. This is the reason, why we cannot execute the same x.exe file in different operating systems.

There is a lot about instruction formats. The example that we have taken is only for illustration purpose.

What does it mean? If we created an .exe file in C or C++ on X processor and Y operating system, then we can execute it on X processor and Y operating system only. If the processor is changed or the operating system is changed, then it is not possible to execute the same code. This means C or C++ programs are executable only on the computer system that has X processor and Y operating system, where they have been developed. They cannot be executed on a different configuration. So they are called system dependent programs. Hence, C or C++ languages are also called system dependent or platform dependent languages.

Now, let us come back to Internet. As we know that Internet is a global network of all the computers existing on the earth and anyone can connect his/her computer to this network. So there will be different types of computers with different processors and different operating systems existing on Internet. It is completely heterogeneous. So, if a software is developed using C/C++ like languages, that software can be distributed on the Internet and people can download the .exe files, but they cannot run those files because of their system dependency. So C/C++ is not suitable for developing software for Internet. We need a language, which is completely system independent so that it can run on any system on Internet. And that is Java!

How Java is suitable for Internet? In Java, if we write a program, it is stored with an extension .java. Let us create a program, say x.java. It contains java source code statements. Now, the first step is to compile this x.java program. To do that, Java compiler first translates the x.java program into x.class file. What will be there in x.class file? Java people coined a group of instructions to express any operation. These instructions are called *byte code* instructions because the size of each instruction is 1 byte (=8 bits) exactly. There are a fixed number of byte code instructions, around 200. Any java program can be rewritten using these few byte code instructions. That file is called x.class. So, we can say that a x.class file contains source code equivalent to byte code.

But the microprocessor cannot understand byte code instructions, neither can it execute them. Then, these byte code instructions are meant for whom? They are for JVM (Java Virtual Machine). These byte code instructions are understandable by JVM, which is a program written to understand the byte code instructions and convert them into machine code. JVM's role is very crucial in a way that it has to first identify the operating system and processor used in the computer system and then convert the byte code instructions in an understandable format for that particular processor and operating system.

Remember, JVM is not a machine—it is a program! JVM program is freely available on Internet and can be downloaded for use in a few minutes. Figure 1.5 shows how a java source code passes through various stages before being executed by the compiler.

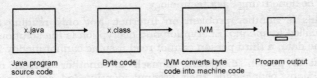

Figure 1.5 Execution of a Java program

So, if we write x.java program on a computer using Pentium processor and compile it, the compiler will produce x.class containing byte code instructions.

These byte code instructions are given to JVM. Now JVM understands that we are using Pentium processor in our system, so it converts byte code into machine code, which is understandable by the Pentium processor. So the processor executes it and displays the results. Similarly, JVM understands the operating system used in the computer and accordingly it forms the instructions, so there will not be any problem for the operating system to understand these instructions. Now, if we send the same x.class file to another computer/system with a different processor, say Spark processor, then the JVM in that system will convert these byte code instructions to machine code understandable by the Spark processor. So Spark processor can execute those instructions and display the results. In this way, we can execute the .class fire on any computer system with any processor and any operating system—provided JVM is available.

Remember byte code is system independent. It can be created on any computer using those predefined 200 instructions only. But JVM is system dependent, since it has to interact with the processor and operating system of the computer. This is the reason behind several flavors of JVM available on Internet. If we are using Windows, then we should download only Windows version of JVM and if we are using Linux, then we should use only Linux version of JVM.

So, if we write a .java program on X processor and Y operating system, then that program is executable on any other computer system with any processor and operating system. This means java programs are system independent or platform independent. That's why Java is called a system independent programming language.

On Internet, different computer systems with different processors and different operating systems are available, but still Java programs will run on any system and produce the same results on all the systems. If we develop a software using Java, the .class files can be downloaded from Internet and can be executed on any other computer system without any problem. Hence, Java is a suitable programming language for software development on Internet.

Important Interview Question

What is the difference between an executable file and a .class file?

.exe file contains machine language instructions for the microprocessor and is system dependent. .class file contains byte code instructions for the JVM and is system independent.

Since Internet is a public network, everyone can connect their computers into Internet and this leads to several security problems for data. Suppose, we are sending an email to a friend. Now, this mail will go through millions of servers on Internet before reaching the destination computer. In between, anybody can open the mail and see the data of the mail. Thus, we can say that data sent over Internet is susceptible to many kinds of security threats. Let us discuss some of the major security problems for data on Internet along with their solutions:

❑ **Eavesdropping**: This means reading others' data illegally on Internet. For example, opening others' emails and reading them comes into this category. The solution for this problem is: encryption and decryption. Converting the data into an unreadable format is called encryption and getting back the original data from the encrypted format is called decryption. When sending the email, we can encrypt the data and send it. If any third person opens it, he cannot read it because it is in an unreadable format. While encrypting the data, we use a password called key. Only the person who knows that key can decrypt it and read it. This key is known to our friend to whom the email is sent, so that only he can open it and read it. Encryption and decryption can be done using Java technology.

❑ **Tampering**: This is another problem on Internet. Not only reading others' data but also modifying it is called *tampering*. Encryption and decryption is the solution for this problem also. If we encrypt the data, a third person cannot read it so he cannot modify it also.

❑ **Impersonation:** A person disguising himself as another person on Internet is called *impersonation*. Many people hide their original identity and act as somebody else to make transactions. The solution for this problem is *digital signature*. Digital signature is a file that contains personal identification information in an encrypted format. Storing the personal information in digital signature and sending this information along with the email assures the receiver of the identity of the sender. Digital signature can be created using Java technology.

❑ **Virus**: Virus represents a program that can cause harm to the data, software, and hardware of a computer system. Most of the viruses spread with .exe, .doc, image (.gif, .jpg), audio, and video files (.mpg, .avi, .mp3). Virus cannot spread with a .txt file (example, the file created in Notepad). In Java, we create .class files, which are similar to .txt files and hence there is no chance of virus affecting these files. Even if somebody intentionally tries to incorporate the virus code into a .class file, JVM can verify its presence before running the program and, if found, can abort the .class file's execution.

From the above discussion, we can say that Java is the language, which can eliminate the above security problems that often occur on Internet. This is another reason why Java is sought after for developing software meant for Internet.

Important Interview Question

Why Java is suitable for Internet?

Java is suitable for Internet because of two main reasons. 1) It is system independent and hence its programs can run on any type of computer system available on Internet. 2) It eliminates a lot of security problems for data on Internet.

Conclusion

By now, you must have gathered information about networks, the Internet, and how Java is suitable for the Internet.

INTRODUCTION TO JAVA

Before starting to learn Java, let us plunge into its history and see how the language originated. In 1990, Sun Microsystems Inc. (US) has conceived a project to develop software for consumer electronic devices that could be controlled by a remote. This project was called *Stealth Project* but later its name was changed to *Green Project*.

In January of 1991, Bill Joy, James Gosling, Mike Sheradin, Patrick Naughton, and several others met in Aspen, Colorado to discuss this project. Mike Sheradin was to focus on business development; Patrick Naughton was to begin work on the graphics system; and James Gosling was to identify the proper programming language for the project. Gosling thought C and C++ could be used to develop the project. But the problem he faced with them is that they were system dependent languages and hence could not be used on various processors, which the electronic devices might use. So he started developing a new language, which was completely system independent. This language was initially called *Oak*. Since this name was registered by some other company, later it was changed to *Java*.

Why the name Java? James Gosling and his team members were consuming a lot of coffee while developing this language. They felt that they were able to develop a better language because of the good quality coffee they consumed. So the coffee had its own role in developing this language and good quality coffee was exported to the entire world from a place called '*Java island*'. Hence they fixed the name of the place for the language as *Java*. And the symbol for *Java* language is coffee cup and saucer.

By September of 1994, Naughton and Jonathan Payne started writing *WebRunner*—a Java-based Web browser, which was later renamed as *HotJava*. By October 1994, HotJava was stable and was demonstrated to Sun executives. HotJava was the first browser, having the capabilities of executing *applets*, which are programs designed to run dynamically on Internet. This time, Java's potential in the context of the World Wide Web was recognized.

Sun formally announced Java and HotJava at SunWorld conference in 1995. Soon after, Netscape Inc. announced that it would incorporate Java support in its browser Netscape Navigator. Later, Microsoft also announced that they would support Java in their Internet Explorer Web browser, further solidifying Java's role in the World Wide Web. On January 23rd 1996, JDK 1.0 version was released. Today more than 4 million developers use Java and more than 1.75 billion devices run Java. Thus, Java pervaded the world.

Features of Java

Apart from being a system independent language, there are other reasons too for the immense popularity of this language. Let us have a look at some of its features.

❑ **Simple:** Java is a simple programming language. Rather than saying that this is the feature of Java, we can say that this is the design aim of Java. When Java is developed, they wanted it to be simple because it has to work on electronic devices, where less memory is available. Now, the question is how Java is made simple? First of all, the difficult concepts of C and C++ have been omitted in Java. For example, the concept of *pointers*—which is very difficult for both learners and programmers—has been completely eliminated from Java. Next, JavaSoft (the team who developed Java is called with this name) people maintained the same syntax of C and C++ in Java, so that a programmer who knows C or C++ will find Java already familiar.

Important Interview Question

Why pointers are eliminated from Java?

1. *Pointers lead to confusion for a programmer.*
2. *Pointers may crash a program easily, for example, when we add two pointers, the program crashes immediately. The same thing could also happen when we forgot to free the memory allotted to a variable and reallot it to some other variable.*
3. *Pointers break security. Using pointers, harmful programs like Virus and other hacking programs can be developed.*

   Because of the above reasons, pointers have been eliminated from Java.

❑ **Object-oriented:** Java is an object-oriented programming language. This means Java programs use objects and classes. What is an object? An object is anything that really exists in the world and can be distinguished from others. Everything that we see physically will come into this definition, for example, every human being, a book, a tree, and so on.

Now, every object has properties and exhibits certain behavior. Let us try to illustrate this point by taking an example of a dog. It got properties like name, height, color, age, etc. These properties are represented by variables. Now, the object dog will have some actions like running, barking, eating, etc. These actions are represented by various methods (functions) in our programming. In programming, various tasks are done by methods only. So, we can conclude that objects contain variables and methods.

A group of objects exhibiting same behavior (properties + actions) will come under the same group called a *class*. A class represents a group name given to several objects. For example, take the dogs: Pinky, Nancy, Tom, and Subbu. All these four dogs exhibit same behavior and hence belong to the same group, called dog. So *dog* is the class name, which contains four objects. In other words, we could define a class as a model or a blueprint for creating the objects. We write the characteristics of the objects in the class: 'dog'. This means, a class can be used as a model in creation of objects. So, just like objects, a class also contains properties and actions, i.e. variables and methods (Figure 2.1).

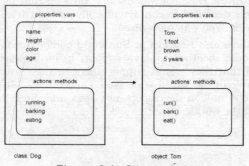

Figure 2.1 Class and object

We can use a class as a model for creating objects. To write a class, we can write all the characteristics of objects which should follow the class. These characteristics will guide us to create the objects. A class and its objects are almost the same with the difference that a class does not exist physically, while an object does. For example, if we say *dog*; it forms a picture into our mind with 4 legs, 2 ears, some length and height. This picture in our mind is *class*. If we tally this picture with the physical things around us, we can find Tom living in our house is satisfying these qualities. So Tom, which physically exists, is an object and not a class.

Let us take another example. Flower is a class but if we take Rose, Lily, Jasmine – they are all objects of *flower* class. The class *flower* does not exist physically but its objects, like Rose, Lily, Jasmine exist physically.

Important Interview Question

What is the difference between a function and a method?

A method is a function that is written in a class. We do not have functions in Java; instead we have methods. This means whenever a function is written in Java, it should be written inside the class only. But if we take C++, we can write the functions inside as well as outside the class. So in C++, they are called member functions and not methods.

Since Java is a purely object-oriented programming language, in order to write a program in Java, we need atleast a class or an object. This is the reason why in every Java program we write atleast one class. C++ is not a purely object-oriented language, since it is possible to write programs in C++ without using a class or an object.

Important Interview Question

Is Java a purely object oriented language or not?

The following reasons are put forward by many people to say Java is not a purely object oriented programming language.

1. *'Purely object oriented' means it should contain only classes and objects. It should not contain primitive datatypes like int, float, char etc, since they are neither classes nor objects.*

2. *In pure object oriented languages, we should access every thing by message passing (through objects). But, Java contains static variables and methods which can be accessed directly without using objects.*

3. *Java does not contain multiple inheritance. It means an important feature of object oriented design is lacking. So how can we say it is purely object oriented?*

No doubt Java is a purely object oriented programming language. The preceding points represent lack of indepth understanding of Java.

1. *Even if Java has primitive datatypes, these types are used inside a class and never outside of it. So, they are part of a class. See the API specification on the class: 'Class'. Java specification says that all the arrays and the primitive Java types (boolean, byte, char, short, int, long, float, and double), and the keyword void are also represented as objects of the class 'Class'.*

2. *Even static variables and static methods are written inside a class. When accessing them from outside, we should use classname. It means they are part and parcel of class definition and should not be considered as individual elements. For reducing memory utilization, only one copy of them will be created in memory and shared by all objects.*

3. *Any purely object oriented language should follow all the 5 features of Object oriented Programming System(OOPS). They are 1. Classes and objects, 2. Encapsulation, 3. Abstraction, 4. Inheritance and 5. Polymorphism. Remember Java contains all these features and hence it is purely object oriented language. Just because Java does not contain multiple inheritance, we should not say it is not purely object oriented language. Multiple inheritance is not the main feature of OOPS, it is only a sub feature under inheritance.*

❑ **Distributed:** Information is distributed on various computers on a network. Using Java, we can write programs, which capture information and distribute it to the clients. This is possible because Java can handle the protocols like TCP/IP and UDP.

❑ **Robust:** Robust means *strong*. Java programs are strong and they don't crash easily like a C or C++ program. There are two reasons for this. Firstly, Java has got excellent inbuilt exception handling features. An *exception* is an error that occurs at run time. If an exception occurs, the program terminates abruptly giving rise to problems like loss of data. Overcoming such problems is called *exception handling*. This means that even though an exception occurs in a Java program, no harm will happen.

Another reason, why Java is robust lies in its memory management features. Most of the C and C++ programs crash in the middle because of not allocating sufficient memory or forgetting the memory to be freed in a program. Such problems will not occur in Java because the user need not allocate or deallocate the memory in Java. Everything will be taken care of by JVM only. For example, JVM will allocate the necessary memory needed by a Java program.

Important Interview Question

Which part of JVM will allocate the memory for a Java program?

Class loader subsystem of JVM will allocate the necessary memory needed by the Java program.

Similarly, JVM is also capable of deallocating the memory when it is not used. Suppose a variable or an object is created in memory and is not used. Then after some time, it is automatically removed by garbage collector of JVM. *Garbage collector* is a form of memory management that checks the memory from time to time and marks the variables or objects not used by the program, automatically. After repeatedly identifying the same variable or object, garbage collector confirms that the variable or object is not used and hence can be deleted.

Important Interview Question

Which algorithm is used by garbage collector to remove the unused variables or objects from memory?

Garbage collector uses many algorithms but the most commonly used algorithm is mark and sweep.

Important Interview Question

How can you call the garbage collector?

Garbage collector is automatically invoked when the program is being run. It can be also called by calling gc() method of Runtime class or System class in Java.

❑ **Secure:** Security problems like eavesdropping, tampering, impersonation, and virus threats can be eliminated or minimized by using Java on Internet.

❑ **System independence:** Java's byte code is not machine dependent. It can be run on any machine with any processor and any operating system.

❑ **Portability:** If a program yields the same result on every machine, then that program is called *portable*. Java programs are portable. This is the result of Java's *System independence* nature.

❑ **Interpreted:** Java programs are compiled to generate the byte code. This byte code can be downloaded and interpreted by the interpreter in JVM. If we take any other language, only an interpreter or a compiler is used to execute the programs. But in Java, we use both compiler and interpreter for the execution.

❑ **High Performance:** The problem with interpreter inside the JVM is that it is slow. Because of this, Java programs used to run slow. To overcome this problem, along with the interpreter,

JavaSoft people have introduced JIT (Just In Time) compiler, which enhances the speed of execution. So now in JVM, both interpreter and JIT compiler work together to run the program.

❑ **Multithreaded:** A thread represents an individual process to execute a group of statements. JVM uses several threads to execute different blocks of code. Creating multiple threads is called 'multithreaded'.

❑ **Scalability:** Java platform can be implemented on a wide range of computers with varying levels of resources—from embedded devices to mainframe computers. This is possible because Java is compact and platform independent.

❑ **Dynamic:** Before the development of Java, only static text used to be displayed in the browser. But when James Gosling demonstrated an animated atomic molecule where the rays are moving and stretching, the viewers were dumbstruck. This animation was done using an *applet* program, which are the dynamically interacting programs on Internet.

The Java Virtual Machine

Java Virtual Machine (JVM) is the heart of entire Java program execution process. It is responsible for taking the `.class` file and converting each byte code instruction into the machine language instruction that can be executed by the microprocessor. Figure 2.2 shows the architecture of Java Virtual Machine.

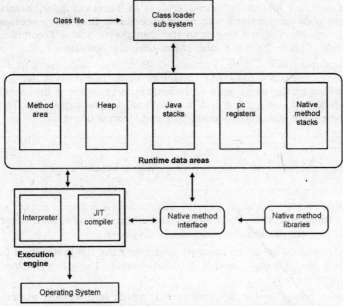

Figure 2.2 Components in JVM architecture

First of all, the `.java` program is converted into a `.class` file consisting of byte code instructions by the java compiler. Remember, this java compiler is outside the JVM. Now this `.class` file is given to the JVM. In JVM, there is a module (or program) called *class loader sub system*, which performs the following functions:

❑ First of all, it loads the `.class` file into memory.

❑ Then it verifies whether all byte code instructions are proper or not. If it finds any instruction suspicious, the execution is rejected immediately.

❏ If the byte instructions are proper, then it allocates necessary memory to execute the program.

This memory is divided into 5 parts, called *run time data areas,* which contain the data and results while running the program. These areas are as follows:

❏ **Method area:** Method area is the memory block, which stores the class code, code of the variables, and code of the methods in the Java program. (Method means functions written in a class)

❏ **Heap:** This is the area where objects are created. Whenever JVM loads a class, a method and a heap area are immediately created in it.

❏ **Java Stacks:** Method code is stored on Method area. But while running a method, it needs some more memory to store the data and results. This memory is allotted on Java stacks. So, *Java stacks* are memory areas where Java methods are executed. While executing methods, a separate frame will be created in the Java stack, where the method is executed. JVM uses a separate thread (or process) to execute each method.

❏ **PC (Program Counter) registers:** These are the registers (memory areas), which contain memory address of the instructions of the methods. If there are 3 methods, 3 PC registers will be used to track the instructions of the methods.

❏ **Native method stacks:** Java methods are executed on Java stacks. Similarly, native methods (for example C/C++ functions) are executed on Native method stacks. To execute the native methods, generally native method libraries (for example C/C++ header files) are required. These header files are located and connected to JVM by a program, called *Native method interface.*

Execution engine contains interpreter and JIT (Just In Time) compiler, which are responsible for converting the byte code instructions into machine code so that the processor will execute them. Most of the JVM implementations use both the interpreter and JIT compiler simultaneously to convert the byte code. This technique is also called *adaptive optimizer.*

Generally, any language (like C/C++, Fortran, COBOL, etc.) will use either an interpreter or a compiler to translate the source code into a machine code. But in JVM, we got interpreter and JIT compiler both working at the same time on byte code to translate it into machine code. Now, the main question is why both are needed and how both work simultaneously? To understand this, let us take some sample code. Assume these are byte code instructions:

```
print a;
print b;
Repeat the following 10 times by changing i values from 1 to 10:
print a;
```

When, the interpreter starts execution from 1st instruction, it converts print a; into machine code and gives it to the microprocessor. For this, say the interpreter has taken 2 nanoseconds time. The processor takes it, executes it, and the value of a is displayed.

Now, the interpreter comes back into memory and reads the 2nd instruction print b; To convert this into machine code, it takes another 2 nanoseconds. Then the instruction is given to the processor and it executes it.

Next, the interpreter comes to the 3rd instruction, which is a looping statement print a; This should be done 10 times and this is known to the interpreter. Hence, the first time it converts print a into machine code. It takes 2 nanoseconds for this. After giving this instruction to the processor, it comes back to memory and reads the print a instruction the 2nd time and converts it to machine code. This will take another 2 nanoseconds. This will be given to the processor and the interpreter comes back and reads print a again and converts it 3rd time taking another 2 nanoseconds. Like this, the interpreter will convert the print a instruction for 10 times, consuming a total of 10 x 2 = 20 nanoseconds. This procedure is not efficient in terms of time. That is the reason why JVM does not allocate this code to the interpreter. It allots this code to the JIT compiler.

Let us see how the JIT compiler will execute the looping instruction. First of all, the JIT compiler reads the `print a` instruction and converts that into machine code. For this, say, it is taking 2 nanoseconds. Then the JIT compiler allots a block of memory and pushes this machine code instruction into that memory. For this, say, it is taking another 2 nanoseconds. This means JIT compiler has taken a total of 4 nanoseconds. Now, the processor will fetch this instruction from memory and executes it 10 times. Just observe that the JIT compiler has taken only 4 nanoseconds for execution, whereas to execute the same loop the interpreter needs 20 nanoseconds. Thus, JIT compiler increases the speed of execution. Recognize that the first two instructions will not be allotted to JIT compiler by the JVM. The reason is clear. Here it takes 4 nanoseconds to convert each instruction, whereas the interpreter actually took only 2 nanoseconds.

After loading the `.class` code into memory, JVM first of all identifies which code is to be left to interpreter and which one to JIT compiler so that the performance is better. The blocks of code allocated for JIT compiler are also called *hotspots*. Thus, both the interpreter and JIT compiler will work simultaneously to translate the byte code into machine code.

Important Interview Question

What is JIT compiler?

JIT compiler is the part of JVM which increases the speed of execution of a Java program.

Differences between C++ and Java

By the way, C++ is also an object-oriented programming language, just like Java. But there are some important feature-wise differences, between C++ and Java. Let us have a glance at them in Table 2.1.

Table 2.1

C++	Java
C++ is not a purely object-oriented programming language, since it is possible to write C++ programs without using a class or an object.	Java is purely an object – oriented programming language, since it is not possible to write a Java program without using atleast one class.
Pointers are available in C++.	We cannot create and use pointers in Java.
Allotting memory and deallocating memory is the responsibility of the programmer	Allocation and deallocation of memory will be taken care of by JVM.
C++ has goto statement.	Java does not have goto statement.
Automatic casting is available in C++.	In some cases, implicit casting is available. But it is advisable that the programmer should use casting wherever required.
Multiple Inheritance feature is available in C++.	No Multiple Inheritance in Java, but there are means to achieve it.
Operator overloading is available in C++.	It is not available in Java.
#define, typedef and header files are available in C++.	#define, typedef and header are not available in Java, but there are means to achieve them.
There are 3 access specifiers in C++: private, public, and protected.	Java supports 4 access specifiers: private, public, protected, and default.

C++	Java
There are constructors and destructors in C++.	Only constructors are there in Java. No destructors are available in this language.

Parts of Java

Sun Microsystems Inc. has divided Java into 3 parts—Java SE, Java EE, and Java ME. Let us discuss them in brief here:

❑ **Java SE**: It is the Java Standard Edition that contains basic core Java classes. This edition is used to develop standard applets and applications.

❑ **Java EE**: It is the Java Enterprise Edition and it contains classes that are beyond Java SE. In fact, we need Java SE in order to use many of the classes in Java EE. Java EE mainly concentrates on providing business solutions on a network.

❑ **Java ME**: It stands for Java Micro Edition. Java ME is for developers who develop code for portable devices, such as a PDA or a cellular phone. Code on these devices needs to be small in size and should take less memory.

Reference

Oracle.com owned Sun Microsystems Inc. So, we can download Java software freely at:

http://www.oracle.com/technetwork/java/javase/downloads/index.html

Or at: https://www.java.com/en/download/

Conclusion

In this chapter, you have learned the features of the Java and got familiar with the JVM architecture along with part of Java. By now, you must have got a glimpse of Java. Along with all this, we have also compared the C++ with Java.

FIRST STEP TOWARDS JAVA PROGRAMMING

Whenever we want to write a program, we should first think about writing comments. What are comments? Comments are description about the features of a program. This means that whatever we write in a program should be described using comments. Why should we write comments? When we write comments, we can understand what the program is doing as well as it helps others to easily follow our code. This means *readability* and *understandability* of a program will be more. If a program is understandable, then only can it be usable in a software. If other members of the software development team cannot understand our program, then they may not be able to use it in the project and will reject it. So writing comments is compulsory in any program. Remember, it is a good programming habit.

There are three types of comments in Java—single line, multi line, and Java documentation. Let us discuss all of them here:

❑ **Single line comments:** These comments are for marking a single line as a comment. These comments start with double slash symbol // and after this, whatever is written till the end of the line is taken as a comment. For example,

```
//This is my comment of one line.
```

❑ **Multi line comments:** These comments are used for representing several lines as comments. These comments start with /* and end with */. In between /* and */, whatever is written is treated as a comment. For example,

```
/* This is a multi line comment. This is line one.
This is line two of the comment.
This is line three of the comment. */
```

❑ **Java documentation comments:** These comments start with /** and end with */. These comments are used to provide description for every feature in a Java program. This description proves helpful in the creation of a .html file called *API* (Application Programming Interface) document. Java documentation comments should be used before every feature in the program as shown here:

```
/** description about a class */
Class code

/** description about a method */
Method code
```

API Document

The API document generated from the .java program is similar to a help file where all the features are available with their descriptions. The user can refer to any feature in this file and get some knowledge regarding how he can use it in his program. To create an API document, we should use a special compiler called javadoc compiler. Figure 3.1 shows the process of creation of an API document.

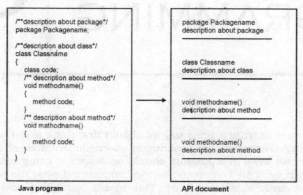

Figure 3.1 API document creation

Important Interview Question

What is an API document?

An API document is a .html file that contains description of all the features of a software, a product, or a technology. API document is helpful for the user to understand how to use the software or technology.

Starting a Java program

Before we start writing our first Java program, let us see how a Java program looks like. Please observe the following program code:

```java
/* This is my first Java program.
To display a message.
Author: DreamTech team
Version: v1.0
Project title: Dream project
Project code: 123
*/
import java.lang.System;
import java.lang.String;
//either the above two statements or below one is enough
//import java.lang.*;
class First
{
  public static void main(String args[ ])
  {
    System.out.print("Welcome to Java");
  }
}
```

So, we are starting our first Java program with multi line comments.

Importing classes

Suppose we are writing a C/C++ program, the first line of the program would generally be:

```
#include<stdio.h>
```

This means, a request is made to the C/C++ compiler to include the header file <stdio.h>. What is a header file? A *header file* is a file, which contains the code of functions that will be needed in a program. In other words, to be able to use any function in a program, we must first include the header file containing that function's code in our program. For example, <stdio.h> is the header file that contains functions, like printf(), scanf(), puts(), gets(), etc. So if we want to use any of these functions, we should include this header file in our C/C++ program.

What happens when we include the header file? After we include the header file, the C/C++ compiler goes to the standard library (generally it is available in tc/lib) and searches for the header file there. When it finds the header file, it copies the entire header file content into the program where the #include statement is written. Thus, if we write a program of 10 lines; then after copying code from the header file, the program size may become, say, 510 lines. From where do these additional 500 lines are coming? They have been copied physically into our program from the header file. Thus, our program size increases unnecessarily, wasting memory and processor time.

A similar but a more efficient mechanism, available in case of Java, is that of importing classes. First, we should decide which classes are needed in our program. Generally, programmers are interested in two things:

❑ Using the classes by creating objects in them.

❑ Using the methods (functions) of the classes.

In Java, methods are available in classes or interfaces. What is an interface? An *interface* is similar to a class that contains some methods. Of course, there is a lot of difference between an interface and a class, which we will discuss later. The main point to be kept in mind, at this stage, is that a class or an interface contains methods. A group of classes and interfaces are contained in a package. A *package* is a kind of directory that contains a group of related classes and interfaces and Java has several such packages in its library.

Java library
|
Packages
|
Classes and interfaces
|
Methods

Note

If a programmer wants to use a class, then that class should be imported into his program. If he wants to use a method, then that corresponding class or interface should be imported into his program.

In our first Java program, we are using two classes namely, System and String. These classes belong to a package called java.lang (here lang represents language). So these two classes must be imported into our program, as shown below:

```
import java.lang.System;
import java.lang.String;
```

Whenever we want to import several classes of the same package, we need not write several import statements, as shown above; instead, we can write a single statement as:

```
import java.lang.*;
```

Here, * means all the classes and interfaces of that package, i.e. java.lang, are imported (made available) into our program. In import statement, the package name that we have written acts like a reference to the JVM to search for the classes there. JVM will not copy any code from the classes or packages. On the other hand, when a class name or a method name is used, JVM goes to the Java library, executes the code there, comes back, and substitutes the result in that place of the program. Thus, the Java program size will not be increased.

Important Interview Question

What is the difference between #include and import statement?

#include directive makes the compiler go to the C/C++ standard library and copy the code from the header files into the program. As a result, the program size increases, thus wasting memory and processor's time.

import statement makes the JVM go to the Java standard library, execute the code there, and substitute the result into the program. Here, no code is copied and hence no waste of memory or processor's time. So, import is an efficient mechanism than #include.

After importing the classes into the program, the next step is to write a class. Since Java is purely an object-oriented programming language, we cannot write a Java program without having at least one class or object. So, it is mandatory that every Java program should have at least one class in it. How to write a class? We should use class keyword for this purpose and then write the class name.

```
class First {
        statements;
}
```

A class code starts with a { and ends with a }. We know that a class or an object contains variables and methods (functions). So we can create any number of variables and methods inside the class.

This is our first program, so we will create only one method, i.e. compulsory, in it—main() method.

Why should we write main() method? Because, if main() method is not written in a Java program, JVM will not execute it. main() is the starting point for JVM to start execution of a Java program.

```
public static void main(String args[])
```

Next to main() method's name, we have written String args[]. Before discussing the main() method, let us first see how a method works. A method, generally, performs two functions.

❑   It can accept some data from outside

❑   It can also return some result

Let us take sqrt() method. This method is used to calculate square root value of a given number. So, at the time of calling sqrt() method, we should pass a number (e.g. 16) for which we want to calculate square root. Then, it calculates square root value and returns the result (e.g. 4) to us. Similarly, main() method also accepts some data from us. For example, it accepts a group of strings, which is also called a *string type array*. This array is String args[], which is written along with the main() method as:

```
public static void main(String args[])
```

Here args[] is the array name and it is of String type. This means that it can store a group of strings. Remember, this array can also store a group of numbers but in the form of strings only. The values passed to main() method are called *arguments*. These arguments are stored into args[] array, so the name args[] is generally used for it.

A method can return some result. If we want the method to return the result in form of an integer, then we should write int before the method name. Similarly, to get the result in string form or as a single character, we can write string or char before it, respectively. If a method is not meant to return any value, then we should write void before that method's name. void means *no value*. main() method does not return any value, so void should be written before that method's name.

A method is executed only when it is called. But, how to call a method? Methods are called using 2 steps in Java.

1.   Create an object to the class to which the method belongs. The syntax of creating the object is:

```
Classname objectname  = new Classname();
```

2.   Then the method should be called using the objectname.methodname().

Since main() method exists in the class First; to call main() method, we should first of all create an object to First class, something like this:

```
First obj = new First();
```

Then call the main() method as:

```
obj.main();
```

So, if we write the statement:

```
First obj = new First()
```

inside the main() method, then JVM will execute this statement and create the object.

```
class First
{
      public static void main(String args[])
      {
             First obj = new First();  //object is created hereafter
JVM executes this.
      }
}
```

By looking at the code, we can understand that an object could be created only after calling the main() method. But for calling the main() method, first of all we require an object. Now, how is it possible to create an object before calling the main() method? So, we should call the main() method without creating an object. Such methods are called static methods and should be declared as static.

Static methods are the methods, which can be called and executed without creating the objects. Since we want to call main() method without using an object, we should declare main() method as static. Then, how is the main() method called and executed? The answer is by using the classname.methodname(). JVM calls main() method using its class name as First.main() at the time of running the program.

JVM is a program written by *JavaSoft* people (Java development team) and main() is the method written by us. Since, main() method should be available to the JVM, it should be declared as public. If we don't declare main() method as public, then it doesn't make itself available to JVM and JVM cannot execute it.

So, the main() method should always be written as shown here:

```
public static void main(String args[])
```

If at all we want to make any changes, we can interchange `public` and `static` and write it as follows:

```
static public void main(String args[])
```

Or, we can use a different name for the string type array and write it as:

```
static public void main(String x[])
```

Important Interview Question

What happens if `String args[]` *is not written in* `main()` *method?*

When `main()` *method is written without* `String args[]` *as:*

```
public static void main()
```

the code will compile but JVM cannot run the code because it cannot recognize the `main()` *method as the method from where it should start execution of the Java program. Remember JVM always looks for* `main()` *method with string type array as parameter.*

Till now, according to our discussion, our Java program looks like this:

```
/* This is my first Java program.
To display a message.
Author: DreamTech team
Version: v1.0
Project title: Dream project
Project code: 123
*/
import java.lang.*;
class First
{
     public static void main(String args[ ])
     {
              statements;   //these are executed by JVM.
     }
}
```

Our aim of writing this program is just to display a string "Welcome to Java". In Java, `print()` method is used to display something on the monitor. So, we can write it as:

```
print("Welcome to Java");
```

But this is not the correct way of calling a method in Java. A method should be called by using `objectname.methodname()`. So, to call `print()` method, we should create an object to the class to which `print()` method belongs. `print()` method belongs to `PrintStream` class. So, we should call `print()` method by creating an object to `PrintStream` class as:

```
PrintStream obj.print("Welcome to Java");
```

But as it is not possible to create the object to `PrintStream` class directly, an alternative is given to us, i.e. `System.out`. Here, *System* is the class name and *out* is a static variable in *System* class. *out* is called a *field* in *System* class. When we call this field, a `PrintStream` class object will be created internally. So, we can call the `print()` method as shown below:

```
System.out.print("Welcome to Java");
```

`System.out` gives the `PrintStream` class object. This object, by default, represents the standard output device, i.e. the monitor. So, the string "Welcome to Java" will be sent to the monitor.

Now, let us see the final version of our Java program:

Program 1: To display a message.

```
/* This is my first Java program.
To display a message.
Author: DreamTech team
Version: v1.0
Project title: Dream project
Project code: 123
*/
import java.lang.*;
class First
{
     public static void main(String args[ ])
     {
     System.out.print("Welcome to Java");
     }
}
```

Output:

```
C:\>javac First.java
C:\>java First
Welcome to Java
```

Save the above program in a text editor like *Notepad* with the name `First.java`. Now, go to *System* prompt and compile it using *javac* compiler as:

```
javac First.java
```

The compiler generates a file called `First.class` that contains byte code instructions. This file is executed by calling the JVM as:

```
java First
```

Then, we can see the result.

We already discussed that JVM is a program. Which program is it? By observing the command `java First`, we can say that JVM is nothing but `java.exe` program. In fact, JVM is written in C language.

Let us write another Java program to find the sum of two numbers. We start this program with a single line comment like this:

```
//To find sum of two numbers
```

Then we should import whatever classes and interfaces we want to use in our program. In this program, we will use two classes: `System` and `String`. These classes are available in the package `java.lang`. So, we should import these classes as:

```
import java.lang.*;
```

Here, * represents all the classes of `java.lang` package. This import statement acts like a reference for the JVM to search for classes when a particular class is used in the program. After writing the import statement, we should write a class, since it is compulsory to create at least one class in every Java program. Let us write the class as shown below:

```
class Sum
{
        statements;
}
```

We know that a class contains variables and methods. Even if we do not create variables or methods, we should write at least one method, i.e. main(). The purpose of writing the main() method is to make JVM execute the statements within it. Let us take an example:

```
class Sum
{
        public static void main(String args[])

        {
                statements;
        }
}
```

Here, main() method is declared as public, static, and void. public because it should be made available to JVM, which is another program; static because it should be called without using any object; and void because it does not return any value. Also, after the method name, we write String args[] which is an array to store the values passed to main() method. These values passed to main() are called *arguments*. These values are stored in args[] array in the form of strings.

Inside the main() method, let us write the code to find the sum of two numbers. Observe the full program now:

Program 2: To find the sum of two numbers.

```
//To find sum of two numbers
import java.lang.*;

class Sum
{
public static void main(String args[])
{
//variables
        int x,y;

        //store values into variables
        x = 10;
        y = 25;

        //calculate sum and store result into z
        int z = x+y;

        //display result
        System.out.print(z);
}
}
```

Output:

```
C:\> javac Sum.java
C:\> java Sum
35
```

In the above program, inside `main()` method, we write the first statement as:

```
int x,y;
```

Here `x,y` are called variables. A variable represents memory location to store data or values. We want to store integer numbers into `x,y`. So before these variables, we write `int`. This `int` represents the type of data to be stored into the variables. It is also called a *data type*. By writing `int x,y`, we are announcing the java compiler that we are going to store integer type data into `x,y` variables. Remember, declaring the data type is always required before using any variable. All data types available in Java are discussed in Chapter 4.

After declaring the `x,y` variables as `int` data type, we have stored integer numbers into `x,y` as:

```
x = 10;
y = 25;
```

`=` represents storing the right hand side value into the left hand side variable. Thus, 10 is stored into `x` and 25 is stored into `y`. So `=` is a symbol that represents assignment (or storage) operation. Such symbols are also called *operators*. All the operators available in Java will be discussed in Chapter 5. The next step is to find the sum of these values. For this purpose, we write:

```
int z = x+y;
```

At the right hand side we got `x+y`, which performs the sum. Here `+` is called *addition operator*. The result of this sum is stored into `z`, which we declared as another `int` type variable. Now, we should display the result using `print()` method as:

```
System.out.print(z);
```

Here, `System` is a class in `java.lang` package and `out` is a field in this class. When we refer to `System.out`, it creates `PrintStream` object, which, by default, represents the standard output device, i.e. monitor. So, by writing `System.out.print(z)`, we are passing z value to `print()` method, which displays that value on the monitor. So in the output, we can see the result as 35.

Formatting the Output

In Program 2, we have used the following statement to display the result:

```
System.out.print(z);
```

This will display the result 35 on the monitor. But, this is not the proper way to display the results to the user. When the user sees 35, he would be baffled as what is this number 35?. So, it is the duty of the programmer to prompt the user with a proper message, something like this:

```
Sum of two numbers= 35
```

This is more clear and avoids any confusion for the user. How can we display the output in the above format? For this purpose, we should add a string "Sum of two numbers=" before the z value in the `print()` method:

```
System.out.print("Sum of two numbers= "+ z);
```

Here, we are using + to join the string "Sum of two numbers=" and the numeric variable z. The reason is that the print() method cannot display more than one value. So if two values, like a string and a numeric value need to be displayed using a single print() method, we should combine them using a + operator.

Now, the output will look like this:

```
Sum of two numbers= 35
```

We know that value of x is 10 and y is 25. Suppose, we use print() method to display directly x+y value in the place of z, we can write:

```
System.out.print("Sum of two numbers="+ x+y);
```

which displays:

```
Sum of two numbers= 1025
```

See the output is wrong. What is the reason? In the print() method's braces, from left to right, we got a string "Sum of two numbers=" and two numeric variables x and y as shown below:

```
"Sum of two numbers= "+ x+y
```

Since left one is a string, the next value, i.e. of x is also converted into a string; thus the value of x, i.e. 10 will be treated as separate characters as 1 and 0 and are joined to the string. Thus, we get the output in the string form:

```
Sum of two numbers= 10
```

The next variable value is 25. Since till now, at left we got a string, so this y value is also converted into a string. Thus 2 and 5 are taken as separate characters and joined to the string, thus we get the result as:

```
Sum of two number= 1025
```

So, how to get the correct result? By using another pair of simple braces inside the print() method, we can get the correct result.

```
System.out.print("Sum of two numbers= "+ (x+y));
```

Here, the execution will start from the inner braces. At left, we got x, which represents a number and at right we got y, which is also a number. Since both are numbers, addition will be done by the + operator, thus giving a result 35. Then the result will be displayed like this:

```
Sum of two numbers= 35
```

To eliminate the above inner braces, we can use two print() methods like this:

```
System.out.print("Sum of two numbers= ");
System.out.print(x+y);
```

This will also give the correct result as:

```
Sum of two numbers= 35
```

Please observe that we have used two print() methods and still we got the result in only one line. What does it mean? First print() method is displaying the string: "Sum of two numbers" and keeping the cursor in the same line. Next print() method is also showing its output in the same line adjacent to the previous string. To conclude, print() method displays the result and then keeps the cursor in the same line.

Suppose, we want the result in two separate lines, then we can use println() method in the place of print() method as:

```
System.out.println("Sum of two numbers= ");
System.out.println(x+y);
```

This will display the result in two lines as:

```
Sum of two numbers= 35
```

println() is also a method belonging to PrintStream class. It throws the cursor to the next line after displaying the result.

Important Interview Question

What is the difference between print() and println() method?

Both methods are used to display the results on the monitor. print() method displays the result and then retains the cursor in the same line, next to the end of the result. println() displays the result and then throws the cursor to the next line.

Let us take the following statement:

```
System.out.print ("Sum of two numbers= "+ (x+y));
```

This will display the output as shown below:

```
Sum of two numbers= 35
```

Now, suppose we want to display the result in two lines using only one println() method, what is the way? For this purpose, we can use a code \n inside the string, as shown here:

```
System.out.println("Sum of two numbers=\n"+(x+y));
```

This will display the result like this:

```
Sum of two numbers=
35
```

This means \n is throwing the cursor into the next line at that place. This is called *backslash code* or *escape sequence*. Table 3.1 lists the noteworthy backslash codes with their meanings.

Table 3.1

Backslash code	Meaning
\n	Next line
\t	Horizontal tab space

Backslash code	Meaning
\r	Enter key
\b	Backspace
\f	Form feed
\\	Displays \
\"	Displays "
\'	Displays '

For example, observe the following statements:

```
System.out.println("Hello");
System.out.println("\\Hello\\");    //Observe \\
System.out.println("\"Hello\"");    //Observe \"
```

The above statements display the output as:

```
Hello
\Hello\
"Hello"
```

Program 3: To understand the effect of `print()` and `println()` methods and the backslash codes.

```
//Formatting the output
class Format
{
    public static void main(String args[])
    {
        int a=1,b=2,c=3,d=4;
        System.out.print(a+"\t"+b);
        System.out.println(b+"\n"+b);
        System.out.print(":"+c);
        System.out.println();   //this throws cursor to the next line
        System.out.println("Hello\\Hi\""+d);
    }
}
```

Output:

```
C:\> javac Format.java
C:\> java Format

1       22
2
:3
Hello\Hi"4
```

By now, you must be finding Java to be very friendly.

Conclusion

In this chapter, we have learned about providing comments in the java program. We have also come across with API documents. While moving towards the end of the chapter we have come across with the creating a program in Java.

NAMING CONVENTIONS AND DATA TYPES

In the previous chapter, we understood Java by writing a couple of programs. In those programs, you might have observed that sometimes we have used small letters and sometimes capital letters. For example, we have written the class System starting with a capital letter. You cannot write this class name as system or SYSTEM. Since Java is a case sensitive programming language, it recognizes capital and small letters as different. So the programmer should take care of upper and lower case while writing a program in Java. But how to know where to use which case—upper or lower? For this purpose, certain conventions (rules) are followed by JavaSoft people while naming the variables, classes, methods, etc. These naming conventions should be followed by every programmer in his programs for maintaining uniformity and also for clarity of distinction between different elements of a program. These rules also reduce the possibility of any spelling mistakes while writing the names of variables, classes, etc. in the programs. For example, a Java program will not compile, if main() method is written as:

```
Public static void Main(String args[])
```

The problem in the preceding statement is using capital P for public and capital M for main(). Such errors can be eliminated if we follow the naming conventions.

Naming Conventions in Java

Naming conventions specify the rules to be followed by a Java programmer while writing the names of packages, classes, methods, etc. Now, let us see some of the major naming conventions to be followed in Java.

❏ A *package* represents a sub directory that contains a group of classes and interfaces. Names of packages in Java are written in small letters as:

```
java.awt
java.io
javax.swing
```

❏ A *class* is a model for creating objects. A class specifies the properties and actions of objects. An interface is also similar to a class. Each word of class names and interface names start with a capital letter as:

```
String
DataInputStream
ActionListener
```

❏ A class and an interface contain methods and variables. The first word of a method name is in small letters; then from second word onwards, each new word starts with a capital letter as shown here:

```
println()
readLine()
getNumberInstance()
```

❏ The naming convention for variables names is same as that for methods as given here:

```
age
empName
employee_Net_Sal
```

> **Note**
>
> *Now, the question that is commonly asked is that if same rule is applied for both variables and methods, how can we distinguish between them? The answer is that since a method's name ends with a pair of simple braces (), it can be distinguished easily from a variable whose name will not have any braces.*

❏ *Constants* represent fixed values that cannot be altered. For example, PI is a constant whose value is 22/7 or 3.14159, which is fixed. Such constants should be written by using all capital letters as shown here:

```
PI
MAX_VALUE
Font.BOLD
```

Here, BOLD is a constant in Font class. This is the way most of the inbuilt constants in Java are referenced.

❏ All keywords should be written by using all small letters as follows:

```
public
void
static
```

Data Types in Java

We know we need variables to store the data. Internally, a variable represents a memory location which holds data. When we want to use a variable in a program, we should first declare it as:

```
int x;
```

Here, we are declaring that x is a variable, which can store int (integer) type data. This means int is representing the nature of data to be stored into x. int is also called a data type. For example, x can store an integer number like 125 as:

```
x = 125;
```

Here, x is a variable and = represents that the value 125 is stored into x. This value 125 stored into x is also called literal. There are various data types and literals defined in Java, which we will be discussing in this chapter.

Integer Data Types

These data types represent integer numbers, i.e. numbers without any fractional parts or decimal points. For example, 125, -225678, 0, 1022, etc. come under this category. Integer data types are again sub divided into byte, short, int, and long types. Table 4.1 lists the data types.

Table 4.1

Data type	Memory size	Minimum and Maximum values
byte	1 byte	-128 to +127
short	2 bytes	-32768 to +32767
int	4 bytes	-2147483648 to +2147483647
long	8 bytes	-9223372036854775808 to +9223372036854775807

Let us try to understand this through an example given here:

```
byte rno=10;
```

In the preceding statement, we are declaring byte data type for the variable rno and the value 10, which is stored into rno. byte represents any value between -128 to +127.

long x=150L;

Here, 150 is stored into x, which is declared as long type. Notice the L at the end of the statement. If this L is not there, then JVM allots only 2 bytes of memory to x as against the usual 8 bytes memory that should be allotted to a long type. The reason for this is that 2 bytes are sufficient to store the value 150. But if we attach l or L at the end of the value as shown in the preceding example, then JVM will consider it as a long value and will allot 8 bytes to it.

Float Data Types

These data types are useful to represent numbers with decimal point. For example, 3.14, 0.0012, -123.11, etc. are called floating point numbers. These are again classified as float (single precision floating point number) and double (double precision floating point number). The difference exists essentially in the number of digits, they can represent accurately after the decimal point. This accuracy is also called *precision*. Table 4.2 depicts the size of float and double.

Table 4.2

Data type	Memory size	Minimum and Maximum values
float	4 bytes	-3.4e38 to -1.4e-45 for negative values and 1.4e-45 to 3.4e38 for positive values
double	8 bytes	-1.8e308 to -4.9e-324 for negative values and 4.9e-324 to 1.8e308 for positive values

What is the difference between float and double?

float can represent up to 7 digits accurately after decimal point, whereas double can represent up to 15 digits accurately after decimal point.

Let us now look at an example given here:

```
float pi=3.142F;
```

Here, the variable pi is containing the value 3.142. If F is not written at the end, then JVM would have allotted 8 bytes assuming the value to be double. The reason for this is that in float and double data types, the default is taken as double. By attaching F or f, we can ask the JVM to consider it as a float value and allot only 4 bytes.

double distance=1.98e8;

Here, e or E represents X 10 to the power. Hence, 1.98e8 means 1.98X108. This is also called *scientific notation* of representing numbers.

Character Data Type

This data type represents a single character like a, P, &, *, etc. Table 4.3 shows char data type details.

Table 4.3

Data type	Memory size	Minimum and Maximum values
char	2 bytes	0 to 65535

Here is an example of character data type:

```
char ch='X';
```

Here, we are storing the single character 'X' into the variable ch. Here, 'X' is also called *character literal*. Whenever character literals are written, they should be enclosed inside the single quotes.

By observing the minimum and maximum values in the table earlier, we shall get a doubt regarding why the range is expressed in integer numbers (0 to 65535). We know that all the characters on the keyboard are translated into integer values called ASCII (American Standard Code for Information Interchange), which is a standard maintained by every keyboard manufacturer. The processor recognizes the character uniquely from its ASCII value. Hence, let us understand the range mentioned in the table is nothing but the ASCII value range only.

The ASCII value range, from 0 to 65535, given in the table can uniquely represent a total of 65536 characters. This means a total of 65536 distinct characters can be recognized by Java. But we never use these many characters since our keyboard contains English alphabets and some other characters whose total does not exceed 256. This means 1 byte is sufficient to represent all the available characters of the keyboard. Then why 2 bytes are used to represent the char data type in Java?

JavaSoft people wanted to provide a facility to include characters not only from English but also from all other human languages to be used in Java programs. This will enable the programmers to write and execute a Java program in any language, which becomes an advantage on Internet. This system is also called *Unicode system*. Unicode uses 2 bytes so that any character from any language can be encoded successfully.

Important Interview Question

What is a Unicode system?

Unicode system is an encoding standard that provides a unique number for every character, no matter what the platform, program, or language is. Unicode uses 2 bytes to represent a single character.

String Data Types

A `String` represents a group of characters, like New Delhi, AP123, etc. The simplest way to create a `String` is by storing a group of characters into a `String` type variable as:

```
String str = "New Delhi";
```

Now, the `String` type variable `str` contains "New Delhi". Note that any string written directly in a program should be enclosed by using double quotes.

There is a class with the name `String` in Java, where several methods are provided to perform different operations on strings. Any string is considered as an object of `String` class. But in C/C++, a string is considered as a character array containing some characters where the last character would be `\0`. This is not valid in Java, since in Java, we got strings and character arrays both separately.

Now the question arises that if `String` is a class, why are we taking it as a data type? The answer is that every class is a data type and is also called *user-defined data type*.

Boolean Data Types

`boolean` data types represent any of the two values—true or false. JVM uses 1 bit to represent a boolean value internally, for example:

```
boolean response=true;
```

As shown earlier, we should not enclose the boolean value `true` (or `false`) in any quotation marks. In C/C++, 0 represents false and any other number represents true. This is not valid in Java.

Literals

A *literal* represents a value that is stored into a variable directly in the program. See the following examples:

```
boolean result = false;
char gender = 'M';
short s = 10000;
int i = -1256;
```

In the preceding statements, the right hand side values are called literals because these values are being stored into the variables shown at the left hand side. As the data type of the variable changes, the type of the literal also changes. So we have different types of literals. These are as follows:

- [ ] Integer literals
- [ ] Float literals
- [ ] Character literals
- [ ] String literals
- [ ] Boolean literals

Read on to get familiar with them.

Integer Literals

Integer literals represent the fixed integer values like 100, -55, 123450, etc. All these numbers belong to decimal system, which uses 10 digits (from 0 to 9) to represent any number. Suppose, we want to write an integer in octal number system (octal number system uses 8 digits, from 0 to 7), then we should prefix 0 before the number. To represent hexadecimal number (hexadecimal number system uses 16 digits from 0 to 9 and from A to F), we should prefix 0x before the value.

```
int decVal = 26;   // The number 26, in decimal
int octVal = 032;  // The number 26, in octal
int hexVal = 0x1a; // The number 26, in hexadecimal
```

Float Literals

Float literals represent fractional numbers. These are the numbers with decimal points like 2.0, -0.005, 3.14, 6.1e-22, etc. which should be used with float or double type variables. While writing these literals, we can use E or e for scientific notation, F or f for float literal, and D or d for double literal (this is the default and generally omitted).

```
double d1 = 123.4;
double d2 = 1.234e2; // same value as d1, but in scientific notation
float  f1 = 123.4f;
```

Character Literals

Character literals indicate the following:

❑ General characters, like A, b, 9, etc.

❑ Special characters, like ?, @, etc.

❑ Unicode characters, like \u0042 (this represents *a* in ISO Latin 1 character set).

❑ Escape sequence (backslash codes) like \n, \b, etc.

Character literals should be enclosed in single quotation marks. The preceding unicode characters and escape sequence can also be represented as strings.

String Literals

String literals represent objects of String class. For example, Hello, Anil Kumar, AP1201, etc. will come under string literals, which can be directly stored into a String object.

Boolean Literals

Boolean literals represent only two values—true and false. It means we can store either true or false into a boolean type variable.

Conclusion

By following naming conventions, a programmer can avoid a lot of mistakes in writing the names of packages, classes, methods, variables, etc. This will improve readability as well as understandability of a program. So maintaining naming conventions is a good programming habit.

A program generally acts on data, processes it, and provides the results. So data is very important element of a program. In this chapter, we also discussed different *data types,* in terms of type of data received, stored, or used in a program.

OPERATORS IN JAVA

A programmer generally wants to do some operations in a program. For example, in a program, you want to perform addition of two numbers. How can you do it? Just by using + symbol, we can add the numbers. This means + is a symbol that performs an operation, i.e. addition. Such symbols are called *operators* and programming becomes easy because of them. Let us discuss about operators in this chapter and how to use them with examples.

Operators

An *operator* is a symbol that performs an operation. An operator acts on some variables, called *operands* to get the desired result, as shown in Figure 5.1.

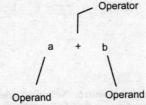

Figure 5.1 Operator and operands

If an operator acts on a single variable, it is called *unary operator;* if it acts on two variables, it is called *binary operator;* and if it acts on three variables, then it is called *ternary operator.* This is one type of classification. Let us now examine various types of operators in detail.

Arithmetic Operators

These operators are used to perform fundamental arithmetic operations like addition, subtraction, etc. There are 5 arithmetic operators in Java. Since these operators act on two operands at a time, these are called *binary operators.* Table 5.1 displays the functioning of these operators. Here, we are assuming the value of a as 13 and b as 5.

Table 5.1

Operator	Meaning	Example	Result
+	Addition operator	a + b	18
-	Subtraction operator	a – b	8
*	Multiplication operator	a * b	65
/	Division operator	a / b	2.6
%	Modulus operator (This gives the remainder of division)	a % b	3

Addition operator (+) is also used to join two strings, as shown in the following code snippet:

❑ `String s1= "wel";`

❑ `String s2= "come";`

❑ `String s3= s1+s2;   //here, '+' is joining s1 and s2.`

Now, we get welcome in s3. In this case, + is called *String concatenation operator*.

Unary Operators

As the name indicates, unary operators act on only one operand. There are 3 kinds of unary operators:

❑ Unary minus operator (-)

❑ Increment operator (++)

❑ Decrement operator (--)

Unary Minus Operator (-)

This operator is used to negate a given value. Negation means converting a negative value into positive and vice versa, for example:

```
int x = 5;
System.out.println(-x);      will display -5.
System.out.println(-(-x));   will display 5.
```

In this code snippet, the unary minus (-) operator is used on variable x to negate its value. The value of x is 5 in the beginning. It became -5 when unary minus is applied on it.

Increment Operator (++)

This operator increases the value of a variable by 1, for example:

```
int x = 1;
++x    will make x = 2
x++    now x = 3
```

Here, the value of the variable x is incremented by 1 when ++ operator is used before or after it. Both are valid expressions in Java. Let us take an example to understand it better:

```
      x = x+1;
```

In this statement, if x is 3, then x+1 value will be 4. This value is stored again in the left hand side variable x. So, the value of x now becomes 4. The same thing is done by ++ operator also.

Writing ++ before a variable is called *pre incrementation* and writing ++ after a variable is called *post incrementation*. In pre incrementation, incrementation is done first and any other operation is done next. In post incrementation, all the other operations are done first and incrementation is done only at the end. To understand the difference between pre and post incremenations, let us take a couple of examples.

Example 1: Finding the difference between pre- and post- increment of x

`int x=1;`
`System.out.println(x);`
`System.out.println(++x);`
`System.out.println(x);`
	`int x=1;`
	`System.out.println(x);`
	`System.out.println(x++);`
	`System.out.println(x);`

Output: 1 2 2	Output: 1 1 2

In this example, see the left-hand side and right-hand side statements. The second statement on the left uses pre-incrementation, while the second statement on the right uses post-incrementation.

At the left hand side:

❑ `System.out.println(x);` // displays the value of x as 1

❑ `System.out.println(++x);` // first increments the value of x and then displays it as 2

❑ `System.out.println(x);` // displays the value of x, which is already incremented, i.e. 2

At the right hand side:

❑ `System.out.println(x);` // displays the value of x, i.e. 1

❑ `System.out.println(x++);` // first displays the value of x as 1 and then increments it.

❑ `System.out.println(x);` // displays the incremented value of x, i.e. 2

Example 2: Finding the difference between pre- and post- increment of a and b

`a=1;`
`b=2;`
`a=++b;`
`what are the values of a and b?`
	`a=1;`
	`b=2;`
	`a=b++;`
	`what are the values of a and b?`

Output: a=3 b=3	Output: a=2

a=1;
b=2;
a=++b;
what are the values of a and b?
	a=1;
	b=2;
	a=b++;
	what are the values of a and b?

	b=3

At the left hand side, `a=++b;`

This is called pre-incrementation. So increment the value of b first (it becomes 3) and then store it into a. Now, the value of a also becomes 3.

At the right hand side, `a=b++;`

This is called post-incrementation. So incrementation of b will not be done first. Without incrementing, the value of b, i.e. 2 is stored into a (so the value of a becomes 2) and then incrementation of b is done (so the value of b becomes 3).

Example 3: Finding the value of the following expression, given that the value of a is 7

`++a*a++;`

Here, the value of a is given as 7. So ++a makes the value of a as 8. Then a++ is there. Since, this is post-incrementation, the value of a will not be incremented in the same statement and hence the value of a, i.e. 8 will stay like that only. As a result, we get 8*8= 64.

Decrement Operator (--)

This operator is used to decrement the value of a variable by 1.

```
int x = 1;
--x   will make the value of x as 0
x--   now, the value of x is -1
```

This means, the value of x is decremented every time we use -- operator on it. This is same as writing x= x-1.

Writing -- before a variable is called *pre-decrementation* and writing -- after a variable is called *post-decrementation*. Like the incrementation operator, here also the same rules apply. Pre-decrementation is done immediately then and there itself and

Post-decrementation is done after all the other operations are carried out.

Assignment Operator (=)

This operator is used to store some value into a variable. It is used in 3 ways:

❑   It is used to store a value into a variable, for example `int x = 5;`

❑   It is used to store the value of a variable into another variable, for example:

```
int x = y;  //here the value of y is stored into x
```

❑ It is used to store the value of an expression into a variable, for example:

```
int x = y+z-4; //here the expression y+z-4 is evaluated and its result is
//stored into x.
```

We cannot use more than one variable at the left hand side of the = operator. For example:

```
x+y = 10;  //this is invalid, since there is doubt for the compiler
//regarding where the value 10 is stored.
```

We cannot use a literal or constant value at the left side of the = operator. For example:

```
15 = x;    //how can we store the value of x into a number?
```

Compact Notation

While using assignment operator (=), sometimes we may have to use same variable at both the sides of the operator. In such cases, we can eliminate repetition of the variable and use compact notation or short cut notation, as shown in Table 5.2.

Table 5.2

Expanded notation	Compact notation	Name of operator
x = x + 10	x +=10	+= is called addition assignment operator
sal = sal * 10.5	sal *=10.5	*= is called multiplication assignment operator
value= value-discount	value -= discount	-= is called subtraction assignment operator
p = p / 1000	p /= 1000	/= is called division assignment operator
num = num % 5.5	num %= 5.5	%= is called modulus assignment operator

Experienced programmers use compact notations. However, both the expanded and compact notations are valid in Java.

Relational Operator

These operators are used for the purpose of comparing. For example, to know which one is bigger or whether two quantities are equal or not. Relational operators are of 6 types:

❑ >   greater than operator
❑ >= greater than or equal to
❑ <   less than operator
❑ <= less than or equal to
❑ == equal to operator
❑ != not equal to operator

The main use of relational operators is in the construction of conditions in statements, like this:

```
if(condition_is_true) statement_to_be_ executed.
```

This statement could be applied in a program as follows:

```
if( a > b) System.out.println(a);
if( a == 100) System.out.println("a value equals to 100");
```

Observe, that in this example the two statements, a>b and a==100, are conditions. If they are true, then the corresponding statements will be executed. Note that = (assignment operator) is for storing the value into a variable and == (equal to operator) is for comparing the two quantities. Both are quite different.

Logical Operators

Logical operators are used to construct compound conditions. A compound condition is a combination of several simple conditions. Logical operators are of three types:

❑   && *and* operator

❑ || *or* operator

❑   ! *not* operator

```
if( a == 1 || b == 1 || c == 1 ) System.out.println("Yes");
```

Here, there are 3 conditions: a==1, b==1, and c==1, which are combined by || (*or* operator). In this case, if either of the a or b or c value becomes equal to 1, Yes will be displayed.

```
if( x > y && y < z ) System.out.print("Hello");
```

In the preceding statement, there are 2 conditions: x>y and y<z. Since they are combined by using && (*and* operator); if both the conditions are true, then only Hello is displayed.

```
if( !(str1.equals(str2)) System.out.println("Not equal");
```

We are assuming that str1 and str2 are two string objects, which are being compared. See the ! (not operator) and the equals() methods in the earlier condition telling that if str1 is not equal to str2, then only Not equal will be displayed.

Boolean Operators

These operators act on boolean variables and produce boolean type result. The following 3 are boolean operators:

❑   &boolean *and* operator

❑ |boolean *or* operator

❑   !boolean *not* operator

Boolean & operator returns *true* if both the variables are *true*. Boolean | operator returns *true* if any one of the variables is *true*. Boolean ! operator converts *true* to *false* and vice versa.

```
boolean a,b; //declare two boolean type variables
```

❑   a= true;   //store boolean value true into a

❑   b= false;   //store boolean value false into b

❑ a & b   //returns false & gives true only if both are true

❑ a | b   //returns true. | gives true if any one is true

❑ a & a   //returns true since both are true

❑ b | b   //returns false since both are false

❑ !a   //gives false

❑ !b   //gives true

Bitwise Operators

There are 7 bitwise operators in Java. These operators act on individual bits (0 and 1) of the operands. They act on only integer datatypes, i.e. byte, short, long, and int. In case of these operators, the internal representation of numbers will be in the form of binary number system, which is different from the decimal number system used in our daily life. Binary number system uses only 2 digits—0 and 1 to represent any number. On the other hand, decimal number system uses 10 digits from 0 to 9. Now, let us see how binary numbers are represented in decimal number system and vice versa.

Example 4: Converting 45 into binary number system

Rule: Divide the number successively by 2 and take the remainders from bottom to top. See Figure 5.2. The decimal number 45 is represented as 101101 in binary. If we use 8 bit representation, we can write it as: 0010 1101.

```
2 │ 45
  ├──────
2 │ 22 - 1
  ├──────
2 │ 11 - 0
  ├──────
2 │ 5 - 1        ↑
  ├──────
2 │ 2 - 1
  ├──────
2 │ 1 - 0        remainders
  ├──────
2 │ 0 - 1
```

Figure 5.2 Converting into binary

Example 5: Converting binary number, 0010 1101, to decimal

Rule: Multiply the individual bits by the powers of 2 and take the sum of the products. See Figure 5.3. Here, the sum is coming to 45. So 0010 1101 in binary is equal to 45 in decimal number system.

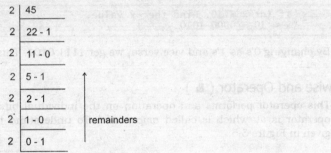

$$0 \quad 0 \quad 1 \quad 0 \quad 1 \quad 1 \quad 0 \quad 1$$
$$2^7 \quad 2^6 \quad 2^5 \quad 2^4 \quad 2^3 \quad 2^2 \quad 2^1 \quad 2^0$$
$$0 + 0 + 32 + 0 + 8 + 4 + 0 + 1 = 45$$

Figure 5.3 Converting from binary to decimal

Let us now understand negative numbers. A negative number is represented as 2's complement of a positive number. For example, take a positive decimal number: 10. It is represented in binary as 0000 1010. We can obtain its 1's complement form by converting the bit 0 as 1 and vice versa. Thus, we get 1111 0101. By adding 1 to this, we can get the 2's complement form as 1111 0110. This is the representation of -10, as shown in Figure 5.4.

```
Decimal 10          =  0000 1010

1's complement      =  1111 0101
(change 0 as 1 and
vice versa)
                            +1
                        _____
2's complement      =
(add 1 to 1's          1111 0110   = Decimal -10
complement)
```

Figure 5.4 Representation of negative numbers

How are positive and negative numbers represented internally?

Positive numbers are represented in binary using 1's complement notation and negative numbers are represented by using 2's complement notation.

There are 7 types of bitwise operators. Read on to understand them. Let us now discuss them one by one.

Bitwise Complement Operator (~)

This operator gives the complement form of a given number. This operator symbol is ~, which is pronounced as *tilde*. Complement form of a positive number can be obtained by changing 0's as 1's and vice versa.

```
If int x = 10. Find the ~x value.
x = 10 = 0000 1010.
```

By changing 0's as 1's and vice versa, we get 1111 0101. This is nothing but -11(in decimal). So, ~x = -11.

Bitwise and Operator (&)

This operator performs and operation on the individual bits of the numbers. The symbol for this operator is &, which is called *ampersand*. To understand the and operation, see the truth table given in Figure 5.5.

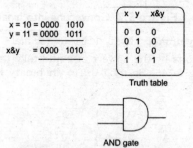

```
x = 10 = 0000  1010
y = 11 = 0000  1011
         _____
x&y    = 0000  1010
```

x	y	x&y
0	0	0
0	1	0
1	0	0
1	1	1

Truth table

AND gate

Figure 5.5 AND operation

Truth table is a table that gives relationship between the inputs and the output. From the table, we can conclude that by multiplying the input bits, we can get the output bit. The AND gate circuit present in the computer chip will perform the and operation.

```
If int x = 10, y = 11. Find the value of x&y.
x = 10 = 0000 1010.
y = 11 = 0000 1011.
```

From the truth table, by multiplying the bits, we can get x&y = 0000 1010. This is nothing but 10 (in decimal).

Bitwise or Operator (|)

This operator performs *or* operation on the bits of the numbers. The symbol is |, which is called *pipe* symbol. To understand this operation, see the truth table given in Figure 5.6. From the table, we can conclude that by adding the input bits, we can get the output bit. The OR gate circuit, which is present in the computer chip will perform the or operation.

```
x = 10 = 0000  1010
y = 11 = 0000  1011
_____
x|y    = 0000  1011
```

x	y	x|y
0	0	0
0	1	1
1	0	1
1	1	1

Truth table

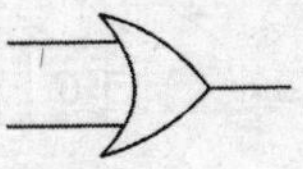

.OR gate

Figure 5.6 OR operation

If int x = 10, y = 11. Find the value of x|y.
x = 10 = 0000 1010.
y = 11 = 0000 1011.

From the truth table, by adding the bits, we can get x|y = 0000 1011. This is nothing but 11 (in decimal).

Bitwise xor Operator (^)

This operator performs *exclusive or (xor)* operation on the bits of the numbers. The symbol is ^, which is called *cap, carat*, or *circumflex* symbol. To understand the *xor* operation, see the truth table given in Figure 5.7. From the table, we can conclude that when we have odd number of 1's in the input bits, we can get the output bit as 1. The *XOR* gate circuit of the computer chip will perform this operation.

```
x = 10 = 0000  1010
y = 11 = 0000  1011
_____
x^y    = 0000  0001
```

x	y	x^y
0	0	0
0	1	1
1	0	1
1	1	0

Truth table

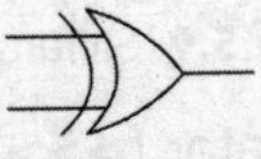

XOR gate

Figure 5.7 XOR operation

If int x = 10, y = 11. Find the value of x^y.
x = 10 = 0000 1010.
y = 11 = 0000 1011.

From the truth table, when odd number of 1's are there, we can get a 1 in the output. Thus, x^y = 0000 0001 is nothing but 1 (in decimal).

Bitwise Left Shift Operator (<<)

This operator shifts the bits of the number towards left a specified number of positions. The symbol for this operator is <<, read as *double less than*. If we write x<<n, the meaning is to shift the bits of x towards left n positions.

`If int x = 10. Calculate x value if we write x<<2.`

Shifting the value of x towards left 2 positions will make the leftmost 2 bits to be lost. The value of x is 10 = 0000 1010. Now x<<2 will be 0010 1000 = 40 (in decimal). The procedure to do this is explained in Figure 5.8.

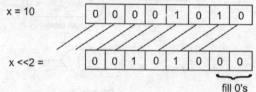

Figure 5.8 Shifting bits towards left 2 times

Bitwise Right Shift Operator (>>)

This operator shifts the bits of the number towards right a specified number of positions. The symbol for this operator is >>, read as *double greater than*. If we write x>>n, the meaning is to shift the bits of x towards right n positions.

>> shifts the bits towards right and also preserves the sign bit, which is the leftmost bit. Sign bit represents the sign of the number. Sign bit 0 represents a positive number and 1 represents a negative number. So, after performing >> operation on a positive number, we get a positive value in the result also. If right shifting is done on a negative number, again we get a negative value only.

`If x = 10, then calculate x>>2 value.`

Shifting the value of x towards right 2 positions will make the rightmost 2 bits to be lost. x value is 10 = 0000 1010. Now x>>2 will be: 0000 0010 = 2 (in decimal) (Figure 5.9).

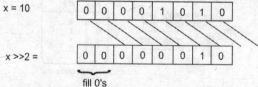

Figure 5.9 Shifting bits towards right 2 times

Bitwise Zero Fill Right Shift Operator (>>>)

This operator also shifts the bits of the number towards right a specified number of positions. But, it stores 0 in the sign bit. The symbol for this operator is >>>, read as *triple greater than*. Since, it always fills 0 in the sign bit, it is called *zero fill right shift* operator. If we apply >>> on a positive number, it gives same output as that of >>. But in case of negative numbers, the output will be positive, since the sign bit is replaced by a 0.

Important Interview Question

What is the difference between >> and >>> ?

Both bitwise right shift operator (>>) and bitwise zero fill right shift operator (>>>) are used to shift the bits towards right. The difference is that >> will protect the sign bit whereas the >>> operator will not protect the sign bit. It always fills 0 in the sign bit.

Program 1: Let us now write a program to observe the effects of various bitwise operators.

```
//Using bitwise operators
class Bits
{
    public static void main(String args[])
    {
        byte x,y;
        x = 10;
        y = 11;

        System.out.println("~x= " + (~x));
        System.out.println("x&y= "+ (x&y));
        System.out.println("x|y= "+ (x|y));
        System.out.println("x^y= "+ (x^y));
        System.out.println("x<<2= "+ (x<<2));
        System.out.println("x>>2= "+ (x>>2));
        System.out.println("x>>>2= "+ (x>>>2));
    }
}

Output:
C:\> javac Bits.java
C:\> java Bits
 ~x= -11
x&y= 10
x|y= 11
x^y= 1
x<<2= 40
x>>2= 2
x>>>2= 2
```

Ternary Operator or Conditional Operator (? :)

This operator is called *ternary* because it acts on 3 variables. The other name for this operator is *conditional operator,* since it represents a conditional statement. Two symbols are used for this operator? and:

Its syntax is `variable = expression1? expression2 expression3;`

This means that first of all, expression1 is evaluated. If it is true, then expression2 value is stored into the variable. If expression1 is false, then expression3 value is stored into the variable. It means:

```
if( expression1 is true )
    variable = expression2;
else variable = expression3;
```

Now, let us put the following condition

```
max = (a>b) ? a : b;
```

Here, (a>b) is evaluated first. If it is true, then the value of a is stored into the variable max, else the value of b is stored into max. This means:

```
if(a>b)
    max = a;
else max = b;
```

Here, we are using 3 variables: a, b, and max—thus, the name *ternary*. The preceding statement, which is called *conditional statement,* is also represented by this operator. So it is also called *conditional operator*. Remember conditional operator is a compact form of conditional statement.

Member Operator (.)

Member operator is also called *dot* operator since its symbol is a. (dot or period). This operator tells about member of a package or a class. It is used in three ways:

❑   We know a package contains classes. We can use . operator to refer to the class of a package.

Syntax:

```
packagename.classname;
```

This could be written as follows:

```
java.io.BufferedReader      // BufferedReader is a class in the package:
                            //java.io.
```

❑   We know that each class contains variables or methods. To refer to the variables of a class, we can use this operator.

Syntax:

```
classname.variablename;
```

Or

```
objectname.variablename;
```

This could be written as:

```
System.out    //out is a static variable in System class
emp.id        //id is a variable in Employee class.
              // emp is Employee class object
```

❑   We know that a class also contains methods. Using dot operator, we can refer to the methods of a class.

Syntax:

```
classname.methodname;
```

Or

```
objectname.methodname;
```

Let us try to understand this with the help of an example.

```
Math.sqrt()   //sqrt() is a method in Math class
br.read()     //read() is a method in BufferedReader class. br is object of
              //BufferedReader class.
```

instanceof Operator

This operator is used to test if an object belongs to a class or not. Note that the word *instance* means *object*. This operator can also be used to check if an object belongs to an interface or not.

Syntax:

```
boolean variable = object instanceof class;
boolean variable = object instanceof interface;
```

This could be written as:

```
boolean x = emp instanceof Employee;
```

Here, we are testing if `emp` is an object of `Employee` class or not. If `emp` is an object of `Employee` class, then `true` will be returned into x, otherwise x will contain `false`.

new Operator

`new` operator is often used to create objects to classes. We know that objects are created on *heap* memory by JVM, dynamically (at runtime).

Syntax:

```
classname  obj = new classname();
```

An example of this is as follows:

```
Employee emp = new Employee();   // emp is an object of the
                                 //Employee class
```

Cast Operator

Cast operator is used to convert one datatype into another datatype. This operator can be used by writing datatype inside simple braces.

```
double  x = 10.54;
        int y = x;  //error - because datatypes of x and y are different.
```

To store x value into y, we have to first convert the datatype of x into the datatype of y. It means double datatype should be converted into `int` type by writing `int` inside the simple braces as: (`int`). This is called *cast* operator.

```
int y = (int)x;  //here, x datayple is converted into int type and then
//stored into y.
```

In the preceding statement, (`int`) is called the cast operator. Cast operator is generally used before a variable or before a method.

Priority of Operators

When several operators are used in a statement, it is important to know which operator will execute first and which will come next. To determine that, certain rules of *operator precedence* are followed:

❑   First, the contents inside the braces: () and [] will be executed.

- ❏ Next, ++ and --.
- ❏ Next, *, /, and % will execute.
- ❏ + and – will come next.
- ❏ Relational operators are executed next.
- ❏ Boolean and bitwise operators
- ❏ Logical operators will come afterwards.
- ❏ Then ternary operator.
- ❏ Assignment operators are executed at the last.

Conclusion

In this chapter, you learnt that operators make programming easy by assisting the programmer to perform any operation by just mentioning a symbol. Just imagine a situation, where we have to add two numbers without any arithmetic or unary operators available to us. In such a case, a mere addition will become a very tedius job. Such programming difficulties can be escaped by using these operators.

CONTROL STATEMENTS IN JAVA

A Java statement is the smallest unit that is a complete instruction in itself. Statements in Java generally contain expressions and end with a semi-colon. The two most commonly used statements in any programming language are as follows:

❏ **Sequential statements**: These are the statements which are executed one by one.

❏ **Control statements**: These are the statements that are executed randomly and repeatedly.

These are followed by Java also. Now, let us see some statements:

```
System.out.println("Hello");
x = y+z;
System.out.println(x);
```

These statements are executed by JVM one by one in a sequential manner. So they are called *sequential statements*. But this type of sequential execution is useful only to write simple programs. If we want to write better and complex programs, we need better control on the flow of execution. This is possible by using *control statements*.

Important Interview Question

What are control statements?

Control statements are the statements which alter the flow of execution and provide better control to the programmer on the flow of execution. They are useful to write better and complex programs.

The following control statements are available in Java:

❏ `if …else` statement

❏ `do…while` loop

❏ `while` loop

❏ `for` loop

❏ `for-each` loop

❏ `switch` statement

❏ `break` statement

❏ `continue` statement

❑ return statement

Note

A statement represents a single time execution from top to bottom and a loop represents repeated execution of several statements.

if...else Statement

This statement is used to perform a task depending on whether a given condition is true or false. Here, *task* represents a single statement or a group of statements.

Syntax:

```
if(condition)
        statements1;
[else statements2;]
```

Here, the condition is written inside the small braces (). The statements written inside the square brackets [ ] represent optional part of the statement. It means that the part within [ ] can be omitted, if not required. This is the convention followed in all control statements.

By observing the syntax, we can understand that if the condition specified after if is true, then statements1 will be executed. If the condition is false, then statements2 will be executed. statements1 and statements2 represent either a single statement or more than one statement. If more than one statement is used, then they should be enclosed in angular brackets { }.

Let us write a program to understand the use of if...else statement.

Program 1: Write a program to test if a number is positive or negative.

Here, actually three combinations arise: +ve, -ve, and neither +ve nor –ve, i.e. zero.

```
//To test if a number is +ve or -ve
class Demo
{
    public static void main(String[] args)
    {
    int num = -5;  //declare and initialize num to -5

        if(num == 0)
            System.out.println("It is zero");
        else if(num > 0)
            System.out.println(num+" is positive");
        else System.out.println(num+" is negative");
    }
}
```

Output:

```
C:\> javac Demo.java
C:\> java Demo
-5 is negative
```

if...else statement can be written in the following different variations as:

```
if(condition1)
        statements1;
        else if(condition2)
            statements2;
            else if(condition3)
```

```
                statements3;
                    else statements4;
```

Here, if `condition1` is true, then `statements1` is executed. If `condition1` is false, then `condition2` is tested. If `condition2` is true, then `statements2` is executed, otherwise `condition3` is tested.

```
    if(condition1)
        if(condition2)
            if(condition3)
                    statements1;
                else statements2;
            else statements3;
        else statements4;
```

Here, if `condition1` is true, then `condition2` is tested. If `condition2` is also true, then `condition3` is tested. If `condition3` is true, then `statements1` will be executed. If `condition3` is false, then `statements2` will be executed. If `condition2` is false, then `statements3` will be executed. If `condition1` itself is false, then `statements4` will be executed.

do...while Loop

This loop is used when there is a need to repeatedly execute a group of statements as long as a condition is true. If the condition is false, the repetition will be stopped and the flow of execution comes out of do...while loop.

Syntax:

```
    do{
            statements;
        }while(condition);
```

We need not use { and } braces, if there is only one statement inside the do...while loop.

Program 2: Write a program to display numbers from 1 to 10.

```java
//To display numbers from 1 to 10
class Demo
{
    public static void main(String[] args)
    {
    int x;
        x = 1;      //starting number is 1

        do{
            System.out.println(x);
            x++;
        }while(x<=10);
    }
}
```

Output:

```
C:\> javac Demo.java
C:\> java Demo
1
2
3
4
5
```

```
6
7
8
9
10
```

In the preceding program, observe the loop:

```
do{
        System.out.println(x);   //display x value
        x++;   //increment x value by 1
    }while(x<=10);  //as long as x <=10
```

Here, already the value of x is 1, so it is displayed. Then x++ will increment the value of x by 1, hence the value of x becomes 2. Then the condition x<=10 is tested. As this condition is true, the flow of execution will go back and the value of x, i.e. 2 will be displayed. Then the x value is incremented and becomes 3. Since 3 is also <= `1`, the flow goes back and displays x value. In this way, as long as x value does not exceed 10, the loop repeats and hence we can see the numbers from 1 to 10.

while Loop

The functioning of this loop is also similar to do...while loop. This loop repeats a group of statements as long as a condition is true. Once the condition is false, the loop is terminated.

Syntax:

```
while(condition)
        {
            statements;
        }
```

In a do...while loop, the statements are executed first and then the condition is tested. Whereas in a while loop, the condition is tested first; if it is true, then only the statements are executed.

Important Interview Question

Out of do...while and while – which loop is efficient?

In a do...while loop, the statements are executed without testing the condition, the first time. From the second time only the condition is observed. This means that the programmer does not have control right from the beginning of its execution. In a while loop, the condition is tested first and then only the statements are executed. This means it provides better control right from the beginning. Hence, while loop is more efficient than do...while loop.

Program 3: Let us rewrite the previous program (Program 2) using while loop.

```
//To display numbers from 1 to 10
class Demo
{
    public static void main(String[] args)
    {
    int x;
        x = 1;    //starting number is 1
        while(x<=10)
        {
            System.out.println(x);  //display x
            x++;   //increment x
```

```
                }
          }
    }
```

In this program, we can also rewrite the `while` loop as:

```
while(x<=10)
        System.out.println(x++);  //display x and increment it
```

for Loop

The `for` loop is also same as `do…while` or `while` loop, but it is more compact syntactically. The `for` loop executes a group of statements as long as a condition is true.

Syntax:

```
for ( expression1; expression2; expression3 )
        {
                statements;
        }
```

To understand the preceding syntax, let us take an example:

```
for( int x = 1;   x <= 10; x++)
{
        System.out.println(x);
}
```

Please compare the expressions in the preceding `for` loop. The first expression represents an initialization expression (`int x = 1`). The second one is a conditional expression

(`x<= 10`). As long as this condition is true, the statements inside `for` loop are executed. The third expression is a modifying expression (`x++`). It may increment or decrement the value of the variable.

Now, let us see how this `for` loop gets executed. `expression1` will be executed only once the first time. So, the value of x becomes 1. Then `expression2` (x<=10) will be evaluated. If it is true, then the statements inside the `for` loop will be executed. It means that the statement:

```
System.out.println(x);
```

is executed. So, the value of x, i.e.1 will be displayed. Then the third expression (x++) will be executed. Now, the x value becomes 2. Second expression is again executed, comparing the x value. Since x<=10 are true, then the statement:

```
System.out.println(x);
```

will be executed again. So, the x value 2 will be displayed. The preceding statement repeatedly executes till the value of x reaches 10. As a result, x values from 1 to 10 will be displayed. From this discussion, we can understand that `expression1` is executed only once in the beginning of the `for` loop. Then `expression2` and `expression3` will be executed repeatedly as long as `expression2` is true.

Do…while or while loops are used when we do not know how many times we have to execute the statements. It just depends on the condition. The execution should continue till the condition is false. But, the for loop is more suitable for situations where the statements should be executed a fixed number of times. Here, we know how many times exactly we want to execute.

Let us now execute for loop to see its effect.

Program 4: Write a program to display the numbers from 1 to 10.

```
//To display numbers from 1 to 10
class Demo
{
    public static void main(String[] args)
    {
    for( int x = 1;   x <= 10; x++)
        {
            System.out.println(x);
        }
    }
}
```

Output:

```
C:\> javac Demo.java
C:\> java Demo
1
2
3
4
5
6
7
8
9
10
```

We can write the for loop without expression1 or expression2 or expression3 or any two expressions or any three expressions and still we can get the same results. As an example, let us rewrite the preceding for loop without expression1 as:

```
int x = 1;
for(;   x <= 10; x++)
{
        System.out.println(x);
}
```

Let us write the same for loop without expression3 as:

```
int x = 1;
for(;   x <= 10; )
{
        System.out.println(x);
        x++;
}
```

Let us now eliminate the second expression also and write it as:

```
int x = 1;
for( ;   ; )
{
        System.out.println(x);
        x++;
}
```

Observe here, there is no condition in the loop that tells where to stop. So the preceding code executes without stoppage. It is called an infinite loop. Infinite loops are drawbacks in a program because when the user is caught in an infinite loop, he would be perplexed and could not understand how to come out of it. So, it is the duty of the programmer to see not to form the infinite loops. By chance, if the programmer got an infinite loop, he should break it when the condition is reached. For this purpose, break statement can be used.

Program 5: Write a program to display numbers from 1 to 10 using infinite for loop.

```
//To display numbers from 1 to 10
class Demo
{
    public static void main(String[] args)
    {
        int x = 1;
    for( ; ; )
        {
            System.out.println(x);
            x++;
            if(x > 10) break; //if x value exceeds 10, then come out of the
                              //loop.
        }
    }
}
```

Output:

```
C:\> javac Demo.java
C:\> java Demo
1
2
3
4
5
6
7
8
9
10
```

break is a statement that can be used to come out of a loop. It can be a for, while or do...while loop. The infinite loops can be formed by using not only for loop but also while or do...while, as shown here:

```
while(true)
{
    statements;
}

do{
    Statements;
}while(true);
```

There is another way of writing a for loop. We can use multiple initialization expressions and modifying expressions in the for loop, as shown here:

```
for(int i=1,j=5; i<=5; i++, j--)
    System.out.println(i+"\t"+j);
```

In the preceding loop, we used two initialization expressions (i=1, j=5) and two modifying expressions (i++,j--), but there is only one conditional expression (i<=5). This for loop displays i values from 1 to 5 whereas j values will simultaneously change from 5 to 1. So, the output of executing the preceding for loop will be:

```
1    5
2    4
3    3
4    2
5    1
```

Nested for Loops

We can write a for loop within another for loop. Such loops are called *nested loops*.

```
for(int i=1; i<=3; i++)
{
        statements1;   //these are executed 3 times
}
```

The preceding for loop gets executed for 3 times by changing i values from 1 to 3. Let us take another for loop as:

```
for(int j=1; j<=4; j++)
{
        statements2;   //these are executed 4 times

}
```

This loop is executed 4 times by changing j values from 1 to 4. If we write this loop inside the preceding for loop, it looks like this:

```
for(int i=1; i<=3; i++)
{
    statements1;    //these are executed 3 times
    for(int j=1; j<=4; j++)
    {
            statements2;    //these are executed 12 times
    }
}
```

In this case, the execution starts from the outer for loop and hence i=1. Then statements1 will be executed once. Now, the execution enters second for loop and j value will be 1. Now statements2 will be executed once. After this, j value will be 2 and statements2 will be executed again. Like this, the inner for loop is executed 4 times, with j values changing from 1 to 4. This means statements2 will be executed 4 times.

When the inner for loop is completed, then the execution goes to the outer for loop and i value will be 2. This time, the execution again comes into the inner for loop and statements2 will be executed 4 times. Then the execution goes to outer for loop and i value will be 3. Again the inner for loop is executed 4 times. It means the i and j values will change like this:

```
i=1,  j=1,2,3,4
i=2,  j=1,2,3,4
i=3,  j=1,2,3,4
```

The preceding sequence represents that the outer for loop is executed totally 3 times and hence statements1 will be executed 3 times. The inner for loop is executed 4 times for each i value and hence statements2 will be executed 12 times.

In the same way, it is also possible to write a while loop or a do...while loop inside a for loop and vice versa. These are called *nested loops*.

Program 6: Write a program to display stars in a triangular form—a single star in the first line, two stars in the second line, three stars in the third line, and so on.

```java
//To display stars in triangular form - nested for loops
class Stars
{
  public static void main(String args[])
  {
     int r = 5; //we want 5 rows

     for(int i=1; i<=r; i++)  //i represents row number
     {
         for(int st=1; st<=i; st++)   //st represents no. of  stars
         {
            System.out.print(" * ");
         }
         System.out.println();
     }
  }
}
```

Output:

```
C:\> javac Stars.java
C:\> java Stars

 *
 *  *
 *  *  *
 *  *  *  *
 *  *  *  *  *
```

for-each Loop

This loop is specifically designed to handle the elements of a collection. Collection represents a group of elements. For example, we can take an array as a collection or any class in java.util package can be considered as a collection. The reason is that an array stores a group of elements like integer values or strings. Similarly, java.util package classes are developed to handle a group of objects.

Important Interview Question

What is a collection?

A collection represents a group of elements like integer values or objects. Examples for collections are arrays and java.util classes (Stack, LinkedList, Vector, etc.)

The for-each loop repeatedly executes a group of statements for each element of the collection. It executes as many times as there are number of elements in the collection.

Syntax:

```java
for(var : collection)
        {
              statements;
        }
```

Here, the var is attached to the collection. This var represents each element of the collection one by one. Suppose, the collection has got 5 elements then this loop will be executed 5 times and the var will represent these elements one by one.

Program 7: Write a program to see the use of for-each loop and retrieve the elements one by one from an array and display it.

```
//Using for-each loop - to display array elements
class Demo
{
  public static void main(String args[])
  {
      //declare an array with 5 elements
      int arr[] = {200, 19, -56, 44, 99};

      //use for each to retrieve elements from array
      for(int i : arr)
      {
          System.out.println(i);        //i represents each element of array
      }
  }
}
```

Output:

```
C:\> javac Demo.java
C:\> java Demo
200
19
-56
44
99
```

switch Statement

When there are several options and we have to choose only one option from the available ones, we can use switch statement. Depending on the selected option, a particular task can be performed. A task represents one or more statements.

Syntax:

```
switch(variable)
      {
          case value1 : statements1;
          case value2 : statements2;
          case value3 : statements3;
          :
          case valuen : statementsn;
          [default    : default_statements;]
      }
```

Here, depending on the value of the variable, a particular task (statements) will be executed. If the variable value is equal to value1, statements1 will be executed. If the variable value is value2, statements2 will be executed, and so on. If the variable value does not equal to value1, value2,...then none of the statements will be executed. In that case, default clause is executed and hence the *default_statements* are executed.

Let us take an example to understand the switch statement. In Program 8, we are taking a variable color, which is initialized to g. Depending on the color value, Red is displayed when the value is r; Green is displayed when the value is g; Blue is displayed when the value is b; and White is displayed when the value is w. If color value is neither of the specified values—r, g, b, or w, then none of the statements are executed. As a result, the default statement is executed and it displays No color.

Program 8: Write a program for using the switch statement to execute a particular task depending on color value.

In this program, since color value is g, we expect that it displays Green as output.

```
//To display a color name depending on color value
class Demo
{
  public static void main(String args[])
  {
      char color = 'g';   //color is set to 'g'

      switch(color)
    {
      case 'r': System.out.println("Red");
      case 'g': System.out.println("Green");
      case 'b': System.out.println("Blue");
      case 'w': System.out.println("White");
      default : System.out.println("No color");
    }
  }
}
```

Output:

```
C:\> javac Demo.java
C:\> java Demo
Green
Blue
White
No color
```

The output of the program is not as expected. We expected that it would display Green, but it is displaying all colors starting from the Green color. What might be the reason? When color value is g, it has displayed Green and after that it has come down to execute the rest of the statements under it leading to the preceding output. The solution is to come out of the switch statement, after displaying Green. For this purpose, we can use break statement.

One of the uses of break is to terminate a loop and come out of it. Another use of break statement is to come out of the switch block. Now, let us rewrite the preceding program using the break statement.

Program 9: Write a program to come out of switch block, after executing a task.

In the following case, g becomes true and hence, JVM displays Green and then executes break, which terminates the switch block.

```
// To display a color name depending on color value
class Demo
{
  public static void main(String args[])
  {
      char color = 'g';   //color is set to 'g'

      switch(color)
    {
      case 'r': System.out.println("Red");
            break;
      case 'g': System.out.println("Green");
            break;
```

```
       case 'b': System.out.println("Blue");
               break;
       case 'w': System.out.println("White");
               break;
       default : System.out.println("No color");
     }
   }
 }
```

Output:

```
C:\> javac Demo.java
C:\> java Demo
Green
```

Remember, we cannot use all the data types along with the switch statement. We can use char, int, byte, short types only. For example, the following switch statement is invalid:

```
String str= "Delhi";
switch(str)    //invalid - String cannot be used with switch.
```

Switch statements are mostly used in menu driven programs. A *menu driven* program is a program where a menu (a list of items) is displayed and the user can select an item from the list of items available in the menu. Depending on the choice of the user, a particular task is done.

```
switch(user_choice)
{
  case 1:  task1;
  case 2: task2;
     :
}
```

break Statement

The break statement can be used in 3 ways:

- ❑ break is used inside a loop to come out of it.
- ❑ break is used inside the switch block to come out of the switch block.
- ❑ break can be used in nested blocks to go to the end of a block. *Nested blocks* represent a block written within another block.

We have already observed the first two uses of break statement. Now, let us see the third use, where break statement is used inside the nested blocks.

```
break label;   //here label represents the name of the block.
```

The meaning of the preceding statement is *go to the end of the block,* whose name is given by the label. See the following example to understand this.

Program 10: Write a program to use a break statement to go to the end of a block.

Here we are using break to go to the end of the Block2.

```
//labeled break to go to end of a block
class Demo
{
  public static void main(String args[])
  {
```

```
        boolean x = true;

    bl1:{
       bl2:{
          bl3:{
             System.out.println("Block3");
             if(x) break bl2; //goto end of bl2
          } //end of bl3
          System.out.println("Block2");
       } //end of bl2
       System.out.println("Block1");
    } //end of bl1
    System.out.println("Out of all blocks");
  }
}
```

Output:

```
C:\>javac Demo.java
C:\>java Demo
Block3
Block1
Out of all blocks
```

In the preceding program, bl1, bl2, bl3 are names of the blocks starting with a { and ending with a }. First, Block3 will be displayed as the control of execution enters that block. Then, it executes:

```
    if(x) break bl2;
```

This represents going to the end of the block, named bl2. After the closing }, we got Block1, which is displayed and then the control jumps out and executes the last statement, so Out of all blocks will be displayed.

This type of break resembles goto statement in C/C++. The goto statement is useful to jump directly from one statement to another statement in the program, but goto is not available in Java due to its certain shortcomings:

❑ goto statements, more often than not, create infinite loops— which are drawbacks in a program.

❑ goto statements make documentation of a program difficult. Documenting a program means preserving a copy of the details of the development of a program. Documentation contains algorithm or logic of the program, flow chart representing the flow of execution and program print out as well as its output. A brief description of the program is done at the end of documentation representing the entire process of development of the program. When several goto statements are used, algorithms, flow charts, and explanation of the program will become unclear and hence the documentation becomes useless.

❑ goto statements are not a part of structured programming. The principles of structured programming do not include goto statements as part of elements of programming. This means, it is perfectly possible to write a program without ever using any goto statement.

Because of the preceding reasons, the use of goto statements has been banned in programming.

Important Interview Question

Why goto *statements are not available in Java?*

goto *statements lead to confusion for a programmer. Especially, in a large program, if several* goto *statements are used, the programmer would be perplexed while understanding the flow from where to where the control is jumping.*

continue Statement

continue is used inside a loop to repeat the next iteration of the loop. When continue is executed, subsequent statements in the loop are not executed and control of execution goes back to the next repetition of the loop.

Syntax:

```
continue;
```

To understand the use of continue, let us write a program using a for loop to display the numbers in descending order from 10 to 1.

Program 11: Write a program using for loop to display the numbers in descending order.

```
//Numbers in descending order
class Demo
{
  public static void main(String args[])
  {
    for(int i=10; i>=1; i--)
    {
        System.out.print(i+"  ");
    }
  }
}
```

Output:

```
C:\> javac Demo.java
C:\> java Demo
10  9  8  7  6  5  4  3  2  1
```

In this program, i value starts at 10. As long as i value is greater or equal to 1, it is decremented by 1. So we get numbers from 10 to 1 in descending order. Now, let's introduce continue in this program as:

```
for(int i=10; i>=1; i--)
    {
        if(i>5) continue;  //go back in the loop
        System.out.print(i+"  ");
    }
```

Here, we are redirecting the flow of execution back to the next iteration of the loop when i>5. So when i value changes from 10 to 6, continue statement will be executed and hence the subsequent statement:

```
System.out.print(i+"  ");
```

will not be executed. So the values of i from 10 to 6 will not be displayed, the output will be as follows:

```
5  4  3  2  1
```

The continue statement can be used along with a label, like break statement as:

```
continue label;  //here label represents name of the loop
```

In this case, the label after `continue` represents the name of the loop to where the flow of execution should jump. This is also called *labeled continue* statement.

Let us write a program using a `for` loop inside a `while` loop, which displays i and j values. It means we are using nested loops. In this program, we can use a label (name) to represent the `while` loop as `lp1` and another label to represent the `for` loop as `lp2`.

Program 12: Write a program for using nested loops (to display i and j values).

In this program, i values change from 1 to 3. When i is 1, then j values change from 1 to 5; when i is 2, j values change from 1 to 5; and when i is 3, j values change from 1 to 5 again.

```
//Using nested loops with labels.
class Demo
{
  public static void main(String args[])
  {
    int i=1,j;

    lp1: while(i<=3)
    {
      System.out.print(i); //i values change from 1 to 3
      lp2: for(j=1; j<=5; j++)
      {
        System.out.println("\t"+j); //j values from 1 to 5 for every i value
      }
      i++;
      System.out.println("-------------");
    }
  }
}
```

Output:

```
C:\> javac Demo.java
C:\> java Demo

1      1
       2
       3
       4
       5
-------------
2      1
       2
       3
       4
       5
-------------
3      1
       2
       3
       4
       5
-------------
```

Now, in the same program, let us introduce a labeled `continue` statement as follows:

```
lp1: while(i<=3)
    {
      System.out.print(i); //i values change from 1 to 3
      lp2: for(j=1; j<=5; j++)
        {
          System.out.println("\t"+j);
          if (j==3) //j values change up to 3 only
```

```
            {
                i++;
                continue lp1; //go back to while loop
            }
        }
        i++;
        System.out.println("-------------");
```

Output:

```
    1       1
            2
            3
    2       1
            2
            3
    3       1
            2
            3
```

Here, we have cut off the values, i.e. 4 and 5 of j, by comparing j value and redirecting the flow of execution to outer `while` loop, using the following statement:

```
    if (j==3) //if j value is 3, then use continue to go back
        {
            i++;
            continue lp1; //go back to while loop
        }
```

return Statement

We know that a method is a function written inside a class. It contains a group of statements and performs a task or processing. It means a method is useful to perform certain calculations or processing of data in the program to yield expected results. Methods can accept the data from outside for their processing and they can also return the results.

A method is executed when called from another method. The first method that is executed in a Java program by the JVM is `main()` method and hence if we want to execute any other method, we should call it from `main()`.

`return` statement is used in a method to come out of it to the calling method. For example, we are calling a method by the name `myMethod()` from the `main()` method. If `return` is used inside `myMethod()`, then the flow of execution comes out of it and goes back to `main()`. While going back from `myMethod()`, we can also return some value to the `main()` method. For this purpose, `return` should be used as follows:

```
    return  1;   //return 1 to calling method
    return  x;   //return x value
    return  (x+y); //calculate x+y and return that value
    return  -5; //return -5
```

In the following example, we have taken a method `myMethod()` that accepts an integer value, calculates square value of it, and returns that value to the `main()` method which is the calling method.

In the `main()` method, we are calling `myMethod()` and passing 10 to it as follows:

```
    Demo.myMethod(10);
```

Here, we are not using an object to call the method. Since it is a static method, we can call it as classname.methodname(), i.e. Demo.myMethod(10).

To receive the result returned from the method, we have taken an int type variable res as follows:

```
int res = Demo.myMethod(10);
```

And we have written myMethod() as:

```
static int myMethod(int num)
{
    return num*num; //return square value
}
```

Here, we declared the method as static and then int before the method name represents the type of value returned by the method. After the method name, we wrote int num, which is useful to receive the integer number into the method. This is nothing but the value 10 passed to the method at the time of calling it from main(). Now to calculate square value and return it, we used:

```
return num*num;
```

Thus, return statement is used to return some value from a method. Figure 6.1 will help to comprehend this.

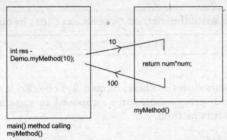

Figure 6.1 Calling a method and getting back result

Program 13: Write a program to return a value from a method.

```
//Calling a method and returning the result from the method.
class Demo
{
  public static void main(String args[])
  {
    //call myMethod() and catch the result into res.
    //since myMethod() is static, we can call it using classname.methodname()
    int res = Demo.myMethod(10);
    //display the result now
    System.out.println("Result= "+ res);
  }

  //this method calculates square value and returns it to main().
  static int myMethod(int num)
  {
    return num*num; //return square value
  }

}
```

Output:

```
C:\> javac Demo.java
```

```
C:\> java Demo
Result = 100
```

If we use `return` statement inside the `main()` method, then the entire program (or application) will be terminated and we come out to the system prompt. Let us try to understand this better with the help of an example.

Program 14: Write a program to demonstrate that the `return` statement in `main()` method terminates the application.

```java
//return inside main()
class Demo
{
  public static void main(String args[])
  {
    int x = 1;
    System.out.println("Before return");
    if(x == 1) return;   //terminate the application
    System.out.println("After return");
  }
}
```

Output:

```
C:\> javac Demo.java
C:\> java Demo
Before return
```

In this program, we can also write the method `System.exit(0);` in place of the statement:

```
if(x==1) return;
```

to terminate the application.

Here, `exit(0)` is a static method in the class, named `System`. So it can be called `System.exit(0)`. When calling `exit()` method, programmers are supposed to pass an `int` value to this method—generally 0 or 1 is passed to this method.

Important Interview Question

What is the difference between `return` *and* `System.exit(0)` *?*

`return` statement is used inside a method to come out of it. `System.exit(0)` is used in any method to come out of the program.

While calling `exit()` method of `System` class, we can give either 0 or 1 to it as `exit(0)` or `exit(1)`. Both will terminate the program, but 0 or 1 indicates the reason for termination. `exit(0)` represents normal termination while `exit(1)` represents termination due to some error in the program.

Important Interview Question

What is the difference between `System.exit(0)` *and* `System.exit(1)` *?*

`System.exit(0)` terminates the program normally. Whereas `System.exit(1)` terminates the program because of some error encountered in the program.

Conclusion

Control statements are very useful to a programmer for writing better and complex programs, since they are designed to implement any sort of logic. Whatever the programmer wishes to do in his program, he can do it with the help of control statements. This is the reason we see the control statements in almost all the languages and not just in Java.

INPUT AND OUTPUT

Input represents data given to a program and output represents data displayed as a result of a program. We are already familiar with the following two statements to display the output:

```
System.out.print();
System.out.println();
```

Both of these statements are used to display the output on the screen. The difference between these two is that `print()` method keeps cursor in the same line after displaying the output and `println()` method throws cursor to the next line after displaying the output.

Input to a program can be given directly inside the program or from outside through the keyboard also. If the input is given in the program itself, every time the same input is used by the program and the same result can be expected. For example, in a program we write:

```
int a,b;
a = 10;
b = 15;
int c = a + b;
System.out.println(c);
```

In this example, the values of a and b are taken as 10 and 15, respectively and the value of c is calculated and displayed. Even if this code is run several times, we get the value of c always as 25. It means that this code is useful to perform addition of the two numbers: 10 and 15 only.

If we want to extend this code to find sum of any two given numbers, we should first accept those two numbers from the keyboard into the program. But how can we accept data from the keyboard and use it in a program? This question is answered in this chapter.

Accepting Input from the Keyboard

A stream is required to accept input from the keyboard. A stream represents flow of data from one place to another place. It is like a water-pipe where water flows. Like a water-pipe carries water from one place to another, a stream carries data from one place to another place. A stream can carry data from keyboard to memory or from memory to printer or from memory to a file. A stream is always required if we want to *move* data from one place to another.

Basically, there are two types of streams: input streams and output streams. Input streams are those streams which receive or read data coming from some other place. Output streams are those streams which send or write data to some other place.

All streams are represented by classes in java.io (input and output) package. This package contains a lot of classes, all of which can be classified into two basic categories: input streams and output streams.

Keyboard is represented by a field, called in in System class. When we write System.in, we are representing a standard input device, i.e. keyboard, by default. System class is found in java.lang (language) package and has three fields as shown below. All these fields represent some type of stream:

❑ **System.in:** This represents InputStream object, which by default represents standard input device, i.e. keyboard.

❑ **System.out:** This represents PrintStream object, which by default represents standard output device, i.e. monitor.

❑ **System.err:** This field also represents PrintStream object, which by default represents monitor.

Note that both System.out and System.err can be used to represent the monitor and hence any of these two can be used to send data to the monitor.

Important Interview Question

What is the difference between System.out and System.err?

System.out and System.err both represent the monitor by default and hence can be used to send data or results to the monitor. But System.out is used to display normal messages and results whereas System.err is used to display error messages.

```
System.out.println("A normal message");
System.err.println("An error message");
```

So, the programmer can indicate what type of message he is displaying by using System.out or System.err.

To accept data from the keyboard, i.e. System.in, we need to connect it to an input stream as some input stream is needed to read data. Figure 7.1 shows the working in detail.

❑ Connect the keyboard to an input stream object. Here, we can use InputStreamReader that can read data from the keyboard.

```
InputStreamReader obj = new InputStreamReader(System.in);
```

In this statement, we are creating InputStreamReader object and connecting the keyboard (System.in) to it.

❑ Connect InputStreamReader to BufferedReader, which is another input type of stream. We are using BufferedReader as it has got methods to read data properly, coming from the stream.

```
BufferedReader br = new BufferedReader(obj);
```

Here, we are creating BufferedReader object (br) and connecting the InputStreamReader object (obj) to it.

In the above two steps, we got BufferedReader object (br). These two steps can be combined and rewritten in a single statement as:

```
BufferedReader br = new BufferedReader(new InputStreamReader(System.in));
```

❑ Now, we can read the data coming from the keyboard using `read()` and `readLine()` methods available in `BufferedReader` class.

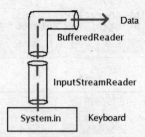

Figure 7.1 Reading data from keyboard

Accepting a Single Character from the Keyboard

Now, follow these steps in order to accept a single character from the keyboard.

❑ Create a `BufferedReader` class object (`br`).

❑ Then, read a single character from the keyboard using `read()` method as:

```
char ch = br.read();
```

Here, the `read()` method reads a single character from the keyboard but it returns its ASCII number, which is an integer. Since, this integer number cannot be stored into character type variable `ch`, we should convert it into `char` type by writing `(char)` before the method as:

```
char ch = (char)br.read();
```

Here, `int` data type is converted into `char` type. Converting one data type into another data type is called *type casting* or simply *casting*. To convert `int` into `char`, we are writing `(char)` before the method or a variable. This is called *cast operator*.

If `read()` method could not accept a character due to some reason (like insufficient memory or illegal character), then it gives rise to a runtime error which is called by the name `IOException`, where `IO` stands for Input/Output) and `Exception` represents runtime error.

So, when `read()` method is giving `IOException`, as a programmer, it is our duty to do something in case of the exception. This is called *exception handling*. Since, at this moment we do not know how to handle exceptions, let us throw this exception without handling it by writing:

`throws IOException` at the side of the method where `read()` is used.

These concepts are used in the following program while receiving a single character from the keyboard.

Program 1: To accept and display a character from the keyboard

```
//Accepting a single character from keyboard
import java.io.*;
class Accept
{
    public static void main(String args[]) throws IOException
    {
        //create BufferedReader object to accept data from keyboard
        BufferedReader br = new BufferedReader(new
        InputStreamReader(System.in));
```

```
                  //ask for char and read it
                  System.out.print("Enter a character: ");
                  char ch = (char)br.read();

                  //display the character
                  System.out.println("You entered: "+ ch);
            }
      }
```

Output:

```
C:\> javac Accept.java
C:\> java Accept
Enter a character: A
You entered: A

C:\> java Accept
Enter a character: XXX
You entered: X
```

If you observe the output, you can understand that read() method is accepting only one character. It cannot be used to accept a string (a group of characters).

To read a string, we need readLine() method of BufferedReader class.

Accepting a String from Keyboard

Observe the statement, where readLine() method is called using BufferedReader object (br):

```
String str = br.readLine();
```

Here, readLine() method accepts a string from the keyboard and returns the string into str. In this case, casting is not needed since readLine() is taking a string and returning the same data type. But this method can give rise to the runtime error: IOException, which can be thrown out without handling by using the statement:

```
throws IOException.
```

Program 2: Accepting a name (string) from the keyboard

```
//Accepting a string from keyboard
import java.io.*;
class Accept
{
    public static void main(String args[]) throws IOException
    {
        //create BufferedReader object to accept data from keyboard
        BufferedReader br = new BufferedReader(new InputStreamReader(System.in));

        //ask for string and read it
        System.out.print("Enter a name: ");
        String name = br.readLine();

        //display the string
        System.out.println("You entered: "+ name);
    }
}
```

Output:

```
C:\> javac Accept.java
C:\> java Accept
Enter a name: Vijay
You entered: Vijay
```

Accepting an Integer Value from the Keyboard

Now, let us follow these steps to accept an integer from the keyboard.

❑ First, we should accept the integer number from the keyboard as a string, using `readLine()` as:

```
String str = br.readLine();
```

❑ Now, the number is in `str`, i.e. in form of a string. This should be converted into an int by using `parseInt()` method of `Integer` class as:

```
int n = Integer.parseInt(str);
```

If needed, the above two statements can be combined and written as:

```
int n = Integer.parseInt(br.readLine());
```

Here, `parseInt()` is a static method in `Integer` class, so it can be called using class name as `Integer.parseInt()`

Let us observe a point here. We are not using casting to convert `String` type into `int` type. The reason is `String` is a class and `int` is a fundamental data type. Converting a class type into a fundamental data type is not possible by using *casting*. It is possible by using the method `Integer.parseInt()`. Remember, casting is useful to convert one fundamental data type into another fundamental data type or one class type into another class type. We cannot use casting to convert a class type into a fundamental data type or vice versa.

Program 3: Accepting an integer from keyboard.

```
//Accepting an int from keyboard
import java.io.*;
class Accept
{
    public static void main(String args[]) throws IOException
    {
        //create BufferedReader object to accept data from keyboard
        BufferedReader br = new BufferedReader(new InputStreamReader(System.in));

        //ask for integer and read it
        System.out.print("Enter an int value: ");
        int num = Integer.parseInt(br.readLine());

        //display the int
        System.out.println("You entered: "+ num);
    }
}
```

Output:

```
C:\> javac Accept.java
C:\> java Accept
```

```
Enter an int value: 457890
You entered: 457890
```

Accepting a Float Value from Keyboard

Just like an integer value, we can also accept a float value in the following way:

```
float n = Float.parseFloat(br.readLine());
```

In this statement, we are accepting a float in the form of a string using `br.readLine()` and then passing the string to `Float.parseFloat()` to convert it into float. `parseFloat()` is a static method in `Float` class.

Program 4: Accepting a float number.

```java
//Accepting a float value from keyboard
import java.io.*;
class Accept
{
   public static void main(String args[]) throws IOException
   {
      //create BufferedReader object to accept data from keyboard
      BufferedReader br = new BufferedReader(new InputStreamReader(System.in));

      //ask for float and read it
      System.out.print("Enter a float value: ");
      float n = Float.parseFloat(br.readLine());

      //display the float
      System.out.println("You entered: "+ n);
   }
}
```

Output:

```
C:\> javac Accept.java
C:\> java Accept
Enter a float value: 44.556
You entered: 44.556
```

Accepting a Double Value

We can accept a double value from the keyboard with the help of the following statement.

```
double n = Double.parseDouble(br.readLine());
```

Here, we are accepting a double in the form of a string using `br.readLine()` and then passing the string to `Double.parseDouble()` to convert it into primitive data type `double`. Let us know that `parseDouble()` is a static method in `Double` class.

Accepting Other Types of Values

Similarly, we can write different statements to accept many other data types from the keyboard as follows:

❑   To accept a byte value:

```
byte n = Byte.parseByte(br.readLine());
```

❑ To accept a short value:

```
short n = Short.parseShort(br.readLine());
```

❑ To accept a long value:

```
long n = Long.parseLong(br.readLine());
```

❑ To accept a boolean value:

```
boolean x = Boolean.parseBoolean(br.readLine());
```

In the above discussion, we used the classes, such as Byte, Short, Integer, Long, Float, Double, and Boolean, which belong to java.lang package. These classes are also called *wrapper classes*. We will have a complete look at wrapper classes in later chapters.

Since we know how to accept various data types, let us write a small program to accept an employee details and display them again.

Program 5: Accepting and displaying employee details.

```
//Employee details
import java.io.*;
class EmpData
{
    public static void main(String args[]) throws IOException
    {
        //create BufferedReader object to accept data
        BufferedReader br = new BufferedReader(new
        InputStreamReader(System.in));

        //accept employee details
        System.out.print("Enter id: ");
        int id = Integer.parseInt(br.readLine());

        System.out.print("Enter sex (M/F): ");
        char sex = (char)br.read();

        System.out.print("Enter name: ");
        String name = br.readLine();

        //display the employee details
        System.out.println("Id= "+ id);
        System.out.println("Sex= "+ sex);
        System.out.println("Name= "+ name);
    }
}
```

Output:

```
C:\> javac EmpData.java
C:\> java EmpData
Enter id: 10
Enter sex (M/F): M
Enter name: Id= 10
Sex= M
Name=
```

Please observe the output of Program 5. After accepting sex of the employee, it is not accepting the name of employee and is displaying blank for name. The reason is that we used read() method to accept the sex value and then readLine() is used to accept the name. When we type M for sex and press Enter, then it releases a \n code. So at sex column, we are giving two characters M and \n.

But, `read()` method takes only the first character and rejects the next character, i.e. \n, which is trapped by the next `readLine()` method, as shown in Figure 7.2. So, name is not accepted by `readLine()` as it already contains \n.

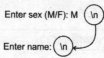

Enter sex (M/F): M \n

Enter name: \n

Figure 7.2 The readLine() method trapping the \n code

There are two ways to overcome this problem.

❑ One solution is to use `readLine()` method to accept the single character while accepting the sex of employee. We can write it as follows:

```
System.out.print("Enter sex (M/F): ");
char sex = br.readLine().charAt(0);
```

In the above statement, we are first accepting the input for sex as a string, i.e. M\n using `readLine()`. Then, we are retrieving the 0th character, i.e. only M from it and returning it into sex variable. This is done by `charAt(0)` method.

❑ Clearing the \n code from `BufferedReader` object, so that the character is not carried into next `readLine()`.

For this purpose, we can use `skip()` method of `BufferedReader`, which helps in skipping a specified number of characters. Suppose we take \n as two characters; now to skip them, we can write `br.skip(2)`;

Now let us see the modified version of the program.

Program 6: Accepting and displaying employee details – version 2

```
//Employee details
import java.io.*;
class EmpData
{
    public static void main(String args[]) throws IOException
    {
        //create BufferedReader object to accept data
        BufferedReader br = new BufferedReader(new
        InputStreamReader(System.in));

        //accept employee details
        System.out.print("Enter id: ");
        int id = Integer.parseInt(br.readLine());

        System.out.print("Enter sex (M/F): ");
        char sex = (char)br.read();
        //Solution1: char sex = br.readLine().charAt(0);

        //Solution2: skip 2 characters
        br.skip(2);

        System.out.print("Enter name: ");
        String name = br.readLine();

        //display the employee details
        System.out.println("Id= "+ id);
        System.out.println("Sex= "+ sex);
        System.out.println("Name= "+ name);
    }
}
```

Output:

```
C:\> javac EmpData.java
C:\> java EmpData
Enter id: 10
Enter sex (M/F): M
Enter name: Kumar
Id= 10
Sex= M
Name= Kumar
```

From the above program, we can understand that in Java if we want to accept input, we can accept only one input at a time. For example, we are accepting id first, then sex, and then name of the employee—one by one. There is no way of accepting all the three types at a time (in a line) from the keyboard in Java. This is possible in C language using scanf() and in C++ using cin functions.

Accepting Different Types of Inputs in a Line

It is possible to simulate scanf() of C language in Java, where we can receive several inputs at a time in a single line. To achieve the effect of scanf(), we can use StringTokenizer class of java.util (utility) package. StringTokenizer is useful to break a string into small pieces called *tokens*. Let us follow these steps to understand how it is done.

❑ First receive a string str from the keyboard, which contains different types of inputs. Assume that the inputs are separated by commas.

```
String str = br.readLine();
```

❑ Pass this string str to StringTokenizer object, so that it will be broken into pieces wherever a comma is found. These tokens will be stored in StringTokenizer object st.

```
StringTokenizer st = new StringTokenizer(str, ",");
```

In the above statement, str is the string which is split into tokens and which represents the character from where to split the string. This comma is also called *delimiter*. Suppose we want to split the string where a space is found, we can use a space as delimiter as:

```
StringTokenizer st = new StringTokenizer(str, " ");
```

❑ Collect the individual tokens from st using nextToken() method of StringTokenizer class.

```
String token = st.nextToken();
```

❑ These individual tokens represent the different types of inputs given. These tokens can be converted into corresponding data types and can be used in the program.

By using these steps, let us now write a Java program to accept name, age, and salary of a person at a time and display them again.

Program 7: To accept different types of input in a line at a time from the keyboard, just like one can do using scanf() in C

We assume that the different values of input are separated by commas.

```
//Accepting different inputs in a line
import java.io.*;
import java.util.*;
class Different
```

```
{
        public static void main(String args[]) throws IOException
        {
                //to accept data from keyboard
                BufferedReader br = new BufferedReader(new
                InputStreamReader(System.in));

                //ask for input - separated by commas
                System.out.print("Enter name, age, salary: ");

                //accept input into a string
                String str = br.readLine();

                //use StringTokenizer to split input at commas
                StringTokenizer st = new StringTokenizer(str, ",");

                //we will have 3 tokens as strings
                //first token represents name, second one age, third one salary
                String s1 = st.nextToken();
                String s2 = st.nextToken();
                String s3 = st.nextToken();

                //trim any spaces before and after the tokens
                s1 = s1.trim();
                s2 = s2.trim();
                s3 = s3.trim();

                //convert s1 into string, s2 into an int and s3 into a float
                String name = s1;
                int age =  Integer.parseInt(s2);
                float sal = Float.parseFloat(s3);

                //display the entered data
                System.out.println("Name= "+ name);
                System.out.println("Age= "+ age);
                System.out.println("Salary= "+ sal);
        }
}
```

Output:

```
C:\> javac Different.java
C:\> java Different
Enter name, age, salary: Vijaya Gopal, 25, 12000.75
Name= Vijaya Gopal
Age= 25
Salary= 12000.75
```

Now let us write a program to accept any two numbers from keyboard and find the results of addition, subtraction, multiplication, and division operations on them.

Program 8: To perform different arithmetic operations on given numbers.

```
//Performing arithmetic operations.
import java.io.*;
import java.util.*;
class Arithmetic
{
        public static void main(String args[]) throws IOException
        {
                //to accept data from keyboard
                BufferedReader br = new BufferedReader(new
                InputStreamReader(System.in));

                //take input into str from keyboard
                System.out.print("Enter two numbers: ");
```

```
            String str = br.readLine();

            //split the string at comma
            StringTokenizer st = new StringTokenizer(str, ",");

            //take the two tokens into s1, s2
            String s1 = st.nextToken();
            String s2 = st.nextToken();

            //trim the spaces in s1, s2
            s1 = s1.trim();
            s2 = s2.trim();

            //convert s1 and s2 into double type and store in n1, n2
            double n1 = Double.parseDouble(s1);
            double n2 = Double.parseDouble(s2);

            //perform the arithmetic operations
            System.out.println("Result of addition: "+ (n1 + n2));
            System.out.println("Result of subtraction: "+ (n1 - n2));
            System.out.println("Result of multiplication: "+ (n1 * n2));
            System.out.println("Result of division: "+ (n1 / n2));
        }
}
```

Output:

```
C:\> javac Arithmetic.java
C:\> java Arithmetic
Enter two numbers: 20.5, 10
Result of addition:  30.5
Result of subtraction: 10.5
Result of multiplication: 205.0
Result of division: 2.05
```

Let us write another program to test whether a given year is leap or not. The following logic can be used for doing so:

❑ If the year is representing the beginning of a new century like 1900, 2000, 2100, 2200, etc. it should be divisible by 400. Then it is called leap year. To know whether the given year is century year or not, we should divide it by 100. If it is divisible by 100, then it is a century year.

❑ If the year is not a century year like 1998, 2007, 2010, etc. it should be divisible by 4. Then it becomes leap year.

❑ If any of the above two cases are satisfied, then that year is called leap year, otherwise it is not a leap year.

From this discussion, we can conclude that a year is leap only when any one of the following two conditions is true.

❑ if (year % 100 ==0 && year % 400 == 0)

❑ if (year % 100 != 0 && year % 4 ==0)

Please observe how the same steps are implemented in the logic of Program 9.

Program 9: To accept a year number from the keyboard and test if it is leap or not.

```
//Leap year or not
import java.io.*;
class Leap
{
      public static void main(String args[]) throws IOException
      {
            //accept year
            BufferedReader br = new BufferedReader(new
```

```
                InputStreamReader(System.in));

        System.out.print("Enter year no: ");
        int year = Integer.parseInt(br.readLine());

        //if it is century year and divisible by 400
        if(year % 100 ==0 && year % 400==0)
        System.out.println("It is leap");
        //if it is not a century year and divisible by 4
        else if(year % 100 !=0 && year % 4==0)
        System.out.println("It is leap");
        //other wise, it is not leap year
        else System.out.println("It is not leap");
    }
}
```

Output:

```
C:\> javac Leap.java
C:\> java Leap
Enter year no: 2007
It is not leap
C:\> java Leap
Enter year no: 1900
It is not leap
C:\> java Leap
Enter year no: 2000
It is leap
```

Let us now write another program in which we will learn to create Fibonacci series. Fibonacci numbers are the numbers which follow the series:

```
0,1,1,2,3,5,8,13,...
```

The first two Fibonacci numbers are taken as 0 and 1. The next Fibonacci number is generated by adding these two. So we get 0+1 = 1. The next Fibonacci number also follows the same rule. Any Fibonacci number is the sum of its two previous Fibonacci numbers.

In order to generate this series, first we should take two Fibonacci numbers as f1 and f2. The next Fibonacci number, say f, will be obtained by adding these two numbers.

```
f1 = 0;
f2 = 1;
f = f1+ f2;   //the next number is sum of the two previous numbers
```

Now, the two recent Fibonacci numbers are f2 and f. So, to get the next Fibonacci number, we should add them by taking them as f1 and f2:

```
f1 = f2;  //take f2 as f1
f2 = f;   //take f as f2
f= f1+ f2; //next Fibonacci no.
```

To repeatedly generate the Fibonacci numbers, we can use the above logic in a loop, as shown below:

```
while(count < n)  //here, count represents the number of fibonaccis generated
{
    f1 = f2;
    f2 = f;
    f = f1+f2;
    System.out.println(f);   //display the new Fibonacci no.
```

```
        count++;  //increment count since one more is generated
}
```

The same logic is shown in Figure 7.3 and also in subsequent Program 10.

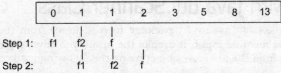

Step 1: f1 f2 f

Step 2: f1 f2 f

Figure 7.3 Logic to display Fibonacci numbers

Program 10: Generating Fibonacci numbers

```java
//Fibonacci number series
import java.io.*;
class Fibo
{
    public static void main(String args[]) throws IOException
    {
        //accept how many fibonaccis needed
        BufferedReader br = new BufferedReader(new
        InputStreamReader(System.in));

        System.out.print("How many fibonaccis? ");
        int n = Integer.parseInt(br.readLine());

        //take first two fibonaccis as 0 and 1
        long f1 =0, f2 =1;

        System.out.println(f1);
        System.out.println(f2);

        //find next fibonacci no.
        long f = f1+f2;
        System.out.println(f);

        //Already 3 fibonaccis are displayed. So count will start at 3
        int count = 3;
        while(count < n)
        {
            f1 = f2;
            f2 = f;
            f = f1+f2;
            System.out.println(f);
            count++;
        }
    }
}
```

Output:

```
C:\> javac Fibo.java
C:\> java Fibo
How many fibonaccis? 10
0
1
1
2
3
5
8
13
21
```

34

Reading Input with java.util.Scanner Class

We can use `Scanner` class of `java.util` package to read input from the keyboard or a text file. When the `Scanner` class receives input, it breaks the input into several pieces, called *tokens*. These tokens can be retrieved from the `Scanner` object using the following methods:

❑ `next()` – to read a string

❑ `next().charAt(0)` – to read a single char

❑ `nextByte()` – to read byte value

❑ `nextInt()` – to read an integer value

❑ `nextFloat()` – to read float value

❑ `nextLong()` – to read long value

❑ `nextDouble()` – to read double value

To read input from keyboard, we can use `Scanner` class as:

```
Scanner sc = new Scanner(System.in);
```

Now, if the user has given an integer value from the keyboard, it is stored into the `Scanner` object (`sc`) as a token. To retrieve that token, we can use the method: `sc.nextInt()`. The following program will make this concept clear.

Program 11: Let us write a program to read different types of data separated by space, from the keyboard using the `Scanner` class.

```
//Scanner to scan the input from keyboard
import java.util.Scanner;
class Ex3
{
     public static void main(String args[])
     {
             System.out.print("Enter id name sal: ");
             Scanner sc = new Scanner(System.in);

             int id = sc.nextInt();
             String name= sc.next();
             float sal = sc.nextFloat();

             System.out.println("Id= "+ id);
             System.out.println("Name= "+ name);
             System.out.println("Sal= "+ sal);
     }
}
```

Output:

```
C:\> javac Ex3.java
C:\> java Ex3
Enter id name sal:10 Gopal 8900.50
Id= 10
Name= Gopal
Sal= 8900.5
```

Displaying Output with System.out.printf()

To format and display the output, `printf()` method is available in `PrintStream` class. This method works similar to `printf()` function in C. We know that `System.out` returns `PrintStream` class object, so to call the `printf()` method, we can use: `System.out.printf()`.

The following format characters can be used in `printf()`:

❑ `%s` - string

❑ `%c` - char

❑ `%d` - decimal integer

❑ `%f` – float number

❑ `%o` – octal number

❑ `%b`, `%B` – boolean value

❑ `%x`, `%X` – hexadecimal number

❑ `%e`, `%E` – number in scientific notation

❑ `%n` – new line character

An example for using `printf()` is given below:

```
System.out.printf("Salary= %f", sal);
```

Here, the string `Salary=` will be displayed as it is in the output. After this, we have `%f`, which represents a format character to display a float value, i.e. `sal` value. So if `sal` variable has `8900.75`, then the output displayed by the above statement will be:

```
Salary= 8900.75
```

Program 12: To understand the use of `printf()`, let us write a Java program.

```
//printf() in Java
class Ex1
{
     public static void main(String args[])
     {
             String s1= "Hello";
             int n= 65;
             float f = 15.1234f;

             System.out.printf("String= %s%nnum= %d%nhexa decimal= %x%nfloat=
             %f", s1, n, n, f);

     }
}
```

Output:

```
C:\> javac Ex1.java
C:\> java Ex1
String= Hello
num=  65
hexa decimal= 41
float= 15.123400
```

Displaying Formatted Output with String.format()

If we want only a string that consists of formatted output, then we can take the help of format() method of String class. The format characters supported by System.out.printf() are also usable with format() method. Since, format() is a static method, we can call it as: String.format(). This method returns a string that contains the formatted output which can be processed and used as the programmer wants it.

Program 13: Understanding format() method to obtain a string that consists of formatted output.

```
//getting formatted output into a string.
class Ex2
{
    public static void main(String args[])
    {
        int i = 65;
        String s = "Hai";
        char ch = 'A';

        //format the output and get into str
        String str = String.format("i=%d%ns=%s%nch=%c", i,s,ch);
        System.out.println(str);
    }
}
```

Output:

```
C:\> javac Ex2.java
C:\> java Ex2
i=65
s=Hai
ch=A
```

Conclusion

We know already that System.out.print() and System.out.println() methods are useful to send output to the monitor. In many programs, the user wants to input values or data required by the program from the keyboard and hence BufferedReader class methods read() and readLine() are very useful. In this chapter, we discussed the techniques to accept input from the keyboard and wrote some programs to illustrate the same.

ARRAYS

Suppose a class contains 50 students, and we want to store their roll numbers, we need 50 separate variables for storing the roll numbers, as shown here:

```
int rno;
int rno1;
int rno2;
:
int rno49;
```

Now to store roll numbers into these variables, we need another 50 statements. Imagine writing 100 statements just to store the roll numbers of students. On the other hand, if we have a single variable which can represent all these 50 variables, it would be very useful to us. Such a variable is called an 'array'.

An array represents a group of elements of same data type. It can store a group of elements. So, we can store a group of int values or a group of float values or a group of strings in the array. But we can not store some int values and some float values in the array.

The advantage of using arrays is that they simplify programming by replacing a lot of statements by just one or two statements. In C /C++, by default, arrays are created on static memory unless pointers are used to create them. In Java, arrays are created on dynamic memory, i.e., allotted at runtime by JVM.

Important Interview Question

On which memory, arrays are created in Java?

Arrays are created on dynamic memory by JVM. There is no question of static memory in Java; every thing (variable, array, object etc.) is created on dynamic memory only.

Types of Arrays

Arrays are generally categorized into two parts as described here:

❑   Single dimensional arrays (or 1D arrays)

❑   Multi dimensional arrays (or 2D, 3D, ... arrays)

Single Dimensional Arrays (1D array)

A one dimensional (1D) or single dimensional array represents a row or a column of elements. For example, the marks obtained by a student in 5 different subjects can be represented by a 1D array, because these marks can be written as a row or as a column.

Creating a Single Dimensional Array

There are some ways of creating a single dimensional array as mentioned here:

❑ We can declare a one dimensional array and directly store elements at the time of its declaration, as:

```
int marks[ ] = {50, 60, 55, 67, 70};//declare marks[] and initialize with  5
                                     //elements
```

Here, 'int' represents integer type elements which can be stored into the array, and the array name is 'marks'. To represent a one dimensional array, we should use a pair of square braces [ ] after the array name. Then the actual elements (integers) are mentioned inside the curly { and } braces. Now JVM creates 5 blocks of memory as there are 5 elements being stored into the array. These blocks of memory can be individually referred to as marks[0], marks[1], marks[2],...marks[4]. Here, 0,1,2,...4 is called 'index' of the array. It refers to the element position in the array. A one dimensional array will have only one index. In general, any element of the array can be shown by writing marks[i], where i = 0,1,2,...4. Please see the Figure 8.1.

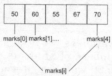

Figure 8.1 Arrangement of elements in a 1D array

❑ Another way of creating a one dimensional array is by declaring the array first and then allotting memory for it by using new operator.

```
int marks[ ];   //declare marks array
marks = new int[5];  //allot memory for storing 5 elements
```

These two statements can also be written by combining them into a single statement, as:

```
int marks[ ] = new int[5];
```

Here, we should understand that JVM allots memory for storing 5 integer elements into the array. But there are no actual elements stored in the array so far. To store the elements into the array, we can use statements like these in the program:

```
marks[0]= 50;
marks[1]= 60;
marks[2]= 55;
marks[3]= 67;
marks[4]= 70;
```

Or, we can pass the values from keyboard to the array by using a loop, as given here:

```
for(int i=0; i<5; i++)
{
        //read integer value from the keyboard and store into marks[i]
        marks[i] = Integer.parseInt(br.readLine());
}
```

Let us examine some more examples for 1D array:

❑   `float salary[ ] = {5670.55f, 12000f, 4500.75f, 3000.50f, 9050f};`

❑   `float salary[ ] = new float[50];`

❑   `char ch[ ] = {'a','b','c','d','e','f'};`

❑   `char ch[ ] = new char[6];`

❑   `String names[ ]= {"Raju", "Vijay", "Gopal", "Kiran"};`

❑   `String names[ ]= new String[10];`

Alternative Way of Writing One Dimensional Array

While writing a one dimensional array, we can write the pair of square braces before or after the array name, as:

❑   `float salary[ ] = {5670.55f, 12000f, 4500.75f, 3000.50f, 9050f};`

❑   `float[ ] salary = {5670.55f, 12000f, 4500.75f, 3000.50f, 9050f};`

The preceding statements are same and valid. Similarly, the following statements are also same:

❑   `String names[ ]= new String[10];`

❑   `String[ ] names = new String[10];`

Program 1: Write a program to create a 1D array and read its elements by using a loop and display them one by one.

To read and display a 1D array:

```
class Arr1
{
        public static void main(String args[])
        {
                //declare and initialize the array
                int arr[] = {50, 60, 55, 67, 70};
                //display all the 5 elements
                for(int i=0; i<5; i++)
                {
                        System.out.println(arr[i]);
                }
        }
}
```

Output:

```
C:\> javac Arr1.java
C:\> java Arr1
50
60
55
67
70
```

Usually a single loop is suitable to read the elements from a 1D array or to store elements into a 1D array. In the following program, let us take the marks obtained by a student from the keyboard and find their total and percentage of marks. Think about the logic to find the total marks. For this purpose, we take a variable 'tot' and initialize it to 0, as initially the total marks will be 0, like this:

```
int tot =0;
```

Then, add the elements one by one to 'tot' and store the result in 'tot', like this:

```
tot = tot + marks[i];
This can be also written as:
tot += marks[i];
```

Now, let us think about the logic to find the percentage. If the maximum mark in any subject is 100, then percentage can be obtained by dividing the total marks (tot) by the number of subjects (n), thus:

```
float percent = tot/n;
```

Since, tot and n are both integers, when an integer value is divided by another integer, by default only int value will be returned. This means if tot = 282 and n = 5, then percent value will be only 56.0. This is definitely wrong result. So to get the correct result, we should convert at least one of the variables tot or n into float type. This can be achieved by using casting, as given here:

```
float percent = (float) tot/n;
```

Here, we are converting the type of tot into float. So float divided by int value gives us correct float value. Now, percent value will be 56.4. Note that the data type of tot, i.e., 'int' is converted into 'float' type here. Converting a data type into another data type is called 'type casting' or simply 'casting'. And for this purpose, we wrote (float) before tot variable. Writing data type like this, in between simple braces before a variable or a method is called 'cast operator'.

Let us have a glance on another program.

Program 2: Write a program which accepts the marks of a student into a 1D array from the keyboard and finds total marks and percentage.

```java
//Total marks and percentage
import java.io.*;
class Arr2
{
    public static void main(String args[]) throws IOException
    {
        //to accept data from keyboard
        BufferedReader br = new BufferedReader(new
        InputStreamReader(System.in));

        //ask how many subjects
        System.out.print("How many subjects? ");
        int n = Integer.parseInt(br.readLine());

        //create 1D array with size n
        int[] marks = new int[n];

        //store elements into the array
        for(int i=0; i<n; i++)
        {
            System.out.print("Enter marks: ");
            marks[i]= Integer.parseInt(br.readLine());
        }

        //find total marks
        int tot = 0;
        for(int i=0; i<n; i++)
        tot += marks[i];

        //display total marks
        System.out.println("Total marks= "+ tot);

        //find percentage
        float percent = (float)tot/n;
        System.out.println("Percentage= "+ percent);
    }
}
```

Output:

```
C:\> javac Arr2.java
```

```
C:\> java Arr2
How many subjects? 5
Enter marks: 50
Enter marks: 60
Enter marks: 55
Enter marks: 50
Enter marks: 67
Total marks= 282
Percentage=  56.4
```

Let us write a program to accept a group of elements into an array and sort them into ascending order. For this purpose, let us use 'bubble sort' technique. In this technique, all the n elements from 0 to n-1 are taken and the first element of the array: arr[j] is compared with the immediate element arr[j+1]. If arr[j] is bigger than arr[j+1], then they are swapped (interchanged) since in ascending order, we expect the smaller elements to be in the first place. When two elements are interchanged, the number of elements to be sorted becomes lesser by 1. When there are no more swaps found, then the 'flag' will become false and we can abort sorting. This logic is implemented in the following Program 3.

Program 3: Write a program which performs sorting of group of integer values using bubble sort technique.

```java
// Sort a group of integers into ascending order
import java.io.*;
class Sort
{
        public static void main(String args[]) throws IOException
        {
                //to accept data from keyboard
                BufferedReader br = new BufferedReader(new
                InputStreamReader(System.in));

                //create an int type array
                System.out.print("How many elements? ");
                int n = Integer.parseInt(br.readLine());
                int arr[] = new int[n];

                //accept integer elements into the array
                for(int i=0; i<n; i++)
                {
                        System.out.print("Enter int: ");
                        arr[i] = Integer.parseInt(br.readLine());
                }

                //use bubble sort technique to sort the integers
                int limit = n-1; //elements from 0 to n-1
                boolean flag = false; //if it is true, swapping done
                int temp; //temporary variable

                for(int i=0; i<limit; i++)
                {
                        for(int j=0; j<limit-i; j++)
                        {
                                //if first element is bigger than second one, then
                                swap
                                if(arr[j] > arr[j+1])
                                {
                                        temp = arr[j];
                                        arr[j] = arr[j+1];
                                        arr[j+1] = temp;
                                        flag = true; //true -> swapping done
                                }
                        }
                        if(flag==false) break; //no swapping, so come out
                        else flag = false; //assign initial value
```

```
                    }

                //display the sorted array
                System.out.println("The sorted array is: ");
                for(int i=0; i<n; i++)
                System.out.println(arr[i]);
        }
    }
```

Output:

```
C:\> javac Sort.java
C:\> java Sort
How many elements? 5
Enter int: 50
Enter int: 23
Enter int: 11
Enter int: 99
Enter int: 23
The sorted array is:
11
23
23
50
99
```

Multi Dimensional Arrays (2D, 3D,... arrays)

Multi Dimensional arrays represent 2D, 3D,...arrays which are combinations of several earlier types of arrays. For example, a two dimensional array is a combination of two or more (1D) one dimensional arrays. Similarly, a three dimensional array is a combination of two or more (2D) two dimensional arrays. Let us understand the two dimensional arrays now.

Two dimensional arrays (2D array)

A two dimensional array represents several rows and columns of data. For example, the marks obtained by a group of students in five different subjects can be represented by a 2D array. If we write the marks of three students as:

❑ 50, 60, 55, 67, 70

❑ 62, 65, 70, 70, 81

❑ 72, 66, 77, 80, 69

The preceding marks represent a 2D array since it got 3 rows (no. of students) and in each row 5 columns (no. of subjects). There are totally 3X5 = 15 elements. We can take the first row itself as a 1D array. Similarly the second row is a 1D array and the third row is another 1D array. So the preceding 2D array contains three 1D arrays within it.

Creating a (2D) Two Dimensional Array

There are some ways of creating (2D) two dimensional array as mentioned here:

❑ We can declare a two dimensional array and directly store elements at the time of its declaration, as:

```
int marks[ ][ ] = {{50, 60, 55, 67, 70},
                   {62, 65, 70, 70, 81},
                   {72, 66, 77, 80, 69}};
```

Here, 'int' represents integer type elements stored into the array, and the array name is 'marks'. To represent a two dimensional array, we should use two pairs of square braces [ ][ ] after the array name. Each row of elements should be written inside the curly braces { and }. The rows and the elements in each row should be separated by commas. There are three rows and five columns in each row, so the JVM creates 3X5= 15 blocks of memory as there are 15 elements being stored into the array. These blocks of memory can be individually referred to as mentioned here:

```
marks[0][0], marks[0][1], marks[0][2], marks[0],[3], marks[0][4]
marks[1][0], marks[1][1], marks[1][2], marks[1],[3], marks[1][4]
marks[2][0], marks[2][1], marks[2][2], marks[2],[3], marks[2][4]
```

By observing the preceding elements, we can understand the rows which are starting from 0 to 2 and the columns are starting from 0 to 4. So any element can be referred in general as marks[i][j], where i represents row position and j represents column position. Thus, a two dimensional array has two indexes: i and j. Similarly we can expect three indexes in case of a three dimensional array. See the Figure 8.2.

	j=0	j=1	j=2	j=3	j=4
i = 0	50	60	55	67	70
i = 1	62	65	70	70	81
i = 2	72	66	77	80	69

Figure 8.2 Arrangement of elements in a 2D array

❑ Another way of creating a two dimensional array is by declaring the array first and then allotting memory for it by using new operator.

```
int marks[ ][ ];   //declare marks array
       marks = new int[3][5];  //allot memory for storing 15 elements
```

The preceding two statements can be written by combining them into a single statement, as:

```
int marks[ ][ ] = new int[3][5];
```

Here, JVM allots memory for storing 15 integer elements into the array. But there are no actual elements stored in the array so far. We can store these elements by accepting them from the keyboard or from within the program also.

Let us take some more examples for 2D arrays:

❑ float x[ ][ ] = {{1.1f, 1.2f, 1.3f, 1.4f},
                    {2.1f, 2.2f, 2.3f, 2.4f},
                    {3.1f, 3.2f, 3.3f, 3.4f}};

❑ double d[ ][ ] = {{20.2, -5.5}, {15.5, 30.331}};

❑ byte b[ ][ ] = new byte[20][50];

❑ String str[ ][ ] = new String[10][20];

Alternative Way of Writing Two Dimensional Arrays

While writing a two dimensional array, we can write the two pairs of square braces before or after the array name, as:

```
String str[ ][ ] = new String[10][20];
String[ ][ ] str = new String[10][20];
```

Let us write a program to take a 2D array and display its elements in a matrix form. A matrix represents a group of elements arranged in several rows and columns. So we can take a 2D array as a matrix.

Program 4: Write a program to take a 2D array and display its elements in the form of a matrix. To display the elements of 2D array, we use two for loops, the outer for loop represents the rows and the inner one represents the columns in each loop.

```
//Displaying a 2D array as a matrix
class Matrix
{
      public static void main(String args[])
      {
      //take a 2D array
      float x[ ][ ] = {{1.1f, 1.2f, 1.3f, 1.4f},
            {2.1f, 2.2f, 2.3f, 2.4f},
            {3.1f, 3.2f, 3.3f, 3.4f}};
            //read and display the array elements
            System.out.println("In matrix form");
            for(int i=0; i<3; i++)    //rows
            {
                  for(int j=0; j<4; j++) //columns in each row
                  {
                        System.out.print(x[i][j]+"\t");
                  }
                  System.out.println();  //next line
            }
      }
}
```

Output:

```
C:\> javac Matrix.java
C:\> java Matrix
1.1  1.2     1.3     1.4
2.1  2.2     2.3     2.4
3.1  3.2     3.3     3.4
```

A two dimensional array can be handled by using two loops. Similarly, a three dimensional array can be handled using three loops.

Let us write a program to find the transpose of a given matrix. The transpose of a matrix is defined as the matrix obtained by converting the rows as columns and columns as rows. Suppose we have a matrix with 3 rows and 4 columns. Its transpose matrix will have 4 rows and 3 columns.

In this program, we are using Scanner class to accept the input from the keyboard. First, connect keyboard to Scanner, as:

```
Scanner sc = new Scanner(System.in);
```

Now, whatever the int values supplied from the keyboard can be accepted by using sc.nextInt() method. This method accepts next integer value from the Scanner. So, by using this method in a loop, it is possible to accept all the integer elements of the array from the keyboard, as shown here:

```
for(int i=0; i<r; i++)
      for(int j=0; j<c; j++)
            arr[i][j] = sc.nextInt();
```

The outer loop is for rows and the inner loop represents columns. In these loops, one by one the elements are received by sc.nextInt() method and are assigned to the array arr[i][j].

Program 5: Write a program which accepts elements of a matrix and displaying its transpose.

```
//Transpose of a matrix.
import java.io.*;
import java.util.Scanner;
class Transpose
{
      public static void main(String args[]) throws IOException
      {
            //use Scanner to accept data from keyboard
            Scanner sc = new Scanner(System.in);
```

```
                    //accept rows, columns of a matrix
                    System.out.print("Enter rows, columns? ");
                    int r = sc.nextInt();
                    int c = sc.nextInt();

                    //create an array with size [r][c]
                    int arr[ ][ ] = new int[r][c];

                    //accept a matrix from keyboard
                    System.out.println("Enter elements of matrix: ");

                    for(int i=0; i<r; i++)
                    for(int j=0; j<c; j++)
                    arr[i][j] = sc.nextInt();

                    System.out.println("The transpose matrix: ");

                    //take columns as rows and vice versa and display
                    for(int i=0; i<c; i++)
                    {
                            for(int j=0; j<r; j++)
                            {
                                    System.out.print(arr[j][i]+ "  ");
                            }
                            System.out.print("\n");
                    }
            }
    }
```

Output:

```
C:\> javac Transpose.java
C:\> java Transpose
Enter rows, columns? 3 4
Enter elements of matrix:
1  2   3   4
5  6   7   8
9  9  -1   2
The transpose matrix:
1  5   9
2  6   9
3  7  -1
4  8   2
```

Three dimensional arrays (3D array)

We can consider a three dimensional array as a combination of several two dimensional arrays. This concept is useful when we want to handle group of elements belonging to another group. For example, a college has 3 departments: Electronics, Computers and Civil. We want to represent the marks obtained by the students of each department in 3 different subjects. We can write these marks as shown here:

Electronics department:

```
    Student1 marks: 50,51,52
    Student2 marks: 60,61,62
```

Computers department:

```
    Student1 marks: 70,71,72
    Student2 marks: 80,81,82
```

Civil department:

```
Student1 marks: 65,66,67
Student2 marks: 75,76,77
```

To store all these marks, department-wise, we need a three dimensional array as shown here:

```
int arr[ ][ ][ ] = {{{50,51,52}, {60,61,62}},
                     {{70,71,72}, {80,81,82}},
                     {{65,66,67}, {75,76,77}}};
```

Here, three pairs of square braces represent a 3D array and there are 3 rows representing the 3 departments. In each department, there are again two groups representing the marks of two students. Observe how the { and } curly braces are used to represent each group. Other ways of creating three dimensional arrays:

```
char x[ ][ ][ ] = new char[10][5][20];
float [ ][ ][ ]f = new float[5][6][10];
```

Program 6: Write a program in which we take a 3D array which consists of department wise student marks. There are 3 departments and in each department, there are 2 students and each student has marks in 3 subjects. We want to calculate total marks of each student.

```
//Three dimensional array
class ThreeD
{
    public static void main(String args[])
    {
        //declare three vars
        int dept, student, marks, tot=0;

        //take the marks of students in a 3D array
        int arr[ ][ ][ ] = {{{50,51,52}, {60,61,62}},
                            {{70,71,72}, {80,81,82}},
                            {{65,66,67}, {75,76,77}}};

        //display the marks from 3D array
        for(dept=0; dept<3; dept++)
        {
            System.out.println("Department "+(dept+1)+": ");
            for(student=0; student<2; student++)
            {
                System.out.print("Student "+(student+1)+" marks: ");
                for(marks=0; marks<3; marks++)
                {
                System.out.print(arr[dept][student][marks]+" ");
                tot += arr[dept][student][marks];
                }
                System.out.println("Total: "+ tot); //display total
                //marks of a student
                tot =0;  //reset total to 0
            }
            System.out.println();
        } //end of for loops
    }
}
```

Output:

```
C:\> javac ThreeD.java
C:\> java ThreeD
Department 1:
Student 1 marks: 50  51  52  Total: 153
```

```
Student 2 marks: 60  61  62  Total: 183

Department 2:
Student 1 marks: 70  71  72  Total: 213
Student 2 marks: 80  81  82  Total: 243

Department 3:
Student 1 marks: 65  66  67  Total: 198
Student 2 marks: 75  76  77  Total: 228
```

arrayname.length

If we want to know the size of any array, we can use the property 'length' of an array. arrayname.length returns an integer number which represents the size of an array.

For example, take the array arr[ ] with size 10 and there are three elements in it, as:

```
int arr[ ] = new int[10];  //size is 10
arr[0]= 50, arr[1]=55, arr[2]=60;  //number of elements is 3.
```

Now, arr.length gives 10. The array arr[ ] contained 3 elements, but 'length' property does not give the number of elements of the array. It gives only its size.

But, in case of a two or three dimensional array, 'length' property gives the number of rows of the array, as given here:

```
int arr[ ][ ] = new int[5][10];
int arr[ ][ ][ ] = new int[5][7][12];
```

In preceding two cases, arr.length gives 5.

Command Line Arguments

We have already learned in the earlier chapters that command line arguments represent the values passed to main() method. To catch and store these values, main() has a parameter, String args[ ] as:

```
public static void main(String args[ ])
```

Here, args[ ] is a one dimensional array of String type. So it can store a group of strings, passed to main() from outside by the user. The user should pass the values from outside, at the time of running the program at command prompt, as:

```
C:\> java  Prog  11  22  Vikas
```

The three values passed to main() at the time of running the program are 11, 22 and Vikas. These three values are automatically stored in the main() method's args[ ] in the form of strings. This is because, args[ ] is a String type array. Thus 11 is stored as a string in args[0], 22 is stored as a string in args[1] and Vikas is stored in args[2]. See the Figure 8.3.

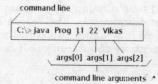

Figure 8.3 Command line and Command line arguments

Command line represents the run command and the values given at the time of running the program. Command line arguments represent the values passed to main() method. If there are three command line arguments, then JVM allots memory for those 3 values only. If there are no command line arguments, then JVM will not allot any memory. So the size of 'args' array is same as the number of arguments passed to it.

Let us write a Java program to understand how the command line arguments are stored in main() and how they can be accessed in main().

Program 7: Write a program to display the command line arguments.

```
//Command line arguments
class Prog
{
    public static void main(String args[ ])
    {
        //find number or arguments
        int n = args.length;
        System.out.println("No. of args= "+ n);

        //display all the arguments
        System.out.println("The args are: ");
        for(int i=0; i<n; i++)
        System.out.println(args[i]);

    }
}
```

Output:

```
C:\> javac Prog.java
C:\> java Prog 11 22 Vikas
No. of args= 3
The args are:
11
22
Vikas
```

Output:

```
C:\> java Prog 10 Subba Rao 5400.55
No. of args= 4
The args are:
10
Subba
Rao
5400.55
```

In Program 7, we passed 3 command line arguments at the time of running the program from command prompt. These 3 values are stored in args[ ] array in the form of strings. It means 11 is stored as a string, not as a number. Suppose we want to use 11 as a number in some arithmetic calculation, it should be converted into 'int' and then used. For this purpose, Integer.parseInt() method can be used. Similarly, we can convert a string into double by using Double.parseDouble() method. These methods were discussed in the Chapter 7.

Please observe the output of second time running the program 7. We passed actually 3 arguments, but the program is storing them in 4 arguments. The reason is the end of an argument which is recognized by the space character. So it is taking Subba Rao as two arguments. Now if we want to take "Subba Rao" as a single argument, we should enclose it in double quotes at the time of passing it, as:

```
C:\> java Prog 10 "Subba Rao" 5400.55
```

Now 10 is stored in `args[0]`, "Subba Rao" is stored in `args[1]` and 5400.55 is stored in `args[2]`. In the next program, we accept 2 numbers from command line and use them to calculate their sum.

Program 8: Write a program which performs addition of two numbers using command line args.

```
//Addition
class Prog
{
        public static void main(String args[])
        {
                //check if 2 args are not entered come out.
                if(args.length != 2)
                {
                        System.out.println("Please enter values");
                        return;
                }

                //take the numbers from args
                //they would be in string form
                String s1 = args[0];
                String s2 = args[1];

                //convert them into numerics
                double d1 = Double.parseDouble(s1);
                double d2 = Double.parseDouble(s2);

                //add them and display
                double d3 = d1+d2;
                System.out.println("The sum= "+ d3);
        }
}
```

Output:

```
C:\> javac Prog.java
C:\> java Prog 10 22.5
The sum= 32.5
```

Command line arguments are a way to provide input for the main() method. The programmer can provide the input and see the output given by the program at the command line. Apart from this, there is another way to provide input for main() method. That is, call the main() method from the main() method of another class and send the input.

Important Interview Question

Can you call the main() method of a class from another class?

Yes. We can call the main() method of a class from another class using Classname.main(). At the time of calling the main() method, we should pass a string type array to it.

In the following program, we write two classes: Class1 and Class2. Both the classes have main() methods. Since main() is a static method, we can call main() method of Class1 from Class2, as:

```
Class1.main();
```

But, at the time of calling the main() method, we should pass a string type array because main() has args[ ] array which is string type. So we create an array like this:

```
String names[ ] = {"Gopi", "Kamal", "Vinay", "Neeta Jain"};
```

And this array is sent to main() method of Class1 as:

```
Class1.main(names);
```

Thus, if we pass the name of the array, the entire array is passed to main() method.

Program 9: Write a program which calls the main() method of Class1 from Class2. In this, we pass names[ ] array to main() method at the time of call. This names[ ] is copied into args[ ] and hence we can display the contents of names[ ] in the main() method of Class1. Since we are calling Class1 from Class2, first of all Class2 should be executed by JVM, so we give this program name as Class2.java.

```
//calling main() of a Class1 from another class: Class2
class Class1
{
    public static void main(String args[ ])
    {
        //args contains names, display them
        for(String s: args)    //we are using for-each loop here
        System.out.println(s);
    }
}
class Class2
{
    public static void main(String args[ ])
    {
        //take a string type array
        String names[] = {"Gopi", "Kamal", "Vinay", "Neeta Jain"};

        //call main() of Class1  and pass the names array
        Class1.main(names);
    }
}
```

Output:

```
C:\> javac Class2.java
C:\> java Class2
Gopi
Kamal
Vinay
Neeta Jain
```

Jagged Arrays

A jagged array is an array that contains a group of arrays within it. It means we can create an array in Java such that other arrays can become its elements. This is a unique feature in Java. A jagged array can store single dimensional (1D) arrays or multi-dimensional (2D, 3D, etc.) arrays and also it can store arrays of any size. Jagged arrays are also called 'irregular multidimensional arrays'. Jagged arrays are useful when dealing with a group of arrays of different sizes.

To create a jagged array that can store two 1D arrays, we can write as:

```
int x[ ][ ] = new int[2][ ];
```

Here, x is the jagged array with size 2. So, its elements will be x[0] and x[1]. Observe last pair of empty square braces in the expression: new int[2][ ]. This last pair of braces represents 1D array. So, x[0] and x[1] can store two 1D arrays. Now, let us allot memory for x[0] and x[1] so that they can store two 1D arrays of different sizes, as:

```
x[0] = new int[2];  //memory for first array
x[1] = new int[3];  //memory for second array
```

So, the first array is represented by x[0] and can have 2 elements which can be referenced as:

```
x[0][0], x[0][1]
```

Similarly, the second array which is represented by x[1] can have 3 elements:

```
x[1][0], x[1][1], x[1][2].
```

The arrangement of memory for this jagged array is shown in the figure 8.4.

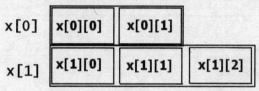

Figure 8.4 Jagged Array with size 2

In the same way, we can also create a jagged array that contains 2D arrays. For example,

```
double arr[ ][ ][ ] = new double[3][ ][ ];
```

Here, arr represents a jagged array with size 3. Observe the last two pairs of empty square braces. They represent 2D arrays. So, this jagged array can store 3 other 2 dimensional arrays. The elements arr[0], arr[1] and arr[2] represent them as:

```
arr[0] = new double[2][3];
arr[1] = new double[2][2];
arr[2] = new double[3][2];
```

The first 2D array can have 2 rows and 3 columns. Its elements can be referenced starting from arr[0][0][0] to arr[0][1][2]. The second 2D array can have 2 rows and 2 columns and its elements can be referenced from arr[1][0]0] to arr[1][1][1]. The third 2D array can have 3 rows and 2 columns and its elements can vary from arr[2][0][0] to arr[2][2][1].

The following program is useful to demonstrate how to create a jagged array that can store two 1D arrays.

Program 10: To create a jagged array that contains two 1D arrays.

```
//Jagged array that contains two 1D arrays
class Jagged
{
    public static void main(String args[])
    {
        //jagged array that can contain two 1D arrays
        int x[][] = new int[2][];

        //create 2 more 1D arrays as part of x
        x[0] = new int[2];  //2 elements in first array
```

```
        x[1] = new int[3];   //3 elements in second array

        //store 2 elements into first array
        x[0][0] = 10;
        x[0][1] = 11;

        //store 3 elements into second array
        x[1][0] = 12;
        x[1][1] = 13;
        x[1][2] = 14;

        //display first array
        for(int i=0; i<2; i++)
          System.out.print(x[0][i]+",");

        System.out.println();

        //display second array
        for(int i=0; i<3; i++)
          System.out.print(x[1][i]+",");

      }
  }
```

Output:

```
C:\> javac Jagged.java
C:\> java Jagged
10,11,
12,13,14,
```

Conclusion

In this chapter, you learnt that arrays are very useful for a programmer to handle a group of elements easily. But the restriction is that all the elements which are to be stored into the array should be of same data type. To store, retrieve and process elements of a 1D array, a single loop is much suitable. Similarly to work with a 2D array, two loops: a loop inside another loop is convenient. The main() method that is written in all Java programs has a parameter: args[ ], which is a String type array. The purpose of this array is to accept input from the user through command line. The same input can be used in the program by the programmer. We also discussed that every array has a property, arrayname.length which gives the size of the array.

STRINGS

Most of the data that transmits on Internet will be in the form of groups of characters. Such groups of characters are called 'strings'. For example, in a business order form, a person enters details like his name, credit card number, address, etc., which are all nothing but strings only. So a string represents a group of characters.

In C/C++ languages, a string represents an array of characters, where the last character will be '\0' (called null character). This last character being '\0' represents the end of the string. But this is not valid in Java. In Java, a string is an object of String class. It is not a character array. In Java, we got character arrays also, but strings are given a different treatment because of their extensive use on Internet. JavaSoft people have created a class separately with the name 'String' in java.lang (language) package with all necessary methods to work with strings.

Even though, String is a class, it is used often in the form of a data type, as:

```
String s = "Java";
```

Here, s is a variable of the data type 'String'.

Important Interview Question

Is String a class or data type?

String is a class in java.lang package. But in Java, all classes are also considered as data types. So we can take String as a data type also.

Can we call a class as a data type?

Yes, a class is also called 'user-defined' data type. This is because a user can create a class.

Creating Strings

There are three ways to create strings in Java:

❑ We can create a string just by assigning a group of characters to a string type variable:

```
String s; //declare String type variable
       s = "Hello"; //assign a group of characters to it
```

❑ Preceding two statements can be combined and written as:

```
String s = "Hello";
```

In this, case JVM creates an object and stores the string: "Hello" in that object. This object is referenced by the variable 's'. Remember, creating object means allotting memory for storing data.

❏ We can create an object to String class by allocating memory using new operator. This is just like creating an object to any class, like given here:

```
String s = new String("Hello");
```

Here, we are doing two things. First, we are creating object using new operator. Then, we are storing the string: "Hello" into the object.

❏ The third way of creating the strings is by converting the character arrays into strings. Let us take a character type array: arr[ ] with some characters, as:

```
char arr[ ] = {'c','h','a','i','r','s'};
```

❏ Now create a string object, by passing the array name to it, as:

```
String s = new String(arr);
```

Now the String object 's' contains the string: "chairs". This means all the characters of the array are copied into the string. If we do not want all the characters of the array into the string, then we can also mention which characters we need, as:

```
String s = new String(arr, 2,3);
```

Here, starting from 2nd character a total of 3 characters are copied into the string s. The original characters are c-h-a-i-r-s. Since counting starts from 0, the 0th character in the array is 'c' and the 2nd character is 'a'. Starting from 'a', a total of three characters implies 'air'. So these three characters are copied into the string s.

String Class Methods

Let us have a look at which methods are available in String class and how they can be used:

❏ String concat(String s)

Here, 'concat' is the method name. Since this method belongs to 'String' class, it can be called using a String class object as s1.concat(). Here, 's1' is a String class object. Please observe the 'String s' in the parenthesis after the method name. It represents that you should pass another String object to the concat() method while it is called. Something like this, s1.concat(s2). Again observe the word 'String' before the method name. This indicates that the method returns a String object, as a result.

So the preceding method can be used as:

```
String s3 = s1.concat(s2);
```

Now concat() method concatenates or joins two strings (s1 and s2) and returns a third string (s3) as a result. So, if s1="Hydera" and s2="bad", then we can expect s3 will be "Hyderabad".

The same concatenation can be done by using '+' operator which is called 'String concatenation operator'.

For example, we can use '+' as: s1+s2+s3. Here the three strings are joined by '+'.

- ❏ int length(): This method returns the length or number of characters of a string. For example, s1.length() gives the number of characters in the string s1.

- ❏ char charAt(int i): This method returns the character at the specified location i. Suppose we call this method as: s1.charAt(5), then it gives the 5th character in the string s1.

- ❏ int compareTo(String s): This method is useful to compare two strings and to know which string is bigger or smaller. This should be used as: s1.compareTo(s2). Now s1 and s2 are compared. If s1 and s2 strings are equal, then this method gives 0. If s1 is greater than s2, then it returns a positive number. If s1 is less than s2, then it returns a negative number.

When we arrange the strings in dictionary order, which ever string comes first is lesser than the string that comes next. Thus "Box" is lesser than "Boy". This method is case sensitive. This means, "BOX" and "box" are not same for this method.

- ❏ int compareToIgnoreCase(String s): This is same as 'compareTo()' method but this does not take the case of strings into consideration. This means "BOX" and "box" look same for this method.

- ❏ boolean equals(String s): This method returns true if two strings are same, otherwise false. This is case sensitive. We can use this method as: s1.equals(s2).

- ❏ boolean equalsIgnoreCase(String s): This is same as preceding but it performs case insensitive comparison.

- ❏ boolean startsWith(String s): This method returns true if a string is beginning with the sub string 's'. To call this method, we use the format s1.startsWith(s2). If s1 starts with s2 then it returns true, otherwise false. This method is case sensitive.

- ❏ boolean endsWith(String s): This method tests the ending of a string. If a string ends with the sub string 's', then it returns true, other wise false. This method is also case sensitive.

- ❏ int indexOf(String s): This method is called in the form, s1.indexOf(s2), and it returns an integer value. If s1 contains s2 as a sub string, then the first occurrence (position) of s2 in the string s1 will be returned by this method. For example, s1= "This is a book", s2= "is", to know the position of the substring s2 in s1, we write

```
int n = s1.indexOf(s2);
```

This method searches for substring "is" in the main string "This is a book". Please observe that the sub string is found at two positions, 2nd and 5th. But this method returns first position only, so it returns 2. If the substring is not found in the main string then this method returns some negative value.

- ❏ int lastIndexOf(String s): This method is similar to the preceding method, but returns the last occurrence of the sub string 's' in the main string. If 's' is not found, then it returns negative value.

- ❏ String replace(char c1, char c2): This method replaces all the occurrences of character 'c1' by a new character 'c2'. For example, s1 = "Hello" and we are using as s1.replace('l', 'x'), then the returned string will be "Hexxo".

- ❏ String substring(int i): This method is useful to extract sub string from a main string. It returns a new string consisting of all characters starting from the position 'i' until the end of the string. For example, s1.substring(5) returns characters starting from 5th character till the end of s1.

- ❏ String substring(int i1, int i2): This method returns a new string consisting of all characters starting from i1 till i2. The character at i2 is excluded. For example, s1.substring(5,10) returns the characters of s1 starting from 5th to 9th positions.

- ❏ String toLowerCase(): This method converts all characters of the string into lower case, and returns that lower-cased string.

❑ String toUpperCase(): This method converts all characters into upper case, and returns that upper-cased string.

❑ String trim(): This method removes spaces from the beginning and ending of a string. If a string is written as " Ravi Kiran ", the spaces before "Ravi" and after "Kiran" are unnecessary and should be removed. This is achieved by trim(). Note that this method does not remove the spaces in the middle of the string. For example, the space between "Ravi" and "Kiran" is not removed.

❑ void getChars(int i1, int i2, char arr[ ], int i3): This method copies characters from a string into a character array. The characters starting from position i1 to i2-1 in the string are copied into the array 'arr' to a location starting from i3. Counting of characters in the string will start from 0th position.

❑ String[ ] split(delimiter): This method is useful to break a string into pieces at places represented by the delimiter. The resultant pieces are returned into a String type array. Suppose, the delimiter is a comma, then the string is cut into pieces wherever a comma (,) is found. Let us have a look on program which will help us to understand strings.

Program 1: Write a program which will help us to understand how to create strings and how to use some important methods of String class.

```java
//Demo of String class methods
class StrDemo
{
    public static void main(String args[ ])
    {
        //create strings in 3 ways
        String s1= "A book on Java";
        String s2= new String("I like it");
        char arr[]= {'D','r','e','a','m','t','e','c','h','
        ','P','r','e','s','s'};
        String s3= new String(arr);

        //display all the 3 strings
        System.out.println(s1);
        System.out.println(s2);
        System.out.println(s3);

        //find length of first string
        System.out.println("Length of s1= "+ s1.length());

        //concatenate two strings
        System.out.println("s1 and s2 joined= "+ s1.concat(s2));

        //concatenate three strings with +
        System.out.println(s1+" from "+ s3);

        //test if string s1 starts with A
        boolean x= s1.startsWith("A");
        if(x) System.out.println("s1 starts with \'A\'");
        else System.out.println("s1 does not start with \'A\'");

        //extract substring from s2, starting from 0th char to 6th char
        String p = s2.substring(0,7);

        //extract substring from s3, starting from 0th char to 8th char
        String q = s3.substring(0,9);

        //concatenate the strings p and q
        System.out.println(p+q);

        //convert s1 into uppercase and lowercase
        System.out.println("Upper s1= "+s1.toUpperCase());
        System.out.println("Lower s1= "+s1.toLowerCase());
    }
}
```

```
        }
```

Output:

```
C:\> javac StrDemo.java
C:\> java StrDemo
A book on Java
I like it
Dreamtech Press
Length of s1= 14
s1 and s2 joined= A book on JavaI like it
A book on Java from Dreamtech Press
s1 starts with 'A'
I like Dreamtech
Upper s1= A BOOK ON JAVA
Lower s1= a book on java
```

To understand how to convert a string into a character array, we can use getChars() method. If the string is 'str' and the array is 'arr', then we can use this method, for example, as:

```
str.getChars(7,21,arr,0);
```

It means we are copying from 7th character to 20th character (21st character is not copied) into 'arr'. These characters are copied starting from the position 0 onwards in the array. Now notice the Program 2.

Program 2: Let us take a string and copy some of the characters of the string into a character array 'arr' using getChars() method.

```java
//Copying a string into an array
class Strcpy
{
    public static void main(String args[ ])
    {
        String str = "Hello, this is a book on Java";
        char arr[ ] = new char[20];

        //copy from str into arr starting from 7th character to 20th
        character
        str.getChars(7,21,arr,0);

        System.out.println(arr);
    }
}
```

Output:

```
C:\> javac Strcpy.java
C:\> java Strcpy
this is a book
```

Let us write another program to understand how to split a string into several pieces. For this purpose, split() method is used. This method is used as:

```
s = str.split("delimiter");
```

Here, "delimiter" is a string that contains a character or group of characters which represent where to split the string. For example, a space as a delimiter splits the string wherever a space is found. A comma splits it at a comma, and a colon splits it at a colon in the string. After splitting is done, the pieces are stored into a String type array 's'. This can be seen in the Program 3.

Program 3: Write a program for splitting a string into pieces wherever a space is found.

```
//Splitting a string
class Strsplit
{
        public static void main(String args[ ])
        {
                //take a string str which is to be broken
                String str = "Hello, this is a book on Java";

                //declare a string type array s to store pieces
                String s[ ];

                //split the string where a space is found in str
                s = str.split(" ");

                //display the pieces from s
                for(int i=0; i<s.length; i++)
                System.out.println(s[i]);
        }
}
```

Output:

```
C:\> javac Strsplit.java
C:\> java Strsplit
Hello,
this
is
a
book
on
Java
```

String Comparison

The relational operators like >, >=, <, <=, == and != cannot be used to compare the strings. On the other hand, methods like: compareTo() and equals() should be used in string comparison.

Program 4: Let us write a program to compare two strings using '==' operator, and see the result.

```
//String comparison using ==
class Strcompare
{
        public static void main(String args[ ])
        {
                String s1= "Hello";
                String s2= new String("Hello");

                if(s1==s2)
                System.out.println("Both are same");
                else System.out.println("Not same");
        }
}
```

Output:

```
C:\> javac Strcompare.java
C:\> java Strcompare
Not same
```

When an object is created by JVM, it returns the memory address of the object as a hexadecimal number, which is called *object reference*. When a new object is created, a new reference number is allotted to it. It means every object will have a unique reference.

What is object reference?

Object reference is a unique hexadecimal number representing the memory address of the object. It is useful to access the members of the object.

Inspite of the fact that both the strings s1 and s2 are same, we are getting wrong output in Program 4. Let us take the first statement:

```
String s1= "Hello";
```

When JVM executes the preceding statement, it creates an object on heap and stores "Hello" in it. A reference number, say 3e25a5 is allotted for this object.

Similarly when the following statement is executed,

```
String s2= new String("Hello");
```

JVM creates another object and hence allots another reference number, say 19821f. So the statement, if(s1==s2) will compare these reference numbers, i.e., 3e25a5 and 19821f. Both are not same and hence the output will be "Not same". Actually, we should compare the contents of the String objects, not their references. This is the reason == is not used to compare the strings. See the Figure 9.1.

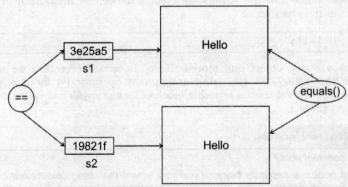

Figure 9.1 Comparing the strings using == and equals()

To compare the contents of String objects, we should use 'equals()'method, as shown here:

```
if(s1.equals(s2))
     System.out.println("Both are same");
     else System.out.println("Not same");
```

Now, we can get the output "Both are same" which is correct.

Important Interview Question

What is the difference between == and equals() while comparing strings? Which one is reliable?

== operator compares the references of the string objects. It does not compare the contents of the objects. equals() method compares the contents. While comparing the strings, equals() method should be used as it yields the correct result.

Program 5: Let us re-write the earlier program with a slight change in creation of strings.

```
//String comparison using ==
class Strcompare
{
     public static void main(String args[ ])
     {
             String s1= "Hello";
             String s2= "Hello";

             if(s1==s2)
             System.out.println("Both are same");
             else System.out.println("Not same");
     }
}
```

Output:

```
C:\> javac Strcompare.java
C:\> java Strcompare
Both are same
```

In Program 5, please notice how the strings are created as well as the output of the program also. The first statement in the program is:

```
String s1 = "Hello";
```

Here, JVM creates a String object and stores "Hello" in it. Observe that we are not using new operator to create the string. We are using assignment operator (=) for this purpose. So, after creating the String object, JVM uses a separate block of memory which is called *string constant pool*, and stores the object there.

Important Interview Question

What is a string constant pool?

String constant pool is a separate block of memory where the string objects are held by JVM. If a string object is created directly, using assignment operator as: String s1= "Hello", then it is stored in string constant pool.

When the next statement, `String s2 = "Hello";` is executed by the JVM, it searches in the string constant pool to know whether the object with same content is already available there or not. Since, the same object is already available there (which is s1), then JVM does not create another object. It simply creates another reference variable (s2) to the same object, and copies the reference number of s1 into s2. So, we have same value in s1 and s2. Hence, the output "Both are same". Please see Figure 9.2.

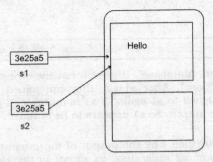

String constant pool

Figure 9.2 String comparison when the strings are created using assignment

Important Interview Question

Explain the difference between the following two statements:

1. String s = "Hello";
2. String s = new String("Hello");

In the first statement, assignment operator is used to assign the string literal to the String variable s. In this case, JVM first of all checks whether the same object is already available in the string constant pool. If it is available, then it creates another reference to it. If the same object is not available, then it creates another object with the content "Hello" and stores it into the string constant pool.

In the second statement, new operator is used to create the string object. In this case, JVM always creates a new object without looking in the string constant pool.

Immutability of Strings

We can divide objects broadly as, mutable and immutable objects. Mutable objects are those objects whose contents can be modified. Immutable objects are those objects, once created can not be modified. And String class objects are *immutable*. Let us take a program to understand whether the String objects are immutable or not.

Program 6: Write a program to test the immutability of strings.

```
//Immutable or Mutable?
class Test
{
    public static void main(String args[])
    {
        String s1 = "data";
        String s2 = "base";

        //join s1 and s2 and store in s1
        s1 = s1+s2;
        System.out.println(s1);

    }
}
```

Output:

```
C:\> javac Test.java
C:\> java Test
Database
```

Please observe the statement:

```
s1 = s1+s2;
```

And the output of the program, "database". It seems that the string s1 content is modified. Earlier s1 got "data" and s2 had "base". After s1+s2, they are joined and the total string becomes "database". This string is assigned to s1 again. If s1 is mutable, it gets the new string "database". This is what we can see in the output. So s1 appears to be mutable. But we learned that strings are immutable.

s1 is definitely immutable. But then why the output of the program is like that? In the program, JVM creates two objects, s1 and s2 separately, as shown in the Figure 9.3. When s1+s2 is done, JVM creates a new object and stores the string "database" in that object. But it does not modify the contents of the string s1. After creating the new object, the reference s1 is adjusted to refer to that new object. The point we should observe here is that the contents of the string s1 are not modified. This is the reason, strings are called immutable. The old object that contains "data" has lost its reference. So it is called 'unreferenced object' and garbage collector will remove it from memory.

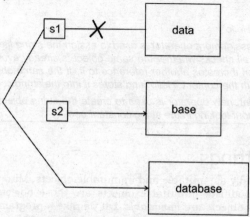

Figure 9.3 Immutability of String objects

Because String class objects are immutable, their contents can not be modified between various applications. So, different applications can share the contents of String class objects. This is the reason why String objects are made immutable. To maintain the immutable nature, none of the String class methods should be able to modify the contents of the objects. So, JavaSoft people did not provide the methods in String class which modify the contents of the same object. Whenever we try to modify the contents, JVM will create a new object with modified data. It will not modify the same object. Also there should not be any scope to override those String class methods. This is the reason, String class is made 'final' class. The methods of a final class cannot be overridden. The concepts of final class and method overriding will be discussed in detail later.

Let us write a program to search for a string in a given group of strings. In this program, first of all, we accept the strings from keyboard and store them in a string type array str[ ]. Then we ask the user to enter the string to be searched. Let this string be 'search'. Then the logic is to compare the 'search' string with each string of the array str[ ] using equals() or equalsIgnoreCase() methods, as:

```
if(search.equalsIgnoreCase(str[i]))
{
        System.out.println("Found at position: "+ (i+1));
}
```

Here, we are making case insensitive comparison. If the search string is found in the array str[ ], then the position of the string in the array will be 'i'. Since i values in the array start from 0 onwards, and our counting will start from 1, we add 1 to i value found. So i+1 gives the position of the string in the array. Here, we are comparing 'search' with str[i], where i represents all the strings in the array one by one. This type of searching is called 'linear search' or 'sequential search'.

Program 7: Search for a given string in an array of strings. This is achieved by comparing the searching string with each of the array elements one by one in a loop.

```java
//Searching for a string - Linear search
import java.io.*;
class Search
{
        public static void main(String args[ ]) throws IOException
        {
                //to accept data from keyboard
                BufferedReader br = new BufferedReader(new
                InputStreamReader(System.in));

                //ask how many strings
                System.out.print("How many strings? ");
                int n = Integer.parseInt(br.readLine());

                //create a string type array with size n
                String str[] = new String[n];

                //store strings into str[ ]
                for(int i=0; i<n; i++)
                        {
                                System.out.print("Enter a string: ");
                                str[i]= br.readLine();
                        }

                //accept the string to search
                System.out.print("Enter string to search: ");
                String search = br.readLine();

                //take a boolean var.
                boolean found = false;

                //search for the string in str[ ]
                for(int i=0; i<n; i++)
                        {
                                if(search.equalsIgnoreCase(str[i]))
                                {
                                        System.out.println("Found at
                                        position: "+ (i+1));
                                        found = true; //string found
                                }
                        }

                //if not found, display message
                if(!found)
                System.out.println("Not found in the group");
        }
}
```

Output:

```
C:\> javac Search.java
C:\> java Search
How many strings? 5
Enter a string: Hyderabad
Enter a string: New Delhi
Enter a string: Bangalore
```

```
Enter a string: HYDERABAD
Enter a string: Bhubaneswar
Enter string to search: Hyderabad
Found at position: 1
Found at position: 4
```

Conclusion

Strings are very important since they are most often used on a network while passing data from one system to another system. The data thus passed will be generally in the form of strings. Java's String class comes with necessary methods to work with strings. Since String class objects are immutable, they can be shared between different applications.

STRINGBUFFER AND STRINGBUILDER

You have learnt in previous chapter that Strings are immutable and cannot be modified. To overcome this, we got another class 'StringBuffer' which represents strings in such a way that their data can be modified. It means StringBuffer class objects are mutable. And there are methods provided in this class which directly manipulate the data inside the object.

Important Interview Question

What is the difference between String and StringBuffer classes?

String class objects are immutable and hence their contents cannot be modified. StringBuffer class objects are mutable, so they can be modified. Moreover the methods that directly manipulate data of the object are not available in String class. Such methods are available in StringBuffer class.

Are there any other classes whose objects are immutable?

Yes, classes like Character, Byte, Integer, Float, Double, Long... called 'wrapper classes' are created as 'immutable'. Classes like Class, BigInteger, BigDecimal are also immutable.

Creating StringBuffer Objects

There are two ways to create a StringBuffer object, and fill the object with a string:

❑ We can create a StringBuffer object by using new operator and pass the string to the object, as:

```
StringBuffer sb = new StringBuffer("Hello");
```

Here, we are passing the string "Hello" to the StringBuffer object 'sb'. So, a statement like:

```
System.out.println(sb);
will display "Hello".
```

❑ Another way of creating a StringBuffer object is to first allotting memory to the StringBuffer object using new operator and later storing the string into it, as:

```
StringBuffer sb = new StringBuffer();
```

Here, we are creating a StringBuffer object as an empty object and not passing any string to it. In this case, a StringBuffer object will be created with a default capacity of 16 characters.

```
StringBuffer sb = new StringBuffer(50);
```

Here, StringBuffer object is created as an empty object with a capacity for storing 50 characters. Of course, even if we declare the capacity as 50, it is possible to store more than 50 characters into this StringBuffer. The reason is that StringBuffer is mutable and can expand dynamically in memory. To store characters, we can use 'append()' method or insert() methods, as:

❏ sb.append("Hello"); //add "Hello" to sb.

❏ sb.insert(0, "Hello"); //insert "Hello" starting from 0th position in sb.

StringBuffer Class Methods

There are some methods in StringBuffer class as given here:

❏ StringBuffer append(x): x may be boolean, byte, int, long, float, double, char, character array, String or another StringBuffer. It will be added to the StringBuffer object. For example,

```
StringBuffer sb = new StringBuffer("Uni");
sb.append("versity");
```

Preceding two statements produce, "University" as the string "versity" is added at the end of "Uni".

❏ StringBuffer insert(int i, x): x may be boolean, byte, int, long, float, double, char, character array, String or another StringBuffer. It will be inserted into the StringBuffer at the position represented by i. For example,

```
StringBuffer sb = new StringBuffer("Intelligent Person");
sb.insert(11, "young");
```

Here, the StringBuffer object sb contains "Intelligent Person". Counting from 0, we find the string, "Intelligent" has 10 characters. So, sb.insert(11, "young") will insert the string, "young" at 11th position, and hence we get "Intelligentyoung Person" in sb.

❏ StringBuffer delete(int i, int j): This removes the characters from ith position till j-1th position in the StringBuffer. For example,

```
StringBuffer sb = new StringBuffer("University");
```

sb.delete(0,3) deletes the characters from the beginning to 2nd character ("Uni") and the resultant string in 'sb' will be "versity".

❏ StringBuffer reverse(): This reverses the character sequence in the StringBuffer. If StringBuffer contains "abc", it becomes "cba".

❏ String toString(): This converts the StringBuffer object into a String object. This will enable us to use String class methods on StringBuffer object, after its conversion.

❏ int length(): This returns the number of characters in the StringBuffer object.

❏ int indexOf(String str): This returns the first occurrence of substring 'str' in the StringBuffer object. For example,

```
StringBuffer sb = new StringBuffer("This is a book");
int n = sb.indexOf("is");
```

Observe the substring "is" occurred starting at 2nd position and 5th positions (counting from 0). indexOf() method returns first occurrence only. So the preceding statement gives 2.

❏ int lastIndexOf(String str): This returns the last occurrence of substring 'str' in the StringBuffer object. For example,

```
StringBuffer sb = new StringBuffer("This is a book");
int n = sb.lastIndexOf("is");
```

Preceding statement returns 5, as the last occurrence of "is " is at 5th position.

❑ `StringBuffer replace(int i, int j, String str)`: This replaces the characters from i to j-1, by the string 'str' in the `StringBuffer` object. For example,

```
StringBuffer sb = new StringBuffer("High cost");
sb.replace(0,4, "Low");
```

We are replacing first 4 characters of sb by the 3 characters, "Low". Now sb contains, "Low cost".

❑ `String substring(int i)`: This retrieves a sub string from the StringBuffer object starting from ith position till the end. For example,

```
StringBuffer sb = new StringBuffer("New Delhi");
String s = sb.substring(4);
```

Preceding statement retrieves characters from 4th position (count from 0) till the end, and hence returns "Delhi" into s.

❑ `String substring(int i, int j)`: This extracts a sub string from the StringBuffer object starting from ith position to j-1th position. For example,

```
StringBuffer sb = new StringBuffer("New Delhi");
String s = sb.substring(0,3);
```

Here, starting from 0th character to 2nd character is extracted from sb and returned into s. So, s contains "New".

To understand some of the StringBuffer class methods, let us write a Java program. In this, we want to receive the name of a person in three parts as sur name, middle name and last name; and display the full name of the person.

Program 1: Write a program to learn how to use some of the `StringBuffer` class methods.

```
//To compose full name of a person
import java.io.*;
class Full
{
        public static void main(String args[])
        throws IOException
        {
                //create empty string buffer object
                StringBuffer sb = new StringBuffer();
                //to accept data from keyboard
                BufferedReader br = new BufferedReader(new
                InputStreamReader(System.in));
                //accept surname
                System.out.print("Enter surname: ");
                String sur = br.readLine();
                //accept middlename
                System.out.print("Enter midname: ");
                String mid = br.readLine();
                //accept lastname
                System.out.print("Enter lastname: ");
                String last = br.readLine();
                //append sur to sb
                sb.append(sur);
                //append last to sb
                sb.append(last);
```

```
                     //display the name till now
                     System.out.println("Name= "+ sb);
                     //insert mid after sur name in sb
                     int n =sur.length();    //n represents no. of chars in sur name
                     sb.insert(n,mid);  //insert mid name after nth character
                     //display full name
                     System.out.println("Full name= "+ sb);
                     //reverse and display the name
                     System.out.println("In reverse= "+ sb.reverse());
            }
        }
```

Output:

```
C:\> javac Full.java
C:\> java Full
Enter surname: Mallipudi
Enter midname: Vijaya
Enter lastname: Lakshmi
Name= MallipudiLakshmi
Full name= MallipudiVijayaLakshmi
In reverse= imhskaLayajiVidupillaM
```

In Program 1, we are accepting sur name, middle name and last name of a person from the keyboard and storing them into sur, mid and last respectively. First of all, we are appending sur name and last name to StringBuffer object, as:

```
sb.append(sur);
sb.append(last);
```

After that, we are calculating the number of characters in sur name and inserting the middle name after those many characters, as:

```
int n =sur.length();
sb.insert(n,mid);
```

So, we got full name in sb in correct sequence: sur name, middle name and last name joined together one by one. This is depicted in the Figure 10.1.

StringBuffer sb = new StringBuffer();

Mallipudi

after executing sb.append(sur)

MallipudiLakshmi

after executing sb.append(last)

MallipudiVijayaLakshmi

after executing sb.insert(n,mid)

imhskaLayajiVidupillaM

after executing sb.reverse()

Figure 10.1 Execution sequence of Program 1

In this program, we can also directly add sur name, middle name and last name one by one. But we are first adding sur name and last name and then inserting the middle name after sur. Why? We did so just to demonstrate the functioning of insert() method of StringBuffer() class.

Let us write another program to check if a given string is a palindrome or not. If a string is palindrome, it gives same string even after reversing it. For example, malayalam, madam, peep, liril etc., are palindromes. The following steps can be followed to check the string:

❑ Let the string be 'str'.

❑ Preserve a copy of the original string 'str' in another string 'temp'.

❑ Convert the string 'str 'into a StringBuffer object 'sb'. Now it is possible to use StringBuffer methods on sb.

❑ Reverse the string in the sb.

❑ Store the reversed string in 'str' again.

❑ Now, compare the original string in 'temp' with the reversed string 'str'. If they are equal, then the string is a palindrome, else it is not a palindrome.

The reason why we are converting a string into a StringBuffer is to use the reverse() method of StringBuffer class. Remember it is not possible to use the methods of a class on the objects of another class.

Program 2: Write a program for testing a string whether it is a palindrome or not.

```
//Palindrome or not
import java.io.*;
class Palindrome
{
        public static void main(String args[]) throws IOException
        {
                //accept the string from keyboard
                BufferedReader br = new BufferedReader(new
                InputStreamReader(System.in));
                System.out.print("Enter a string: ");
                String str = br.readLine();
                //store a copy of original string in temp
                String temp = str;
                //convert the string into StringBuffer
                StringBuffer sb = new StringBuffer(str);
                //now reverse the string in StringBuffer
                sb.reverse();
                //convert the StringBuffer into a string
                str = sb.toString();
                //compare the original string available in
                //temp with this reversed string
                if(temp.equalsIgnoreCase(str))
                System.out.println(temp+" is Palindrome");
                else System.out.println(temp+" is not a palindrome");
        }
}
```

Output:

```
C:\> javac Palindrome.java
C:\> java Palindrome
Enter a string: Malayalam
Malayalam is Palindrome
```

StringBuilder Class

StringBuilder class has been added in jdk1.5 which has same features like StringBuffer class. StringBuilder class objects are also mutable as are the StringBuffer objects. For example, to create objects to StringBuilder class, we can use any of the following statements:

❑ StringBuilder sb = new StringBuilder ("Hello");
❑ StringBuilder sb = new StringBuilder ();
❑ StringBuilder sb = new StringBuilder (50);

StringBuilder Class Methods

The following are the important methods in StringBuilder class, which are functionally similar to methods of StringBuffer class discussed previously:

❑ StringBuilder append(x)
❑ StringBuilder insert(int i, x)
❑ StringBuilder delete(int i, int j)
❑ StringBuilder reverse()
❑ String toString()
❑ int length()
❑ int indexOf(String str)
❑ int lastIndexOf(String str)
❑ StringBuilder replace(int i, int j, String str)
❑ String substring(int i)
❑ String substring(int i, int j)

The main difference between StringBuffer and StringBuilder classes is that the StringBuffer class is synchronized by default and StringBuilder class is not. This means, when several threads process or act on a StringBuffer class object, they are executed one by one on the object, thus ensuring reliable results. But in case of StringBuilder object, since it is not synchronized, it allows several threads to act on it simultaneously. This may lead to inaccurate results in some cases.

Synchronizing the object is like locking the object. This means, when a thread acts on the object, it is locked and any other thread should wait till the current thread completes and unlocks the object. Thus, synchronization does not allow more than 1 thread to act simultaneously on the object. Implementing the synchronization mechanism (like locking and unlocking of the object) will take some time for the JVM. Hence StringBuffer class will take more execution time than the StringBuilder, which does not implement this mechanism. We discuss more about threads later in the chapter on 'Threads'.

So, it is recommended that when a programmer wants to use a single thread as is the case generally, he should use StringBuilder class instead of StringBuffer class, to get faster execution.

Important Interview Question

What is the difference between StringBuffer and StringBuilder classes?

StringBuffer class is synchronized and StringBuilder is not. When the programmer wants to use several threads, he should use StringBuffer as it gives reliable results. If only one thread is used, StringBuilder is preferred, as it improves execution time.

Conclusion

StringBuffer and StringBuilder classes differ from String class in their mutability of objects. These classes provide methods which directly modify the contents of the objects, and hence these objects are called 'mutable'. Some methods like insert(), delete() and reverse() which are not available in String class are very valuable for the programmers.

CHAPTER 11

INTRODUCTION TO OOPs

The languages like C, Pascal, Fortran etc., are called Procedure oriented programming languages since in these languages, a programmer uses procedures or functions to perform a task. When the programmer wants to write a program, he will first divide the task into separate sub tasks, each of which is expressed as a function. So a C program generally contains several functions which are called and controlled from a main() function. This approach is called *Procedure oriented approach*. Please see Figure 11.1.

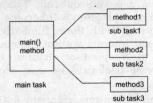

Figure 11.1 Procedure oriented approach

On the other hand, languages like C++ and Java use classes and objects in their programs and are called Object Oriented Programming languages. A class is a module which itself contains data and methods (functions) to achieve the task. The main task is divided into several modules, and these are represented as classes. Each class can perform some tasks for which several methods are written in a class. This approach is called *Object oriented approach*. See Figure 11.2.

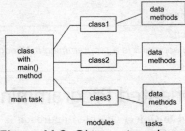

Figure 11.2 Object oriented approach

Programmers have firmly followed Procedure oriented approach for several decades, but as experience and observation teaches new lessons, there is a sudden shift in the software industry for a new approach, called Object oriented approach. First of all, let us discuss the point, why one should go for Object oriented approach when already one has Procedure oriented approach?

Problems in Procedure Oriented Approach

In procedure oriented approach, the programmer concentrates on a specific task, and writes a set of functions to achieve it. When there is another task to be added to the software, he would be writing another set of functions. This means his concentration will be only on achieving the tasks. He perceives the entire system as fragments of several tasks. Whenever he wants to perform a new task, he would be writing a new set of functions. Thus, there will be no reusability of previous functions, in most of the cases. If the programmer can construct the new modules with the help of old modules, i.e., reusing the old modules, programming will become easy. With this view, computer scientists have thought about developing a new approach.

When the software is developed, naturally code size will also be increased. It has been observed in most of the softwares developed following procedure oriented approach, when the code size exceeds 10,000 lines and before reaching 100,000 lines, suddenly at a particular point, the programmers were losing control on the code. This means, the programmers could not understand the exact behavior of the code and could neither debug it, nor extend it. This posed many problems, especially when the software was constructed to handle bigger and complex systems. For example, to create software to send satellites into the sky and control their operations from the ground stations, we may have to write millions of lines of code. In such systems, procedure oriented approach fails and we need another approach.

There is another problem with procedure oriented approach. Programming in this approach is far way from human being's life, and hence considered to be unnatural. Any thing that is not natural leads to certain problems. For example, take the activity, talking. A man talks in his own voice effortlessly. It does not need any special effort on his part. But if the man is asked to imitate the speech of some body else, he feels it is very difficult. Talking in some body else's tone is not a natural activity. Similarly, developing a program will become easy when it is natural. For example, in our life, we have friends. We interact with them. Similarly, a code will have friendly code. Both interact with each other. We will not interact with our enemies. Similarly a code will have enemy code and does not interact with it. We produce children, become aged and die. Similarly code produces new code and may become useless. Like this, programming should stem from human being's life.

Because of the preceding reasons, computer scientists felt the need of a new approach where programming will have several modules. Each module represents a 'class' and the classes can be reusable and hence maintenance of code will become easy. This approach is suitable not only to develop bigger and complex applications but also to manage them easily. Moreover, this approach is built from a single root concept 'object', which represents any thing that physically exists in this world. It means all human beings are objects. All animals are objects. All existing things will become objects. This new approach is called 'Object oriented approach'. Programming in this approach is called 'Object Oriented Programming System (OOPS).

Important Interview Question

What is object oriented approach?

Object oriented programming approach is a programming methodology to design computer programs using classes and objects.

Features of Object Oriented Programming System (OOPS)

There are many features related to Object Oriented approach is discussed in the chapter. Some of the features are:

❑ Class/Object
❑ Encapsulation
❑ Abstraction
❑ Inheritance
❑ Polymorphism

Let us move further to have clear understanding of each feature of Object Oriented Approach.

Class/object

Entire OOP methodology has been derived from a single root concept, called 'object'. An object is anything that really exists in the world and can be distinguished from others. This definition specifies that every thing in this world is an object. For example, a table, a ball, a car, a dog, a person, etc., every thing will come under objects. Then what is not an object? If something does not really exist, then it is not an object. For example, our thoughts, imagination, plans, ideas etc., are not objects, because they do not physically exist.

Every object has properties and can perform certain actions. For example, let us take a person whose name is 'Raju'. Raju is an object because he exists physically. He has properties like name, age, sex, etc. These properties can be represented by variables in our programming. For example,

```
String name;
int age;
char sex;
```

Similarly, Raju can perform some actions like talking, walking, eating and sleeping. We may not write code for such actions in programming. But, we can consider calculations and processing of data as actions. These actions are performed by methods (functions). So an object contains variables and methods.

It is possible that some objects may have similar properties and actions. Such objects belong to same category called a 'class'. For example, not only Raju, but also Ravi, Sita, Vijay, etc., persons have same properties and actions. So they are all objects of same class, 'Person'. Now observe that the 'Person' will not exist physically but only Raju, Ravi, Sita etc. exist physically. This means, a class is a group name and does not exist physically, but objects exist physically. See Figure 11.3.

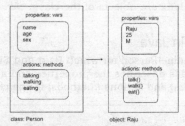

Figure 11.3 Person class and Raju object

To understand a class, take a pen and paper and write down all the properties and actions of any person. That paper contains a model that depicts a person. So it is called a class. We can find a person with the name 'Raju', who got all the properties and actions written on the paper. So 'Raju' becomes an object of the class, Person. This gives a definition for the class. A class is a model or blueprint for creating objects. By following the class, one can create objects. So we can say, whatever is there in the class, will be seen in its objects also.

Important Interview Question

What is the difference between a class and an object?

A class is a model for creating objects and does not exist physically. An object is any thing that exists physically. Both the class and objects contain variables and methods.

We can use a class as a model for creating objects. To write a class, we can write all the characteristics of objects which should follow the class. These characteristics will guide us to create the objects. A class and its objects are almost the same with the difference that a class does not exist physically, while an object does. For example, if we say *dog*; it forms a picture into our mind with 4 legs, 2 ears, some length and height. This picture in our mind is *class*. If we tally this picture with the physical things around us, we can find Tom living in our house is satisfying these qualities. So Tom, which physically exists, is an object and not a class.

Let us take another example. Flower is a class but if we take Rose, Lily, Jasmine – they are all objects of *flower* class. The class *flower* does not exist physically but its objects, like Rose, Lily, Jasmine exist physically.

Let us take another example. We want some shirts stitched by a tailor. First of all, the tailor takes the measurements and makes a plan for the shirt, according to the measurements. He may also draw a model shirt in his note book. This plan or model is called a 'class'. Following this model, he stitches the shirts which we can wear. These shirts are called 'objects'. To stitch the shirts, we need the material 'cloth'. The cloth represents the memory allotted by the JVM for the objects. Remember, objects are created on heap memory by JVM at run time. See Figure 11.4. It is also possible to create several objects from the same class. An object cannot exist without a class. But a class can exist without any object.

We can think that a class is a model and if it physically forms, then it becomes an object. So an object is called 'instance' (the thing physically happens) of a class.

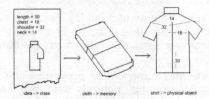

Figure 11.4 Creation of a class and object

Let us take some more examples, like table, chair, cot and sofa are objects of the class, furniture. Similarly, Maruti, Santro and Benz are objects of the class, car. Red, Blue and Green are objects of the class, color.

Creating Classes and Objects in Java

Let us create a class with the name Person for which Raju and Sita are objects. A class is created by using the key word, class. A class describes the properties and actions performed by its objects. So, we write the properties (variables) and actions (methods) in the class, as:

```java
class Person
{
        //properties of a person — variables
        String name;
        int age;
        //actions done by a person - methods
        void talk()
        { }
        void eat()
        { }
}
```

Observe the preceding code. Person class has two variables and two methods. This class code is stored in JVM's method area. When we want to use this class, we should create an object to the class, as:

```java
Person Raju = new Person();
```

Here, Raju is an object of Person class. Object represents memory to store the actual data. Preceding 'new' operator tells the JVM to allot necessary memory to the object of the Person class. Objects are created by JVM on heap memory.

Encapsulation

Encapsulation is a mechanism where the data (variables) and the code (methods) that act on the data will bind together. For example, if we take a class, we write the variables and methods inside the class. Thus, class is binding them together. So class is an example for encapsulation.

The variables and methods of a class are called 'members' of the class. Generally, the variables in the class are declared by using a keyword 'private'. This means the variables are not directly available to any other class. The methods of a class are declared as 'public'. This means the methods can be called and used from any where outside the class. To use the variables from outside, we should take the help of methods. There is no other way of interacting with the variables. This means outsiders do not know what variables are declared in a class, and what code is written in the method that is giving the result. Others can only use them and obtain the results. Encapsulation thus protects the inner implementation of the members of the class from outside environment.

Encapsulation isolates the members of a class from the members of another class. The reason is when objects are created, each object shares different memory and hence there will not be any overwriting of data. This gives an advantage to the programmer to use same names for the members of two different classes. For example, a programmer can declare and use the following variables in two different classes: Employee and Student.

```
int id;
String name;
```

Now in the variable 'id' of Employee class, the programmer can store 1001 and in the 'id' of Student class, he can store 12. Similarly, in the 'name' of Employee class, he can store "Visal" and in the 'name' of Student class, he can store "Lakshmi". Thus the data of one class will not spoil the data of another.

Encapsulation in Java

In a program if we write a variable as:

```
num = 100;
```

And, after some statements in the program, again we write:

```
num = 200;
```

Now which value will be available in the variable num? The value 100 is overwritten by the new value 200 and hence num contains 200 now. This means the previous data is lost. Sometimes, this is unwanted in a software project, especially when the data is important. Two programmers may use same names for two variables and store different data. Then one programmer's data will be lost or modified. This problem is solved with the concept of encapsulation. According to encapsulation a class protects its own members. So, even though same names are used for the members of two different classes, there will not be any overwriting or losing the data.

For example, two programmers are writing Employee and Student classes with same variables: id and name. Also, they can write same method displayDetails() in both the classes. It is possible to store different data in the variables. The data of one class will not spoil the data of another class. The displayDetails() method of Employee class will display the employee details, i.e. 1001 and "Visal". Similarly, the displayDetails() method of Student class will display the student's details, i.e. 12 and "Lakshmi".

```
class Employee {
        int id = 1001;
        String name = "Visal";
        void displayDetails()
```

```
            {
       System.out.println("Id= "+ id);
            System.out.println("Name= "+ name);
       }
   }
class Student {
       int id = 12;
       String name = "Lakshmi";
       void displayDetails()
       {
       System.out.println("Id= "+ id);
            System.out.println("Name= "+ name);
       }
   }
```

Abstraction

There may be a lot of data, a class contains and the user does not need the entire data. The user requires only some part of the available data. In this case, we can hide the unnecessary data from the user and expose only that data that is of interest to the user. This is called abstraction.

A good example for abstraction is a car. Any car will have some parts like engine, radiator, mechanical and electrical equipment etc. The user of the car (driver) should know how to drive the car and does not require any knowledge of these parts. For example driver is never bothered about how the engine is designed and the internal parts of the engine. This is why, the car manufacturers hide these parts from the driver in a separate panel, generally at the front.

The advantage of abstraction is that every user will get his own view of the data according to his requirements and will not get confused with unnecessary data. A bank clerk should see the customer details like account number, name and balance amount in the account. He should not be entitled to see the sensitive data like the staff salaries, profit or loss of the bank, interest amount paid by the bank and loans amount to be recovered etc,. So such data can be abstracted from the clerk's view. Where as the bank manager is interested to know this data, it will be provided to the manager. Here is an example for abstraction in Java:

```
class Bank {
       private int accno;
       private String name;
       private float balance;
       private float profit;
       private float loan;
       public void display_to_clerk()
       {
            System.out.println("Accno= "+ accno);
            System.out.println("Name= "+ name);
            System.out.println("Balance= "+ balance);
       }
   }
```

In the preceding class, inspite of several data items, the `display_to_clerk()` method is able to access and display only the accno, name and balance values. It can not access profit and loan of the customer. This means the profit and loan data is hidden from the view of the bank clerk.

Inheritance

It creates new classes from existing classes, so that the new classes will acquire all the features of the existing classes is called Inheritance. A good example for Inheritance in nature is parents producing the children and children inheriting the qualities of the parents.

Let us take a class A with some features (members i.e., variables and methods). If we feel another class B wants almost same features, then we can derive or create the class B from A, as:

```
class B extends A
{
}
```

Now, all the features of A are available to B. If an object to B is created, it contains all the members of classes A and also its own members. Thus, the programmer can access and use all the members of both the classes A and B. Thus, class B becomes more useful. This is called inheritance. The original class (A) is called the *super class* and the derived class (B) is called the *sub class*.

There are three advantages of inheritance. First, we can create more useful classes needed by the application (software). Next, the process of creating the new classes is very easy, since they are built upon already existing classes. The last, but very important advantage is managing the code becomes easy, since the programmer creates several classes in a hierarchical manner, and segregates the code into several modules.

An Example for Inheritance in Java

Here, we take a class A with two variables a and b and a method, method1(). Now all these members are needed by another class B, we extend class B from A. We want some additional members in B, for example a variable c and a method, method2(). So, these are written in B. Now remember, class B can use all the members of both A and B. This means the variables a,b,c and also the methods method1() and method2() are available to class B. Please observe 'protected' is another *access specifier* in Java that is generally used in inheritance.

```
class A
{
        protected int a;
        protected int b;
        public void method1()
        {
        }
}
class B extends A
{
        private int c;
        public void method2()
        {
        }
}
```

Polymorphism

The word 'Polymorphism' came from two Greek words 'poly' meaning 'many' and 'morphos' meaning 'forms'. Thus, polymorphism represents the ability to assume several different forms. In programming, we can use a single variable to refer to objects of different types and thus, using that variable we can call the methods of the different objects. Thus a method call can perform different tasks depending on the type of the object.

Polymorphism provides flexibility in writing programs in such a way that the programmer uses same method call to perform different operations depending on the requirement.

Example code for Polymorphism in Java:

Let us take a super class 'One' and a sub class 'Two' as shown here:

```
class One
{
        void calculate(int x)
        {
                System.out.println("Square value= "+ (x*x));
        }
}
```

```
class Two extends One
{
        void calculate(int x)
        {
                System.out.println("Cube value= "+ (x*x*x));
        }
}
```

Let us take obj1 and obj2 are objects of classes One and Two respectively. Let us create a reference variable 'ref' for class One as:

```
One ref;
```

If we use this 'ref' to refer to the object of class One, as:

```
ref = obj1;
```

and then call the calculate() method, as:

```
ref.calculate(2);
```

It will calculate the square value.

If on the other hand, we use 'ref' to refer to the object of class Two, then 'ref' will call the method of the class Two, as:

```
ref = obj2;
ref.calculate(2);
```

This will calculate the cube value. Observe that the same method call is performing two different tasks.

We should remember that Object oriented approach is a methodology to accomplish tasks in a better way in programming. Languages like C++ and Java which are created based on this methodology are called 'Object oriented programming languages'.

Important Interview Question

What is the difference between object oriented programming languages and object based programming languages?

Object oriented programming languages follow all the features of Object Oriented Programming System (OOPS). Smalltalk, Simula-67, C++, Java are examples for OOPS languages.

Object based programming languages follow all the features of OOPS, except Inheritance. For example, JavaScript and VBScript will come under object based programming languages.

Conclusion

Since the Procedure oriented approach is not suitable for managing bigger and complex projects, another approach called Object oriented approach is invented. Object oriented approach advocates using classes and objects in writing programs. It comes with features like encapsulation, abstraction, inheritance as well as polymorphism. Using these features, if programs are written, it is called Object Oriented Programming System (OOPS). The practical implementation and impact of OOPS in programming will be visited in subsequent chapters.

CLASSES AND OBJECTS

We know a class is a model for creating objects. This means the properties and actions of the objects are written in the class. Properties are represented by variables and actions of the objects are represented by methods. So a class contains variables and methods. The same variables and methods are also available in the objects because they are created from the class. These variables are also called 'instance variables' because they are created inside the object (instance).

If we take Person class, we can write code in the class that specifies the properties and actions performed by any person. For example, a person has properties like name, age, etc. Similarly a person can perform actions like talking, walking, etc. So, the class Person contains these properties and actions, as shown here:

```
class Person
{
        //properties - instance variables
        String name;
        int age;

        //actions - methods
        void talk()
        {
                System.out.println("Hello Iam "+ name);
                System.out.println("My age is "+ age);
        }
}
```

Observe that the key word 'class' is used to declare a class. After this, we should write the class name. In the class, we write instance variables and methods. See the method: void talk(). This method does not return any result (void) and it does not accept any data from us. So we did not declare any variables after the method name. Through this method, the person is talking with us; he is introducing himself to us, as shown here:

```
Hello Iam Raju
My age is 22
```

This is what we are displaying in the method. Writing a class like this is not sufficient. It should be used. To use a class, we should create an object to the class. Object creation represents allotting memory necessary to store the actual data of the variables, i.e., Raju and 22. To create an object, the following syntax is used:

```
Classname objectname = new Classname();
```

So, to create Raju object to Person class, we can write as:

```
Person Raju = new Person();
```

Here, 'new' is an operator that creates the object to Person class, hence the right hand side part of the statement is responsible for creating the object. What about the left side statement, which is:

```
Person Raju;
```

Here, Person is the class name and Raju is the object name. Raju is actually a variable of Person class. This variable stores the reference number of the object returned by JVM, after creating the object. If Raju is a variable, then what is 'Person'? It is, of course the class name, but class is also a data type. So we can say that Raju is a variable of Person class type.

Object Creation

We know that the class code along with method code is stored in 'method area' of the JVM. When an object is created, the memory is allocated on 'heap'. After creation of an object, JVM produces a unique reference number for the object from the memory address of the object. This reference number is also called hash code number.

To know the hashcode number (or reference) of an object, we can use hashCode() method of Object class, as shown here:

❏ Employee e1 = new Employee(); //e1 is reference of Employee object.

❏ System.out.println(e1.hashCode()); //displays hash code stored in e1.

Important Interview Question

What is hash code?

Hash code is a unique identification number allotted to the objects by the JVM. This hash code number is also called reference number which is created based on the location of the object in memory, and is unique for all objects, except for String objects.

How can you find the hash code of an object?

The hashCode() method of 'Object' class in java.lang package is useful to find the hash code of an object.

The object reference (hash code) internally represents heap memory where instance variables are stored. There would be a pointer (memory address) from heap memory to a special structure located in method area. In method area, a table is available which contains pointers to static variables and methods. This is how the instance variables and methods are organized by JVM internally at run time. Please see Figure 12.1.

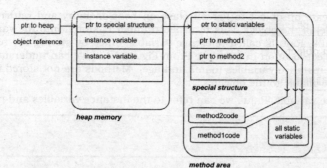

object reference

Figure 12.1 Memory organization for members of a class

Program 1: Write a program to create Person class and an object Raju to Person class. Let us display the hash code number of the object, using hashCode().

```
//Creating a class and object
class Person
{
       //properties - variables
       String name;
       int age;

       //actions - methods
       void talk()
       {
              System.out.println("Hello Iam "+ name);
              System.out.println("My age is "+ age);
       }
}
class Demo
{
       public static void main(String args[ ])
       {
              //create Person class object: Raju
              Person Raju = new Person();

              //find the hash code of object
              System.out.println("Hash code= "+Raju.hashCode());
       }
}
```

Output:

```
C:\> javac Demo.java
C:\> java Demo
Hash code= 1671711
```

In the preceding program, there are two classes. In this case, on which class name we should store the program? The class name which contains main() method should be used for this. Since Demo class contains main(), JVM starts execution from there and hence the program should be saved as "Demo.java".

The hash code displayed by the preceding program may vary from system to system and dependent on the internal memory address by the JVM. Observe the code in Demo class. We created an object to Person class, as:

```
Person Raju = new Person();
```

Here, JVM will create an object to Person class on heap memory and returns a unique reference number (hash code) of the object. This returned number is stored into the variable Raju, as shown in Figure 12.2. Thus, Raju is called reference variable, since by storing the reference number, it is referring to the object location in memory. From Figure 12.2, we can understand that the object on heap contains the instance variables (name and age). Methods are not stored in the object on heap. But methods are available to the object.

Using the reference variable 'Raju', we can refer to the instance variables and methods, as:

```
Raju.name;
Raju.age;
Raju.talk();
```

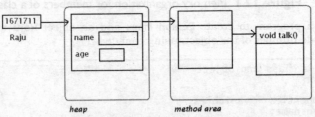

Figure 12.2 Creation of Raju object

Program 2: Let us rewrite the program 1, where we want to call the talk() method.

```
//class and object
class Person
{
        //properties - variables
        String name;
        int age;
        //actions - methods
        void talk()
        {
                System.out.println("Hello Iam "+ name);
                System.out.println("My age is "+ age);
        }
}
class Demo
{
        public static void main(String args[ ])
        {
                //create Person class object: Raju
                Person Raju = new Person();
                //call the talk() method
                Raju.talk();
        }
}
```

Output:

```
C:\> javac Demo.java
C:\> java Demo
Hello Iam null
My age is 0
```

Please observe the output of the preceding program. In this program, we created the object 'Raju', but did not initialize the instance variables. Initialization means storing the starting data. Since we did not initialize the instance variables, Java compiler adds some additional code to Person class, as:

```
        name = null;
        age = 0;
```

When JVM executes the preceding code, it stores null into name and 0 into age. 'null' represents 'nothing'. Table 12.1 summarizes the default values of the instance variables as used by Java compiler.

Table 12.1

Data type	Default value
byte	0
short	0
int	0
long	0
float	0.0
double	0.0
char	a space
String	null
any class type	null
boolean	false

Initializing the Instance Variables

It is the duty of the programmer to initialize the instance variables, depending on his requirements. There are various ways to do this. First way is to initialize the instance variables of Person class in the other class, i.e., Demo class. For this purpose, the Demo class can be rewritten like this:

```
class Demo
{
      public static void main(String args[ ])
      {
              //create Person class object: Raju
              Person Raju = new Person();
              //initialize the instance variables using the reference
              Raju. name = "Raju";
              Raju.age = 22;
              //call the talk() method
              Raju.talk();
      }
}
```

When the preceding code is executed, the output will be:

```
Hello Iam Raju
My age is 22
```

In this way, we are initializing the instance variables of Person class in some other class, i.e., Demo. This violates the security of data of Person class. If Person class is written by a programmer and the Demo class is written by some other programmer, then the other programmer is accessing the

Person class instance variables and directly storing data into them. This will overwrite the originally stored data of Person class.

For example, in Person class, we stored "Venkat" and 30. The other programmer is storing "Raju" and 22 again in the same variables. The output shows only "Raju" and 22. This means the data "Venkat" and 30 are overwritten. Thus, there is no security for data, "Venkat" and 30. Observe this in the following program.

Program 3: Write a program to initialize the Person class instance variables in Demo class.

```
//Initializing the instance variables
class Person
{
        //instance variables are initialized here
        String name = "Venkat";
        int age = 30;
        //methods
        void talk()
        {
                System.out.println("Hello Iam "+ name);
                System.out.println("My age is "+ age);
        }
}

class Demo
{
        public static void main(String args[ ])
        {
                //create Person class object: Raju
                Person Raju = new Person();
                //initialize Person class variables again here
                Raju. name = "Raju";
                Raju.age = 22;
                //call the talk() method
                Raju.talk();
        }
}
```

Output:

```
C:\> javac Demo.java
C:\> java Demo
Hello Iam Raju
My age is 22
```

Protection for data is always needed. All companies are worried about security of data, which is compulsory. Just think, in an organization's database, an employee salary is stored as 12,500.00 and this is modified as 22,500.00. This is sensitive data and should not be modified by any external source. For this purpose, we can use 'private' access specifier while declaring the variables in Person class, as:

```
private String name = "Venkat";
private int age = 30;
```

'private' key word does not allow name and age to be accessed by any other class or program from outside. Thus, it protects data. We also use 'public' access specifier for methods as this 'public' key word allows the methods to be accessed by any outside program. Since programmers want to access the methods to perform various tasks, we declare the methods as 'public'. 'private' and 'public' are called 'access specifiers'.

Access Specifiers

An access specifier is a key word that specifies how to access the members of a class or a class itself. We can use access specifiers before a class and its members. There are four access specifiers available in Java:

❑ **private:** 'private' members of a class are not accessible any where outside the class. They are accessible only within the class by the methods of that class.

❑ **public:** 'public' members of a class are accessible every where outside the class. So any other program can read them and use them.

❑ **protected:** 'protected' members of a class are accessible outside the class, but generally, within the same directory.

❑ **default:** If no access specifier is written by the programmer, then the Java compiler uses a 'default' access specifier. 'default' members are accessible outside the class, but within the same directory.

We generally use private for instance variables, and public for methods. In Java, classes cannot be declared by using 'private'.

Important Interview Question

Can you declare a class as 'private'?

No, if we declare a class as private, then it is not available to Java compiler and hence a compile time error occurs. But, inner classes can be declared as private.

You may feel public, protected and default – all are same. But there is some difference between them. We reserve a complete discussion on access specifiers till the chapter on 'Packages' in Chapter 20.

If the instance variables of Person class are declared as private, then they are not available in Demo class to be initialized. Then how can we initialize them? There is another way. Let us initialize them directly within the Person class at the time of their declaration, as:

```
private String name = "Raju";
private int age = 30;
```

But, the problem in this way of initialization is that all the objects are initialized with same data. Please observe Program 4, where we are creating two objects and both are initialized with same data.

Program 4: Write a program to initialize the instance variables directly within the Person class.

```
//Initializing the instance variables at the time declaration
class Person
{
    //instance variables are initialized here
    private String name = "Raju";
    private int age = 30;
    //methods
    void talk()
    {
        System.out.println("Hello Iam "+ name);
        System.out.println("My age is "+ age);
    }
}

class Demo
{
    public static void main(String args[ ])
    {
```

```
                    //create Person class object: Raju
                    Person Raju = new Person();
                    //call the talk() method
                    Raju.talk();
                    //create another Person class object: Sita
                    Person Sita = new Person();
                    //call the talk() method
                    Sita.talk();

        }
    }
```

Output:

```
    C:\> javac Demo.java
    C:\> java Demo
    Hello Iam Raju
    My age is 30
    Hello Iam Raju
    My age is 30
```

Please observe that we are creating two objects, 'Raju' and 'Sita'. But both the objects are initialized with same data, Raju and 30. We need Sita object should get Sita's data, not Raju's data.

This way of initialization is suitable for declaring constants. The reason is that constants' value will not change even though we create several objects. A constant is like a variable, but its value is fixed and cannot be changed. To declare constants, we use the key word 'final', as:

```
    final double PI = 3.14159;
```

Since constants are written by using all capitals letters, PI is written in all caps and the final key word indicates that PI value is fixed. When PI is used any where in the rest of the program, Java compiler simply substitutes the value 3.14159 in the place of PI.

Constructors

The third possibility of initialization is using constructors. A constructor is similar to a method that is used to initialize the instance variables. The sole purpose of a constructor is to initialize the instance variables. A constructor has the following characteristics:

❑ The constructor's name and class name should be same. And the constructor's name should end with a pair of simple braces.

For example, in Person class, we can write a constructor as:

```
    Person()
    {
    }
```

❑ A constructor may have or may not have parameters. Parameters are variables to receive data from outside into the constructor. If a constructor does not have any parameters, it is called 'default constructor'. If a constructor has 1 or more parameters, it is called 'parameterized constructor'. For example, we can write a default constructor as:

```
    Person()
    {
    }
```

And a parameterized constructor with two parameters, as:

```
        Person(String s, int i)
        {
        }
```

❑ A constructor does not return any value, not even 'void'. Recollect, if a method does not return any value, we write 'void' before the method name. That means the method is returning 'void' which means 'nothing'. But in case of a constructor, we should not even write 'void' before the constructor.

❑ A constructor is automatically called and executed at the time of creating an object. While creating an object, if nothing is passed to the object, the default constructor is called and executed. If some values are passed to the object, then the parameterized constructor is called. For example, if we create the object as:

* `Person Raju = new Person();` //here default constructor is called,

* `Person Raju = new Person("Raju", 22);` //here parameterized constructor will receive "Raju" and 22.

❑ A constructor is called and executed only once per object. This means when we create an object, the constructor is called. When we create second object, again the constructor is called second time.

Important Interview Question

When is a constructor called, before or after creating the object?

A constructor is called concurrently when the object creation is going on. JVM first allocates memory for the object and then executes the constructor to initialize the instance variables. By the time, object creation is completed, the constructor execution is also completed.

Program 5: Rewrite the previous program by using a default constructor to initialize the instance variables of Person class.

```
        //Initializing the instance variables using a default constructor
        class Person
        {
                //instance variables
                private String name;
                private int age;
                //default constructor
                Person()
                {
                        name = "Raju";
                        age = 22;
                }
                //method
                void talk()
                {
                        System.out.println("Hello Iam "+ name);
                        System.out.println("My age is "+ age);
                }
        }
        class Demo
        {
                public static void main(String args[ ])
                {
                        //create Person class object: Raju
                        Person Raju = new Person();
                        //call the talk() method
                        Raju.talk();
                        //create another object: Sita
                        Person Sita = new Person();
                        //call the talk() method
```

```
                    Sita.talk();
        }
    }
```

Output:

```
C:\> javac Demo.java
C:\> java Demo
Hello Iam Raju
My age is 22
Hello Iam Raju
My age is 22
```

From the output, we can understand that the same data "Raju" and 22 are stored in both the objects Raju and Sita. Sita object should get Sita's data, not Raju's data. Isn't it? To mitigate this problem, let us try parameterized constructor, which accepts data from outside and initializes the instance variables with that data. This is what we did in Program 6.

Program 6: Write a program to initialize the instance variables of Person class, using parameterized constructor.

```
//Initializing the instance variables using a parameterized constructor
class Person
{
    //instance variables
    private String name;
    private int age;
    //default constructor
    Person()
    {
        name = "Raju";
        age = 22;
    }
    //parameterized constructor
    Person(String s, int i)
    {
        name = s;
        age = i;
    }
    //method
    void talk()
    {
        System.out.println("Hello Iam "+ name);
        System.out.println("My age is "+ age);
    }
}
class Demo
{
    public static void main(String args[ ])
    {
        //create Raju object. Here default constructor is called.
        Person Raju = new Person();
        //call the talk() method
        Raju.talk();
        //create Sita object. Here parameterized constructor is called.
        Person Sita = new Person("Sita", 20);
        //call the talk() method
        Sita.talk();
    }
}
```

Output:

```
C:\> javac Demo.java
```

```
C:\> java Demo
Hello Iam Raju
My age is 22
Hello Iam Sita
My age is 20
```

In the preceding program, we achieved our target of initializing the objects with different data. Observe the following code:

```
//parameterized constructor
Person(String s, int i)
{
    name = s;
    age = i;
}
```

This is a parameterized constructor with two parameters, String s and int i. These parameters are useful to receive data from outside. So while creating the object, we are supposed to pass a string and an integer number, as:

```
Person Sita = new Person("Sita", 20);
```

Now, "Sita" is copied into the first parameter s, and 20 is copied into the second parameter i. From there, these values are copied into the instance variables, name and age in the parameterized constructor. So in Sita, object receives the data, "Sita" and 20.

When we do not pass any values at the time of creating an object, then the default constructor is called. For example, when the object is created as:

```
Person Raju = new Person();
```

Here, the following default constructor is called:

```
//default constructor
Person()
{
    name = "Raju";
    age = 22;
}
```

And hence, Raju object is initialized with "Raju" and 22.

Important Interview Question

What is the difference between default constructor and parameterized constructor?

Please observe the Table 12.2 given here.

Table 12.2

Default constructor	Parameterized constructor
Default constructor is useful to initialize all objects with same data.	Parameterized constructor is useful to initialize each object with different data.
Default constructor does not have any parameters.	Parameterized constructor will have 1 or more parameters.
When data is not passed at the time of creating an object, default constructor is called.	When data is passed at the time of creating an object, parameterized constructor is called.

What is the difference between a constructor and a method?

Please see the Table 12.3 given here.

Table 12.3

Constructors	Methods
A constructor is used to initialize the instance variables of a class.	A method is used for any general purpose processing or calculations.
A constructor's name and class name should be same.	A method's name and class name can be same or different.
A constructor is called at the time of creating the object.	A method can be called after creating the object.
A constructor is called only once per object.	A method can be called several times on the object.
A constructor is called and executed automatically.	A method is executed only when we call it.

Please observe Program 6, where we have written two constructors. Both the constructors have same name, but there is a difference in the parameters. This is called constructor overloading.

Important Interview Question

What is constructor overloading?

Writing two or more constructors with the same name but with difference in the parameters is called constructor overloading. Such constructors are useful to perform different tasks.

When the programmer does not write any constructor in a class, then Java compiler writes a default constructor and initializes the instance variables with the default values which are shown in Table 12.1. This is the reason, we got null and 0 in the output of Program 2.

Let us write another program to understand how to use classes and objects. In this program, we take Person class with name and age. Then we accept the name and age from keyboard with the help of `BufferedReader` in `accept()` method. We check the age in `check()` method. `BufferedReader` belongs to `java.io` package. `readLine()` method of `BufferedReader` class can give `IOException` which we do not want to handle. Since we are calling `readLine()` method in `accept()` method, we should attach 'throws IOException' after `accept()` method, and since we are calling `accept()` from `main()` method, we should again attach 'throws IOException' after `main()` method.

Program 7: Write a Java program to understand the use of methods in a class.

```
/* To accept a person's name and age and display if he is
    young, middle aged or old
*/
import java.io.*;
class Person
{
  //instance variables
  private String name;
  private int age;
  //to accept the name and age
  public void accept() throws IOException
  {
      //to accept data from keyboard
      BufferedReader br = new BufferedReader(new InputStreamReader(System.in));

      //accept name and age
```

```
            System.out.print("Enter name: ");
            name = br.readLine();

            System.out.print("Enter age: ");
            age = Integer.parseInt(br.readLine());
    }

    //to check the age and display he is young, middle aged or old
    public void check()
    {
            if(age<=30)
            System.out.println(name+" is young");
            else if(age<=50)
            System.out.println(name+" is middle aged");
            else System.out.println(name+" is old");
    }
}
class Demo
{
        public static void main(String args[ ]) throws IOException
        {

                //create Person class object
                Person p = new Person();

                //accept person data
                p.accept();

                //check the age
                p.check();
        }
}
```

Output:

```
C:\> javac Demo.java
C:\> java Demo
Enter name: Vijay
Enter age: 32
Vijay is middle aged
```

In this program, we can observe that the instance variables of Person class are available within that class to the methods accept() and check().

Let us rewrite the preceding program, this time using a parameterized constructor to initialize the instance variables. In this program, we accept the name (s) and age (i) of the person from command line arguments and send them to the constructor at the time of creating the object, as:

```
    Person p = new Person(s,i);
```

Here, the parameterized constructor will receive the data, s and i and store them into the instance variables.

Program 8: Write a program to accept a person's name and age through command line arguments and display if he is young, middle aged or old - version 2.

```
    //Program 7 rewritten using constructor and command line arguments
    import java.io.*;
    class Person
    {
        //instance variables
        private String name;
        private int age;
        //parameterized constructor
```

```
        Person(String s, int i)
        {
                name = s;
                age = i;
        }

        //to check the age and display he is young, middle aged or old
        public void check()
        {
                if(age<=30)
                System.out.println(name+" is young");
                else if(age<=50)
                System.out.println(name+" is middle aged");
                else System.out.println(name+" is old");
        }
}
class Demo
{
        public static void main(String args[ ]) throws IOException
        {
        //create BufferedReader object
        BufferedReader br = new BufferedReader(new InputStreamReader(System.in));

        //accept person name and age from command line arguments
        //name and age are stored in args[0] and args[1] as strings
        String s = args[0];
        int i = Integer.parseInt(args[1]);

        //create Person class object and pass name and age to the constructor
        Person p = new Person(s,i);

        //check the age
        p.check();
        }
}
```

Output:

```
C:\> javac Demo.java
C:\> java Demo "Vinod Kumar"  20
Vinod Kumar is young
```

Conclusion

We introduced the concepts of creating classes and objects in this chapter. A class contains instance variables and methods. When the object is created, a copy of instance variables is available in the object and methods are also accessible. It is the duty of the programmer to initialize the instance variables of a class. Constructors are very useful to initialize the instance variables with required data. If the programmer does not write any constructor, then the Java compiler adds a default constructor to the class code and initializes the instance variables with default values. We also discussed the characteristics of constructors and contrasted them with methods.

METHODS IN JAVA

A method represents a group of statements that performs a task. Here 'task' represents a calculation or processing of data or generating a report etc., For example, take sqrt() method. It calculates square root value and returns that value. A method has two parts:

❑ Method header or Method prototype

❑ Method body

Method Header or Method Prototype

It contains method name, method parameters and method return data type. Method prototype is written in the form:

```
returndatatype  methodname(parameter1, parameter2,…)
```

Here, method name represents the name given to the method. After the method name, we write some variables in the simple braces. These variables are called parameters. Method parameters are useful to receive data from outside into the method. This data can be used by the method. Return data type is written before the method name to represent what type of result/data the method is returning. Let us examine some method prototypes:

❑ double sqrt(double num): Here, sqrt is the method name. num is method parameter that represents that this method accepts a double type value. This method calculates square root value of num and returns that result which is again double type. We can call this method something like:

```
double result = obj.sqrt(25.6);
```

❑ void sum(): This method is not accepting any data from outside. So after the method name we write empty braces (). This method does not return any value. So void is written before the method name. 'void' means 'no value'. Probably this method is doing its own calculations and displaying the result (but not returning it). We can call this method as:

```
obj.sum();
```

❑ long factorial(int x): This method is calculating factorial value of given value x which is an integer. So at the time of calling this method, we should pass x value to the method. It is returning long type value which is factorial value of x. We can call this method as:

```
long result = obj.factorial(10);
```

❑ `double power(double x, int n)`: This method calculates power value of a number when it is raised to a particular power. When it is called, we should pass two values, the number (x) and its power (n). It then calculates x^n value and returns that result as double value. So double is written before the method name. We can call this method as:

```
double result = obj.power(5.12, 3);
```

❑ `Employee calculateTax(Employee obj)`: This method is intended to calculate income tax of an employee. It accepts Employee object which contains salary of an employee. By taking the salary, it calculates the tax and stores it again in Employee object which is returned. So while calling this method, we should pass an Employee object e2 and it returns another Employee object e3, as shown here:

```
Employee e3 = e1.calculateTax(Employee e2);
```

❑ `int[ ][ ] matrixSum(int a[ ][ ], int b[ ][ ])`: This method is taking two integer type 2D arrays which represent two matrices. It calculates sum of these two matrices and returns the sum matrix, which is again a 2D array of integer type. Hence, before this method name, we wrote `int[ ][ ]`. If arr1 and arr2 are two matrices being passed to this method, we can call this method as:

```
arr3 = obj.matrixSum(arr1, arr2);
```

Method Body

Below the method header, we should write the method body. Method body consists of a group of statements which contains logic to perform the task. Method body can be written in the following format:

```
{
        statements;
}
```

For example, we want to write a method that calculates sum of two numbers. It may contain the body, as shown here:

```
{
        double c = a+b;
        System.out.println("Sum of two= "+ c);
}
```

If a method returns some value, then a return statement should be written within the body of the method, as:

```
return x;     //return x value
return (x+y);    //return sum of x and y
return -1;  //return -1
return  obj;  //return object obj
return arr;    //return array arr
```

For example, a method that calculates sum of two numbers can return the result using return statement, as:

```
{
        double c = a+b;
        return c;
}
```

A method can never return more than one value. Hence the following statements will be invalid:

❑   `return x,y;`   `//invalid` – returning two values

❑   `return x; return y;`   `//invalid` - two executable return statements

Understanding Methods

To understand how to write methods, let us take an example program. In this program, we write Sample class with two instance variables num1 and num2. To find the sum of these values, we can write a method as:

```
void sum()
{
      double res = num1+ num2;
      System.out.println("Sum= "+ res);
}
```

Observe the method header. Since this method does not accept any values, we did not declare any parameters in the braces ( ). This method does not return any result, so 'void' is written before the method.

Observe the method body. The sum of num1 and num2 is stored in a variable 'res' and that it displayed. Displaying the result does not mean that it is returned. To return the result, a method needs a return statement in the body. To call the preceding method, we can use a statement like:

```
s.sum();
```

Here, we are not passing any values to the method and also not catching any result from the method.

Program 1: Write a program for a method without parameters and without return type.

```
//Understanding the methods
class Sample
{
   //instance variables
   private double num1, num2;
   //parameterized constructor
   Sample(double x, double y)
   {
      num1 = x;
      num2 = y;
   }
   //method to calculate sum of num1, num2
   //this method does not accept any values and
   //does not return result
   void sum()
   {
      double res = num1+ num2;
      System.out.println("Sum= "+ res);
   }
}
class Methods
{
   public static void main(String args[ ])
   {
      //create the object and pass values 10 and 22.5 to constructor.
      //they will be stored into num1, num2.
      Sample s = new Sample(10, 22.5);
      //call the method and find sum of num1, num2
      s.sum();
   }
}
```

Output:

```
C:\> javac Methods.java
C:\> java Methods
Sum= 32.5
```

In the preceding program, the sum() method is acting on num1 and num2 which are instance variables of the Sample class. Since instance variables are available in the object, while calling this method we created an object to Sample class, and using the object we called the method. Such methods are called 'instance methods'.

Important Interview Question

What are instance methods?

Instance methods are the methods which act on the instance variables of the class. To call the instance methods, we should use the form: objectname.methodname().

Let us rewrite the Program1, this time using sum() method with a return type. This method is written as:

```
double sum()
{
    double res = num1+ num2;
    return res; //return result
}
```

Observe the return statement where the result 'res' is returned from the method. This result can be caught into a variable x, as:

```
double x = s.sum();
```

Remember a method always returns the result to the calling method. A method call is replaced by the returned result. In the following program, we called the sum() method of Sample class from the main() method of Methods class. So sum() method will return the result to main() method. In the main() method, we can receive the result into x.

Note

It is not compulsory in Java to catch the value returned by a method.

Program 2: Write a program for a method without parameters but with return type.

```
//Understanding the methods
class Sample
{
    //instance variables
    private double num1, num2;
    //parameterized constructor
    Sample(double x, double y)
    {
        num1 = x;
        num2 = y;
    }
    //method to calculate sum of num1, num2
    //this method does not accept any values
    //but returns the result
    double sum()
    {
        double res = num1+ num2;
        return res; //return result
```

```
      }
    }
    class Methods
    {
      public static void main(String args[ ])
      {
        //create the object and pass values 10 and 22.5 to constructor.
        //they will be stored into num1, num2.
        Sample s = new Sample(10, 22.5);
        //call the method and store the result in x
        double x = s.sum();
        System.out.println("Sum= "+ x);
      }
    }
```

Output:

```
C:\> javac Methods.java
C:\> java Methods
Sum= 32.5
```

Let us rewrite the Program2, where the sum() method not only return the result, but also receives the values from outside, as:

```
double sum(double num1, double num2)
{
    double res = num1+ num2;
    return res; //return result
}
```

The preceding method has two parameters num1 and num2. They receive double type values from outside. So we should pass double type values to this method at the time of calling it, as:

```
double x = s.sum(10,22.5);
```

Here, 10 is stored into num1 as 10.0 and 22.5 is stored into num2.

Program 3: Write a program for a method with two parameters and return type.

```
//Understanding the methods
class Sample
{
//method to calculate sum of num1, num2
  //this method accepts two double values
  //and also returns the double type result
  double sum(double num1, double num2)
  {
    double res = num1+ num2;
    return res; //return result
  }
}
class Methods
{
  public static void main(String args[ ])
  {
    //create the object to Sample class.
    Sample s = new Sample();
    //call the method and pass two values to
    //the method. Store the returned result in x.
    double x = s.sum(10,22.5);
    System.out.println("Sum= "+ x);
  }
}
```

Output:

```
C:\> javac Methods.java
C:\> java Methods
Sum= 32.5
```

Please observe that in Program3, the sum() method is not acting on any instance variables. In fact, there are no instance variables defined in the Sample class. We know instance variables are available in the object. Since sum() method is not using any instance variables, there is no need to create an object to call this method. Such methods are called 'static methods'.

Important Interview Question

What are static methods?

Static methods are the methods which do not act upon the instance variables of a class. Static methods are declared as 'static'.

So, to call the static methods, we need not create an object. We can call a static method, as:

```
Classname. methodname();
```

For example, to call the sum() method, we can write as, Sample.sum(10,22.5). Let us write the preceding program again, to use the static method.

Program 4: Write a program for a static method that accepts data and returns the result.

```
//Understanding the methods
class Sample
{
//static method should be declared as static
  static double sum(double num1, double num2)
  {
      double res = num1+ num2;
      return res; //return result
  }
}
class Methods {
  public static void main(String args[ ])
  {
      //call the static method using Classname.methodname().
      double x = Sample.sum(10,22.5);
      System.out.println("Sum= "+ x);

  }
}
```

Output:

```
C:\> javac Methods.java
C:\> java Methods
Sum= 32.5
```

Static Methods

A static method is a method that does not act upon instance variables of a class. A static method is declared by using the keyword 'static'. Static methods are called using Classname.methodname(). The reason why static methods can not act on instance variables is that the JVM first executes the static methods and then only it creates the objects. Since the objects are not available at the time of calling the static methods, the instance variables are also not available.

In the following program, we are trying to read and display the instance variable 'x' of Test class in a static method 'access()'. This gives an error at compile time. See the output.

Program 5: Write a program to test whether a static method can access the instance variable or not.

```
//static method trying to access instance variable
class Test
{
//instance var
  int x;
  //parameterized constructor
  Test(int x)
  {
    this.x = x;
  }
  //static method accessing x value
  static void access()
  {
    System.out.println("x= "+ x);
  }
}
class Demo
{
  public static void main(String args[])
  {
    Test obj = new Test(55);
    Test.access();
  }
}
```

Output:

```
C:\> javac Demo.java
Demo.java:16: non-static variable x cannot be referenced from a static context
    System.out.println("x= "+ x);
                               ^
1 error
```

But a static method can access static variables. Static variables are also declared as 'static'. In the following program, we are declaring x as a static variable. Now it is accessible in the static method access().

Program 6: Write a program to test whether a static method can access the static variable or not.

```
//static method accessing static variable
class Test
{
  //static var
  static int x = 55;
  //static method accessing x value
  static void access()
  {
    System.out.println("x= "+ x);
  }
}
class Demo
{
public static void main(String args[])
{
    Test.access();
  }
}
```

Output:

```
C:\> javac Demo.java
C:\> java Demo
x= 55
```

The other name for static variable is 'class variable' and for static method is 'class method'.

Important Interview Question

What is the difference between instance variables and class variables (static variables)?

1. An instance variable is a variable whose separate copy is available to each object. A class variable is a variable whose single copy in memory is shared by all objects.

2. Instance variables are created in the objects on heap memory. Class variables are stored on method area.

Since, instance variable will have a separate copy in each object, when the value of an instance variable is modified in an object, it does not affect the instance variables in other objects. This is proved in Program 7. Also see the Figure 13.1.

Program 7: Let us make a program by taking an instance variable x in the Test class.

```
//instance variables
class Test
{
  //instance var
  int x = 10;
  //display the variable
  void display()
  {
    System.out.println(x);
  }
}
class InstanceDemo
{
  public static void main(String args[ ])
  {
    //create two references
    Test obj1, obj2;
    //create two objects
    obj1 = new Test();
    obj2 = new Test();
    //increment x in obj1
    ++obj1.x;
    System.out.print("x in obj1: ");
    obj1.display();
    //display x in obj2
    System.out.print("x in obj2: ");
    obj2.display();
  }
}
```

Output:

```
C:\> javac InstanceDemo.java
C:\> java InstanceDemo
x in obj1: 11
x in obj2: 10
```

Here we create two objects obj1, obj2 to Test class. When x value in obj1 is incremented, it does not change the x value in obj2.

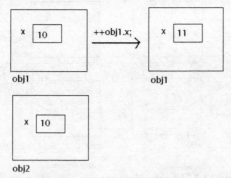

Figure 13.1 Each object gets a separate copy of instance variable

Since a class variable (static variable) will have only one copy in memory and that is shared by all the objects, any modification to it will also affect other objects. This is proved in Program 8. Also see Figure 13.2.

Program 8: Let us make a program by taking a static variable x in the Test class.

```java
//class variables
class Test
{
//class var
  static int x = 10;
  //display the variable
  static void display()
  {
    System.out.println(x);
  }
}
class StaticDemo
{
  public static void main(String args[ ])
  {
      //create two references
      Test obj1, obj2;
      //create two objects
      obj1 = new Test();
      obj2 = new Test();
      //increment x in obj1
      ++obj1.x;
      System.out.print("x in obj1: ");
      obj1.display();
      //display x in obj2
      System.out.print("x in obj2: ");
      obj2.display();
  }
}
```

Output:

```
C:\> javac StaticDemo.java
C:\> java StaticDemo
x in obj1: 11
x in obj2: 11
```

Here in this program, we create two objects obj1, obj2 to Test class. When x value in obj1 is incremented, the incremented value is seen in obj2 also.

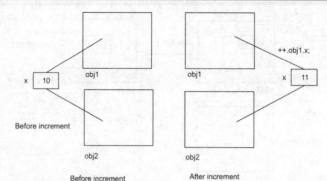

Before increment   After increment

Figure 13.2 All objects share same copy of a static variable

Why instance variables are not available to static methods?

After executing static methods, JVM creates the objects. So the instance variables of the objects are not available to static methods.

The execution sequence of JVM is the process where JVM executes first of all any static blocks in the Java program. Then it executes static methods (remember `main()` is a static method) and then it creates any objects needed by the program. Finally, it executes the instance methods.

Static Block

A static block is a block of statements declared as 'static', some thing like this:

```
static {
    statements;
}
```

JVM executes a static block on a highest priority basis. This means JVM first goes to static block even before it looks for the `main()` method in the program. This can be understood from the Program 9.

Program 9: Write a program to test which one is executed first by JVM, the static block or the static method.

```
//Static block or Static method?
class Test
{
  static {
     System.out.println("Static block");
  }
  public static void main(String args[ ])
  {
     System.out.println("Static method");
  }
}
```

Output:

```
C:\> javac Test.java
C:\> java Test
Static block
Static method
```

So far, we thought that the `main()` method is the first one that is given attention by the JVM. This is ok if static block is not present in the program. If a static block is present, then JVM executes it first of all. After that, it searches for the `main()` method. If `main()` method is not found, it will display an error as shown in the output of the program 10.

Program 10: Write a Java program without `main()` method. This program compiles but gives an error at runtime.

```
//No main() method
class Test
{
  static {
     System.out.println("Static block");
  }
}
```

Output:

```
C:\> javac Test.java
C:\> java Test
Static block
Exception in thread "main" java.lang.NoSuchMethodError: main
```

Now, we can cheat the JVM by terminating it before it realizes that there is no `main()` method in the program, as shown here.

Program 11: Write a Java program without `main()` method. This program compiles and also runs.

```
//No main() method
class Test
{
  static {
     System.out.println("Static block");
     System.exit(0);
  }
}
```

Output:

```
C:\> javac Test.java
C:\> java Test
Static block
```

Important Interview Question

Is it possible to compile and run a Java program without writing `main()` *method?*

Yes, it is possible by using a static block in the Java program.

So far, we discussed about instance variables and static variables. There are other types of variables, called 'local variables'. A local variable is a variable that is declared locally inside a method or a constructor and is available only within that method or constructor. It means a local variable cannot be accessed outside the method or constructor. For example,

```
void modify(int a)
{
    x = a;
}
```

In the preceding code, we declared 'a' inside the `modify()` method. It is a local variable. It cannot be accessed outside of `modify()` method. The other variable 'x' is not declared within it. It may be an instance variable. Instance variables are accessible any where within the class. See the Program 12.

Program 12: Let us make a program to access an instance variable 'x' and a local variable 'a' from the method `access()`.

```
//local variables
class Sample
{
    //x is instance variable
    private int x;
    //a is local variable
    void modify(int a)
    {
        x = a;
    }
    //we can access x, but not a.
    void access()
    {
        System.out.println("x= "+x);
        System.out.println("a= "+a);
    }
}
class Local
{
    public static void main(String args[ ])
    {
        Sample s = new Sample();
        s.modify(10);
        s.access();
    }
}
```

Output:

```
C:\> javac Local.java
Local.java:17: cannot find symbol
Symbol   : variable a
Location: class Sample
      System.out.println("a= "+a);
                                 ^
1 error
```

By observing the output, we can understand that there is an error while accessing 'a'. This clearly tells that a local variable cannot be accessed outside the method where it is declared. But the instance variable 'x' is accessible by `access()` method.

Sometimes a local variable has the same name as that of an instance variable. This leads to problems regarding their accessibility. For example,

```
void modify(int x)
{
    x = x;  //both the x refer only local variable
}
```

In the preceding code, the local variable is 'x' and the instance variable is also 'x'. Inside the `modify()` method, if we write 'x', it denotes by default the local variable only. Now the question is how to refer to the instance variable. For this purpose, we should use 'this' keyword.

The keyword 'this'

'this' is a keyword that refers to the object of the class where it is used. In other words, 'this' refers to the object of the present class. Generally, we write instance variables, constructors and methods in a class. All these members are referenced by 'this'. When an object is created to a class, a default reference is also created internally to the object, as shown in the Figure 13.3. This default reference is nothing but 'this'. So 'this' can refer to all the things of the present object.

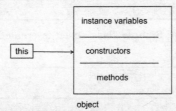

object

Figure 13.3 The keyword 'this' is a reference to class object

Now modify() method can be written as:

```
void modify(int x)
{
   this.x = x;  //store local variable x into present class instance variable x.
}
```

In the preceding code 'this.x' refers to the present class instance variable and just 'x' refers to the local variable. To understand the use of 'this', let us take a sample program.

Program 13: Write a program to use this to refer the current class parameterized constructor as 'this()', its method as 'this.method()' and its instance variable as 'this.variable'.

```
//this - refers to all the members of present class
class Sample
{
   //x is instance variable
   private int x;
   //default constructor
   Sample()
   {
     this(55); //call present class para constructor and send 55
     this.access(); //call present class method
   }
   //parameterized constructor
   Sample(int x)
   {
      this.x = x; //refer present class instance variable
   }
   //method
   void access()
   {
     System.out.println("x= "+x);
   }
}
class ThisDemo
{
   public static void main(String args[])
   {
     Sample s = new Sample();

   }
}
```

Output:

```
C:\> javac ThisDemo.java
C:\> java ThisDemo
x= 55
```

In the preceding program, we created an object to Sample class, as:

```
Sample s = new Sample();
```

Here, two things will happen. First, Sample class object is created and then its default constructor is also executed. Hence the code:

```
this(55);
this.access();
```

is executed. In the first statement, present class (Sample) constructor is called and 55 is passed to it. This value is used by parameterized constructor to initialize the present class instance variable as:

```
this.x = x;
```

Here, 'this.x' represents present class instance variable 'x'. Similarly to call the present class access() method, we can use 'this.access()', which displays the x value 55 as output.

Instance Methods

Instance methods are the methods which act upon the instance variables. To call the instance methods, object is needed, since the instance variables are contained in the object. We call the instance methods by using objectname.methodname(). The specialty of instance methods is that they can access not only instance variables but also static variables directly.

There are two types of instance methods:

❑   Accessor methods, and

❑   Mutator methods.

Accessor methods are the methods that simply access or read the instance variables. They do not modify the instance variables. Mutator methods not only access the instance variables but also modify them.

Suppose, we take a 'Person' class with name and age as instance variables. To store data into these instance variables, we can use setName() and setAge() methods. These methods are called mutator methods. Similarly to read and return the instance variables, we can write methods like getName() and getAge(). These are called accessor methods. These are demonstrated in the next program.

Program 14: Write a program to create Person class object.

```
//Accessor and mutator methods
class Person
{
    //instance variables
    private String name;
    private int age;
    //mutator methods to store data
    public void setName(String name)
    {
        this.name = name;
    }
    public void setAge(int age)
```

```
    {
       this.age = age;
    }
    //accessor methods to read data
    public String getName()
    {
       return name;
    }
    public int getAge()
    {
       return age;
    }
}
class Methods
{
  public static void main(String args[ ])
  {
    //create an empty Person class object
    Person p1 = new Person();
    //store some data into the object
    p1.setName("Raju");
    p1.setAge(20);
    //access data from object
    System.out.println("Name= "+ p1.getName());
    System.out.println("Age= "+ p1.getAge());
  }
}
```

Output:

```
C:\> javac Methods.java
C:\> java Methods
Name= Raju
Age= 20
```

In this program, we use setter methods to set some values into the instance variables. We also use getter methods to return the same.

Passing Primitive Data Types to Methods

Primitive data types or fundamental data types represent single entities or single values. For example, char, byte, short, int, long, float, double and boolean are called primitive data types, because they store single values. They are passed to methods *by value*. This means when we pass primitive data types to methods, a copy of those will be passed to methods. Therefore, any changes made to them inside the method will not affect them outside the method.

Let us take an example. There is a method 'swap()' to interchange two values, num1 and num2. The logic for this can be taken as:

❏ Take a temporary variable temp.

❏ Preserve a copy of num1 into temp.

❏ Now store num2 into num1.

❏ Store the previous copy of num1 from temp into num1.

In the following program, we pass two integer numbers 10 and 20 to the swap method. Let us display the output to know whether they are interchanged or not.

Program 15: Let us try to interchange two integers 10 and 20 by passing them to swap() method.

```
//Primitive data types are passed to methods by value
class Check
{
    //to interchange num1 and num2 values
```

```
        void swap(int num1, int num2)
        {
          int temp; //take a temporary variable
          temp = num1;
          num1 = num2;
          num2 = temp;
        }
      }
      class PassPrimitive
      {
       public static void main(String args[ ])
       {
          //take two primitive data types
          int num1 = 10, num2 = 20;
          //create Check class object
          Check obj = new Check();
          //display data before calling
          System.out.println(num1+"\t"+num2);
          //call swap and pass primitive data types
          obj.swap(num1, num2);
          //display data after calling
          System.out.println(num1+"\t"+num2);
       }
      }
```

Output:

```
C:\> javac PassPrimitive.java
C:\> java PassPrimitive
10    20
10    20
```

The output indicates that the two integers are not interchanged. From `main()` method, we passed 10 and 20 to `swap()` method. Inside the method, they are interchanged. But when we come out of `swap()` method, again we find the previous values as they are, not interchanged.

When we send primitive data types like int, float, char, etc., to a method, a copy of their values will be sent to the method. So any modifications to them inside the method will not affect their original copy. This is also called pass *by value* or call *by value*.

Passing Objects to Methods

We can also pass class objects to methods, and return objects from the methods. For example,

```
Employee myMethod(Employee obj)
{
        statements;
        return obj;
}
```

Here, `myMethod()` is a method that accepts Employee class object. So reference of Employee class is declared as parameter in `myMethod()`. After doing some processing on the object, if it returns the same object, we can write a statement like:

```
return obj;
```

Even the objects are also passed to methods *by value*. This means, when we send an object to a method, its bit by bit copy will be sent to the method. Any modifications to the object inside the method will not affect the original copy outside the method. So when we come out of the method, we find the original value unchanged.

In the following program, we take Employee class with employee identification number 'id' as an instance variable. We pass two Employee class objects to `swap()` method written in Check class, as:

```
void swap(Employee obj1, Employee obj2)
```

To interchange the Employee class objects inside the `swap()` method, we can call the `swap()` method by passing two Employee objects as:

```
obj.swap(obj1, obj2);
```

When we pass objects obj1 and obj2 to a method as shown earlier, actually a copy of the references obj1 and obj2 are passed to the method where they will be interchanged. Outside the method, the original obj1 and obj2 will remain same. See Figure 13.4. So, when we come out of `swap()` method, we find the 'id' values are not changed. This is the effect of pass *by value*.

Program 16: Let us try to make a program to interchange two Employee objects by passing them to `swap()` method.

```
//Objects are also passed to methods by value
class Employee
{
  //instance variable
  int id;
  //to initialize id value
  Employee(int id)
  {
    this.id = id;
  }
}
class Check
{
  //to interchange Employee class objects
  void swap(Employee obj1, Employee obj2)
  {
    Employee temp; //take a temporary reference
    temp = obj1;
    obj1 = obj2;
    obj2 = temp;
  }
}
class PassObjects
{
 public static void main(String args[ ])
  {
    //take two Employee class objects
    Employee obj1 = new Employee(10);
    Employee obj2 = new Employee(20);
    //create Check class object
    Check obj = new Check();
    //display data before calling
    System.out.println(obj1.id+"\t"+obj2.id);
    //call swap and pass Employee class objects
    obj.swap(obj1, obj2);
    //display data after calling
    System.out.println(obj1.id+"\t"+obj2.id);
  }
}
```

Output:

```
C:\> javac PassObjects.java
C:\> java PassObjects
10    20
10    20
```

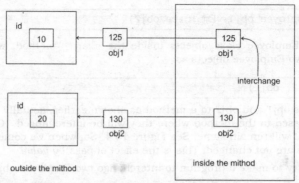

Figure 13.4 Interchanging the objects will interchange the references

Some authors have written out of confusion that primitive data types are passed to methods *by value* and objects are passed to methods *by reference*. This confusion primarily stems from applying C/C++ concept of 'pass by reference' in Java where the memory address (pointer) of the variables is passed to the methods. Since Java does not support creation and use of pointers, there is no question of passing memory addresses. So 'pass by reference' is not valid in Java.

Important Interview Question

How are objects are passed to methods in Java?

Primitive data types, objects, even object references – every thing is passed to methods using 'pass by value' or 'call by value' concept. This means their bit by bit copy is passed to the methods.

So, how can we interchange the 'id' values of Employee class objects by using swap() method? One possible solution is to use only one object and take two variables id1 and id2, and interchange their values in the object. This is shown in Program 17. In this program, we call the swap() method as:

```
obj.swap(obj1);
```

Here, a copy of obj1 is sent to the method and from there still, it can refer to the same object. So using it, if we modify the instance variables, we can have the data really modified in the original object. This is shown in Figure 13.5.

Program 17: Write a program to interchange the values inside an object, since the same object data is modified, we can see the data has been interchanged.

```java
//Interchanging the values should be done in a single object
class Employee
{
    //instance variables
    int id1, id2;
    //to initialize id values
    Employee(int id1, int id2)
    {
        this.id1 = id1;
        this.id2 = id2;
    }
}
class Check
{
    //to interchange id values in the same Employee object
    void swap(Employee obj)
    {
        int temp; //take a temporary variable
        temp = obj.id1;
        obj.id1 = obj.id2;
```

```
        obj.id2 = temp;
    }
}
class PassObjects
{
    public static void main(String args[ ])
    {
        //take Employee class object with id values
        Employee obj1 = new Employee(10, 20);
        //create Check class object
        Check obj = new Check();
        //display data before calling
        System.out.println(obj1.id1+"\t"+obj1.id2);
        //call swap and pass Employee class object
        obj.swap(obj1);
        //display data after calling
        System.out.println(obj1.id1+"\t"+obj1.id2);
    }
}
```

Output:

```
C:\> javac PassObjects.java
C:\> java PassObjects
10    20
20    10
```

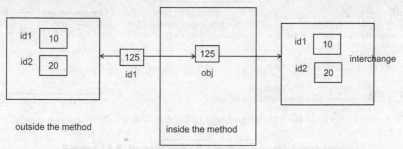

Figure 13.5 Interchanging the instance variables of the object

Passing Arrays to Methods

Just like the objects are passed to methods, it is also possible to pass arrays to methods and return arrays from methods. In this case, an array name should be understood as an object reference. For example,

```
int[ ] myMethod(int arr[ ])
```

This is the way, we can pass a one dimensional array 'arr' to 'myMethod()'. We can also return a one dimensional array of int type as shown in the preceding statement.

```
int[ ][ ] myMethod(int arr[ ][ ])
```

Here, we are passing and returning a two dimensional array of int type. Let us write a Java program to understand this concept further. In this program, we want to find the sum of two matrices. We take two 2D arrays of int type which represent the two matrices. We add them and get another 2D array of int type which represents the sum matrix. This sum matrix is finally displayed. We want to perform these tasks by using the following methods:

❏ Accept array (matrix) elements from keyboard by using getMatrix() method.

❏ Accept second array (matrix) elements from keyboard. For this also, same getMatrix() method can be used.

❏ Add the two matrices by using findSum() method.

❏ Finally, display the sum matrix by using displayMatrix() method.

Program 18: Write a program to add two matrices and display sum matrix.

```java
//Matrix addition using methods.
//Passing arrays to methods and returning them.
import java.io.*;
import java.util.*;
class Matrix
{
  //take a 2D array for matrix and rows,cols
  int arr[ ][ ];
  int r,c;
  //Initialize r,c and allot memory for array
  Matrix(int r,int c)
  {
    this.r = r;
    this.c = c;
    arr = new int[r][c];
  }
  //accept 2D array from keyboard and return it
  int[ ][ ] getMatrix() throws IOException
  {
    BufferedReader br = new BufferedReader(new InputStreamReader(System.in));
    //StringTokenizer is useful to accept each row as a single string and then
    // divide it into tokens. Each token represents an array element.
    StringTokenizer st;

      for(int i=0; i<r; i++)
      {
          String s = br.readLine();
          st = new StringTokenizer(s," ");
          for(int j=0; j<c; j++)
          arr[i][j] = Integer.parseInt(st.nextToken());
      }

      return arr;
  }
  //accept two 2D arrays and find sum matrix and return it.
  int[ ][ ] findSum(int a[ ][ ], int b[ ][ ])
  {
    int temp[ ][ ] = new int[r][c];

    for(int i=0; i<r; i++)
      for(int j=0; j<c; j++)
        temp[i][j]= a[i][j]+b[i][j];

    return temp;
  }
  //display the resultant 2D array as a matrix.
  void displayMatrix(int res[ ][ ])
  {
    for(int i=0; i<r; i++)
    {
      for(int j=0; j<c; j++)
      {
        System.out.print(res[i][j]+"\t");
      }
      System.out.println();
    }
  }
}
```

```
class MatrixSum
{
  public static void main(String args[ ])
  throws IOException
  {
    //create 2 objects to Matrix class, since each object
    //contains an array.
    Matrix obj1 = new Matrix(3,3);   //3X3 matrix
    Matrix obj2 = new Matrix(3,3); //3X3 matrix
    //take 3 references for 2D arrays.
    int x[ ][ ],y[ ][ ],z[ ][ ];
    System.out.println("\nEnter elements for first matrix: ");
    x = obj1.getMatrix();
    System.out.println("\nEnter elements for second matrix: ");
    y = obj2.getMatrix();
    //add the matrices and return sum matrix into z
    z = obj1.findSum(x,y);
    System.out.println("\nThe sum matrix is: ");
    obj2.displayMatrix(z);
  }
}
```

Output:

```
C:\> javac MatrixSum.java
C:\> java MatrixSum
Enter elements for first matrix:
1  2  3
4  5  6
7  8  9

Enter elements for second matrix:
1  1  1
2  2  3
0  0  -2

The sum matrix is:
2  3  4
6  7  9
7  8  7
```

Here in preceding program, we take a matrix as a 2D array of int type. This program assumes 3X3 matrices. But the same logic can be applied to add mXn matrices also.

Let us write another program by using methods to generate prime number series. A prime number is a number that is not divisible by any other number except by 1 and itself. For example, the prime numbers may start from 2 and proceed as: $2, 3, 5, 7, 11, 13, \ldots$

In this program, we write a static method prime() to test if a number is prime or not. Suppose 5 is a prime number, then it should not be divisible by any number from 2 to 4 (except 1 and itself). This logic is used in prime() method. prime() method returns true if a number passed to it is a prime, else it returns false. Another static method generate() generates a sequence of numbers and passes each number to prime() method for testing. If it is prime, it is displayed other wise, next number is tested.

Program 19: Write a program to generate required number of primes using methods.

```
//Prime number series
import java.io.*;
class Primes
{
  //to test and return true if num is prime
  static boolean prime(long num)
  {
    //initially isPrime is true, it becomes false if
    //num is not prime
```

```
            boolean isPrime = true;
            //from 2 to num-1, if any number divides num, it is not prime
            for(int i=2; i<=num-1; i++)
                if(num % i ==0) isPrime = false;
            return isPrime;
        }
        //accept how many primes required into max.
        // c is counter for no. of primes generated.
        static void generate(long max)
        {
            long c=1, num=2;
            while(c<= max)
            {
                if(prime(num))    //call prime() method directly
                {
                    System.out.println(num);
                    ++c;
                }
                ++num;
            }
        }
    }
    class PrimeDemo
    {
        public static void main(String args[ ]) throws IOException
        {
            //accept the number of primes are needed
            BufferedReader br= new BufferedReader(new InputStreamReader(System.in));
            System.out.print("How many primes? ");
            int max = Integer.parseInt(br.readLine());
            //generate max number of primes
            Primes.generate(max);
        }
    }
```

Output:

```
C:\> javac PrimeDemo.java
C:\> java PrimeDemo
How many primes? 10
2
3
5
7
11
13
17
19
23
29
```

Recursion

A method calling itself is known as 'recursive method', and that phenomenon is called 'recursion'. It is possible to write recursive methods in Java. Let us take an example to find factorial value of a given number. Factorial value for a number num is defined as: num* (num-1)* (num-2)…..* 1. For example, factorial of 5 will be 5*4*3*2*1 = 120. As long as num value is >0, we should decrement num value and take the products into some other variable say 'fact'. This can be written as:

```
long fact = 1;
while(num>0)
{
    fact = fact * num ;
```

```
        num = num -1;
    }
```

This logic is represented in Program 20.

Program 20: Write a program to find factorial value without using recursion.

```
//Factorial without Recursion
class NoRecursion
{
    static long factorial(int num)
    {
      long fact = 1;
      while(num>0)
        fact *= num--;
      return fact;
    }
    public static void main(String args[])
    {
        System.out.println("Factorial of 5: ");
        System.out.println(NoRecursion.factorial(5));

    }
}
```

Output:

```
C:\> javac Recursion.java
C:\> java Recursion
Factorial of 5:
120
```

In the next program, we calculate the factorial value by using recursion. The logic is to call the factorial method from within the same factorial method, as:

```
result = factorial(num-1)*num;
```

this is because, factorial of 5 = factorial(4) * 5

and factorial of 4 = factorial(3) *4

and factorial of 3 = factorial(2) *3

and factorial of 2 = factorial(1) *2

and factorial of 1 = 1.

Hence, substituting in the first statement, we get:

```
factorial of 5 = 1*2*3*4*5 = 120.
```

So, we write the logic something like this:

```
if(num==1) return 1;
    result =factorial(num-1)*num;
```

Program 21: Write a program to calculate factorial value by using Recursion.

```
//Factorial using Recursion
class Recursion
{
    static long factorial(int num)
    {
      long result;
```

```
        if(num==1) return 1;
        result =factorial(num-1)*num;
        return result;
      }
     public static void main(String args[ ])
     {
        System.out.println("Factorial of 5: ");
        System.out.println(Recursion.factorial(5));
     }
   }
```

Output:

```
C:\> javac Recursion.java
C:\> java Recursion
Factorial of 5:
120
```

Factory Methods

Factory methods are static methods only. But their intension is to create an object depending on the user choice. Precisely, a factory method is a method that returns an object to the class, to which it belongs. For example, getNumberInstance() is a factory method. Why? Because it belongs to NumberFormat class and returns an object to NumberFormat class.

At the time of creating objects, if the user has several types of options (values) to be passed to the object, then several overloaded constructors should be written in the class. For example, there are 10 different types of values to be passed, then 10 constructors are needed to accept those 10 types of options. This can be eliminated by using factory methods. A single factory method gives provision to pass any type of value through a parameter. Generally, the parameter is used to pass different types of values. Based on the value passed, the object is created by the factory method.

Important Interview Question

What are factory methods?

A factory method is a method that creates and returns an object to the class to which it belongs. A single factory method replaces several constructors in the class by accepting different options from the user, while creating the object.

To understand how to use a factory method, let us take an example program to calculate the area of a circle.

Program 22: Write a program for calculating and displaying area of a circle. The area is not formatted and displayed as it is.

```
//Area of a circle
class Circle
{
  public static void main(String args[])
  {
    final double PI = (double)22/7;  //constant
    double r = 15.5;  //radius
    double area = PI*r*r;
    System.out.println("Area= "+ area);
  }
}
```

Output:

```
C:\> javac Circle.java
C:\> java Circle
Area= 755.0714285714286
```

The digits before the decimal point are called 'integer digits' and the digits after the decimal point are called 'fraction digits'. In the output of the preceding program, there are 13 digits displayed after the decimal point. For most of the general purposes, these many digits are not needed. For example, in an electricity bill, we need not display more than 2 digits after the decimal point to indicate paise. So the question is how to format the output (area) of the preceding program to display as many digits as we want in the integer and fraction parts. This is achieved by NumberFormat class. NumberFormat class of java.text package is useful to format the numerical values. The way to do this is:

❑ Create NumberFormat object. For this, we should use the factory method getNumberInstance().

❑ Decide how to format the area value. Depending on this, we should use any of the NumberFormat class methods:

```
setMaximumIntegerDigits();
setMinimumIntegerDigits();
setMaximumFractionDigits();
setMinimumFractionDigits();
```

These methods specify how many integer digits or fraction digits to be displayed in the output.

❑ Apply the format to the area value using format() method. This method returns a string that contains formatted area value.

These steps can be seen in the following program.

Program 23: Write a program for calculating and displaying area of a circle. The area is formatted to have 7 maximum integer digits and 2 minimum fraction digits.

```
//Area of a circle
import java.text.*;
class Circle
{
  public static void main(String args[])
  {
    final double PI = (double)22/7;
    double r = 15.5;
    double area = PI*r*r;
    System.out.println("Area= "+ area);
    //create NumberFormat class object
    NumberFormat obj = NumberFormat.getNumberInstance();
    //store the format information into obj
    obj.setMaximumFractionDigits(2);
    obj.setMinimumIntegerDigits(7);
    //apply the format to area value
    String str = obj.format(area);
    //display formatted area value
    System.out.println("Formatted area= "+ str);

  }
}
```

Output:

```
C:\> javac Circle.java
C:\> java Circle
Area= 755.0714285714286
Formatted area= 0,000,755.07
```

Please observe the formatted area value in the output. It has 7 integer digits separated properly by commas and 2 fraction digits as specified by the methods:

```
obj.setMaximumFractionDigits(2);
obj.setMinimumIntegerDigits(7);
```

Also observe using the getNumberInstance() method to create an object to NumberFormat class. We used the default format of this method. There is another way of using getNumberInstance() method as:

```
getNumberInstance(Locale constant);
```

Here, the parameter represents a constant that represents the name of a country (locality) as Locale.CANADA, Locale.CHINA, Locale.FRANCE, Locale.GERMANY, Locale.ITALY, Locale.JAPAN, Locale.US, Locale.UK, etc., For example, to format a number according to the numerical format of United States, we can pass that constant to the NumberFormat object, as:

```
NumberFormat obj = NumberFormat.getNumberInstance(Locale.US);
```

In the place of getNumberInstance() method, if constructors are provided in the NumberFormat class, they should be created something like: NumberFormat(Locale.CANADA), NumberFormat(Locale.CHINA),...

In this way, several constructors should be created. This awkwardness is avoided by using a single factory method getNumberInstance() and passing the required name of the country to it.

We can consider factory methods as alternative way to create objects, other than the new operator. So, new operator is not the only way to create objects in Java. There are other ways for that, which are discussed here in the important interview questions.

Important Interview Question

In how may ways can you create an object in Java?

There are four ways of creating objects in Java:

1. Using new operator.

```
Employee obj = new Employee();
```

Here, we are creating Employee class object 'obj' using new operator.

2. Using factory methods:

```
NumberFormat obj = NumberFormat.getNumberInstance();
```

Here, we are creating NumberFormat *object using the factory method* getNumberInstance().

3. Using newInstance() *method. Here, we should follow two steps, as:*

(a) First, store the class name 'Employee' as a string into an object. For this purpose, factory method forName() *of the class 'Class' will be useful:*

```
Class c = Class.forName("Employee");
```

We should note that there is a class with the name 'Class' in java.lang *package.*

(b) Next, create another object to the class whose name is in the object c. For this purpose, we need newInstance() *method of the class 'Class', as:*

```
Employee obj = (Employee)c.newInstance();
```

4. By cloning an already available object, we can create another object. Creating exact copy of an existing object is called 'cloning':

```
Employee obj1 = new Employee();
Employee obj2 = (Employee)obj1.clone();
```

Earlier, we created obj2 by cloning the Employee object obj1. `clone()` *method of Object class is used to clone an object. We should note that there is a class by the name 'Object' in* `java.lang` *package.*

Methods with Variable Arguments

If we write a method in the form: sum(int a, int b), since this method has only 2 parameters, we can pass only 2 arguments or values to this method. It is not possible to pass more than 2 values to this method. Suppose we want to find sum of 3 numbers, then to pass 3 values, we can write another method in the form: sum(int a, int b, int c). Similarly, if we want to find sum of 4 numbers, again another method with 4 arguments like sum(int a, int b, int c, int d) is needed. The problem is this: We should write a new method every time, when we change the number of arguments. On the other hand, think that if the same method can accept any number of arguments, then that method would be very useful to the programmer.

Observe the following methods:

```
int sum(int a, int b)
int sum(int a, int b, int c)
int sum(int a, int b, int c, int d)
```

Instead of writing the previous three methods, we can write a single method, as:

```
int sum(int x[])
```

This method can accept a group of integer values and finds their sum. But, there is a restriction while using this method. When we call this method, we must pass an array. We cannot pass individual values. For example, calling this method as:

```
sum(2, 4);
```

will give an error.

There is a solution for this problem. We can write a method which can accept arbitrary number of arguments in such a way that it can take 0 or more arguments. For this purpose, we can write:

```
int sum(int … x)
```

Please observe the three dots between the datatype and the variable. These dots represent that it is not an ordinary parameter but a parameter that can accept any number of arguments. This type of method is called 'method with variable arguments' or simply 'method with varargs'. So, a method with variable arguments is a method that accepts 0 or more number of arguments. We can pass individual elements or an array also to this method.

The following rules should be observed to write methods with varargs:

❑ We should write the method name followed by simple braces. In the braces, we can specify the datatype and then three dots and then the variable or object. For example,

```
int sum(int … x)
```

❑ We can also specify other arguments along with vararg. In that case, the vararg should be the last one in the method parameters. For example,

```
int sum(int a, int b, int … x)
```

Here, 'a' and 'b' represent ordinary arguments and 'x' represents vararg.

❑ We can use only one variable argument in a method.

❑ Internally, the vararg is treated as a one dimensional array. For example, if we pass individual elements to sum() method, the vararg 'x' will become an array and stores them all. Suppose, if we pass an array to this method, then all the elements of the array are copied into 'x' array.

Program 24: Write a method with variable arguments that accepts a group of numbers and returns biggest number among them.

```
//Demo of varargs method to find biggest number.
class VArgs
{
    /* This is varargs method. It can accept arbitrary number of arguments. */
    static int max(int ... x)
    {
        //take the first number in the array as biggest
        int max = x[0];
        //compare the biggest number with other numbers
        for(int i=1; i<x.length; i++)
            /* If the biggest is less than the other number then
               take that other number as biggest. */
            if(max < x[i]) max = x[i];
        //return the biggest number
        return max;
    }
    public static void main(String  args[])
    {
        //pass an arry of 5 elements to varargs method
        int arr1[] = {20, 10, 5, 35, 40};
        int result = max(arr1);
        System.out.println("Maximum= "+ result);
        //pass an array of 3 elements to varargs method
        int arr2[] = {1, 2, 3};
        result = max(arr2);
        System.out.println("Maximum= "+ result);
        //pass 2 individual elements to varargs method
        result = max(10, 30);
        System.out.println("Maximum= "+ result);
    }
}
```

The output of this program can be seen here:

```
C:\> javac VArgs.java
C:\> java VArgs
Maximum= 40
Maximum= 3
Maximum= 30
```

Conclusion

Methods are very important components of a program. The programmer should divide the main task into sub tasks and represent each sub task in the form of a method. In Java, we got Static methods, Instance methods and Factory methods. Again, Instance methods are divided into two methods and these are Accessor and Mutator methods.

We also discussed different variables available in Java. An instance variable is directly declared in the class and available anywhere in the class. A separate copy of an instance variable is available to each object. A static variable is a variable whose single copy is shared by all the objects. A local variable is a variable whose scope is limited only to that method or constructor, where it is declared.

Also, we examined the key word 'this', which is a reference to the class object, where it is used, and hence it can refer to all the members of that class object.

RELATIONSHIP BETWEEN OBJECTS

It is possible to create objects for different classes and establish relationship between them. When the objects are related, it is possible to access and use members of one object in another object. This becomes an advantage when an object should start processing data where another object has left. It is also helpful to pass data from one object to another object and from there to another object in a chained form.

There are three ways to relate objects in Java:

❑ Using references

❑ Using inner class concept

❑ Using inheritance

We take up a discussion of the first two in this chapter. The third one will be discussed in the next chapter as it needs an entirely different treatise.

Relating Objects using References

Let us create two classes, 'One' and 'Two'. Suppose we want to access the members of class Two, in class One, we should relate their objects. For this, just declare the reference variable of class Two as an instance variable in class One.

```
class One
{
        Two t;   //t is a reference of class Two
}
```

Now this reference variable 't' can be used to refer to all the members of class Two from class One. For example, to call class Two's display() method, we can write:

```
t.display();
```

And to access class Two's instance variable 'y', unless it is private, we can write as:

```
t.y;
```

To understand this, we can take the example of following program.

Program 1: Write a program to take class One and class Two, and create the reference of class Two in class One. Using this reference, let us refer to the instance variables and methods of class Two.

```
//Relating class Two with class One
class One
{
        //instance variables
        int x;
        Two t;    //class Two's reference
        //constructor that receives Two's reference
        One(Two t)
        {
                //copy Two's reference into t
                this.t = t;
                x = 10;
        }
        //method to display class One and class Two vars
        void display()
        {
                System.out.println("One's x= "+x);
                //call class Two's method
                t.display();
                //access class Two's var
                System.out.println("Two's var= "+t.y);
        }
}
class Two
{
        //instance variable
        int y;
        //initialize y
        Two(int y)
        {
                this.y = y;
        }

        //method to display y
        void display()
        {
                System.out.println("Two's y= "+y);

        }
}

class Relate
{
        public static void main(String args[])
        {
                //create class Two object and store 22 there.
                Two obj2 = new Two(22);
                //create class One object and pass class Two object to it
                One obj1 = new One(obj2);
                //call class One's method
                obj1.display();
        }
}
```

Output:

```
C:\> javac Relate.java
C:\> java Relate
One's x= 10
Two's y= 22
Two's var= 22
```

In preceding program, we followed the following steps:

❑ At the time of creating class One's object, we passed reference of class Two's object, as:

```
One obj1 = new One(obj2);
```

Here, reference of Two's object obj2 is passed to One's object obj1.

❑ This reference obj2's value is copied into class One's constructor and there, it initializes the reference 't' which is declared at class One, as:

```
this.t = t;
```

Here, this.t refers to class Two's reference 't' declared at class One.

❑ Now, 't' refers to class Two's object. So it can access class Two's members. For example, to call class Two's method, we can use:

```
t.display();
```

And, to access class Two's variable, we can use:

```
t.y;
```

This discussion achieves clarity if you see Figure 14.1.

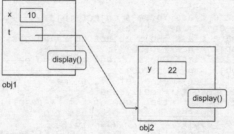

Figure 14.1 't' in obj1 can access members of obj2

In Figure 14.1, we have shown the relation between obj1 and obj2 which are objects of two different classes. Similarly, it is also possible to relate several objects of various classes. This is what, we attempt in the following program.

Program 2: Write a program to call cube() method in class One.

```
//Relating the objects of three classes.
class One
{
    //obj2 is class Two's reference
    Two obj2;
    //initialize obj2
    One(Two obj2)
    {
        this.obj2 = obj2;
    }
    double cube(double x)
    {
        //call class Two's method using obj2
        double result = x*obj2.square(x);
        //return result to Relate class
        return result;
    }
}
class Two
```

```
{
        //obj3 is class Three's reference
        Three obj3;
        //initialize obj3
        Two(Three obj3)
        {
                this.obj3 = obj3;
        }
        double square(double x)
        {
                //call class Three's method using obj3
                double result = x*obj3.get(x);
                //return result to class One
                return result;
        }
}
class Three
{
        double get(double x)
        {
                //just return x value to class Two
                return x;
        }
}
class Relate
{
        public static void main(String args[ ])
        {
                //create class Three's object obj3
                Three obj3 = new Three();
                //create class Two's object obj2 and pass obj3
                Two obj2 = new Two(obj3);
                //create class One's object obj1 and pass obj2
                One obj1 = new One(obj2);
                //call cube() method of class One
                double result1 = obj1.cube(5);
                System.out.println("Cube of 5 = "+ result1);
                //call square() method of class Two
                double result2 = obj2.square(6);
                System.out.println("Square of 6 = "+ result2);
        }
}
```

Output:

```
C:\> javac Relate.java
C:\> java Relate
Cube of 5 = 125.0
Square of 6 = 36.0
```

In preceding program, cube() method of class One calls square() method of class Two, which in turn calls get() method of class Three. Let us discuss this program in detail, we create three classes, One, Two and Three. Class Three's reference obj3 is declared as variable in class Two. Similarly, class Two's reference obj2 is taken as a variable in class One. So from class One, we can access class Two's members. Similarly from class Two, we can access class Three's members.

Please observe the main() method in Relate class. In this method, first we created class Three object obj3. This obj3 is passed to class Two's object obj2. Then obj2 is passed to class One's object obj1. For this, we write:

```
Three obj3 = new Three();
Two obj2 = new Two(obj3);
One obj1 = new One(obj2);
```

The preceding three statements can be combined and written as:

```
One obj1 = new One(new Two(new Three()));
```

Please compare this with the statement for creating the BufferedReader object to accept data from keyboard, which we have been already using, as:

```
BufferedReader br = new BufferedReader(new InputStreamReader(System.in));
```

Here, System.in gives InputStream object which represents the keyboard. This is passed to InputStreamReader object which is again passed to BufferedReader object (br). So the data from the keyboard can be received by the InputStreamReader object, and from there it can be received into br. This is the reason BufferedReader is able to read the data coming from the keyboard.

The relationship between the obj1, obj2 and obj3 in memory is shown in Figure 14.2. From this figure, we can understand that obj1 can call the method of obj2 as: obj2.square()   //in class One

And obj2 can call the method of ob3, as:

❑   obj3.get()   // in class Two

In this way, relationship between objects will be advantageous to access the members of the related objects. The relationship diagram shown in Figure 14.2 is called 'object graph'.

Important Interview Question

What is object graph?

Object graph is a graph showing relationship between different objects in memory.

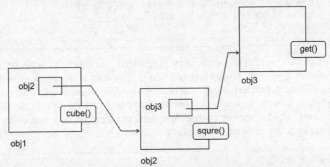

Figure 14.2 Object graph of three objects of classes One, Two and Three

Inner Class

Inner class is a class written within another class. Inner class is basically a safety mechanism, since it is hidden from other classes in its outer class.

To make instance variables not available outside the class, we use 'private' access specifier before the variables. This is how we provide the security mechanism to variables. Similarly, in some cases, we want to provide security for the entire class. In this case, can we use 'private' access specifier before the class? The problem is, if we use private access specifier before a class, the class is not available to the Java compiler or JVM. So it is illegal to use 'private' before a class name in Java.

But, private specifier is allowed before an inner class and thus it is useful to provide security for the entire inner class. Once private is used before the inner class, it is not available to other classes. This means an object to inner class cannot be created in any other class.

Suppose we are writing `BankAcct` class with bank account details like 'balance' and 'rate' of interest as instance variables and `calculateInterest()` method to calculate interest amount and add it to balance amount, as shown here:

```
class BankAcct
{
      //balance and rate of interest
      private double bal;
      private double rate;
      //calculate interest and update balance
      void calculateInterest()
      {
            double interest= bal*rate/100;
            bal += interest;
            System.out.println("Balance= "+bal);
      }
}
```

There is no security for this code. Since we did not use any access specifier before `BankAcct` class, it comes under `default` access specifier. `default` indicates that the class is available to any other class outside. So any other programmer can easily create an object to this class and access the members of the class. Hence, there is no security for the `BankAcct` class. For example, a programmer can write another class, where he can create an object to `BankAcct` class and call the `calculateInterest()` method, as:

```
class Myclass
{
      public static void main(String args[ ])
      {
            BankAcct account = new BankAcct(10000);
            account.calculateInterest(9.5);
      }
}
```

The `calculateInterest()` method is a very sensitive method. It should be protected from outsiders. If it is available to other programmers, they may call it as shown earlier and the balance amounts in the bank will be updated. Only authorized people should be able to update the balance amounts, and hence `calculateInterest()` method should not be available to others. The way to provide security to `calculateInterest()` method and the rate of interest is to write them inside a class `Interest` and make it an private inner class in `BankAcct` class, as shown here:

```
private class Interest
{
      private double rate;
      void calculateInterest()
      {
            double interest= bal*rate/100;
            bal += interest;
            System.out.println("Balance= "+bal);
      }
}
```

Since `Interest` class is declared as private, an object to it cannot be created in any other class. Then how to use the inner class? We can create an object to the inner class in its outer class. For this purpose, a method `contact()` can be written in outer class where the inner class object is created. Any programmer should interact with the inner class by calling `contact()`. Some authentication procedure to verify the user can be implemented in `contact()` method. When the user calls this method, he is verified, and if he is a legitimate user, then only the inner class object is created. Then the user will be able to use the inner class. The contact() method can be designed some thing like this:

```java
//in this method, inner class object is created after validating.
//the authenticity of the user. r is the rate of interest.
void contact(double r) throws IOException
{
    //accept the password from keyboard and verify
    BufferedReader br = new BufferedReader(new InputStreamReader(System.in));
    System.out.print("Enter password: ");
    String passwd = br.readLine();
    if(passwd.equals("xyz123"))
    {
        //if password is correct then calculate interest
        Interest in = new Interest(r);
        in.calculateInterest();
    }
    else {
        System.out.println("Sorry, you are not an authorized person");
        return;
    }
}
```

Now, see the complete program to create an inner class Interest in the outer class BankAcct. Also, in this program, we are showing that a user can use inner class by calling the contact() method of the outer class, where authentication is checked. Thus, outer class is acting like a fire wall (implementer of security mechanism) between the user and the inner class.

Program 3: Let us make a program to create the outer class BankAcct and the inner class Interest in it.

```java
//Inner class example
//this is the outer class
import java.io.*;
class BankAcct
{
    //balance amount is the variable
    private double bal;
    //initialize the balance
    BankAcct(double b)
    {
        bal = b;
    }
    //in this method, inner class object is created after verifying
    //the authentication of user. r is rate of interest
    //this method accepts rate of interest r
    void contact(double r) throws IOException
    {
    //accept the password from keyboard and verify
    BufferedReader br = new BufferedReader(new InputStreamReader(System.in));
    System.out.print("Enter password: ");
    String passwd = br.readLine();
    if(passwd.equals("xyz123"))
    {
        //if password is correct then calculate interest
        Interest in = new Interest(r);
        in.calculateInterest();
    }
    else {
        System.out.println("Sorry, you are not an authorized person");
        return;
    }
    }
    //inner class
    private class Interest
```

```
        {
                //rate of interest
                private double rate;
                //initialize the rate
                Interest(double r)
                {
                        rate = r;
                }
                //calculate interest amount and update balance
                void calculateInterest()
                {
                        double interest= bal*rate/100;
                        bal += interest;
                        System.out.println("Updated Balance= "+bal);
                }
        }
}
//Using inner class
class InnerClass
{
        public static void main(String args[]) throws IOException
        {
                //bank account is holding a balance of 10000
                BankAcct account = new BankAcct(10000);
                //update balance amount by adding interest at 9.5%
                account.contact(9.5);
        }
}
```

Output:

```
C:\> javac InnerClass.java
C:\> java InnerClass
Enter password: xyz123
Updated Balance= 10950.0
```

When the objects for `BankAcct` and `Interest` classes are created, they are created in memory separately, but they will have some relation between them, as shown in the Figure 14.3.

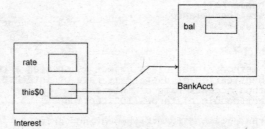

Figure 14.3 Relation between Interest and BankAcct objects

The inner class object will contain an additional field by the name `this$0` which stores the reference number of the outer class object in memory. `this$0` is an invisible field and created in the object as an additional field. Because reference of outer class object is available to inner class object, now inner class is able to refer to all the members of the outer class. For example, in our Program 3, the outer class balance is directly available to inner class.

It is also possible to use same names for the members of both the outer class and inner classes. In that case, there may be confusion while referring to the outer and inner class members separately. Then it is convenient to use the following notation to refer to the members in the inner class:

❏ Outer class members can be referred as `Outerclassname.this.member`. For example, to refer to `BanckAcct` class's `bal` in the inner class, we can write: `BankAcct.this.bal`.

- Inner class members can be referred as `this.member`. For example, to refer to `Inner` class interest, we can write: `this.interest`.

Let us now summarize the points regarding the inner classes:

- An inner class is a class that is defined inside another class.
- Inner class is a safety mechanism.
- Inner class is hidden from other classes in its outer class.
- An object to inner class can not be created in other classes.
- An object to inner class can be created only in its outer class.
- Inner class can access the members of outer class directly.
- Inner class object and outer class objects are created in separate memory locations.
- Inner class object contains an additional invisible field 'this$0' that refers to its outer class object.
- When same names are used, we can refer to outer class members in the inner class, as:

```
outerclassname.this.member;
```

and, the inner class members can be referred in the inner class, as:

```
this.member;
```

- Inner classes decrease readability (understanding) of a program. This is against to the design principle of Java to be a simple programming language.

Anonymous Inner Class

It is an inner class without a name and for which only a single object is created. Anonymous inner classes are very useful in writing implementation classes for listener interfaces in graphics programming. To understand the use of anonymous inner class, let us take a program, where we display a push button, which will terminate the application when clicked. For this purpose, we should follow the steps:

- Add `ActionListener` interface to the push button 'b'. This is done by `addActionListener()` method. But this method expects an object of `ActionListener` interface. Since it is not possible to create an object to an interface, we create an object to the implementation class of the interface.

```
b.addActionListener(new Myclass());
```

Here, `Myclass` is assumed to be the implementation class of the `ActionListener` interface.

- Now we write the `Myclass` as:

```
class Myclass implements ActionListener
{
        //this method is executed when button is clicked
        public void actionPerformed(ActionEvent ae)
        {
                //exit the application
                System.exit(0);
        }
}
```

Since, `Myclass` is an implementation class of `ActionListener` interface, the method `actionPerformed()` should be implemented in this class. This method code is executed when the push button is clicked by the user.

Program 4: Write a program to create a push button and add it to a frame.

```
//Creating a push button and providing action to it.
import java.awt.*;   //for Button
import java.awt.event.*; //for ActionListener
class But extends Frame
{
        But ()
        {
                //create a push button b
                Button b = new Button("OK");
                //add push button to frame
                add(b);
                //add action listener to button.
                //Myclass is implementation class of ActionListener interface
                b.addActionListener(new Myclass());
        }
        public static void main(String args[ ])
        {
                //create a frame by creating But class object
                But obj = new But();
                //set the size of frame to width: 400 px and height: 300 px
                obj.setSize(400,300);
                //display the frame
                obj.setVisible(true);
        }
}
//Myclass should implement the methods of ActionListener.
class Myclass implements ActionListener
{
        //this method is executed when button is clicked
        public void actionPerformed(ActionEvent ae)
        {
                //exit the application
                System.exit(0);
        }
}
```

Output:

```
C:\> javac But.java
C:\> java But
```

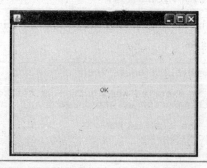

In preceding program, we add ActionListener interface to provide some action to the button. Here, ActionListener needs an implementation class. We write Myclass as the implementation class of ActionListener interface.

As done in Program 4, we need not write a separate Myclass and pass its object to `addActionListener()` method, as:

```
b.addActionListener(new Myclass());
```

Instead, we can directly copy the code of Myclass into this method parameter, as shown here:

```
b.addActionListener(new ActionListener()
{
        //this method is executed when button is clicked
        public void actionPerformed(ActionEvent ae)
        {
                //exit the application
                System.exit(0);
        }
} );
```

Please do not think that we are creating an object to `ActionListener` in the preceding method. We are, in fact, creating an object of Myclass and copying the entire class code into the method parameter. This is possible only with anonymous inner class. Here, we did not write the name of the class in the method parameter. Such a class is called 'anonymous inner class' so, we call 'Myclass' as an anonymous inner class.

Let us understand the following points from the preceding discussion:

❑   Myclass is inner class inside But class.

❑   The name 'Myclass' is not written in its outer class, i.e., But class.

❑   Myclass object is created only once.

❑   Myclass code is directly copied into the method parameter.

Important Interview Question

What is anonymous inner class?

It is an inner class whose name is not written in the outer class and for which only one object is created.

Please see Program 5, which is the anonymous inner class version of the Program 4.

Program 5: Write a program by taking Myclass as an anonymous inner class whose name is not mentioned in the But class's `addActionListener()` method.

```
//Creating a push button and providing action to it using inner class.
import java.awt.*;
import java.awt.event.*;
class But extends Frame
{
        But ()
        {
                //create a push button b
                Button b = new Button("OK");

                //add push button to frame
                add(b);

                //add action listener to button.
                //Myclass is hidden inner class of ActionListener interface,
                //whose name is not written but an object to it created.
```

```
                b.addActionListener(new ActionListener()
                {
                        //this method is executed when button is clicked
                        public void actionPerformed(ActionEvent ae)
                        {
                                //exit the application
                                System.exit(0);
                        }
                } );
        }

        public static void main(String args[ ])
        {
                //create a frame by creating But class object
                But obj = new But();
                //set the size of frame to width: 400 px and height: 300 px
                obj.setSize(400,300);
                //display the frame
                obj.setVisible(true);
        }
}
```

Output:

```
C:\> javac But.java
C:\> java But
```

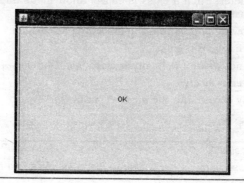

Conclusion

To relate the objects of two classes, we declare the reference of one class as an instance variable in another class. This is useful to access the members of that class whose object is referenced. Another way of relating the objects is by using inner class concept. When the programmer wants to restrict the access of entire code of a class, he creates an inner class as a private class. The way to access the inner class is through its outer class only. So any authentication mechanism is implemented in the outer class. Finally, anonymous inner class is helpful when we want to pass entire class code to a method, where the class name is not written but an object is created to it.

Another way of relating objects is using inheritance, which we discuss in the next chapter.

INHERITANCE

I t is possible to acquire all the members of a class and use them in another class by relating the objects of the two classes. This is possible by using inheritance concept. When a class is written by a programmer and another programmer wants the same features (members) in his class also, then the other programmer will go for inheritance. This is done by deriving the new class from the existing class. This chapter deals with how to derive new classes from existing classes and the advantage of inheritance.

Important Interview Question

What is inheritance?

Deriving new classes from existing classes such that the new classes acquire all the features of existing classes is called inheritance.

Inheritance

Inheritance is a concept where new classes can be produced from existing classes. The newly created class acquires all the features of existing class from where it is derived.

Let us take an example to understand the inheritance concept. A programmer in a software development team has written the Teacher class as shown here:

```java
//Teacher class
class Teacher
{
        //instance variables
        int id;
        String name;
        String address;
        float sal;

        //setter method to store id
        void setId(int id)
        {
                this.id=id;
        }

        //getter method to retrieve id
        int getId()
        {
                return id;
```

```
        }

        //to store name
        void setName(String name)
        {
                this.name=name;
        }

        //to retrieve name
        String getName()
        {
                return name;
        }

        //to store address
        void setAddress(String address)
        {
                this.address=address;
        }

        //to retrieve address
        String getAddress()
        {
                return address;
        }

        //to store salary
        void setSal(float sal)
        {
                this.sal= sal;
        }

        //to retrieve salary
        float getSal()
        {
                return sal;
        }
}
```

In the preceding code, observe that all the setter() methods are mutator methods, and the getter() methods are accessor methods. Save the preceding code as Teacher.java and compile it to get Teacher.class. These files are then copied into a central database that is available to every programmer in the project development team. So other programmers also know that Teacher.class is available in the database. This situation is shown in Figure 15.1.

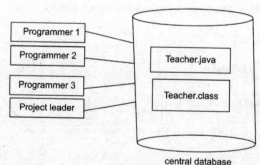

Figure I5.I The central database is available to project team members

Now, another programmer wants to develop a Student class as part of the project. The programmer is not considering the Teacher class which is already available in the central database, and writing the Student class as shown here:

```
//Student class - version 1
class Student
{
    //instance variables
    int id;
    String name;
    String address;
    int marks;

//setter method to store id
void setId(int id)
{
    this.id=id;
}

//getter method to retrieve id
int getId()
{
    return id;
}

//to store name
void setName(String name)
{
    this.name=name;
}

//to retrieve name
String getName()
{
    return name;
}

//to store address
void setAddress(String address)
{
    this.address=address;
}

//to retrieve address
String getAddress()
{
    return address;
}

//to store marks
void setMarks(int marks)
{
    this.marks=marks;
}

//to retrieve marks
int getMarks()
{
    return marks;
}
}
```

Save the preceding code as Student.java and compile it to get Student.class. Now, if the programmer wants to use Student.class, he can write another program where he can create an object to Student and use the features available, as shown in the next program.

Program 1: Write a program to create an object to Student class, then store data into it and then retrieve and display the data.

Note

Already created Student class is used in this program.

```
//Using Student class
class Use
{
        public static void main(String args[ ])
        {
                //create an object to Student class
                Student s = new Student();

                //store data into object- for this use setter methods
                s.setId(1001);
                s.setName("Chandra Sekhar");
                s.setAddress("MIG-12, Kukatpally, Hyderabad");
                s.setMarks(950);

                //retrieve data using getter methods and display
                System.out.println("Id= "+s.getId());
                System.out.println("Name= "+s.getName());
                System.out.println("Address= "+s.getAddress());
                System.out.println("Marks= "+s.getMarks());
        }
}
```

Output:

```
C:\> javac Use.java
C:\> java Use
Id= 1001
Name= Chandra Sekhar
Address= MIG-12, Kukatpally, Hyderabad
Marks= 950
```

In this program, an object to Student class is created by JVM, as shown in the Figure 15.2.

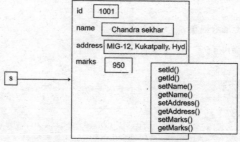

Figure 15.2 Student class object

Just compare the Teacher class and Student class. You can find 75% similarities in both the classes. While developing the Student class, if the programmer has thought of reusing Teacher class code, developing Student class would have been very easy. With this idea, let us rewrite Student class again. Whatever code is available in Teacher class will be omitted in writing the Student class as that code will be automatically available to Student class. For this purpose, simply use the keyword 'extends' as:

```
class Student extends Teacher
```

The preceding statement means all the members of Teacher class are available to Student class without rewriting them in Student class. Only additional members should be written in Student class. So, developing the Student class will become easy as shown in Program 2.

Program 2: Write a program to use 'extends' keyword to create Student class by reusing Teacher class code. We should write only additional members in Student class which are not available in Teacher class.

```
//Student class - version 2
class Student extends Teacher
{
        //since id, name, address are available from Teacher class, we omit
        //those instance variables and the corresponding methods.
        int marks;

        //to store marks
        void setMarks(int marks)
        {
                this.marks=marks;
        }

        //to retrieve marks
        int getMarks()
        {
                return marks;
        }
}
```

Save the preceding code as Student.java and compile it to get Student.class. In other words, we can say Student class is created based on Teacher class.

Like this, creating new classes from existing classes is called inheritance. The original class, i.e., Teacher class is called super class and the newly created class, i.e., Student class is called subclass. We created Student class by extending the Teacher class, as:

```
class Student extends Teacher
```

So, the syntax (correct format) of inheritance is:

```
class subclass extends superclass
```

Now, please go through Use.java again. Execute it, and you will see the same result. In Use.java, we create Student class object, as:

```
Student s = new Student();
```

When an object to Student class is created, it contains a copy of Teacher class within it. This means there is a relation between the Teacher class and Student class objects. This is the reason why Teacher class members are available to Student class. Note that we do not create Teacher class object, but still a copy of it is available to Student class object. Please see the object diagram of Student class in Figure 15.3. You can understand that all the members (i.e., variables and methods) of Teacher class as well as Student class are available in it.

Why super class members are available to sub class?

Because, the sub class object contains a copy of super class object.

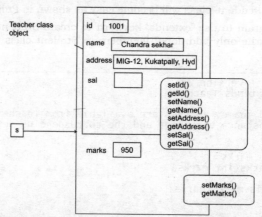

Figure 15.3 Student class object contains a copy of Teacher class

Then, what is the advantage of inheritance? Please look at Student class version 1 and Student class version 2. Clearly, second version is smaller and easier to develop. By using inheritance, a programmer can develop the classes very easily. Hence programmer's productivity is increased. He can deliver more code in less time. This will increase the overall productivity of the Organization, and hence more growth for the Organization.

What is the advantage of inheritance?

In inheritance, a programmer reuses the super class code without rewriting it, in creation of sub classes. So, developing the classes becomes very easy. Hence, the programmer's productivity is increased.

The Keyword 'super'

If we create an object to super class, we can access only the super class members, but not the sub class members. But if we create sub class object, all the members of both super and sub classes are available to it. This is the reason, we always create an object to sub class in inheritance. Some times, the super class members and sub class members may have same names. In that case, by default only sub class members are accessible. This is shown in the following example program.

Program 3: Write a program where the names of instance variables and methods in super and sub classes are same. Hence, by default only sub class members are accessible.

```
//By default sub class members are accessible
//to subclass object
class One
{
    //super class var
    int i=10;

    //super class method
    void show()
```

```
            {
                    System.out.println("super class method:i= "+i);
            }
    }
    class Two extends One
    {
            //sub class var
            int i=20;

            //sub class method
            void show()
            {
                    System.out.println("sub class method:i= "+i);
            }
    }

    class Super1
    {
            public static void main(String args[ ])
            {
                    //create sub class object
                    Two t = new Two();

                    //This will call sub class method only
                    t.show();
            }
    }
```

Output:

```
    C:\> javac Super1.java
    C:\> java Super1
    sub class method:i= 20
```

Please observe that a call to sub class method, `t.show();` calls and executes only sub class method. And hence the sub class instance variable i value 20 is displayed. In such a case, how to access the super class members from sub class is the question. For this purpose, super key word has been invented. super refers to super class members from a sub class. For example,

❑ super can be used to refer to super class variables, as:

```
    super.variable
```

❑ super can be used to refer to super class methods, as:

```
    super.method()
```

❑ super can be used to refer to super class constructor.

We need not call the default constructor of the super class, as it is by default available to sub class.

To call the parameterized constructor, we can write:

```
    super(values);
```

In the next program, we want to access super class instance variable and super class method directly in sub class using super key word.

Program 4: Write a program to access the super class method and instance variable by using super key word from sub class.

```
    //super - to access the super class method and variable
```

```
class One
{
      //super class var
      int i=10;

      //super class method
      void show()
      {
            System.out.println("super class method:i= "+i);
      }
}
class Two extends One
{
      //sub class var
      int i=20;

      //sub class method
      void show()
      {
            System.out.println("sub class method:i= "+i);

            //using super to call super class method
            super.show();

            //using super to access super class var
            System.out.println("super i= "+ super.i);
      }
}

class Super1
{
      public static void main(String args[ ])
      {
            //create sub class object
            Two t = new Two();

            //This will call sub class method only
            t.show();
      }
}
```

Output:

```
C:\> javac Super1.java
C:\> java Super1
sub class method:i= 20
super class method:i= 10
super i= 10
```

Now the next thing is to access the constructors of the super class. We need not access the default constructor of the super class, as it is available to sub class by default. This is illustrated in the following program.

Program 5: Write a program to prove that the default constructor of the super class is available to sub class by default.

```
//Calling super class default constructor from sub class.
class One
{
      //super class default constructor
      One()
      {
            System.out.println("One");
      }
}
class Two extends One
```

```
{
        //sub class default constructor
        Two()
        {
                System.out.println("Two");
        }
}

class Super1
{
        public static void main(String args[])
        {
                //create sub class object
                Two t = new Two();
        }
}
```

Output:

```
C:\> javac Super1.java
C:\> java Super1
One
Two
```

Please observe that when sub class object is created, first of all the super class default constructor is called and then only the sub class constructor is called.

In the following program, we take a parameterized constructor in the super class. This is not available to sub class by default. So it should be called by using super keyword.

Program 6: Write a program to understand that the parameterized constructor of the super class can be called from sub class using super().

```
//Calling super class parameterized constructor from sub class.
class One
{
        //super class var
        int i;

        //super class para constructor
        One(int i)
        {
                this.i = i;
        }

}
class Two extends One
{
        //sub class var
        int i;

        //sub class para constructor
        Two(int a,int b)
        {
                super(a); //call super class constructor and pass a.
                i = b; //initialize sub class var
        }

        //sub class method
        void show()
        {
                System.out.println("sub class i= "+ i);
                System.out.println("super class i= "+ super.i);
        }

}
class Super1
```

```
        {
                public static void main(String args[ ])
                {
                        //create sub class object
                        Two t = new Two(11, 22);

                        //call sub class method
                        t.show();

                }
        }
```

Output:

```
C:\> javac Super1.java
C:\> java Super1
sub class i= 22
super class i= 11
```

In the preceding program, there is a parameterized constructor in super class which initializes the instance variable i, as:

```
One(int i)
{
        this.i = i;
}
```

This constructor can be called from sub class by writing another parameterized constructor in sub class and passing two values to it, as:

```
Two(int a, int b)
{
        super(a); //call super class constructor and pass a.
        i = b; //initialize sub class var
}
```

The preceding constructor will receive data when the sub class object is created, as:

```
Two t = new Two(11, 22);
```

So, the values 11 and 22 are copied into a and b respectively. And then, the value 'a' is sent to the super class parameterized constructor by using the statement:

```
super(a);
```

One condition is that the statement calling the super class constructor should be the first one in sub class constructor. This implies that the super class constructor should be given priority over the sub class constructor.

The Protected Specifier

The private members of the super class are not available to sub classes directly. But some times, there may be a need to access the data of super class in the sub class. For this purpose, protected specifier is used. protected is commonly used in super class to make the members of the super class available directly in its sub classes. We can think that the protected specifier works like public with respect to sub classes. See the program 7.

Program 7: Write a program to understand private members are not accessible in sub class, but protected members are available in sub class.

```
//private and protected
class Access
{
      private int a;
      protected int b;
}
class Sub extends Access
{
      public void get()
      {
              System.out.println(a);  //error - a is private
              System.out.println(b);
      }
}

class Test
{
      public static void main(String args[])
      {
              Sub s = new Sub();
              s.get();
      }
}
```

Output:

```
C:\> javac Test.java
Test.java:11: a has private access in Access
      System.out.println(a);
                         ^
1 error
```

In the next program, we create Shape class with a protected instance variable '1'. From Shape class, we derive Square class and from Square class, we derive Rectangle class. We want to calculate areas of Square and Rectangle classes. For this purpose, in Square class we can directly use '1' of the Shape class and calculate the area of square as l*l. We can also calculate area of rectangle, by taking another variable 'b' and using the '1' of Shape, as l*b.

Program 8: Write a program to find the areas of Square and Rectangle by deriving them from Shape.

```
//Shape is the super class for Square
//And Square is the super class for Rectangle
class Shape
{
      //take protected type var
      protected double 1;

      //parameterized constructor
      Shape(double 1)
      {
              this.1 = 1;
      }
}

class Square extends Shape
{
      //call Shape's constructor and send 1 value
      Square(double 1)
      {
              super(1);
      }

      //calcuTate area of square
```

```
        void area()
        {
                //because of inheritance, 'l' of Shape class is available
                System.out.println("Area of Square= "+ (l*l));
        }
}

class Rectangle extends Square
{
        //var
        private double b;

        //call Square's constructor and send x value
        Rectangle(double x,double y)
        {
                super(x);
                b = y;
        }

        //calculate area of rectangle
        void area()
        {
                //because of inheritance,  'l' of Shape class is available
                System.out.println("Area of Rectangle= "+ (l*b));
        }
}

class Inherit
{
        public static void main(String args[])
        {
                //display area of square
                Square s = new Square(5.5);
                s.area();

                //display area of rectangle
                Rectangle r = new Rectangle(5.5, 6);
                r.area();
        }
}
```

Output:

```
C:\> javac Inherit.java
C:\> java Inherit
Area of Square= 30.25
Area of Rectangle= 33.0
```

Types of Inheritance

So far, we discussed about inheritance and the advantage of using inheritance in software development. Let us now look at the types of inheritance. There are two types of inheritance, Single and Multiple.

❑ **Single Inheritance:** Producing sub classes from a single super class is called single inheritance. In this, a single super class will be there. There can be one or more sub classes. See the examples in Figure 15.4.

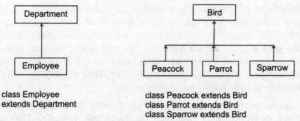

class Employee
extends Department

class Peacock extends Bird
class Parrot extends Bird
class Sparrow extends Bird

Figure 15.4 Single inheritance

❑ **Multiple Inheritance:** Producing sub classes from multiple super classes is called multiple inheritance. In this case, there will be more than one super class and there can be one or more sub classes. See the examples in Figure 15.5.

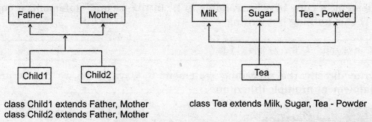

class Child1 extends Father, Mother
class Child2 extends Father, Mother

class Tea extends Milk, Sugar, Tea - Powder

Figure 15.5 Multiple inheritance.

Only Single inheritance is available in Java. There is no multiple inheritance in Java. The following are the reasons:

❑ Multiple inheritance leads to confusion for the programmer. For example, class A has got a member x and class B has also got a member x. When another class C extends both the classes, then there is a confusion regarding which copy of x is available in C. See the Figure 15.6.

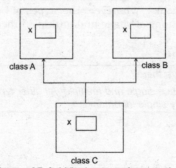

Figure 15.6 Which copy of x is in class C ?

❑ Multiple inheritance is available in C++, which is not available in Java. This leads to disappointment in Java programmers. A Java programmer wishes to use multiple inheritance in some cases. Fortunately, JavaSoft people have provided interface concept, expecting the programmers to achieve multiple inheritance by using multiple interfaces. For example, we can write:

```
class Myclass implements interface1, interface2,…
```

In this case, all the members of interface1, interface2,... are accessible in Myclass. This is the way, we can achieve multiple inheritance in an indirect way. But this is lacking in real flexibility offered by multiple inheritance. In multiple inheritance, we can use multiple classes where complete methods are available, which can be called and directly used in the sub classes. But in case of interfaces, none of the methods will have method body. So, the programmers should provide body for all the methods of the interfaces in the implementation class, i.e., Myclass. Hence, achieving multiple inheritance by using interfaces is not so useful.

❑ The programmer feels achieving multiple inheritance by using classes would be practically useful to him. This need is also fulfilled by JavaSoft people. The way to achieve multiple inheritance is by repeating the use of single inheritance. For example,

```
class B extends A    //single inheritance
class C extends B    //single inheritance
```

In the first statement, a copy of A is available in B. In the second statement, a copy of A plus B is available to C. This is nothing but writing:

```
class C extends A,B    //invalid
```

We can not write directly the preceding statement in Java. But, we can write the earlier two statements to implement multiple inheritance.

Important Interview Question

Why multiple inheritance is not available in Java?

Multiple inheritance is not available in Java for the following reasons:

1. It leads to confusion for a Java program.

2. The programmer can achieve multiple inheritance by using interfaces.

3. The programmer can achieve multiple inheritance by repeatedly using single inheritance.

There are only two types of inheritance. But some authors have fancied other types of inheritance and included them also in their books. Whatever other types of inheritance the authors are claiming are none other than the combinations of single and multiple inheritance.

Important Interview Question

How many types of inheritance are there?

There are two types of inheritance single and multiple. All other types are mere combinations of these two. However, Java supports only single inheritance.

Conclusion

Parents producing the children and children acquiring the qualities of parents have inspired the creators of OOPS to include inheritance concept into Object Oriented approach. Inheritance is a very powerful concept, as it makes programming easy by reusing the available classes in creation of new classes. Reusability is achieved because of the sub class object containing a copy of super class object within it. The programmer can use 'super' keyword if he wants to access all the members of a super class directly in the subclasses. There are two types of inheritance single and multiple. But in Java, only single inheritance is available. This does not make Java handicapped, because there are ways to achieve multiple inheritance by other means.

CHAPTER
POLYMORPHISM
16

Polymorphism came from the two Greek words 'poly' meaning many and morphos meaning forms. The ability to exist in different forms is called 'polymorphism'. In Java, a variable, an object or a method can exist in different forms, thus performing various tasks depending on the context. Because same variable or method can perform different tasks, the programmer has the advantage of writing flexible code.

Polymorphism with Variables

When using variables, some times inherently the data type of the result is decided by the compiler and accordingly execution proceeds. For example, in the statement:

```
System.out.println(a+b);
```

Java compiler decides the data type of the result of the expression a+b depending on the data types of a and b. If a and b are int type, then a+b will also be taken as int type. If a and b are float type variables, then a+b will be taken as float type. If a is int and b is float, then the compiler converts a also into float and then sum is found. Thus, the result a+b is exhibiting polymorphic nature. It may exist as an int or as a float or as some other data type depending on the context. This is also called 'Coercion'.

Important Interview Question

What is coercion?
Coercion is the automatic conversion between different data types done by the compiler.

Let us take a different example. See the following code:

```
float a = 15.5f;
int x = (int)a;
```

In the second line, the actual data type of the variable is changed by using a cast operator. Even if 'a' is float type, it is converted into int type. If 'a' is taken as it is, it becomes float type and because we converted, it can take the form of an int. This means 'a' exists in two different forms. This also comes under polymorphism, which is called 'Conversion'.

Important Interview Question

What is conversion?
Conversion is an explicit change in the data type specified by the cast operator.

Polymorphism using Methods

If the same method performs different tasks, then that method is said to exhibit polymorphism. This statement is tricky. Let us stop and think again, how is it possible for a method to perform different tasks? It is possible only when the method assumes different bodies. It is something like this, take two persons with the same name 'Ravi'. Because the name is same but the persons are different, they can perform different tasks. In the same way, there may be two methods with the same name and they can perform different tasks. When we call the methods, we use same name but the task will be different depending on which method (body) is called.

Now, the crucial thing is to decide which method is called in a particular context. This decision may happen either at compile time or at runtime. This will lead to two types of polymorphism, Static polymorphism and Dynamic polymorphism. The words 'static' represents at compile time and 'dynamic' represents at run time. Let us discuss dynamic polymorphism first.

Dynamic Polymorphism

The polymorphism exhibited at runtime is called dynamic polymorphism. This means when a method is called, the method call is bound to the method body at the time of running the program, dynamically. In this case, Java compiler does not know which method is called at the time of compilation. Only JVM knows at runtime which method is to be executed. Hence, this is also called 'runtime polymorphism' or 'dynamic binding'.

Let us take a class 'Sample' with two instance methods having same name as:

```
void add(int a, int b)
{
      System.out.println("Sum of two= "+ (a+b));
}
void add(int a, int b, int c)
{
      System.out.println("Sum of three= "+ (a+b+c));
}
```

The bodies of these methods are different and hence they can perform different tasks. For example, the first method adds two integer numbers and the second one adds three integer numbers. However, to call these methods, we use the same method name. Suppose, we called the method as:

❏   s. add(10, 15);   //s is the object of Sample class.

Now, who will decide which method is to be executed? Is it Java compiler or JVM? Because the methods are called by using an object, the Java compiler can not decide at the time of compilation which method is actually called by the user. It has to wait till the object is created for Sample class. And the creation of object takes place at runtime by JVM. Now, JVM should decide which method is actually called by the user at runtime (dynamically).

The question is how JVM recognizes which method is called, when both the methods have same name. For this, JVM observes the signature of the methods. Method signature consists of a method name and its parameters. Even if, two methods have same name, their signature may vary. For example, two human beings may have same name but their signatures will differ.

Important Interview Question

What is method signature?

Method signature represents the method name along with method parameters.

When there is a difference in the method signatures, then the JVM understands both the methods are different and can call the appropriate method. The difference in the method signatures will arise because of one of the following reasons:

❑   There may be a difference in the number of parameters passed to the methods.

For example,

```
void add(int a, int b)
void add(int a, int b, int c)
```

In this case, if we call add(10, 15) then JVM executes the first method and if we call add(10, 15, 22) then it runs the second method.

❑   Or, there may be a difference in the data types of parameters.

For example,

```
void add(int a, float b)
void add(double a, double b)
```

In this case, if we call the method add(10, 5.5f) then JVM goes for the first method and if it is add(10.5, 22.9) then JVM runs the second one.

❑   Or, there may be a difference in the sequence (orderliness) of the parameters.

For example,

```
void add(int a, float b)
void add(float a, int b)
```

In this case, if we call add(10, 5.55) then JVM executes the first method and if it is add(5.5, 20) then it goes for the second method.

JVM matches the values passed to the method at the time of method call with the method signature and picks up the appropriate method. In this way, difference in the method signatures helps JVM to identify the correct method and execute it. Please see Program 1 to understand this.

Program 1: Write a program to create Sample class which contains two methods with the same name but with different signatures.

```
//Dynamic polymorphism
class Sample
{
       //method to add two values
       void add(int a,int b)
       {
              System.out.println("Sum of two= "+ (a+b));
       }
       //method to add three values
       void add(int a, int b, int c)
       {
              System.out.println("Sum of three= "+ (a+b+c));
       }
}
class Poly
{
       public static void main(String args[ ])
       {
              //create Sample class object
              Sample s = new Sample();
              //call add() and pass two values
              s.add(10,15);   //This call is bound with first method
              //call add() and pass three values
              s.add(10,15,20);  //This call is bound with second method
       }
}
```

Output:

```
C:\> javac Poly.java
C:\> java Poly
Sum of two= 25
Sum of three= 45
```

In the preceding program, JVM can understand and bound the method call with the appropriate method by observing the difference in the method signatures. Two methods with the same name but with different signatures have been written in Sample class. Such methods are called overloaded methods and this concept is referred to as method overloading.

Important Interview Question

What is method overloading?

Writing two or more methods in the same class in such a way that each method has same name but with different method signatures – is called method overloading.

In Program 1, we did method overloading using instance methods. And hence, Java compiler does not know which method is called at compilation time. But JVM knows and binds the method call with the correct method at the time of running the program. So, this is an example for dynamic polymorphism.

We understood that in method overloading JVM recognizes methods separately by observing the difference in the method signatures that arises due to the difference either in the number of parameters or in the data types of parameters or in the sequence of parameters. It is not possible if the programmer wants to write two methods in the same class without any of these differences. Doing so will come under writing duplicate methods and Java compiler will reject that code.

But it is always possible for the programmer to write two or more methods with same name and same signature in two different classes. This can be done in super and sub classes also. See Program 2. In this program, the super class 'One' has calculate() method which calculates square value. The sub class 'Two' is derived from class One. But the programmer who is creating the sub class does not want to calculate square value. His requirement is to calculate square root value. So he writes another method with the same name and same signature in the sub class but with a different body i.e., to calculate the square root value.

Observe the methods in the super and sub classes, written as:

```
void calculate(double x)    //in super class One
void calculate(double x)    //in sub class Two
```

These two methods have same name and same signatures and there is no difference any where in the parameters. When calculate() method is called by using the sub class object 't' as:

```
t.calculate(25);
```

The sub class method is only executed by the JVM, but not the super class method. In other words, the sub class calculate() method 'overrides' the super class calculate() method. This concept is also called 'method overriding'.

Important Interview Question

What is method overriding?

Writing two or more methods in super and sub classes such that the methods have same name and same signature - is called method overriding.

In method overriding, the Java compiler does not decide which method is called by the user, since it has to wait till an object to sub class is created. After creating the object, JVM has to bind the method call to an appropriate method. But the methods in super and sub classes have same name and same method signatures. Then how JVM decides which method is called?

Here, JVM calls the method depending on the class name of the object which is used to call the method. For example, we are calling the method by using the sub class object 't' as:

```
t.calculate(25);
```

So, the sub class method is only executed by the JVM. In Inheritance, we always create an object to sub class and hence only sub class method is called. In this way, method overriding using instance methods is an example for dynamic polymorphism.

In Program 2, JVM calls the sub class `calculate()` method as the object used to call the method is of sub class type.

Program 2: Write a program where `calculate()` method of super class is overridden by the `calculate()` method of sub class. The behavior of the `calculate()` method is dynamically decided.

```java
//Dynamic polymorphism
class One
{
    //method to calculate square value
    void calculate(double x)
    {
        System.out.println("Square value= "+ (x*x));
    }
}
class Two extends One
{
    //method to calculate square root value
    void calculate(double x)
    {
        System.out.println("Square root= "+ Math.sqrt(x));
    }
}
class Poly
{
    public static void main(String args[ ])
    {
        //create sub class object t.
        Two t = new Two();
        //call calculate() method using t.
        t.calculate(25);
    }
}
```

Output:

```
C:\> javac Poly.java
C:\> java Poly
Square root= 5.0
```

Remember, when a super class method is overridden by the sub class method, JVM calls only the sub class method and never the super class method. In other words, we can say the sub class method is replacing the super class method.

Important Interview Question

What is the difference between method overloading and method overriding?

See the table 16.1.

Table 16.1

Method Overloading	Method Overriding
Writing two or more methods with the same name but with different signatures is called method overloading.	Writing two or more methods with the same name and same signatures is called method overriding.
Method overloading is done in the same class.	Method overriding is done in super and sub classes.
In method overloading, method return type can be same or different.	In method overriding, method return types should also be same.
JVM decides which method is called depending on the difference in the method signatures.	JVM decides which method is called depending on the data type (class) of the object used to call the method.
Method overloading is done when the programmer wants to extend the already available feature.	Method overriding is done when the programmer wants to provide a different implementation (body) for the same feature.
Method overloading is code refinement. Same method is refined to perform a different task.	Method overriding is code replacement. The sub class method overrides (replaces) the super class method.

Static Polymorphism

The polymorphism exhibited at compilation time is called static polymorphism. Here the Java compiler knows without any ambiguity which method is called at the time of compilation. Of course, JVM executes the method later, but the compiler knows and can bind the method call with method code (body) at the time of compilation. So, it is also called 'static binding' or 'compile time polymorphism'.

In the previous section, we discussed that the method overloading and the method overriding using instance methods are examples for dynamic polymorphism. Similarly, achieving method overloading and method overriding by using static methods, private methods, and final methods are examples for static polymorphism. The reason is that all of these methods maintain only one copy in memory that is available to the objects of the class. So the Java compiler knows which method is called at the time of compilation and it needs not wait till the objects are created. Since at the time of compilation, the method call can be bound with actual method body, this comes under static polymorphism.

Polymorphism with Static Methods

A static method is a method whose single copy in memory is shared by all the objects of the class. Static methods belong to the class rather than to the objects. So they are also called class methods. When static methods are overloaded or overridden, since they do not depend on the objects, the Java compiler need not wait till the objects are created to understand which method is called.

Let us re-write the Program 2 using static methods to understand how to override them.

Program 3: Write a program to use super class reference to call the calculate() method.

```
//static polymorphism
class One
{
    //method to calculate square value
    static void calculate(double x)
```

```
                {
                        System.out.println("Square value= "+ (x*x));
                }
        }
        class Two extends One
        {
                //method to calculate square root value
                static void calculate(double x)
                {
                        System.out.println("Square root= "+ Math.sqrt(x));
                }
        }
        class Poly
        {
                public static void main(String args[ ])
                {
                        //Super class reference refers to sub class object
                        One o = new Two();
                        //call calculate() method using super class reference
                        o.calculate(25);
                }
        }
```

Output:

```
C:\> javac Poly.java
C:\> java Poly
Square value= 625.0
```

In preceding program, the super class method is called. If sub class reference is used to call the `calculate()` method, then sub class method is called. In class Poly, we created super class reference to sub class object, as:

```
One o = new Two();
```

Here 'o' is super class reference variable. Using this variable, we are calling the `calculate()` method as `o.calculate(25)`. So the super class `calculate()` method is executed. Suppose, we created a sub class reference as,

```
Two t = new Two();
```

and called the `calculate()` method using this sub class reference as `t.calculate(25)`, then the sub class `calculate()` is executed by the JVM. The point is, when static methods are overridden, the JVM decides which method is to be executed depending on the reference type used to call the method.

Polymorphism with Private Methods

Private methods are the methods which are declared by using the access specifier 'private'. This access specifier makes the method not to be available outside the class. So other programmers cannot access the private methods. Even private methods are not available in the sub classes. This means, there is no possibility to override the private methods of the super class in its sub classes. So only method overloading is possible in case of private methods.

What happens if a method is written in the sub class with the same name as that of the private method of the super class? It is possible to do so. But in this case, the method in the super class and the method in the sub class act as different methods. The super class will get its own copy and the sub class will have its own copy. It does not come under method overriding.

Can you override private methods?

> *No. Private methods are not available in the sub classes, so they cannot be overridden.*

The only way to call the private methods of a class is by calling them within the class. For this purpose, we should create a public method and call the private method from within it. When this public method is called, it calls the private method.

Polymorphism with Final Methods

Methods which are declared as 'final' are called final methods. Final methods cannot be overridden, because they are not available to the sub classes. Therefore, only method overloading is possible with final methods.

There are two uses of declaring a method as 'final' given here:

❑ When a method is declared as final, the performance will be better. For example, take the following classes. In class A, we got a final method, method1(). This method is being called from class B's method2():

```
class A
{
    final void method1()
    {
        System.out.println("Hello");
    }
}
class B
{
    void method2()
    {
        A.method1();  //call the final method
    }
}
```

Now, JVM physically copies the code of method1() into method2() of class B, as:

```
class B
{
    void method2()
    {
        System.out.println("Hello");  //body of final method copied
    }
}
```

Copying the code like this is called 'inline operation'. Previously, when we call method2(), it had to call method1() again. But now, in this version, we have avoided that method call. Every method call takes some time of the JVM. This overhead is avoided here, and hence the time of execution improves. In this way, final methods improve performance. Remember, JVM performs inline operation only if it feels there would be improvement in the performance. Otherwise, JVM does not perform this inline operation, even if a final method is written.

❑ When the programmer does not want others to override his method, he should declare his method as 'final'.

Can we take private methods and final methods as same?

Yes. The Java compiler assigns the value for the private methods at the time of compilation. Also, private methods can not be modified at run time. This is the same case with final methods also. Neither the private methods nor the final methods can be overridden. So, private methods can be taken as final methods.

final Class

A final class is a class which is declared as `final`. `final` keyword before a class prevents inheritance. This means sub classes cannot be created to a final class. For example,

```
final class A
class B extends A    //invalid
```

What is final?

'final' keyword is used in two ways:

- *It is used to declare constants, as:*

`final double PI = 3.14159;` *//PI is constant.*

It is used to prevent inheritance, as:

- `final class A` *//sub class to A cannot be created.*

What is the difference between dynamic polymorphism and static polymorphism?

Dynamic polymorphism is the polymorphism exhibited at runtime. Here, Java compiler does not understand which method is called at compilation time. Only JVM decides which method is called at runtime. Method overloading and method overriding using instance methods are the examples for dynamic polymorphism.

Static polymorphism is the polymorphism exhibited at compile time. Here, Java compiler knows which method is called. Method overloading and method overriding using static methods; method overloading using private or final methods are examples for static polymorphism.

Let us write a program where we take a class with the name 'Commercial' that contains code for calculating electricity bill for a commercial user. In this class, `setName()` method is used for storing the customer name into the instance variable. `getName()` method is useful to return the name. If we write a 'Domestic' class for calculating the electricity bill for a domestic user, `setName()` and `getName()` methods of the Commercial class are also needed by the 'Domestic' class.

Commercial class contains another method `calculateBill()` which calculates bill amount at a charge of Rs. 5.00 per unit. This method should be overridden by the Domestic class because, the charge varies for a domestic customer at Rs. 2.50 per unit.

Program 4: Let us make a program to show how to override the `calculateBill()` method of Commercial class inside the Domestic class.

```
//Electricity bill for commercial connection
class Commercial
{
      //take customer name
      private String name;
      //store customer name into name
      void setName(String name)
```

```
        {
                this.name = name;
        }
        //retrieve the name
        String getName()
        {
                return name;
        }
        //to calculate bill taking Rs. 5.00 per unit
        void calculateBill(int units)
        {
                System.out.println("Customer: "+ getName());
                System.out.println("Bill amount= "+ units*5.00);
        }
}
//Electricity bill for domestic connection
class Domestic extends Commercial
{
        //override the calculateBill() of Commercial class, to calculate
        //bill at Rs. 2.50 per unit
        void calculateBill(int units)
        {
                System.out.println("Customer: "+ getName());
                System.out.println("Bill amount= "+units*2.50);
        }
}
//Calculate electricity bill for commercial and domestic users
class ElectricityBill
{
        public static void main(String args[])
        {
                //call calculateBill() using the Commercial object
                Commercial c = new Commercial();
                c.setName("Raj Kumar");
                c.calculateBill(100);
                //call calculateBill() using the Domestic object
                Domestic d = new Domestic();
                d.setName("Vijaya Laxmi");
                d.calculateBill(100);
        }
}
```

Output:

```
C:\> javac ElectricityBill.java
C:\> java ElectricityBill
Customer: Raj Kumar
Bill amount= 500.0
Customer: Vijaya Laxmi
Bill amount= 250.0
```

Conclusion

If the same variable or method or an object performs different tasks, it is said to exhibit polymorphism. In this chapter, we have seen how variables and methods can exhibit polymorphism. A programmer goes for method overloading when he wants to extend the available features of the class. A programmer does method overriding when he wants to perform a different task with the same method. Even the objects can also change their form at runtime and can perform different tasks depending on how they are referenced. This is possible by casting the object types. This concept is discussed in the next chapter.

TYPE CASTING

C onverting one data type into another data type is called 'type casting' or simply 'casting'. Whenever we assign a value to a variable using assignment operator, the Java compiler checks for uniformity and hence the data types at both the sides should be same. If the data types are not same, then we should convert the types to become same at the both sides. To convert the data type, we use 'cast operator'. Cast operator means writing the data type between simple braces, before a variable or method whose value is to be converted.

Let us revise what is a data type. Data type represents the type of data being stored into a variable (memory). For example, int x;

Here, 'int' represents that we can store an integer value into the variable x. So it is called a data type.

Types of Data Types

There are two types of data types, as given here:

❏ Primitive Data Types or Fundamental Data Types

The data types which represent a single entity (or value) are called 'primitive data types'. For example, take 'int' type, it can store only one integer value. Take 'boolean' value, it can store either true or false - only one value. So they come under primitive data types. The following are the primitive data types:

> char, byte, short, int, long, float, double, boolean.

❏ Referenced Data Types or Advanced Data Types

These data types represent several values. For example, take an array. It can store several values. Similarly take a class. It can store different values. So they are called advanced data types. We can access an array or an object of a class in memory through references. So, they are also called 'referenced data types'. The following are examples for referenced data types:

> any array, any class (String, StringBuffer, Employee, Manager etc.)

Important Interview Question

What is the difference between primitive data types and advanced data types?

Primitive data types represent single values. Advanced data types represent a group of values. Also, methods are not available to handle the primitive data types. In case of advanced data types, methods are available to perform various operations.

We can convert a primitive data type into another primitive data type using casting. Similarly, it is possible to convert a referenced data type into another referenced data type by using casting. But we cannot convert a primitive data type into a referenced data type by using casting. For this purpose, methods of Wrapper classes should be used. Wrapper classes will be discussed later in Wrapper Classes chapter.

Casting Primitive Data Types

It is possible to convert one primitive data type into another primitive data type. This is done in two ways, widening and narrowing. The primitive data types are classified into two types, lower types and higher types. Naturally, the lower types are the types which use less memory and which can represent lesser number of digits in the value. The higher types use more memory and can represent more number of digits. To recognize the lower and higher types, the following diagram is useful:

```
byte, short, char, int, long, float, double
lower <---------------------------------> higher
```

Thus, char is a lower type than int. float is a higher type than long. `boolean` is not included earlier, because it cannot be converted into any other type.

Widening in Primitive Data Types

Converting a lower data type into a higher data type is called widening. See the examples:

❏   char ch = 'A';

int num = (int)ch;   //num contains 65, the ASCII value of 'A'.

Here, we are converting char type variable 'ch' into int type. For this purpose, we used the cast operator by writing 'int' in the simple braces before the variable 'ch'. Now that ch is converted into int type, it can be assigned to the variable num. This is an example for widening.

❏   int x = 9500;

float sal = (float)x;   //sal contains 9500.0.

Here, we are converting int type variable 'x' into float. So, we wrote (float) before the variable x.

Widening is safe because there will not be any loss of data or precision or accuracy. This is the reason, even though the programmer does not use cast operator, Java compiler does not complain. Of course, in this case, Java compiler does the casting operation internally and hence this is also called 'implicit casting'. For example, writing the preceding statements without using cast operator, as shown here will compile properly:

❏   char ch = 'A';

int num = ch;

❏   int x = 9500;

float sal = x;

What is implicit casting?

Automatic casting done by the Java compiler internally is called implicit casting. Implicit casting is done to convert a lower data type into a higher data type.

Narrowing in Primitive Data Types

Converting a higher data type into a lower data type is called 'narrowing'. Take the example:

□   `int n = 66;`

     `char ch = (char)n;  //ch contains 'B'.`

Here, we are converting int type n value into char type. The value of n is 66 which is when converted into char type represents the character 'B', since 66 is the ASCII value of 'B'. This character is stored into ch.

□   `double d = 12.6789;`

     `int n = (int)d;   //n stores 12.`

Observe, we are converting double type into int type by using the cast operator (int) before the variable d. The value in d is 12.6789. Since it is converted into int type, the fraction part of the number is lost and only 12 is stored in n. Here, we are losing some digits. So narrowing is not safe. This is the reason, Java compiler forces the programmer to use cast operator when going for narrowing. The programmer should compulsory cast the data type. So, narrowing is also called explicit casting.

What is explicit casting?

The casting done by the programmer is called explicit casting. Explicit casting is compulsory while converting from a higher data type to a lower data type.

Casting Referenced Data Types

A class is a referenced data type. Converting a class type into another class type is also possible through casting. But the classes should have some relationship between them by the way of inheritance. For example, you can not convert a Dog class into a Horse class, as those classes do not have any relationship between them. But you can convert a College class into a University class, since College is derived from University. And you can convert a Department class into a College, since Department is a sub class of College class. See Figure 17.1 which shows that the classes Department, College and University have relationship by the way of inheritance.

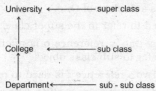

Figure 17.1 Relationship of classes by the way of Inheritance

Generalization and Specialization

Let us take a super class Fruit and the sub classes Citrus and Non-Citrus, as shown in the Figure 17.2.

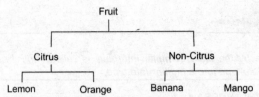

Figure 17.2 The hierarchy of inherited classes from Fruit class

When we talk about a fruit, remember we are talking in general terms and it may represent any kind of fruit. So, here the scope is widened. Suppose, we talk about citrus fruit, then we came down one step in inheritance hierarchy and thus, we have eliminated other types of fruit. So, we are becoming more specific. When we still come down to lemon, we are pin-pointing the type of the fruit. It is lemon only and not any other fruit. This is very specific. This means when we come down from super class to sub classes, we are becoming more and more specific. When we go back from sub classes to super class, we are becoming more general.

Converting a sub class type into a super class type is called 'generalization', because we are making the sub class to become more general and its scope is widening. This is also called widening or up-casting. Widening is safe because the classes will become more general. For example, if we say lemon is a fruit, there will be no objection. Hence, Java compiler will not ask for cast operator in generalization. It will do implicit casting. Similarly, converting a super class type into a sub class type is called 'specialization'. Here, we are coming down from more general form to a specific form and hence the scope is narrowed. Hence, this is also called narrowing or down-casting. Narrowing is not safe because, the classes will become more and more specific thus giving rise to more and more doubts. For example, if we say so and so fruit is a citrus fruit, we should show proof for the statement, since we are becoming more specific. In this case, Java compiler specifically asks the programmer to use cast operator.

Important Interview Question

What is generalization and specialization?

Generalization is a phenomenon where a sub class is promoted to a super class, and hence becomes more general. Generalization needs widening or up-casting. Specialization is phenomenon where a super class is narrowed down to a sub class. Specialization needs narrowing or down-casting.

Generally, any class reference can be used to refer to that class object only. For example,

❑   `Employee e;` //e is the reference variable of Employee class.

❑   `e= new Employee();` //here, e is used to refer to Employee class object.

Suppose class One and class Two are two related classes:

❑   class One   //One is super class.

❑   class Two extends One //Two is sub class of One.

Now, the super class reference is used to refer to the super class object.

❑   `One o = new One();` //class One's reference o is referring to One's object. Similarly, sub class reference can be used to refer to sub class object.

❑   `Two t = new Two();` //class Two's reference t is used to refer to Two's object

In the preceding two cases, we do not require any casting. The reason is that at the left side and at the right side of the assignment operator, we have same data types. For example,

```
One o = new One();
```

Here, 'o' is the reference of class One. So the data type of 'o' is One. At the right side of assignment, we got class One's object. So the data type (class) of the object is also One. So casting is not needed here.

But when, we try to use a reference to refer to a different class object, we need casting. For example, if class One's reference is used to refer to class Two's object, as:

```
One o = new Two();
```

At the left side, we got the reference 'o' whose data type is class One. At the right side, we got the object whose data type is class Two. Now it is essential, we convert the object's data type into class One using cast operator, as:

```
One o = (One) new Two();   //convert class Two's type as class One
```

Here, sub class object type is converted into super class. This is an example for widening or up-casting. In this case, even if we do not use cast operator, there will not be any error message, as the Java compiler will do implicit casting. Similarly, we can convert class One's type as class Two's type in this case:

```
Two t = (Two) new One();   //convert class One's type as class Two
```

Here, we are converting from super class to sub class, which comes under narrowing or down-casting. In this case, cast operator is compulsory as this is unsafe operation.

Widening in Referenced Data Types

Let us observe the difference between widening and narrowing in case of referenced data types. In the program 1, we take class One as super class and class Two is its sub class. We do widening by using super class reference to refer to sub class object. In this case, we convert the sub class object type as super class type.

Program 1: Write a program to see the widening effect where super class reference is used to refer to sub class object.

```
//Widening using referenced data types
class One
{
        void show1()
        {
                System.out.println("Super class method");
        }
}
class Two extends One
{
        void show2()
        {
                System.out.println("Sub class method");
        }
}
class Cast
{
        public static void main(String args[ ])
        {
                One o;  //o is super class reference
                o = (One)new Two(); //o is referring to sub class object
                //the above is widening
                o.show1();
        }
}
```

Output:

```
C:\> javac Cast.java
C:\> java Cast
Super class method
```

In program 1, we used super class reference to refer to sub class object. In this case, the sub class object type is converted into super class type, as:

```
O = (One) new Two();
```

Please observe that, we are able to call the show1() method of the super class. But in this case, it is not possible to call the show2() method of the sub class. For example, if we call the sub class show2() method as:

```
o.show2();
```

There would be an error message during compilation time, as:

```
Cast.java:26: cannot find symbol
symbol: method show2()
location: class One
        o.show2();
1 error
```

So, in widening, the programmer can access all the super class methods, but not the sub class methods. Suppose, we override the super class methods in sub class, as shown here in Program 2, then it is possible to access the sub class methods but not the super class methods. Any how, the programmer will get only 50% functionality into his hands.

Program 2: Let us make a program to override the super class show1() method in sub class. Now only the sub class method is executed.

```
//Widening in referenced data types
class One
{
      void show1()
      {
            System.out.println("Super class method");
      }
}
class Two extends One
{
      void show1()  //override the super class method
      {
            System.out.println("Sub class method");
      }
}

class Cast
{
      public static void main(String args[ ])
      {
            One o;  //o is super class reference
            o = (One)new Two(); //o is referring to sub class object
            //the above is widening
            o.show1();

      }
}
```

Output:

```
C:\> javac Cast.java
C:\> java Cast
Sub class method
```

Narrowing in Referenced Data Types

Narrowing represents converting super class type into sub class type. In the following program, we attempt to go for narrowing by taking sub class reference to refer to super class object. See the Program 3.

Program 3: Write a program for creating sub class reference which is used to refer to the super class object.

```
//Narrowing using super class object
class One
{
    void show1()
    {
        System.out.println("Super class method");
    }
}
class Two extends One
{
    void show2()
    {
        System.out.println("Sub class method");
    }
}

class Cast
{
    public static void main(String args[ ])
    {
        Two t;  //t is sub class reference
        t = (Two)new One(); //t is referring to super class object
        //the above is narrowing
        t.show1();

    }
}
```

Output:

```
C:\> javac Cast.java
C:\> java Cast
Exception in thread "main" java.lang.ClassCastException:
One cannot be cast to Two
```

By observing the output of Program 3, we can understand that the method call t.show1() is not executing the super class method. Similarly, write another statement and call the sub class method show2() as:

```
t.show2()
```

which will also give the same error. So, in narrowing using super class object, we cannot access any of the methods of the super class or sub class. So the programmer will get 0% functionality in this case.

There is a solution for this problem. Let us not create an object to super class, as we did in the previous case. This time, we create an object to sub class and use narrowing, as shown in the Program 4.

Program 4: Write a program for creating super class reference to refer to sub class object.

```
//Narrowing using sub class object
class One
{
        void show1()
        {
                System.out.println("Super class method");
        }
}
class Two extends One
{
        void show2()
        {
                System.out.println("Sub class method");
        }
}

class Cast
{
        public static void main(String args[ ])
        {

                One o;
                o = new Two(); //super class reference to refer to sub class object
                Two t = (Two)o; //this is narrowing - convert class One's reference
                //type as class Two's type
                t.show1();
                t.show2();
        }
}
```

Output:

```
C:\> javac Cast.java
C:\> java Cast
Super class method
Sub class method
```

In program 4, we convert the super class reference type into sub class reference type. Then using the sub class reference, we try to call the methods. From the preceding code, it is evident that if an object to sub class is created, it is possible to access all the methods of the super class as well as the sub class. Narrowing using sub class object will provide 100% functionality to be accessible to the programmer. This is the reason in inheritance, we create an object always to sub class, but not to the super class.

Summary

So the following points can be summarized from the preceding discussion:

☐ If the super class reference is used to refer to super class object, naturally all the methods of super class are accessible.

☐ If the sub class reference is used to refer to sub class object, all the methods of the super class as well as sub class are accessible since the sub class object avails a copy of the super class.

☐ If widening is done by using sub class object, only the super class methods are accessible. If they are overridden, then only the sub class methods are accessible.

❏ If narrowing is done by using super class object, then none of the super class or sub class methods are accessible. This is useless.

❏ If narrowing is done by using sub class object, then all the methods of both the super and sub classes are available to the programmer.

From the preceding points, we can understand that since an object behavior is changed depending on which reference is used to refer the object, we can say that the object is exhibiting polymorphism.

Important Interview Question

What is widening and narrowing?

Converting lower data type into a higher data type is called widening and converting a higher data type into a lower type is called narrowing. Widening is safe and hence even if the programmer does not use cast operator, the Java compiler does not flag any error. Narrowing is unsafe and hence the programmer should explicitly use cast operator in narrowing.

The Object Class

There is a class with the name 'Object' in `java.lang` package which is the super class of all classes in Java. Every class in Java is a direct or indirect sub class of the Object class. The Object class defines the methods to compare objects, to convert an object into a string, to notify threads (processes) regarding the availability of an object, etc.

Important Interview Question

Which is the super class for all the classes including your classes also?

Object class

Object class reference can store any reference of any object. This becomes an advantage when we want to write a method that needs to handle objects of unknown type. If we define a parameter of Object type, any class object can be passed to the method. Thus, the method can receive any type of object and handle it. The methods of Object class are given in the Table 17.1.

Table 17.1

Method	Description
equals()	This method compares the references of two objects and if they are equal, it returns true, otherwise false. The way it compares the objects is dependent on the objects.
toString()	This method returns a string representation of an object. For example, the string representation of an Integer object is an integer number displayed as string.
getClass()	This method gives an object that contains the name of a class to which an object belongs.
hashCode()	This method returns hash code number of an object.
notify()	This method sends a notification to a thread which is waiting for an object.
notifyAll()	This method sends a notification for all waiting threads for the object.

Method	Description
wait()	This method causes a thread to wait till a notification is received from a notify() or notifyAll() methods.
clone()	This method creates a bit wise exact copy of an existing object.
finalize()	This method is called by the garbage collector when an object is removed from memory.

Let us see how to compare two objects by using equals() method of Object class. This method normally compares the references of two objects. If both the references refer to same object, then it gives true, otherwise it gives false. But in case of String objects and wrapper class objects (Character, Integer, Float, Double etc. classes are called wrapper classes), it compares the contents of the objects. If the contents are same then it returns true, otherwise false. In Program 5, we are using equals() method to compare two objects of a general class 'Myclass' and two objects of wrapper class 'Integer'. In case of Myclass objects, if the references are same, then equals() method gives true, otherwise false. In case of Integer class objects, it gives true if the contents are same, otherwise false.

Program 5: Write a program where equals() method compares Myclass objects' references. The same equals() method is used to compare Integer class objects' contents.

```
//equals() method
//take Myclass that stores an int value
class Myclass
{
        int x;

        Myclass(int x)
        {
                this.x = x;
        }
}

class Compare
{
        public static void main(String args[ ])
        {
                //create two Myclass objects with same content.
                //In this case, references of  objects will be different.
                Myclass obj1 = new Myclass(15);
                Myclass obj2 = new Myclass(15);

                //create two wrapper class objects and store same content.
                //In this case, references of objects will be different.
                Integer obj3 = new Integer(15);
                Integer obj4 = new Integer(15);


                if(obj1.equals(obj2))
                System.out.println("obj1 and obj2 are same");
                else System.out.println("obj1 and obj2 are not same");

                if(obj3.equals(obj4))
                System.out.println("obj3 and obj4 are same");
                else System.out.println("obj3 and obj4 are not same");

        }

    }
```

Output:

```
C:\> javac Compare.java
C:\> java Compare
obj1 and obj2 are not same
obj3 and obj4 are same
```

Let us use getClass() method to know the name of the class to which an object belongs. In Program 6, we are taking Myclass which contains an int value. There is another class KnowName which contains a static method printName() as:

```
static void printName(Object obj)
{
        Class c = obj.getClass();
        String name = c.getName();
        System.out.println("The classname= "+ name);
}
```

Observe that this method has a parameter which is the reference variable of Object class. Object class reference can be used to refer to any other class object. So it is possible to send Myclass object to this method, and then the Object class reference will refer to Myclass object.

❑ Observe the code in printName() method:

```
Class c = obj.getClass();
```

Here, getClass() method gets the class name of the object and it stores that class name in the object of the class Class. Please note that there is a class with the name 'Class' in Java. This class exists in java.lang package. Now using c.getName(), we can find the class name.

Program 6: Write a program where an object is passed to printName() method and the class name of the object is displayed by the method.

```
//Using getClass() to know the classname
//Myclass stores an int value
class Myclass
{
        int x;
        Myclass(int x)
        {
                this.x = x;
        }
}
//This class contains method to receive an object and display the classname
class KnowName
{
        static void printName(Object obj)
        {
                //get the class name into an object c of the class Class
                Class c = obj.getClass();
                //get the name of the class using getName()
                String name = c.getName();
                System.out.println("The classname= "+ name);
        }
}
class Demo
{
        public static void main(String args[ ])
        {
                //create Myclass object obj
                Myclass obj = new Myclass(10);
                //know the class name of the object obj by calling printName().
                KnowName.printName(obj);
```

```
        }
    }
```

Output:

```
C:\> javac Demo.java
C:\> java Demo
The classname= Myclass
```

Cloning the Class Objects

The process of creating an exact copy of an existing object is called 'cloning'. In cloning, already an object should exist and when we clone the object, a bit wise copy of the object will result. The original object and the cloned object will be exactly the same bit to bit. If the original object has some data in it, it also automatically comes into cloned object.

There are two types of cloning. When the cloned object is modified, same modification will also affect the original object. This is called 'shallow cloning'. When the cloned object is modified, if the original object is not modified, then it is called 'deep cloning'.

When we have new operator to create the objects, why do we need the cloning technology? Let us take an example of object1 which is created by using new operator. There is a lot of processing done on this object, so the content of the object has been drastically changed. Let us call it object2. At this intermediate stage, we want another copy of this object. There are two ways to perform this:

❑ Using new operator, we can create another object. But, when new operator is used to create the object, the object is created by using the initial values as object1. So, the same processing should be repeated on this object to get the intermediate object, i.e., object2.

❑ The other way is to clone the object2, so that we get exact copy of the object. This preserves a copy of the intermediate object and hence the original object and the cloned objects can be processed separately. This method is easy because, we can avoid a lot of processing to be done on the object.

From the preceding discussion, we can understand that cloning is advantageous than using new operator while creating objects.

Let us discuss the steps to clone the object of a class:

❑ The class whose objects to be cloned should implement Cloneable interface. This interface belongs to `java.lang` package. Cloneable interface indicates that the class objects are cloneable. If this interface is not implemented, then that class objects can not be cloned and it gives `CloneNotSupportedException`.

❑ `clone()` method of Object class is used for cloning. Object is the super class for every class. So, let us write our own method in the class and call the `clone()` method, something like this:

```
public Object myClone()  //our own method
{
    return super.clone();  //create cloned object and return it
}
```

❑ It is also possible to create a cloned object, by overriding the `clone()` method of Object class. Since `clone()` method is defined as protected Object `clone()` in Object class, we can write our `clone()` method overriding this, as:

```
protected Object clone()  //This method overrides clone() method of Object class
{
    return super.clone();
}
```

Here, we are overriding the `clone()` method and again we are calling the `clone()` method from it. These concepts are used in Program 7 to clone Employee object. In this program, we are creating Employee class with id and name details. The Employee class should implement Cloneable interface because we are going to clone Employee class objects. There is `myClone()` method which calls the super class (Object class) `clone()` method to clone the Employee class object.

Program 7: Write a program to make cloning Employee class object by writing our own `myClone()` method, from where Object class `clone()` method is called.

```java
//Cloning example
class Employee implements Cloneable
{
        //instance vars
        int id;
        String name;

        //constructor to initialize vars
        Employee(int id, String name)
        {
                this.id = id;
                this.name = name;
        }

        //method to display the details
        void getData()
        {
                System.out.println("Id= "+ id);
                System.out.println("Name= "+ name);
        }

        //clone the present class object
        public Object myClone() throws CloneNotSupportedException
        {
                return super.clone();
        }
}


class CloneDemo
{
        public static void main(String args[ ])  throws CloneNotSupportedException
        {
                //create Employee class object using new operator
                Employee e1 = new Employee(10, "Srinivas");

                System.out.println("Original object:");
                e1.getData();

                //create another object by cloning e1. As myClone() method returns
                //object of Object class type, it should be converted into
                //Employee type
                Employee e2 = (Employee)e1.myClone();

                System.out.println("Cloned object: ");
                e2.getData();
        }
}
```

Output:

```
C:\> javac CloneDemo.java
C:\> java CloneDemo
Original object:
Id= 10
Name= Srinivas
```

```
Cloned object:
Id= 10
Name= Srinivas
```

We can also rewrite the preceding program, by overriding the `clone()` method of Object . Replace the `myClone()` method code with the following code:

```
protected Object clone() throws CloneNotSupportedException
  {
    return super.clone();
  }

And call this method from main() as:
Employee e2 = (Employee)e1.clone();
```

Important Interview Question

Which method is used in cloning?

   `clone()` *method of Object class is used in cloning.*

In cloning the objects, the class should implement Cloneable interface. In fact, the Cloneable interface does not have any members. It means, this interface does not have any variables or methods. Such an interface is called 'marking interface' or 'tagging interface'. This interface behaves like a 'tag' indicating the class objects are cloneable. Or, we can say that this interface is 'marking' the class so that any body can clone the class objects. If we do not implement Cloneable interface then that class objects are not cloneable and `clone()` method gives CloneNotSupportedException.

Important Interview Question

Can you write an interface without any methods?

   Yes.

What do you call the interface without any members?

   An interface without any members is called marking interface or tagging interface. It marks the class objects for a special purpose. For example, Cloneable (`java.lang`) and Serializable (`java.io`) are two marking interfaces. Cloneable interface indicates that a particular class objects are cloneable while Serializable interface indicates that a particular class objects are serializable.

We shall discuss the `wait()`, `notify()` and `notifyAll()` methods of Object class later in a chapter on Threads.

Conclusion

Generally, a class reference can be used to refer to any of that class objects. By casting the reference, we can use it to refer to its sub or super class objects. In this case, the behavior of the object will change exhibiting the polymorphic nature. We can cast primitive data types in two ways, widening and narrowing. Similarly, the advanced data types also can be casted in two ways, widening and narrowing. Finally, the universal super class 'Object' comes into picture as all other classes in Java have been derived from Object class. So, Object class reference can be used to refer to any other class.

CHAPTER
18

ABSTRACT CLASSES

W e know that a class is a model for creating the objects. A class contains description of properties or variables and actions or methods of its objects. If an object has the properties and actions as mentioned in the class, then that object belongs to the class. The rule is that any thing is written in the class is applicable to all of its objects. If a method is written in the class, it is available as it is to all of the class objects. For example, take a class Myclass that contains a method calculate() that calculates square value of a given number. If we create three objects to this class, all the three objects get the copy of this method and hence, from any object, we can call and use this method. See Program 1.

Program 1: Write a program where Myclass's calculate() method is available to all the objects and hence every object can calculate the square value.

```
        //All the objects sharing the same method
        class Myclass
        {
                //method to calculate square value
                void calculate(double x)
                {
                        System.out.println("Square= "+ (x*x));
                }
        }
        class Common
        {
                public static void main(String args[ ])
                {
                        //create 3 objects
                        Myclass obj1 = new Myclass();
                        Myclass obj2 = new Myclass();
                        Myclass obj3 = new Myclass();

                        //call calculate() method from the objects
                        obj1.calculate(3);
                        obj2.calculate(4);
                        obj3.calculate(5);
                }
        }
```

Output:

```
C:\> javac Common.java
C:\> java Common
Square= 9.0
Square= 16.0
```

```
Square= 25.0
```

Of course, in the preceding program, the requirement of all the objects is same, i.e., to calculate square value. But, some times the requirement of the objects will be different and entirely dependent on the specific object only. For example, in the preceding program, if the first object wants to calculate square value, the second object wants the square root value and the third object wants cube value. In such a case, how to write the `calculate()` method in Myclass ?

Since, calculate() method has to perform three different tasks depending on the object, we cannot write the code to calculate square value in the body of calculate() method. On the other hand, if we write three different methods like `calculate_Square()`, `calculate_Sqrt()`, and `calculate_Cube()` in Myclass, then all the three methods are available to all the three objects which is not advisable. When each object wants one method, providing all the three does not look reasonable. To serve each object with the one and only required method, we can follow the steps:

1. First, let us write a `calculate()` method in Myclass. This means every object wants to calculate something.

2. If we write body for `calculate()` method, it is commonly available to all the objects. So let us not write body for `calculate()` method. Such a method is called abstract method. Since, we write abstract method in Myclass, it is called abstract class.

3. Now derive a sub class `Sub1` from `Myclass`, so that the `calculate()` method is available to the sub class. Provide body for `calculate()` method in Sub1 such that it calculates square value. Similarly, we create another sub class `Sub2` where we write the `calculate()` method with body to calculate square root value. We create the third sub class `Sub3` where we write the `calculate()` method to calculate cube value. This hierarchy is shown in Figure 18.1.

4. It is possible to create objects for the sub classes. Using these objects, the respective methods can be called and used. Thus, every object will have its requirement fulfilled.

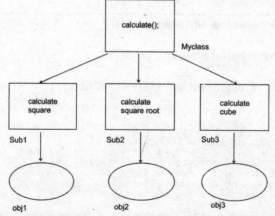

Figure 18.1 Defining a method in sub classes to suit the objects

Abstract Method and Abstract Class

An abstract method does not contain any body. It contains only the method header. So we can say it is an incomplete method. An abstract class is a class that generally contains some abstract methods. Both the abstract class and the abstract methods should be declared by using the key word 'abstract'.

Since, abstract class contains incomplete methods, it is not possible to estimate the total memory required to create the object. So, JVM can not create objects to an abstract class. We should create sub classes and all the abstract methods should be implemented (body should be written) in the sub classes. Then, it is possible to create objects to the sub classes since they are complete classes.

Important Interview Question

What is abstract method?

An abstract method is a method without method body. An abstract method is written when the same method has to perform different tasks depending on the object calling it.

What is abstract class?

An abstract class is a class that contains 0 or more abstract methods.

In Program   we create Myclass as the abstract super class with an abstract method calculate(). This method does not have any body within it. Sub1, Sub2 and Sub3 are the three sub classes where the abstract method is implemented as per the requirement of the objects. Since, the same abstract method is implemented differently for different objects, they can perform different tasks.

Program 2: Let us make a program where the abstract class Myclass has one abstract method which has got various implementations in sub classes.

```java
//All the objects need different implementations of the same method
abstract class Myclass
{
        //this is abstract method
        abstract void calculate(double x);

}
class Sub1 extends Myclass
{
        //calculate square value
        void calculate(double x)
        {
                System.out.println("Square= "+ (x*x));
        }
}
class Sub2 extends Myclass
{
        //calculate square root value
        void calculate(double x)
        {
                System.out.println("Square root= "+ Math.sqrt(x));
        }
}

class Sub3 extends Myclass
{
        //calculate cube value
        void calculate(double x)
        {
                System.out.println("Cube= "+ (x*x*x));
        }
}

class Different
{
        public static void main(String args[ ])
        {
                //create sub class objects
                Sub1 obj1 = new Sub1();
                Sub2 obj2 = new Sub2();
                Sub3 obj3 = new Sub3();
```

```
                    //let the objects call and use calculate() method
                    obj1.calculate(3);   //calculate square
                    obj2.calculate(4);   //calculate square root
                    obj3.calculate(5);   //calculate cube value

          }
     }
```

Output:

```
     C:\> javac Different.java
     C:\> java Different
     Square= 9.0
     Square root= 2.0
     Cube= 125.0
```

We cannot create an object to abstract class, but we can create a reference variable to it, as this variable will not take any memory. Once the reference is created, it can be used to refer to the objects of sub classes, as shown here:

```
     Myclass ref;   //ref is the reference of Myclass
     ref = obj1;    //ref is referring to obj1
     ref.calculate(3);  //call obj1' s calculate() method
     ref = obj2;    //now ref is referring to obj2
     ref.calculate(4);  //call obj2's calculate() method
     ref = obj3;    //now ref is referring to obj3
     ref.calculate(5);  //call obj3's calculate() method
```

Let us take another example to understand the abstract class concept in a better way. We see many cars on the road. These cars are all objects of car class. For example, Maruti, Santro, Benz are all objects of car class. Suppose, we plan to write Car class, it contains all the properties (variables) and methods (actions) of any car object in the world. For example, we can write the following members in Car class:

❑ **Registration number:** Every car will have a registration number and hence we write this as an instance variable in Car class. All cars whether it is Maruti or Santro should have a registration number. It means registration number is a common feature to all the objects. So, it can be written in the Car class.

❑ **Fuel tank:** Every car will have a fuel tank, opening and filling the tank is an action. To represent this action, we can write a method like:

```
     void openTank()
```

How do we open and fill the tank? Take the key, open the tank and fill fuel. Let us assume that all cars have same mechanism of opening the tank. So, the code representing the opening mechanism can be written in openTank() method's body. So it becomes a concrete method. A concrete method is a method with body.

❑ **Steering:** Every car will have a steering and steering the car is an action. For this, we write a method as:

```
     void steering(int direction, int angle)
```

How do we steer the car? All the cars do not have same mechanism for steering. Maruti cars have manual steering. Santro cars have power steering. So, it is not possible to write a particular mechanism in steering() method. So, this method should be written without body in Car class. It becomes an abstract method.

❑ **Brakes:** Every car will have brakes. Applying brakes is an action and hence it can be represented as a method, as:

```
void braking(int force)
```

How do we apply brakes? All cars do not have same mechanism for brakes. Maruti cars have hydraulic brakes. Santro cars have gas brakes. So, we cannot write a particular braking mechanism in this method. This method, hence, will not have a body in Car class, and hence becomes abstract. See Figure 18.2.

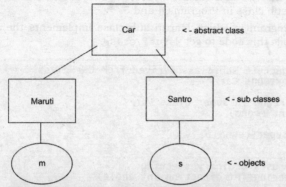

Figure 18.2 Abstract class and its sub classes

So, the Car class has an instance variable, one concrete method and two abstract methods. Hence, Car class will become abstract class. See this class in Program 3 given here.

Program 3: Write a program in which abstract class Car contains an instance variable, one concrete method and two abstract methods. Compile this code to get Car.class. We can not run it because it does not have a main() method.

```
//This is an abstract class
abstract class Car
{
      //every car will have a registration number
      int regno;

      //initialize the value of regno
      Car(int r)
      {
            regno=r;
      }

      //all cars will have a fuel tank and same mechanism to open the tank
      void openTank()
      {
            System.out.println("Fill the tank");
      }

      //all cars will have steering but different cars will have different
      //steering mechanisms.
      abstract void steering(int direction,int angle);

      //all cars will have brakes but different cars will have different
      //braking mechanisms.
      abstract void braking(int force);
}
```

```
C:\> javac Car.java
C:\>
```

Now, we have written the abstract class, the next step is to derive sub classes from the Car class. In the sub classes, we should take the abstract methods of the Car class and implement (writing body in) them. The reason why we implement the abstract methods in the sub classes is that the implementation of these methods is dependent on the sub classes. In our program, let us write Maruti and Santro as the two sub classes where the two abstract methods will be implemented accordingly. See these sub class in Programs 4 and 5.

Program 4: Write a program in which Maruti sub class implements the abstract methods of the super class, Car. Compile this code to get Maruti.class.

```
//This is a concrete sub class derived from Car class
class Maruti extends Car
{
        //store regno in super class var
        Maruti(int regno)
        {
                super(regno);
        }

        //Maruti uses ordinary steering
        void steering(int direction,int angle)
        {
                System.out.println("Take a turn");
                System.out.println("This is ordinary steering");
        }

        //Maruti uses hydraulic brakes
        void braking(int force)
        {
                System.out.println("Brakes applied");
                System.out.println("These are hydraulic brakes");
        }
}
```

Output:

```
C:\> javac Maruti.java
C:\>
```

Program 5: Write a program in which Santro sub class implements the abstract methods of the super class, Car. Compile this code to get Santro.class.

```
//This is a concrete class derived from class Car
class Santro extends Car
{
        //store regno at super class
        Santro(int regno)
        {
                super(regno);
        }

        //Santro uses power steering
        void steering(int direction,int angle)
        {
                System.out.println("Take a turn");
                System.out.println("This car uses power steering");
        }
}
```

```
                //Santro uses gas breaks
                void braking(int force)
                {
                        System.out.println("Brakes applied");
                        System.out.println("This cars uses gas brakes");
                }
        }
```

Output:

```
C:\> javac Santro.java
C:\>
```

The next step is to use the sub classes by creating objects. Since, we cannot create an object to `Car` class, we can create a reference to it, as:

```
Car ref;
```

This reference can be used to refer to any of the sub class objects. Through this reference, all features of Maruti and Santro can be used. This can be seen in Program 6.

Program 6: Let us create a program to use all the features of abstract class by creating a reference to it and referring to the sub class objects. Abstract class reference can be used to call the methods of the sub classes.

```
//Using cars
class UseCar
{
    public static void main(String args[ ])
    {
            //create sub class objects
            Maruti m = new Maruti(1001); //1001 is regno.
            Santro s = new Santro(5005); //5005 is regno.

            //create a reference to super class: Car
            Car ref;

            //to use the Maruti car
            ref=m; //to use Santro car: ref=s;

            //use the features of the car
            ref.openTank();
            ref.steering(1,90);
            ref.braking(500);
    }
}
```

Output:

```
C:\> javac UseCar.java
C:\>java UseCar
Fill the tank
Take a turn
This is ordinary steering
Brakes applied
These are hydraulic brakes
```

In the preceding program, if reference is used to refer to Santro object, as:

```
ref = s;
```

Then, the following output can be expected:

```
Fill the tank
Take a turn
This car uses power steering
Brakes applied
This cars uses gas brakes
```

In the preceding program, we created a reference of the super class and using this reference, we are accessing all the features of the sub classes in main() method. Why should we create a reference of the super class? Can't we access the features of the sub classes by individually creating sub class objects?

It is perfectly possible to access all the members of the sub classes by using sub class objects. But we prefer to use super class reference to access the sub class features because, the reference variable can access only those features of the sub classes which have been already declared in super class. If we write an individual method in the sub class, the super class reference cannot access that method. This is to enforce discipline in the programmers not to add any of their own features in the sub classes other than whatever is given in super class. For example, a programmer has added the following method in Maruti class:

```
void wings()
{
    System.out.println("I can fly");
}
```

This method declaration is not found in super class (Car), so super class reference cannot refer to this method. When wings are added to Maruti car, there is doubt whether it still belongs to Car class or not. When wings are there, it may belong to Bird class or Aeroplane class, who knows!

Important Interview Question

How can you force your programmers to implement only the features of your class?

  By writing an abstract class or an interface.

We take another program where abstract class can be used practically. Suppose, we are writing a program to calculate electricity bills. There are two types of electricity connections, commercial and domestic. Depending on the type of connection, the rate per unit will vary. So, we take an abstract class Plan with instance variables rate and to store rate, we write an abstract method getRate(). Then, we create a sub class CommercialPlan where rate per unit is taken as Rs. 5.00 per unit. Another sub class DomesticPlan will store Rs. 2.60 per unit as rate. Then, we write a separate class with the name Calculate to calculate the electricity bill and display the bill amount. In this class, we use abstract class reference to refer to CommercialPlan class object to calculate the bill according to commercial plan. Similarly, we use abstract class reference to refer to DomesticPlan class object to calculate the bill according to domestic plan.

Program 7: Let us make a program to write abstract class with an instance variable: rate, a concrete method: getRate() and an abstract method:calculateBill().

```
//Calculating electricity bill for commercial and domestic plans
abstract class Plan
{
    //take rate as protected to access it in sub classes
    protected double rate;

    //accept rate into rate variable. Since rate will change
    //depending on plan, we declare abstract method
    public abstract void getRate();
```

```java
        //calculate the electricity bill by taking units
        public void calculateBill(int units)
        {
                System.out.print("Bill amount for "+ units + " units: ");
                System.out.println(rate*units);
        }
}

class CommercialPlan extends Plan
{
        //store commercial rate as Rs.5.00 per unit
        public void getRate()
        {
                rate = 5.00;
        }

}

class DomesticPlan extends Plan
{
        //store domestic rate as Rs.2.60 per unit
        public void getRate()
        {
                rate = 2.60;
        }
}

class Calculate
{
        public static void main(String args[])
        {
                //create reference p to abstract class
                Plan p;

                //calculate commercial bill for 250 units
                System.out.println("Commercial connection: ");
                p = new CommercialPlan();    //use reference to refer to sub class
                //object
                p.getRate();
                p.calculateBill(250);

                //calculate domestic bill for 150 units
                System.out.println("Domestic connection: ");
                p = new DomesticPlan();    //use reference to refer to sub class
                // object
                p.getRate();
                p.calculateBill(150);
        }
}
```

Output:

```
C:\> javac Calculate.java
C:\> java Calculate
Commercial connection:
Bill amount for 250 units: 1250.0
Domestic connection:
Bill amount for 150 units: 390.0
```

Summary

Let us summarize the points on abstract class:

❏   An abstract class is a class that contains 0 or more abstract methods.

❏   An abstract class can contain instance variables and concrete methods in addition to abstract methods.

❏   Abstract class and the abstract methods should be declared by using the key word 'abstract'.

❏   All the abstract methods of the abstract class should be implemented (body) in its sub classes.

❏   If any abstract method is not implemented, then that sub class should be declared as 'abstract'. In this case, we cannot create an object to the sub class. We should create another sub class to this sub class and implement the remaining abstract method there.

❏   We cannot create an object to abstract class.

❏   But, we can create a reference of abstract class type.

❏   The reference of abstract class can be used to refer to objects of its subclasses.

❏   The reference of abstract class can not refer to individual methods of its subclasses.

❏   It is possible to derive an abstract class as a sub class from a concrete super class.

❏   We cannot declare a class as both abstract and final. For example,

```
abstract final class A     //invalid
```

The key word `abstract` represents an incomplete class which depends on the sub classes for its implementation. Creating sub class is compulsory for abstract class. `final` key word prevents inheritance. This means, we cannot create sub class to a final class. So, the key words `abstract` and `final` are contradictory and hence both can not be used simultaneously for a class.

Important Interview Question

Can you declare a class as abstract and final also?

No. `abstract` *class needs sub classes.* `final` *key word represents sub classes which can not be created. So, both are quite contradictory and cannot be used for the same class.*

Conclusion

Any class will have all concrete methods implemented to perform a particular task. So a class can perform only that task and hence it is rigid. Abstract class will make programming more flexible by giving scope to write abstract methods. It is possible to implement the abstract methods differently in the sub classes of an abstract class. These different implementations will help the programmer to perform different tasks depending on the need of the sub classes. Moreover, the common members of the abstract class are also shared by the sub classes. Thus, abstract class is useful to write better and flexible programs. Also, because of several levels followed like abstract class, its sub classes, sub-sub classes, etc., the programmer can manage the code easily.

INTERFACES

I n the last chapter, we learned that an abstract class is a class which contains some abstract methods as well as concrete methods also. Imagine there is a class that contains only abstract methods and there are no concrete methods. It becomes an interface. This means an interface contains methods which are all abstract and hence none of the methods will have body. Only method prototypes will be written in the interface. So an interface can be defined as a specification of method prototypes. Since, we write only abstract methods in the interface, there is possibility for providing different implementations (body) for those abstract methods depending on the requirements of objects.

Interface

An interface contains only abstract methods which are all incomplete methods. So it is not possible to create an object to an interface. In this case, we can create separate classes where we can implement all the methods of the interface. These classes are called implementation classes. Since, implementation classes will have all the methods with body, it is possible to create objects to the implementation classes. The flexibility lies in the fact that every implementation class can have its own implementation of the abstract methods of the interface. See Figure 19.1.

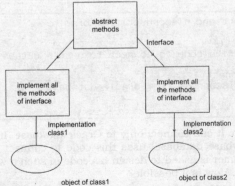

Figure 19.1 Interface and its implementation classes

Important Interview Question

What is an interface?

An interface is a specification of method prototypes. All the methods of the interface are public and abstract.

Since, none of the methods have body in the interface, we may tend to think that writing an interface is mere waste. This is not correct. In fact, an interface is more useful when compared to the class owing to its flexibility of providing necessary implementation for the objects. Let us elucidate this point further with an example. You have some rupees in your hands. You can spend in rupees only by going to a shop where billing is done in rupees. Suppose you have gone to a shop where only dollars are accepted, you can not use your rupees there. This money is like a 'class'. A class satisfies the only requirement intended for it. It is not useful to handle a different situation.

Suppose, you have a credit card. Now, you can pay by using your credit card in rupees in a shop. If you go to another shop where they expect you to pay in dollars, you can pay in dollars. The same credit card can be used to pay in pounds also. Here, the credit card is like an interface which performs several tasks. In fact, the credit card is a plastic card and does not hold any money physically. It contains just your name, your bank name and perhaps some number. But how the shop keepers are able to draw the money from the credit card? Behind the credit card, you got your bank account which holds the money from where it is transferred to the shop keepers. This bank account can be taken as an implementation class which actually performs the task. See Figure 19.2.

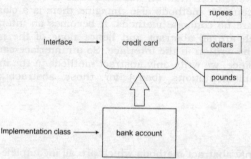

Figure 19.2 Interface and Implementation class

Let us see how the interface concept is advantageous in software development. A programmer is asked to write a Java program to connect to a database and retrieve the data from the database, process the data and display the results in the form of some reports. For this purpose, the programmer has written a class to connect to Oracle database, some thing like this:

```
//class to connect and disconnect from oracle
class Myclass {
        void connect() {
                //write code to connect to oracle database
        }
        void disconnect() {
                //disconnect from oracle database
        }
}
```

This class has a limitation. It can connect only to Oracle database. If a client (user) using any other database (for example, Sybase database) uses this code to connect to his database, this code will not work. So, the programmer is asked to design his code in such a way that it is used to connect to any database in the world. How is it possible?

One way is to write several classes, each to connect to a particular database. Thus, considering all the databases available in the world, the programmer has to write a lot of classes. This takes a lot of time and effort. Even though, the programmer spends a lot of time and writes all the classes, by the time the software is released into the market, all the versions of the databases will change and the programmer is supposed to rewrite the classes again to suit the latest versions of databases. This is very cumbersome.

Interface helps to solve this problem. The programmer writes an interface with abstract methods as shown here:

```
interface MyInter
{
    //All the methods of an interface are by default public and abstract.
    //So, we need not declare them explicitly as public abstract.
    void connect();
    void disconnect();
}
```

Important Interview Question

Why the methods of interface are public and abstract by default?

Interface methods are public since they should be available to third party vendors to provide implementation. They are abstract because their implementation is left for third party vendors.

We cannot create objects to the interface. So, we need implementation classes where all these methods of the interface are implemented to suit the needs of objects. So, the programmer releases a notification inviting the programmers of all other companies (third party vendors) to provide implementation classes for his `MyInter` interface. He also specifies in the terms of usage to the user that the user should purchase the implementation class related to his database and use it along with his program.

Now, the third party vendors will provide implementation classes to MyInter interface. These implementation classes are also called database drivers. For example, Oracle Corp people may provide an implementation class (driver) where the code related to connecting to the oracle database and disconnecting from the database will be provided, as:

```
class OracleDB implements MyInter {
    public void connect() {
        //code to connect to oracle database
    }
    public void disconnect() {
        //code to disconnect from oracle
    }
}
```

Note that OracleDB is an implementation class of MyInter interface. `implements` keyword should be used with implementation class, as:

```
class Classname implements Interfacename
```

Similarly, the Sybase people may provide another implementation class SybaseDB, where code related to connect to Sybase database and disconnect from Sybase will be provided, as:

```
class SybaseDB implements MyInter {
    public void connect() {
        //code to connect to sybase database
    }
    public void disconnect() {
        //code to disconnect from sybase
    }
}
```

Now, it is possible to create objects to the implementation classes and call the `connect()` method and `disconnect()` methods from a main program. This program is also written by the same programmer who develops the interface. Since the programmer does not know the names of implementation classes at the time of writing the main program, he should create object to implementation class without knowing its name. For this, the following steps can be followed:

❑ Take the driver name (e.g., OracleDB) from the client (user) through command line arguments and pass it to `forName()` method. This method belongs to the class 'Class' which is in `java.lang` package. `forName()` accepts the name of a class as a string, creates an object and stores the class name in that object. This object belongs to the class `Class`, as:

```
Class c = Class.forName(args[0]);
```

Simply speaking, the object 'c' preceding contains the driver name (e.g., OracleDB).

❑ Now create an object to the class (e.g., OracleDB) whose name is in c. This can be done by `newInstance()` method of the class `Class`. We can create a reference to the interface MyInter which can be used to refer to this object.

```
MyInter mi = (MyInter)c.newInstance();
```

Simply speaking, mi refers to the object of driver class (e.g., OracleDB). This object is created by `newInstance()` method as an object of Object class type. To use MyInter reference to refer to this object, the object type should be converted as MyInter type by using casting.

❑ Call the `connect()` and `disconnect()` methods of the driver class using mi, as:

```
mi.connect();
mi.disconnect();
```

`connect()` method establishes connection with the particular database and `disconnect()` method disconnects from the database. The complete program is shown in Program 1.

Program 1: Write a program to create an interface MyInter that connects to a database and retrieves the data from the database.

```java
//interface example - Connecting to any Database
interface MyInter
{
    void connect(); //abstract public
    void disconnect();
}
class OracleDB implements MyInter {
    public void connect() {
        System.out.println("Connecting to Oracle database...");
    }
    public void disconnect() {
        System.out.println("Disconnected from Oracle.");
    }
}
class SybaseDB implements MyInter {
    public void connect() {
        System.out.println("Connecting to Sybase database...");
    }
    public void disconnect() {
        System.out.println("Disconnected from Sybase.");
    }
}
class InterfaceDemo {
    public static void main(String args[ ]) throws Exception {
        //accept the implementation classname from Commandline argument
        //and store it in the object c.
        Class c = Class.forName(args[0]);
        //create an object to the class whose name is in c.
        //let the reference variable of interface point to it.
        MyInter mi = (MyInter)c.newInstance();
        //call methods of the object using mi.
        mi.connect();
        mi.disconnect();
    }
}
```

Output:

```
C:\> javac InterfaceDemo.java
C:\> java InterfaceDemo OracleDB
Connecting to Oracle database...
Disconnected from Oracle.

C:\> java InterfaceDemo SybaseDB
Connecting to Sybase database...
Disconnected from Sybase.
```

In preceding program, the implementation classes OracleDB and SybaseDB are supposed to be provided by third party vendors. An object to OracleDB or SybaseDB is created and connect() and disconnect() methods are called by using MyInter reference mi. There are two more concerns in the preceding program. The first one, why third party vendors provide implementation classes for our interface? They definitely provide implementation classes because it is profitable for them. Every client who ever purchases our software (interface) will definitely purchase the implementation classes from the third party vendor because they want to use our software in connection with the database. Thus, the third party vendors can sell the implementation classes. Also, the database vendor can promote their business by providing the implementation classes.

The second concern is how the third party vendors know which methods to implement? The third party people know which interface we wrote and which methods were written there along with their description through API (Application Programming Interface) document. API document is a hyper text mark up language (html) file that contains the description of all the features of a software, a product or a technology. After creating the software, we create an API document which works like a reference manual to the third party vendor to understand which methods to implement. API document creation is explained in Chapter 20. This entire discussion is represented in Figure 19.3.

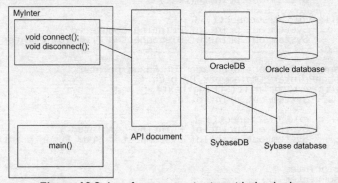

Figure 19.3 Interface communicating with the databases

Let us take another example where interface is used. We want to write Printer interface which is used to send data to different printers. This interface has a method printit() that sends text to the printer and disconnect() method that disconnects the printer after printing is done. Of course, this program is a model how the printer interface can be used. It does not send the text to a real printer. On the other hand, it displays the text on the screen.

Printer interface is implemented by IBM people such that it sends text to IBM printer. Similarly, Epson people provide a different implementation to the Printer interface such that it sends text to Epson printer. These implementation classes (printer drivers) are written as IBMPrinter and EpsonPrinter.

To use a printer, first of all we should know which printer is used by the client. We assume that the printer driver name is generally stored in the config.txt file at the time of installing the driver (implementation class). So, open notepad (or any text editor) and create a file with the name config.txt and store a single line that represents the printer driver name, as:

```
EpsonPrinter
```

And then save the file. Alternately, you can store the name IBMPrinter in the `config.txt` file.

Now, this `config.txt` file should be connected to an input stream which can read data from this file. We can use `FileReader` for this purpose. We can connect another stream like `LineNumberReader` to read line by line from the stream. This stream can read the first line available in `config.txt` file. This line will be, of course, the line stored by us, i.e., `EpsonPrinter`.

Store the printer name 'EpsonPrinter' in an object using `Class.forName()` method. Taking EpsonPrinter as a class name (which represents implementation class), create another object to it by using `newInstance()` method. Using this object, we can call and use the methods of Printer interface.

Program 2: Write a program which contains a Printer interface and its implementation classes to send text to any printer.

```java
//An interface Printer to send text to any printer
import java.io.*;
//creating an interface for printing
 interface Printer {
      //to print the text sent to printer
      void printit(String text);  //public abstract
      //to disconnect from printer
      void disconnect();
}
//Implementing Printer interface for IBM printer
 class IBMPrinter implements Printer {
      public void printit(String text) {
            System.out.println(text);
      }
      public void disconnect() {
            System.out.println("Printing completed");
            System.out.println("Disconnected from IBM Printer");
      }
}
//Implementing Printer interface for Epson printer
 class EpsonPrinter implements Printer {
      public void printit(String text) {
            System.out.println(text);
      }
      public void disconnect() {
            System.out.println("Printing completed");
            System.out.println("Disconnected from Epson printer");
      }
}
//Using a printer
 class UsePrinter {
      public static void main(String args[ ]) throws Exception {
            //attach FileReader to config.txt file to read data from it
            FileReader fr = new FileReader("config.txt");
            //connect LineNumberReader to FileReader to read one line at a time
            LineNumberReader lnr= new LineNumberReader(fr);
            //read the first line from config.txt file
            String printername =  lnr.readLine();
            //The read line represents the printer name
            System.out.println("Loading the driver for: "+printername);
            //store the printername in an object c
            Class c =Class.forName(printername);
            //create an object to that class represented by printername in c
            Printer ref = (Printer)c.newInstance();
            //send text to printit using Printer reference
            ref.printit("Hello, This is printed on the printer");
            //disconnect afeter printing
            ref.disconnect();
      }
}
```

Output:

```
C:\> javac UsePrinter.java
C:\> java UsePrinter
Loading the driver for: EpsonPrinter
Hello, This is printed on the printer
Printing completed
Disconnected from Epson printer
```

Summary

Now, let us summarize the following points on interfaces, before we proceed further:

- *An interface is a specification of method prototypes. This means, only method names are written in the interface without method bodies.*
- *An interface will have 0 or more abstract methods which are all public and abstract by default.*
- *An interface can have variables which are public static and final by default. This means all the variables of the interface are constants.*
- *None of the methods in Interface can be private, protected or static.*
- *We cannot create an object to an interface, but we can create a reference of interface type.*
- *All the methods of interface should be implemented in its implementation classes. If any method is not implemented, then that implementation class should be declared as 'abstract'.*
- *Interface reference can refer to the objects of its implementation classes.*
- *When an interface is written, any third party vendor can provide implementation classes to it.*
- *An interface can extend another interface.*
- *An interface cannot implement another interface.*
- *It is possible to write a class within an interface.*
- *Interface forces the implementation classes to implement all of its methods compulsory. Java compiler checks whether all the methods are implemented in the implementation classes or not.*

A class can implement (not extend) multiple interfaces. For example, we can write:

```
class Myclass implements Interface1, Interface2,...
class Myclass extends Class1 implements Interface1, Interface2
```

Important Interview Question

Can you implement one interface from another?

   No, we can't. Implementing an interface means writing body for the methods. This can not be done again in an interface, since none of the methods of the interface can have body.

Can you write a class within an interface?

   Yes, it is possible to write a class within an interface.

Multiple Inheritance using Interfaces

We know that in multiple inheritance, sub classes are derived from multiple super classes. If two super classes have same names for their members (variables and methods) then which member is inherited into the sub class is the main confusion in multiple inheritance. This is the reason, Java does not support the concept of multiple inheritance. This confusion is reduced by using multiple interfaces to achieve multiple inheritance. Let us take two interfaces as:

```
interface A
{
      int X = 20;   //public static final
      void method();  //public abstract
```

```
        }
interface B
{
        int X= 30;
        void method();
}
```

And there is an implementation class Myclass as:

```
class Myclass implements A,B
```

Now, there is no confusion to refer to any of the members of the interfaces from Myclass. For example, to refer to interface A's X, we can write:

```
A.X
```

And to refer to interface B's X, we can write:

```
B.X
```

Similarly, there will not be any confusion regarding which method is available to the implementation class, since both the methods in the interfaces do not have body, and the body is provided in the implementation class, i.e., Myclass.

The way to achieve multiple inheritance by using interfaces is shown in Program 3. In this program, interface Father has a constant HT which represents the height of father and interface Mother has another constant HT which represents the height of mother. Both the interfaces have an abstract method height(). If Child is the implementation class of these interfaces, we can write:

```
class Child implements Father, Mother
```

Now, in Child class, we can use members of Father and Mother interfaces without any confusion. The height() method can be implemented in Child class to calculate child's height which we assume being the average height of both of its parents.

Program 3: Write a program to illustrate how to achieve multiple inheritance using multiple interfaces.

```
//Multiple inheritance using interfaces
interface Father {
        float HT = 6.2f;
        void height();
}
interface Mother {
        float HT = 5.8f;
        void height();
}
class Child implements Father, Mother {
        public void height() {
                //child got average height of its parents
                float ht = (Father.HT+ Mother.HT)/2;
                System.out.println("Child's height= "+ ht);
        }
}
class Multi {
        public static void main(String args[ ]) {
                Child ch = new Child();
                ch.height();
        }
}
```

Output:

```
C:\> javac Multi.java
C:\> java Multi
Child's height= 6.0
```

Callbacks using Interfaces

The mechanism of calling a function from another function is called 'callback'. Suppose function1() should be called from function2(). For this purpose, function2() should know the location of function1() in memory. Then only, function2() can call it. Hence we should pass the memory address of function1() to function2(). Using that memory address, function2() will be able to call function1().

Memory address of a function is represented as 'function pointer' in the languages like C and C++. So, callback is achieved by passing function pointer of function1() to function2(). But, the picture is slightly different in Java. Since we do not have pointer concept in Java, we can achieve callbacks with the help of interfaces. Instead of passing memory address of a function, we can pass interface reference that refers to the location of a function.

Important Interview Question

What is callback?

The mechanism of calling a function from another function by passing its memory address is known as 'callback'. Callbacks are achieved in Java with the help of interface references.

Let us take an example to understand where callbacks can be used. Suppose a programmer wants to design a tax calculator that calculates total commercial tax for a state. Assume central tax and state tax - are the only two types of taxes levied by the Government. The central tax is common for all states where as the state tax will vary from one state to another. The total tax will be sum of these two taxes.

```
static void calculateTax() {
    calculate central tax (ct).
    calcualte state tax for AP (st).
    display total tax = ct+st;
}
```

The preceding method represents a rigid design since it can calculate total tax for AP(Andhra Pradesh) Government only. It cannot be applied to calculate tax for other states like Karnataka or Uttar Pradesh. What we want is a flexible design which can calculate tax for any state.

Suppose, there is a separate method like stateTax() which is implemented separately for every state. We can call this method from calculateTax() method, as:

```
static void calculateTax(address of stateTax() function) {
    calculate central tax (ct).
    calcualte state tax for any state depending on the address (st).
    display total tax = ct+st;
}
```

In the preceding code, the address of stateTax() method is passed to calculateTax(). The calculateTax() method will use that address to call stateTax() method of a particular state and the state tax 'st' is calculated. This makes the code more flexible since it can be used to calculate total tax for any state.

Since the code of stateTax() method changes from one state to another state, we should declare it as an abstract method in an interface, as:

```
interface Tax {
    double stateTax();
}
```

The following is the implementation (body) of stateTax() method for AP state:

```
class AP implements Tax {
    public double stateTax() {
        System.out.println("According to AP Govt rules");
        return 5000.50;
    }
}
```

Similarly, the following is the implementation of stateTax() method for Karnataka state:

```
class Karnataka implements Tax {
    public double stateTax() {
        System.out.println("According to Karnataka Govt rules");
        return 2000.00;
    }
}
```

Now, the calculateTax() method can be designed as:

```
static void calculateTax(Tax t)
{
        //calculate central tax
        double ct = 1000.00;
        //calculate state tax
        double st = t.stateTax();
        //display total tax
        System.out.println("Total tax= "+ (ct+st));
}
```

Here, observe the parameter 'Tax t' in the calculateTax() method. 't' is a reference of the 'Tax' interface which is passed as a parameter to the method. Using this reference, the stateTax() method is called, as:

```
double st =  t.stateTax();
```

Here, if 't' refers to stateTax() method of class AP, then that method is called and AP state tax is calculated. If 't' refers to stateTax() method of class Karnataka, then that method is called and Karnataka state tax is calculated. In this way, by passing interface reference to calculateTax() method, we can call stateTax() method of any state. This is known as callback mechanism. Please note that the reference 't' in this case is working like a function pointer.

Callbacks are useful to provide flexible design to the software. By passing the interface reference that refers to a method, it is possible to call and use that method from another method. For example, we can call and use stateTax() method of any state from calculateTax() method.

Program 4: Write a program to understand how to achieve callback mechanism through interfaces in Java.

```
//callback mechanism using interfaces in Java
//create an interface
interface Tax
{
    double stateTax();
}
//implementation class for AP state tax
class AP implements Tax {
    public double stateTax() {
        System.out.println("According to AP Govt rules");
        return 5000.50;
    }
}
//implementation class for Karnataka state tax
class Karnataka implements Tax {
    public double stateTax() {
        System.out.println("According to Karnataka Govt rules");
```

```
                return 2000.00;
        }
}
class TaxApp {
    public static void main(String args[]) throws Exception {
        /* Accept the state name through command line args.
        The state name is stored in an object c */
        Class c = Class.forName(args[0]);
        /* Create a new object to that class whose name is in c.
        Tax interface reference is referencing that new object. */
        Tax ref = (Tax)c.newInstance();
        /* Call the method to calculate total tax
        and pass interface reference - this is callback.
        Here, ref may refer to stateTax() of AP or Karnataka classes
        depending on the class for which the object is created in the previous
        step */
        calculateTax(ref);
    }
    static void calculateTax(Tax t) {
        //calculate central tax
        double ct = 1000.00;
        //calculate state tax
        double st = t.stateTax();
        //display total tax
        System.out.println("Total tax= "+ (ct+st));
    }
}
```

The output of the Program 4 is as follows:

```
C:\> javac TaxApp.java
C:\> java TaxApp AP
According to AP Govt rules
Total tax= 6000.5
```

Abstract Classes vs. Interfaces

It is the discretion of the programmer to decide when to use an abstract class and when to go for an interface. Generally, abstract class is written when there are some common features shared by all the objects as they are. For example, take a class WholeSaler which represents a whole sale shop with text books and stationery like pens, papers and note books, as:

```
class WholeSaler {
        void text_books() {
                //text books of X class
        }
        void stationery();  //this can be pens, papers or note books.
}
```

Let us take Retailer1, a class which represents a retail shop. Retailer1 wants text books of X class and some pens. Similarly, Retailer2 also wants text books of X class and some papers. In this case, we can understand that the void text_books() is the common feature shared by both the retailers. But the stationery asked by the retailers is different. This means, the stationery has different implementations for different retailers but there is a common feature, i.e., the text books. So in this case, the programmer designs the WholeSaler class as an abstract class. Retailer1 and Retailer2 are sub classes.

On the other hand, the programmer uses an interface if all the features need to be implemented differently for different objects. Suppose, Retailer1 asks for VII class text books and Retailer2 asks for X class text books, then even the text_books() method of WholeSaler class needs different implementations depending on the retailer. It means, the void text_books() method and also void stationery() methods should be implemented differently depending on the retailer. So, in this case, the programmer designs the WholeSaler as an interface and Retailer1 and Retailer2 become implementation classes.

There is a responsibility for the programmer to provide the sub classes whenever he writes an abstract class. This means the same development team should provide the sub classes for the abstract class. But if an interface is written, any third party vendor will take the responsibility of providing implementation classes. This means, the programmer prefers to write an interface when he wants to leave the implementation part to the third party vendors.

In case of an interface, every time a method is called, JVM should search for the method in the implementation classes which are installed elsewhere in the system and then execute the method. This takes more time. But when an abstract class is written, since the common methods are defined within the abstract class and the sub classes are generally in the same place along with the software, JVM will not have that much overhead to execute a method. Hence, interfaces are slow when compared to abstract classes.

From this discussion, you can understand that it is possible to convert an abstract class into an interface and vice versa.

Complete differences between an abstract class and interface are provided here.

Table 19.1

Abstract class	Interface
1. An abstract class is written when there are some common features shared by all the objects.	An interface is written when all the features are implemented differently in different objects.
2. When an abstract class is written, it is the duty of the programmer to provide sub classes to it.	An interface is written when the programmer wants to leave the implementation to the third party vendors.
3. An abstract class contains some abstract methods and also some concrete methods.	An interface contains only abstract methods.
4. An abstract class can contain instance variables also.	An interface can not contain instance variables. It contains only constants.
5. All the abstract methods of the abstract class should be implemented in its sub classes.	All the (abstract) methods of the interface should be implemented in its implementation classes.
6. Abstract class is declared by using the keyword `abstract`.	Interface is declared using the keyword `interface`.

Important Interview Question

What is the difference between an abstract class and an interface?
  See the Table 19.1.

Conclusion

Interfaces are very important, especially when the programmer wants to customize the features of the software differently for different objects. In this case, an interface should be written so that the features will not have any specific implementation. These features are then implemented in the implementation classes by the third party vendors according to the task to be performed in a particular context. The third party vendors get the description of features of the interface from a document, called API document. So, it is the duty of the programmer to create an API document after completion of his software.

PACKAGES

I t is necessary in software development to create several classes and interfaces. After creating these classes and interfaces, it is better if they are divided into some groups depending on their relationship. Thus, the classes and interfaces which handle similar or same task are put into the same directory. This directory or folder is also called a package.

Package

A package represents a directory that contains related group of classes and interfaces. For example, when we write statements like:

```
import java.io.*;
```

We are importing classes of java.io package. Here, java is a directory name and io is another sub directory within it. And the '*' represents all the classes and interfaces of that io sub directory. Please look at the Figure 20.1.

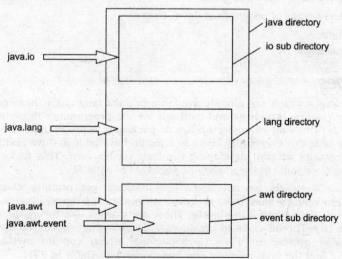

Figure 20.1 Package is a directory

Important Interview Question

A programmer is writing the following statements in a program:

1. `import java.awt.*;`

2. `import java.awt.event.*;`

Should he write both the statements in his program or the first one is enough?

`event` *is a sub package of* `java.awt` *package. But, when a package is imported, its sub packages are not automatically imported into a program. So, for every package or sub package, a separate import statement should be written. Hence if the programmer wants the classes and interfaces of both the* `java.awt` *and* `java.awt.event` *packages, then he should write both the preceding statements in his program.*

There are several following advantages of package concept:

❑ Packages are useful to arrange related classes and interfaces into a group. This makes all the classes and interfaces performing the same task to put together in the same package. For example, in Java, all the classes and interfaces which perform input and output operations are stored in `java.io` package.

❑ Packages hide the classes and interfaces in a separate sub directory, so that accidental deletion of classes and interfaces will not take place.

❑ The classes and interfaces of a package are isolated from the classes and interfaces of another package. This means that we can use same names for classes of two different classes. For example, there is a Date class in `java.util` package and also there is another Date class available in `java.sql` package.

❑ A group of packages is called a library. The classes and interfaces of a package are like books in a library and can be reused several times. This reusability nature of packages makes programming easy. Just think, the packages in Java are created by JavaSoft people only once, and millions of programmers all over the world are daily by using them in various programs.

Different Types of Packages

There are two different types of packages in Java. They are:

❑ Built-in packages
❑ User-defined packages

Built-in Packages

These are the packages which are already available in Java language. These packages provide all most all necessary classes, interfaces and methods for the programmer to perform any task in his programs. Since, Java has an extensive library of packages, a programmer need not think about logic for doing any task. For everything, there is a method available in Java and that method can be used by the programmer without developing the logic on his own. This makes the programming easy. Here, we introduce some of the important packages of Java SE:

❑ `java.lang:` `lang` stands for language. This package got primary classes and interfaces essential for developing a basic Java program. It consists of wrapper classes which are useful to convert primitive data types into objects. There are classes like String, StringBuffer to handle strings. There is a Thread class to create various individual processes. Runtime and System classes are also present in `java.lang` package which contain methods to execute an application and find the total memory and free memory available in JVM.

How can you call the garbage collector?

We can call garbage collector of JVM to delete any unused variables and unreferenced objects from memory using gc() *method. This* gc() *method appears in both Runtime and System classes of* java.lang *package. For example, we can call it as:*

System.gc();

Runtime.getRuntime().gc();

- ❑ java.util: util stands for utility. This package contains useful classes and interfaces like Stack, LinkedList, Hashtable, Vector, Arrays, etc. These classes are called collections. There are also classes for handling date and time operations.

- ❑ java.io: io stands for input and output. This package contains streams. A stream represents flow of data from one place to another place. Streams are useful to store data in the form of files and also to perform input-output related tasks.

- ❑ java.awt: awt stands for abstract window toolkit. This package helps to develop GUI (Graphics User Interface) where programs with colorful screens, paintings and images etc., can be developed. It consists of an important sub package, java.awt.event, which is useful to provide action for components like push buttons, radio buttons, menus etc.

- ❑ javax.swing: This package helps to develop GUI like java.awt. The 'x' in javax represents that it is an extended package which means it is a package developed from another package by adding new features to it. In fact, javax.swing is an extended package of java.awt.

- ❑ java.net: net stands for network. Client-Server programming can be done by using this package. Classes related to obtaining authentication for a network, creating sockets at client and server to establish communication between them are also available in java.net package.

- ❑ java.applet: Applets are programs which come from a server into a client and get executed on the client machine on a network. Applet class of this package is useful to create and use applets.

- ❑ java.text: This package has two important classes, DateFormat to format dates and times, and NumberFormat which is useful to format numeric values.

- ❑ java.sql: sql stands for structured query language. This package helps to connect to databases like Oracle or Sybase, retrieve the data from them and use it in a Java program.

User-defined Packages

Just like the Built-in packages shown earlier, the users of the Java language can also create their own packages. They are called user-defined packages. User-defined packages can also be imported into other classes and used exactly in the same way as the Built-in packages.

Let us see how to create a package of our own and use it in any other class. To create a package the keyword package used as:

```
package packagename;  //to create a package
package packagename.subpackagename;  //to create a sub package within a
                                      //package
```

The preceding statements in fact create a directory with the given package name. We should of course add our classes and interfaces to this directory. In program 1, we are creating a package with the name pack and adding a class Addition to it. This Addition class has a method void sum() which performs addition of two given numbers. One point we should understand while creating the class in a package is to declare all the members and the class itself as public, except the instance variables. The reason is only that the public members are available outside the package to other programs.

Program 1: Write a program to create a package with the name pack and store Addition class in it.

```
//STEP 1: creating a package pack with Addition class
package pack;   //pack is the package name
public class Addition
{
        //instance vars
        private double d1,d2;

        public Addition(double a, double b)
        {
                d1=a;
                d2=b;
        }

        //method to find sum of two numbers
        public void sum()
        {
                System.out.println("Sum= "+(d1+d2));
        }
}
```

Output:

```
C:\> javac -d . Addition.java
C:\>
```

See the output to understand how to compile a Java program that contains a package. The -d option (switch) tells the Java compiler to create a separate sub directory and place the .class file there. The dot (.) after -d indicates that the package should be created in the current directory i.e., C:\. We have written as:

```
javac -d . Addition.java
```

The preceding command means create a package (-d) in the current directory (.) and store Addition.class file there in the package. The package name is specified in the program as pack. So the Java compiler creates a directory in C:\ with the name as pack and stores Addition.class there. Please observe it by going to pack sub directory which is created in C:\.

So, our package with Addition class is ready. The next step is to use the Addition class and its sum() method in a program. For this purpose, we write another class Use as shown in Program 2. In this program, we can refer to the Addition class of package pack using membership operator (.) as,

```
pack.Addition
```

Now, to create an object to Addition class, we can write as:

```
pack.Addition obj = new pack.Addition(10, 15.5);
```

Program 2: Write a program which depicts how to use the Addition class of package pack.

```
//STEP 2: Using the package pack
class Use
{
        public static void main(String args[ ])
```

```
        {
                //create Addition class object
                pack.Addition obj = new pack.Addition(10, 15.5);

                //call the sum() method
                obj.sum();
        }
}
```

Output:

```
C:\> javac Use.java
C:\> java Use
Sum= 25.5
```

Every time we refer to a class of a package, we should write the package name before the class name as pack.Addition in the preceding program. This is inconvenient for the programmer. To overcome this, we can use import statement only once in the beginning of the program, as:

```
import pack.Addition;
```

Once the import statement is written as shown earlier, we need not to use the package name before the class name in the rest of the program and we can create the object to Addition class, in a normal way as:

```
Addition obj = new Addition(10, 15.5);
```

This is shown in Program 3, given here.

Program 3: Write a program which is using the import statement to import a package and it's classes into a program.

```
//STEP 2: Using the package pack
import pack.Addition;
class Use
{
        public static void main(String args[ ])
        {
                //create Addition class object
                Addition obj = new Addition(10, 15.5);

                //call the sum() method
                obj.sum();
        }
}
```

Output:

```
C:\> javac Use.java
C:\> java Use
Sum= 25.5
```

Of course, we have seen how to create a package pack and add a class Addition to it. Similarly, we can add another class Subtraction with sub() method which performs subtraction of two numbers. To add another class to the package, the same procedure should be repeated. First of all, write the Subtraction class with the package statement, as shown in Program 4. And then write Subtraction class and its members as public.

Program 4: Write a program to add another class Subtraction to the same `package pack`.

```
//Adding another class to the package :pack
package pack;
public class Subtraction
{
      //a static method to return result of subtraction
      public static double sub(double a, double b)
      {
            return (a - b);
      }
}
```

Output:

```
C:\> javac -d . Subtraction.java
C:\>
```

See the preceding output. Here, the Java compiler checks whether the package with the name pack already exists or not. If it is existing, then it adds `Subtraction.class` to it. If the package pack does not exist then Java compiler creates a sub directory with the name pack in the current directory and adds `Subtraction.class` to it. Since package pack is already existing, the `Subtraction.class` file is also added to the existing package where already `Addition.class` file is available.

Let us see how to use the `Subtraction` class in our `Use.java` program. The Program 3 can be rewritten as shown here.

Program 5: Let us make a program using both the Addition and Subtraction classes of the package pack.

```
//Using the package pack
import pack.Addition;
import pack.Subtraction;
class Use
{
      public static void main(String args[ ])
      {
            //create Addition class object
            Addition obj = new Addition(10, 15.5);

            //call the sum() method
            obj.sum();

            //call the sub() method and pass values
            double res = Subtraction.sub(10, 15.5);

            System.out.println("Result= "+ res);
      }
}
```

Output:

```
C:\> javac Use.java
C:\> java Use
Sum= 25.5
Result= -5.5
```

We should understand that generally a package is created by a programmer and it is used by another programmer in some other program. For example, the package pack with Addition class and Subtraction class is created by a programmer and another user is using that package in

Use.java program. Now the question is how the other user knows that the package pack has got Addition class and Subtraction class, and there are sum() and sub() methods available in those classes? For this purpose, the user takes the help of API (application programming interface) document which contains the description of all the packages, classes, methods etc. The API document is discussed later in this chapter.

Observe in Program 5, we are using multiple import statements as:

```
import pack.Addition;
import pack.Subtraction;
```

When we want to use classes of the same package, we need not write separate import statements as shown earlier. We can write a single import statement as:

```
import pack.*;
```

Here, '*' represents all the classes and interfaces of a particular package, in this case, it is the package pack.

Important Interview Question

What is the difference between the following two statements:

1) import pack.Addition;

2) import pack.;*

In statement 1, only the Addition class of the package pack is imported into the program and in statement 2, all the classes and interfaces of the package pack are available to the program.

If a programmer wants to import only one class of a package say BufferedReader *of* java.io *package, he can write:*

```
import java.io.BufferedReader;
```

This is straight and the Java compiler links up the BufferedReader of java.io package with the program. But, if he writes import statement as:

```
import java.io.*;
```

In this case, the Java compiler conducts a search for BufferedReader class in java.io package, every time it is used in the rest of the program. This increases load on the compiler and hence compilation time increases. However, there will not be any change in the runtime.

Let us rewrite Program 5, as shown here. Here, we are using import statement to represent all the classes of the package pack, as:

```
import pack.*;
```

In this case, please be sure that any of the Addition.java and Subtraction.java programs will not exist in the current directory. Delete them from the current directory as they cause confusion for the Java compiler. The compiler looks for byte code in Addition.java and Subtraction.java files and there is no byte code available there and hence it flags some errors.

Program 6: Write a program to use import statement in a different way. Remove Addition.java and Subtraction.java from current directory and then test this program.

```
//Using the package pack
import pack.*;
class Use
```

```
{
        public static void main(String args[ ])
        {
                //create Addition class object
                Addition obj = new Addition(10, 15.5);

                //call the sum() method
                obj.sum();

                //call the sub() method and pass values
                double res = Subtraction.sub(10, 15.5);

                System.out.println("Result= "+ res);
        }
}
```

Output:

```
C:\> javac Use.java
C:\> java Use
Sum= 25.5
Result= -5.5
```

Of course, the package pack is available in the current directory. If the package is not available in the current directory, then what happens? Suppose our program is running in C:\ and the package pack is available in the directory D:\sub. In this case, the compiler should be given information regarding the package location by mentioning the directory name of the package in class path.

Class path represents an operating system's environment variable which stores active directory path such that all the files in those directories are available to any programs in the system. Generally, it is written in all capital letters as CLASSPATH.

Important Interview Question

What is CLASSPATH?

The CLASSPATH *is an environment variable that tells the Java compiler where to look for class files to import.* CLASSPATH *is generally set to a directory or a JAR (Java Archive) file.*

To see what is there currently in the CLASSPATH variable in your system, you can type in Windows 98/2000/Me/NT/XP/Vista:

```
C:\> echo %CLASSPATH%
```

Suppose, preceding command has displayed class path as:

```
c:\rnr;.
```

This means the current class path is set to rnr directory in C:\ and also to the current directory represented by dot (.). Our package pack does not exist in either rnr or current directory. Our package exists in D:\sub. This information should be provided to the Java compiler by setting the class path to d:\sub, as shown here:

```
C:\>set CLASSPATH=D:\sub;.;%CLASSPATH%
```

In the preceding command, we are setting the class path to sub directory and current directory (.). And then we typed %CLASSPATH% which means retain the already available class path as it is. This is necessary especially when the class path in your system is already set to an important application that should not be disturbed.

Please create a new directory in D:\ with the name sub and copy our package pack directory into that directory. Now, set the class path to that sub directory as:

```
C:\>set CLASSPATH=D:\sub;.;%CLASSPATH%
```

Then execute our program Use.java which is in C:\, by typing:

```
C:\> javac Use.java
C:\> java Use
```

Alternately, you can mention the class path at the time of executing the program at command line using –cp (classpath) option, as:

```
C:\> javac –cp D:\sub;.  Use.java
C:\> java –cp D:\sub;.   Use
```

Remember, here our Use.java program is in the current directory and the package pack is available in D:\sub directory. So, it is possible to use the package by setting the class path to D:\sub;. and execute the program.

The JAR Files

A JAR (Java Archive) file is a file that contains compressed version of .class files, audio files, image files or directories. We can imagine a .jar file as a zipped file (.zip) that is created by using WinZip software. Even, WinZip software can be used to extract the contents of a .jar file. The difference is that a .jar file can be used as it is but whereas the .zip file can not be used directly. The files should be extracted first from a .zip file, and then used.

Important Interview Question

What is a JAR file?

A Java Archive file (JAR) is a file that contains compressed version of several .class files, audio files, image files or directories. JAR file is useful to bundle up several files related to a project and use them easily.

Let us see how to create a .jar file and related commands which help us to work with .jar files:

❑ To create .jar file, JavaSoft people have provided jar command, which can be used in the following way:

```
jar cf jarfilename inputfiles
```

Here, cf represents create file. For example, assuming our package pack is available in C:\ directory, to convert it into a jar file with the name pack.jar, we can give the command as:

```
C:\> jar cf pack.jar pack
```

Now, pack.jar file is created.

❑ To view the contents of a .jar file, we can use the jar command as:

```
jar tf jarfilename
```

Here, tf represents `table view of file` contents. For example, to view the contents of our `pack.jar` file, we can give the command:

```
C:\> jar tf pack.jar
```

Now, the contents of `pack.jar` are displayed as:

```
META-INF/
META-INF/MANIFEST.MF
pack/
pack/Addition.class
pack/Subtraction.class
```

The first two entries represent that there is a manifest file created and added to `pack.jar` file. The third entry represents the sub directory with the name pack and the last two represent the file names in the directory `pack`.

When we create a `.jar` file, it automatically receives the default manifest file. There can be only one manifest file in an archive, and it always has the pathname

```
META-INF/MANIFEST.MF
```

This manifest file is useful to specify the information about other files which are packaged.

❑ To extract the files from a .jar file, we can use:

```
jar xf jarfilename
```

Here, xf represents `extract files` from the jar file. For example, to extract the contents of our `pack.jar` file, we can write:

```
C:\> jar xf pack.jar
```

This will create the following directories in `C:\`

```
META-INF
```

pack //in this directory, we can see `Addition.class` and `Subtraction.class`.

Now, we know how to create a `.jar` file, let us see how it can be used. In software development, any package is converted into a `.jar` file and stored in a separate sub directory. For example, convert our package pack into `pack.jar` file and store it in a sub directory `e:\temp`.

Now set the CLASSPATH permanently to the `pack.jar` file by following the procedure shown here:

❑ First, go to Start -> Settings -> Control Panel

❑ In Control Panel, select System and double click on it, System properties dialog box appears

❑ In this, select Advanced tab and then click on Environment variables button

❑ Go to User variables and click on New button

❑ Set the CLASSPATH variable to pack.jar and also to the current directory, by typing at:

❑ Variable name: CLASSPATH

❑ Variable value: E:\temp\pack.jar;

❑ Then click on OK button

❑ Then click on OK in the Environment variables window and System Properties windows.

❑ Close the Control Panel.

After setting the CLASSPATH permanently as shown in the preceding steps to the pack.jar file, it is available any where in that computer system. Our program (Use.java) which uses the package may present in any directory, it can be compiled and run without any problem.

Interfaces in a Package

It is also possible to write interfaces in a package. But whenever, we create an interface the implementation classes are also should be created. We cannot create an object to the interface but we can create objects for implementation classes and use them. Let us see how to do this. We write an interface to display system date and time in the package mypack as shown in the following Program 7.

Program 7: Write a program to create an interface with a single method to display system date and time.

```
//Create MyDate interface in the package mypack
package mypack;
public interface MyDate
{
        void showDate(); //public abstract
}
```

Output:

```
C:\> javac -d . MyDate.java
C:\>
```

Compile the preceding code and observe that the Java compiler creates a sub directory with the name mypack and stores MyDate.class file there. This MyDate.class file denotes the byte code of the interface. The next step is to create implementation class for MyDate interface where showDate() method body should be written. This is done in Program 8. DateImpl is an implementation class where the body for showDate() method is written. Here, we create an object to Date class (of java.util package) which by default stores the system date and time.

Program 8: Write a program to create an implementation class for the MyDate interface with the name DateImpl and storing it in the same package mypack.

```
//This is implementation class of MyDate interface
package mypack; //store DateImpl class also in mypack
import mypack.MyDate;
import java.util.*;

public class DateImpl implements MyDate
{
        public void showDate()
        {
                //Date class object by default stores system date and time
                Date d = new Date();
                System.out.println(d);
        }
}
```

Output:

```
C:\> javac -d . DateImpl.java
C:\>
```

When the preceding code is compiled, `DateImpl.class` file is created in the same package mypack. `DateImpl` class contained `showDate()` method which can be called and used in any other program. This is shown in Program 9. In this program, `DateDisplay` is a class where we want to use `DateImpl` class. So, an object to `DateImpl` is created and the `showDate()` method is called. This displays system date and time.

Program 9: Write a program which shows how to use the DateImpl which is an implementation class of MyDate interface.

```
//Using the DateImpl of mypack
import mypack.DateImpl;
class DateDisplay
{
        public static void main(String args[ ])
        {
                //create DateImpl object
                DateImpl obj = new DateImpl();
                //call showDate()
                obj.showDate();
        }
}
```

Output:

```
C:\> javac DateDisplay.java
C:\> java DateDisplay
Tue Aug 07 21:14:43 IST 2007
```

An alternative approach where the `MyDate` interface reference can be used to refer to the `DateImpl` class object to access all the methods of the `DateImpl` class is shown in Program 10.

Program 10: Write a program where `MyDate` interface reference is used to object of `DateImpl` class.

```
//This is another version of Program 9.
import mypack.MyDate;
import mypack.DateImpl;
class DateDisplay
{
        public static void main(String args[ ])
        {
                //MyDate interface reference is used to refer to DateImpl object
                MyDate obj = new DateImpl();
                //call showDate()
                obj.showDate();
        }
}
```

Output:

```
C:\> javac DateDisplay.java
C:\> java DateDisplay
Tue Aug 07 21:14:43 IST 2007
```

Creating Sub Package in a Package

We can create sub package in a package in the format:

```
package pack1.pack2;
```

Here, we are creating pack2 which is created inside pack1. To use the classes and interfaces of pack2, we can write import statement as:

```
import pack1.pack2;
```

This concept can be extended to create several sub packages. In the following program, we are creating tech package inside dream package by writing the statement:

```
package dream.tech;
```

And in this sub package, we are storing Sample class with a method show().

Program 11: Let us make a program to learn how to create a sub package in a package.

```
//Creating a sub package tech in the package dream
package dream.tech;
public class Sample
{
    public void show()
    {
            System.out.println("Welcome to Dream tech");
    }
}
```

Output:

```
C:\> javac -d . Sample.java
C:\>
```

When the preceding program is compiled, the Java compiler creates a sub directory with the name dream. Inside this, there would be another sub directory with the name tech is created. In this tech directory, Sample class is stored. Suppose the user wants to use the Sample class of dream.tech package, he can write a statement as:

```
import dream.tech.Sample;
```

Program 12: Let us make a program using Sample class of dream.tech package.

```
//Using the package dream.tech
import dream.tech.Sample;
class Use
{
  public static void main(String args[])
  {
    //create an object to Sample class
    Sample s = new Sample();
    //call the show() method
    s.show();
  }
}
```

Output:

```
C:\> javac Use.java
C:\> java Use
Welcome to Dream tech
```

Suppose, in the preceding program, we want to use the import statement by using a '*' to refer to all the classes of the package, we can write:

```
import dream.tech.*;
```

In this case, any source code related to Sample class (e.g. `Sample.java`) should be deleted from the current directory (i.e., from `C:\`). Then compiling Program 11 and executing it will yield the correct result.

If the `dream.tech` package is not in the current directory, then we should set the class path to that directory which holds the `dream.tech` package. For example, copy `dream.tech` package into some other directory, say `e:\temp`. To link up this package with `Use.java` program, we should set the class path in the current directory as:

```
C:\> set CLASSPATH=E:\temp;.;%CLASSPATH%
```

Now compile and run the `Use.java` program to yield correct output.

Access Specifiers in Java

We have seen that any class and its members within a package should be declared as public. Then, only the class and its members will be available for use outside the package. Let us discuss what exact difference is there among various access specifiers in Java.

An access specifier is a key word that is used to specify how to access a member of a class or the class itself. It means, we can use access specifiers with the members of a class or with the class also. There are four access specifiers in Java: private, public, protected and default. We do not use `default` key word for specifying the default access specifier. If no other access specifier is used, then Java compiler will take it as default access specifier.

In the Figure 20.2, we are taking three classes, class A, class B and class C. Whereas class A and class B exists in the same package (same directory), class C is away from them in another package (another directory). Let us assume that there are four members with private, public, protected and default specifiers in class A. Now let us discuss which of these members will be available to class B and class C.

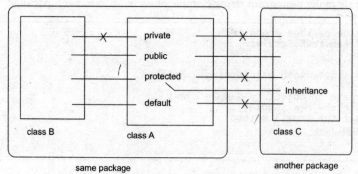

Figure 20.2 Availability of access specifiers in packages

❏ private members of class A are not available to class B or class C. This means, any private member's scope is limited only to that class where it is defined. So the scope of private access specifier is `class scope`.

❏ public members of class A are available to class B and also class C. This means, public members are available every where and their scope is `global scope`.

❑ protected members of class A are available to class B, but not in class C. But if, class C is a sub class of class A, then the protected members of class A are available to class C. So, protected access specifier acts as public with respect to sub classes.

❑ When no access specifier is used, it is taken as default specifier. Default members of class A are accessible to class B which is within the same package. They are not available to class C. This means, the scope of default members is package scope.

Important Interview Question

What is the scope of default access specifier?

Default members are available within the same package, but not outside of the package. So their scope is package scope.

Let us create class A with private, public, protected and default instance variables, as shown here.

Program 13: Write a program to create class A with different access specifiers.

```
//class A of same package
package same;
public class A
{
      private int a=1;
      public int b=2;
      protected int c=3;
      int d=4; //default
}
```

Output:

```
C:\> javac -d . A.java
C:\
```

Now, create another class B in the same package as class A, as shown here. In class B, we are trying to access class A's members. When class B is compiled there would be 1 error saying that the private member of class A is not accessible in class B. It means, the public, protected and default members are accessible in class B. This is verified in Program 13.

Program 14: Write a program for creating class B in the same package.

```
//class B of same package
package same;
import same.A;
public class B
{
      public static void main(String args[ ])
      {
              //access the members of class A
              A obj = new A();
              System.out.println(obj.a);
              System.out.println(obj.b);
              System.out.println(obj.c);
              System.out.println(obj.d);
      }
}
```

Output:

```
C:\> javac -d . B.java
B.java: 10: a has private access in same.A
      System.out.println(obj.a);
                  ^
```

```
        1 error
```

Let us create class C in another package. We want to access all the members of class A from C. In this case, only the public member of class A will be available to class C. Other members such as private, protected and default are not available to C.

Program 15: Write a program for creating class C of another package

```
//class C of another package
package another;
import same.A;
public class C
{
        public static void main(String args[ ])
        {
                //access the members of class A
                A obj = new A();
                System.out.println(obj.a);
                System.out.println(obj.b);
                System.out.println(obj.c);
                System.out.println(obj.d);
        }
}
```

Output:

```
C:\> javac -d . C.java
C.java: 10: a has private access in same.A
        System.out.println(obj.a);
                           ^
C.java: 12: c has protected access in same.A
        System.out.println(obj.c);
                           ^
C.java: 13: d is not public in same.A; cannot be accessed from outside package
        System.out.println(obj.d);
                           ^
        3 errors
```

If class C is a sub class of class A, then the protected members of class A will be available to class C in addition to public members. This is shown in Program 15.

Program 16: Write a program for creating class C is a sub class of class A.

```
//class C of another package
package another;
import same.A;
public class C extends A
{
        public static void main(String args[])
        {
                //access the members of class A
                C obj = new C();
                System.out.println(obj.a);
                System.out.println(obj.b);
                System.out.println(obj.c);
                System.out.println(obj.d);
        }
}
```

Output:

```
C:\> javac -d . C.java
C.java:10: a has private access in same.A
        System.out.println(obj.a);
                           ^
```

```
C.java:10: d is not public in same.A; cannot be accessed from outside package
        System.out.println(obj.d);
                           ^
2 errors
```

Creating API Document

Application Programming Interface (API) document is a hypertext markup language (html) file that contains description of all the features of a software, a product or a technology. API document is like a reference manual that is useful to all the users of the product to understand all the features and how to use them. For example, JavaSoft people have created API document separately for the three parts, Java SE, Java EE and Java ME after they created Java language. In Figure 20.3, we have shown some part of original API document of Java SE. The Java documentation can be downloaded from the following page of Sun Micro systems site, http://java.sun.com/javase/downloads/index.jsp.

Every feature of Java language is described in API document. We can select any package, any class in that package and the description of the class along with the fields, constructors, methods will appear. When we click on any of these features, a detailed description of the feature is displayed. We can also click on Index of the first row to see the index of all items in alphabetical order. For example, to know about Math class, we can simply click on Math in the index to have a page , as shown in Figure 20.3

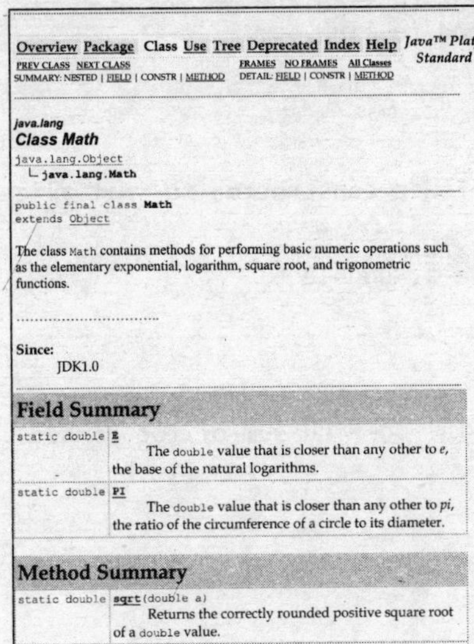

Overview **Package** **Class** **Use** **Tree** **Deprecated** **Index** **Help**	*Java™ Platform*
PREV CLASS NEXT CLASS	*Standard Ed. 6*
SUMMARY: NESTED	FIELD	CONSTR	METHOD DETAIL: FIELD	CONSTR	METHOD	

java.lang
Class Math

java.lang.Object
　└ **java.lang.Math**

public final class **Math**
extends Object

The class Math contains methods for performing basic numeric operations such as the elementary exponential, logarithm, square root, and trigonometric functions.

....

Since:
　　JDK1.0

Field Summary

static double	**E**
	The double value that is closer than any other to *e*, the base of the natural logarithms.
static double	**PI**
	The double value that is closer than any other to *pi*, the ratio of the circumference of a circle to its diameter.

Method Summary

static double	**sqrt**(double a)
	Returns the correctly rounded positive square root of a double value.
static double	**tan**(double a)
	Returns the trigonometric tangent of an angle.
static double	**tanh**(double x)
	Returns the hyperbolic tangent of a double value.
static double	**toDegrees**(double angrad)
	Converts an angle measured in radians to an approximately equivalent angle measured in degrees.
static double	**toRadians**(double angdeg)
	Converts an angle measured in degrees to an approximately equivalent angle measured in radians.
static double	**ulp**(double d)
	Returns the size of an ulp of the argument.
static float	**ulp**(float f)
	Returns the size of an ulp of the argument.

Methods inherited from class java.lang.Object

clone, equals, finalize, getClass, hashCode, notify, notifyAll, toString, wait, wait, wait

Figure 20.3 API document of Java SE

There are three important uses of API document:

❑ API document is useful for the user to understand all the features of the product. The user can understand how to create an object to a class, which fields and methods are available in the class and how to use them.

❑ API document makes programming easy. By understanding the methods of the API, the programmer will be able to use those methods and construct his programs easily.

❑ Any third party vendor can provide implementation classes for the interfaces depending on the information available on the interfaces in the API.

Let us now see how to create an API document for any software:

❑ First of all, we should copy all the source code files (.java) into a directory. For example, copy Addition.java and Subtraction.java of the package pack into a directory e:\temp.

❑ We should open each of the source code files and provide Java documentation comments by using /** and */. When documentation comments are written, the Addition.java and Subtraction.java files look like shown here:

```java
//Addition.java

/** This package is useful to perform some arithmetic calculations. It has two
classes by the name Addition and Subtraction.*/

package pack;

/** This class is useful to find sum of two numbers. It has a parameterized
constructor and a method to find sum */

public class Addition
{
 private double d1,d2;

/** This is a parameterized constructor to initialize the instance variables of
the class. */

 public Addition(double a, double b)
 {
   d1=a;
   d2=b;
 }

/** This method is useful to find sum of two numbers. It does not accept any
parameters.

<br>Parameters: nil
<br>Return type: void
<br>Exceptions: nil
*/

 public void sum()
 {
   System.out.println("Sum= "+(d1+d2));
 }
}
```

```java
//Subtraction.java
//Adding another class to package: pack

/** This package is useful to perform some arithmetic calculations. It has two
classes by the name Addition and Subtraction.*/

package pack;
```

```
/** This class is useful to calculate subtraction on two values */

public class Subtraction
{

/* This method is useful to subtract a number from another and return the result

<br> Parameters: double x, double y
<br> Return type: double
<br> Exceptions: nil
 */
   public static double sub(double x,double y)
   {
     return x-y;
   }
}
```

❑ After adding Java documentation comments, we should save the `Addition.java` and `Subtraction.java` files. Then, to generate API document, we should give the following command:

```
E:\temp> javadoc  *.java
```

Here, we are calling `javadoc` compiler to create the API document. When the preceding command is typed, then several `.html` files are created in `E:\temp` directory. Among them, observe `index.html` file and open it in the browser. It looks as shown here in Figure 20.4.

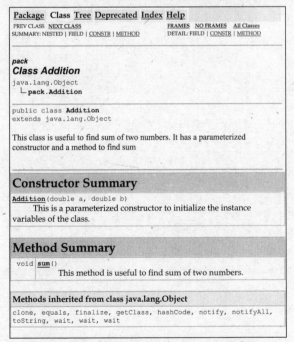

Figure 20.4 API document for our own software

Conclusion

A package is a directory that stores all the related classes and interfaces. As part of the software development, several packages are developed which are collectively called a library. These libraries are reusable in further projects and make programming very easy. But the question is how the users know about all the packages and their members available in the libraries? To solve this problem, API document is provided by the programmers. API document is developed by the programmers at the end of software development which helps like a reference manual to understand all the features of the software.

EXCEPTION HANDLING

'To err is human'—as human beings, we commit many errors. A software engineer may also commit several errors while designing the project or developing the code. These errors are also called 'bugs' and the process of removing them is called 'debugging'. Let us take a look at different types of errors that are possible in a program.

Errors in a Java Program

There are basically three types of errors in the Java Program:

❑ **Compile-time errors:** These are syntactical errors found in the code, due to which a program fails to compile. For example, forgetting a semicolon at the end of a Java statement, or writing a statement without proper syntax will result in compile-time error. Let us see the following program to understand this better.

Program 1: Write a program to demonstrate compile-time error.

```
//Compile-time error
class Err
{
    public static void main(String args[ ])
    {
        System.out.println("Hello")
        System.out.println("Where is error")
    }
}
```

Output:

```
C:\> javac Err.java
Err.java:6: ';' expected
    System.out.println("Hello")
                               ^
Err.java:7: ';' expected
    System.out.println("Where is error")
                                        ^
2 errors
```

In this program, we are not writing a semicolon at the end of the statements. This is will be detected by the Java compiler.

Detecting and correcting compile-time errors is easy as the Java compiler displays the list of errors with the line numbers along with their description. The programmer can go to the statements, check them word by word and line by line to understand where he has committed the errors.

❑ **Run-time errors:** These errors represent inefficiency of the computer system to execute a particular statement. For example, insufficient memory to store something or inability of the microprocessor to execute some statement come under run-time errors. The following program explains this further.

Program 2: Write a program to write `main()` method without its parameter: `String args[ ]`. Hence JVM cannot detect it and cannot execute the code.

```
    //Run-time error
class Err
{
    public static void main()
    {
        System.out.println("Hello");
        System.out.println("Where is error");
    }
}
```

Output:

```
C:\> javac Err.java
C:\> java Err
Exception in thread "main" java.lang.NoSuchMethodError: main
```

Run-time errors are not detected by the Java compiler. They are detected by the JVM, only at runtime.

Important Interview Question

What happens if main() method is written without String args[ ] ?

The code compiles but JVM cannot run it, as it cannot see the main() method with String args[ ].

❑ **Logical errors:** These errors depict flaws in the logic of the program. The programmer might be using a wrong formula or the design of the program itself is wrong. Logical errors are not detected either by Java compiler or JVM. The programmer is solely responsible for them. In the following program, the programmer wants to calculate incremented salary of an employee, but he gets wrong output, since he uses wrong formula.

Program 3: An employee got an increment of 15% in his salary and the programmer wants to calculate his incremented salary. The programmer has used wrong formula where he is calculating the increment only and not the incremented salary. Write a program related to this problem.

```
    //Logical error
class Err
{
    public static void main(String args[ ])
    {
        double sal = 5000.00;
        sal = sal * 15/100;    //wrong. Use: sal += sal*15/100;
        System.out.println("Incremented salary= "+ sal);
    }
}
```

Output:

```
C:\> javac Err.java
C:\> java Err
Incremented salary= 750.0
```

By comparing the output of a program with manually calculated results, a programmer can guess the presence of a logical error.

Exceptions

Basically, an exception is a runtime error. Then there arises a doubt: Can't I call a compile time error an exception? The answer is: "No, you can not call compile-time errors also exceptions". They come under errors. All exceptions occur only at runtime but some exceptions are detected at compile time and some others at runtime. The exceptions that are checked at compilation time by the Java compiler are called 'checked exceptions' while the exceptions that are checked by the JVM are called 'unchecked exceptions'.

Important Interview Question

What are checked exceptions?

The exceptions that are checked at compilation-time by the Java compiler are called 'checked exceptions'. The exceptions that are checked by the JVM are called 'unchecked exceptions'.

Unchecked exceptions and errors are considered as unrecoverable and the programmer cannot do any thing when they occur. The programmer can write a Java program with unchecked exceptions and errors and can compile the program. He can see their effect only when he runs the program. So, Java compiler allows him to write a Java program without handling the unchecked exceptions and errors. In case of other exceptions (checked), the programmer should either handle them or throw them without handling them. He cannot simply ignore them, as Java compiler will remind him of them. Let us now consider a statement:

```
public static void main(String args[ ]) throws IOException
```

Here, IOException is an example for checked exception. So, we threw it out of main() method without handling it. This is done by throws clause written after main() method in the above statement. Of course, we can also handle it. Suppose, we are not handling it and not even throwing it, then the Java compiler will give an error.

The point is that an exception occurs at run time but in case of checked exceptions, whether you are handling it or not, it is detected at compilation time. So let us define an exception as a runtime error that can be handled by a programmer. This means a programmer can do something to avoid any harm caused by the rise of an exception. In case of an error, the programmer cannot do any thing and hence if error happens, it causes some damage.

All exceptions are declared as classes in Java. Of course, everything is a class in Java. Even the errors are also represented by classes. All these classes are descended from a super class called Throwable, as shown in Figure 21.1.

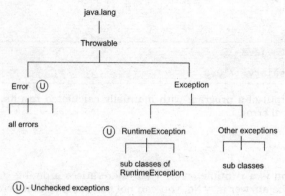

Figure 21.1 The exception hierarchy in Java

Important Interview Question

What is Throwable?

Throwable is a class that represents all errors and exceptions which may occur in Java.

Which is the super class for all exceptions?

Exception is the super class of all exceptions in Java.

What is the difference between an exception and an error?

An exception is an error which can be handled. It means when an exception happens, the programmer can do something to avoid any harm. But an error is an error which cannot be handled, it happens and the programmer cannot do any thing.

Let's now discuss what happens when there is an exception. Generally, in any program, any files or databases are opened in the beginning of the program. The data from the files is retrieved and processed in the middle of the program. At the end of the program, the files are closed properly, so that the data in the files is not corrupted. The following program shows this situation.

Program 4: Write a program that opens the files in the beginning. Then the number of command line arguments is accepted into n. This n divides a number 45 and the result is stored into a. Finally the files are closed.

```
//An exception example
class Ex
{
      public static void main(String args[ ])
      {
            //open the files
            System.out.println("Open files");

            //do some processing
            int n = args.length;
            System.out.println("n= "+ n);
            int a = 45/n;
            System.out.println("a= "+ a);

            //close the files
            System.out.println("Close files");
      }
}
```

Output:

```
C:\> javac Ex.java
C:\> java Ex 11 22 44
Open files
n= 3
a= 15
Close files

C:\> java Ex
Open files
n= 0
Exception in thread "main" java.lang.ArithmeticException: / by zero
        at Ex.main(Ex.java:12)
C:\>
```

Please observe the outputs of this program. When we passed 3 command line arguments, then the program executed without any problem. But when we run the program without passing any arguments, then n value became zero. Hence, execution of the following expression fails:

```
int a = 45/n;
```

Here, division by zero happens and this value represents infinity. This value cannot be stored in any variable. So there will be an exception at runtime in the above statement. In this case, JVM displays exception details and then terminates the program abnormally. The subsequent statements in the program are not executed. This means that the files which are open in the program will not be closed and hence the data in the files will be lost. This is the major problem with exceptions. When there is an exception, the files may not be closed or the threads may abnormally terminate or the memory may not be freed properly. These things lead to many other problems in the software. Closing the opened files, stopping any running threads in the program, and releasing the used memory are called 'cleanup operations'. Therefore, it is compulsory to design the program in such a way that even if there is an exception, all the clean up operations are performed and only then the program should be terminated. This is called exception handling.

Exception Handling

When there is an exception, the user data may be corrupted. This should be tackled by the programmer by carefully designing the program. For this, he should perform the following 3 steps:

Step 1: The programmer should observe the statements in his program where there may be a possibility of exceptions. Such statements should be written inside a try block. A try block looks like as follows:

```
try{
    statements;
}
```

The greatness of try block is that even if some exception arises inside it, the program will not be terminated. When JVM understands that there is an exception, it stores the exception details in an exception stack and then jumps into a catch block.

Step 2: The programmer should write the catch block where he should display the exception details to the user. This helps the user to understand that there is some error in the program. The programmer should also display a message regarding what can be done to avoid this error. Catch block looks like as follows:

```
catch(Exceptionclass ref)
{
```

```
            Statements;
    }
```

The reference `ref` above is automatically adjusted to refer to the exception stack where the details of the exception are available, as shown in Figure 21.2. So, we can display the exception details using any one of the following ways:

❑ Using `print()` or `println()` methods, such as `System.out.println(ref);`

❑ Using `printStackTrace()` method of `Throwable` class, which fetches exception details from the exception stack and displays them.

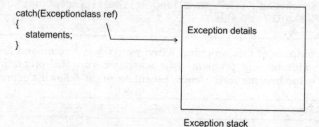

Figure 21.2 Exception class reference referring to exception stack

Step 3: Lastly, the programmer should perform clean up operations like closing the files and terminating the threads. The programmer should write this code in the `finally` block. Finally block looks like as follows:

```
finally{
    Statements;
}
```

The specialty of `finally` block is that the statements inside the `finally` block are executed irrespective of whether there is an exception or not. This ensures that all the opened files are properly closed and all the running threads are properly terminated. So, the data in the files will not be corrupted and the user is at the safe-side.

Performing the above three tasks is called 'exception handling'. Remember, in exception handling the programmer is not preventing the exception, as in many cases it is not possible. But the programmer is avoiding any damage that may happen to user data.

Now, let's rewrite Program 4 using `try`, `catch`, and `finally` blocks where we want to handle the `ArithmeticException`.

Program 5: Write a program which tells the use of try, catch and finally block.

```
//Exception handling using try, catch and finally blocks
class Ex
{
    public static void main(String args[ ])
    {
        try
        {
            //open the files
            System.out.println("Open files");

            //do some processing
            int n = args.length;
            System.out.println("n= "+ n);
            int a = 45/n;
            System.out.println("a= "+ a);
        }
```

```
                    catch(ArithmeticException ae)
                    {
                            //display the exception details
                            System.out.println(ae);

                            //display any message to the user
                            System.out.println("Please pass data while running this
                            program");
                    }
                    finally
                    {
                            //close the files
                            System.out.println("Close files");
                    }
            }
    }
```

Output:

```
C:\> javac Ex.java
C:\> java Ex 11 22 44
Open files
n= 3
a= 15
Close files

C:\> java Ex
Open files
n= 0
java.lang.ArithmeticException: / by zero
Please pass data while running this program
Close files
```

In this program, the `try` block contains the statements where there is possibility for an exception. When there is an exception, JVM jumps into `catch` block. The `finally` block is executed even if there is exception or not.

Observe the output of the program. When there is no exception, we can see normal execution and the files are closed properly; but when there is an exception, the exception details are displayed along with a message to the user. Then, `finally` block is executed which closes the files. This prevents any loss to user data.

Handling Multiple Exceptions

Most of the times there is possibility of more than one exception present in the program. In this case, the programmer should write multiple `catch` blocks to handle each one of them.

In the previous program, we can intentionally create another exception by adding the code:

```
int b[ ] = {10, 20, 30};
b[50] = 100;
```

Above, we are creating an array `b[ ]` with 3 elements. Index of the array represents the element position in the array. So, in this case the index is from 0 to 2, since there are 3 elements. There is no index like 50. But we are trying to store 100 at index position 50 in the second statement. This leads to an exception called `ArrayIndexOutOfBoundsException`. To handle this, we should write another `catch` block as shown here:

```
catch(ArrayIndexOutOfBoundsException aie)
{
        //display exception details
        aie.printStackTrace();
```

```
        //display a message to user
        System.out.println("Please see that the array index is within the range");
    }
```

Program 6: Write a program which shows how to handle the `ArithmeticException` and `ArrayIndexOutOfBoundsException`.

```
//Handling multiple exceptions using try, catch and finally blocks
class Ex
{
    public static void main(String args[ ])
    {
        try
        {
            //open the files
            System.out.println("Open files");
            //do some processing
            int n = args.length;
            System.out.println("n= "+ n);
            int a = 45/n;
            System.out.println("a= "+ a);
            int b[] = {10, 20, 30};
            b[50] = 100;
        }
        catch(ArithmeticException ae)
        {
            //display the exception details
            System.out.println(ae);
            //display any message to the user
            System.out.println("Please pass data while running this
            program");
        }
        catch(ArrayIndexOutOfBoundsException aie)
        {
            //display exception details
            aie.printStackTrace();
            //display a message to user
            System.out.println("Please see that the array index is
            within the range");
        }
        finally
        {
            //close the files
            System.out.println("Close files");
        }
    }
}
```

Output:

```
C:\> javac Ex.java
C:\> java Ex
Open files
n= 0
java.lang.ArithmeticException: / by zero
Please pass data while running this program
Close files

C:\> java Ex 11 22
Open files
n= 2
a= 22
java.lang.ArrayIndexOutOfBoundsException: 50
    at Ex.main(Ex.java:18)
Please see that the array index is within the range
```

> ### Close files

In this program, there is provision for two exceptions—ArithmeticException and ArrayIndexOutOfBoundsException. These exceptions are handled with the help of two catch blocks.

Observe the output. When we did not pass any values while running this program, we got ArithmeticException and when we pass some values, then there is another exception called ArrayIndexOutOfBoundsException. This means, even if there is scope for multiple exceptions, only one exception at a time will occur.

From the preceding discussion, we can conclude that:

❑ An exception can be handled using try, catch, and finally blocks.

❑ It is possible to handle multiple exceptions using multiple catch blocks.

❑ Even though there is possibility for several exceptions in try block, at a time only one exception will be raised.

❑ A single try block can be followed by several catch blocks.

❑ We cannot write a catch without a try block, but we can write a try without any catch block.

❑ It is not possible to insert some statements between try and catch.

❑ It is possible to write a try block within another try. They are called nested try blocks.

throws Clause

Even if the programmer is not handling runtime exceptions, the Java compiler will not give any error related to runtime exceptions. But the rule is that the programmer should handle checked exceptions. In case the programmer does not want to handle the checked exceptions, he should throw them out using throws clause. Otherwise, there will be an error flagged by Java compiler. See Program 7 to understand this better, where there is an IOException raised by readLine() method of BufferedReader class. This is checked exception and hence the compiler checks it at the compilation time. If it is not handled, the compiler expects at least to throw it out.

Program 7: Write a program that shows the compile time error for IOException.

```java
//Not handling the exception
import java.io.*;
class Sample
{
    //instance variable
    private String name;
    //method to accept name
    void accept()
    {
        //to accept data from keyboard
        BufferedReader br = new BufferedReader(new
        InputStreamReader(System.in));
        System.out.print("Enter name: ");
        name = br.readLine();
    }
    //method to display name
    void display()
    {
        System.out.println("Name: "+ name);
    }
}
class Ex1
{
    public static void main(String args[ ])
    {
```

```
                Sample s = new Sample();
                s.accept();
                s.display();
        }
}
```

Output:

```
C:\> javac Ex1.java
Ex1.java:15: unreported exception java.io.IOException; must be caught or
declared to be thrown
        name = br.readLine();
                  ^
1 error
```

In this program, the Java compiler expects the programmer to handle the IOException using try and catch blocks; else, he should throw out the IOException without handling it. But the programmer is not performing either. So there is a compile time error displayed.

Here, we are not handling the IOException given by readLine() method. Since it is a checked exception, we should throw it out of the method using throws clause as:

```
throws IOException
```

The throws clause is written at the side of accept() method since in this method the readLine() is called. Also, we should write throws clause next to main() method since in this method, the accept() is called, as shown here:

```
void accept() throws IOException
public static void main(String args[ ]) throws IOException
```

Now, if the above code is inserted into the program, the preceding program executes without any problem. This version of the program is shown in Program 8. Note that since in this program, we are not handling the exception, it is not a robust program. This means that if exception happens, the program goes for abnormal termination.

Program 8: Write a program which shows the use of throws clause.

```
//Not handling the exception -using throws clause
import java.io.*;
class Sample
{
    //instance variable
    private String name;
    //method to accept name
    void accept() throws IOException
    {
            //to accept data from keyboard
            BufferedReader br = new BufferedReader(new
            InputStreamReader(System.in));
            System.out.print("Enter name: ");
            name = br.readLine();
    }
    //method to display name
    void display()
    {
            System.out.println("Name: "+ name);
    }
}
class Ex1
{
    public static void main(String args[ ]) throws IOException
```

```
                {
                        Sample s = new Sample();
                        s.accept();
                        s.display();
                }
        }
```

Output:

```
C:\> javac Ex1.java
C:\> java Ex1
Enter name: Kumar
Name: Kumar
```

In this program, we are using throws clause to throw out an exception without handling it, from a method.

throw Clause

There is also a throw statement available in Java to throw an exception explicitly and catch it. Let us see how it can be used.

In the following program, we are creating an object of NullPointerException class and throwing it out of try block, as shown here:

```
throw new NullPointerException("Exception data");
```

In the above statement, NullPointerException class object is created and 'Exception data' is stored into its object. Then it is thrown using throw statement. Now, we can catch it using catch block as:

```
catch(NullPointerException ne)
{
}
```

Program 9: Write a program that shows the use of throw clause for throwing the NullPointerException.

```
//using throw
class Sample
{
        static void demo()
        {
                try{
                System.out.println("Inside demo()");
                throw new NullPointerException("Exception data");
        }
        catch(NullPointerException ne)
        {
                System.out.println(ne);
        }
        }
}
class ThrowDemo
{
        public static void main(String args[ ])
        {
                Sample.demo();
        }
}
```

Output:

```
C:\> javac ThrowDemo.java
C:\> java ThrowDemo
Inside demo()
java.lang.NullPointerException: Exception data
```

In this program, we are using throw clause to throw NullPointerException class object. Then it is caught and its details are displayed in catch block.

Above, we used throw to throw out an exception object and handle it. This activity is useful in software development in the following two ways:

1. throw clause is used in software testing to test whether a program is handling all the exceptions as claimed by the programmer. Now, let us see how this is done. Suppose a programmer has written a program to handle some 5 exceptions properly. Now, the software tester has to test and certify whether the program is handling all the 5 exceptions as said by the programmer or not. For this, the tester should plan the input data such that if he provides that input, the said exceptions will occur. Causing the exceptions intentionally like this will be at times very difficult. In this case, the tester can take the help of the throw clause. Suppose the tester wants to test whether IOException is handled by the program or not, he can introduce a statement in the source code as:

```
throw new IOException("My IOException");
```

Then he will compile and run the program. Then the above statement will raise the IOException and the rest of the program should handle it. How the program handles it will be noted down by the tester for a feedback to the programmer. This is the way throw will help the tester to test a program for exceptions.

2. throw clause can be used to throw our own exceptions also. Just like the exceptions available in Java, we can also create our own exceptions which are called 'user-defined exceptions'. We need the throw clause to throw these user defined exceptions.

Types of Exceptions

As you have already read about the exceptions in the preceding paragraphs, let us move on further to understand the types of exceptions. Following are the exceptions available in Java:

❑ Built-in exceptions
❑ User-defined exceptions.

Built-in Exceptions

Built-in exceptions are the exceptions which are already available in Java. These exceptions are suitable to explain certain error situations. Table 21.1 lists the important built-in exceptions.

Table 21.1

Exception class	Meaning
ArithmeticException	Thrown when an exceptional condition has occurred in an arithmetic operation.
ArrayIndexOutOfBoundsException	Thrown to indicate that an array has been accessed with an illegal index. The index is either negative or greater than or equal to the size of the array.

Exception class	Meaning
ClassNotFoundException	This exception is raised when we try to access a class whose definition is not found.
FileNotFoundException	Raised when a file is not accessible or does not open.
IOException	Thrown when an input-output operation failed or interrupted.
InterruptedException	Thrown when a thread is waiting, sleeping, or doing some processing, and it is interrupted.
NoSuchFieldException	Thrown when a class does not contain the field (or variable) specified.
NoSuchMethodException	Thrown when accessing a method which is not found.
NullPointerException	Raised when referring to the members of a null object. null represents nothing.
NumberFormatException	Raised when a method could not convert a string into a numeric format.
RuntimeException	This represents any exception which occurs during runtime.
StringIndexOutOfBoundsException	Thrown by String class methods to indicate that an index is either negative or greater than the size of the string.

User-defined Exceptions

Sometimes, the built-in exceptions in Java are not able to describe a certain situation. In such cases, like the built-in exceptions, the user (programmer) can also create his own exceptions which are called 'user-defined exceptions'. The following steps are followed in creation of user-defined exceptions:

❏ The user should create an exception class as a subclass to Exception class. Since all exceptions are subclasses of Exception class, the user should also make his class a subclass to it. This is done as:

```
class MyException extends Exception
```

❏ The user can write a default constructor in his own exception class. He can use it, in case he does not want to store any exception details. If the user does not want to create an empty object to his exception class, he can eliminate writing the default constructor.

```
MyException() {}
```

❏ The user can create a parameterized constructor with a string as a parameter. He can use this to store exception details. He can call super class (Exception) constructor from this and send the string there.

```
MyException(String str)
{
    super(str);  //call Exception class constructor and store str there.
}
```

❑ When the user wants to raise his own exception, he should create an object to his exception class and throw it using throw clause, as:

```
MyException me = new MyException("Exception details");
throw me;
```

To understand how to create user-defined exceptions, let us write a program. In program 10, we are creating our own exception class MyException. In this program, we are taking the details of account numbers, customer names, and balance amounts in the form of three arrays. Then in main() method, we display these details using a for loop. At this time, we check if in any account the balance amount is less than the minimum balance amount to be kept in the account. If it is so, then MyException is raised and a message is displayed "Balance amount is less".

Program 10: Write a program to throw a user defined exception.

```
//User defined exception
//to throw whenever balance amount is below Rs. 1000
class MyException extends Exception
{
  //store account information
  private static int accno[] = {1001,1002,1003,1004,1005};

  private static String name[] = {"Raja Rao", "Rama Rao", "Subba Rao", "Appa
Rao", "Laxmi Devi"};

  private static double bal[] = {10000.00,12000.00,5600.50,999.00,1100.55};

  //default constructor
  MyException()
  {
  }

  //parameterized constructor
  MyException(String str)
  {
    super(str);
  }

  //write main()
  public static void main(String args[ ])
  {
    try{
    //display the heading for the table
    System.out.println("ACCNO"+"\t"+"CUSTOMER"+"\t"+ "BALANCE");

      //display actual account information
      for(int i=0; i<5; i++)
      {
        System.out.println(accno[i]+"\t"+name[i]+"\t"+ bal[i]);

        //display own exception if balance < 1000
        if(bal[i]<1000)
        {
          MyException me = new MyException("Balance amount is less");
          throw me;
        }
      } //end of for
    } //end of try
    catch(MyException me){
      me.printStackTrace();
    }
  } //end of main
}//end of MyException class
```

Output:

```
C:\> javac MyException.java
C:\> java MyException
ACCNO CUSTOMER        BALANCE
1001          Raja Rao       10000.0
1002          Rama Rao       12000.0
1003          Subba Rao      5600.5
1004          Appa Rao       999.0
MyException: Balance amount is less
        at MyException.main(MyException.java:39)
```

In this program, we are throwing our own exception when the balance amount in a bank account is less than Rs. 1000.

Here, we created our own exception since there is no exception class available to describe situation where the balance amount in a bank account is less than the prescribed minimum. Also note that we are throwing our own exception using throw statement.

Important Interview Question
_____

What is the difference between throws and throw ?

throws clause is used when the programmer does not want to handle the exception and throw it out of a method. throw clause is used when the programmer wants to throw an exception explicitly and wants to handle it using catch block. Hence, throws and throw are contradictory.

Re-throwing an Exception

When an exception occurs in a try block, it is caught by a catch block. This means that the thrown exception is available to the catch block. The following code shows how to re-throw the same exception out from the catch block:

```
try{
     throw exception;
}
catch(Exception obj)
{
     throw exception;   //re-throw the exception out
}
```

Suppose there are two classes A and B. If an exception occurs in A, we want to display some message to the user and then we want to re-throw it. This re-thrown exception can be caught in class B where it can be handled. Hence re-throwing exceptions is useful especially when the programmer wants to propagate the exception details to another class. In this case (Program 11), the exception details are sent from class A to class B where some appropriate action may be performed.

Program 11: Write a program to throw the StringIndexOutOfBoundsException.

```
//Rethrowing an exception.
class A
{
     void method1()
     {
          try
          {
          //take a string with 5 chars. Their index will be from 0 to 4.
          String str = "Hello";

          //exception is thrown in below statement because there is
```

```
                              //no index with value 5.
                              char ch = str.charAt(5);
                              }
                              catch(StringIndexOutOfBoundsException sie)
                              {
                              System.out.println("Please see the index is within the range");
                              throw sie; //rethrow the exception
                              }
                      }
              }

          class B
          {
                  public static void main(String args[ ])
                      {
                              //create an object to A and call method1().
                              A a = new A();
                              try{
                                      a.method1();
                              }
                              //the rethrown exception is caught by the below catch block
                              catch(StringIndexOutOfBoundsException sie){
                              System.out.println("I caught rethrown exception");
                              }
                      }
              }
```

Output:

```
C:\> javac B.java
C:\> java B
Please see the index is within the range
I caught rethrown exception
```

In this program, StringIndexOutOfBoundsException is thrown in method1() of class A which is caught by catch block in that method. Then the catch block is re-throwing it into main() method of class B.

Important Interview Question

Is it possible to re-throw exceptions?

Yes, we can re-throw an exception from catch block to another class where it can be handled.

Conclusion

Errors in a program are nightmares to the programmer. The errors that can be identified and handled are called exceptions. By handling exceptions, a programmer can make his programs 'robust'. It means the Java program will not abnormally terminate if all the possible exceptions have been handled properly. This is a great boon to the user since there will not be any loss of data. There are two types of exceptions—Built-in and User-defined. Further, the exceptions checked by the compiler are called checked exceptions and the remaining are called unchecked. The programmer should compulsorily handle the checked exceptions or at least write a throws statement to throw them out, if he does not want to handle them. In Unchecked exceptions, he has been given freedom not to handle them. But it is advisable to handle every possible exception in case of a Java program.

WRAPPER CLASSES

We see many applications on Internet which receive data from the user and send it to the server. For example, in a business application, we type our details like name, credit card number, address, etc. and send them to the server. The server expects this data in the form of objects and hence we are supposed to send objects. In our data, 'name' is a String type object, but credit card number is just an int type value, which is not an object. This primitive datatype should also be converted into an object and then sent to the server. To do this conversion, we need wrapper classes.

A wrapper class contains a field where it stores the primitive datatype. When we create an object to a wrapper class, it carries the primitive datatype within it and hence the object can be sent to the server. The server can retrieve the primitive datatype from the object and use it.

There is another reason why we need wrapper classes. In Java, collection classes are defined in java.util package which handle only objects, not the primitives. Hence, if we want to use collection classes on primitives, we should convert them into objects. Here, also we need the help of wrapper classes.

Wrapper Classes

A wrapper class is a class whose object wraps or contains a primitive data type. When we create an object to a wrapper class, it contains a field and in this field, we can store a primitive data type. In other words, we can wrap a primitive value into a wrapper class object. For example, if we create an object to Character wrapper class, it contains a single field char and it is possible to store a character like A there, as shown in the Figure 22.1. So, Character is a wrapper class of char data type.

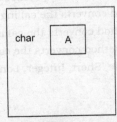

char   A

Character object

Figure 22.1 Character class object contains char type field in it

Important Interview Question

Why do we need wrapper classes?

    1. They convert primitive data types into objects and this is needed on Internet to communicate between two applications.

    2. The classes in java.util package handle only objects and hence wrapper classes help in this case also.

Table 22.1 contains the list of wrapper classes that are defined in `java.lang` package. They are useful to convert the primitive data types into object form.

Table 22.1

Primitive data type	Corresponding Wrapper class
char	Character
byte	Byte
short	Short
int	Integer
long	Long
float	Float
double	Double
boolean	Boolean

Number Class

`Number` is an abstract class whose subclasses are Byte, Short, Integer, Long, Float, and Double. So the methods of `Number` class are commonly available in all these subclasses.

Number Class Methods

`Number` class includes following methods:

- `byte byteValue()`: This method converts the calling object into byte value. The calling object can be an object of Byte, Short, Integer, Long, Float, or Double class.
- `short shortValue()`: This method converts the calling object into short value.
- `int intValue()`: This method converts the calling object into int value.
- `long longValue()`: This method converts the calling object into long value.
- `float floatValue()`: This method converts the calling object into float value.
- `double doubleValue()`: This method converts the calling object into double value.

All these methods are available to Byte, Short, Integer, Long, Float, and Double classes.

Character Class

The `Character` class wraps a value of the primitive type `char` in an object. If we create `Character` class object, it contains a `char` type field. In this field, we can store a primitive `char` value like A. `Character` class has only one constructor which accepts primitive data type.

```
Character(char ch)
```

So, we can create `Character` class object and store A there, as:

```
Character obj = new Character('A');
```

Important Methods of Character Class

`Character class` includes following important methods:

❑ `char charValue()`:This method is useful to convert `Character` class object again into primitive char value and returns that value. For example, we can use it as:

```
Character obj = new Character('A');
char ch = obj.charValue();
Now, ch contains 'A'.
```

❑ `int compareTo(Character obj)`: This method is useful to compare two Character objects. It is called as:

```
int x = obj1.compareTo(obj2);
```

❑ where, `obj1` and `obj2` are `Character` class objects.
❑ If `obj1 == obj2`, then this method returns 0.
❑ If `obj1 < obj2`, then it returns negative value.
❑ If `obj1 > obj2`, then it returns positive value.
❑ `String toString()`: This method converts Character object into String object and returns that String object.
❑ `static Character valueOf(char ch)`: This method converts a single character `ch` into Character object and returns that object.
❑ `static boolean isDigit(char ch)`: This method returns true if `ch` is a digit (0 to 9) otherwise returns false.
❑ `static boolean isLetter(char ch)`: This method returns true if `ch` is a letter (A to Z or a to z).
❑ `static boolean isUpperCase(char ch)`: This method returns true if `ch` is an uppercase letter (A to Z).
❑ `static boolean isLowerCase(char ch)`: This method returns true if `ch` is a lowercase letter (a to z).
❑ `static boolean isSpaceChar(char ch)`: This method returns true if `ch` represents a space which is coming from spacebar.
❑ `static boolean isWhitespace(char ch)`: This method returns true if `ch` represents white space. White space is a space that comes on pressing tab, enter, or backspace buttons.
❑ `static boolean isLetterOrDigit(char ch)`: This method returns true if `ch` is either a letter or digit.
❑ `static char toUpperCase(char ch)`: This method converts `ch` into uppercase and returns that upper case letter.
❑ `static char toLowerCase(char ch)`: This method converts `ch` into lowercase and returns that lower case letter.

Now, let us write a program to accept a character from keyboard and test what type of character it is. Program 1 represents the logic for this, where the character is tested repeatedly using Character class methods to know the type of the character. This program executes till the user presses the Enter button.

Program 1: Write a program that accepts the character from the keyboard and displays its type.

```
//Accept a character from keyboard and display what it is
import java.io.*;
class CharTest
{
    public static void main(String args[ ])
    throws IOException
    {
        //to accept a char from keyboard
        char ch;
        BufferedReader br = new BufferedReader(new
        InputStreamReader(System.in));

        while(true)  //execute repeatedly
        {
            System.out.print("Enter a character: ");
            ch = (char)br.read();

            //test and display the type of character
            System.out.print("You entered: ");
            if(Character.isDigit(ch))
            System.out.println("a digit");
            else if (Character.isUpperCase(ch))
            System.out.println("an uppercase letter");
            else if (Character.isLowerCase(ch))
            System.out.println("a lowercase letter");
            else if(Character.isSpaceChar(ch))
            System.out.println("a spacebar character");
            else if(Character.isWhitespace(ch)){
            System.out.println("a whitespace character");
            return;
            }
        else System.out.println("Sorry, I dont know that");
        br.skip(2); //to skip \n code from br
    }

    }
}
```

Output:

```
C:\> javac CharTest.java
C:\> java CharTest
Enter a character: y
You entered: a lowercase letter
Enter a character:
You entered: a spacebar character
Enter a character: 9
You entered: a digit
Enter a character:      [Press Enter]
You entered: a whitespace character
C:\>
```

In this program, we first accept a character from keyboard and display what type of character it is. This is done repeatedly in while loop till Enter button is pressed by the user.

Byte Class

The Byte class wraps a value of the primitive type 'byte' in an object. The `Byte` class object contains a byte type field. In this field, we can store a primitive byte number. Remember byte number ranges from -128 to +127.

Constructors

`Byte` class has two constructors. The first one takes byte number as its parameter and converts it into `Byte` class object and the next one takes a String type parameter and converts that string into `Byte` class object.

❑ `Byte(byte num)`

So, we can create Byte object as: `Byte obj = new Byte(120);`

❑ `Byte(String str)`

This constructor suggests that we can create a Byte object by converting a string that contains a byte number, as:

❑ `Byte obj = new Byte("120");`

Please try to understand that these two constructors can be seen in every wrapper class. This means every wrapper class contains two constructors—the first one takes the corresponding primitive data type and the other takes a string parameter. Apart from this, some wrapper classes have a third constructor also. But `Character` class has only the first type of constructor.

Important Interview Question

Which of the wrapper classes contains only one constructor?

   (or) Which of the wrapper classes does not contain a constructor with String as parameter?

A) Character.

Important Methods of Byte Class

`Byte class` includes following important methods:

❑ `int compareTo(Byte b)`

This method is useful to compare the contents of two `Byte` class objects. It is called as:

```
int x = obj1.compareTo(obj2);
```

where, obj1 and obj2 are Byte class objects.

If obj1 == obj2, then this method returns 0.

If obj1 < obj2, then it returns negative value.

If obj1 > obj2, then it returns positive value.

boolean equals(Object obj)

This method compares the Byte object with any other object `obj`. If both have same content, then it returns true otherwise false.

❑ `static byte parseByte(String str)`: This method returns the primitive byte number contained in the string `str`.

❑ `String toString()`: This method converts Byte object into String object and returns that String object.

❑ `static Byte valueOf(String str)`: This method converts a string `str` that contains some byte number into `Byte` class object and returns that object.

❏ `static Byte valueOf(byte b)`: This method converts the primitive byte b into Byte object.

Let us write a program to see how one can create `Byte` class objects. Then we want to compare them and display which object has less or more contents when compared to another.

Program 2: Write a program which shows the use of `Byte` class objects.

```
//Creating Byte class objects and comparing them
import java.io.*;
class ByteDemo
{
        public static void main(String args[]) throws IOException

        {
                //to accept data from keyboard
                BufferedReader br = new BufferedReader(new
                InputStreamReader(System.in));

                //accept a byte number as string s1
                System.out.print("Enter a byte no: ");
                String s1 = br.readLine();

                //create Byte object b1 using s1
                Byte b1 = new Byte(s1);

                //accept another byte number as string s2
                System.out.print("Enter a byte no: ");
                String s2 = br.readLine();

                //create Byte object b2 using s2
                Byte b2 = new Byte(s2);

                //compare both the Byte objects contents
                int n= b1.compareTo(b2);

                if(n==0) System.out.println("Both bytes are same");
                else if(n<0) System.out.println(b1 + " is less");
                else System.out.println(b2+ " is less");

        }
}
```

Output:

```
C:\> javac ByteDemo.java
C:\> java ByteDemo
Enter a byte no: 120
Enter a byte no: 124
120 is less
```

Short Class

`Short` class wraps a value of primitive data type 'short' in its object. Short class object contains a short type field that stores a short number.

Constructors

Short class has two constructors. The first one takes short number as its parameter and converts it into Short class object and the next one takes a String type parameter and converts that string into Short class object.

❏ `Short(short num)`

This constructor is useful to construct the Short class object by supplying a short number to it, as:

```
short s = 14007;
Short  obj = new Short(s);
```

❑ Short(String str)

This constructor is useful to construct the Short class object by passing a string str to it as:

```
String str = "14007";
Short obj = new Short(str);
```

Important Methods of Short Class

Short class includes following important methods:

❑ int compareTo(Short obj): This method compares the numerical value of two Short class objects and returns 0, -ve value, or +ve value.

❑ boolean equals(Object obj): This method compares the Short object with any other object obj. If both have the same content then it returns true otherwise false.

❑ static short parseShort(String str): This method returns int equivalent of the string str.

❑ String toString(): This method returns a string form of the Short object.

❑ static Short valueOf(String str): This method converts a string str that contains some short number into Short class object and returns that object.

Integer Class

The Integer class wraps a value of the primitive type int in an object. The Integer class object contains an int type field. In this field, we can store a primitive int number.

Constructors

Integer class has two constructors. The first one takes int number as its parameter and converts it into Integer class object and the next one takes a String type parameter and converts that string into Integer class object.

❑ Integer(int num): This means Integer object can be created, as:

Integer obj = new Integer(123000);   Here, we are converting a primitive int value into Integer object. This is called 'boxing'.

Important Interview Question

What is boxing?

Converting a primitive datatype into an object is called 'boxing'.

❑ Integer(String str): This constructor suggests that we can create an Integer object by converting a string that contains an int number, as:

```
Intcger obj = new Integer("198663");
```

Important Methods of Integer Class

`Integer` class includes following important methods:

❏ `int compareTo(Integer obj)`: This method compares the numerical value of two Integer class objects and returns 0,-ve value, or +ve value.

❏ `boolean equals(Object obj)`: This method compares the Integer object with any other object obj. If both have the same content, then it returns true otherwise false.

❏ `static int parseInt(String str)`: This method returns `int` equivalent of the string `str`.

❏ `String toString()`: This method returns a string form of the Integer object.

❏ `static Integer valueOf(String str)`: This method converts a string `str` that contains some `int` number into Integer class object and returns that object.

❏ `static String toBinaryString(int i)`: This method converts decimal integer number `i` into binary number system and returns that binary number as a string.

❏ `static String toHexString(int i)`: This method converts decimal integer number `i` into hexadecimal number system and returns that hexadecimal number as a string.

❏ `static String toOctalString(int i)`: This method converts decimal integer number `i` into octal number system and returns that octal number as a string.

❏ `int intValue()`: This method converts Integer object into primitive `int` type value. This is called 'unboxing'.

Important Interview Question

What is unboxing?

Converting an object into its corresponding primitive datatype is called unboxing.

What happens if a string like "Hello" is passed to parseInt() method?

Ideally, a string with an integer value should be passed to parseInt() method. So, on passing "Hello", an exception called 'NumberFormatException' occurs since the parseInt() method cannot convert the given string "Hello" into an integer value.

Program 3: Write a program to accept an integer number from keyboard and convert it into other number systems.

```
//Convert int into binary, hexadecimal, and octal format
import java.io.*;
class Convert
{
    public static void main(String args[ ] )
    throws IOException
    {
        BufferedReader br = new BufferedReader(new
        InputStreamReader(System.in));
        System.out.print("Enter an integer: ");
        String str = br.readLine();

        //convert string into int
        int i = Integer.parseInt(str);
        System.out.println("In decimal: "+ i);

        //convert int into other systems
        str = Integer.toBinaryString(i);
        System.out.println("In binary: "+str);

        str = Integer.toHexString(i);
        System.out.println("In hexadecimal: "+str);
```

```
                    str = Integer.toOctalString(i);
                    System.out.println("In octal: "+str);
        }
    }
```

Output:

```
C:\> javac Convert.java
C:\> java Convert
Enter an integer: 456
In decimal: 456
In binary: 111001000
In hexadecimal: 1c8
In octal: 710
```

Long Class

The Long class contains a primitive 'long' type data. The object of Long class contains a field where we can store a long value.

Constructors

Long class has two constructors. The first one takes long number as its parameter and converts it into Long class object and the next one takes a String type parameter and converts that string into Long class object.

❑ Long(long num): This means Long object can be created as: Long obj = new Long(12300044);

❑ Long(String str): This constructor suggests that we can create Long object by converting a string that contains a long number, as:

```
String str = "12300044";
Long obj = new Long(str);
```

Important Methods of Long Class

Long class includes following important methods:

❑ int compareTo(Long obj): This method compares the numerical value of two Long class objects and returns 0, -ve value, or +ve value.

❑ boolean equals(Object obj): This method compares the Long object with any other object obj. If both have same content, then it returns true otherwise false.

❑ static long parseLong(String str): This method returns long equivalent of the string str.

❑ String toString(): This method converts Long object into String object and returns the String object.

❑ static Long valueOf(String str): This method converts a string str that contains some long number into Long object and returns that object.

Float Class

The Float class wraps a value of the primitive type float in an object. The Float class object contains a float type field that stores a primitive float number.

Constructors

Float class has three constructors. The first one takes float number as its parameter and converts it into Float class object and the next one takes a double type number and converts into Float class object and then the third one takes a String type parameter and converts that string into Float class object.

❑ Float(float num): This means Float object can be created as:

```
float f = 12.987f;
Float obj = new Float(f);
```

❑ Float(double num): This constructor is useful to create Float class object with a double type value converted into float.

❑ Float(String str): This constructor suggests that we can create a Float object by converting a string that contains a float number, as:

```
Float obj = new Float("12.987");
```

Important Methods of Float Class

Float class includes following important methods:

❑ int compareTo(Float obj): This method compares the numerical value of two Float class objects and returns 0, -ve value, or +ve value.

❑ boolean equals(Object obj): This method compares the Float object with any other object obj. If both have same content then it returns true otherwise false.

❑ static float parseFloat(String str): This method returns float equivalent of the string str.

❑ String toString(): This method returns a string form of the Float object.

❑ static Float valueOf(String str): This method converts a string str that contains some float number into Float object and returns that object.

Double Class

The Double class wraps a value of the primitive type double in an object. The Double class object contains a double type field that stores a primitive double number.

Constructors

Double class has two constructors. The first one takes double number as its parameter and converts it into Double class object and the next one takes a String type parameter and converts that string into Double class object.

❑ Double(double num): This means Integer object can be created as:

```
double d = 12.1223;
Double obj = new Double(d);
```

❑ Double(String str): This constructor is useful to create a Double object by converting a string that contains a double number, as:

```
String str = "12.1223";
Double obj = new Double(str);
```

Important Methods of Double Class

`Double class` includes following important methods:

❑ `int compareTo(Double obj)`: This method compares the numerical value of two Double class objects and returns 0, -ve value, or +ve value.

❑ `boolean equals(Object obj)`: This method compares the Double object with any other object `obj`. If both have same content then it returns true otherwise false.

❑ `static double parseDouble(String str)`: This method returns double equivalent of the string `str`.

❑ `String toString()`: This method returns a string form of the Double object.

❑ `static Double valueOf(String str)`: This method converts a string `str` that contains a double number into Double class object and returns that object.

Boolean Class

The Boolean class object contains a primitive 'boolean' type data. The object of Boolean class contains a field where we can store a boolean value.

Constructors

`Boolean` class has two constructors. The first one takes boolean number as its parameter and converts it into Boolean class object and the next one takes a String type parameter and converts that string into Boolean class object.

❑ `Boolean(boolean value)`: This means Boolean object can be created, as:

```
Boolean obj = new Boolean(true);
```

❑ `Boolean(String str)`: This constructor suggests that we can create Boolean object by converting a string that contains a boolean value, as:

```
String str = "false";
Boolean obj = new Boolean(str);
```

Important Methods of Boolean Class

`Boolean class` includes following important methods:

❑ `int compareTo(Boolean obj)`: This method compares the numerical value of two Boolean class objects and returns 0, -ve value, or +ve value.

❑ `boolean equals(Object obj)`: This method compares the Boolean object with any other object `obj`. If both have same content then it returns true, otherwise false.

❑ `static boolean parseBoolean(String str)`: This method returns boolean equivalent of the string `str`.

❑ `String toString()`: This method converts Boolean object into a String object and returns the String object.

❑ static Boolean valueOf(String str): This method converts a string str that contains a boolean value into Boolean object and returns that object.

We can observe that most of the methods are common in all the wrapper classes. There is another class called Math in java.lang package that contains methods to perform mathematical operations.

Math Class

The class Math contains methods for performing basic numeric operations, such as the elementary exponential, logarithm, square root, and trigonometric methods. Note that all the methods of Math class are 'static' and hence we need not create an object to Math class to call them. Let us have a look at the methods available in Math class.

Important Methods of Math Class

Math class includes following important methods:

❑ static double sin(double arg): This method returns the sine value of the arg. arg is given in radians, as:

    Math.sin(0.5) gives 0.479425538604203

❑ static double cos(double arg): This method returns the cosine value of the arg. arg is in radians, as:

    Math.cos(0.5) gives 0.8775825618903728

❑ static double tan(double arg): This method returns the tangent value of the arg. arg is in radians, as:

    Math.tan(0.5) gives 0.5463024898437905

❑ static double log(double arg): This method returns the natural logarithm value (base e) of arg, as:

    Math.log(0.5) gives -0.6931471805599453

❑ static double log10(double arg): This method returns the base 10 logarithm value of arg, as:

    Math.log10(0.5) gives -0.3010299956639812

❑ static double pow(double x, double n): This method returns x to the power of n value, as:

    Math.pow(5,3) gives 125.0

❑ static double sqrt(double arg): This method returns the square root of arg, as:

    Math.sqrt(25) gives 5.0

❑ `static double abs(double arg)`: This method returns the absolute value of arg. Absolute value represents the positive quantity of the given number, as:

> `Math.abs(-4.55) gives 4.55`

❑ `static double ceil(double arg)`: This method raises the given arg value to the next integer value. If integer is given to this method, it gives the same value, as:

> `Math.ceil(4.5) is 5.0`

❑ `static double floor(double arg)`: This method decreases the given arg value to the previous integer value. If integer is given to this method, then it gives the same value, as:

> `Math.floor(4.5) is 4.0`

❑ `static double min(arg1,arg2)`: This method returns the minimum of arg1 and arg2, as:

> `Math.min(5,10) gives 5.0`

❑ `static double max(arg1,arg2)`: This method returns the maximum of arg1 and arg2, as:

> `Math.max(5,10) gives 10.0`

❑ `static long round(arg)`: This method returns the rounded value of arg. If the fraction part of the number is more or equal to 0.5, then 1 is added to the integer part; otherwise, the same integer part is returned, as:

> `Math.round(4.6) gives 5  or  Math.round(4.4) gives 4.`

❑ `static double random()`: This method returns a random number between 0 and 1. A random number is a number that cannot be guessed by any one. This method gives any number which cannot be guessed, as:

> `Math.random() gives 0.2230762209884291`

❑ `static double toRadians(double angle)`: This method converts the given angle value in degrees into radians, as:

> `Math.toRadians(180) gives 3.141592653589793`

❑ `static double toDegrees(double angle)`: This method converts angle in radians into degrees, as:

> `Math.toDegrees(3.14159) gives 179.99984796050427`

Let us see how to create some random numbers using `random()` method of `Math` class. A random number is a number that cannot be guessed by any one. `Random()` method generates random numbers between 0 and 1. Suppose we want to generate them between 0 and 10, then we ought to multiply the method's output by 10. This is shown in Program 4.

Program 4: Write a program that generates random numbers repeatedly between '0' and '10'. You need to also ensure that if the generated number is '0' then program gets terminated.

```
//Generating random nos. between 0 and 10
class Random
```

```
{
        public static void main(String args[ ])
        throws Exception
        {
                System.out.println("Random no.s between 0 and 10: ");

                while(true)
                {
                        /*random() returns double type between 0 and 1. But we want
                        the no. as integer and between 0 and 10. So multiply it
                        by 10 and convert into int. */

                        double d= 10*Math.random();
                        int i = (int)d;
                        System.out.println(i);

                        //Let the execution wait till 2000 milli seconds = 2 second
                        Thread.sleep(2000);

                        if(i==0) System.exit(0); //come out
                } //end of while
        }
}
```

Output:

```
C:\> javac Random.java
C:\> java Random
4
3
5
5
4
3
3
9
0
```

In the above program, we used a method:

```
Thread.sleep(2000);
```

which made processing to be suspended for 2000 milli seconds time. This means the JVM stops execution for 2 seconds (2000 milli seconds= 2 sec) and then starts again with the next statement. Thread class is found in `java.lang` package.

Note

For more information about threads, refer Chapter 26.

Conclusion

Since OOPS is all about objects, it is necessary to convert every thing into objects. Wrapper classes are useful to convert primitive data types into objects. Moreover, they contain methods to reconvert an object into primitive data. The methods of a wrapper class facilitate a programmer to work with objects easily and effectively.

THE COLLECTION FRAMEWORK

CHAPTER

23

How can we handle a group of elements? This is a very easy question. We use an array to store a group of elements and handle them easily. OK, then how can we handle a group of objects? Can we use an array to store a group of objects? Yes, It is possible to use an array to store a group of objects.

Using an Array to Store a Group of Objects

It is possible to store a group of objects into an array. Let us take an example where we want to store 100 objects of Employee class into an array. For this purpose, we need to create an array of Employee type as:

```
Employee arr[ ] = new Employee[100];
```

This array can store 100 Employee objects. This can be achieved using a single loop as:

```
for(int i=0; i<100; i++)
{
    arr[i] = new Employee(data);
}
```

In Program 1, we create an Employee class with id and name details. Next, in the Group class, we create an array of Employee type with size 5. We accept 5 objects data from the keyboard and store the data into the array using a loop. Then we display the data once again by reading it from the array. In this program, the array arr[ ] is storing the Employee object references. So arr[0] represents first object reference, arr[1] represents second object reference, and so on.

Program 1: Write a program to store a group of objects into an array and retrieve the object data and display.

```
//To store and a group of objects in an array
import java.io.*;
class Employee
{
    //instance vars
    int id;
    String name;

    //to store data
    Employee(int i, String n)
```

```
            {
                    id = i;
                    name = n;
            }

        //a method to display data
        void displayData()
        {
                System.out.println(id+"\t"+ name);
        }
}
class Group
{
        public static void main(String args[ ]) throws IOException
        {
                //to accept data from keyboard
                BufferedReader br = new BufferedReader(new
                InputStreamReader(System.in));

                //create Employee type array with size 5
                Employee arr[ ] = new Employee[5];

                //store 5 employees' data into the array
                for(int i=0; i<5; i++)
                {
                        System.out.print("Enter id: ");
                        int id = Integer.parseInt(br.readLine());

                        System.out.print("Enter name: ");
                        String name = br.readLine();

                        arr[i] = new Employee(id, name);
                }

                System.out.println("\nThe employee data is: ");

                //display the Employee data from the array
                for(int i=0; i<arr.length; i++)
                {
                        arr[i].displayData();
                }

        }

}
```

Output:

```
C:\> javac Group. java
C:\> java Group
Enter id: 10
Enter name: Nagesh
Enter id: 11
Enter name: Vijaya
Enter id: 22
Enter name: Ganesh
Enter id: 33
Enter name: Kumar
Enter id: 20
Enter name: Chandu

The employee data is:
10              Nagesh
11              Vijaya
22              Ganesh
```

33	Kumar
20	Chandu

So, here we have seen how to store a group of objects into an array and retrieve them again easily. But there are also certain inconveniences in this mechanism. They are as follows:

❑ Arrays cannot grow dynamically. This means, once an array is created, its size is fixed and at runtime its size cannot be increased or decreased.

❑ We cannot store different class objects into the same array. The reason is that an array can store only one data type of elements.

❑ Adding the objects at the end of an array is easy. But, inserting and deleting the elements in the middle of the array is difficult. In this case, we have to re-arrange all the elements of the array.

❑ Retrieving the elements from an array is easy but after retrieving the elements, if we want to process them, then there are no methods available to carry out this.

Due to these problems, programmers want a better mechanism to store a group of objects. The alternative is using an object to store a group of other objects. It means that we can use a class object as an array. Such an object is called 'collection object' or 'container object'.

Collection Objects

A collection object or a container object is an object which can store a group of other objects. In Figure 23.1, we are using a collection object to store 4 objects. A collection object has a class called as 'collection class' or 'container class'. All the collection classes are available in the package— java.util. (Util stands for utility). A group of collection classes is called a 'collection framework'.

Important Interview Question

what is a collection framework?

A collection framework is a class library to handle groups of objects. Collection framework is implemented in java.util package.

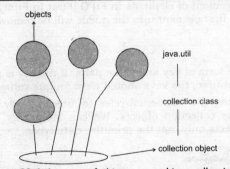

Figure 23.1 A group of objects stored in a collection object

In fact, collection object does not store the physical copies of other objects. Since the other objects are already available in memory, storing another copy of them into the collection object would be a mere wasting of memory. So, JVM does not store the copies of other objects, it simply stores the references of other objects into a collection object.

Important Interview Question

Does a collection object store copies of other objects or their references?

A collection object stores references of other objects.

All the collection classes in `java.util` package are the implementation classes of different interfaces as shown in the Table 23.1.

Table 23.1

Interface type	Implementation classes
Set<T>	HashSet<T>
	LinkedHashSet<T>
List<T>	Stack<T>
	LinkedList<T>
	ArrayList<T>
	Vector<T>
Queue<T>	LinkedList<T>
Map<K,V>	HashMap<K,V>
	Hashtable<K,V>

Sets

A set represents a group of elements arranged just like an array. The set will grow dynamically when the elements are stored into it. A set will not allow duplicate elements. If we try to pass the same element that is already available in the set, then it is not stored into the set.

Lists

Lists are like sets. They store a group of elements. But lists allow duplicate values to be stored.

Queues

A Queue represents arrangement of elements in FIFO (First In First Out) order. This means that an element that is stored as a first element into the queue will be removed first from the queue.

Maps

Maps store elements in the form of key and value pairs. If the key is provided then its corresponding value can be obtained. Of course, the keys should have unique values.

Remember, in all the cases the 'elements' refer to 'objects' only. This means we cannot store primitive data types in the collection objects. We can store only objects since the main aim of collections is to handle objects only, not the primitive data types.

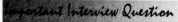
Important Interview Question

Can you store a primitive data type into a collection?
  No, Collections store only objects.

Retrieving Elements from Collections

Following are the 4 ways to retrieve any element from a collection object:

❑ Using `for-each` loop.

❑ Using `Iterator` interface.

❑ Using `ListIterator` interface.

❑ Using `Enumeration` interface.

for-each Loop

`for-each` loop is like `for` loop which repeatedly executes a group of statements for each element of the collection. The format is:

```
for(variable: collection-object)
{
    Statements;
}
```

Here, the variable assumes each element of the collection-object and the loop is executed as many times as there are number of elements in the collection-object. If collection-object has n elements the loop is executed exactly n times and the variable stores each element in each step.

Iterator Interface

`Iterator` is an interface that contains methods to retrieve the elements one by one from a collection object. It has 3 methods:

❑ `boolean hasNext()`: This method returns true if the iterator has more elements.

❑ `element next()`: This method returns the next element in the iterator.

❑ `void remove()`: This method removes from the collection the last element returned by the iterator.

ListIterator Interface

`ListIterator` is an interface that contains methods to retrieve the elements from a collection object, both in forward and reverse directions. It has the following important methods:

❑ `boolean hasNext()`: This returns true if the ListIterator has more elements when traversing the list in the forward direction.

❑ `boolean hasPrevious()`: This returns true if the ListIterator has more elements when traversing the list in the reverse direction.

❑ `element next()`: This returns the next element in the list.

❑ `element previous()`: This returns the previous element in the list.

❑ `void remove()`: This removes from the list the last element that was returned by the `next()` or `previous()` methods.

Important Interview Question

What is the difference between Iterator and ListIterator?

Both are useful to retrieve elements from a collection. Iterator can retrieve the elements only in forward direction. But ListIterator can retrieve the elements in forward and backward direction also. So ListIterator is preferred to Iterator.

Enumeration Interface

This interface is useful to retrieve one by one the elements like the Iterator. It has 2 methods:

❑ `boolean hasMoreElements()`: This method tests if the Enumeration has any more elements or not.

❑ `element nextElement()`: This returns the next element that is available in Enumeration.

Important Interview Question

What is the difference between Iterator and Enumeration?

Both are useful to retrieve elements from a collection. Iterator has methods whose names are easy to follow and Enumeration methods are difficult to remember. Also Iterator has an option to remove elements from the collection which is not available in Enumeration. So, Iterator is preferred to Enumeration.

HashSet Class

A `HashSet` represents a set of elements (objects). It does not guarantee the order of elements. Also it does not allow the duplicate elements to be stored.

We can write the `HashSet` class as:

```
class HashSet<T>
```

Here, `<T>` represents the generic type parameter. It represents which type of elements are being stored into the `HashSet`. Suppose, we want to create a `HashSet` to store a group of Strings, then we can create the object as:

```
HashSet<String> hs = new HashSet<String>();
```

The following constructors are available in `HashSet`:

❑ `HashSet();`

❑ `HashSet(int capacity);`

Here, `capacity` represents how many elements can be stored into the `HashSet` initially. This capacity may increase automatically when more number of elements are being stored.

❑ `HashSet(int capacity, float loadfactor);`

Here, `loadfactor` determines the point where the capacity of `HashSet` would be increased internally. For example, the product of `capacity` and `loadfactor` is 101*0.5 = 50.5. This means after storing the 50th element into the `HashSet`, its capacity will be internally increased to accommodate more elements. The default initial capacity is 16 and the default load factor is 0.75.

HashSet Class Methods

`HashSet` class provides the following methods:

❑ `boolean add(obj)`:This method adds an element `obj` to the `HashSet`. It returns `true` if the element is added to the `HashSet`, else it `returns` false. If the same element is already available in the `HashSet`, then the `present` element is not added.

❑ `boolean remove(obj)`: This method removes the element `obj` from the `HashSet`, if it is present. It returns true if the element is removed successfully otherwise false.

❑ `void clear()`: This removes all the elements from the `HashSet`.

❑ `boolean contains(obj)`: This returns true if the HashSet contains the specified element obj.

❑ `boolean isEmpty()`: This returns true if the HashSet contains no elements.

❑ `int size()`: This returns the number of elements present in the HashSet.

Let us take a program to understand how to construct a HashSet with String type elements and how to retrieve the elements using an Iterator. In this program, we store "America" and the same string is stored second time into the HashSet. The set will not store it second time, since a set will not allow the duplicate data. Also we can observe that the set will not maintain the same order of elements as in which they were entered.

Program 2: Write a program which shows the use of HashSet and Iterator.

```java
//HashSet demo
import java.util.*;
class HS
{
        public static void main(String args[ ])
        {
                //create a HashSet to store strings
                HashSet<String> hs = new HashSet<String>();

                //store some string elements
                hs.add("India");
                hs.add("America");
                hs.add("Japan");
                hs.add("China");
                hs.add("America");

                //view the HashSet
                System.out.println("Hash set = "+ hs);

                //add an Iterator to hs.
                Iterator it = hs.iterator();

                //display element by element using Iterator
                System.out.println("Elements using Iterator: ");
                while(it.hasNext())
                {
                        String s = (String)it.next();
                        System.out.println(s);
                }
        }
}
```

Output:

```
C:\> javac HS.java
C:\> java HS
Hash set = [America, China, Japan, India]
Elements using Iterator:
America
China
Japan
India
```

In this program, we store a group of strings into a HashSet. Then we retrieve the elements one by one using an Iterator.

LinkedHashSet Class

This is a subclass of HashSet class and does not contain any additional members on its own. It is a generic class that has the declaration:

```
class LinkedHashSet<T>
```

Here, <T> represents the generic type parameter. It represents the data type of elements being stored into the LinkedHashSet. LinkedHashSet internally uses a linked list to store the elements.

Stack Class

A stack represents a group of elements stored in LIFO (Last In First Out) order. This means that the element which is stored as a last element into the stack will be the first element to be removed from the stack. Inserting elements (objects) into the stack is called 'push operation' and removing elements from stack is called 'pop operation'. Searching for an element in the stack is called 'peep operation'. Insertion and deletion of elements take place only from one side of the stack, called 'top' of the stack, as shown in Figure 23.2.

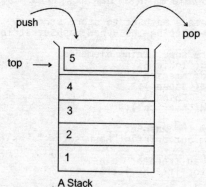

Figure 23.2 A stack with some elements

A pile of plates in a cafeteria where the lastly washed plate will be coming out first can be taken as an example for a stack. For example, if we take the top plate (the 3rd plate) from the pile, the weight on the spring will be lessened and the next plate (2nd one) will come up. Similarly, a Compact Disk holder where the CDs are arranged such that the last CD is available first is also an example for a stack (Figure 23.3). This means if the objects are logically arranged in the form of the plates or CDs in the memory, it becomes a stack. Generally, stacks are used to evaluate the expressions like ax^2+bx+c, and rarely for storing data into memory.

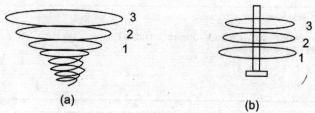

Figure 23.3 (a) A pile of plates (b) A group of CDs

We can write a Stack class as:

```
class Stack<E>
```

where E stands for element type. Suppose, we want to create a Stack object that contains Integer objects, we can do so as shown here:

```
Stack<Integer> obj = new Stack<Integer>();
```

Stack Class Methods

Stack class includes the following methods:

- boolean empty(): This method tests whether the stack is empty or not. If the stack is empty then true is returned otherwise false.
- element peek(): This method returns the top-most object from the stack without removing it.
- element pop(): This method pops the top-most element from the stack and returns it.
- element push(element obj): This method pushes an element obj onto the top of the stack and returns that element.
- int search(Object obj): This method returns the position of an element obj from the top of the stack. If the element (object) is not found in the stack then it returns -1.

Let us write a program to perform different operations on a stack. First, we want to create a stack that can store Integer type objects as:

```
Stack<Integer> st = new Stack<Integer>();
```

Suppose, in this stack we want to store some integer elements. Since int is a primitive data type, we should convert the int values into Integer objects and then store into the stack. For this purpose, we can write a statement as:

```
st.push(element);
```

Here, we can pass int type element to push() method. But the method automatically converts it into Integer object and then stores it into the stack st. This is called 'auto boxing'.

Important Interview Question

What is auto boxing?

Converting a primitive data type into an object form automatically is called 'auto boxing'. Auto boxing is done in generic types.

To remove the top-most element (object) from the stack, we can use pop() method, as:

```
Integer obj = st.pop();
```

The code to search the position of an element in the stack is as:

```
position = st.search(element);
```

Program 3: Write a program to perform different operations on a stack through a menu.

```
//Pushing, popping, searching elements in a stack.
import java.io.*;
import java.util.*;

class StackDemo
{
    public static void main(String args[]) throws Exception
    {
        //create an empty stack to contain Integer objects
        Stack<Integer> st = new Stack<Integer>();
```

```
                    //take vars
                    int choice =0;
                    int position,element;
                    BufferedReader br = new BufferedReader(new
                    InputStreamReader(System.in));

                    //display the menu as long as user choice < 4
                    while(choice<4)
                    {
                            System.out.println("STACK OPERATIONS");
                            System.out.println("1 Push an element");
                            System.out.println("2 Pop an element");
                            System.out.println("3 Search an element");
                            System.out.println("4 Exit");
                            System.out.print("Your choice: ");

                            choice = Integer.parseInt(br.readLine());

                            //perform a task depending on user choice
                            switch(choice)
                            {
                                    case 1: System.out.print("Enter element: ");
                                            element = Integer.parseInt(br.readLine());
                                            //int type element is converted into Integer
                                            //object and
                                            //then pushed into the stack
                                            st.push(element);
                                            break;

                                    case 2: //the top-most Integer object is popped
                                            Integer obj = st.pop();
                                            System.out.println("Popped= "+ obj);
                                            break;

                                    case 3: System.out.print("Which element? ");
                                            element = Integer.parseInt(br.readLine());
                                            //int type element is converted into Integer
                                            //object and
                                            //then searched in the stack
                                            position = st.search(element);
                                            if(position == -1)
                                            System.out.println("Element not found");
                                            else System.out.println("Position:
                                            "+position);
                                            break;

                                            default: //come out if user choice is other
                                            //than 1,2 or 3
                                            return;
                            }
                            //view the contents of stack
                            System.out.println("Stack contents: "+st);

                    }
            }
    }
```

Output:

```
C:\> javac StackDemo.java
C:\> java StackDemo
STACK OPERATIONS
1 Push an element
2 Pop an element
3 Search an element
4 Exit
Your choice: 1
```

```
Enter element: 11
Stack contents: [11]
STACK OPERATIONS
1 Push an element
2 Pop an element
3 Search an element
4 Exit
Your choice: 1
Enter element: 20
Stack contents: [11, 20]
STACK OPERATIONS
1 Push an element
2 Pop an element
3 Search an element
4 Exit
Your choice: 3
Which element? 20
Position: 1
Stack contents: [11, 20]
STACK OPERATIONS
```

LinkedList Class

A Linked list contains a group of elements in the form of nodes. Each node will have three fields—the data field contains data and the link fields contain references to previous and next nodes. Figure 23.4 displays that how the traversing in the linked list is done using these link fields.

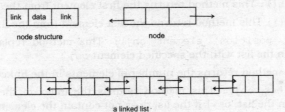

Figure 23.4 Node structure and a linked list with nodes

Linked list is very convenient to store data. Inserting the elements into the linked list and removing the elements from the linked list is done quickly and takes the same amount of time.

Important Interview Question

What is the difference between a Stack and LinkedList?

1. A Stack is generally used for the purpose of evaluation of expressions. A LinkedList is used to store and retrieve data.

2. Insertion and deletion of elements only from the top of the Stack is possible. Insertion and deletion of elements from any where is possible in case of a LinkedList.

A linked list is written in the form of:

```
class LinkedList<E>
```

We can create an empty linked list for storing String type elements (objects) as:

```
LinkedList<String> ll = new LinkedList<String>();
```

LinkedList Class Methods

LinkedList class includes the following methods:

- ❏ boolean add(element obj): This method adds an element to the linked list. It returns true if the element is added successfully.
- ❏ void add(int position, element obj): This method inserts an element obj into the linked list at a specified position.
- ❏ void addFirst(element obj): This method adds the element obj at the first position of the linked list.
- ❏ void addLast(element obj): This method appends the specified element to the end of the linked list.
- ❏ element removeFirst(): This method removes the first element from the linked list and returns it.
- ❏ element removeLast(): This method removes the last element from the linked list and returns it.
- ❏ element remove(int position): This method removes an element at the specified position in the linked list.
- ❏ void clear(): This method removes all the elements from the linked list.
- ❏ element get(int position): This method returns the element at the specified position in the linked list.
- ❏ element getFirst(): This method returns the first element from the list.
- ❏ element getLast(): This method returns the last element from the list.
- ❏ element set(int position, element obj): This method replaces the element at the specified position in the list with the specified element obj.
- ❏ int size(): This method returns the number of elements in the linked list.
- ❏ int indexOf(Object obj): This method returns the index of the first occurrence of the specified element in the list, or -1 if the list does not contain the element.
- ❏ int lastIndexOf(Object obj): This method returns the index of the last occurrence of the specified element in the list, or -1 if the list does not contain the element.
- ❏ Object[ ] toArray(): This method converts the linked list into an array of Object class type. All the elements of the linked list will be stored into the array in the same sequence.

Let us create a linked list to store a group of strings and perform some important operation on the list. In Program 4, we create a linked list as:

```
LinkedList<String> ll= new LinkedList<String>();
```

Now, we can add any string type elements to the list using add() method, as:

```
ll.add(position-1,element);
```

In case of linked list, the counting will start from 0 and we start counting from 1. Hence, we deducted 1 from the position number to get the position number maintained by the list.

To remove a particular element, we can use remove() method, as:

```
ll.remove(position-1);
```

To replace an existing element with a new element, the set() method can be used as:

```
ll.set(position-1,element);
```

Program 4: Write a program that shows the use of LinkedList class

```java
//A LinkedList with strings
import java.io.*;
import java.util.*;
class LLDemo
{
    public static void main(String args[ ]) throws IOException
    {
        //create an empty linked list to store strings
        LinkedList<String> ll= new LinkedList<String>();

        //add some names to linked list
        ll.add("America");
        ll.add("India");
        ll.add("Japan");

        //display the elements in the linked list
        System.out.println("List= "+ ll);

        //vars
        BufferedReader br = new BufferedReader(new
        InputStreamReader(System.in));
        String element;
        int position, choice=0;

        //menu

        while(choice<4)
        {
            System.out.println("\nLINKEDLIST OPERATIONS");
            System.out.println("1 Add an element");
            System.out.println("2 Remove an element");
            System.out.println("3 Change an element");
            System.out.println("4 Exit");

            System.out.print("Your choice: ");
            choice = Integer.parseInt(br.readLine());

            //perform a task depending on user choice
            switch(choice)
            {
                case 1: System.out.print("Enter element: ");
                        element = br.readLine();
                        System.out.print("At what position? ");
                        position= Integer.parseInt(br.readLine());
                        ll.add(position-1,element);
                        break;

                case 2: System.out.print("Enter position: ");
                        position= Integer.parseInt(br.readLine());
                        ll.remove(position-1);
                        break;

                case 3: System.out.print("Enter position: ");
                        position= Integer.parseInt(br.readLine());
                        System.out.print("Enter new element: ");
                        element= br.readLine();
                        ll.set(position-1,element);
                        break;

                default: return;
```

```
                                }
                                //Use Iterator to retrieve the elements
                                System.out.print("List= ");
                                Iterator it = ll.iterator();
                                while(it.hasNext())
                                System.out.print(it.next()+" ");

                        }//end of while
                }
        }
```

Output:

```
C:\> javac LLDemo.java
C:\> java LLDemo
List= [America, India, Japan]

LINKEDLIST OPERATIONS
1 Add an element
2 Remove an element
3 Change an element
4 Exit
Your choice: 1
Enter element: China
At what position? 1
List= China America India Japan
LINKEDLIST OPERATIONS
1 Add an element
2 Remove an element
3 Change an element
4 Exit
Your choice: 2
Enter position: 2
List= China India Japan
LINKEDLIST OPERATIONS
```

In this program, we create a linked list with some strings. Then we display a menu to the user to opt any option he wants and the specified operation is carried on the list.

ArrayList Class

An ArrayList is like an array, which can grow in memory dynamically. It means that when we store elements into the ArrayList, depending on the number of elements, the memory is dynamically allotted and re-allotted to accommodate all the elements. ArrayList is not synchronized. This means that when more than one thread acts simultaneously on the ArrayList object, the results may be incorrect in some cases. Please see the chapter on Threads for synchronization concepts.

The ArrayList class can be written as:

```
class ArrayList<E>
```

where E represents the type of elements to be stored into the ArrayList. For example, to store String type elements, we can create an object to ArrayList as:

```
ArrayList<String> arl = new ArrayList<String>();
```

The preceding statement constructs an ArrayList with a default initial capacity of 10. We can also mention the capacity at the time of creating ArrayList object as:

```
ArrayList<Double>arl = new ArrayList<Double>(101);
```

The preceding ArrayList can store Double type objects and initial capacity is declared to be 101.

ArrayList Class Methods

ArrayList class includes the following methods:

- ❑ boolean add(element obj): This method appends the specified element to the end of the ArrayList. If the element is added successfully then the preceding method returns true.
- ❑ void add(int position, element obj): This method inserts the specified element at the specified position in the ArrayList.
- ❑ element remove(int position): This method removes the element at the specified position in the ArrayList. This method also returns the element which was removed from the ArrayList.
- ❑ boolean remove(Object obj): This method removes the first occurrence of the specified element obj from the ArrayList, if it is present.
- ❑ void clear(): This method removes all the elements from the ArrayList.
- ❑ element set(int position, element obj): This method replaces an element at the specified position in the ArrayList with the specified element obj.
- ❑ boolean contains(Object obj): This method returns true if the ArrayList contains the specified element obj.
- ❑ element get(int position): This method returns the element available at the specified position in the ArrayList.
- ❑ int indexOf(Object obj): This method returns the position of the first occurrence of the specified element obj in the list, or -1 if the element is not found in the list.
- ❑ int lastIndexOf(Object obj): This method returns the position of the last occurrence of the specified element obj in the list, or -1 if the element is not found in the list.
- ❑ int size(): This method returns the number of elements present in the ArrayList.
- ❑ Object[ ] toArray(): This method returns an Object class type array containing all the elements in the ArrayList in proper sequence.

Let us write a program to understand the way to create an ArrayList with some String type elements and perform various operations on it. For example, we can add the elements to ArrayList using:

```
arl.add("Apple");
```

We can remove 3rd element using remove() method as:

```
Arl.remove(3);
```

We can use an Iterator or ListIterator to retrieve elements from the ArrayList. These things are demonstrated in Program 5.

Program 5: Write a program to create an ArrayList with strings and perform various operations on it.

```java
//ArrayList with String objects
import java.util.*;
class ArrayListDemo
{
        public static void main(String args[ ])
        {
                //create ArrayList
                ArrayList<String> arl = new ArrayList<String>();

                //add four objects
                arl.add("Apple");
                arl.add("Mango");
                arl.add("Grapes");
                arl.add("Guava");

                //display contents
                System.out.println("Contents: "+arl);

                //remove two objects
                arl.remove(3);
                arl.remove("Apple");

                //display again
                System.out.println("Contents after Removing: "+arl);

                //display its size
                System.out.println("Size of ArrayList: "+arl.size());

                //extract elements using Iterator
                System.out.println("Extracting using Iterator:");

                //add an  Iterator to ArrayList to retrieve elements
                Iterator it = arl.iterator();

                while(it.hasNext())
                {
                        System.out.println(it.next());
                }
        }
}
```

Output:

```
C:\> javac ArrayListDemo.java
C:\> java ArrayListDemo
Contents: [Apple, Mango, Grapes, Guava]
Contents after Removing: [Mango, Grapes]
Size of ArrayList: 2
Extracting using Iterator
Mango
Grapes
```

Vector Class

A Vector also stores elements (objects) similar to ArrayList, but Vector is synchronized. It means even if several threads act on Vector object simultaneusly, the results will be reliable.

We can write a Vector class as:

```
class Vector<E>
```

Here, E represents the type of elements stored into the Vector. For example, if we want to create an empty Vector that can be used to store Float type objects, we can write:

```
Vector<Float> v = new Vector<Float>();
```

The preceding statement creates a Vector object v which can be used to store Float type objects. The default capacity will be 10.

```
Vector<Integer> v = new Vector<Integer>(101);
```

This vector v can store Integer objects. The capacity of Vector is given as 101. Another way of creating a Vector object is by specifying a 'capacity increment' which specifies how much the capacity should be incremented when the Vector is full with elements.

```
Vector<Integer> v = new Vector<Integer>(101, 20);
```

Here, 101 is the capacity of the Vector and capacity increment is 20. Should the Vector is full with elements; the capacity automatically goes to 121.

Vector Class Methods

Vector class includes the following methods:

- [ ] boolean add(element obj): This method appends the specified element to the end of the Vector. If the element is added successfully then the preceding method returns true.
- [ ] void add(int position, element obj): This method inserts the specified element at the specified position in the Vector.
- [ ] element remove(int position): This method removes the element at the specified position in the Vector. This method also returns the element which was removed from the Vector.
- [ ] boolean remove(Object obj): This method removes the first occurrence of the specified element obj from the Vector, if it is present.
- [ ] void clear(): This method removes all the elements from the Vector.
- [ ] element set(int position, element obj): This method replaces an element at the specified position in the Vector with the specified element obj.
- [ ] boolean contains(Object obj): This method returns true if the Vector contains the specified element obj.
- [ ] element get(int position): This method returns the element available at the specified position in the Vector.
- [ ] int indexOf(Object obj): This method returns the position of the first occurrence of the specified element obj in the Vector, or -1 if the element is not found in the list.
- [ ] int lastIndexOf(Object obj): This method returns the position of the last occurrence of the specified element obj in the Vector, or -1 if the element is not found in the list.
- [ ] int size(): This method returns the number of elements present in the Vector.
- [ ] Object[ ] toArray(): This method returns an Object class type array containing all the elements in the Vector in proper sequence.

❏ `int capacity()`: This method returns the current capacity of the Vector.

To understand the Vector concept, let us take an example. In Program 6, we take a Vector to store Integer objects as:

```
Vector<Integer> v = new Vector<Integer>();
```

Our idea is to take an `int` type array `x[ ]` and store the elements of this array into the vector v. In this case, since `x[ ]` has `int` type elements, we should convert them all to Integer type objects and then store them into the vector v. This is done by the statement:

```
v.add(x[i]);
```

In fact, here we are storing `x[i]` directly into v. The Java compiler converts internally the `int` type elements of `x[i]` into Integer type objects. This is called auto boxing.

Program 6: Write a program that shows the use of Vector Class.

```java
//Creating a vector with Integer elements
import java.util.*;
class VectorDemo
{
    public static void main(String args[ ])
    {
        //take a vector to store Integer objects
        Vector<Integer> v = new Vector<Integer>();

        //take an int type array
        int x[ ]={22,20,10,40,15,60};

        //when x[i] is stored into v below. x[i] values are converted into
        //Integer objects and stored into v. This is auto boxing.
        for(int i=0; i<x.length; i++)
        {
            v.add(x[i]);
        }

        //retrieve the elements using get()
        System.out.println("Vector elements: ");
        for(int i=0; i<v.size(); i++)
        {
            System.out.println(v.get(i));
        }

        //retrieve using ListIterator
        System.out.println("Elements using ListIterator:");
        ListIterator lit = v.listIterator();

        System.out.println("In forward direction:");
        while(lit.hasNext())
        System.out.print(lit.next()+"\t");

        System.out.println("\nIn backward direction:");
        while(lit.hasPrevious())
        System.out.print(lit.previous()+"\t");

    }
}
```

Output:

```
C:\> javac VectorDemo.java
C:\> java VectorDemo
Vector elements:
22
20
10
40
15
60
Elements using ListIterator:
In forward direction:
22      20      10      40      15      60
In backward direction:
60      15      40      10      20      22
```

In this program, we create a Vector and store the elements of x[i] into the Vector. Then we retrieve the elements from Vector using get(). ListIterator is used later to retrieve the elements in forward and reverse directions from Vector.

Important Interview Question

What is the difference between ArrayList and Vector?

See Table 23.2.

Table 23.2

ArrayList	Vector
ArrayList object is not synchronized by default.	Vector object is synchronized by default.
In case of a single thread, using ArrayList is faster than the Vector.	In case of multiple threads, using Vector is advisable. With a single thread, Vector becomes slow.
ArrayList increases its size every time by 50 percent (half).	Vector increases its size every time by doubling it.

Important Interview Question

Can you synchronize the ArrayList object?

Yes, we can use synchronizedList() method to synchronize the ArrayList, as:

Collections.synchronizedList(new ArrayList());

HashMap Class

HashMap is a collection that stores elements in the form of key-value pairs. If key is provided later, its corresponding value can be easily retrieved from the HashMap. Keys should be unique. This means we cannot use duplicate data for keys in the HashMap. However, HashMap is not synchronized and hence while using multiple threads on HashMap object, we get unreliable results.

We can write HashMap class as:

```
class HashMap<K,V>
```

where K represents the type of key element and V represents the type of value element. For example, to store a String as key and an Integer object as its value, we can create the HashMap as,

```
HashMap<String, Integer> hm = new HashMap<String, Integer>();
```

Here, we did not mention any capacity for the HashMap. The default initial capacity of this HashMap will be taken as 16 and the load factor as 0.75. Load factor represents at what level the HashMap capacity should be doubled. For example, the product of capacity and load factor = 16 * 0.75 = 12. This represents that after storing the 12th key-value pair into the HashMap, its capacity will become 32.

Important Interview Question

What is the load factor for a HashMap or Hashtable?
  0.75

We can also create HashMap in the following ways:

❑ `HashMap<String, Integer> hm = new HashMap<String, Integer>(81);`

Here, 81 is the initial capacity of HashMap.

❑ `HashMap<String, Integer> hm = new HashMap<String, Integer>(81, 0.5);`

Here, 81 is the initial capacity and 0.5 is the load factor.

HashMap Class Methods

HashMap class includes the following methods:

❑ `value put(key, value)`: This method stores key-value pair into the HashMap.

❑ `value get(Object key)`: This method returns the corresponding value when key is given. If the key does not have a value associated with it, then it returns null.

❑ `Set<K> keySet()`: This method, when applied on a HashMap converts it into a Set where only keys will be stored.

❑ `Collection<V> values()`: This method, when applied on a HashMap object returns all the values of the HashMap into a Collection object.

❑ `value remove(Object key)`: This method removes the key and corresponding value from the HashMap.

❑ `void clear()`: This method removes all the key-value pairs from the map.

❑ `boolean isEmpty()`: This method returns true if there are no key-value pairs in the HashMap.

❑ `int size()`: This method returns number of key-value pairs in the HashMap.

We take a case where we want to create a telephone book using a HashMap. In this book, we store name of a person and his telephone number. Since the name is a String and the telephone number is taken as Long type object, we can create a HashMap as:

```
HashMap<String, Long> hm = new HashMap<String, Long>();
```

Here, String type name is key and the telephone number which is Long type is its value. Using put() method, we can store the key-value pair as:

```
hm.put(name,phno);
```

If we provide the key, that is name, we can get its value, that is phno. This is done by get() method as:

```
phno= hm.get(name);
```

Finally, to display all the keys (names), we can use keySet() method which returns all the keys into a HashSet object.

Program 7: Write a program that shows the use of HashMap class.

```java
//HashMap used as telephone book
import java.io.*;
import java.util.*;

class HashMapDemo
{
    public static void main(String args[ ])
    throws IOException
    {
        //create HashMap
        HashMap<String, Long> hm = new HashMap<String, Long>();

        //vars
        String name,str;
        Long phno;
        BufferedReader br = new BufferedReader(new
        InputStreamReader(System.in));

        //menu
        while(true)
        {
            System.out.println("1 Enter Phone entries");
            System.out.println("2 Lookup in the book");
            System.out.println("3 Display Names in book");
            System.out.println("4 Exit");

            System.out.print("Your choice: ");
            int n=Integer.parseInt(br.readLine());

            switch(n)
            {
                case 1: System.out.print("Enter name: ");
                        name= br.readLine();
                        System.out.print("Enter phno: ");
                        str= br.readLine();
                        phno= new Long(str);
                        //store name and phno into HashMap
                        hm.put(name,phno);
                        break;

                case 2: System.out.print("Enter name: ");
                        name = br.readLine();
                        name= name.trim();  //remove unnecessary
                        //spaces
                        //pass name and get phno
                        phno= hm.get(name);
                        System.out.println("Phno: "+phno);
                        break;
```

```
                                        case 3: //use keySet() to display the names
                                                //create HashSet object to store names and
                                                //refer it by Set reference
                                                Set<String> set = new HashSet<String>();
                                                set = hm.keySet();
                                                System.out.println(set);
                                                break;

                                        case 4: return;

                                }
                        }

                }
        }
```

Output:

```
C:\> javac HashMapDemo.java
C:\> java HashMapDemo
1 Enter Phone entries
2 Lookup in the book
3 Display Names in book
4 Exit
Your choice: 1
Enter name: Laxmi
Enter phno: 9866633445
1 Enter Phone entries
2 Lookup in the book
3 Display Names in book
4 Exit
Your choice: 1
Enter name: Ganesh
Enter phno: 22340056
1 Enter Phone entries
2 Lookup in the book
3 Display Names in book
4 Exit
Your choice: 3
[Laxmi, Ganesh]
1 Enter Phone entries
2 Lookup in the book
3 Display Names in book
4 Exit
Your choice: 2
Enter name: Laxmi
Phno: 9866633445
1 Enter Phone entries
2 Lookup in the book
3 Display Names in book
4 Exit
Your choice: 4
```

This program creates a HashMap to store name and phone number. When name is given, we can get back the corresponding phone number.

Hashtable Class

Hashtable is similar to HashMap which can store elements in the form of key-value pairs. But Hashtable is synchronized assuring proper results even if multiple threads act on it simultaneously.

We can write Hashtable class as:

```
class Hashtable<K,V>
```

where K represents the type of key element and V represents the type of value element. For example, to store a String as key and an Integer object as its value, we can create the Hashtable as,

```
Hashtable<String, Integer> hm = new Hashtable<String, Integer>();
```

Here, we did not mention any capacity for the Hashtable. The default initial capacity of this Hashtable will be taken as 11 and the load factor as 0.75. Load factor represents at what level the HashMap capacity should be doubled. For example, the product of capacity and load factor = 11 * 0.75 = 8.25. This represents that after storing 8th key-value pair into the Hashtable, its capacity will become 22.

We can also create Hashtable in the following ways:

❑ `Hashtable<String, Integer> ht = new Hashtable<String, Integer>(81);`

Here, 81 is initial capacity of Hashtable

❑ `Hashtable<String, Integer> hm = new Hashtable<String, Integer>(81, 0.5);`

Here, 81 is initial capacity and 0.5 is load factor.

Hashtable Class Methods

Hashtable class includes the following methods:

❑ `value put(key, value)`: This method stores key-value pair into the Hashtable.

❑ `value get(Object key)`: This method returns the corresponding value when key is given. If the key does not have a value associated with it, then it returns null.

❑ `Set<K> keySet()`: This method, when applied on a Hashtable converts it into a Set where only keys will be stored.

❑ `Collection<V> values()`: This method, when applied on a Hashtable object returns all the values of the Hashtable into a Collection object.

❑ `value remove(Object key)`: This method removes the key and corresponding value from the Hashtable.

❑ `void clear()`: This method removes all the key-value pairs from the Hashtable.

❑ `boolean isEmpty()`: This method returns true if there are no key-value pairs in the Hashtable.

❑ `int size()`: This method returns the number of key-value pairs in the Hashtable.

In Program 8, we create a Hashtable with the names of cricket players and their scores. For this purpose, the Hashtable can be created as:

```
Hashtable<String, Integer> ht = new Hashtable<String, Integer>();
```

Then using `put()` method, we can store the key-value pairs. Here, key is the player name and the value is his score.

```
ht.put("Ajay", 50);
```

Here, the primitive int value 50 will be converted into Integer object and then stored into the Hashtable. To retrieve all the keys (names), we can use `keys()` method which returns the keys of the Hashtable into an Enumeration object.

```
Enumeration  e = ht.keys();
```

Then using `get()` method, we can retrieve the score of a player.

```
Integer score= ht.get(name);
```

Program 8: Write a program that shows the use of HashTable class.

```
//Hashtable with cricket player names and their scores
import java.io.*;
import java.util.*;
class HashtableDemo
{
      public static void main(String args[ ])
      throws IOException
      {
            //create Hashtable with names and scores
            Hashtable<String, Integer> ht = new Hashtable<String, Integer>();
            ht.put("Ajay", 50);
            ht.put("Sachin", 77);
            ht.put("Gavaskar", 44);
            ht.put("Kapil", 60);
            ht.put("Dhoni", 88);

            //display all player names using enumerator
            System.out.println("The player names: ");
            Enumeration  e = ht.keys();
            while (e.hasMoreElements())
            System.out.println(e.nextElement());

            //accept player name from keyboard
            BufferedReader br = new BufferedReader(new
            InputStreamReader(System.in));
            System.out.print("Enter player name: ");
            String name= br.readLine();
            name= name.trim();   //remove unnecessary spaces

            //get score of the player
            Integer score= ht.get(name);
            if(score != null)
            {
                  //convert score from Integer object to int value
                  int sc=score.intValue();
                  System.out.println(name +" Scored: "+sc);
            }
            else System.out.println("Player not found");
      }
}
```

Output:

```
C:\> javac HashtableDemo.java
C:\> java HashtableDemo
The player names:
Ajay
Dhoni
Sachin
Gavaskar
Kapil
Enter player name: Sachin
Sachin Scored: 77
```

In this program, we are creating Hashtable that stores the cricket players' names as keys and their scores as values.

Important Interview Question

What is the difference between HashMap and Hashtable ?

The difference between a HashMap and a Hashtable is given in Table 23.3

Table 23.3

HashMap	Hashtable
HashMap object is not synchronized by default.	Hashtable object is synchronized by default.
In case of a single thread, using HashMap is faster than the Hashtable.	In case of multiple threads, using Hashtable is advisable. With a single thread, Hashtable becomes slow.
HashMap allows null keys and null values to be stored.	Hashtable does not allow null keys or values.
Iterator in the HashMap is fail-fast. This means Iterator will produce exception if concurrent updates are made to the HashMap.	Enumeration for the Hashtable is not fail-fast. This means even if concurrent updations are done to Hashtable, there will not be any incorrect results produced by the Enumeration.

Important Interview Question

Can you make HashMap synchronized ?

Yes, we can make HashMap object synchronized using synchronizedMap() method as shown here:

Collections.synchronizedMap(new HashMap());

What is the difference between a Set and a List?

The difference between a Set and a List is given in Table 23.4.

Table 23.4

Set	List
A set represents a collection of elements. Order of the elements may change in the set.	A List represents ordered collection of elements. List preserves the order of elements in which they are entered.
Set will not allow duplicate values to be stored.	List will allow duplicate values.
Accessing elements by their index (position number) is not possible in case of sets.	Accessing elements by index is possible in lists.
Sets will not allow null elements.	Lists allow null elements to be stored.

Arrays Class

Arrays class provides methods to perform certain operations on any one dimensional array. All the methods of the Arrays class are static, so they can be called in the form of `Arrays.methodname()`.

Arrays Class Methods

`Arrays class` includes the following methods:

❑ `static void sort(array)`: This method sorts all the elements of an array into ascending order. This method internally uses QuickSort algorithm.

❑ `static void sort(array, int start, int end)`: This method sorts the elements in the range from 'start' to 'end' within an array into ascending order.

❑ `static int binarySearch(array, element)`: This method searches for an element in the array and returns its position number. If the element is not found in the array, it returns a negative value. Note that this method acts only on an array which is sorted in ascending order. This method internally uses BinarySearch algorithm.

❑ `static boolean equals(array1, array2)`: This method returns true if two arrays, that is array1 and array2 are equal, otherwise false.

❑ `static array copyOf(source-array, int n)`: This method copies n elements from the source-array into another array and returns that array.

❑ `static void fill(array, value)`: This method fills the array with the specified value. It means that all the elements in the array will receive that value.

To understand how to sort the elements of an array and how to search for a specific element in the array, let us write a program now. In this program, we can take an example array that contains some elements. To sort all the elements into ascending order, we can use `sort()` method of Arrays class as:

```
Arrays.sort(arr);
```

Arrays class also offers `binarySearch()` method to search for an element in the array. This method returns the position of an element in the array and can be called as:

```
int index = Arrays.binarySearch(arr,element);
```

If the element is not found, then the preceding method returns a negative value. This method counts the position of the element in the array starting from 0. But we count starting from 1. So, we should add 1 to the position number (index+1) given by this method while displaying the element position in the array, as shown in Program 9.

Program 9: Write a program that shows the use of Arrays.

```
//Sorting and searching an array
import java.io.*;
import java.util.*;

class ArraysDemo
{
    public static void main(String args[ ])
    throws IOException
    {
        //to accept data from keyboard
        BufferedReader br = new BufferedReader(new
        InputStreamReader(System.in));

        //create an array
```

```
            int arr[ ] = new int[5];

            //store elements into arr[ ]
            for(int i=0; i<5; i++)
            {
                    System.out.print("Enter an integer: ");
                    arr[i] = Integer.parseInt(br.readLine());
            }

            //display the arr[ ] contents
            System.out.println("Contents of the array: ");
            display(arr);

            //sort the arr[ ] into ascending order
            Arrays.sort(arr);

            //display the sorted contents
            System.out.println("The Sorted array: ");
            display(arr);

            //Now search for an element
            System.out.print("Which element to search? ");
            int element = Integer.parseInt(br.readLine());
            int index = Arrays.binarySearch(arr,element);
            if(index<0) System.out.println("Element not found");
            else System.out.println("Element found at location: "+(index+1));

    }
    //display method- uses for each loop
    static void display(int arr[ ])
    {
            for(int i:arr)
            System.out.println(i);
    }
}//end of ArraysDemo class
```

Output:

```
C:\> javac ArraysDemo.java
Enter an integer: 22
Enter an integer: 44
Enter an integer: 10
Enter an integer: 67
Enter an integer: 30
Contents of the array:
22
44
10
67
30
The Sorted array:
10
22
30
44
67
Which element to search? 22
Element found at location: 2
```

In this program, we take an int type array and store 5 elements into it. Then we sort the elements and then search for an element also in the array.

Using Comparator to Sort an Array

java.util package offers an interface, called Comparator that is useful to impose a total ordering on a collection of elements. It can be used to sort the elements (objects) of an array into ascending order or descending order. Comparator is written as:

```
interface Comparator<T>
```

where T represents the type of elements (objects) compared by the Comparator. For example, to compare Integer objects, we can write a class that implements the Comparator as:

```
class Ascend implements Comparator<Integer>
```

The Comparator interface contains a method compare() that should be implemented in such a way that the two objects should be compared using compareTo() method in its body as:

```
public int compare(Integer i1, Integer i2)
{
    return i1.compareTo(i2);
}
```

Here, the compareTo() method returns a positive number if i1>i2 and a negative value if i1<i2. It returns 0 if i1==i2. This logic can be applied to a group of objects when we want to arrange them in ascending order. Similarly, the reverse order is needed to sort the elements in descending order. Now the Ascend class object should be passed to Arrays class sort() method as:

```
Arrays.sort(arr, new Ascend());
```

Then all the elements (objects) of the array arr[ ] will be sorted into ascending order. In Program 10, we want to sort a group of Integer objects. The objects are first stored into an array arr[ ]. Then using Comparator, we compare only two objects of the array and decide the order. In Ascend class we write the code of ascending order and in Descend class, we write the code for descending order. Then the objects of Ascend class and Descend classes are passed to the sort() method of Arrays class as:

```
Arrays.sort(arr, new Ascend()); //for sorting into ascending order
Arrays.sort(arr, new Descend()); // for sorting into descending order
```

Program 10: Write a program that shows sorting using comparator.

```
//Sorting an array with a group of Integer objects
import java.io.*;
import java.util.*;

//to sort into ascending order
 class Ascend implements Comparator<Integer>
 {
      public int compare(Integer i1, Integer i2)
      {
            return i1.compareTo(i2);
      }
 }

//to sort into descending order
 class Descend implements Comparator<Integer>
 {
      public int compare(Integer i1, Integer i2)
```

```
            {
                    return i2.compareTo(i1);
            }
    }

class Arrays1
{
    public static void main(String args[ ])
    throws IOException
        {
                //to accept array elements from keyboard
                BufferedReader br = new BufferedReader(new
                InputStreamReader(System.in));

                System.out.print("How many elements? ");
                int size = Integer.parseInt(br.readLine());

                //create an array to store Integer type objects.
                Integer arr[ ] = new Integer[size];

                //Below, we pass int values to the array but they are
                //converted into Intege objects and then stored
                for(int i=0; i<size; i++)
                {
                        System.out.print("Enter int: ");
                        arr[i]= Integer.parseInt(br.readLine());
                }

                //sort the array in ascending order
                Arrays.sort(arr, new Ascend());

                //display the sorted array
                System.out.println("\nSorted in Ascending order: ");
                display(arr);

                //in descending order
                Arrays.sort(arr, new Descend());
                System.out.println("\nSorted in Descending order: ");
                display(arr);
        }

    static void display(Integer arr[ ])
        {
                for(Integer i: arr)
                System.out.print(i+"\t");

        }
}
```

Output:

```
C:\> javac Arrays1.java
C:\> java Arrays1
How many elements? 5
Enter int: 55
Enter int: 60
Enter int: 12
Enter int: 30
Enter int: 12

Sorted in Ascending order:
12      12      30      55      60
Sorted in Descending order:
60      55      30      12      12
```

In this program, we are demonstrating, how to sort objects into ascending and descending orders using Comparator.

StringTokenizer Class

This class is useful to break a string into pieces, called 'tokens'. These tokens are then stored in the StringTokenizer object from where they can be retrieved. The code to create an object to StringTokenizer class is:

```
StringTokenizer st = new StringTokenizer(str, "delimiter");
```

In the preceding statement, the actual string str is broken into pieces at the positions marked by a group of characters, called 'delimiters'. For example, to break the string wherever a comma is found, we can write:

```
StringTokenizer st = new StringTokenizer(str, ",");
```

Similarly, to break the string wherever a comma or colon or both are found, we can use:

```
StringTokenizer st = new StringTokenizer(str, ",:");
```

StringTokenizer Class Methods

StringTokenizer class includes the following methods:

❑ int countTokens(): This method counts and returns the number of tokens available in a StringTokenizer object.

❑ boolean hasMoreTokens(): This method tests if there are more tokens available in the StringTokenizer object or not. If next token is there then it returns true.

❑ String nextToken(): This method returns the next token from the StringTokenizer.

Program 11: Write a program that shows the use of StringTokenizer object.

```
//A string broken into pieces at spaces
import java.util.*;
class STDemo
{
    public static void main(String args[ ])
    {
        //take a string
        String str = "He is a gentle man";

        //break into tokens at spaces. Here delimiter is a space
        StringTokenizer st = new StringTokenizer(str," ");

        //retrieve tokens from st and display
        System.out.println("The tokens are:");

        while(st.hasMoreTokens())
        {
            String one=st.nextToken();
            System.out.println(one);
        }
    }
}
```

Output:

```
C:\> javac STDemo.java
C:\> java STDemo
The tokens are:
He
is
a
gentle
man
```

In this program, we take a string and break it into tokens wherever a space is found in the string. The tokens are then retrieved from StringTokenizer object and then displayed.

Calendar Class

Calender class is useful in two ways:

❑ It helps in knowing the system date and time.

❑ It helps in storing a date and time value so that it can be transported to some other application. To create an object to Calendar class, we can write:

```
Calendar cl = Calendar.getInstance();
```

Then the object cl is created to Calendar object which stores the current system date and time by default.

Calendar Class Methods

`Calendar class` includes the following methods:

❑ `int get(int field)`: This method returns the value of the given Calendar field. For example,

❑ `Calendar.DATE` gives the date number from 1 to 31.

❑ `Calendar.MONTH` gives the month number from 0 to 11. (January is taken as 0)

❑ `Calendar.YEAR` gives the year number.

❑ `Calendar.HOUR` gives the hour number from 0 to 11.

❑ `Calendar.MINUTE` gives the minute number from 0 to 59.

❑ `Calendar.SECOND` gives the second number from 0 to 59.

❑ `Calendar.AM_PM` gives 0 if it is AM. Gives 1 if it is PM.

❑ `void set(int field, int value)`

This method sets the given field in Calendar object to the given value. For example, we can set a date like 15th March 2007 to Calendar object as:

```
cl.set(Calendar.DATE, 15);
cl.set(Calendar.MONTH, 2);
cl.set(Calendar.YEAR, 2007);
```

❑ `String toString()`: This method returns the String representation of the Calendar object.

❑ `boolean equals(Object obj)`: This method compares the Calendar object with another object `obj` and returns true if they are same, otherwise false.

Program 12: Write a program that shows the use of Calendar class.

```
//To display System date and time
import java.util.*;

class CalendarDemo
{
    public static void main(String args[ ])
    {
        //create Calendar class object. By default it
        //contains the system date and time
        Calendar cl = Calendar.getInstance();

        //display date separately
        System.out.print("Current date: ");
        int dd= cl.get(Calendar.DATE);
        int mm= cl.get(Calendar.MONTH);
        ++mm;
        int yy= cl.get(Calendar.YEAR);
        System.out.println(dd+ "-" + mm + "-" +yy);

        //display time alone
        System.out.print("Current time: ");
        int h= cl.get(Calendar.HOUR);
        int m= cl.get(Calendar.MINUTE);
        int s= cl.get(Calendar.SECOND);
        System.out.println(h+ ":" + m +":" +s);

        int x = cl.get(Calendar.AM_PM);
        if(x == 0) System.out.println("Good morning");
        else System.out.println("Good evening");

    }
}
```

Output:

```
C:\> javac CalendarDemo.java
C:\> java CalendarDemo
Current date: 19-9-2007
Current time: 11:9:10
Good morning
```

In this program, we create a Calendar class object and by default it contains the date and time as shown by the local system. From the Calendar object, we get the date and time separately using get() method and display them.

Date Class

Date class is useful to display the date and time at a particular moment. When an object to Date class is created, it contains the system date and time by default. To create an object, we write:

```
Date d = new Date();
```

Now, d contains the system date and time. Once Date class object is created, it should be formatted using the following methods of DateFormat class of java.text package.

❑   DateFormat fmt = DateFormat. getDateInstance(formatconst, region);

This method is useful to store format information for date value into DateFormat object fmt.

❏ `DateFormat fmt = DateFormat. getTimeInstance(formatconst, region);`

This method is useful to store format information for time into DateFormat object `fmt`.

❏ DateFormat fmt = DateFormat.getDateTimeInstance(formatconst,formatconst,region);

This method stores the format information for date and time into the DateFormat class object `fmt`.

The DateFormat object `fmt` contains the formatting information which the programmer wants to format the date and time of Date class object. This can be done using `format()` method as:

```
String str = fmt.format(d);
```

The preceding `format()` method will apply the format which is in `fmt` object to the Date class object `d`. The formatted date and time will appear as a string in `str`. In the preceding DateFormat methods, we used 'formatconst' parameter which represents one of the following values:

```
DateFormat.FULL
DateFormat.LONG
DateFormat.MEDIUM
DateFormat.SHORT
```

And the 'region' parameter represents one of the following values for countries in the world: Locale.US, Locale.UK, Locale.US, Locale.UK, Locale.CHINA, Locale.CANADA, Locale.ITALY, Locale.JAPAN, Locale.KOREA, Locale.TAIWAN, Locale.FRANCE, Locale.GERMANY. All these are defined as constants in Locale class which is available in `java.util` package.

Please see Table 23.5 to understand how the 'formatconst' will modify the appearance of the Date class object for the 'region' Locale.UK.

Table 23.5

Formatconst	Example (region= Locale.UK)
`DateFormat.FULL`	`03 September 2007 19:43:14 O'clock GMT + 05:30`
`DateFormat.LONG`	`03 September 2007 19:43:14 GMT + 05:30`
`DateFormat.MEDIUM`	`03-Sep-07 19:43:14`
`DateFormat.SHORT`	`03/09/07 19:43`

Program 13: Write a program that shows the use of Date class.

```java
//Display System date and time using Date class
import java.util.*;
import java.text.*;
class MyDate
{
        public static void main(String args[ ])
        {
                //Creat Date class object- this contains system date and time
                Date d = new Date();

                //Format the date to medium format and time to short format
                DateFormat fmt = DateFormat.getDateTimeInstance(DateFormat.MEDIUM,
                DateFormat.SHORT, Locale.UK);

                //Apply the above format to the Date object
                String str = fmt.format(d);

                //Now display the formatted date and time
                System.out.println(str);
        }
}
```

```
    }
```

Output:

```
C:\> javac MyDate.java
C:\> java MyDate
19-Sep-2007 23:46
```

In this program, first we create a Date class object and then format the object contents using DateFormat class method and finally display the formatted date and time in string form.

Let us see one application of collection objects to store and handle groups of objects. We take an ArrayList to hold a group of Employee class objects in Program 14.

Let us write create several Employee class objects and store them in an ArrayList. For this purpose, we can create the ArrayList object as:

```
ArrayList<Employee> arl = new ArrayList<Employee>();
```

Then store the Employee class object obj into the ArrayList as:

```
arl.add(obj);
```

Let us then search for a specific employee id in the ArrayList and pick up that employee details and display them. For this purpose, get() method of ArrayList can be used as:

```
Employee obj = arl.get(i);
```

In the preceding statement, by changing the i values, the objects from ArrayList can be retrieved one by one. After retrieving an Employee object, the id number is checked and if it is the one we are searching for, then the details of that employee will be displayed. This is seen in Program 14.

Program 14: An ArrayList handling a group of Employee class objects

```java
//To create an ArrayList of Employee objects and search for a particular
Employee //object based on id number.

import java.io.*;
import java.util.*;
class Employee
{
      //take variables
      int id;
      String name;
      String address;

      //initialize them
      Employee(int i, String n, String a)
      {
            id = i;
            name = n;
            address = a;
      }

      //display employee details
      void display()
      {
            System.out.println("Id: "+ id);
            System.out.println("Name: "+ name);
            System.out.println("Address: "+ address);
      }
}
```

```
class EmpList
{
    public static void main(String args[ ]) throws IOException
    {
        //vars
        BufferedReader br = new BufferedReader(new
        InputStreamReader(System.in));
        int id;
        String name;
        String address;

        //create an ArrayList arl to store Employee objects
        ArrayList<Employee> arl = new ArrayList<Employee>();

        //accept 5 employee's details and store into arl
        for(int i=0; i<5; i++)
        {
            System.out.print("Enter id: ");
            id = Integer.parseInt(br.readLine());

            System.out.print("Enter name: ");
            name = br.readLine();

            System.out.print("Enter address: ");
            address = br.readLine();

            //create Employee object with accepted data
            Employee obj = new Employee(id, name, address);

            //store Employee object into arl
            arl.add(obj);
        }

        //Now search for an employee id
        System.out.print("Enter id to search: ");
        id = Integer.parseInt(br.readLine());

        //found becomes true if employee id is found in arl
        boolean found = false;

        //search all elements in arl
        for(int i=0;  i<arl.size();  i++)
        {
            //get() method of ArrayList will return i-th Employee
            //object
            Employee obj = arl.get(i);

            //check if given id is equal to id of Employee object
            if(id == obj.id)
            {
                obj.display();  //display that Employee data
                found = true;
            }
        }

        if(!found)
        System.out.println("Employee not found");
    }
}
```

Output:

```
C:\> javac EmpList.java
C:\> java EmpList
Enter id: 10
Enter name: Vijaya
```

```
    Enter address: Hyderabad
    Enter id: 11
    Enter name: Kumar
    Enter address: New Delhi
    Enter id: 12
    Enter name: Ganesh
    Enter address: Mumbai
    Enter id: 13
    Enter name: Nehru
    Enter address: Chennai
    Enter id: 14
    Enter name: Chandana
    Enter address: Kolkata
    Enter id to search: 13
    Id: 13
    Name: Nehru
    Address: Chennai
```

Study Program 14 keenly and observe Figure 23.5 to understand the logic used in the program.

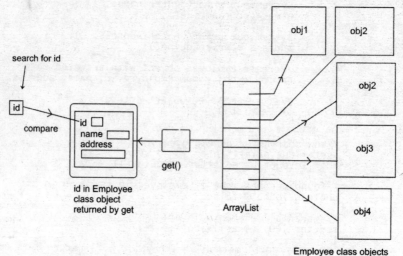

Figure 23.5 Retrieving objects using get() from an ArrayList

Conclusion

Collection framework contains classes exclusively to handle groups of objects. This is very essential because all the applications which are designed in OOPS extensively interchange data in the form of objects. Since generic classes are useful to handle any class type objects, all the collection classes of java.util package are written as generic classes. So they can handle any class type objects. Each collection class has a different mechanism of storing data in memory and has methods to perform various operations on the data. The programmer has to exercise discretion as to which collection is helpful to properly handle the data which he has planned in his software.

CHAPTER 24

STREAMS AND FILES

Streams facilitate transporting data from one place to another. Different streams are needed to send or receive data through different sources, such as to receive data from keyboard, we need a stream and to send data to a file, we need another stream. Without streams, it is not possible to move data in Java.

Stream

A stream carries data just as a water pipe carries water from one place to another (Figure 24.1). Streams can be categorized as 'input streams' and 'output streams'. Input streams are the streams which receive or read data while output streams are the streams which send or write data. All streams are represented by classes in java.io (input-output) package.

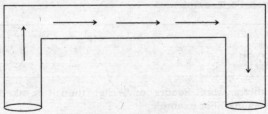

Figure 24.1 A stream to move data

Now, let us see how a stream works. We know an input stream reads data. So, to read data from keyboard, we can attach the keyboard to an input stream, so that the stream can read the data typed on the keyboard.

```
DataInputStream dis = new DataInputStream(System.in);
```

In the above statement, we are attaching the keyboard to DataInputStream object. The keyboard is represented by System.in. Now, DataInputStream object can read data coming from the keyboard. Here, System is a class and in is a field in System class. In fact, the System class has the following 3 fields:

❑ System.in: represents InputStream object. This object represents the standard input device, that is keyboard by default.

❑ System.out: represents PrintStream object. This object by default represents the standard output device, that is monitor.

❑   `System.err`: represents `PrintStream` object. This object by default represents the standard output device, that is monitor.

So, we can also use `System.err` to print something on the monitor, just like `System.out`.

Important Interview Question

What is the difference between System.out and System.err ?

Both are used to display messages on the monitor. System.out is used to display normal messages as:

System.out.println("Hello");

System.err is used to display any error messages in the program as:

System.err.println("This is an error");

Please observe that the keyboard is represented by `System.in` which internally creates `InputStream` object. It means the keyboard is an `InputStream`. Similarly, the monitor is represented by `PrintStream`. In this way, streams represent input/output devices in Java. Even if we change the keyboard or monitor, we can still use the same streams to handle those devices. In this way, streams are useful to handle the input/output devices irrespective of their make.

Important Interview Question

What is the advantage of stream concept?

Streams are mainly useful to move data from one place to another place. This concept can be used to receive data from an input device and send data to an output device.

Another classification of streams is 'byte streams' and 'text streams'. Byte streams represent data in the form of individual bytes. Text streams represent data as characters of each 2 bytes. If a class name ends with the word 'Stream', then it comes under byte streams. `InputStream` reads bytes and `OutputStream` writes bytes. For example:

```
FileInputStream
FileOutputStream
BufferedInputStream
BufferedOutputStream
```

If a class name ends with the word 'Reader' or 'Writer' then it is taken as a text stream. Reader reads text and Writer writes text. For example,

```
FileReader
FileWriter
BufferedReader
BufferedWriter
```

Byte streams are used to handle any characters (text), images, audio, and video files. For example, to store an image file (`.gif` or `.jpg`), we should go for a byte stream. The important classes of byte streams are shown in Figure 24.2(a) and 24.2(b).

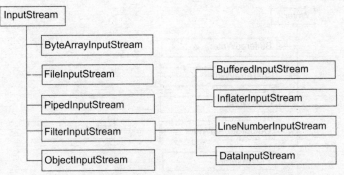

Figure 24.2(a) byte stream classes for reading data

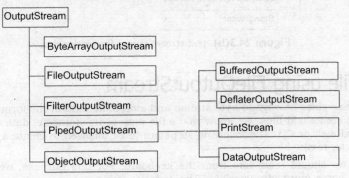

Figure 24.2(b) byte stream classes for writing data

Character or text streams can always store and retrieve data in the form of characters (or text) only. It means text streams are more suitable for handling text files like the ones we create in Notepad. They are not suitable to handle the images, audio, or video files. The important classes of character streams are shown in Figure 24.3(a) and 24.3(b).

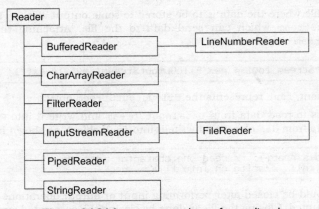

Figure 24.3(a) text stream classes for reading data

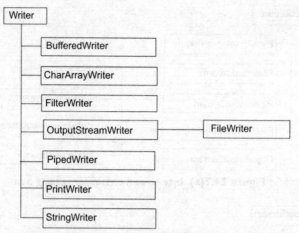

Figure 24.3(b) text stream classes for writing data

Creating a file using FileOutputStream

FileOutputStream class belongs to byte stream and stores the data in the form of individual bytes. It can be used to create text files. We know that a file represents storage of data on a second storage media like a hard disk or CD. The following steps are to be followed to create a text file that stores some characters (or text):

❑ First of all, we should read data from the keyboard. For this purpose, we should attach the keyboard to some input stream class. The code for using DataInputStream class for reading data from the keyboard is as:

```
DataInputStream dis = new DataInputStream(System.in);
```

Here, System.in represents the keyboard which is linked with DataInputStream object, that is, dis.

❑ Now, attach a file where the data is to be stored to some output stream. Here, we take the help of FileOutputStream which can send data to the file. Attaching the file myfile.txt to FileOutputStream can be done as:

```
FileOutputStream fout = new FileOutputStream("myfile.txt");
```

In the above statement, fout represents the FileOutputStream object.

❑ The next step is to read data from DataInputStream and write it into FileOutputStream. It means read data from dis object and write it into fout object, as shown here:

```
ch =(char)dis.read();  //read one character into ch
fout.write(ch);  //write ch into file
```

Finally, any file should be closed after performing input or output operations on it, else the data of the file may be corrupted. Closing the file is done by closing the associated streams. For example, fout.close(); will close the FileOutputStream, hence there is no way to write data into the file.

These steps are shown in Figure 24.4 and implemented in Program 1.

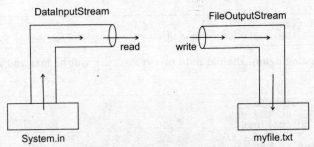

Figure 24.4 Creating a text file

Program 1: Write a program which shows how to read data from the keyboard and write it to myfile.txt file.

```java
//Creating a text file using FileOutputStream
import java.io.*;
class CreateFile
{
    public static void main(String args[ ])
    throws IOException
    {

        //attach keyboard to DataInputStream
        DataInputStream dis = new DataInputStream(System.in);

        //attach myfile to FileOutputStream
        FileOutputStream fout = new FileOutputStream("myfile.txt");

        System.out.println("Enter text (@ at the end): ");

        char ch;

        //read characters from dis into ch. Then write them into fout.
        //repeat this as long as the read character is not @
        while((ch =(char)dis.read()) != '@')
        fout.write(ch);

        //close the file
        fout.close();
    }
}
```

Output:

```
C:\> javac CreateFile.java
C:\> java CreateFile
Enter text (@ at the end):
This is my file line one
This is my file line two
@

C:\> type myfile.txt
This is my file line one
This is my file line two
```

In this program, we read data from the keyboard and write it to myfile.txt file. This program accepts data from the keyboard till the user types @ when he does not want to continue.

Here, we stored two lines of text into myfile.txt. To view the contents of myfile.txt, we can use type command in DOS or cat command in UNIX. For example,

```
    Type myfile.txt
    will display the contents of myfile.txt.
```

If Program 1 is executed again, the old data of `myfile.txt` will be lost and any recent data is only stored into the file.

```
    C:\> java CreateFile
    Enter text (@ at the end):
    This is my third line
    @
    C:\> type myfile.txt
    This is my third line
```

Notice that the file `myfile.txt` has now stored only the third line which has been entered in the preceding code output. The previous two lines have been deleted from the file and the file has been created as a fresh file. If we do not want to lose the previous data of the file, and just append the new data at the end of already existing data, then we should open the file by writing `true` along with the filename as:

```
    FileOutputStream fout = new FileOutputStream("myfile.txt", true);
```

When the above statement is used—even though the program is run several times—all previous data will be preserved and new data will be added to the old data.

Improving Efficiency using BufferedOutputStream

Normally, whenever we write data into a file using `FileOutputStream` as:

```
    fout.write(ch);
```

Here, we call write() method on 'fout' which is FileOutputStream object, to write a character (ch) into the file. Here, the FileOutputStream is invoked to write the character into the file.

Let us estimate how much time it takes to read 100 characters from the keyboard and write all of them into a file. Let us assume we read data from the keyboard into memory using DataInputStream and it takes 1 second time to read 1 character into memory. Let us assume that this character is written into the file by FileOutputStream by spending another 1 second time. So, for reading and writing a single character, a total time of 2 seconds are used. Thus, to read and write 100 characters, it takes 200 seconds time. This is wasting a lot of time.

On the other hand, if Buffered classes are used, they provide a buffer (temporary block of memory), which is first filled with characters and then all the characters from the buffer can be at once written into the file. Buffered classes should be used always in connection to other stream classes. For example, BufferedOutputStream can be used along with FileOutputStream to write data into a file.

First, the DataInputStream reads data from keyboard by spending 1 second time for each character. This character is written into the buffer. Thus, to read 100 characters into the buffer, it will take 100 seconds time. When the buffer is full, then the FileOutputStream will write the entire buffer full of characters in a single step into the file. This is like writing a single character into the file and hence the FileOutputStream will spend only 1 second time. So, to read and write 100 characters, it takes 101 seconds time which is very less when compared to the previous time of 200 seconds. Thus, by using Buffered classes, the speed of writing is improved. In the same way, we can use Buffered classes for improving the speed of reading operation also. See the behavior of Buffered classes in the Figure 24.5.

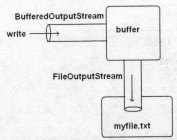

Figure 24.5 Using BufferedOutputStream to improve performance

In Program 1, we can attach FileOutputStream to BufferedOutputStream as:

```
BufferedOutputStream bout = new BufferedOutputStream(fout, 1024);
```

Here, the buffer size is declared as 1024 bytes. If the buffer size is not specified, then a default buffer size of 512 bytes is used.

Important Interview Question

What is the default buffer size used by any buffered class?

   512 bytes.

Program 2: Write a program to improve the efficiency of writing data into a file using `BufferedOutputStream`.

Note

Here, we are rewriting Program 1 using BufferedOutputStream where the file is opened for appending data

```
//Creating a text file using BufferedOutputStream
import java.io.*;
class CreateFile
{
        public static void main(String args[ ])
        throws IOException
        {

                //attach keyboard to DataInputStream
                DataInputStream dis = new DataInputStream(System.in);
                //attach myfile to FileOutputStream in append mode
                FileOutputStream fout = new FileOutputStream("myfile.txt",true);
                //attach FileOutputStream to BufferedOutputStream
                BufferedOutputStream bout = new BufferedOutputStream(fout, 1024);
                System.out.println("Enter text (@ at the end): ");
                char ch;
                //read characters from dis into ch. Then write them into bout.
                //repeat this as long as the read character is not @
                while((ch =(char)dis.read()) != '@')
                bout.write(ch);
                //close the file
                bout.close();
        }
}
```

Output:

```
C:\> javac CreateFile.java
C:\> java CreateFile
Enter text (@ at the end):
This is my file line four
This is last line
@

C:\> type myfile.txt
This is my third line
This is my file line four
This is last line
```

Reading Data from a File using FileInputStream

FileInputStream is useful to read data from a file in the form of sequence of bytes. It is possible to read data from a text file using `FileInputStream`. Let us see how it is done:

❑   First, we should attach the file to a `FileInputStream` as shown here:

```
FileInputStream fin = new FileInputStream("myfile.txt");
```

This will enable us to read data from the file. Then, to read data from the file, we should read data from the `FileInputStream` as:

```
ch= fin.read();
```

When the `read()` method reads all the characters from the file, it reaches the end of the file. When there is no more data available to read further, the `read()` method returns -1.

❑   Then, we should attach the monitor to some output stream, example `PrintStream`, so that the output stream will send data to the monitor. For displaying the data, we can use `System.out` which is nothing but `PrintStream` object.

```
System.out.print(ch);
```

❑   Finally, we read data from the `FileInputStream` and write it to `System.out`. This will display all the file data on the screen.

These steps are shown in Figure 24.6 and implemented in Program 3.

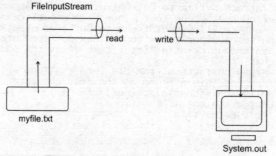

Figure 24.6 Reading data from a text file

Program 3: Write a program to read data from `myfile.txt` using `FileInputStream` and display it on the monitor.

```java
//Reading textfile using FileInputStream
import java.io.*;
class ReadFile
{
      public static void main(String args[ ])
      throws IOException
      {

              //attach the file to FileInputStream
              FileInputStream fin = new FileInputStream("myfile.txt");
              System.out.println("File contents: ");

      //read characters from FileInputStream and write them
      //to monitor. Repeat this till the end of file.
      int ch;

      while((ch= fin.read()) != -1)
        System.out.print((char)ch);

      //close the file
      fin.close();
   }
}
```

Output:

```
C:\> javac ReadFile.java
C:\> java ReadFile
File contents:
This is my third line
This is my file line four
This is last line
```

There are some improvements suggestible in the above program. First, the above program works with `myfile.txt` only. To make this program work with any file, we should accept the filename from the keyboard. For this purpose, create `BufferedReader` object as:

```java
BufferedReader br = new BufferedReader(new InputStreamReader(System.in));
```

Here, the keyboard (`System.in`) is attached to `InputStreamReader` which is attached to `BufferedReader`. So if we read data from the `BufferedReader`, then that is actually read from the keyboard. Using `readLine()` method of `BufferedReader` class we can read the filename from the keyboard as:

```java
String fname = br.readLine();
```

This filename should be attached to `FileInputStream` for reading data as:

```java
FileInputStream fin = new FileInputStream(fname);
```

What happens if the file being opened is not available? There would be `FileNotFoundException`. By handling this exception, it is possible to know whether the file is available or not.

```java
try{
      fin = new FileInputStream(fname);
}
```

```
        catch(FileNotFoundException fe) {
                System.out.println("File not found");
                return;
        }
```

As another improvement, we can use `BufferedInputStream` to read a buffer full of data at a time from the file. This improves the speed of execution. These improvements can be found in Program 4.

Program 4: Write a program which is used to read data from any text file.

```
//Reading data from text file - version 2
import java.io.*;
class ReadFile
{
        public static void main(String args[ ])
        throws IOException
        {
                        //to accept filename from keyboard
                BufferedReader br = new BufferedReader(new
                InputStreamReader(System.in));
                System.out.print("Enter file name: ");
                String fname = br.readLine();

                //attach the file to FileInputStream
                FileInputStream fin = null;  //assign nothing to fin

                //check if file exists or not
                try{
                        fin = new FileInputStream(fname);
                }
                catch(FileNotFoundException fe) {
                System.out.println("File not found");
                return;
                }

                //attach FileInputStream to BufferedInputStream
                BufferedInputStream bin = new BufferedInputStream(fin);

                System.out.println("File contents: ");

                //read characters from BufferedInputStream and write them
                //to monitor. Repeat this till the end of file.
                int ch;

                while((ch= bin.read()) != -1)
                System.out.print((char)ch);

                //close the file
                bin.close();
        }
}
```

Output:

```
C:\> javac ReadFile.java
C:\> java ReadFile
Enter file name: myfile.txt
File contents:
This is my third line
This is my file line four
This is last line
C:\> java ReadFile
Enter file name: jjjjjj
File not found
```

Creating a File using FileWriter

`FileWriter` is useful to create a file by writing characters into it. The following program depicts how to create a text file using `FileWriter`.

Program 5: Write a program to create a text file using FileWriter.

```
//Creating a text file using FileWriter
import java.io.*;
class CreateFile1
{
        public static void main(String args[ ])
        throws IOException
        {
                //take a string
                String str="This is a book on Java."+"\nIam a learner of Java.";

                //attach file to FileWriter
                FileWriter fw = new FileWriter("text");

                //read character wise from string and write into FileWriter
                for(int i=0; i<str.length(); i++)
                fw.write(str.charAt(i));

                //close the file
                fw.close();
        }
}
```

Output:

```
C:\> javac CreateFile1.java
C:\> java CreateFile1
C:\>
C:\> type text
This is a book on Java.
Iam a learner of Java.
```

In this program, we are taking a string from where the characters are read and written into a `FileWriter`, which is attached to a file named `text`.

Here, we could also use `BufferedWriter` along with `FileWriter` to improve speed of execution as:

```
BufferedWriter bw = new BufferedWriter(fw, 1024);
```

Reading a File using FileReader

`FileReader` is useful to read data in the form of characters from a 'text' file.

Program 6: Write a program to show how to read data from the 'text' file using FileReader.

```
//Reading data from a file using FileReader
import java.io.*;
class ReadFile1
{
        public static void main(String args[ ])
        throws IOException
        {
                //var
                int ch;
```

```
                    //check if file exists or not
                    FileReader fr = null;

                    //check if file exists or not
                    try{
                            fr = new FileReader("text");
                    }
                    catch(FileNotFoundException fe) {
                            System.out.println("File not found");
                            return;
                    }

                    //read from FileReader till the end of file
                    while((ch=fr.read()) != -1)
                    System.out.print((char)ch);

                    //close the file
                    fr.close();
            }
    }
```

Output:

```
    C:\> javac ReadFile1.java
    C:\> java ReadFile1
    This is a book on Java.
    Iam a learner of Java.
```

In this program, the 'text' file is attached to `FileReader` for reading data. It is read using `read()` method and is displayed on the monitor.

Here, we could also use `BufferedReader` to improve the speed of execution as:

```
    BufferedReader br = new BufferedReader(fr, 512);
```

The data will be then read from the `BufferedReader` object `br`, instead of the `FileReader` object `fr`.

Zipping and Unzipping Files

We know that some software like 'winzip' provide zipping and unzipping of file data. In zipping the file contents, following two things could happen:

❑   The file contents are compressed and hence the size will be reduced.

❑   The format of data will be changed making it unreadable.

While zipping a file content, a zipping algorithm (logic) is used in such a way that the algorithm first finds out which bit pattern is most often repeated in the original file and replaces that bit pattern with a 0. Then the algorithm searches for the next bit pattern which is most often repeated in the input file. In its place, a 1 is substituted. The third repeated bit pattern will be replaced by 01, the fourth by 10, the fifth by 100, and so on. In this way, the original bit patterns are replaced by lesser number of bits. This file with lesser number of bits is called 'zipped file' or 'compressed file'.

To get back the original data from the zipped file, we can follow a reverse algorithm, which substitutes the original bit pattern wherever particular bits are found. This is shown in Figure 24.7.

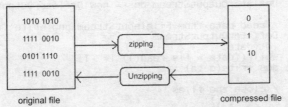

Figure 24.7 Zipping and Unzipping a file

In Java, classes are provided to zip and unzip the file contents. We can use `DeflaterOutputStream` class for zipping a file content and `InflaterInputStream` class for unzipping the file contents. These classes are found in `java.util.zip` package.

Zipping a File using DeflaterOutputStream

Let us now learn how to compress data in a file, say 'file1' by following these steps:

❏ Attach the input file 'file1' to `FileInputStream` for reading data.

❏ Take the output file 'file2' and attach it to `FileOutputStream`. This will help to write data into 'file2'.

❏ Attach `FileOutputStream` to `DeflaterOutputStream` for compressing the data.

❏ Now, read data from `FileInputStream` and write it into `DeflaterOutputStream`. It will compress the data and send it to `FileOutputStream` which stores the compressed data into the output file. These steps are shown in Figure 24.8 and implemented in Program 7.

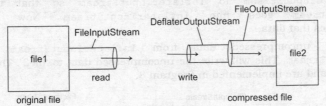

Figure 24.8 Zipping a file

Program 7: Write a program to compress the data contained in a file using `DeflaterOutputStream`.

Note

Before running this program, create 'file1' with some data.

```
//Compressing a file using a DeflaterOutputStream
import java.io.*;
import java.util.zip.*;
class Zip
{
      public static void main(String args[ ]) throws Exception
      {
            //attach the original file:file1 to
            FileInputStream for reading data
            FileInputStream fis = new FileInputStream("file1");

            //attach compressed file:file2 to FileOutputStream
            FileOutputStream fos = new FileOutputStream("file2");

            //attach FileOutputStream to DeflaterOutputStream
```

```
                DeflaterOutputStream dos = new DeflaterOutputStream(fos);

                //read data from FileInputStream and write it into
                DeflaterOutputStream
                int data;
                while((data = fis.read()) != -1)
                dos.write(data);

                //close the files
                fis.close();
                dos.close();
            }
        }
```

Output:

```
C:\> javac Zip.java
C:\> java Zip
```

Unzipping a File using InflaterInputStream

Now, the file with the name 'file2' contains compressed data and suppose we want to obtain original uncompressed data from this file. Let us follow these steps to uncompress data from this file.

❑ Attach the compressed file 'file2' to FileInputStream. This helps to read data from 'file2'.

❑ Attach the output file 'file3' to FileOutputStream. This will help to write uncompressed data into 'file3'.

❑ Attach FileInputStream to InflaterInputStream so that the data read from FileInputStream goes into InflaterInputStream. Now InflaterInputStream uncompresses that data.

❑ Now, read uncompressed data from InflaterInputStream and write it into FileOutputStream. This will write the uncompressed data to 'file3'. These steps are shown in Figure 24.9 and are implemented in Program 8.

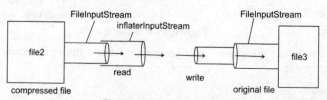

Figure 24.9 Unzipping a file

Program 8: Write a program to uncompress data from a compressed file by using InflaterInputStream.

```
        //Uncompressing a file using an InflaterInputStream
        import java.io.*;
        import java.util.zip.*;
        class UnZip
        {
            public static void main(String args[ ]) throws Exception
            {
                //attach input file: file2 to FileInputStream for reading data
                FileInputStream fis = new FileInputStream("file2");

                //attach output file: file3 to FileOutputStream for writing data
                into it
                FileOutputStream fos = new FileOutputStream("file3");
```

```
                        //attach InflaterInputStream to FileInputStream for uncompressing
                        the data
                        InflaterInputStream iis = new InflaterInputStream(fis);

                        //read data from InflaterInputStream and write it into
                        FileOutputStream
                        int data;
                        while((data = iis.read()) != -1)
                        fos.write(data);

                        //close the files
                        fos.close();
                        iis.close();
                }
        }
```

Output:

```
        C:\> javac UnZip.java
        C:\> java UnZip
```

In this program, we take the compressed file 'file2' from where data is read and uncompressed by InflaterInputStream. The output of this program is 'file3' which contains the original uncompressed data.

Serialization of Objects

So far, we wrote some programs where we stored only text into the files and retrieved same text from the files. These text files are useful when we do not want to perform any calculations on the data. What happens if we want to store some structured data in the files? For example, we want to store some employee details like employee identification number (int type), name (String type), salary (float type) and date of joining the job (Date type) in a file. This data is well structured and got different types. To store such data, we need to create a class Employee with the instance variables id, name, sal, doj as shown here:

```
        class Employee implements Serializable
        {
                //instance var
                private int id;
                private String name;
                private float sal;
                private Date doj;
        }
```

Then create an object to this class and store actual data into that object. Later, this object should be stored into a file using ObjectOutputStream. Please observe that the Serializable interface should be implemented by the class whose objects are to be stored into the file. This is the reason why Employee class implements Serializable interface.

To store the Employee class objects into a file, follow these steps:

❑   First, attach objfile to FileOutputStream. This helps to write data into objfile.

```
        FileOutputStream fos = new FileOutputStream("objfile");
```

❑   Then, attach FileOutputStream to ObjectOutputStream.

```
        ObjectOutputStream oos = new ObjectOutputStream(fos);
```

❑ Now, `ObjectOutputStream` can write objects using `writeObject()` method to `FileOutputStream`, which stores them into the `objfile`.

Storing objects into a file like this is called 'serialization'. The reverse process where objects can be retrieved back from a file is called 'de-serialization'.

Important Interview Question

What is serialization?

Serialization is the process of storing object contents into a file. The class whose objects are stored in the file should implement 'Serializable' interface of java.io package.

Serializable interface is an empty interface without any members in it. It does not contain any methods also. Such an interface is called 'marking interface' or 'tagging interface'. Marking interface is useful to mark the objects of a class for a special purpose. For example, 'Serializable' interface marks the class objects as 'serializable' so that they can be written into a file. If Serializable interface is not implemented by the class, then writing that class objects into a file will lead to `NotSerializableException`. However, any static and transient variables of the class cannot be serialized. Suppose, we declare variables in the class as:

```
static int x = 15;
transient String str= "mypassword";
```

Now, these variables cannot be written into the file. Such variables are useful when the programmer wants to restrain from storing some sensitive data into the file.

Important Interview Question

Which type of variables cannot be serialized?

static and transient variables cannot be serialized.

Once the objects are stored into a file, they can be later retrieved and used as and when needed. This is called de-serialization.

What is de-serialization?

De-serialization is a process of reading back the objects from a file.

To read `Employee` class objects from `objfile`, follow these steps:

❑ Attach `objfile` to `FileInputStream`. This helps to read objects from `objfile`.

```
FileInputStream fis = new FileInputStream("objfile");
```

❑ Attach `FileInputStream` to `ObjectInputStream`. This `ObjectInputStream` gets the objects from `FileInputStream`.

```
ObjectInputStream ois = new ObjectInputStream(fis);
```

❑ Now, read objects from `ObjectInputStream` using `readObject()` method as:

```
Employee e = (Employee) ois.readObject();
```

The serialization process is shown in Programs 9 and 10 while Program 11 is showing the de-serialization.

Program 9: Write a program to create `Employee` class whose objects are to be stored into a file.

```java
//Employee class
import java.io.*;
import java.util.Date;
class Employee implements Serializable
{
        //instance var
        private int id;
        private String name;
        private float sal;
        private Date doj;

        //initialize the var
        Employee(int i, String n, float s, Date d)
        {
                id = i;
                name = n;
                sal = s;
                doj = d;
        }
        //to display employee details
        void display()
        {
                System.out.println(id+"\t"+name+"\t"+sal+"\t"+doj);
        }
        //to accept data from keyboard and store into Employee object
        static Employee getData() throws IOException
        {

                //to accept data from keyboard
                BufferedReader br = new BufferedReader(new
                InputStreamReader(System.in));

                //accept employee id number, name and salary
                System.out.print("Enter emp id: ");
                int id= Integer.parseInt(br.readLine());

                System.out.print("Enter name: ");
                String name = br.readLine();

                System.out.print("Enter salary: ");
                float sal = Float.parseFloat(br.readLine());

                //take current system date and time as for joining
                Date d = new Date();

                //create Employee object with the accepted data
                Employee e= new Employee(id, name, sal, d);

                //return the Employee object
                return e;
        }
}
```

Output:

```
C\>javac Employee.java
```

Program 10: Write a program to show serialization of objects.

```java
//ObjectOutputStream is used to store objects to a file
import java.io.*;
import java.util.*;
class StoreObj
```

```
    {
        public static void main(String args[ ]) throws Exception
        {
            //to accept data from keyboard
            BufferedReader br = new BufferedReader(new
            InputStreamReader(System.in));

            //to store objects into objfile
            FileOutputStream fos = new FileOutputStream("objfile");
            ObjectOutputStream oos = new ObjectOutputStream(fos);

            //ask how many objects to store
            System.out.print("How many objects? ");
            int n =Integer.parseInt(br.readLine());

            //store n objects into objfile
            for(int i=0; i<n; i++)
            {
                //create Employee object with data from keyboard
                Employee e1= Employee.getData();

                //store Employee object into ObjectOutputStream
                oos.writeObject(e1);
            }
            //close the objfile
            oos.close();
        }
    }
```

Output:

```
C:\> javac StoreObj.java
C:\> java StoreObj
How many objects? 3
Enter emp id: 10
Enter name: Suresh
Enter salary: 9800.50
Enter emp id: 11
Enter name: Rajani
Enter salary: 5000.75
Enter emp id: 12
Enter name: Swapna
Enter salary: 3000.00
```

Program 11: Write a program showing de-serialization of objects.

```
//ObjectInputStream is used to read objects from a file
import java.io.*;
class GetObj
{
    public static void main(String args[ ]) throws Exception
    {
        //to read objects from objfile
        FileInputStream fis = new FileInputStream("objfile");
        ObjectInputStream ois = new ObjectInputStream(fis);

        //read objects and display till a null object is read
        try{
            Employee e;
            while((e = (Employee) ois.readObject())!= null)
            {
                e.display();
            }
        }catch(EOFException ee){
            System.out.println("End of file reached");
        }
}
```

```
                    finally{
                    //close the objfile
                    ois.close();
                    }
            }
    }
```

Output:

```
C:\> javac GetObj.java
C:\> java GetObj
10    Suresh  9800.5          Tue Sep 25 19:56:44 GMT+05:30 2007
11    Rajani       5000.75 Tue Sep 25 19:57:03 GMT+05:30 2007
12    Swapna  3000.0          Tue Sep 25 19:57:20 GMT+05:30 2007
End of file reached
```

In this program, we read `Employee` class objects from `objfile` using `readObject()` method of `ObjectInputStream` class.

Counting Number of Characters in a File

Let us write a program to count number of characters, words, and lines of a text file. To count the number of characters, we take a counter `char_count` that is incremented whenever a character is read using `read()` method. To count non-space characters, we can use the logic:

```
if(ch != ' ')  ++char_count;
```

To count the number of words, we take a counter `word_count` that is incremented whenever a space is found, since words are separated by spaces. But, we should not count repeated spaces between words. For this purpose, we use:

```
if(!prev && ch == ' ')  ++word_count;
if(ch == ' ')  prev=true; else prev= false;
```

where, `prev` is a boolean variable that becomes `true` if there is a space encountered previously.

To count the number of lines, we take a counter `line_count` that is incremented whenever a \n is found. This \n is released when Enter button is pressed at the end of a line.

```
if(ch == '\n')  ++line_count;
```

Pressing Enter button releases two characters at the end of each line. They are \r and \n. These characters are counted as 2 characters by our program. So these excess characters (2 per a line) should be deducted from the character count. Similarly, when three words are there in a line, they get 2 spaces between. Since, we count only spaces to judge the number of words, we should add the number of lines to the `word_count` to get correct number of words. This logic is used in Program 12.

Program 12: Write a program which accepts a filename from command line argument and displays the number of characters, words, and lines in the file.

```
//Counting no. of chars in a text file
import java.io.*;
class Count
{
    public static void main(String args[ ])
    throws IOException
    {
```

```
                //vars
                int ch;
                boolean prev= true;

                //counters
                int char_count=0;
                int word_count=0;
                int line_count=0;
                //attach the file: args[0] to FileInputStream to read data
                FileInputStream fin = new FileInputStream(args[0]);
                //read characters from the file till the end
                while((ch= fin.read()) != -1)
                {
                        if(ch != ' ') ++char_count;
                        if(!prev && ch == ' ') ++word_count;
                        //dont count if previous char is space
                        if(ch == ' ') prev=true; else prev= false;
                        if(ch == '\n') ++line_count;

                }
                //display the count of characters, words and lines
                char_count -= line_count*2;
                word_count += line_count;
                System.out.println("No. of chars= "+ char_count);
                System.out.println("No. of words= "+ word_count);
                System.out.println("No. of lines= "+ line_count);

                //close the file
                fin.close();

        }
}
```

Output:

```
C:\> javac Count.java
C:\> java Count myfile
No. of chars= 44
No. of words= 12
No. of lines= 6
```

File Copy

Sometimes we need to copy the entire data of a text file into another text file. Streams are useful in this case. To understand how to use streams for copying a file content to another file, we can use the following logic:

❑ For reading data from the input file, attach it to `FileInputStream`.

❑ For writing data into the output file, which is to be created, attach it to `FileOutputStream`.

❑ Now, read data from `FileInputStream` and write into `FileOutputStream`. This means, the data is read from the input file and send to output file.

These steps are implemented in Program 13. Please note that this program can copy not only text files, but also image (`.gif` or `.jpg`) files.

Program 13: Write a program to read the contents of the input file and write them into an output file. The input file needs to be already available.

```
//Copying a file contents as another file.
import java.io.*;
class CopyFile
{
```

```
        public static void main(String args[ ])
        throws IOException
        {

                //take a var
                int ch;

                //for reading data from args[0]
                FileInputStream fin = new FileInputStream(args[0]);

                //for writing data into args[1]
                FileOutputStream fout = new FileOutputStream(args[1]);

                //read from FileInputStream and write into FileOutputStream
                while((ch= fin.read()) != -1)
                fout.write(ch);

                //close the files
                fin.close();
                fout.close();

                System.out.println("1 file copied");
        }
}
```

Output:

```
C:\> javac CopyFile.java
C:\> java CopyFile  car.gif  car11.gif
1 file copied
```

The output file is created by this program. The names of both the input file and output file are passed from command line arguments.

File Class

File class of `java.io` package provides some methods to know the properties of a file or a directory. First of all, we should create the File class object by passing the filename or directory name to it.

```
File obj = new File(filename);
File obj = new File(directoryname);
File obj = new File("path", filename);
File obj= new File("path", directoryname);
```

Remember, when we pass a filename or directory name, it need not necessarily exist on our computer. We can also judge whether it really exists on our computer system or not using File class methods.

File Class Methods

`File class` includes the following methods:

❑ `boolean isFile()`: This method returns true if the File object contains a filename, otherwise false.

❑ `boolean isDirectory()`: This method returns true if the File objects contains a directory name.

❑ `boolean canRead()`: This method returns true if the File object contains a file which is readable.

❑ `boolean canWrite()`: This method returns true if the file is writeable.

- ❏ `boolean can Execute()`: This method returns true if the file is executable.
- ❏ `boolean exists()`: This method returns true when the File object contains a file or directory which physically exists in the computer.
- ❏ `String getParent()`: This method returns the name of the parent directory of a file or directory.
- ❏ `String getPath()`: This method gives the name of directory path of a file or directory.
- ❏ `String getAbsolutePath()`: This method gives the absolute directory path of a file or directory location. Absolute path is mentioned starting from the root directory.
- ❏ `long length()`: This method returns a number that represents the size of the file in bytes.
- ❏ `boolean delete()`: This method deletes the file or directory whose name is in File object.
- ❏ `boolean createNewFile()`: This method automatically creates a new, empty file indicated by File object, if and only if a file with this name does not yet exist.
- ❏ `boolean mkdir()`: This method creates the directory whose name is given in File object.
- ❏ `boolean renameTo(File newname)`: This method changes the name of the file as `newname`.
- ❏ `String[ ] list()`: This method returns an array of strings naming the files and directories in the directory.

Let us write a program that accepts a file or directory name from command line arguments. Then the program checks if that file or directory physically exists or not and it displays the properties of that file or directory. This is shown in Program 14.

Program 14: Write a program that accepts a file or directory name from command line arguments.

Pass the filename or directory name at command line to this program. This program will display its properties.

```
//Displaying file properties
import java.io.*;
class FileProp
{
    public static void main(String args[ ])
    {
        //accept file name or directory name through command line args
        String fname = args[0];
        //pass the filename or directory name to File object
        File f = new File(fname);
        //apply File class methods on File object
        System.out.println("File name: "+ f.getName());
        System.out.println("Path: "+ f.getPath());
        System.out.println("Absolute path: "+ f.getAbsolutePath());
        System.out.println("Parent: "+ f.getParent());
        System.out.println("Exists: "+ f.exists());
        if(f.exists())
        {
            System.out.println("Is writeable: "+ f.canWrite());
            System.out.println("Is readable: "+ f.canRead());
            System.out.println("Is a directory: "+ f.isDirectory());
            System.out.println("File size in bytes: "+ f.length());
        }
    }
}
```

Output:

```
C:\> javac FileProp.java
C:\> java FileProp myfile.txt
File name: myfile.txt
Path: myfile.txt
Absolute path: D:\rnr\myfile.txt
```

```
Parent: null
Exists: true
Is writeable: true
Is readable: true
Is a directory: false
File size in bytes: 61
```

We write another program, where we want to accept a directory name from the keyboard and then display all the contents of the directory. For this purpose, list() method can be used as:

```
String arr[ ] = f.list();
```

In the preceding statement, the list() method causes all the directory entries copied into the array arr[ ]. Then we pass these array elements arr[i] to File object and test them to know if they represent a file or directory.

```
File f1 = new File(arr[i]);
if(f1.isFile()) System.out.println(": is a file");
if(f1.isDirectory()) System.out.println(": is a directory");
```

This logic is implemented in Program 15.

Program 15: Write a program to accept a directory name and display its contents into an array.

```
//Display the contents of a directory.
import java.io.*;
class Contents
{
      public static void main(String args[ ]) throws IOException
      {
            // enter the path and dirname from keyboard
            BufferedReader br = new BufferedReader(new
            InputStreamReader(System.in));

            System.out.print("Enter dirpath: ");
            String dirpath = br.readLine();
            System.out.print("Enter dirname: ");
            String dname = br.readLine();

            //create File object with dirpath and dname
            File f = new File(dirpath, dname);

            //if directory exists, then
            if(f.exists())
            {
                  //get the contents into arr[ ]
                  //now arr[i] represents either a file or sub directory
                  String arr[ ] = f.list();

                  //find no.of entries in the directory
                  int n = arr.length;

                  //display the entries
                  for(int i=0; i<n; i++)
                  {
                        System.out.print(arr[i]);
                        //create File object with the entry and test
                        //if it is a file or directory
                        File f1 = new File(arr[i]);
                        if(f1.isFile()) System.out.println(": is a file");
                        if(f1.isDirectory()) System.out.println(": is a
                        directory");
                  }
```

```
                        System.out.println("No of entries in this directory: "+ n);
        }
        else System.out.println("Directory does not exist");
    }
}
```

Output:

```
C:\> javac Contents.java
C:\> java Contents
Enter dirpath: c:\
Enter dirname: rnr
DIAMONDS.GIF: is a file
MyMessage.java: is a file
Myclass.class: is a file
textfile: is a file
twist.gif: is a file
same: is a directory
pool: is a directory
pack: is a directory
oracle: is a directory
misc: is a directory
jdbc: is a directory
advjava: is a directory
Thumbs.db: is a file
Search.class: is a file
mypack: is a directory
App.java: is a file
Palindrome.java: is a file
One.class: is a file
Table.java: is a file
Table.class: is a file
:
:

No of entries in this directory: 320
```

In this program, we accept the directory name and get its contents into an array `arr[ ]`. Then we pass these array elements arr[i] to File object and test them each to know if it is a file or directory.

Conclusion

Streams are needed to move data from one place to another. Input streams help to receive data coming from another place, whereas output streams help to send data to some other place. Byte streams handle data in the form of individual bytes and Character streams are useful to receive and send characters. Using streams, it is possible to store data permanently in the form of files on a secondary storage medium. If the programmer wants to store structured data, he should store the data first in a class object and then the object contents should be written to a file. This is called serialization. However, these techniques are not suitable for handling large volumes of data. For this purpose, the programmer should go for a database like Oracle or Sybase where the data is stored in the form of tables, and then a Java program can be constructed to retrieve and use the data of the database.

NETWORKING IN JAVA

CHAPTER

25

When we have several computers and each one's resources should be available to the other computers, then we should connect all the computers. This is called a network. A network represents interconnection of computers either by using a cable or a satellite where no cable is needed. In a network, there may be several computers—some of them receiving the services and some providing the services to others. The computer which receives service is called a 'client' and the computer which provides the service is called a 'server'. Remember, a client sometimes acts as a server and a server acts as a client.

There are 3 requirements to establish a network:

❑ Hardware: includes the computers, cables, modems, hubs, etc.

❑ Software: includes programs to communicate between servers and clients.

❑ Protocol: represents a way to establish connection and helps in sending and receiving data in a standard format.

Let us now discuss Protocol in some detail.

TCP/IP Protocol

A protocol represents a set of rules to be followed by every computer on the network. Protocol is useful to physically move data from one place to another place on a network. TCP (Transmission Control Protocol) / IP (Internet Protocol) is the standard protocol model used on any network, including Internet.

TCP/IP model has got the following 5 layers:

❑ Application layer

❑ TCP

❑ IP

❑ Data link layer

❑ Physical layer

Application layer is the topmost layer of the TCP/IP model that directly interacts with an application (or data). This layer receives data from the application and formats the data. Then it sends that data to the next layer called TCP in the form of continuous stream of bytes. The TCP, upon receiving the data from the Application layer, will divide it into small segments called 'packets'. A packet contains a group of bytes of data. These packets are then sent to the next IP layer. IP layer inserts the packets into envelopes called 'frames'. Each frame contains a packet, the IP address of destination computer, the IP address of source computer, and some additional bits useful in error detection and correction. These frames are then sent to Data link layer which dispatches them to correct destination computer on the network. The last layer, which is called the Physical layer, is used to physically transmit data on the network using the appropriate hardware. See Figure 25.1.

Of course, to send data from one place to another, first of all the computers should be correctly identified on the network. This is done with the help of IP addresses. An IP address is a unique identification number given to every computer on the network. It contains four integer numbers in the range of 0 to 255 and separated by a dot as:

> 87.248.113.14

This IP address may represent, for example a website on a server machine on Internet as:

www.yahoo.com

Therefore, to open 'yahoo.com' site, we can type the site address as 'www.yahoo.com' or its IP address as '87.248.113.14'. But when we type the IP address in numeric form, that number is mapped to the website automatically. This mapping service is available on Internet, which is called 'DNS' (Domain Naming service).

Important Interview Question

What is IP address?

An IP address is a unique identification number allotted to every computer on a network or Internet. IP address contains some bytes which identify the network and the actual computer inside the network.

What is DNS?

Domain Naming Service is a service on Internet that maps the IP addresses with corresponding website names.

On Internet, IP addresses of 4 bytes are used and this version is called IP address version 4. The next new version of IP address is version 6, which uses 16 bytes to identify a computer.

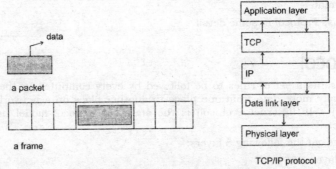

Figure 25.1 Packet, frame, TCP/IP layers

TCP/IP takes care of number of bits sent and whether all the bits are received duly by the destination computer. So it is called 'connection oriented reliable protocol'. Every transmitted bit is accountable in this protocol. Hence, this protocol is highly suitable for transporting data reliably on a network. Almost all the protocols on Internet use TCP/IP model internally.

HTTP (hyper text transfer protocol) is the most widely used protocol on Internet, which is used to transfer web pages (.html files) from one computer to another computer on Internet. FTP (file transfer protocol) is useful to download or upload files from and to the server. SMTP (simple mail transfer protocol) is useful to send mails on network. POP (post office protocol) is useful to receive mails into the mail boxes.

User Datagram Protocol (UDP)

UDP is another protocol that transfers data in a connection less and unreliable manner. It will not check how many bits are sent or how many bits are actually received at the other side. During transmission of data, there may be loss of some bits. Hence, UDP is used to send images, audio files, and video files. Even if some bits are lost, still the image or audio file can be composed with a slight variation that will not disturb the original image or audio.

Sockets

It is possible to establish a logical connecting point between a server and a client so that communication can be done through that point. This point is called 'socket'.

Important Interview Question

What is a socket?

A socket is a point of connection between a server and a client on a network.

Each socket is given an identification number, which is called 'port number'. Port number takes 2 bytes and can be from 0 to 65,535. Establishing communication between a server and a client using sockets is called 'socket programming'.

Important Interview Question

What is port number?

Port number is a 2 byte number which is used to identify a socket uniquely.

We should use a new port number for each new socket. Similarly, we should allot a new port number depending on the service provided on a socket. Every new service on the net should be assigned a new port number. Please have a look at some already allotted port numbers for the services shown in Table 25.1. Avoid using same port numbers, which are already used by applications running in your system.

Table 25.1

Port number	Application or service
13	Data and time services
21	FTP which transfers files
23	Telnet, which provides remote login
25	SMTP, which delivers mails
67	BOOTP, which provides configuration at boot time
80	HTTP, which transfers web pages
109	POP, which accesses mail boxes

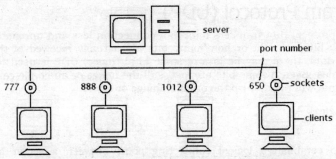

Figure 25.2 A server connected with clients using sockets

A socket, at server side is called 'server socket ' and is created using ServerSocket class in Java. A socket, at client side is called 'Socket' and is created using Socket class. Both the ServerSocket and Socket classes are available in java.net package. Of course, a server socket may not be necessarily at server side; it may be created at client side also, if the client acts as server. Similarly, a client socket may also exist at server side, if the server acts as client.

Knowing IP Address

It is possible to know the IP Address of a website on Internet with the help of getByName() method of InetAddress class of java.net package. The getByName() method takes host name (server name) and returns InetAddress, which is nothing but the IPAddress of that server. See the following program.

Program 1: Write a program to accept a website name and return its IPAddress, after checking it on Internet.

Note

This program should be executed on a system which is connected to Internet.

```
//Knowing IPAddress of a website
import java.io.*;
import java.net.*;
class Address
{
      public static void main(String args[ ]) throws IOException
      {
            //accept name of website from keyboard
            BufferedReader br = new BufferedReader(new
             InputStreamReader(System.in));
            System.out.print("Enter a website name: ");
            String site = br.readLine();
            try{
                  //getByName() method accepts site name and returns its IP
                  //Address
                  InetAddress ip = InetAddress.getByName(site);
                  System.out.println("The IP Address is: "+ ip);
            }catch(UnknownHostException ue)
            {
                  System.out.println("Website not found");
            }
      }
}
```

Output:

```
C:\> javac Address.java
C:\> java Address
Enter a website name: www.yahoo.com
The IP Address is: www.yahoo.com/87.248.113.14
```

URL

URL (Uniform Resource Locator) represents the address that is specified to access some information or resource on Internet. Look at the example URL:

`http://www.dreamtechpress.com:80/index.html`

The URL contains 4 parts:

❑ The protocol to use (`http://`).

❑ The server name or IP address of the server (`www.dreamtechpress.com`).

❑ The third part represents port number, which is optional (`:80`).

❑ The last part is the file that is referred. This would be generally `index.html` or `home.html` file (`/index.html`).

URL is represented by a class 'URL' in `java.net` package. To create an object to URL, we can use the following formats:

```
URL obj = new URL(String protocol, String host, int port, String path);
```

Or,

```
URL obj = new URL(String protocol, String host, String path);
```

The following program accesses the different parts of the URL supplied to URL object and displays them.

Program 2: Write a program to retrieve different parts of a URL supplied to URL class object.

```
//URL
import java.net.*;
class MyURL
{
    public static void main(String args[ ]) throws Exception
    {
        URL obj = new URL("http://dreamtechpress.com/index.html");
        System.out.println("Protocol: "+ obj.getProtocol());
        System.out.println("Host: "+ obj.getHost());
        System.out.println("File: "+ obj.getFile());
        System.out.println("Port: "+ obj.getPort());
        System.out.println("Path: "+ obj.getPath());
        System.out.println("External form: "+ obj.toExternalForm());
    }
}
```

Output:

```
C:\> javac MyURL.java
C:\> java MyURL
Protocol: http
Host: dreamtechpress.com
File: /index.html
```

```
Port: -1
Path: /index.html
External form: http://dreamtechpress.com/index.html
```

Please note that port number is displayed as -1 in the output, which represents that no port number is passed in the URL.

URLConnection Class

URLConnection class is useful to actually connect to a website or resource on a network and get all the details of the website. For example, to know the details of www.yahoo.com, we should pass its URL to the object of URL class. Then using openConnection() method, we should establish a contact with the site on Internet. This method returns URLConnection object. Then using URLConnection class methods, we can display all the details of the website and also content of the webpage whose name is given in URL. This is shown in Program 3. Note that this program should be executed on a computer where the Internet connection is enabled.

Program 3: Write a program to display the details and the index.html page contents of www.yahoo.com.

```java
//connecting to www.yahoo.com and getting the details.
import java.io.*;
import java.net.*;
import java.util.*;
class Details
{
    public static void main(String args[ ]) throws Exception
    {
        //pass the site url to URL object
        URL obj = new URL("http://www.yahoo.com/index.html");
        //open a connection with the site on Internet
        URLConnection conn = obj.openConnection();
        //display the date
        System.out.println("Date: "+ new Date(conn.getDate()));
        //display the content type whether text or html
        System.out.println("Content-type: "+ conn.getContentType());
        //display expiry date
        System.out.println("Expiry: "+ conn.getExpiration());
        //display last modified date
        System.out.println("Last modified: "+ new
         Date(conn.getLastModified()));
        //display how many bytes the index.html page has
        int l = conn.getContentLength();
        System.out.println("Length of content: "+ l);
        if(l == 0)
        {
            System.out.println("Content not available");
            return;
        }
        else {
            int ch;
            InputStream in = conn.getInputStream();
            //display the content of the index.html page
            while((ch = in.read())!= -1)
            System.out.print((char)ch);
        }
    }
}
```

Output:

```
C:\> javac Details.java
```

```
C:\> java Details
Date: Thu Sep 27 20:04:49 GMT+05:30 2007
Content-type: text/html; charset=utf-8
Expiry: 0
Last modified: Thu Sep 27 19:47:52 GMT+05:30 2007
Length of content: 9431
<html>
<head>
<title>Yahoo!</title>
<meta http-equiv="Content-Type" content="text/html; charset=UTF-8">
<meta http-equiv="PICS-Label" content='(PICS-1.1
 "http://www.icra.org/ratingsv02.html"

l r (cz 1 lz 1 nz 1 oz 1 vz 1) gen true for "http://www.yahoo.com" r
 (cz 1 lz 1 nz 1

oz 1 vz 1) "http://www.rsac.org/ratingsv01.html" l r (n 0 s 0 v 0 l 0)
 gen true for

"http://www.yahoo.com" r (n 0 s 0 v 0 l 0))'>
<base
    href="http://www.yahoo.com/_ylh=
X3oDMTFnN2Rkcmg4BF9TAzI3MTYxNDkEcGlkAzExOTA5MDI0ODUEdG
    VzdAMwBHRtcGwDdGFibGUuaHRtbA--/" target="_top">
<style type="text/css">
a{color:#16387c;}
a:link,a:visited{text-decoration:none;}
a:hover{text-decoration:underline;}
</style>
<style type="text/css" media="all">
#p{width:310px;}
form{margin:0;}
</style>
</head>
<body link="#16387c" vlink="#16387c">
<center>
<table cellpadding="0" cellspacing="0" border="0" bgcolor="#EEF3F6" width="760">
<tr><td colspan="3">
<table cellpadding="0" cellspacing="0" border="0" width="0"><tr><td width="0"
    height="7"><spacer type="block" width="0" height="7"></td></tr></table>
</td></tr>
<tr>
<td width="10" height="0" rowspan="2"><spacer type="block" width="10"
 height="0"></td>
<td height="56" valign="top">
<img src="http://us.a1.yimg.com/us.yimg.com/i/ww/beta/y3.gif" width="232"
 height="44"
    alt="Yahoo!" title="Yahoo">
</td>
<td rowspan="2">
<table cellpadding="1" cellspacing="0" border="0" bgcolor="#BFCFD7"><tr><td>
<table cellpadding="20" cellspacing="0" border="0"
 bgcolor="#F4F6F5"><tr><td><font
    face="arial" size="-1">
<form name="sf1" action="r/sx/*-http://search.yahoo.com/search">
<input type="hidden" name="ei" value="UTF-8" />
<input type="hidden" name="fr" value="yfp-t-501" />
<input type="hidden" name="cop" value="mss" />
:
:
```

Creating a Server That Sends Data

We can create a socket that can be used to connect a server and a client. Once the socket is created, the server can send data to the client and the client can receive it. All we have to do is to just send the data from the server to the socket. The socket will take care of whom to send data on the network. Let us follow these steps to create a server that sends some strings (messages) to the client:

❑ At server side, create a server socket with some port number. This is done using `ServerSocket` class as:

```
ServerSocket ss = new ServerSocket(777);
```

❑ Now, we should make the server wait till a client accepts connection. This is done using `accept()` method.

```
Socket s = ss.accept();
```

❑ Attach output stream to the server socket using `getOutputStream()` method. This method returns `OutputStream` object. This stream is used by the socket to send data to client.

```
OutputStream obj = s.getOutputStream();
```

❑ Take another stream like `PrintStream` to send data till the socket.

```
PrintStream ps = new PrintStream(obj);
```

❑ Finally, this `PrintStream` is used by the server to send data to the client. To send data, we have `print()` or `println()` methods available in `PrintStream`.

```
ps.println(str);
```

❑ Then close the connection. This can be done by closing all the streams and sockets at sever side as:

```
ss.close();   //close ServerSocket
s.close();    //close Socket
ps.close();   //close PrintStream
```

All these steps are shown in Figure 25.3 and also implemented in Program 4.

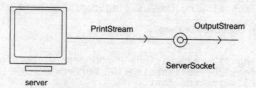

Figure 25.3 A server that sends data

Program 4: Write a program to create a server for the purpose of sending some strings to the client.

```
//Server1 - to send strings
import java.io.*;
import java.net.*;
class Server1
{
     public static void main(String args[ ])
     throws Exception
     {
          //Create a server socket with some port number
          ServerSocket ss = new ServerSocket(777);
```

```
                      //let the server wait till a client accepts connection
                      Socket s = ss.accept();
                      System.out.println("Connection established");
                      //attach output stream to the server socket
                      OutputStream obj = s.getOutputStream();
                      //attach print stream to send data to the socket
                      PrintStream ps = new PrintStream(obj);
                      //send 2 strings to the client
                      String str = "Hello client";               \
                      ps.println(str);
                      ps.println("Bye");
                      //close connection by closing the streams and sockets
                      ps.close();
                      ss.close();
                      s.close();
                }
          }
```

Ouput:

```
      D:\rnr> javac Server1.java
      D:\rnr>
      DO NOT RUN THIS PROGRAM TILL CLIENT IS ALSO CREATED...
```

Creating a Client That Receives Data

We can write a client program that receives all the strings sent from the server. Let us follow these steps to do this:

❑   First, we should create a socket at client side using `Socket` class as:

```
      Socket s = new Socket("IPAddress", port number);
```

Here, the `IPAddress` represents the IPAddress of the server machine where `Server1.java` program is running. To know the IPAddress, we can use DOS command, as:

```
      C:\> ipconfig
```

This will display the IPAddress of the machine where the command is applied.

Or, we can follow the commands:

Start -> settings -> control panel -> Network connections ->right click on this to see the 'local area connection' dialog box and there double click on Internet protocol (TCP/IP).

It opens Internet protocol properties dialog box where we can see the IPAddress. See Figure 25.4.

It is possible to run the `Server1.java` and `Client1.java` programs on two different computers connected in a network. But, at `Client1.java`, we should pass the server machine's IPAddress. Then the port number at `Client1.java` should be same as the port number with which the server socket has been created. In case, you do not have your computer in a network, you have to run both the server and client programs in the same system. In that case, you can use `localhost` in place of `IPAddress`. The word `localhost` represents that the server is also locally available in the same system.

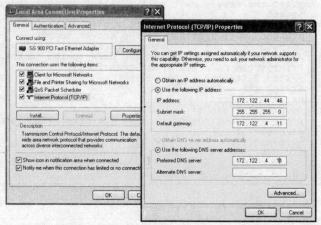

Figure 25.4 IPAddress of a computer system

❑ We should add InputStream to the socket so that the socket will be able to receive the data on the InputStream.

```
    InputStream obj = s.getInputStream();
```

❑ To read the data from the socket into the client, we can take the help of BufferedReader as:

```
    BufferedReader br = new BufferedReader(new InputStreamReader(obj));
```

❑ Now we can read data from the BufferedReader object, using read() or readLine() methods. Read() method can read a single character at a time, where as readLine() can read a string.

```
    str = br.readLine();
```

❑ Close the connection by closing all the streams and sockets.

```
    br.close();  //close the BufferedReader
    s.close();   //close the Socket
```

All these steps are shown in Figure 25.4 and also implemented in Program 5.

Figure 25.5 A client that receives data

Program 5: Write a program to create client side program, which accepts all the strings sent by the server.

```
    //Client1 - to receive strings
    import java.io.*;
    import java.net.*;
```

```
class Client1
{
    public static void main(String args[ ])
    throws Exception
    {
        //create client socket with same port number
        Socket s = new Socket("localhost", 777);
        //to read data coming from server, attach InputStream to the socket
        InputStream obj = s.getInputStream();
        //to read data from the socket into the client, use BufferedReader
        BufferedReader br = new BufferedReader(new InputStreamReader(obj));
        //receive strings
        String str;
        while((str = br.readLine()) != null)
        System.out.println("From server: "+str);
        //close connection by closing the streams and sockets
        br.close();
        s.close();
    }
}
```

Output:

```
D:\rnr> javac Client1.java
D:\rnr>
```

To run the server and client in the same system:

After compiling server1.java and client1.java, run these programs in two separate dos windows, as shown in the output.

To run in different systems:

Run the server1.java in a computer and client1.java in another. They should have been connected in a network.

Run the Server1.java in a DOS window, the server would be in waiting state, expecting a connection from a client. Then run Client1.java in another DOS window. Immediately the connection is established, and at server side it displays "Connection established". Then it sends two strings "Hello client" and "Bye" to the client, which are received and displayed at client terminal. When the server disconnects, it sends a null string to the client. When client receives null, it also disconnects.

Two-way Communication between Server and Client

It is possible to send data from the server and receive the response from the client. Similarly, the client can also send and receive the data to-and-fro. For this purpose, we need additional streams both at server and client. For example, to receive data into the server, it is a better idea to use `BufferedReader` as:

```
InputStream obj = s.getInputStream();
BufferedReader br = new BufferedReader(new InputStreamReader(obj);
```

Then `read()` or `readLine()` methods of `BufferedReader` class can be used to read data.

To send data from the client, we can take the help of `DataOutputStream` as:

```
OutputStream obj = s.getOutputStream();
DataOutputStream dos = new DataOutputStream(obj);
```

Then `writeBytes()` method of `DataOutputStream` can be used to send strings in the form of group of bytes.

Program 6: Write a program to create a server such that the server receives data from the client using `BufferedReader` and then sends reply to the client using `PrintStream`.

```
//Server2 - A server that receives data and sends data
import java.io.*;
import java.net.*;
class Server2
{
      public static void main(String args[ ])
      throws Exception
      {
            //Create server socket
            ServerSocket ss = new ServerSocket(888);
            //connect it to client socket
            Socket s = ss.accept();
            System.out.println("Connection established");
            //to send data to the client
            PrintStream ps = new PrintStream(s.getOutputStream());
            //to read data coming from the client
            BufferedReader br = new BufferedReader(new
             InputStreamReader(s.getInputStream()));
            //to read data from the key board
            BufferedReader kb = new BufferedReader(new
             InputStreamReader(System.in));
            while(true)  //server executes continuously
            {
                  String str,str1;
                  //repeat as long as client does not send null string
                  while((str = br.readLine()) != null)  //read from client
                  {
                        System.out.println(str);
                        str1 = kb.readLine();
                        ps.println(str1); //send to client
                  }
                  //close connection
                  ps.close();
                  br.close();
                  kb.close();
                  ss.close();
                  s.close();
                  System.exit(0); //terminate application
            } //end of while
      }
}
```

Output:

```
D:\rnr> javac Sever2.java
```

```
D:\rnr>
```

Program 7: Write a program to create a client which first connects to a server, then starts the communication by sending a string to the server. The server sends response to the client. When 'exit' is typed at client side, the program terminates.

```java
//Client2 - a client that sends data and receives also
import java.io.*;
import java.net.*;
class Client2
{
    public static void main(String args[ ])
    throws Exception
    {
        //create client socket
        Socket s = new Socket("localhost", 888);
        //to send data to the server
        DataOutputStream dos = new DataOutputStream(s.getOutputStream());
        //to read data coming from the server
        BufferedReader  br = new BufferedReader(new
         InputStreamReader(s.getInputStream()));
        //to read data from the key board
        BufferedReader kb = new BufferedReader(new
         InputStreamReader(System.in));
        String str,str1;
        //repeat as long as exit is not typed at client
        while(!(str = kb.readLine()).equals("exit"))
        {
            dos.writeBytes(str+"\n");   //send to server
            str1 = br.readLine(); //receive from server
            System.out.println(str1);
        }
        //close connection.
        dos.close();
        br.close();
        kb.close();
        s.close();
    }
}
```

Output:

```
D:\rnr> javac Client2.java
D:\rnr>
```

Run the `server2.java` and `client2.java` in two dos windows.

See the output while running these programs.

Retrieving a file at server

Let us write client and server programs, such that the client sends the name of a file to the server. After receiving the filename, the server searches for the file to know if it exists or not. If the file exists, the server sends the file contents to the client. This is shown in Programs 8 and 9, which are self-explanatory.

Program 8: Write a program that accepts the filename and checks for its existence. When the file exists at server side, it sends its contents to the client.

```java
//A server that sends a file content to the client
import java.io.*;
import java.net.*;
class FileServer
{
        public static void main(String args[ ]) throws Exception
        {
                //create server socket
                ServerSocket ss = new ServerSocket(8888);

                //make the server wait till a client accepts connection
                Socket s = ss.accept();
                System.out.println("Connection established");

                //to accept file name from client
                BufferedReader in = new BufferedReader(new
                 InputStreamReader(s.getInputStream()));

                //to send file contents to client
                DataOutputStream out = new DataOutputStream(s.getOutputStream());

                //read the filename from the client
                String fname = in.readLine();

                FileReader fr = null;
                BufferedReader file = null;
                boolean flag;

                //create File class object with filename
                File f = new File(fname);

                //test if file exists or not
                if(f.exists()) flag = true;
                else flag = false;

                //if file exists, send "Yes" to client, else send "No"
                if(flag == true) out.writeBytes("Yes"+"\n");
                else out.writeBytes("No"+"\n");

                if(flag == true)
                {
                        //attach file to the FileReader to read data
                        fr = new FileReader(fname);

                        //attach FileReader to BufferedReader
                        file = new BufferedReader(fr);

                        String str;

                        //read from BufferedReader and write to DataOutputStream
                        while((str = file.readLine()) != null)
                        {
                                out.writeBytes(str+"\n");
                        }
                }
                file.close();
```

```
                                    out.close();
                                    in.close();
                                    fr.close();
                                    s.close();
                                    ss.close();
                    }
            }
    }
```

Output:

```
D:\rnr> javac FileServer.java
D:\rnr>
```

This is a server program that receives the file name from the client and if file exists, it sends "Yes", otherwise "No" to the client. This helps the client to understand whether the file really exists at server or not. Then this server program sends the file contents to the client if the file exists.

Program 9: Write a client program to accept a file name from the keyboard and send that name to the server. The client receives the file contents from the server.

```
//FileClient - receiving  a file content
import java.io.*;
import java.net.*;

class FileClient
{
        public static void main(String args[ ]) throws Exception
        {
                //Create client socket
                Socket s = new Socket("localhost", 8888);
                //accept filename from keyboard
                BufferedReader kb = new BufferedReader(new
                 InputStreamReader(System.in));

                System.out.print("Enter filename: ");
                String fname = kb.readLine();

                //send filename to the server using DataOutputStream
                DataOutputStream out = new DataOutputStream(s.getOutputStream());
                out.writeBytes(fname+"\n");

                //to read data coming from the server
                BufferedReader  in = new BufferedReader(new
                 InputStreamReader(s.getInputStream()));

                String str;

                //read first line from server into str
                str = in.readLine();

                //if file is found server returns "Yes", else "No"
                if(str.equals("Yes"))
                {
                        //read and display the file contents coming from server
                        while((str = in.readLine()) != null)
                        System.out.println(str);

                        //close connection by closing the streams.
                        kb.close();
                        out.close();
                        in.close();
                        s.close();
```

```
        }
        else System.out.println("File not found");

    }
}
```

Output:

```
D:\rnr> javac FileClient.java
D:\rnr>
```

This is a client program that accepts a file name from the keyboard and sends that name to the server. Then it reads the first line sent by the server. If it is Yes, then the file exists at server. If it is No then the file is not found at server. If file exists, then its contents are displayed at the client.

Run the fileserver.java and fileclient.java programs in two dos windows.

Conclusion

The classes of java.net package internally use TCP/IP and UDP protocols that are responsible for sending and receiving data. We can also establish communication between a server and a client by creating server socket and client socket. This is called 'socket programming'. The data can be then sent or received between sockets, with the help of streams. However, socket programming offers only basic networking. If we want to achieve sophisticated client-server communication, we should look forward to servlets, JSPs (Java Server Pages), etc.

THREADS

A thread represents a separate path of execution of a group of statements. In a Java program, if we write a group of statements, then these statements are executed by JVM one by one. This execution is called a thread, because JVM uses a thread to execute these statements. This means that in every Java program, there is always a thread running internally. This thread is used by JVM to execute the program statements. What is this thread? Let us write a program to see what that thread is:

Program 1: Write a program to find the thread used by JVM to execute the statements.

```
//To find currently running thread in this program
class Current
{
    public static void main(String args[ ])
    {
        System.out.println("Let us find current thread");
        Thread t = Thread.currentThread();
        System.out.println("Current thread= "+t);
        System.out.println("Its name= "+t.getName());
    }
}
```

Output:

```
C:\> javac Current.java
C:\> java Current
Let us find current thread
Current thread= Thread[main,5,main]
Its name= main
```

In the preceding program, currentThread() is a static method in Thread class. So we called it as Thread.currentThread(). Then this method gave an object t of Thread class. When we displayed this object t, it displayed its contents as:

    Thread[main,5,main]

Here, Thread indicates that t is a Thread class object. And the first main indicates the name of the thread running the current code. We get 5 which is a number representing the priority of the thread. Every thread will have a priority number associated with it. These priority numbers will range from 1 to 10. 1 is the minimum priority, and 10 is the maximum priority of a thread. If the priority number of a thread is more, it is given more preference while execution by JVM. The default priority number of a thread is 5.

The next main indicates the thread group name to which this thread belongs. A thread group represents a group of threads as a single unit. The 'main' thread belongs to 'main' thread group. See the last line in the output of the program. We are displaying the currently running thread's name which is 'main'. If a thread is t, its name can be known using t.getName() method.

What does the preceding program indicate? When we write any program in Java, JVM internally uses a thread called 'main thread' to run the statements of the program. This thread is responsible for executing our statements and displaying the results.

Important Interview Question

Which thread always runs in a Java program by default?

main thread.

A thread represents execution of statements. The way the statements are executed is of two types: 1) Single tasking 2) Multi tasking.

Single Tasking

A task means doing some calculation, processing, etc. Generally, a task involves execution of a group of statements, for example executing a program. In 'single tasking' environment, only one task is given to the processor at a time. See Figure 26.1. Here, let us take an example of a student who goes to the lab to write some programs. He types his first program. It may be taking some 10 minutes. When he is typing his program, the micro processor is sitting idle, without any work. After typing is completed, he gives the program to the processor. The processor executes it within a millisecond. Since now-a-days processors can execute millions of instructions per second, even if the student has written a program of 100 lines, the processor will not take more than a fraction of a second to complete its execution. After verifying the results, the student has started typing the second program. It may take another 10 or 15 minutes. Within this time, the processor sits idle, waiting for the job. When the student submits the second program, then it works for a fraction of a second on the program. Then again it goes into idle state. From this discussion, we can understand that the processor is sitting idle without any work for most of the time.

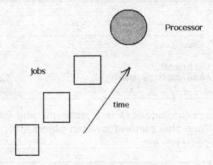

Figure 26.1 Single tasking

In single tasking, only one task is given to the processor at a time. This means we are wasting a lot of processor time and microprocessor has to sit idle without any job for a long time. This is the drawback in single tasking.

Multi Tasking

To use the processor's time in an optimum way, we can give it several jobs at a time. This is called multi tasking. But how can we give several jobs at a time? Suppose there are 4 tasks that we want to execute. We load them into the memory, as shown in Figure 26.2. The memory is divided into 4 parts and the jobs are loaded there. Now, the micro processor has to execute them all at a time. So the processor will take small time duration, like a millisecond and divide this time between the number of jobs. Here, 4 jobs are there. So we get ¼ millisecond time for each job. This small part of the processor time is called 'time slice'. It will allot exactly ¼ millisecond time for executing each of the jobs. Within this time slice, it will try to execute each job. Suppose, it started at first job, it will spend exactly ¼ millisecond time executing the first job. Within this time duration, if it could not complete the first job, then what it does? In that case, it stores the intermediate results till then it obtained in a temporary memory, and then it goes to the second task. It then spends exactly ¼ millisecond time executing the second task. Within this time, if it can complete this task, no problem. Suppose it could not complete this task, then it goes to the third task, storing the results in a temporary memory. Similarly, it will spend exactly ¼ millisecond for third task, and another ¼ millisecond for the fourth task. After executing the fourth task, it will come back to the first task, in a circular manner. This is called 'round robin' method.

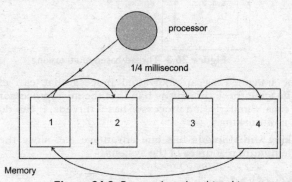

Figure 26.2 Process-based multi tasking

The processor, after returning to the first task, again starts execution from the point, where it has left that task earlier. It will execute the first task exactly for ¼ millisecond this time, and proceeds for the second task and then third and fourth before coming back to the first task in a round robin way. So if you have submitted the first job, you can understand that the processor is executing your job for ¼ millisecond and then keeping you waiting for another ¾ millisecond, while it is going and executing the other tasks. After ¾ millisecond, it is again coming back to your job and executing your job for another ¼ millisecond time. But you will not be aware that you are kept waiting for ¾ millisecond time, as this time is very small. You will feel that the processor is spending its time executing your job only. Similarly, the second person who submitted the second job will also feel that only his job is being executed by the processor. The third and fourth persons will also feel the same way. It is something like all the 4 jobs are executed by the processor simultaneously. This is called multi tasking.

Generally, we have only one processor in our Computer systems. One processor has to execute several tasks means that it has to execute them in a round robin method. Strictly speaking, this is not multi tasking, since the processor is quickly executing the tasks one by one, so quickly that we feel all the jobs are executed by the processor at a time. Multitasking cannot be a real phenomenon with single processor systems. If we want to really achieve multi tasking, we need Computers with multiple processors.

The main advantage of multi tasking is to use the processor time in a better way. We are engaging most of the processor time and it is not sitting idle. In this way, we can complete several tasks at a time, and thus achieve good performance.

Multi tasking is of two types: a) Process-based multi tasking b) Thread-based multi tasking. So far, we discussed the first type, i.e. Process-based multi tasking. Now let us think about Thread-based multi tasking.

In Process-based multi tasking, several programs are executed at a time, by the microprocessor. In Thread-based multi tasking, several parts of the same program is executed at a time, by the microprocessor. See Figure 26.3. Here, we have a program. In this program, there are 2 parts. These parts may represent two separate blocks of code or two separate methods containing code. Each part may perform a separate task. The processor should execute the two parts (tasks) simultaneously. So the processor uses 2 separate threads to execute these two parts.

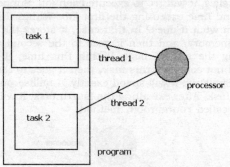

Figure 26.3 Thread-based multi tasking

Each thread can be imagined as an individual process that can execute a separate set of statements. We can imagine these threads as hands of the microprocessor. We have 2 hands, so we can do 2 things at a time. Similarly, if a processor has 2 threads, it can do 2 tasks at a time. This is called Thread-based multitasking.

Achieving multi tasking with threads has one advantage ,i.e. since the threads are light weight processes, they use minimum resources of the system.

Important Interview Question
___

Why threads are called light-weight?

   Threads are light-weight because they utilize minimum resources of the system. This means they take less memory and less processor time.

What is the difference between single tasking and multi tasking?

   Executing only one job at a time is called single tasking. Executing several jobs at a time is called multi tasking. In single tasking, the processor time is wasted, but in multi tasking, we can utilize the processor time in an optimum way.
___

Uses of Threads

Threads can be used for multiple purposes. Some of the uses of threads are:

❑ Threads are mainly used in server-side programs to serve the needs of multiple clients on a network or Internet. On Internet, a server machine has to cater the needs of thousands of clients, at a time. For this purpose, if we use threads in the server, they can do various jobs at a time, thus they can handle several clients.

❑ Threads are also used to create games and animation. Animation means moving the objects from one place to another. In many games, generally we have to perform more than one task simultaneously. There, threads will be of invaluable help. For example, in a game, a flight may be moving from left to right. A machine gun should shoot it, releasing the bullets at the flight. These 2 tasks should happen simultaneously. For this purpose, we can use 2 threads, one thread will move the flight and the other one will move the bullet, simultaneously towards the flight.

Creating a Thread and Running it

We know that in every Java program, there is a main thread available already. Apart from this main thread, we can also create our own threads in a program. The following steps should be used:

❑ Create a class that extends Thread class or implements Runnable interface. Both the Thread class and Runnable interface are found in java.lang package.

```
class Myclass extends Thread
Or, class Myclass implements Runnable
```

❑ Now in this class, write a run() method as:

```
public void run()
{
        statements;
}
```

By default, this run() method is recognized and executed by a thread.

❑ Create an object to Myclass, so that the run() method is available for execution.

```
Myclass obj = new Myclass();
```

❑ Now, create a thread and attach the thread to the object obj.

```
Thread t = new Thread(obj);
Or,  Thread t = new Thread(obj, "threadname");
```

❑ Run the thread. For this purpose, we should use start() method of Thread class.

```
t.start();
```

Now, the thread will start execution on the object of Myclass. In that object, run() method is found, hence it will execute the statements inside that run() method.

By following these steps, let us write a sample program to understand how to create a thread.

Program 2: Write a program to create MyThread class with run() method and then attach a thread to this MyThread class object.

```
//To create a thread and run it
//let the class extends Thread or implements Runnable
class  MyThread extends Thread
{
        //write run() method inside this class
        public void run()
        {
                //only this code is executed by the thread
                for(int i=1; i<=100000; i++)
                {
                        System.out.println(i);
                }
        }
}
```

```
        }
//another class
class Demo1
{
        public static void main(String args[ ])
        {
                //create an object to MyThread class.
                MyThread obj = new MyThread();

                //create a thread and attach it to the object of MyThread class.
                Thread t = new Thread(obj);

                //now run the thread on the object.
                t.start();    //now this thread will execute the code inside run()
                //method of  MyThread object
        }
}
```

Output:

```
C:\> javac Demo1.java
C:\> java Demo1
1
2
3
4
5
:
:
```

In this program, we create MyThread class with run() method and then attach a thread to this MyThread class object. When we run the thread, it runs the run() method of MyThread object.

Here, the class MyThread extends Thread class. We can also replace this statement with a statement like class MyThread implements Runnable. Thread class and Runnable interface both have public void run() method in them. By writing class MyThread extends Thread, we are overriding the run() method of Thread class. By writing class MyThread implements Runnable interface, we are implementing the run() method of the Runnable interface.

In Demo1 class, we created an object to MyThread class. This means that object contains run() method. Then we attached this object to thread t, as:

```
Thread t = new Thread(obj);
```

If we give t.start(), then the thread t starts running the code inside the run() method of the object obj. In the run() method, we wrote code to print numbers from 1 to 100000 using a for loop. As a result, the numbers will be displayed starting from 1 to 100000. If you want to terminate the program in the middle, you can press Ctrl+C from the keyboard. This leads to abnormal program termination. It means the entire program is terminated, not just the thread.

If we want to terminate only the thread that is running the code inside run() method, we should devise our own mechanism. If we press Ctrl+C, we are abnormally terminating the program. This is dangerous. Abnormal program termination may cause loss of data and lead to unreliable results. So we should terminate the thread only, not the program. How can we terminate the thread smoothly is the question now.

Terminating the Thread

A thread will terminate automatically when it comes out of run() method. To terminate the thread on our own, we have to device our own logic. For this purpose, the following steps can be used:

❑ Create a `boolean` type variable and initialize it to `false`.

```
boolean stop = false;
```

❑ Let us assume that we want to terminate the thread when the user presses <Enter> key. So, when the user presses that button, make the `boolean` type variable as `true`

```
stop = true;
```

❑ Check this variable in `run()` method and when it is true, make the thread return from the `run()` method.

```
public void run()
{
    if(stop == true) return;
}
```

Important Interview Question

How can you stop a thread in Java?

First of all, we should create a boolean type variable which stores 'false'. When the user wants to stop the thread, we should store 'true' into the variable. The status of the variable is checked in the run() method and if it is true, the thread executes 'return' statement and then stops.

Now, let us re-write the previous program, incorporating the logic to stop the thread smoothly.

Program 3: Re-write Program 2 showing how to terminate the thread by pressing the Enter button.

```
//To create a thread and run it, then stop it
import java.io.*;
class MyThread extends Thread
{
    boolean stop = false;
    public void run()
    {
        for(int i=1; i<=100000; i++)
        {
            System.out.println(i);
            if(stop) return;       //come out of run()
        }
    }
}
class Demo1
{
    public static void main(String args[]) throws IOException
    {
        MyThread obj = new MyThread();
        Thread t = new Thread(obj);
        t.start();
        //stop the thread when Enter key is pressed
        System.in.read();  //wait till Enter key pressed
        obj.stop = true;
    }
}
```

Output:

```
C:\> javac Demo1.java
C:\> java Demo1
```

```
1
2
3
4
5
6
:
:
Press <Enter> to stop the thread at any time.
```

This is same as Program 2, except that here we terminate the thread when the user presses the Enter button.

What is the difference between 'extends Thread' and 'implements Runnable' ? Which one is advantageous?

extends Thread and implements Runnable – both are functionally same. But when we write extends Thread, there is no scope to extend another class, as multiple inheritance is not supported in Java.

class Myclass extends Thread, AnotherClass //invalid

If we write implements Runnable, then still there is scope to extend another class.

class Myclass extends AnotherClass implements Runnable //valid

This is definitely advantageous when the programmer wants to use threads and also wants to access the features of another class.

Single Tasking Using a Thread

A thread can be employed to execute one task at a time. Suppose there are 3 tasks to be executed. We can create a thread and pass the 3 tasks one by one to the thread. For this purpose, we can write all these tasks separately in separate methods: task1(), task2(), task3(). Then these methods should be called from run() method, one by one. Remember, a thread executes only the code inside the run() method. It can never execute other methods unless they are called from run().

Which method is executed by the thread by default?
public void run() method.

Program 4: Write a program showing execution of multiple tasks with a single thread.

```
//single tasking using a thread
class MyThread implements Runnable
{
    public void run()
    {
        //execute the tasks one by one by calling the methods.
        task1();
        task2();
        task3();
    }
    void task1()
    {
```

```
                  System.out.println("This is task 1");
          }
          void task2()
          {
                  System.out.println("This is task 2");
          }
          void task3()
          {
                  System.out.println("This is task 3");
          }
}
class Single
{
      public static void main(String args[])
      {
              //create an object to MyThread class.
              MyThread obj = new MyThread();
              //create a thread t1 and attach it to that object
              Thread t1 = new Thread(obj);
              //execute the thread t1 on that object's run() method.
              t1.start();
      }
}
```

Output:

```
C:\> javac Single.java
C:\> java Single
This is task 1
This is task 2
This is task 3
```

In this program, a single thread `t1` is used to execute three tasks.

Multi Tasking Using Threads

In multi tasking, several tasks are executed at a time. For this purpose, we need more than one thread. For example, to perform 2 tasks, we can take 2 threads and attach them to the 2 tasks. Then those tasks are simultaneously executed by the two threads. Using more than one thread is called 'multi threading'.

When we go to a movie theatre, generally a person is there at the door—checking and cutting the tickets. When we enter the hall, there is another person who shows the seats to us. Suppose there is only one person (1 thread) doing these two tasks. He has to first cut the ticket and then come along with us to show the seat. Then he goes back to the door to cut the second ticket and then again enter the hall to show the seat for the second ticket. Like this, if he is does the things one by one, it takes a lot of time, and even though the show is over, there will be still a few people left outside the door waiting to enter the hall! This is pretty well known to the theatre management. So what they do? They employ two persons (2 threads) for this purpose. The first person will cut the ticket, and the second one will show the seat. When the second person is showing the seat, the first person cuts the second ticket. Like this, both the persons can act simultaneously and hence there will be no wastage of time. This is shown in Program 5.

Program 5: Write a program showing two threads working simultaneously upon two objects.

```
//Two threads performing two tasks at a time - Theatre example
class MyThread implements Runnable
{
      //declare a string to represent the task
      String str;
      MyThread(String str)
      {
```

372 | Chapter 26

```
                        this.str = str;
            }

        public void run()
        {
                for(int i=1; i<=10; i++)
                {
                        System.out.println(str+ " : "+i);
                        try{
                                Thread.sleep(2000);
                                //cease thread execution for 2000 milliseconds
                        } catch(InterruptedException ie)
                {
                        ie.printStackTrace();
                }
                } //end of for

        } //end of run()
}

class Theatre
{
        public static void main(String args[])
        {
                //create two objects to represent two tasks
                MyThread obj1 = new MyThread("Cut the ticket");
                MyThread obj2 = new MyThread("Show the seat");

                //create two threads and attach them to the two objects
                Thread t1 = new Thread(obj1);
                Thread t2 = new Thread(obj2);

                //start the threads
                t1.start();
                t2.start();

        }
}
```

Output:

```
C:\> javac Theatre.java
C:\> java Theatre
Cut the ticket: 1
Show the seat: 1
Cut the ticket: 2
Show the seat: 2
Cut the ticket: 3
Show the seat: 3
:
Cut the ticket: 10
Show the seat: 10
```

In the preceding example, first we have taken a string variable str in MyThread class. Then we passed two strings—Cut the ticket and Show the seat—into that variable from Theatre class. When t1.start() is executed, it starts execution on run() method code showing Cut the ticket. Just behind it, t2.start() will make the thread t2 also execute on run() method, almost simultaneously. So it will display Show the seat. In this manner, both the threads are simultaneously doing the two tasks. Note that in run() method, we used:

```
try{
        Thread.sleep(2000);
}
catch(InterruptedException ie)
{
```

```
                ie.printStackTrace();
    }
```

Here, `sleep()` is a static method in `Thread` class, which is used to suspend execution of a thread for some specified milliseconds. For example, `Thread.sleep(2000)` will stop the execution of the thread for 2000 milliseconds, i.e. 2 seconds. (1000 milliseconds = 1 second). Since this method can throw `InterruptedException`, we caught it in `catch` block.

Multiple Threads Acting on Single Object

In theatre example, we have used 2 threads on the 2 objects of `MyThread` class. It is also possible to use 2 or more threads on a single object. But in this case, sometimes we get unreliable results.

First let us see why 2 threads should share the same object (same `run()` method). We write an object to represent one task. If there is a different task, we take another object. When two people (threads) perform same task, then they need same object (`run()` method) to be executed each time. Take the case of railway reservation. Every day several people want reservation of a berth for them. The procedure to reserve the berth is same for all the people. So we need same object with same `run()` method to be executed repeatedly for all the people (threads).

Let us think that only one berth is available in a train, and two passengers (threads) are asking for that berth. In reservation counter no.1, the clerk has sent a request to the server to allot that berth to his passenger. In counter no.2, the second clerk has also sent a request to the server to allot that berth to his passenger. Let us see now see to whom that berth is allotted.

Program 6: Write a program showing two threads acting upon a single object.

```java
//Thread unsafe - Two threads acting on same object
class Reserve implements Runnable
{
        //available berths are 1
        int available=1;
        int wanted;

        //accept wanted berths at run time
        Reserve(int i)
        {
                wanted=i;
        }

        public void run()
        {
                //display available berths
                System.out.println("Available Berths= "+available);
                //if available berths are more than wanted berths
                if(available >= wanted)
                {
                        //get the name of passenger
                        String name= Thread.currentThread().getName();
                        //allot the berth to him
                        System.out.println(wanted +" Berths reserved for " +name);
                        try{
                        Thread.sleep(1500); //wait for printing the ticket
                        available = available - wanted;
                        //update the no. of available berths
                        }catch(InterruptedException ie){}

                }
                //if available berths are less, display sorry
                else System.out.println("Sorry, no berths");

        }
}
```

```
class Unsafe
{
        public static void main(String args[])
        {
                //tell that 1 berth is needed
                Reserve obj = new Reserve(1);

                //attach first thread to the object
                Thread t1 = new Thread(obj);
                //attach second thread to the same object
                Thread t2 = new Thread(obj);

                //take the thread names as persons names
                t1.setName("First person");
                t2.setName("Second person");

                //send the requests for berth
                t1.start();
                t2.start();
        }
}
```

Output:

```
C:\> javac Unsafe.java
C:\> java Unsafe
Available Berths = 1
1 Berths reserved for First Person
Available Berths = 1
1 Berths reserved for Second Person
```

Please observe the output in the preceding program. It is absurd. It has allotted the same berth to both the passengers. In this program, already we have taken available berths as 1. When thread t1 enters the run() method, it sees available number of berths as 1 and hence, it allots it to First Person, and displays:

```
1 Berths reserved for First Person
```

Then it enters try{ } block inside run() method, where it will sleep for 1.5 seconds. In this time, the ticket will be printed on the printer. When the first thread is sleeping, thread t2 also enters the run() method, it also sees that there is 1 berth remaining. The reason is for this is that the available number of berths is not yet updated by the first thread. So the second thread also sees 1 berth as available, and it allots the same berth to the Second Person. Then the thread t2 will also go into sleep state.

Thread t1 wakes up first, and then it updates the available number of berths as:

```
available = available - wanted;
```

Now available number of berths will become 0. But by this time, the second thread has already allotted the same berth to the Second Person also. Since both the threads are acting on the same object simultaneously, the result is unreliable.

What is the solution for this problem? Let us keep the second thread t2 wait till the first thread t1 completes and comes out. Let us not allow any other thread to enter the object till t1 comes out. This means we are preventing the threads to act on the same object simultaneously. This is called Thread Synchronization or Thread safe. See Figure 26.4.

What is Thread synchronization?

When a thread is already acting on an object, preventing any other thread from acting on the same object is called 'Thread synchronization' or 'Thread safe' The object on which the threads are synchronized is called 'synchronized object'. Thread synchronization is recommended when multiple threads are used on the same object (in multithreading).

Synchronized object is like a locked object, locked on a thread. It is like a room with only one door. A person has entered the room and locked from it from behind. The second person who wants to enter the room should wait till the first person comes out. In this way, a thread also locks the object after entering it. Then the next thread cannot enter it till the first thread comes out. This means the object is locked mutually on threads. So, this object is called 'mutex' (mutually exclusive lock).

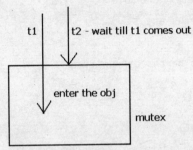

Figure 26.4 Thread synchronization

How can we synchronize the object? There are two ways of doing this.

❑ Using synchronized block: Here, we can embed a group of statements of the object (inside run() method) within a synchronized block, as shown here:

```
synchronized(object)
{
      statements;
}
```

Here, object represents the object to be locked or synchronized. The statements inside the synchronized block are all available to only one thread at a time. They are not available to more than one thread simultaneously.

❑ Using synchronized keyword: We can synchronize an entire method by using synchronized keyword. For example, if we want to synchronize the code of display() method, then add the synchronized keyword before the method name as shown here:

```
synchronized void display()
{
    statements;
}
```

Now the statements inside the display() method are not available to more than one thread at a time. This method code is synchronized.

What is the difference between synchronized block and synchronized keyword?

Synchronized block is useful to synchronize a block of statements. Synchronized keyword is useful to synchronize an entire method.

Let us re-write the above program, by putting the code inside run() method into a synchronized block. Observe that there is no change in the program, except that we introduced the synchronized block in run() method.

Program 7: Write a program to synchronize the threads acting on the same object. The synchronized block in the program can be executed by only one thread at a time.

```java
//Thread synchronization - Two threads acting on same object
class Reserve implements Runnable
{
        //available berths are 1
        int available=1;
        int wanted;

        //accept wanted berths at run time
        Reserve(int i)
        {
                wanted=i;
        }

        public void run()
        {
                synchronized(this)  //synchronize the current object
                {
                        //display available berths
                        System.out.println("Available Berths= "+available);
                        //if available berths are more than wanted berths
                        if(available >= wanted)
                        {
                                //get the name of passenger
                                String name= Thread.currentThread().getName();
                                //allot the berth to him
                                System.out.println(wanted +" Berths reserved for "
                                 +name);
                                try{
                                Thread.sleep(1500); //wait for printing the ticket
                                available = available - wanted;
                                //update the no. of available berths
                                }catch(InterruptedException ie){}

                        }
                        //if avaiable berths are less, display sorry
                        else System.out.println("Sorry, no berths");
                } //end of synchronized block
        }
}
class Safe
{
        public static void main(String args[])
        {
                //tell that 1 berth is needed
                Reserve obj = new Reserve(1);

                //attach first thread to the object
                Thread t1 = new Thread(obj);
                //attach second thread to the same object
                Thread t2 = new Thread(obj);

                //take the thread names as persons names
                t1.setName("First person");
```

```
                    t2.setName("Second person");
                    //send the requests for berth
                    t1.start();
                    t2.start();
            }
    }
```

Output:

```
C:\> javac Safe.java
C:\> java Safe
Available Berths = 1
1 Berths reserved for First Person
Available Berths = 0
Sorry, no berths
```

Thread Class Methods

So far, we discussed some concepts of threads, it is time we listed out some important methods of `java.lang.Thread` class:

To create a thread, we can use the following forms:

```
Thread t1 = new Thread();     //thread is created without any name
Thread t2 = new Thread(obj); //here, obj is target object of the thread
Thread t3 = new Thread(obj, "thread-name");    //target object and thread name
//are given
```

❑ To know the currently running thread:

```
Thread t = Thread.currentThread();
```

❑ To start a thread:

```
t.start();
```

❑ To stop execution of a thread for a specified time:

```
Thread.sleep(millseconds);
```

❑ To get the name of a thread:

```
String name = t.getName();
```

❑ To set a new name to a thread:

```
t.setName("new name");
```

❑ To get the priority of a thread:

```
int priority_no= t.getPriority();
```

❑ To set the priority of a thread:

```
t.setPriotity(int priority_no);
```

Thread priorities can change from 1 to 10. We can also use the following constants to represent priorities:

Thread.MAX_PRIORITY value is 10

Thread.MIN_PRIORITY value is 1

Thread.NORM_PRIORITY value is 5

❑ To test if a thread is still alive:

```
t.isAlive()  returns true/false.
```

❑ To wait till a thread dies:

```
t.join();
```

Deadlock of Threads

Even if we synchronize the threads, there is possibility of other problems like 'deadlock'. Let us understand this with an example.

Daily, thousands of people book tickets in trains and cancel tickets also. If a programmer is to develop code for this, he may visualize that booking tickets and canceling them are reverse procedures. Hence, he will write these 2 tasks as separate and opposite tasks, and assign 2 different threads to do these tasks simultaneously.

To book a ticket, the thread will enter the train object to verify that the ticket is available or not. When there is a ticket, it updates the available number of tickets in the train object. For this, it takes, say 150 milliseconds. Then it enters the compartment object. In compartment object, it should allot the ticket for the passenger and update its status to 'reserved'. This means the thread should go through both the train and compartment objects.

Similarly, let us think if a thread has to cancel a ticket, it will first enter compartment object, and updates the status of the ticket as 'available'. For this it is taking, say 200 milliseconds. Then it enters train object and updates the available number of tickets there. So, this thread also should go through both the compartment and train objects.

When the BookTicket thread is at train object for 150 milliseconds, the CancelTicket thread will be at compartment object for 200 milliseconds. Because we are using multiple (more one) threads, we should synchronize them. So, the threads will lock those objects. When 150 milliseconds time is over, BookTicket thread tries to come out of train object and wants to lock on compartment object, by entering it. At that time, it will find that the compartment object is already locked by another thread (CancelTicket) and hence it will wait. BookTicket thread will wait for compartment object for another 50 milliseconds.

After 200 milliseconds time is up, the CancelTicket thread which is in compartment object completes its execution and wants to enter and lock on train object. But it will find that the train object is already under lock by BookTicket thread and hence is not available. Now, CancelTicket will wait for the train object which should be unlocked by BookTicket.

In this way, BookTicket thread keeps on waiting for the CancelTicket thread to unlock the compartment object and the CancelTicket thread keeps on waiting for the BookTicket to unlock the train object. Each thread is expecting the other thread to release the object first, and then only it is willing to release its own object. Both the threads will wait forever in this way, suspending any further execution. This situation is called 'Thread deadlock'. See Figure 26.5.

What is Thread deadlock?

When a thread has locked an object and waiting for another object to be released by another thread, and the other thread is also waiting for the first thread to release the first object, both the threads will continue waiting forever. This is called 'Thread deadlock'.

When Thread deadlock occurs, any further execution is stopped and the program will come to a halt. Thread deadlock is a drawback in a program. The programmer should take care to avoid any such deadlocks in his programs.

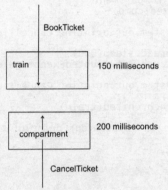

Figure 26.5 Thread deadlock

Program 8: Write a program depicting a situation in which a deadlock can occur.

```java
// Thread Deadlock
class BookTicket extends Thread
{
    //we are assuming train, compartment as objects
    Object train,comp;

    BookTicket(Object train, Object comp)
    {
        this.train = train;
        this.comp = comp;
    }

    public void run()
    {
        //lock on train
        synchronized(train)
        {
            System.out.println("BookTicket locked on train");
            try{
            Thread.sleep(150);
            }catch(InterruptedException e ){}

            System.out.println("BookTicket  now waiting to lock on
             compartment...");

            synchronized(comp)
            {
                System.out.println("BookTicket locked on
                    compartment");
            }
        }
    }
```

```
        class CancelTicket extends Thread
        {
                //we are assuming train, compartment as objects
                Object train,comp;

                CancelTicket(Object train, Object comp)
                {
                        this.train = train;
                        this.comp = comp;
                }

        public void run()
        {
                //lock on compartment
                synchronized(comp)
                {
                        System.out.println("CancelTicket locked on compartment");
                        try{
                        Thread.sleep(200);
                        }catch(InterruptedException e ){}

                        System.out.println("CancelTicket  now waiting to lock on
                         train...");
                        synchronized(train)
                        {
                                System.out.println("CancelTicket locked on train");
                        }
                }
        }
}
class DeadLock
{
        public static void main(String[ ] args) throws Exception
        {
                //take train, compartment as objects of Object class
                Object train = new Object();
                Object compartment = new Object();

                //create objects to BookTicket, CancelTicket classes
                BookTicket obj1 = new BookTicket (train,compartment);
                CancelTicket obj2 = new CancelTicket (train,compartment);
                //attach 2 threads to these objects
                Thread t1= new Thread(obj1);
                Thread t2= new Thread(obj2);
                //run the threads on the objects
                t1.start();
                t2.start();
        }
}
```

Output:

```
C:\> javac DeadLock.java
C:\> java DeadLock
BookTicket locked on train
CancelTicket locked on compartment
BookTicket now waiting to lock on compartment...
CancelTicket now waiting to lock on train...
```

In this program, BookTicket thread and CancelTicket threads act in reverse direction creating a deadlock situation.

Please observe the output, the program is not terminated, BookTicket thread is waiting for the compartment object and CancelTicket thread is waiting for train object. This waiting continues forever.

Avoiding Deadlocks in a Program

There is no specific solution for the problem of deadlocks. It depends on the logic used by the programmer. The programmer should design his program in such a way, that it does not form any deadlock. For example, in the preceding program, if the programmer used the threads in such a way that the CancelTicket thread follows the BookTicket, then he could have avoided the deadlock situation.

For this, we change the code in the CancelTicket class, so that it also follows the same sequence like BookTicket thread. Then what happens? First of all, BookTicket will enter the train object. After it processes the object, it comes out and finds that the compartment is freely available. So it enters compartment object and finally releases both the objects and comes out. Till then, CancelTicket thread will wait and once BookTicket comes out, the CancelTicket thread also follows the same sequence. Hence, there will not be any deadlock. So the run() method inside the CancelTicket should be changed as shown here:

```
public void run()
{
    //first lock on train like the BookTicket does
    synchronized(train)
    {
        System.out.println("CancelTicket locked on train");
        try{
        Thread.sleep(200);
        }catch(InterruptedException e ){}

        System.out.println("CancelTicket  now waiting to lock on
         compartment...");
        synchronized(comp)
        {
            System.out.println("CancelTicket locked on compartment");
        }
    }
}
```

Now run the program again to see the output:

```
BookTicket locked on train
BookTicket now waiting to lock on compartment...
BookTicket locked on compartment
CancelTicket locked on train
CancelTicket now waiting to lock on train...
CancelTicket locked on compartment
```

Thread Communication

In some cases, two or more threads should communicate with each other. For example, a Consumer thread is waiting for a Producer to produce the data (or some goods). When the Producer thread completes production of data, then the Consumer thread should take that data and use it. Let us now see how to plan the Producer class.

In the Producer class, we take a StringBuffer object to store data; in this case, we take some numbers from 1 to 10. These numbers are added to StringBuffer object. We take another boolean variable dataprodover, and initialize it to false. The idea is to make this dataprodover true when the production of numbers is completed. Producing data is done by appending numbers to StringBuffer using a for loop. This may take some time. When appending is over, we come out of for loop and then store true into dataprodover. This is shown in the following code:

```
//go on appending data (numbers) to string buffer
    for(int i= 1; i<=10; i++)
    {
            sb.append(i + ":");
            Thread.sleep(100);
            System.out.println("appending");
    }
    //data production is over, so store true into dataprodover
    dataprodover = true;
```

When the Producer is busy producing the data, now and then the Consumer will check if `dataprodover` is true or not. If `dataprodover` is true, the Consumer takes the data from `StringBuffer` and uses it. If the `dataprodover` shows false, then Consumer will sleep for some time and then again checks the `dataprodover`. The way to implement this logic is:

```
//sleep for 10 milliseconds while data production is not over. This while loop
//will be broken if dataprodover is true.

while( ! prod.dataprodover)
    Thread.sleep(10);
```

In this way, the Producer and Consumer can communicate with each other. But this is not an efficient way of communication. Why? Consumer checks the `dataprodover` at some point of time, and finds it false. So it goes into sleep for the next 10 milliseconds. Meanwhile, the data production may be over. But Consumer comes out of sleep after 10 milliseconds and then only it can find `dataprodover` is true. This means that there may be a time delay of 1 to 9 milliseconds to receive the data after its actual production is completed. Please see Figure 26.6.

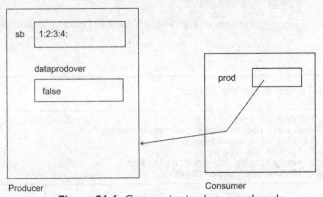

Figure 26.6 Communication between threads

Program 9: Write a program where the Consumer thread checks whether the data production is over or not every 10 milliseconds.

```
/*This program shows how two threads can communicate with each other.
        This is inefficient way of communication */
class Communicate
{
        public static void main(String[ ] args) throws Exception
        {
                //Producer produces some data which Consumer consumes
                Producer obj1 = new Producer();
                //Pass Producer object to Consumer  so that it is then available to
                Consumer
                Consumer obj2 = new Consumer(obj1);
```

```
                    //create 2 threads and attach to Producer and Consumer
                    Thread t1 = new Thread(obj1);
                    Thread t2 = new Thread(obj2);

                    //Run the threads
                    t2.start();  //Consumer waits
                    t1.start(); //Producer starts production
        }
}

class Producer  extends Thread
{
        //to add data, we use string buffer object
        StringBuffer sb;

        //dataprodover will be true when data production is over
        boolean dataprodover = false;

        Producer()
        {
                sb = new StringBuffer(); //allot memory
        }

        public void run()
        {
                //go on appending data (numbers) to string buffer
                for(int  i= 1; i<=10;  i++)
                {
                        try{
                        sb.append(i+":");
                        Thread.sleep(100);
                        System.out.println("appending");
                        }catch(Exception e){}
                }
                //data production is over, so store true into dataprodover
                dataprodover = true;
        }
}

class Consumer extends Thread
{
        //create Producer reference to refer to Producer object from
        //Consumer class
        Producer prod;

        Consumer(Producer prod)
        {
                this.prod = prod;
        }

        public void run()
        {
                //if data production is not over, sleep for 10 milliseconds
                //and check
                //again. Here there is a time delay of several milliseconds to
                //receive data
                try{
                while( ! prod.dataprodover)
                Thread.sleep(10);
                }catch(Exception e){}

                //when data production is over, display data of stringbuffer
                System.out.println(prod.sb);
        }
}
```

Output:

```
C:\> javac Communicate.java
C:\> java Communicate
appending
appending
appending
appending
appending
appending
appending
appending
appending
appending
1:2:3:4:5:6:7:8:9:10:
```

How can we improve the efficiency of communication between threads? java.lang.Object class provides 3 methods for this purpose.

❏ obj.notify(): This method releases an object (obj) and sends a notification to a waiting thread that the object is available.

❏ obj.notifyAll(): This method is useful to send notification to all waiting threads at once that the object (obj) is available.

❏ obj.wait(): This method makes a thread wait for the object (obj) till it receives a notification from a notify() or notifyAll() methods.

It is recommended to use the above methods inside a synchronized block.

Let us re-write the Producer-Consumer program using the above methods so that there will not be any wastage of a single millisecond time to receive the data by the Consumer. In this program, there is no need to use dataprodover variable at Producer side. We can directly send a notification immediately after the data production is over, as shown here:

```
synchronized(sb)
{
        //go on appending data (numbers) to string buffer
        for(int  i= 1; i<=10;  i++)
        {
                try{
                        sb.append(i+":");
                        Thread.sleep(100);
                        System.out.println("appending");
                }catch(Exception e){}
        }
        //data production is over, so notify to Consumer thread
        sb.notify();
}
```

Here, sb.notify() is sending a notification to the Consumer thread that the StringBuffer object sb is available, and it can be used now. Meanwhile, what the Consumer thread is doing? It is waiting for the notification that the StringBuffer object sb (of Producer class) is available. We should refer to the sb object at Consumer class as prod.sb.

```
synchronized(prod.sb)
{
        //wait till the sb object is released and a notification is sent
        try{
                prod.sb.wait();
        }catch(Exception e){}
}
```

Here, there is no need of using `sleep()` method to go into sleep for sometime. `wait()` method stops waiting as soon as it receives the notification. So there is no time delay to receive the data from the Producer.

Important Interview Question

What is the difference between the sleep() and wait() methods ?

Both the sleep() and wait() methods are used to suspend a thread execution for a specified time. When sleep() is executed inside a synchronized block, the object is still under lock. When wait() method is executed, it breaks the synchronized block, so that the object lock is removed and it is available.

Generally, sleep() is used for making a thread to wait for some time. But wait() is used in connection with notify() or notifyAll() methods in thread communication.

Program 10: Write a program such that the Consumer thread is informed immediately when the data production is over.

```
/* This program shows how to use wait and notify
      This is the most efficient way of thread communication */

class Communicate
{
      public static void main(String[ ] args) throws Exception
      {
            //Producer produces some data which Consumer consumes
            Producer obj1 = new Producer();
            //Pass Producer object to Consumer so that it is then available to
            //consumer
            Consumer obj2 = new Consumer(obj1);

            //create 2 threads and attach to Producer and Consumer
            Thread t1 = new Thread(obj1);
            Thread t2 = new Thread(obj2);

            //Run the threads
            t2.start();  //Consumer waits
            t1.start(); //Producer starts production
      }
}

class Producer  extends Thread
{
      //to add data, we use string buffer object
      StringBuffer sb;

      Producer()
      {
            sb = new StringBuffer(); //allot memory
      }

      public void run()
      {
            synchronized(sb)
            {
                  //go on appending data (numbers) to string buffer
                  for(int  i= 1; i<=10;  i++)
                  {
                        try{
                        sb.append(i+":");
                        Thread.sleep(100);
                        System.out.println("appending");
                        }catch(Exception e){}
                  }
```

```
                                //data production is over, so notify to Consumer thread
                                sb.notify();
                        }
                }
        }

        class Consumer extends Thread
        {
                //create Producer reference to refer to Producer object from
                //Consumer class
                Producer prod;

                Consumer(Producer prod)
                {
                        this.prod = prod;
                }

                public void run()
                {
                        synchronized(prod.sb)
                        {
                                //wait till a notification is received from Producer
                                //thread. Here
                                //there is no wastage of time of even a single millisecond

                                try{
                                prod.sb.wait();
                                }catch(Exception e){ }

                                //when data production is over, display data of
                                //stringbuffer
                                System.out.println(prod.sb);
                        }
                }
        }
```

Output:

```
C:\> javac Communicate.java
C:\> java Communicate
appending
appending
appending
appending
appending
appending
appending
appending
appending
appending
1:2:3:4:5:6:7:8:9:10:
```

Thread Priorities

When the threads are created and started, a 'thread scheduler' program in JVM will load them into memory and execute them. This scheduler will allot more JVM time to those threads which are having higher priorities. The priority numbers of a thread will change from 1 to 10. The minimum priority (shown by Thread.MIN_PRIORITY) of a thread is 1, and the maximum priority (Thread.MAX_PRIORITIY) is 10. The normal priority of a thread (Thread.NORM_PRIORITY) is 5.

What is the default priority of a thread?
When a thread is created, by default its priority will be 5.

When two tasks are assigned to two threads with different priorities, example, 2 and 5, then the thread with priority number 5 will be given more JVM time and hence it will complete the task earlier than the thread with priority number 2. See this effect in the following example to understand thread priorities. In Program 11, two threads are counting numbers from 1 to 10000. The thread with priority number 5 is completing the counting first, even if it has been started later than the thread with priority number 2.

Program 11: Write a program to understand the thread priorities. The thread with higher priority number will complete its execution first.

```
//Thread priorities
class Myclass extends Thread
{
     int count=0;    //this counts numbers

     public void run()
     {
          for(int i=1; i<=10000; i++)
          count++;    //count numbers upto 10000

          //display which thread has completed counting and its priority
          System.out.println("Completed thread: "+
           Thread.currentThread().getName());
          System.out.println("Its priority: "+
           Thread.currentThread().getPriority());

     }
}

class Prior
{
     public static void main(String args[])
     {
          Myclass obj = new Myclass();

          //create two threads
          Thread t1 = new Thread(obj, "One");
          Thread t2 = new Thread(obj, "Two");

          //set priorities for them
          t1.setPriority(2);
          t2.setPriority(Thread.NORM_PRIORITY);   //this means priority no. 5

          //start first t1 and then t2.
          t1.start();
          t2.start();
     }
}
```

Output:

```
C:\> javac Prior.java
C:\> java Prior
Completed thread: Two
Its priority: 5
Completed thread: One
Its priority: 2
```

Thread Group

A thread group represents several threads as a single group. The main advantage of taking several threads as a group is that by using a single method, we will be able to control all the threads in the group.

❑ To create a thread group, we should simply create an object to `ThreadGroup` class as:

```
ThreadGroup tg = new ThreadGroup("groupname");
```

Here, `tg` is the thread group object, and `groupname` is its name.

❑ To add a thread to this group (`tg`):

```
Thread t1 = new Thread(tg, targetobj, "threadname");
```

Here, `t1` thread is created and added to the thread group `tg`. This thread acts on `targetobj`, which is the target object for the thread. The `threadname` represents the name of the thread `t1`.

❑ To add another thread group (`tg1`) to this group (`tg`):

```
ThreadGroup tg1 = new ThreadGroup(tg, "groupname");
```

Here we are creating and adding the thread group `tg1` to the thread group `tg`. The name of the added thread group is represented by `groupname`.

❑ To know the parent of a thread or a thread group, we can use `getParent()`.

```
tg.getParent();
```

This method returns `ThreadGroup` object which is the parent of `tg`.

❑ To know the parent thread group of a thread, we can use:

```
t.getThreadGroup();
```

This returns a `ThreadGroup` object to which the thread `t` belongs.

❑ To know the number of threads actively running in a thread group:

```
tg.activeCount();
```

This method returns an integer number that gives the number of threads in `tg` which are currently running in memory.

❑ To change the maximum priority of a thread group tg:

```
tg.setMaxPriority();
```

Normally, the maximum priority of a thread group will be 10. But this method can set it as any other number between 1 and 10.

In the following program, we are taking a thread group `tg` and in that we are adding two threads `t1` and `t2`. Then we are creating another thread group `tg1`, and adding it to `tg`. The threads `t3` and `t4` are added to the thread group `tg1`. We also used some methods which act on thread groups.

Program 12: Write a program to demonstrate the creation of thread groups and some methods which act on thread groups.

```java
// Using thread groups
class TGroups
{

    public static void main(String[ ] args) throws Exception
    {
            //We should understand that the following statements are
             executed by
            //the main thread.

            Reservation res = new Reservation();
            Cancellation can = new Cancellation();

            //create a Thread group with name
            ThreadGroup tg = new ThreadGroup("First Group");

            //create 2 threads and add them to First Group
            Thread t1 = new Thread(tg, res, "First thread");
            Thread t2 = new Thread(tg, res, "Second thread");

            //create another thread group tg1 as a child to tg
            ThreadGroup tg1 = new ThreadGroup(tg, "Second Group");

            //create 2 threads and add them to Second group
            Thread t3 = new Thread(tg1, can, "Third thread");
            Thread t4 = new Thread(tg1, can, "Fourth thread");

            //find parent group of tg1
            System.out.println("Parent of tg1= "+tg1.getParent());

            //set maximum priority to tg1 as 7
            tg1.setMaxPriority(7);

            //know the thread group of t1 and t3
            System.out.println("Thread group of t1= "+ t1.getThreadGroup());
            System.out.println("Thread group of t3= "+ t3.getThreadGroup());

            //start the threads
            t1.start();
            t2.start();
            t3.start();
            t4.start();

            //find how many threads are actively running
            System.out.println("No of threads active in tg =
            "+tg.activeCount());
    }
}
class Reservation extends Thread
{
    public void run()
    {
            System.out.println("I am reservation thread");
    }
}
class Cancellation extends Thread
{
    public void run()
    {
            System.out.println("I am cancellation thread");
    }
}
```

Output:

```
C:\> javac TGroups.java
C:\> java TGroups
Parent of tg1= java.lang.ThreadGroup[name=First Group,maxpri=10]
Thread group of t1= java.lang.ThreadGroup[name=First Group,maxpri=10]
Thread group of t3= java.lang.ThreadGroup[name=Second Group,maxpri=7]
No of threads active in tg= 4
I am reservation thread
I am reservation thread
I am cancellation thread
I am cancellation thread
```

Daemon Threads

Sometimes, a thread has to continuously execute without any interruption to provide services to other threads. Such threads are called daemon threads. For example, oracle.exe is a program (a thread) that continuously executes in a computer. When the system is switched on, it also starts running and will terminate only when the system is off. Any other threads like SQL+ can communicate with it to store or retrieve data.

Important Interview Question

What is a daemon thread?

A daemon thread is a thread that executes continuously. Daemon threads are service providers for other threads or objects. It generally provides a background processing.

❏ To make a thread t as a daemon thread, we can use setDaemon() method as:

```
t. setDaemon(true);
```

❏ To know if a thread is daemon or not, isDaemon() is useful.

```
boolean x = t.isDaemon();
```

If isDaemon() returns true, then the thread t is a daemon thread, otherwise not.

Applications of Threads

In a network, a server has to render its services to several clients at a time. So, by using threads at server side programs, we can make the threads serve several clients at a time. In the following program, we are creating a server using 2 threads that can send messages to two clients at a time. First thread will contact first client, at the same time second thread will contact the second client. If third client comes, then again first thread will provide service to it. Like this, 2 threads will contact the clients one by one, thus they can serve several clients. Here, we are combining the java.net features with threads.

Program 13: Write a program to create a server with 2 threads to communicate with several clients.

```
//A server with 2 threads to contact multiple clients
import java.io.*;
import java.net.*;
class MultiServe implements Runnable
{
        static ServerSocket ss;
```

```
        static Socket s;

        public void run()
        {
                //find thread name
                String name= Thread.currentThread().getName();
                for(;;)  //server runs continuously
                {
                        try{
                        System.out.println("Thread "+name+" ready to accept...");
                        s = ss.accept();
                        System.out.println("Thread "+name+" accepted a
                         connection");
                        //for sending message
                        PrintStream ps = new PrintStream(s.getOutputStream());
                        ps.println("Thread "+name+" contacted you");

                        //close connection
                        ps.close();
                        s.close();
                        //do not close ServerSocket.
                        }
                        catch(Exception e) {}
                }
        }

        public static void main(String args[ ]) throws Exception
        {
                MultiServe ms = new MultiServe();

                //create server socket with 999 as port number
                ss = new ServerSocket(999);

                //create 2 threads
                Thread t1 = new Thread(ms,"One");
                Thread t2 = new Thread(ms,"Two");

                //start the threads
                t1.start();
                t2.start();

        }
}
```

Output:

```
C:\> javac MultiServe.java
C:\>
-------------------------------------------------------
```

Program 14: Write a program to create a client that receives message from the server.

```
//A Client that receives the messages from the server above
import java.io.*;
import java.net.*;
class MultiClient
{
        public static void main(String args[ ]) throws Exception
        {
                //create Client socket with port number 999
                Socket s = new Socket("localhost", 999);

                //to accept data from server
                BufferedReader br = new BufferedReader(new  InputStreamReader
                  ( s.getInputStream()));
                //receive data as long as server does not close client socket
```

```
                        String str;
                        while((str = br.readLine()) != null)
                        System.out.println(str);

                        //close connection
                        br.close();
                        s.close();
                }
        }
```

Output:

```
        C:\> javac MultiClient.java
        C:\>
```

Now run `MultiServe` server in a DOS window. Run several copies of `MultiClient` in several DOS windows. You can see the server communicating with all the clients at a time by sending a message to them.

See the Screen shot of the output of the preceding program.

Another application of threads is animation, where an object, an image or some text is moved from one place to another on the screen. Here is an example program to see a moving banner using a thread. The logic is to extract the first character from a banner string and add it at the end of the string. When the screen contents are refreshed, it appears as if the entire string will move towards left. Now extract the leftmost character and place it at the end of the banner string. Like this, repeat the same to get the effect of a moving banner.

Program 15: Write a program to understand how threads can be used to animate the things. Here, we animate a banner text.

```
        //a moving banner using a thread
        import java.awt.*;  //for GUI

        class Banner extends Frame implements Runnable
        {
                //this is the banner string
```

```
                String str= " DREAM TECH PUBLICATIONS ";

        Banner()
        {
                setLayout(null); //dont set Layout manager
                setBackground(Color.cyan);
                setForeground(Color.red);

        }//end of constructor

        public void paint(Graphics g)
        {
                //set a font and display the banner string
                Font f = new Font("Courier", Font.BOLD, 40);
                g.setFont(f);
                g.drawString(str, 10,100);
        }

        public void run()
        {

                for(;;) {          //move banner continuously
                repaint();   //refresh the frame contents
                try{
                        Thread.sleep(400);  //give a gap of 400 millis between each
                        //movement
                        }catch(InterruptedException ie){}
                        char ch = str.charAt(0);    //extract first char from string
                        str = str.substring(1, str.length()); //add to str from second
                        // char till end
                        str = str+ch;  //attach first char at the end of str
                }
        }

        public static void main(String args[ ])
        {
                Banner b = new Banner();  //b represents the frame
                b.setSize(400,400);
                b.setTitle("My banner");
                b.setVisible(true);
                //create a thread and run it
                Thread t = new Thread(b);
                t.start();
        }
}
```

Output:

```
C:\> javac Banner.java
C:\> java Banner
```

Thread Life Cycle

Starting from the birth of a thread, till its death, a thread exists in different states which are collectively called 'Thread Life cycle'. Please see Figure 26.7.

A thread will be born when it is created using `Thread` class as:

```
Thread t = new Thread();
```

Then the thread goes into runnable state when `start()` method is applied on it. `Yield()` method may pause a thread briefly, but the thread will be still in runnable state only.

From runnable state, a thread may get into not-runnable state, when `sleep()` or `wait()` methods act on it. A thread may be occasionally blocked on some Input-Output device where it is expecting some input-output from the user. The thread would be in not-runnable state till the user provides the required input or output. After coming out from not-runnable state, again the thread comes back to runnable state.

Finally, a thread is terminated from memory only when it comes out of `run()` method. This happens when the thread completely executes the `run()` method and naturally comes out, or when the user forces it to come out of `run()` method.

All these state transitions of a thread, starting from its birth till its death are called 'thread life cycle'.

Important Interview Question

What is thread life cycle?

A thread is created using new Thread() statement and is executed by start() method. The thread enters 'runnable' state and when sleep() or wait() methods are used or when the thread is blocked on I/O, it then goes into 'not runnable' state. From 'not runnable' state, the thread comes back to the 'runnable' state and continues running the statements. The thread dies when it comes out of run() method. These state transitions of a thread are called 'life cycle of a thread'.

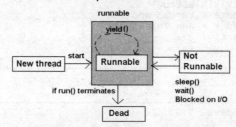

Figure 26.7 Life cycle of a thread

Conclusion

In most of the applications, different segments (parts) of the application run independently performing their duties almost at a time and thus improving performance. In such a case, we need threads to run those segments individually and at the same time. For example, a server on a network or Internet provides its services to several clients at a time. In such cases, we can use threads at the server so that a group of threads will be able to serve hundreds of clients at a time.

Threads are also useful where a process should run continuously. For example, a continuously running animation or continuously running server application needs a daemon thread which keeps it running for ever. Being light weight, threads use minimal system resources and hence they are highly preferred to actual heavy weight processes.

GRAPHICS PROGRAMMING USING AWT

W henever an application (or software) is created, the user can work with it in two ways. The first way is where the user can remember some commands on which the application is built and type those commands to achieve the respective tasks. For example, the user may have to type a PRINT command to send a file contents to a printer. Here, the user should know the syntax and correct usage of the PRINT command. Then only he can interact with the application properly. This is called CUI (Character User Interface) since the user has to use characters or commands to interact with the application. The main disadvantage in CUI is that the user has to remember several commands and their use with correct syntax. Hence, CUI is not user-friendly. A person who does not know any thing about computers will find this CUI very difficult.

The second way is where the user need not remember any commands but interacts with any application by clicking on some images or graphics. For example, if the user wants to print a file, he can click on a printer image and the rest of the things will be taken care of by the application. The user has to tell how many copies he wants and printing continues. This is very easy for the user since the user remembers only some symbols or images, like a magnifying glass symbol for searching, a briefcase symbol for a directory, etc. This environment where the user can interact with an application through graphics or images is called GUI (Graphics User Interface). GUI has the following advantages:

❏ It is user-friendly. The user need not worry about any commands. Even a layman will be able to work with the application developed using GUI.

❏ It adds attraction and beauty to any application by adding pictures, colors, menus, animation, etc. We can observe almost all websites lure their visitors on Internet since they are developed attractively using GUI.

❏ It is possible to simulate the real life objects using GUI. For example, a calculator program may actually display a real calculator on the screen. The user feels that he is interacting with a real calculator and he would be able to use it without any difficulty or special training. So, GUI eliminates the need of user training.

❏ GUI helps to create graphical components like push buttons, radio buttons, check boxes, etc. and use them effectively in our programs.

AWT

Abstract Window Toolkit (AWT) represents a class library to develop applications using GUI. The java.awt package got classes and interfaces to develop GUI and let the users interact in a more friendly way with the applications. Figure 27.1 shows some important classes of java.awt package.

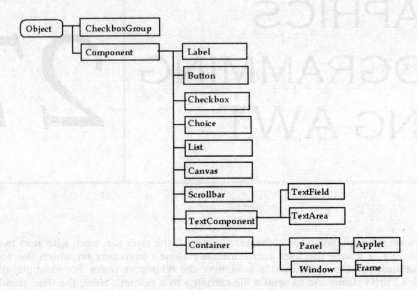

Figure 27.1 Classes of AWT

Components

A Component represents an object which is displayed pictorially on the screen. For example, we create an object of Button class as:

```
Button b = new Button();
```

Now, b is the object of Button class. If we display this b on the screen, it displays a push button. Therefore, the object b, on going to the screen is becoming a component called 'Push button'. In the same way, any component is a graphical representation of an object. Push buttons, radio buttons, check boxes, etc. are all components.

Window and Frame

A window represents any imaginary rectangular area on the screen without any borders or title bar. A frame represents a window with some title and borders. See Figure 27.2. In any application, we create frames to represent various screens like input screens where the user can type some data for the application and output screens where the result may be displayed in a particular form. Such screens are nothing but frames only.

Important Interview Question

What is the difference between a window and a frame?

A window is a frame without any borders and title, whereas a frame contains borders and title.

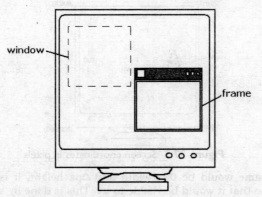

window

frame

Figure 27.2 A window and a frame on the monitor

Creating a Frame

A frame becomes the basic component in AWT. The frame has to be created before any other component. The reason is that all other components can be displayed in a frame. There are three ways to create a frame, which are as follows:

❑ Create a Frame class object,

```
Frame f = new Frame();
```

❑ Create a Frame class object and pass its title also,

```
Frame f = new Frame("My frame");
```

❑ The third way is to create a subclass MyFrame to the Frame class and create an object to the subclass as:

```
class MyFrame extends Frame
MyFrame f = new MyFrame();
```

Since, MyFrame is a subclass of Frame class, its object f contains a copy of Frame class and hence f represents the frame.

In all these cases, a frame with initial size of 0 pixels width and 0 pixels height will be created, which is not visible on the screen. You may be wondering what these pixels are. A pixel (short for picture element) represents any single point or dot on the screen. Any data or pictures which are displayed on the screen are composed of several dots called pixels. Nowadays, monitors can accommodate 800 pixels horizontally and 600 pixels vertically. So the total pixels seen on one screen would be 800x600 = 480,000 pixels. This is called 'screen resolution'. See Figure 27.3. The more the screen resolution, the more clarity a picture will have on the screen when displayed. This is the reason most laptops use 1024x768 pixels resolution.

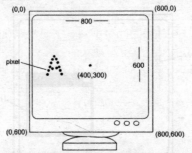

Figure 27.3 Screen coordinates in pixels

Since, the size of our frame would be 0px width and 0px height, it is not visible and hence we should increase its size so that it would be visible to us. This is done by setSize() method, as:

```
f.setSize(400,350);
```

Here, the frame's width is set to 400 px and height to 350 px. Then, we can display the frame, using setVisible() method, as:

```
f.setVisible(true);
```

Program 1: Write a program to create a frame by creating an object to Frame class.

```
//Creating a frame - version 1
import java.awt.*;
class MyFrame
{
        public static void main(String args[])
        {
                //create a frame
                Frame f = new Frame("My AWT frame");
                //set the size of the frame
                f.setSize(300,250);
                //display the frame
                f.setVisible(true);
        }
}
```

Output:

```
C:\> javac MyFrame.java
C:\> java MyFrame
```

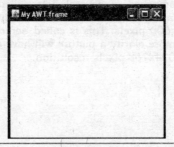

The same program can be rewritten in a different way, as shown in Program 2.

Program 2: Write a program to create a frame by creating an object to the subclass of `Frame` class.

```
//Creating a frame - version 2
import java.awt.*;
class MyFrame extends Frame
{
        //call super class constructor to store title
        MyFrame(String str)
        {
                super(str);
        }

        public static void main(String args[])
        {
                //create a frame with title
                MyFrame f = new MyFrame("My AWT frame");

                //set the size of the frame
                f.setSize(300,250);

                //display the frame
                f.setVisible(true);

        }
}
```

Output:

```
C:\> javac MyFrame.java
C:\> java MyFrame
```

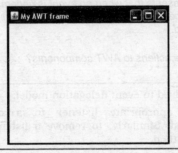

This frame can be minimized, maximized and resized, but cannot be closed. Even if we click on close button of the frame, it will not perform any closing action. Now the question is how to close the frame? Closing a frame means attaching action to the component. To attach actions to the components, we need 'event delegation model'. Let us discuss what it is.

Event Delegation Model

When we create a component, generally the component is displayed on the screen but is not capable of performing any actions. For example, we created a push button, which can be displayed but cannot perform any action, even when someone clicks on it. But user expectation will be different. A user wants the push button to perform some action. Hence, he clicks on the button. Clicking like this is called event. An event represents a specific action done on a component. Clicking, double clicking, typing data inside the component, mouse over, etc. are all examples of events.

When an event is generated on the component, the component will not know about it because it cannot listen to the event. To let the component understand that an event is generated on it, we should add some listener to the components. A listener is an interface which listens to an event coming from a component. A listener will have some abstract methods which need to be implemented by the programmer.

When an event is generated by the user on the component, the event is not handled by the component. On the other hand, the component sends (delegates) that event to the listener attached to it. The listener will not handle the event. It hands over (delegates) the event to an appropriate method. Finally, the method is executed and the event is handled. This is called 'event delegation model'. See Figure 27.4.

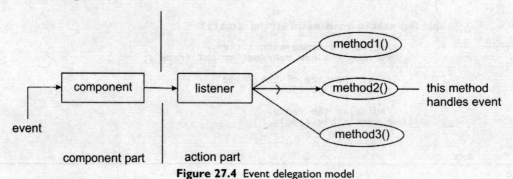

Figure 27.4 Event delegation model

Important Interview Question

What is event delegation model?

Event delegation model represents that when an event is generated by the user on a component, it is delegated to a listener interface and the listener calls a method in response to the event. Finally, the event is handled by the method.

Which model is used to provide actions to AWT components?

Event delegation model.

So, the following steps are involved in event delegation model:

❑ We should attach an appropriate listener to a component. This is done using `addxxxListener()` method. Similarly, to remove a listener from a component, we can use `removexxxListener()` method.

❑ Implement the methods of the listener, especially the method which handles the event.

❑ When an event is generated on the component, then the method in step 2 will be executed and the event is handled.

What is the advantage of event delegation model? In this model, the component is separated from the action part. So there are two advantages:

❑ The component and the action parts can be developed in two separate environments. For example, we can create the component in Java and the action logic can be developed in VisualBasic.

❑ We can modify the code for creating the component without modifying the code for action part of the component. Similarly, we can modify the action part without modifying the code for the component. Thus, we can modify one part without effecting any modification to other part. This makes debugging and maintenance of code very easy.

Closing the Frame

We know Frame is also a component. We want to close the frame by clicking on its close button. Let us follow these steps to see how to use event delegation model to do this:

❑ We should attach a listener to the frame component. Remember, all listeners are available in java.awt.event package. The most suitable listener to the frame is 'window listener'. It can be attached using addWindowListener() method as:

```
f.addWindowListener(WindowListener obj);
```

Please note that the addWindowListener() method has a parameter that is expecting object of WindowListener interface. Since it is not possible to create an object to an interface, we should create an object to the implementation class of the interface and pass it to the method.

❑ Implement all the methods of the WindowListener interface. The following methods are found in WindowListener interface:

```
public void windowActivated(WindowEvent e)
public void windowClosed(WindowEvent e)
public void windowClosing(WindowEvent e)
public void windowDeactivated(WindowEvent e)
public void windowDeiconified(WindowEvent e)
public void windowIconified(WindowEvent e)
public void windowOpened(WindowEvent e)
```

In all the preceding methods, WindowListener interface calls the public void windowClosing() method when the frame is being closed. So, implementing this method alone is enough, as:

```
public void windowClosing(WindowEvent e)
{
        //close the application
        System.exit(0);
}
```

For the remaining methods, we can provide empty body.

❑ So, when the frame is closed, the body of this method is executed and the application gets closed. In this way, we can handle the frame closing event.

These steps are shown in Program 3.

Program 3: Write a program which first creates a frame and then closes it on clicking the close button.

```
//Creating a frame and closing it.
import java.awt.*;
import java.awt.event.*;
class MyFrame extends Frame
{
        public static void main(String args[])
        {
                //create a frame with title
                MyFrame f = new MyFrame();

                //set a title for the frame
                f.setTitle("My AWT frame");

                //set the size of the frame
                f.setSize(300,250);
```

```
                    //display the frame
                    f.setVisible(true);

                    //close the frame
                    f.addWindowListener(new Myclass());

            }
    }
class Myclass implements WindowListener
{
    public void windowActivated(WindowEvent e){}
    public void windowClosed(WindowEvent e){}
    public void windowClosing(WindowEvent e)
    {
            System.exit(0);
    }
    public void windowDeactivated(WindowEvent e){}
    public void windowDeiconified(WindowEvent e){}
    public void windowIconified(WindowEvent e){}
    public void windowOpened(WindowEvent e){}

}
```

Output

```
C:\> javac MyFrame.java
C:\> java MyFrame
CLICK ON CLOSE BUTTON, THE FRAME CLOSES
```

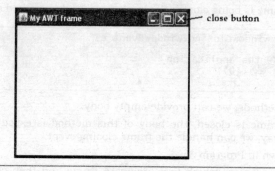
close button

In this program, we not only create a frame but also close the frame when the user clicks on the close button. For this purpose, we use `WindowListener` interface.

Here, we had to mention all the methods of `WindowListener` interface, just for the sake of one method. This is really cumbersome. There is another way to escape this. There is a class `WindowAdapter` in `java.awt.event` package, that contains all the methods of the `WindowListener` interface with an empty implementation (body). If we can extend `Myclass` from this `WindowAdapter` class, then we need not write all the methods with empty implementation. We can write only that method which interests us. This is shown in Program 4.

Program 4: Write a program to close the frame using `WindowAdapter` class.

```
//Creating a frame and closing it.
import java.awt.*;
import java.awt.event.*;
class MyFrame extends Frame
{

    public static void main(String args[])
```

```
            {
                        //create a frame with title
                        MyFrame f = new MyFrame();

                        //set a title for the frame
                        f.setTitle("My AWT frame");

                        //set the size of the frame
                        f.setSize(300,250);

                        //display the frame
                        f.setVisible(true);

                        //close the frame
                        f.addWindowListener(new Myclass());

            }
    }
    class Myclass extends WindowAdapter
    {
            public void windowClosing(WindowEvent e)
            {
                        System.exit(0);
            }
    }
```

Output

```
    C:\> javac MyFrame.java
    C:\> java MyFrame
    CLICK ON CLOSE BUTTON, THE FRAME CLOSES
```

Important Interview Question

What is an adapter class?

An adapter class is an implementation class of a listener interface which contains all methods implemented with empty body. For example, WindowAdapter is an adapter class of WindowListener interface. Adapter classes reduce overhead on programming while working with listener interfaces.

Please observe Program 4. In this, even the code of `Myclass` can be copied directly into `addWindowListener()` method, as:

```
    f.addWindowListener(new WindowAdapter()
    {
            public void windowClosing(WindowEvent e)
            {
                        System.exit(0);
            }
    });
```

This looks a bit confusing, but it is correct. We copy the code of `Myclass` into the method of `MyFrame` class. But, in the preceding code, we cannot find the name of `Myclass` anywhere in the code. It means the name of `Myclass` is hidden in `MyFrame` class and hence `Myclass` is an inner class in `MyFrame` class whose name is not mentioned. Such an inner class is called 'anonymous inner class'.

Important Interview Question

What is anonymous inner class?

Anonymous inner class is an inner class whose name is not mentioned, and for which only one object is created.

Let us now rewrite Program 4 again using anonymous inner class concept to close the frame.

Program 5: Write a program to close the frame using an anonymous inner class.

```
//Creating a frame and closing it.
import java.awt.*;
import java.awt.event.*;
class MyFrame extends Frame
{

    public static void main(String args[])
    {
        //create a frame with title
        MyFrame f = new MyFrame();

        //set a title for the frame
        f.setTitle("My AWT frame");

        //set the size of the frame
        f.setSize(300,250);

        //display the frame
        f.setVisible(true);

        //close the frame. Here Myclass name is not mentioned
        //but its object is passed to the method.
        f.addWindowListener(new WindowAdapter()
        {
            public void windowClosing(WindowEvent e)
            {
                System.exit(0);
            }
        });
    }
}
```

So far, we discussed the following three ways to close the frame:

❑ By implementing all the methods of `WindowListener` interface.

❑ By using `WindowAdapter` class and by implementing only the required method.

❑ By directly copying the code of an anonymous inner class.

Uses of a Frame

Once, the frame is created, we can use it for any of the purposes mentioned here:

❑ To draw some graphical shapes like dots, lines, rectangles, etc. in the frame.

❑ To display some text in the frame.

❑ To display pictures or images in the frame.

❑ To display components like push buttons, radio buttons, etc. in the frame.

Drawing in the Frame

Graphics class of `java.awt` package has the following methods which help to draw various shapes.

❑ `drawLine(int x1, int y1, int x2, int y2)`

This method is useful to draw a line connecting (x1,y1) and (x2,y2).

❑ `drawRect(int x, int y, int w, int h)`

This method draws outline of a rectangle. The left top corner of the rectangle starts at (x,y), the width is w, and the height is h.

❑ drawRoundRect(int x, int y, int w, int h, int arcw, int arch): This method draws the outline of a rectangle with rounded corners. The rectange's top left corner starts at (x,y), the width is w, and height is h. The rectangle will have rounded corners. The rounding is specified by arcw and arch. arcw represents horizontal diameter of the arc at the corner and arch represents vertical diameter of the arc at the corner.

❑ drawOval(int x, int y, int w, int h): This method draws a circle or ellipse bounded in the region of a rectangle starting at (x,y), with width w and height h.

❑ drawArc(int x, int y, int w, int h, int sangle, int aangle): Draws an arc bounded by a rectangle region of (x,y), with width w and height h. Here, sangle represents the beginning angle measured from 3 o'clock position in the clock. aangle represents the arc angle relative to start angle. sangle + aangle = end angle. If the sangle is positive, the arc is drawn counter clock wise and if it is negative, then it is drawn clockwise. To understand the arcs, see Figure 27.5

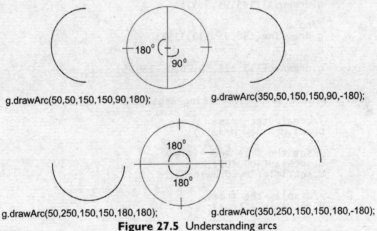

g.drawArc(50,50,150,150,90,180);   g.drawArc(350,50,150,150,90,-180);

g.drawArc(50,250,150,150,180,180);   g.drawArc(350,250,150,150,180,-180);

Figure 27.5 Understanding arcs

❑ drawPolygon(int x[], int y[], int n): This method draws a polygon that connects pairs of coordinates mentioned by the arrays x[] and y[]. Here, x[] is an array which holds x coordinates of points and y[] is an array which holds y coordinates. n represents the number of pairs of coordinates.

To draw any of these shapes, we need paint() method of Component class, which refreshes the frame contents automatically when a drawing is displayed. This method is useful whenever we want to display some new drawing or text or images in the frame. The paint() method is automatically called when a frame is created and displayed.

Program 6: Write a program to draw a smiling face using the methods of Graphics class.

```
//Drawing a smiling face in a frame
import java.awt.*;
import java.awt.event.*;
class Draw1 extends Frame
{
        Draw1()
        {
                //close the frame
                this.addWindowListener(new WindowAdapter()
                {
```

```
                    public void windowClosing(WindowEvent e)
                    {
                            System.exit(0);
                    }
            });
    }

    //to refresh the frame contents
    public void paint(Graphics g)
    {
            //set blue color for drawing
            g.setColor(Color.blue);

            //display a rectangle to contain drawing
            g.drawRect(40,40,200,200);

            //face
            g.drawOval(90,70,80,80);

            //eyes
            g.drawOval(110,95,5,5);
            g.drawOval(145,95,5,5);

            //nose
            g.drawLine(130,95,130,115);

            //mouth
            g.drawArc(113,115,35,20,0,-180);
    }

    public static void main(String args[])
    {
            //create the frame
            Draw1 d = new Draw1();

            //set the size and title
            d.setSize(400,400);
            d.setTitle("My drawing");

            //display the frame
            d.setVisible(true);
    }
}
```

Output:

```
C:\> javac Draw1.java
C:\> java Draw1
```

Filling with Colors

To fill any shape with a desired color, first of all we should set a color using setColor() method. Then any of the following methods will draw those respective shapes by filling with the color.

❑ fillRect(int x, int y, int w, int h): This method draws a rectangle and fills it with the specified color.

❑ fillRoundRect(int x, int y, int w, int h, int arcw, int arch): This method draws filled rectangle with rounded corners.

❑ fillOval(int x, int y, int w, int h): This method is useful to create an oval (circle or ellipse) which is filled with a specified color.

❑ fillArc(int x, int y, int w, int h, int sangle, int aangle): This method draws an arc and fills it with a specified color.

❑ fillPolygon(int x[], int y[], int n) : This method draws and fills a polygon with a specified color.

Let us rewrite Program 6, using filled shapes and see the output.

Program 7: Write a program that allows you to fill the shapes with some colors.

```java
//Drawing a smiling face in a frame with filled colors
import java.awt.*;
import java.awt.event.*;
class Draw2 extends Frame
{
        Draw2()
        {
                //close the frame
                this.addWindowListener(new WindowAdapter()
                {
                        public void windowClosing(WindowEvent e)
                        {
                                System.exit(0);
                        }
                });
        }

        public void paint(Graphics g)
        {
                //set blue color
                g.setColor(Color.blue);

                //display a rectangle to contain drawing
                g.fillRect(40,40,200,200);

                //set yellow color
                g.setColor(Color.yellow);

                //face
                g.fillOval(90,70,80,80);

                //set black color
                g.setColor(Color.black);

                //eyes
                g.fillOval(110,95,5,5);
                g.fillOval(145,95,5,5);

                //nose
                g.drawLine(130,95,130,115);

                //set red color
                g.setColor(Color.red);
```

```
                    //mouth
                    g.fillArc(113,115,35,20,0,-180);
        }

        public static void main(String args[])
        {
                    //create the frame
                    Draw2 d = new Draw2();

                    //set the size and title
                    d.setSize(400,400);
                    d.setTitle("My drawing");

                    //display the frame
                    d.setVisible(true);
        }
}
```

Output:

```
C:\> javac Draw2.java
C:\>java Draw2
```

Let us write a Java program to see how to create a polygon. Now, a polygon has several sides and to create each side, we need x and y coordinates to connect by a straight line. All the x coordinates and y coordinates can be stored in two arrays as:

```
int x[] = {40,200,40,100};
int y[] = {40,40,200,200};
```

Now, if a polygon is drawn, it starts at (40, 40) and connects it with (200,40), from there a line connects it to (40, 200) and finally ends at (100,200). So here, totally 4 pairs of coordinates are there, and hence the polygon can be drawn using:

```
g.drawPolygon(x,y,4);
```

Or, to get a filled polygon, we can use:

```
g.fillPolygon(x, y, 4);
```

Program 8: Write a program to create a polygon that is filled with green color. This polygon must be created inside a rounded rectangle which is filled with red color.

```
//Drawing a smilie in a frame
import java.awt.*;
import java.awt.event.*;
class DrawPoly extends Frame
{
        DrawPoly()
        {
                //close the frame
                this.addWindowListener(new WindowAdapter()
                {
                        public void windowClosing(WindowEvent e)
                        {
                                System.exit(0);
                        }
                });
        }

        public void paint(Graphics g)
        {
                //set red color
                g.setColor(Color.red);

                //display a filled rounded rectangle
                g.fillRoundRect(30,30,250,250,30,30);

                //set green color
                g.setColor(Color.green);

                //take x and y coordinates in arrays
                int x[] = {40,200,40,100};
                int y[] = {40,40,200,200};

                //there are 4 pairs of x,y coordinates
                int num = 4;

                //create filled polygon connecting the coordinates
                g.fillPolygon(x, y, num);

        }

        public static void main(String args[])
        {
                //create the frame
                DrawPoly d = new DrawPoly();

                //set the size and title
                d.setSize(400,400);
                d.setTitle("My Polygon");

                //display the frame
                d.setVisible(true);
        }
}
```

Output:

```
C:\> javac DrawPoly.java
C:\> java DrawPoly
```

Finally, another Java program to depict a small figure is shown in Program 9.

Program 9: Write a program to draw a home with moon at back ground.

```
//My Home
import java.awt.*;
import java.awt.event.*;
class Home extends Frame
{
        Home()
        {
                this.addWindowListener(new WindowAdapter()
                {
                        public void windowClosing(WindowEvent e)
                        {
                                System.exit(0);
                        }
                });
        }

        public void paint(Graphics g)
        {
                //store x,y coordinates in x[] and y[]
                int x[] = {375,275,475};
                int y[] = {125,200,200};
                int n = 3; //no. of pairs

                //set gray background for frame
                this.setBackground(Color.gray);


                //set yellow color for rectangle - house
                g.setColor(Color.yellow);
                g.fillRect(300,200,150,100);

                //set blue color for another rectangle - door
                g.setColor(Color.blue);
                g.fillRect(350,210,50,60);

                //draw a line - line below the door
                g.drawLine(350,280,400,280);

                //set dark gray for polygon - roof
                g.setColor(Color.darkGray);
                g.fillPolygon(x,y, n);

                //set cyan color for oval - moon
                g.setColor(Color.cyan);
```

```
                    g.fillOval(100,100,60,60);

                    //set green for arcs - grass
                    g.setColor(Color.green);
                    g.fillArc(50,250,150,100,0,180);
                    g.fillArc(150,250,150,100,0,180);
                    g.fillArc(450,250,150,100,0,180);

                    //draw a line - the bottom most line of drawing
                    g.drawLine(50,300,600,300);

                    //display some text
                    g.drawString("My Happy Home", 275, 350);
            }

            public static void main(String args[])
            {
                    //create the frame
                    Home h = new Home();

                    //set the size and title
                    h.setSize(500,400);
                    h.setTitle("My Home");

                    //display the frame
                    h.setVisible(true);
            }
    }
```

Output:

```
C:\> javac Home.java
C:\> java Home
```

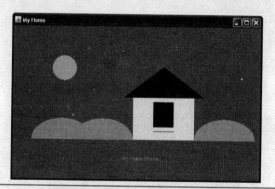

Displaying Dots

To display a dot or point on the screen, we can take the help of drawLine() method. For example, to display a point at (300,300) coordinates, we should use drawLine() method in such a way that the line is drawn starting from the same point and ending at the same point, as:

```
    drawLine(300,300,300,300);
```

This will display a dot at (300,300). The following program illustrates how to draw several white dots on the black screen.

Program 10: Write a program to display several dots on the screen continuously.

```
    //Displaying a group of dots on black screen
    import java.awt.*;
    import java.awt.event.*;
    class Points extends Frame
    {
        public void paint(Graphics g)
        {
            //set white color for dots
            g.setColor(Color.white);

            for (;;) //display dots forever
            {
            //generate x, y coordinates randomly. Maximum 800 and 600 px
            int x = (int) (Math.random() * 800);
            int y = (int) (Math.random() * 600);

            //Use drawLine() to display a dot
            g.drawLine(x, y, x, y);
            try{
                    //make a time delay of 20 milliseconds
                    Thread.sleep(20);
            }catch(InterruptedException ie){}

            }
        }
        public static void main(String args[])
        {
            //create frame
            Points obj = new Points();
            //set black background color for frame
            obj.setBackground(Color.black);
            //set the size and title for frame
            obj.setSize(500,400);
            obj.setTitle("Random dots");
            //display the frame
            obj.setVisible(true);

        }
    }
```

Output:

```
    C:\> javac Points.java
    C:\> java Points
```

Displaying text in the frame

To display some text or strings in the frame, we can take the help of drawString() method of Graphics class, as:

```
g.drawString("Hello", x,y);
```

Here, the string "Hello" will be displayed starting from the coordinates (x,y).

If we want to set some color for the text, we can use setColor() method of Graphics class, as:

```
g.setColor(Color.red);
```

There are two ways to set a color in AWT. The first way is by directly mentioning the needed color name from Color class, as Color.red, Color.yellow, Color.cyan, etc. All the standard colors are declared as constants in Color class, as shown in the Table 27.1:

Table 27.1

Color.black	Color.blue	Color.cyan
Color.pink	Color.red	Color.orange
Color.magenta	Color.darkGray	Color.gray
Color.lightGray	Color.green	Color.yellow
Color.white		

The second way to mention any color is by combining the three primary colors: red, green, and blue while creating Color class object, as:

```
Color c = new Color(r,g,b);
```

Here, r,g,b values can change from 0 to 255. 0 represents no color. 10 represents low intensity whereas 200 represents high intensity of color. Thus,

```
Color c = new Color(255,0,0); //red color
Color c = new Color(255,255,255); //white color
Color c = new Color(0,0,0); //black color
```

This Color class object c should be then passed to setColor() method to set the color.

To set some font to the text, we can use setFont() method of Graphics class, as:

```
g.setFont(Font object);
```

This method takes Font class object, which can be created as:

```
Font f = new Font("SansSerif", Font.BOLD, 30);
```

Here, "SansSerif" represents the font name, Font.BOLD represents the font style and 30 represents the font size in pixels. There are totally 3 styles that we can use:

```
Font.BOLD
Font.ITALIC
Font.PLAIN
```

We can also combine any two styles, for example, to use bold and italic, we can write Font.BOLD + Font.ITALIC

Program 11: Write a program to display some text in the frame using drawString() method.

```
//Frame with background color and message
import java.awt.*;
import java.awt.event.*;
class Message extends Frame
{
        Message()
        {
                //close the frame when close button clicked
                addWindowListener(new WindowAdapter(){
                public void windowClosing(WindowEvent we)
                {
                        System.exit(0);
                }
                });
        }//end of constructor

        public void paint(Graphics g)
        {
                //set background color for frame
                this.setBackground(new Color(100,20,20));

                //set font for the text
                Font f = new Font("Arial", Font.BOLD+Font.ITALIC,30);
                g.setFont(f);

                //set foreground color
                g.setColor(Color.green);

                //display the message
                g.drawString("Hello, How are U? ", 100,100);

        }

        public static void main(String args[])
        {
                Message m = new Message();
                m.setSize(400,300);
                m.setTitle("This is my text");
                m.setVisible(true);
        }
}
```

Output:

```
C:\> javac Message.java
C:\> java Message
```

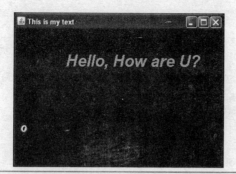

Knowing the Available Fonts

It is possible to know which fonts are available in our system. When we know the available fonts, we can use any of the font names to create Font class object. First of all, we should get the local graphics environment, as: GraphicsEnvironment ge = GraphicsEnvironment .getLocalGraphicsEnvironment();

Now, this ge contains the available font names which can be retrieved as:

```
String fonts[] = ge.getAvailableFontFamilyNames();
```

Program 12: Write a program to know which fonts are available in a local system.

```
//knowing the available fonts
import java.awt.*;
class Fonts
{
      public static void main(String args[])
      {

            //get the local graphics environment information into
            //GraphicsEnvironment object ge
            GraphicsEnvironment ge =
            GraphicsEnvironment.getLocalGraphicsEnvironment();

            //From ge, get available font family names into fonts[]
            String fonts[] = ge.getAvailableFontFamilyNames();

            System.out.println("Available fonts on this system: ");

            //retreive one by one the font names from fonts[] and display
            for(int i=0; i<fonts.length; i++)
            System.out.println(fonts[i]);
      }
}
```

Output:

```
C:\> javac Fonts.java
C:\> java Fonts
Available fonts on this system:
Agency FB
Arial
Arial Black
Arial Narrow
Arial Rounded MT Bold
```

```
          AS-TTDurga
          Astro
          Blackadder ITC
          BN-TTDurga
          Bodoni MT
          Bodoni MT Black
          Bodoni MT Condensed
          Book Antiqua
          Bookman Old Style
          Bookshelf Symbol 7
          Bradley Hand ITC
          Calisto MT
          Castellar
          Century Gothic
          Century Schoolbook
          Comic Sans MS
          Courier New
          :
          :
```

Displaying Images in the Frame

We can display images like .gif and .jpg files in the frame. For this purpose, we should follow these steps:

❏ Load the image into Image class object using getImage() method of Toolkit class.

```
    Image img = Toolkit.getDefaultToolkit().getImage("diamonds.gif");
```

Here, Toolkit.getDefaultToolkit() method creates a default Toolkit class object. Using this object, we call getImage() method and this method loads the image diamonds.gif into img object.

❏ But, loading the image into img will take some time. JVM uses a separate thread to load the image into img and continues with the rest of the program. So, there is a possibility of completing the program execution before the image is completely loaded into img. In this case, a blank frame without any image will be displayed. To avoid this, we should make JVM wait till the image is completely loaded into img object. For this purpose, we need MediaTracker class. Add the image to MediaTracker class and allot an identification number to it starting from 0,1,...

```
    MediaTracker track = new MediaTracker(this);
    track.addImage(img,0);  //0 is the id number of image
```

❏ Now, MediaTracker keeps JVM waiting till the image is loaded completely. This is done by waitForID() method.

```
    track.waitForID(0);
```

This means wait till the image with the id number 0 is loaded into img object. Similarly, when several images are there, we can use waitForID(1), waitForID(2), etc.,

❏ Once the image is loaded and available in img, then we can display the image using drawImage() method of Graphics class, as:

```
    g.drawImage(img,50,50,null);
```

Here, img is the image that is displayed at (50,50) coordinates and 'null' represents ImageObserver class object which is not required. ImageObserver is useful to store history of how the image is loaded into the object. Since, this is not required, we can use just null in its place. Another alternative for drawImage() is:

```
g.drawImage(img,50,50, 200, 250, null);
```

Here, additional 200, 250 represent the width and height of the image. They help to increase or decrease the size of the image to fit in the area allotted for it in the frame.

❑ To display an image in the title bar of the frame, we can use setIconImage() method of Frame class, as:

```
setIconImage(img);
```

Program 13: Write a program to display an image in the frame and also in the title bar of the frame.

```
//Displaying an image in the frame and also in the title bar
import java.awt.*;
import java.awt.event.*;
class Images extends Frame
{
        //take a static type Image class object
        static Image img;

        Images()
        {
                //load an image into Image object
                img=Toolkit.getDefaultToolkit().getImage("diamonds.gif");

                //wait till the image is loaded into img object
                //for this purpose, create MediaTracker
                MediaTracker track = new MediaTracker(this);

                //add image to MediaTracker
                track.addImage(img,0);
                try{
                        //let the JVM wait till the image is loaded completely
                        track.waitForID(0);
                }catch(InterruptedException ie){}

                //close the frame
                addWindowListener(new WindowAdapter()
                {
                        public void windowClosing(WindowEvent we)
                        {
                                System.exit(0);
                        }
                });
        }

        public void paint(Graphics g)
        {
                //display the image in the frame at 50,50 pixels
                g.drawImage(img,50,50,null);

        }

        public static void main(String args[])
        {
                //create the frame
                Images i = new Images();

                //set the size and title
```

```
                    i.setSize(500,400);
                    i.setTitle("My images");

                    //display the same image in the title bar of frame
                    i.setIconImage(img);

                    //display the frame
                    i.setVisible(true);
            }
        }
```

Output:

```
C:\> javac Images.java
C:\>java Images
```

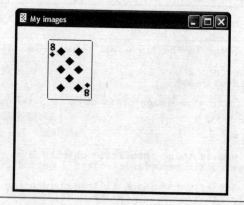

Component Class Methods

A component is a graphical representation of an object on the screen. For example, push buttons, radio buttons, menus, etc. are components. Even frame is also a component. There is Component class available in `java.awt` package which contains the following methods which are applicable to any component.

❑ `Font getFont()`: This method returns the font of the component.

❑ `void setFont(Font f)`: This method sets a particular font `f` for the text of the component.

❑ `Color getForeground()`: This method gives the foreground color of the component.

❑ `void setForeground(Color c)`: This method sets a foreground color `c` to the component.

❑ `Color getBackground()`: Gets the background color of the component.

❑ `void setBackground(Color c)`: Sets the background color `c` for the component.

❑ `String getName()`: Returns the name of the component.

❑ `void setName(String name)`: Sets a new name for the component.

❑ `int getHeight()`: Returns the height of the component in pixels as an integer.

❑ `int getWidth()`: Returns the width of the component in pixels as an integer.

❑ `Dimension getSize()`: Returns the size of the component as an object of `Dimension` class. `Dimenison.width` and `Dimenision.height` will provide the width and height of the component.

❑ `int  getX()`: Returns the current x coordinate of the component's origin.

❑ `int  getY()`: Returns the current y coordinate of the component's origin.

❑ `Point getLocation()`: Gets the location of the component in the form of a point specifying the component's top-left corner.

❑ `void setLocation(int x, int y)`: Moves the component to a new location specified by (x,y).

❑ `void setSize(int width, int height)`: Resizes the component so that it has new width and height as passed to `setSize()` method.

❑ `void setVisible(boolean b)`: Shows or hides the component depending on the value of parameter b. `setVisible(true)` will display the component and `setVisible(false)` hides the component.

❑ `void setEnabled(boolean b)`: Enables or disables the component, depending on the value of the parameter b. `setEnabled(true)` will enable the component to function and `setEnabled(false)` will disable it.

❑ `void setBounds(int x, int y, int w, int h)`: This method allots a rectangular area starting at (x,y) coordinates and with width w and height h. The component is resized to this area before its display. This method is useful to specify the location of the component in the frame.

After creating a component, we should add the component to the frame. For this purpose, `add()` method is used.

```
f.add(component);
```

Similarly, to remove a component from the frame, we can use `remove()` method, as:

```
f.remove(component);
```

Push Buttons

Button class is useful to create Push buttons. A Push button is useful to perform a particular action.

❑   To create a push button with a label, we can create an object to `Button` class, as:

```
Button b = new Button();  //a button without any label is created.
Button b = new Button("label");  //a button with label is created.
```

❑   To get the label of the button, use `getLabel()`:

```
String l = b.getLabel();
```

❑   To set the label of the button:

```
b.setLabel("label");
```

Here, the "label" is set to the button b.

❑   When, there are several buttons, naturally the programmer should know which button is clicked by the user. For this purpose, `getActionCommand()` method of `ActionEvent` class is useful.

```
        String s = ae.getActionCommand();
```

Here, s represents the label of the button clicked by the user.

❏ To know the source object which has been clicked by the user, we can use, getSource() method of ActionEvent class, as:

```
        Object obj = ae.getSource();
```

Remember that only displaying the push buttons will not perform any actions. This means they cannot handle any events. To handle the events, we should use event delegation model. According to this model, an appropriate listener should be added to the push button. When the button is clicked, the event is passed to the listener and the listener calls a method which handles the event. With the push buttons, ActionListener is a suitable listener. To handle ActionListener to the button, we can use addxxxListener() method, as:

```
        b.addActionListener(ActionListener obj);
```

Similarly, to remove action listener from the button, we can use removexxxListener() method, as:

```
        b.removeActionListener(ActionListener obj);
```

In the two methods, addActionListener() and removeActionListener(), we are passing ActionListener object. Since ActionListener is an interface, we cannot directly create an object to it, we should pass object of implementation class of the interface in this case.

Let us write a program to create push buttons and also add some actions to the buttons. The following steps can be followed:

❏ First, set a layout manager using setLayout() method. In our program, we do not want to set any layout, hence we can pass null to setLayout() as:

```
        this.setLayout(null);
```

Since our class Mybuttons extends Frame class, this represents Mybuttons class object or Frame class.

❏ Then create the push buttons by creating objects to Button class.

❏ Since, we are not using any layout manager, we should specify where to attach the buttons in the frame using setBounds() method.

❏ Then add the buttons to the frame using add() method.

❏ Add ActionListener to the buttons so that when we click on any button, the listener will handle the event by calling actionPerformed() method.

Program 14: Write a program that helps in creating 3 push buttons bearing the names of 3 colors. When a button is clicked, that particular color is set as background color in the frame.

```
//Push buttons
import java.awt.*;
import java.awt.event.*;
class Mybuttons extends Frame implements ActionListener
{
    //vars
    Button b1,b2,b3;

    Mybuttons()
    {
```

```
                    //do not set any layout
                    this.setLayout(null);

                    //create 3 push buttons
                    b1 = new Button("Yellow");
                    b2 = new Button("Blue");
                    b3 = new Button("Pink");

                    //set the locations of buttons in the frame
                    b1.setBounds(100,100,70,40);
                    b2.setBounds(100,160,70,40);
                    b3.setBounds(100,220,70,40);

                    //add the buttons to the frame
                    this.add(b1);
                    this.add(b2);
                    this.add(b3);

                    //add action listener to the buttons
                    b1.addActionListener(this);
                    b2.addActionListener(this);
                    b3.addActionListener(this);

                    //close the frame
                    addWindowListener(new WindowAdapter()
                    {
                            public void windowClosing(WindowEvent we)
                            {
                                    System.exit(0);
                            }
                    });

        }//end of constructor

        //this method is called when a button is clicked
        public void actionPerformed(ActionEvent ae)
        {
                    //know the label of the button clicked by user
                    String str= ae.getActionCommand();

                    //change the frame's background color depending on the button
                    //clicked
                    if(str.equals("Yellow")) this.setBackground(Color.yellow);
                    if(str.equals("Blue")) this.setBackground(Color.blue);
                    if(str.equals("Pink")) this.setBackground(Color.pink);

        }

        public static void main(String args[])
        {
                    //create the frame
                    Mybuttons mb = new Mybuttons();
                    mb.setSize(400,400);
                    mb.setTitle("My buttons");
                    mb.setVisible(true);
        }
}
```

Output:

```
C:\> javac Mybuttons.java
C:\> java Mybuttons
```

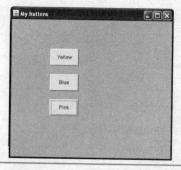

In the preceding program, observe the following statement:

```
this.setLayout(null);
```

Here, this represents current class object. Since the current class Mybuttons is a subclass of Frame class, we know that Mybuttons class object has a copy of Frame class object within it. So any Frame class methods can be invoked using this. So, setLayout() method of Frame class can be called using

```
this.setLayout()
```

In fact, even if this is also not used, there will not be any problem, since anyhow a method by default acts on present class object only.

setLayout() is useful to set a layout for the frame. What is this layout? A layout represents a manner of arranging components in the frame. All layouts are represented as implementation classes of LayoutManager interface. For example, the following layouts are available in AWT:

- FlowLayout
- BorderLayout
- GridLayout
- CardLayout
- GridBagLayout
- BoxLayout (belongs to javax.swing package)

We will discuss about layout managers in a later chapter. The following points are helpful to understand how to work with a layout manager:

- To set a layout for our components, we can pass the layout class object to the setLayout() method as:

```
setLayout( new  FlowLayout());
```

The preceding statement will set FlowLayout to the frame. It means FlowLayout will take the responsibility of arranging the components in the frame as a flow or as a line one after the other.

- Suppose, we do not want to set any layout, then we should pass null to the setLayout() method as:

```
setLayout(null);
```

- Suppose, we do not use setLayout() method at all, then the Java compiler assumes a default layout manager. The default layout in case of a frame is BorderLayout.

What is the default layout in a frame?
  BorderLayout.

What is the default layout in an applet?
  FlowLayout.

The previous program can be rewritten with two variations. First, we want to use `FlowLayout` manager to arrange the components in the frame in a line one after the other. When a line is filled with components, automatically the components are arranged into the second line. `FlowLayout` is the simplest layout manager of all. When we use some layout manager like this, there is no need to use `setBounds()` method to specify the location of push buttons. The second change in this program is that instead of using `getActionCommand()` we use `getSource()` method to find which button is clicked. Another thing is that we are not using `this` in this version. Thus, when we call a method directly, as:

```
setLayout(new FlowLayout());
```

we should understand that, since we did not use any object to call the method, it is by default called with the present class object or Frame object.

Program 15: Write a program to create the push buttons, arrange them using `FlowLayout` manager and setting the background color for the frame depending on the button clicked by the user.

```
//Push buttons - version 2
import java.awt.*;
import java.awt.event.*;
class Mybuttons extends Frame implements ActionListener
{
      //vars
      Button b1,b2,b3;

      Mybuttons()
      {
            //do not set any layout
            setLayout(new FlowLayout());

            //create 3 push buttons
            b1 = new Button("Yellow");
            b2 = new Button("Blue");
            b3 = new Button("Pink");

            //add the buttons to the frame
            add(b1);
            add(b2);
            add(b3);

            //add action listener to the buttons
            b1.addActionListener(this);
            b2.addActionListener(this);
            b3.addActionListener(this);

            //close the frame
            addWindowListener(new WindowAdapter()
            {
                  public void windowClosing(WindowEvent we)
                  {
                        System.exit(0);
```

```
                                    }
                });

        }//end of constructor

        //this method is called when a button is clicked
        public void actionPerformed(ActionEvent ae)
        {
                //know the the button clicked by user

                if(ae.getSource() == b1) setBackground(Color.yellow);
                if(ae.getSource() == b2) setBackground(Color.blue);
                if(ae.getSource() == b3) setBackground(Color.pink);

        }

        public static void main(String args[])
        {
                //create the frame
                Mybuttons mb = new Mybuttons();
                mb.setSize(400,400);
                mb.setTitle("My buttons");
                mb.setVisible(true);
        }
}
```

Output:

```
C:\> javac Mybuttons.java
C:\> java Mybuttons
```

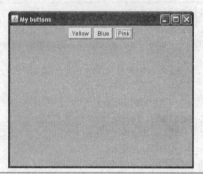

Listeners and Listener Methods

For working with push buttons, `ActionListener` is more suitable. Similarly, for other components, other listeners are also available. All listeners are available in `java.awt.event` package. Table 27.2 summarizes the components, suitable listeners for the component, and the methods in the listener interface to be implemented when using that listener

Table 27.2

Component	Listener	Listener methods
Button	ActionListener	public void actionPerformed(ActionEvent e)
CheckBox	ItemListener	public void itemStateChanged(ItemEvent e)

Component	Listener	Listener methods
CheckBoxGroup	ItemListener	public void itemStateChanged(ItemEvent e)
TextField	ActionListener FocusListener	public void actionPerformed(ActionEvent e) public void focusGained(FocusEvent e) public void focusLost(FocusEvent e)
TextArea	ActionListener FocusListener	public void actionPerformed(ActionEvent e) public void focusGained(FocusEvent e) public void focusLost(FocusEvent e)
Choice	ActionListener ItemListener	public void actionPerformed(ActionEvent e) public void itemStateChanged(ItemEvent e)
List	ActionListener ItemListener	public void actionPerformed(ActionEvent e) public void itemStateChanged(ItemEvent e)
Scrollbar	AdjustmentListener MouseMotionListener	public void adjustmentValueChanged(AdjustmentEvent e) public void mouseDragged(MouseEvent e) public void mouseMoved(MouseEvent e)
Frame	WindowListener	public void windowActivated(WindowEvent e) public void windowClosed(WindowEvent e) public void windowClosing(WindowEvent e) public void windowDeactivated(WindowEvent e) public void windowDeiconified(WindowEvent e) public void windowIconified(WindowEvent e) public void windowOpened(WindowEvent e)
Key board	KeyListener	public void keyPressed(KeyEvent e) public void keyReleased(KeyEvent e) public void keyTyped(KeyEvent e)
Label	No listener is needed	

Check Boxes

A check box is a square shaped box which displays an option to the user. The user can select one or more options from a group of check boxes. Let us see how to work with check boxes.

❑ To create a check box, we can create an object to Checkbox class, as:

```
Checkbox cb = new Checkbox();  //create a check box without any label
Checkbox cb = new Checkbox("label");  //with a label
Checkbox cb = new Checkbox("label", state); // if state is true, then the check
//box appears as if it is selected by default, else not selected.
```

❏ To get the state of a check box:

```
boolean b = cb.getState();
```

If the check box is selected, this method returns true, else false.

❏ To set the state of a check box:

```
cb.setState(true);
```

The check box cb will now appear as if it is selected.

❏ To get the label of a check box:

```
String s = cb.getLabel();
```

If cb is the check box object, then getLabel() will give its label.

❏ void setLabel(String label)

This method sets a new label to the check box.

❏ To get the selected check box label into an array we can use getSelectedObjects() method. This method returns an array of size 1 only.

```
Object x[ ] = cb.getSelectedObjects();
```

Here, x[0] stores the label of the check box selected by the user, if selected. Other wise, it stores null.

For example, there are 2 check boxes as:

```
Checkbox c1 = new Checkbox("One");
Checkbox c2 = new Checkbox("Two");

x = c1.getSelectedObjects();  //x is an array of Object type
if(x[0] == null) System.out.println("The check box is not selected");
else System.out.println("Selected check box label is : "+ x[0]);
```

Program 16: Write a program to create 3 check boxes to display Bold, Italic, and Underline to the user.

```
//Checkbox demo
import java.awt.*;
import java.awt.event.*;
class Mycheckbox extends Frame implements ItemListener
{
        //vars
        String msg="";
        Checkbox c1,c2,c3;

        Mycheckbox()
        {
                //set flow layout manager
                setLayout(new FlowLayout());
```

```
                        //display 3 checkboxes
                        c1 = new Checkbox("Bold",true);
                        c2 = new Checkbox("Italic");
                        c3 = new Checkbox("Underline");

                        //add the check boxes to the frame
                        add(c1);
                        add(c2);
                        add(c3);

                        //add item listener to the check boxes
                        c1.addItemListener(this);
                        c2.addItemListener(this);
                        c3.addItemListener(this);

                        //close the frame
                        addWindowListener(new WindowAdapter()
                        {
                                public void windowClosing(WindowEvent we)
                                {
                                        System.exit(0);
                                }
                        });
        } //end of constructor

        //this method is called the user clicks on a check box
        public void itemStateChanged(ItemEvent ie)
        {
                repaint(); //call paint() method
        }

        //display current state of checkboxes
        public void paint(Graphics g)
        {
                g.drawString("Current state: ", 10,100);
                msg = "Bold: "+c1.getState();
                g.drawString(msg, 10,120);
                msg = "Italic: "+c2.getState();
                g.drawString(msg, 10,140);
                msg = "Underline: "+c3.getState();
                g.drawString(msg, 10, 160);
        }

        public static void main(String args[])
        {
                //create the frame
                Mycheckbox mc = new Mycheckbox();
                mc.setTitle("My checkbox");
                mc.setSize(400,400);
                mc.setVisible(true);
        }
}
```

Output:

```
C:\> javac Mycheckbox.java
C:\>java Mycheckbox
```

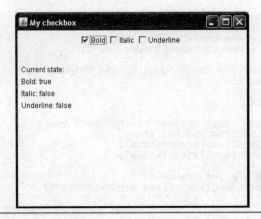

In this program, when the user clicks on any check box, the event is handled by `ItemListener` attached to the check boxes and hence the code of `itemStateChanged(ItemEvent ie)` gets executed.

Radio Button

A radio button represents a round shaped button, such that only one can be selected from a group of buttons. Radio buttons can be created using `CheckboxGroup` class and `Checkbox` classes. First of all, we should create a `CheckboxGroup` class object. While creating a radio button, we should pass CheckboxGroup object to the Checkbox class. It represents the group to which the radio button belongs. When the same CheckboxGroup object is passed to different radio buttons, then all those radio buttons will be considered as belonging to same group and hence the user is allowed to select only one from them.

❑ To create a radio button, pass `CheckboxGroup` object to `Checkbox` class object:

```
CheckboxGroup cbg = new CheckboxGroup();
Checkbox cb = new Checkbox("label", cbg, state);
```

Here, if state is true then the radio button appears to be already selected by default. If the state is false, then the radio button appears normal as if it is not selected.

❑ To know which radio button is selected by the user:

```
Checkbox cb = cbg.getSelectedCheckbox();
```

❑ To know the selected radio button's label:

```
String label = cbg.getSelectedCheckbox().getLabel();
```

Program 17: Write a program that creates 2 radio buttons 'Yes' and 'No'. The user selects a button from them, and displays the selected button label.

```
//Radio buttons demo
import java.awt.*;
import java.awt.event.*;
class Myradio extends Frame implements ItemListener
{
    //vars
```

```
        String msg="";
        CheckboxGroup cbg;
        Checkbox y,n;

        Myradio()
        {
                //set the layout to flow layout
                setLayout(new FlowLayout());

                //create CheckboxGroup object
                cbg = new CheckboxGroup();

                //create 2 radio buttons
                y = new Checkbox("Yes",cbg,true);
                n = new Checkbox("No", cbg,false);

                //add the radio buttons to frame
                add(y);
                add(n);

                //add item listener to the radio buttons
                y.addItemListener(this);
                n.addItemListener(this);

                //close the frame
                addWindowListener(new WindowAdapter()
                {
                        public void windowClosing(WindowEvent we)
                        {
                                System.exit(0);
                        }
                });
        } //end of constructor

        //this method is called when a radio button is clicked
        public void itemStateChanged(ItemEvent ie)
        {
                repaint();   //call paint()
        }

        //display the selected radio label
        public void paint(Graphics g)
        {
                msg= "Current selection: ";
                msg+= cbg.getSelectedCheckbox().getLabel();
                g.drawString(msg,10,100);
        }

        public static void main(String args[])
        {
                //create frame
                Myradio mr = new Myradio();
                mr.setTitle("My radio buttons");
                mr.setSize(400,400);
                mr.setVisible(true);
        }
}
```

Output:

```
C:\> javac Myradio.java
C:\> java Myradio
```

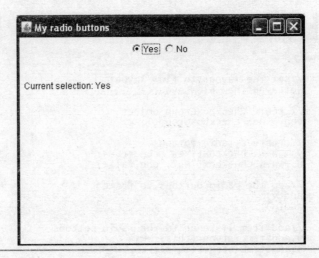

TextField

A TextField represents a long rectangular box where the user can type a single line of text. We can also display a line of text in the text field also.

❑   To create a TextField:

```
TextField tf = new TextField();  // a blank text field is created
TextField tf = new TextField(25);  //25 characters width of text field
TextField tf = new TextField("default text", 25);  //default text is displayed
//when the text field is displayed.
```

❑   To retrieve the text from a `TextField`:

```
String s = tf.getText();
```

❑   To set the text to a `TextField`:

```
tf.setText("text");
```

❑   To hide the text being typed into the `TextField` by a character `char`:

```
tf.setEchoChar('char');
```

Now, the original characters typed in the text field are not displayed. In their place, the `char` is displayed. This is useful to hide important text like credit card numbers, passwords, etc.

TextArea

A TextArea is similar to a text field, but it can accommodate several lines of text. For example, if the user wants to type his address which contains several lines, he can use a text area.

❑   To create a TextArea:

```
TextArea ta = new TextArea(); //an empty text area
TextArea ta = new TextArea(rows,cols); //text area with some rows and
//columns
TextArea ta = new TextArea("string"); //text area with predefined string
```

❏ To retrieve the text from a TextArea:

```
String s = ta.getText();
```

❏ To set the text to a TextArea:

```
ta.setText("text");
```

❏ To append the given text to the text area's current text:

```
ta.append("text");
```

❏ To insert the specified text at the specified position in this text area:

```
ta.insert("text", position);
```

Label

A Label is a constant text that is generally displayed along with a TextField or TextArea.

❏ To create a label:

```
Label l = new Label();    //create an empty label
Label l = new Label("text", alignment constant);
Here, the alignmentconstant may be one of the following:
Label.RIGHT, Label.LEFT, Label.CENTER
```

When the label is displayed, there would be some rectangular area allotted for the label. In this area, the label is aligned towards right, left, or center as per the alignment constant.

Program 18: Write a program to create two labels and two text fields for entering name and passwords. The password typed by the user in the text field is hidden.

```
//TextFields with a Labels
import java.awt.*;
import java.awt.event.*;
class MyText extends Frame implements ActionListener
{
      //vars
      TextField name,pass;

      MyText()
      {
            //set layout to flow layout
            setLayout(new FlowLayout());

            //create 2 labels
            Label n = new Label("Name: ", Label.LEFT);
            Label p = new Label("Pass word: ", Label.LEFT);

            //create text fields for name and password
            name = new TextField(20);
            pass = new TextField(20);
```

```
                    //hide the password by *
                    pass.setEchoChar('*');

                    //use background,foreground colors and font for name textfield
                    name.setBackground(Color.yellow);
                    name.setForeground(Color.red);
                    Font f = new Font("Arial",Font.PLAIN,25);
                    name.setFont(f);

                    //add the labels and textfields to frame
                    add(n);
                    add(name);
                    add(p);
                    add(pass);

                    //add action listener to text fields
                    name.addActionListener(this);
                    pass.addActionListener(this);

                    //close the frame
                    addWindowListener(new WindowAdapter()
                    {
                            public void windowClosing(WindowEvent we)
                            {
                                    System.exit(0);
                            }
                    });

            }//end of constructor

            //this method is executed when enter is clicked
            //display the text entered into the text fields
            public void actionPerformed(ActionEvent ae)
            {
                    //create Graphics class object
                    Graphics g = this.getGraphics();

                    g.drawString("Name: "+name.getText(), 10,200);
                    g.drawString("Pass word:"+pass.getText(),10,240);
            }


            public static void main(String args[])
            {
                    //create the frame
                    MyText mt = new MyText();
                    mt.setTitle("My text field");
                    mt.setSize(400,400);
                    mt.setVisible(true);
            }
    }
```

Output:

```
C:\> javac MyText.java
C:\> java MyText
```

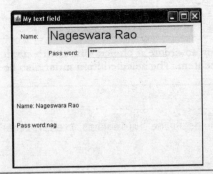

Choice Class

Choice class is useful to display a choice menu. It is a pop-up list of items and the user can select only one item from the available items.

❑ To create a Choice menu:

```
Choice ch = new Choice(); //create empty choice menu
```

❑ Once a choice menu is created, we should add items to it using add() method, as:

```
ch.add("item");
```

❑ To know the name of the item selected from the Choice menu:

```
String s = ch.getSelectedItem();
```

❑ Index of items in the Choice menu starts from 0 onwards. To know the index of the currently selected item:

```
int i = ch.getSelectedIndex();
This method returns -1 if nothing is selected.
```

❑ To get the item string, given the item index number,

```
String item = ch.getItem(int index);
```

❑ To know the number of items in the Choice menu,

```
int n = ch.getItemCount();
```

❑ To remove an item from the choice menu at a specified position,

```
ch.remove(int position)
```

❑ To remove an item from the choice menu,

```
ch.remove(String item)
```

❑ To remove all items from the choice menu,

```
        ch.removeAll();
```

Program 19: Write a program to create a choice menu with names of some languages from where the user has to select any one item. The selected item must also be displayed in the frame.

```java
//Choice box demo
import java.awt.*;
import java.awt.event.*;
class Mychoice extends Frame implements ItemListener
{
    //vars
    String msg;
    Choice ch;

    Mychoice()
    {
        //set flow layout to frame
        setLayout(new FlowLayout());

        //create an empty choice menu
        ch = new Choice();

        //add some items to choice menu
        ch.add("English");
        ch.add("Hindi");
        ch.add("Telugu");
        ch.add("Sanskrit");
        ch.add("French");

        //add the choice menu to frame
        add(ch);

        //add item listener to choice menu
        ch.addItemListener(this);

        //close the frame
        addWindowListener(new WindowAdapter()
        {
            public void windowClosing(WindowEvent we)
            {
                System.exit(0);
            }
        });

    }

    //this method is called when any item is clicked
    public void itemStateChanged(ItemEvent ie)
    {

        //call paint() method
        repaint();

    }

    //display selected item from the choice menu
    public void paint(Graphics g)
    {
        g.drawString("Selected language: ", 10,100);
        msg = ch.getSelectedItem();
        g.drawString(msg,10,120);
    }

    public static void main(String args[])
    {
        //create a frame
```

```
        Mychoice mc = new Mychoice();
        mc.setTitle("My choice box");
        mc.setSize(400,350);
        mc.setVisible(true);
    }
}
```

Output:

```
C:\> javac Mychoice.java
C:\> java Mychoice
```

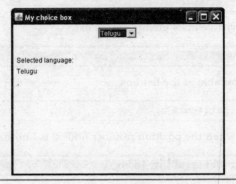

List Class

This class is useful to create a list box which is similar to choice menu. A list box presents the user with a scrolling list of text items. The user can select one or more items from the list box.

❏   To create a list box, we can create an object to List class:

```
    List lst = new List();
```

This statement creates a list box. The user can select only one item from the available items.

```
    List lst = new List(3);
```

This statement creates a list box which displays initially 3 rows. The rest of the rows can be seen by clicking on the scroll button.

```
    List lst = new List(3, true);
```

This list box initially displays 3 items. The next parameter `true` represents that the user can select more than one item from the available items. If it is `false`, then the user can select only one item.

❏   To add items to the list box, we can use `add()` method, as:

```
    lst.add("item");
```

❏   To get all the selected items from the list box:

```
    String x[] = lst.getSelectedItems();
```

❑ To get a single selected item from the list box:

```
String x = lst.getSelectedItem();
```

❑ To get the selected items' position numbers:

```
int x[] = lst.getSelectedIndexes();
```

❑ To get a single selected item position number:

```
int x = lst.getSelectedIndex();
```

❑ To get the number of visible lines (items) in this list:

```
int x = lst.getRows();
```

❑ To get all the items available in the list box:

```
String x[] = lst.getItems();
```

❑ To get the item name when the position number (index) is known:

```
String item = lst.getItem(int index);
```

❑ To know how many number of items are there in the list box:

```
int x = lst.getItemCount();
```

❑ To remove an item at a specified position from the list:

```
lst.remove(int position);
```

❑ To remove an item whose name is given:

```
lst.remove(String item);
```

❑ To remove all items from the list:

```
lst.removeAll();
```

Program 20: Write a program to create a list box with names of some languages from where the user can select one or more items.

```java
//List box demo
import java.awt.*;
import java.awt.event.*;

class Mylist extends Frame implements ItemListener
{
        //vars
        int[] msg;
        List lst;

        Mylist()
        {
                //set flow layout manager
```

```
                    setLayout(new FlowLayout());

                    //create an empty list box that displays 4 items initially
                    //and multiple selection is also enabled
                    lst = new List(4,true);

                    //add items to the list box
                    lst.add("English");
                    lst.add("Hindi");
                    lst.add("Telugu");
                    lst.add("Sanskrit");
                    lst.add("French");

                    //add the list box to frame
                    add(lst);

                    //add item listener to the list box
                    lst.addItemListener(this);

                    //frame closing
                    addWindowListener(new WindowAdapter()
                    {
                            public void windowClosing(WindowEvent we)
                            {
                                    System.exit(0);
                            }
                    });

            } //end of constructor

            public void itemStateChanged(ItemEvent ie)
            {
                    //call the paint() method
                    repaint();
            }

            public void paint(Graphics g)
            {
                    g.drawString("Selected languages: ",100,200);

                    //get the selected items position numbers into msg[]
                    msg = lst.getSelectedIndexes();

                    //know each selected item's name and display
                    for(int i=0; i<msg.length; i++)
                    {
                            String item = lst.getItem(msg[i]);
                            g.drawString(item, 100, 220+i*20);
                    }
            }
            public static void main(String args[])
            {
                    //create the frame
                    Mylist ml = new Mylist();
                    ml.setTitle("my list box");
                    ml.setSize(400,400);
                    ml.setVisible(true);
            }
    }
```

Output:

```
C:\> javac Mylist.java
C:\> java Mylist
```

In this program, the position numbers of the selected items are stored in an array and then displayed in the frame.

Scrollbar Class

Scrollbar class is useful to create scrollbars that can be attached to a frame or text area. Scrollbars are used to select continuous values between a specified minimum and maximum. Scrollbars can be arranged vertically or horizontally.

❑ To create a scrollbar we can create an object to Scrollbar class , as:

```
Scrollbar sb = new Scrollbar(alignment, start, step, min, max);
```

Here,

```
alignment:  Scrollbar.VERTICAL, Scrollbar.HORIZONTAL
start: starting value (Ex: 0)
step: step value (Ex: 30)   //represents scrollbar length
min: minimum value (Ex: 0)
max: maximum value (Ex: 300)
```

❑ To know the location of a scrollbar, we can use getValue() method that gives the position of the scrollbar in pixels, as:

```
int n = sb.getValue();
```

❑ To update the scrollbar position to a new position, we can use setValue() method, as:

```
sb.setValue(int position);
```

❑ To get the maximum value of the scrollbar:

```
int x = sb.getMaximum();
```

❑ To get the minimum value of the scrollbar:

```
int x = sb.getMinimum();
```

❑ To get the alignment of the scrollbar:

```
int x = getOrientation();
```

This method returns 0 if the scrollbar is aligned HORIZONTAL and returns 1 if it is aligned VERTICAL.

Program 21: Write a program to create a vertical scrollbar with scroll button length 30 px and with the starting and ending positions ranging from 0 to 400px.

```java
//Creating a vertical scrollbar
import java.awt.*;
import java.awt.event.*;

class Myscroll extends Frame implements AdjustmentListener
{
        //vars
        String msg="";
        Scrollbar s1;

        Myscroll()
        {
                //do not set any layout
                setLayout(null);

                //create a vertical scrollbar
                s1 = new Scrollbar(Scrollbar.VERTICAL, 0,30,0,400);

                //set the location of scrollbar in the frame
                s1.setBounds(250,50,30,200);

                //add it to frame
                add(s1);

                //add adjustment listener to scrollbar
                s1.addAdjustmentListener(this);

                //frame Closing
                addWindowListener(new WindowAdapter()
                {
                        public void windowClosing(WindowEvent we)
                        {
                                System.exit(0);
                        }
                });
        }

        public void adjustmentValueChanged(AdjustmentEvent ae)
        {
                repaint();  //call paint()
        }

        public void paint(Graphics g)
        {
                //display the position of scrollbar
                g.drawString("SCROLLBAR POSITION: ", 20,150);
                msg += s1.getValue();
                g.drawString(msg, 20,180);
                msg="";
        }

        public static void main(String args[])
        {
                //create the frame
                Myscroll ms = new Myscroll();
                ms.setTitle("My scroll bar");
                ms.setSize(400,400);
```

```
                ms.setVisible(true);
        }
}
```

Output:

```
C:\> javac Myscroll.java
C:\> java Myscroll
```

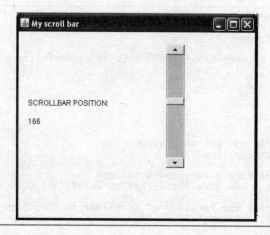

Knowing the Keys on Keyboard

To know which key is pressed on the keyboard, we can take the help of `KeyListener` interface. This interface has the following methods:

❑ `public void keyPressed(KeyEvent ke)`: This method is called when a key on the keyboard is pressed.

❑ `public void keyTyped(KeyEvent ke)`: This method is called when a key on the keyboard is typed. This method is applicable to the keys, which can be displayed and generally does not denote the special keys like function keys, control keys, shift keys, etc.

❑ `public void keyReleased(KeyEvent ke)`: This method is called when a key on the keyboard is released.

Program 22: Write a program to trap the key code and key name typed by the user on the keyboard and display them in a text area.

```
//Catching which key is pressed
import java.awt.*;
import java.awt.event.*;

class Keys extends Frame implements KeyListener
{
        //vars
        TextArea ta;
        String msg="";

        Keys()
        {
                //set flow layout
                setLayout(new FlowLayout());
```

```
                //create a text area to display the key code
                ta= new TextArea(5,25);

                //set some font and foreground color to text area
                Font f = new Font("SansSerif", Font.BOLD, 25);
                ta.setFont(f);
                ta.setForeground(Color.red);

                //add text area to frame
                add(ta);

                //add key listener to text area
                ta.addKeyListener(this);

                //close the frame
                addWindowListener(new WindowAdapter()
                {
                        public void windowClosing(WindowEvent we)
                        {
                                System.exit(0);
                        }
                });
        }
        public void keyPressed(KeyEvent ke)
        {
                //get the code of the key pressed
                int keycode= ke.getKeyCode();
                msg += "\nKey code: "+keycode;

                //get the name of the key from the code
                String keyname= ke.getKeyText(keycode);
                msg += "\nKey pressed: "+ keyname;

                //display the key code and key name in text area
                ta.setText(msg);
                msg="";
        }

        public void keyTyped(KeyEvent ke)
        {  }

        public void keyReleased(KeyEvent ke)
        {
                //get the key code released
                int keycode= ke.getKeyCode();
                msg += "\nKey code: "+keycode;

                //get the key name from the code
                String keyname= ke.getKeyText(keycode);
                msg += "\nKey Released: "+ keyname;

                //display key code and key name in text area
                ta.setText(msg);
                msg="";
        }

        public static void main(String args[])
        {
                //create the frame
                Keys ks = new Keys();
                ks.setTitle("Catch the key");
                ks.setSize(400,400);
                ks.setVisible(true);
        }
}
```

```
C:\> javac Keys.java
C:\> java Keys
```

Key code: 10
Key Released: Enter

Working with Several Frames

In software development, it is necessary to create several frames to display some screens to the user and to accept user input. Similarly, there may be several other screens which display the results to the user. So, we should know how to generate one frame from the other one.

Suppose, we create a frame with the name 'Frame1'. When a button like 'Next' is clicked on Frame1 then it should display 'Frame2'. There is another button 'Back' in Frame2, which when clicked takes us back to the first frame.

To create a new frame 'Frame2', we should write the following code in `Frame1` class:

```
Frame2 f2 = new Frame2();
f2.setSize(400,400);
f2.setVisible(true);
```

To make Frame2 terminate from memory, we can use `dispose()` method. To do this, write the following code in `Frame2` class:

```
this.dispose();
```

Program 23: Write a program to create a frame 'Frame1' with Next and Close buttons.

```
//This is Frame1
import java.awt.*;
import java.awt.event.*;
class Frame1 extends Frame implements ActionListener
{
    //vars
    Button b1,b2;
    Frame1()
    {
        setLayout(null);

        //create two buttons
        b1= new Button("Next");
        b2= new Button("Close");

        //set the location of buttons
        b1.setBounds(100,100,70,40);
        b2.setBounds(200,100,70,40);

        //add them to frame
```

```
                add(b1);
                add(b2);

                //add action listener to buttons
                b1.addActionListener(this);
                b2.addActionListener(this);

        }
        public void actionPerformed(ActionEvent ae)
        {
                //if Next button is clicked, display Frame2
                if(ae.getSource() == b1)
                {
                        //create Frame2 object and display
                        Frame2 f2 = new Frame2();
                        f2.setSize(400,400);
                        f2.setVisible(true);
                }
                else {
                        //if Close button is clicked, close application
                        System.exit(0);
                }
        }
        public static void main(String args[])
        {
                //create Frame1
                Frame1 f1 = new Frame1();
                f1.setSize(500,500);
                f1.setTitle("First frame");
                f1.setVisible(true);
        }
}
```

Note

DO NOT COMPILE THIS CODE TILL FRAME2.JAVA IS COMPILED.

Here, in this program when the user clicks the Next button, Frame2 is displayed. When the user clicks the Close button, the application is closed.

Program 24: Write a program to create Frame2 with Back button, such that when the user clicks Back button, Frame2 is closed and we see the Frame1 only.

```
//This is Frame2
import java.awt.*;
import java.awt.event.*;
class Frame2 extends Frame implements ActionListener
{
        //create a button
        Button b;

        Frame2()
        {
                //set layout to flow layout
                setLayout(new FlowLayout());

                //create the button
                b= new Button("Back");

                //add it to frame
                add(b);

                //add action listener to button
                b.addActionListener(this);
        }
```

```
        public void actionPerformed(ActionEvent ae)
        {
                //remove this frame from memory
                this.dispose();
        }
}
```

Output:

```
C:\> javac Frame2.java
C:\> java Frame1.java
C:\> java Frame1
```

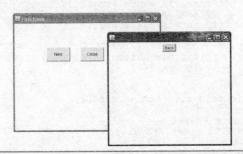

Is it possible to send some data from Frame1 to Frame2 ? Yes, it is. Now, suppose we want to pass the roll number (10) and name 'Srinu' of a student to Frame2. We can do that at the time of creating Frame2 object by passing the data as shown here:

```
//this code should be written in Frame1
Frame2 f2 = new Frame2(10, "Srinu");
f2.setSize(400,400);
f2.setVisible(true);
```

Now, to catch the data in Frame2, we should take a parameterized constructor with two parameters which accepts the values coming from Frame1 as:

```
//instance vars in Frame2
int rno;
String name;

//constructor in Frame2
Frame2(int rno, String name)
{
    this.rno = rno;
    this.name = name;
}
```

Now, the values 10 and "Srinu" will be received by the constructor through its parameters and stored into the instance variables. These values can be used in Frame2 class as the user wishes.

Conclusion

AWT provides the features to create and use graphics, images, components, etc. in our Java programs. These graphics features are very important especially in making the application more user-friendly and more attractive on Internet. We can also use javax.swing package for developing graphics programs which we see in later chapters.

GRAPHICS PROGRAMMING USING SWING

In the previous chapter, we learned about Abstract Window Toolkit (AWT), which is used in GUI programming. However, the AWT components internally depend on native methods like C functions and hence problems related to portability arise. Let us have a look at these problems first.

❑ When a component is created in AWT, it internally calls a native method (for example, a C function) that creates the component internally. This component is called 'peer component'. This peer component is given back and displayed on the screen in AWT. This means AWT internally depends on C code and this is not desirable as we know that C is a system dependant language. AWT is also called 'peer component based' model for this reason.

❑ The appearance of a component is called its 'look' and how the user interacts with the component is called its 'feel'. The look-and-feel of AWT components change depending on the platform (or operating system). For example, refer code to create a push button in AWT (discussed in Chapter 27). code When this code is executed in Windows it will display windows-type of push button whereas the same code in Unix will display unix-style of push button. It means when a programmer creates a screen with different components, he cannot be sure how his screen will look on a particular system. Its appearance changes from system to system.

❑ Moreover, AWT components are heavy-weight. It means these components take more system resources like more memory and more processor time.

Due to these reasons, JavaSoft people felt it better to redevelop AWT package without internally taking the help of native methods. Hence, all the classes of AWT are extended to form new classes and a new class library is created. This library is called JFC (Java Foundation Classes).

Java Foundation Classes (JFC)

JFC is an extension of the original AWT. It contains classes that are completely portable, since the entire JFC is developed in pure Java. Noteworthy features of JFC are as follows:

❑ JFC components are light-weight. This means, they utilize minimum system resources. Their speed is comparatively good and hence JFC programs execute much faster.

❑ JFC components have same look-and-feel on all platforms. Once a component is created, it looks same on any Operating system. So the programmer can be sure of the look of his screen.

❑ JFC offers 'pluggable look-and-feel' feature, which allows the programmer to change the look and feel as suited for a platform. Suppose, the programmer wants to display Windows-style push buttons on Windows operating system, and Unix-style buttons on Unix, it is possible.

❑ JFC offers a rich set of components with lots of features. In fact, this is the reason behind why JFC is very popular all over the world.

❑ JFC does not replace AWT. JFC is an extension to AWT. All the classes of JFC are derived from AWT and hence all the methods that we have seen in AWT are also applicable in JFC.

Important Interview Question

What are Java Foundation classes?

Java Foundation classes (JFC) represent a class library developed in pure Java which is an extension to AWT.

Packages of JFC

The following packages are found in JFC, which are very useful to the programmer in designing GUI.

❑ `javax.swing`: This package helps to develop components like push buttons, radio buttons, menus, etc. The x in `javax` represents that it is an 'extended package' whose classes are derived from `java.awt` package.

❑ `javax.swing.plaf`: `plaf` stands for pluggable look and feel. This package helps to provide a native look-and-feel to swing components. It means the look-and-feel of components will change depending on Operating system.

❑ `java.awt.dnd`: `dnd` stands for drag and drop. This package helps to drag and drop the components and data from one place to another place in the application.

❑ `javax.accessibility`: One of the important aims of Internet is to reach everyone, including the physically challenged persons. `javax.accessibility` package is useful to develop applications in such a way that physically challenged people are able to use the applications. For example, a blind person will be able convert a printer report into Braille language so that he can read it or a deaf person will be able to enjoy the music which is converted and sent to his ears through his hearing-aid.

❑ `java.awt.geom`: `geom` stands for geometrical shapes. This package helps to draw 2D graphics, filling with colors, rotating the shapes, etc.

javax.swing and MVC

javax.swing is the most important and most-commonly used package among all the other packages of JFC. This package provides classes to create components like push buttons, check boxes, radio buttons, menus, etc. All the components of this package are developed in pure java and hence are light weight.

All the components in swing follow a model-view-controller (MVC) architecture. 'model' represents the data that represents the state of a component. For example, if we take a push button, its state information, such as whether the button is pressed or not or whether it is selected or not will be stored in an object called 'model'. By looking at the model, we can understand the state of the push button. The model of the push button can be inspected with the help of some methods. For example, to know whether a push button is selected or not, we can use isSelected() method on the model of the button which gives true if the button is selected otherwise false.

'view' represents visual appearance of the component based on the model data. For example, if isSelected() returns true, the button is selected by the user and hence the view will change with a dotted line around the push button which represents that the button is selected.

When the user interacts with the component, first of all 'controller' will understand this and modifies the model data accordingly. For example, when a user clicks on push button, the controller decides whether to change the model or not. When the model is changed, it tells the view to update itself.

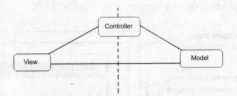

Figure 28.1 MVC architecture

The goal of the MVC architecture is to separate the application object (model), its representation to the user (view), and the way it is controlled by the user (controller). See Figure 28.1.

Before MVC, user interface designs tended to lump such objects together. MVC separates them thus allowing greater flexibility and possibility for reuse. Separating view and model has several advantages, which are as follows:

❑ **Multiple views using the same model:** Since, the view and model are separated in MVC, it is possible to represent the same model data in several views. For example, the same employee data can be represented in the form of a table or as a histogram or a pie chart. This forms the basis for 'pluggable look and feel' since the user can change the view on different platforms without changing the inner details.

❑ **Efficient modularity:** It is possible to develop view and model in different environments. For example, we can develop a push button in Java and its model data can be stored using Visual Basic. Also, it is possible to make changes to view or model without affecting the other. Thus debugging will become easy.

❑ **Easier support for new types of clients:** To support a new type of client, we can simply write a view and controller for it and wire them into the existing enterprise model.

Important Interview Question

Discuss about the MVC architecture in JFC/ swing ?

Model-View-Controller is a model used in swing components. Model represents the data of the component. View represents its appearance and controller is a mediater between the model and the view. MVC represents the separation of model of an object from its view and how it is controlled.

Window Panes

A window pane represents a free area of a window where some text or components can be displayed. For example, we can create a frame using JFrame class in `javax.swing`, which contains a free area inside it, as shown in Figure 28.2. This free area is called 'window pane'.

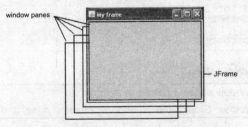

Figure 28.2 Window panes are part of JFrame

We have four types of window panes available in javax.swing package. These panes can be imagined like transparent sheets lying one below the other. So, if we attach any components to any pane, they all will be finally displayed on the screen. See Figure 28.3.

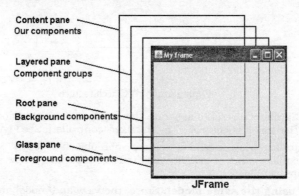

Figure 28.3 Window panes and their use

Let us now have a brief discussion of all the four panes available in swing:

❑ **Glass pane:** This is the first pane and is very close to the monitor's screen. Any components to be displayed in the foreground are attached to this glass pane. To reach this glass pane, we use getGlassPane() method of JFrame class. This method returns Component class object.

❑ **Root pane:** This pane is below the glass pane. Any components to be displayed in the background are displayed in this pane. Root pane and glass pane are used in animation also. For example, suppose we want to display a flying aeroplane in the sky. The aeroplane can be displayed as a .gif or .jpg file in the glass pane whereas the blue sky can be displayed in the root pane in the background. To go to the root pane, we can use getRootPane() method of JFrame class which returns an object of JRootPane class.

❑ **Layered pane:** This pane lies below the root pane. When we want to take several components as a group, we attach them in the layered pane. We can reach this pane by calling getLayeredPane() method of JFrame class which returns an object of JLayeredPane class object.

❑ **Content pane:** This is the bottom most pane of all. Individual components are attached to this pane. To reach this pane, we can call getContentPane() method of JFrame class which returns Container class object.

Remember, in swing, the components are attached to the window panes only. For example, if we want to attach a push button (but object) to the content pane, first of all we should create the content pane object by calling getContentPane() method as:

```
JFrame jf = new JFrame();  //create JFrame object
Container c = Jf.getContentPane();
//create the content pane, i.e. Container object
c.add(but);
//add button to content pane
```

Important Interview Question

What are the various window panes available in swing?

There are 4 window panes: Glass pane, Root pane, Layered pane, and Content pane.

Important Classes of javax.swing

Let us have a look at the important classes available in javax.swing package. They are shown in Figure 28.4. From the figure, we can understand that the classes of javax.swing are derived from the classes of java.awt package.

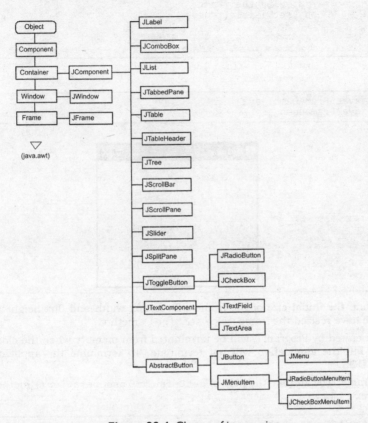

Figure 28.4 Classes of javax.swing

Creating a Frame in Swing

We know that a frame represents a window with a title bar and borders. Frame becomes the basis for creating the screens for an application because all the components go into the frame. To create a frame, we have to create an object to JFrame class in swing, as:

❑ JFrame jf = new JFrame();, //create a frame without any title

❑ JFrame jf = new JFrame("title"); //create frame with title

Program 1: Write a program to create a frame by creating an object to JFrame class.

```
//A simple frame
import javax.swing.*;
class FrameDemo
{
      public static void main(String args[ ])
```

```
        {
                //create the frame with title
                JFrame obj = new JFrame("My frame");

                //set the size to 200 by 200 px
                obj.setSize(200,200);

                //display the frame
                obj.setVisible(true);
        }
    }
```

Output:

```
    C:\> javac FrameDemo.java
    C:\> java FrameDemo
```

In this program, the initial size of the frame will be 0px width and 0px height and hence it is not visible. So, we have resized the frame using setSize() method.

The frame generated by Program 1 will be terminated from memory when the close button is clicked by the user, but the application will not terminate. To terminate the application forcibly, press Control+C in DOS.

To close the frame, we can take the help of getDefaultCloseOperation() method of JFrame class, as shown here:

```
    getDefaultCloseOperation(constant);
```

where the constant can be any one of the following:

❑ JFrame.EXIT_ON_CLOSE: This closes the application upon clicking on close button.

❑ JFrame.DISPOSE_ON_CLOSE: This disposes the present frame which is visible on the screen. The JVM may also terminate.

❑ JFrame.DO_NOTHING_ON_CLOSE: This will not perform any operation upon clicking on close button.

❑ JFrame.HIDE_ON_CLOSE: This hides the frame upon clicking on close button.

Program 2: Rewrite Program 1 to show how to terminate an application by clicking on the close button of the frame.

```
    //A simple frame
    import javax.swing.*;
    class FrameDemo extends JFrame
    {
```

```
            public static void main(String args[])
            {
                    //create the frame
                    FrameDemo obj = new FrameDemo();

                    //set a title for the frame
                    obj.setTitle("My swing frame");

                    //set the size to 200 by 200 px
                    obj.setSize(200,200);

                    //display the frame
                    obj.setVisible(true);

                    //close the application upon clicking on close button of frame
                    obj.setDefaultCloseOperation(JFrame.EXIT_ON_CLOSE);

            }
    }
```

Output:

```
    C:\> javac FrameDemo.java
    C:\> java FrameDemo
```

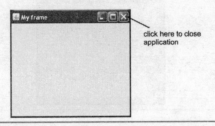

Let us now think about how to display some text in the frame. We know that the content pane is the free area of the frame. To show some background color in the frame, we should set the background color to the content pane. The code to do this is as follows:

```
    c.setBackground(Color.green);   //c represents the content pane object
```

Program 3: Write a program to create the frame and display green color in its background.

Note

For this purpose, we should set the background color to content pane.

```
        //A simple frame with background color
        import javax.swing.*;
        import java.awt.*; //Container class
        class FrameDemo extends JFrame
        {
                public static void main(String args[])
                {
                        //create the frame
                        FrameDemo obj = new FrameDemo();

                        //create content pane. It is nothing but Container object c
                        Container c = obj.getContentPane();
```

```
                        //set green back ground color to c
                        c.setBackground(Color.green);

                        //set a tsitle for the frame
                        obj.setTitle("My swing frame");

                        //set the size to 200 by 200 px
                        obj.setSize(200,200);

                        //display the frame
                        obj.setVisible(true);

                        //close the application upon clicking on close button of frame
                        obj.setDefaultCloseOperation(JFrame.EXIT_ON_CLOSE);
                }
        }
```

Output:

```
C:\> javac FrameDemo.java
C:\> java FrameDemo
```

Displaying Text in Frame

Swing package provides us the following two ways to display text in an application:

❏   paintComponent(Graphics g) method of JPanel class is used to paint the portion of a component in swing. We should override this method in our class. In the following example, we are writing our class MyPanel as a subclass to JPanel and override the paintComponent() method as:

```
class MyPanel extends JPanel
{
        public void paintComponent(Graphics g)
        {
                super.paintComponent(g);    //call JPanel's method
                g.setColor(Color.red);
                g.setFont(new Font("Helvetica", Font.BOLD, 34));
                g.drawString("Hello Learners!", 50,100);
        }
}
```

But, we should again call the paintComponent() method of JPanel from our method using super.paintComponent(). This will enable the super class to paint the component's area. The following program depicts how to use paintComponent() method to display some text in the frame.

Program 4: Write a program to display text in the frame by overriding paintComponent() method of JPanel class.

```java
//A simple frame with background color and text
import javax.swing.*;
import java.awt.*; //Container class
class MyPanel extends JPanel
{
        MyPanel()
        {
                this.setBackground(Color.green);
        }
        public void paintComponent(Graphics g)
        {
                super.paintComponent(g);
                g.setColor(Color.red);
                g.setFont(new Font("Helvetica", Font.BOLD, 34));
                g.drawString("Hello Learners!", 50,100);

        }
}
class FrameDemo extends JFrame
{
        FrameDemo()
        {
                //create content pane
                Container c = this.getContentPane();

                //create MyPanel object and add it to c
                MyPanel mp = new MyPanel();
                c.add(mp);
        }

        public static void main(String args[])
        {
                //create the frame
                FrameDemo obj = new FrameDemo();

                //set a title for the frame
                obj.setTitle("My swing frame");

                //set the size to 300 by 300 px
                obj.setSize(300,300);

                //display the frame
                obj.setVisible(true);

                //close the application upon clicking on close button of frame
                obj.setDefaultCloseOperation(JFrame.EXIT_ON_CLOSE);

        }
}
```

Output:

```
C:\> javac FrameDemo.java
C:\> java FrameDemo
```

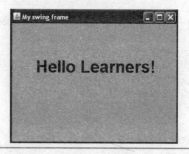

❑ The second way to display some text in swing frame is by using a label. A label represents some constant text to be displayed in the frame. We can use JLabel class to create a label as:

```
JLabel lbl = new JLabel("text");
```

Now, this label should be attached to the content pane to display the text in the frame. This is shown in the following program.

Program 5: Write a program to display some text in the frame with the help of a label.

```java
//A simple frame with background color and text
import javax.swing.*;
import java.awt.*; //Container class

class FrameDemo extends JFrame
{
        //vars
        JLabel lbl;

        FrameDemo()
        {
                //create content pane
                Container c = this.getContentPane();

                //set the layout manager to c
                c.setLayout(new FlowLayout());

                //set background color for content pane c
                c.setBackground(Color.green);

                //create a label with some text
                lbl = new JLabel("Hello Learners!");

                //set font for label
                lbl.setFont(new Font("Helvetica", Font.BOLD, 34));

                //set red color for label
                lbl.setForeground(Color.red);

                //add the label to content pane
                c.add(lbl);

        }

        public static void main(String args[])
        {
                //create the frame
                FrameDemo obj = new FrameDemo();

                //set a title for the frame
                obj.setTitle("My swing frame");
```

```
                //set the size to 300 by 300 px
                obj.setSize(300,300);

                //display the frame
                obj.setVisible(true);

                //close the application upon clicking on close button of frame
                obj.setDefaultCloseOperation(JFrame.EXIT_ON_CLOSE);

        }
}
```

Output:

```
C:\> javac FrameDemo.java
C:\> java FrameDemo
```

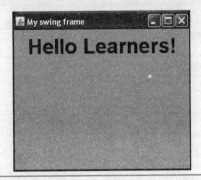

JComponent Class Methods

JComponent class of javax.swing package is the subclass of the Component class of java.awt. So, whatever methods are available in Component class are also available to JComponent. This is the reason why almost all the methods of AWT are useful in swing also. Additional methods found in JComponent are also applicable for the components created in swing.

When a component is created, to display it in the frame, we should not attach it to the frame directly as we did in AWT. On the other hand, the component should be attached to a window pane. For example, to add the component to the content pane, we can write, as:

```
c.add(component);
where c represents the content pane which is represented by Container object.
```

Similarly, to remove the component, we can use remove() method, as:

```
c.remove(component);
```

removeAll() method removes all the components from the content pane and can be used as:

```
c.removeAll();
```

When components are to be displayed in the frame, we should first set a layout manager which arranges the components in a particular manner in the frame. Layout manager should be set for the content pane, as:

```
c.setLayout(new FlowLayout());
```

Here, c is the Container class object which represents the content pane.

The following methods of JComponent class are very useful while handling the components:

❏ To set some background color to the component, we can use setBackground() method, as:

```
component.setBackground(Color.yellow);
```

❏ To set the foreground color to the component, we can use setForeground() method, as:

```
component.setForeground(Color.red);
```

❏ To set some font for the text displayed on/in the component, we can use setFont() method. We should pass Font class object to this method, as:

```
component.setFont(Font obj);
```

where, Font class object can be created as:

```
Font obj = new Font("fontname", style, size);
```

For example, Font obj =new Font("Dialog", Font.BOLD, 30);

❏ Tool tip text is the text that is displayed automatically when the mouse is placed on the component. Tool tip text helps to provide some help text about the component. To set the tool tip text, we can use setToolTipText() method, as:

```
component.setToolTipText("This is a swing component.");
```

❏ Sometimes when the mouse is not useful, the user can use the keyboard to interact with the components. For example, to invoke 'Cancel' button, the user can press Alt+C where C represents the first character of the label of the button. This 'C' is called short cut key or mnemonic. To set a mnemonic, we can use setMnemonic() method, as:

```
component.setMnemonic('C');
```

The preceding statement means that the component can be activated by pressing Alt+C on the keyboard.

❏ To enable or disable a component, we can use setEnabled() method, as:

```
component.setEnabled(true);
```

Here, true will enable the component to be ready to perform an action, whereas false will disable it.

❏ To make a component to be visible or invisible, we can use setVisible() method, as:

```
component.setVisible(true);
```

Here, true will make component to be visible, whereas false will make it invisible.

❑ To know the border of a component, we can use getBorder() method, as:

```
component.getBorder();
```

This method returns Border object which represents the border of the component. It returns null if no border is set.

❑ To know the current height of the component, use getHeight() method, as:

```
component.getHeight();
```

This method returns an integer which represents height of component in pixels.

❑ To know the current width of the component, use getWidth() method, as:

```
component.getWidth();
```

This method returns an integer which represents the width of component.

❑ To know the current x coordinate of the component,

```
component.getX();
```

This method returns integer which represents x coordinate of component in pixels.

❑ To know the current y coordinate of the component,

```
component.getY();
```

This method returns integer which represents y coordinate of component.

❑ To set location of the component in the frame, we can use setBounds() method, as:

```
component.setBounds(x, y, width, height);
```

This method specifies the x,y coordinates of the component, which represent the width and height of the rectangular area allotted for displaying the component.

❑ It is possible to set border around the components in swing. The javax.swing.BorderFactory class has got methods which are useful to set different borders for the component. These methods return Border interface object. Border interface belongs to javax.swing.border package. Border object should be passed to setBorder() method to set the border to the component, as:

```
component.setBorder(Border obj);
```

The following are BorderFactory methods:

❑ createBevelBorder() Method: To set bevel border, we can use createBevelBorder() method. Bevel border is the border which either raises or lowers around the component in 3D form. It has the following forms:

```
BorderFactory.createBevelBorder(BevelBorder.RAISED);
BorderFactory.createBevelBorder(BevelBorder.LOWERED);
```

The above methods will draw bevel border with current background color for highlighting and a bit darker color for shading the shadows around the component.

```
BorderFactory.createBevelBorder(BevelBorder.RAISED, Color.red, Color.green);
```

This method uses raised bevel border with red color for highlighting and green for shading purpose.

❑ createEtchedBorder() Method: Etched border is the border around the component which appears with a shade. To set etched border, we use createEtchedBorder() method, as:

```
BorderFactory.createEtchedBorder();
```

The above method creates a border with an etched look using the component's current background color for highlighting and shading.

```
BorderFactory.createEtchedBorder(Color.red, Color.green);
```

This method cretes etched border with red color for high lighting and green for shading purpose.

```
BorderFactory.createEtchedBorder(EtchedBorder.RAISED);
BorderFactory.createEtchedBorder(EtchedBorder.LOWERED);
```

These methods create raised or lowered etched borders.

```
BorderFactory.createEtchedBorder(EtchedBorder.RAISED, Color.red, Color.green);
```

The above method creates an etched border with raised border in red color for highlighting and green for shading.

❑ createLineBorder() Method: To set a simple line as border around the component, we can use createLineBorder() method, as:

```
BorderFactory.createLineBorder(Color.red);
```

This method creates a line border with red color.

```
BorderFactory.createLineBorder(Color.red, 5);
```

This method creates a line border with red color and 5 px thickness of the border.

❑ createMatteBorder() Method: Matte border is like line border except that it can be distributed unevenly around the component. To set matte border, we can use createMatteBorder() method, as:

```
BorderFactory.createMatteBorder(5,10,15,20, Color.red);
```

This method creates a matte border with thickness 5,10,15,20 px at top, left, bottom, and right of the component. The border appears in red color.

❑ createCompoundBorder() Method: Compound border can use other borders at outside and inside edges of component. To set a compound border, we can use createCompoundBorder() method, as:

```
BorderFactory.createCompoundBorder();
```

This will create a compound border without using any other borders at edges of the component.

```
BorderFactory.createCompoundBorder(Border out, Border in);
```

This method creates a compound border with 'out' at outside edge of the component and 'in' at inside edge of component.

❑ createEmptyBorder() Method: To set an empty border which does not take any space around the component, we can use createEmptyBorder() method, as:

```
BorderFactory.createEmptyBorder();
```

This creates an empty border without any space around the component.

```
BorderFactory.createEmptyBorder(5,10,15,20);
```

This creates an empty border that takes up space but which does no drawing, specifying the width of the top, left, bottom, and right sides as 5,10,15, and 20 px.

Program 6: Write a program to create some push buttons using JButton class and draw different borders around the buttons.

```java
//Understanding the borders
import java.awt.*;
import javax.swing.*;
import javax.swing.border.*;

class BorderDemo extends JFrame
{
    //vars
    JButton b1,b2,b3,b4,b5,b6,b7,b8;

    BorderDemo()
    {
        //create content pane c
        Container c = getContentPane();

        //set a layout for content pane
        c.setLayout(new FlowLayout());

        //Create push buttons
        b1 = new JButton("Raised Bevel Border");
        b2 = new JButton("Lowered Bevel Border");
        b3 = new JButton("Raised Etched Border");
        b4 = new JButton("Lowered Etched Border");
        b5 = new JButton("Line Border");
        b6 = new JButton("Matte Border");
        b7 = new JButton("Compound Border");
        b8 = new JButton("Empty Border");

        //set raised bevel border for b1 with high light color:
        //red and shadow color: green
        Border bd = BorderFactory.createBevelBorder(BevelBorder.RAISED,
         Color.red, Color.green);
        b1.setBorder(bd);

        //set lowered bevel border for b2 with its current background
        //color for high light and shadow
        bd = BorderFactory.createBevelBorder(BevelBorder.LOWERED);
        b2.setBorder(bd);

        //set raised etched border for b3 with high light color: red
        //and shadow color: green
```

```
                        bd = BorderFactory.createEtchedBorder(EtchedBorder.RAISED,
                         Color.red, Color.green);
                        b3.setBorder(bd);

                        //set lowered etched border for b4 with its current background
                        //color for highlight and shadow
                        bd = BorderFactory.createEtchedBorder(EtchedBorder.LOWERED);
                        b4.setBorder(bd);

                        //set line border for b5 with red color and width 5 px
                        bd = BorderFactory.createLineBorder(Color.red, 5);
                        b5.setBorder(bd);

                        //set matte border for b6 with top, left, bottom, right widths as
                        //5,10,15,20 px and in red color
                        bd = BorderFactory.createMatteBorder(5,10,15,20, Color.red);
                        b6.setBorder(bd);

                        //set compound border for b7 without any borders inside or outside
                        //edges
                        bd = BorderFactory.createCompoundBorder();
                        b7.setBorder(bd);

                        //set empty border for b8 without any space for border
                        bd = BorderFactory.createEmptyBorder();
                        b8.setBorder(bd);
                        //add the buttons to the container
                        c.add(b1);
                        c.add(b2);
                        c.add(b3);
                        c.add(b4);
                        c.add(b5);
                        c.add(b6);
                        c.add(b7);
                        c.add(b8);
                        //close the frame upon clicking
                        setDefaultCloseOperation(JFrame.EXIT_ON_CLOSE);
                }

        public static void main(String args[])
        {
                //create a frame
                BorderDemo obj = new BorderDemo();
                //set the title and size for frame
                obj.setTitle("Borders");;
                obj.setSize(500,400);
                //display the frame
                obj.setVisible(true);
        }

    }
```

Output:

```
C:\> javac BorderDemo.java
C:\> java BorderDemo
```

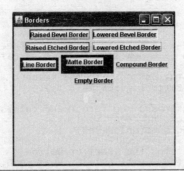

Where are the borders available in swing?

All borders are available in BorderFactory class in javax.swing.border package.

Creating a Push Button with All Features

Let us create a push button in swing and apply different features available in swing like setting colors and font for the button, setting border, short cut key, and tool tip text. We can create a push button using JButton class in swing, as:

```
JButton b = new JButton("OK");
```

Here, a push button with the label "OK" will be created.

```
JButton b = new JButton(ImageIcon ii);
```

This will create a push button with an image on it. The image is specified by ImageIcon class object.

```
JButton b = new JButton("OK", ImageIcon ii);
```

Here, the button is created with label "OK" and image ii.

It is possible to create components in swing with images on it. It is also possible to create a component in/on another component in swing.

Program 7: Write a program in which we create a push button with a label and image on it and then set different features for the button.

Note

This push button will not perform any action, since there is no action attached to it.

```
//Button with an image, colors, border, tool tip text and shortcut key
import java.awt.*;
import javax.swing.*;
import javax.swing.border.*;
class ButtonDemo extends JFrame
{
    JButton b;
    ButtonDemo()
    {
        //create container
        Container c = getContentPane();
```

```
                    //set a layout for container
                    c.setLayout(new FlowLayout());

                    //store the image into ImageIcon object
                    ImageIcon ii = new ImageIcon("car2.gif");

                    //create the button with the image
                    b = new JButton("Click Me", ii);

                    //set background and foreground colors for button
                    b.setBackground(Color.yellow);
                    b.setForeground(Color.red);

                    //set font for the label of button
                    b.setFont(new Font("Arial", Font.BOLD, 30));

                    //set bevel border for button
                    Border bd = BorderFactory.createBevelBorder(BevelBorder.RAISED);
                    b.setBorder(bd);
                    //set tool tip text for button
                    b.setToolTipText("This is a button");
                    //set a short cut key for button. Alt+C from keyboard will invoke
                    //the button
                    b.setMnemonic('C');
                    //add the button to the container
                    c.add(b);
                    //close the frame upon clicking
                    setDefaultCloseOperation(JFrame.EXIT_ON_CLOSE);
            }
        public static void main(String args[])
        {
                    //create a frame
                    ButtonDemo obj = new ButtonDemo();
                    obj.setTitle("My Button");;
                    obj.setSize(500,400);
                    obj.setVisible(true);
        }
    }
```

Output:

```
    C:\> javac ButtonDemo.java
    C:\> java ButtonDemo
```

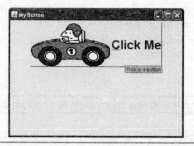

Displaying Image in Swing

Suppose we want to make the push button to perform some action when clicked by the user. For this purpose, we should add action listener to the button and implement actionPerformed()

method. When the button is clicked, this method is executed. So the action part should be written in this method.

Let us now see how to display an image when the button is clicked. First of all, we take an empty label. A label can be used to display some constant text or an image in the frame. For example,

```
JLabel lbl = new JLabel() ;
```

The above statement will create an empty label. Later, we can send text to this label using setText() method. We can also set some image to this label using setIcon() method.

```
JLabel lbl = new JLabel("text");
```

This will create the label with text.

```
JLabel lbl = new JLabel("text", alignment);
```

This will create a label with text and the text will be aligned. The alignment can be JLabel.CENTER, JLabel.LEFT, and JLabel.RIGHT.

```
JLabel lbl = new JLabel(ImageIcon ii);
```

This will create a label with an image on it. The image is provided by the ImageIcon object.

```
JLabel lbl = new JLabel("text", ImageIcon ii);
```

This will create the label with text as well as image.

Program 8: Write a program to create a push button as we did in Program 7. When the button is clicked an image is displayed in the frame.

```
//Button which displays image when clicked
import java.awt.*;
import java.awt.event.*;
import javax.swing.*;
import javax.swing.border.*;

class ButtonDemo1 extends JFrame implements ActionListener
{
        JButton b;
        JLabel lbl;

        ButtonDemo1()
        {
                //create container
                Container c = getContentPane();

                //set a layout for container
                c.setLayout(new FlowLayout());

                //store the image into ImageIcon object
                ImageIcon ii = new ImageIcon("car2.gif");

                //create the button with the image
                b = new JButton("Click Me", ii);

                //set background and foreground colors for button
                b.setBackground(Color.yellow);
                b.setForeground(Color.red);

                //set font for the label of button
```

```
                b.setFont(new Font("Arial", Font.BOLD, 30));

                //set bevel border for button
                Border bd = BorderFactory.createBevelBorder(BevelBorder.RAISED);
                b.setBorder(bd);

                //set tool tip text for button
                b.setToolTipText("This is a button");

                //set a short cut key for button. Alt+C will invoke the button
                b.setMnemonic('C');
                //add the button to the container
                c.add(b);

                //add action listener to button
                b.addActionListener(this);

                //create an empty label and add to the content pane
                lbl = new JLabel();
                c.add(lbl);

                //close the frame upon clicking
                setDefaultCloseOperation(JFrame.EXIT_ON_CLOSE);
        }
        public void actionPerformed(ActionEvent ae)
        {
                //set some image to the label. This image is displayed when the
                //button is clicked
                ImageIcon ii = new ImageIcon("car2.gif");
                lbl.setIcon(ii);
        }

        public static void main(String args[])
        {
                //create a frame
                ButtonDemo1 obj = new ButtonDemo1();

                obj.setTitle("My Button");;
                obj.setSize(500,400);
                obj.setVisible(true);
        }
}
```

Output:

```
C:\> javac ButtonDemo1.java
C:\> java ButtonDemo1
```

Creating Components in Swing

Let us now discuss some common components and how to create them in swing. Already we have seen how to create a push button and a label. To create check boxes, we can use JCheckBox class, as:

```
JCheckBox cb = new JCheckBox();
```

This statement creates a check box without any label and image.

```
JCheckBox cb = new JCheckBox("label");
```

This creates a check box with the label.

```
JCheckBox cb = new JCheckBox(ImageIcon ii);
```

This creates a check box with an image. The image is loaded from ImageIcon object.

```
JCheckBox cb = new JCheckBox("label", ImageIcon ii);
```

This creates the check box with label and image.

```
JCheckBox cb = new JCheckBox("label", status);
```

Here, status can be 'true' or 'false'. If it is 'true', the check box appears as if it is selected by default.

To know which check box is selected by the user, we should first go to the model of the check box by calling getModel() method, as:

```
Model m = cb.getModel();
```

Now this model object contains the information on whether the check box is selected or not. This information can be obtained by using isSelected() method on Model object as:

```
boolean x = m.isSelected();
```

This method returns true if the check box is selected, otherwise it returns false.

We can combine both the methods and write, as:

```
cb.getModel().isSelected();
```

To create radio buttons, we can use JRadioButton class, as:

```
JRadioButton rb = new JRadioButton();
```

This will create a radio button without any label or image.

```
JRadioButton rb = new JRadioButton("label");
```

This creates a radio button with the indicated label.

```
JRadioButton rb = new JRadioButton(ImageIcon ii);
```

This creates a radio button with an image.

```
JRadioButton rb = new JRadioButton("label", ImageIcon ii);
```

This creates a radio button with label and image.

```
JRadioButton rb = new JRadioButton("label", status);
```

This creates a radio button with label and the status can be 'true' or 'false'. If it is 'true', the radio button appears as if it is selected by default.

After creating the radio buttons, we should add them to ButtonGroup. This specifies that the radio buttons form a group and hence JVM will allow the user to select only one button from the group. This can be done as:

```
ButtonGroup bg = new ButtonGroup();
bg.add(rb);   //add radio button to button group.
```

To know whether a radio button is selected by the user or not, we can use:

```
rb.getModel().isSelected();
```

This method gives true if the radio button is selected otherwise false.

To create a text field, we can take the help of JTextField class, as:

```
JTextField tf = new JTextField();
```

This constructs a text field without any text within it.

```
JTextField tf = new JTextField("text");
```

This creates a text field with text displaying in it.

```
JTextField tf = new JTextField(15);
```

This creates a text field with a width of 15 characters.

```
JTextField tf = new JTextField("text", 15);
```

This creates a text field with text and a width of 15 characters.

A text field can accommodate only one line of text, whereas a text area can display or accept several lines of text. A text area can be created as:

```
JTextArea ta = new JTextArea();
```

This creates a text area without any text in it.

```
JTextArea ta = new JTextArea("text");
```

This creates a text area with text within it.

```
JTextArea ta = new JTextArea(5, 15);
```

This creates a text area with 5 rows and 15 characters in each row.

```
JTextArea ta = new JTextArea("text", 5, 15);
```

This creates a text area with text and with 5 rows and 15 characters per row.

Program 9: Write a program that helps in creating some check boxes and radio buttons. When the user clicks on a check box or radio button, the selected option text will be displayed in a text area.

```
//Check boxes, radio buttons and Text area
import java.awt.*;
import javax.swing.*;
import java.awt.event.*;

class CheckRadio extends JFrame implements ActionListener
{
        //vars
        JCheckBox cb1, cb2;
        JRadioButton rb1, rb2;
        JTextArea ta;
        ButtonGroup bg;
        String msg="";

        CheckRadio()
        {
                //create the content pane
                Container c = getContentPane();

                //set flow layout to content pane
                c.setLayout(new FlowLayout());

                //create a text area with 10 rows and 20 chars per row
                ta = new JTextArea(10,20);

                //create two check boxes
                cb1 = new JCheckBox("Java", true);
                cb2 = new JCheckBox("J2EE");

                //create two radio buttons
                rb1 = new JRadioButton("Male", true);
                rb2 = new JRadioButton("Female");

                //create a button group and add the radio buttons to it
                bg = new ButtonGroup();
                bg.add(rb1);
                bg.add(rb2);

                //add the checkboxes, radio buttons, textarea to the container
                c.add(cb1);
                c.add(cb2);
                c.add(rb1);
                c.add(rb2);
                c.add(ta);

                //add action listeners. We need not add listener to text area
                //since the user clicks on the checkboxes or radio buttons only
                cb1.addActionListener(this);
                cb2.addActionListener(this);
                rb1.addActionListener(this);
                rb2.addActionListener(this);

                //close the frame upon clicking
                setDefaultCloseOperation(JFrame.EXIT_ON_CLOSE);
        }

        public void actionPerformed(ActionEvent ae)
```

```
        {
                //know which components are selected by user
                if(cb1.getModel().isSelected()) msg+="\nJava";
                if(cb2.getModel().isSelected()) msg+="\nJ2EE";
                if(rb1.getModel().isSelected()) msg+="\nMale";
                else msg+="\nFemale";
                //display the selected message in text area
                ta.setText(msg);

                //reset the message to empty string
                msg="";
        }

        public static void main(String args[])
        {
                //create frame
                CheckRadio cr = new CheckRadio();
                cr.setTitle("My checkboxes and Radio buttons");
                cr.setSize(500,400);
                cr.setVisible(true);
        }
}
```

Output:

```
C:\> javac CheckRadio.java
C:\> java CheckRadio
```

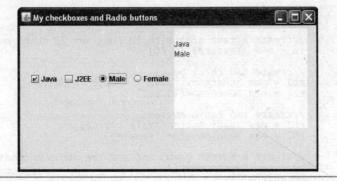

Setting the Look and Feel of Components

Swing provides the programmer the facility to change the look and feel of components being displayed on any system. This is called 'plaf' (pluggable look and feel). 'Look' refers to the appearance of the component on the screen and 'feel' represents how the user can interact with the component. There are 3 types of look and feel available in swing—Metal look and feel, Motif look and feel, and Window look and feel. They are defined as classes in `javax.swing.plaf` package. By default, swing programs use 'metal' look and feel. It is possible to set any look and feel for the swing components. For this purpose, we should use `UIManager.setLookAndFeel()` method. To this method we should pass one of the following strings:

❑ For getting metal look and feel, we use:

```
"javax.swing.plaf.metal.MetalLookAndFeel"
```

❏ For getting motif look and feel, we use:

```
"com.sun.java.swing.plaf.motif.MotifLookAndFeel"
```

❏ For getting windows look and feel, we use:

```
"com.sun.java.swing.plaf.windows.WindowsLookAndFeel"
```

After this, we should update the contents on the content pane, using `updateComponentTreeUI()` method, as:

```
SwingUtilities.updateComponentTreeUI(c);
```

Where, c represents the content pane which is nothing but the Container object.

Program 10: Write a program that changes the look and feel of the component.

```
//Changing the look and feel of components
import java.awt.*;
import java.awt.event.*;
import javax.swing.*;
import javax.swing.plaf.*;
class LookFeel extends JFrame implements ItemListener
{
        //vars
        JButton b;
        JCheckBox cb;
        JTextField t;
        JRadioButton r1, r2, r3;
        ButtonGroup bg;
        Container c;

        LookFeel()
        {
                //create content pane
                c = this.getContentPane();

                //set flow layout to c
                c.setLayout(null);

                //create components
                b = new JButton("Button");
                cb = new JCheckBox("CheckBox");
                t = new JTextField("TextField", 15);
                r1 = new JRadioButton("Metal");
                r2 = new JRadioButton("Motif");
                r3 = new JRadioButton("Windows");

                //create ButtonGroup object and add radio buttons to specify
                //that they belong to same group
                bg = new ButtonGroup();
                bg.add(r1);
                bg.add(r2);
                bg.add(r3);

                //set the location of components in content pane
                b.setBounds(100,50,75,40);
                cb.setBounds(100,100,100,40);
                t.setBounds(100,150,100,40);
```

```
                r1.setBounds(50,250,100,30);
                r2.setBounds(150,250,100,30);
                r3.setBounds(250,250,100,30);

                //add the components to content pane
                c.add(b);
                c.add(cb);
                c.add(t);
                c.add(r1);
                c.add(r2);
                c.add(r3);
                //add item listeners to radio buttons
                r1.addItemListener(this);
                r2.addItemListener(this);
                r3.addItemListener(this);

                //close the frame
                this.setDefaultCloseOperation(JFrame.EXIT_ON_CLOSE);
        }

        public void itemStateChanged(ItemEvent ie)
        {

                try{
                //know which radio button is selected and accordingly change
                //the look and feel

                if(r1.getModel().isSelected())
                UIManager.setLookAndFeel("javax.swing.plaf.metal.
                 MetalLookAndFeel");
                if(r2.getModel().isSelected())
                UIManager.setLookAndFeel(
                 "com.sun.java.swing.plaf.motif.MotifLookAndFeel");
                if(r3.getModel().isSelected())
                UIManager.setLookAndFeel
                ("com.sun.java.swing.plaf.windows.WindowsLookAndFeel");

                //change the look and feel in the content pane
                SwingUtilities.updateComponentTreeUI(c);
                }catch(Exception e){}
        }

        public static void main(String args[])
        {
                //create the frame
                LookFeel lf = new LookFeel();
                lf.setSize(400,400);
                lf.setTitle("Look and Feel");
                lf.setVisible(true);
        }
}
```

Output:

```
C:\> javac LookFeel.java
C:\> java LookFeel
```

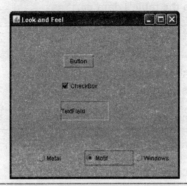

In this program, we create 3 components: a push button, a check box and a text field. Their look and feel will be changed when the user selects one of the radio buttons labeled as 'Metal', 'Motif' and 'Windows'.

JTable Class

JTable class is useful to create a table. A table represents several rows and columns of data. To create a table, we can create JTable class object as:

```
JTable tab = new JTable(data, columnnames);
```

Here, `data` represents the data of the table in the form of a two-dimensional array and `columnnames` represents the names of the individual columns that can be a one-dimensional array. Alternately, we can also use a Vector class object to represent data and another Vector object to represent columnnames.

Suppose we want to create a row for the table using a Vector, we can create an object to Vector class as:

```
Vector row = new Vector();
```

Now, using `add()` method, we can add column data to this row, as:

```
row.add(columndata);
```

Now this row should be added to the table's data part, as:

```
Vector data = new Vector();
data.add(row);
```

Let us see the methods which help us to work with `JTable`.

❑ To know the number of rows in the table:

```
int n = tab.getRowCount();
```

❑ To know the number of columns in the table:

```
int n = tab.getColumnCount();
```

❑ To know the name of the column when column position number is given:

```
String name = tab.getColumnName(int columnnumber);
```

❑ To know the height of a table row, in pixels:

```
int n = tab.getRowHeight();
```

❑ To set the rows height in pixels in the table:

```
tab.setRowHeight(int height);
```

❑ To know the index of the first selected column:

```
int n = tab.getSelectedColumn();
```

This method returns –1 if no column is selected.

❑ To know the indices of all selected columns:

```
int x[] = tab.getSelectedColumns();
```

❑ To know the index of the first selected row:

```
int n = tab.getSelectedRow();
```

This method returns -1 if no row is selected.

❑   To know the indices of all selected rows:

```
int x[] = tab.getSelectedRows();
```

❑   To know which object is there in the table at particular row and column position:

```
Object x = tab.getValueAt(int row, int column);
```

❑   To set an object in a particular row and column of the table:

```
tab.setValueAt(Object obj, int row, int column);
```

❑   A grid represents rows and columns of the table. To set the grid color:

```
tab.setGridColor(Color.red);
```

❑   To return the table header used by the table, we can use getTableHeader() method as:

```
JTableHeader  head = tab.getTableHeader();
```

Please note that JTableHeader class is defined in javax.swing.table package.

Program 11: Write a program that creates a table with some rows and columns.

```
//JTable demo
import java.awt.*;  //Container
import javax.swing.*;   //JTable
import javax.swing.table.*;  //JTableHeader
import javax.swing.border.*; //Border
import java.util.*; //Vector

class JTableDemo extends JFrame
{

    JTableDemo()
    {
            //take Vector object to represent data of table
            Vector<Vector> data= new Vector<Vector>();

            //take another Vector object to represent a row
            Vector<String> row= new Vector<String>();

            //add 3 column's data to row
            row.add("Rama Rao");
            row.add("Analyst");
            row.add("22,000.00");

            //add the row to data of the table
            data.add(row);

            //create another row
            row= new Vector<String>();
            row.add("Srinivas Kumar");
            row.add("Programmer");
            row.add("18,000.50");

            //add the second row also to data
            data.add(row);

            //create third row
            row= new Vector<String>();
```

```
                        row.add("Vinaya Devi");
                        row.add("Programmer");
                        row.add("16,000.75");

                        //add the second row also to data
                        data.add(row);

                        //Create another vector object for column names
                        Vector<String> cols = new Vector<String>();
                        cols.add("Employee Name");
                        cols.add("Designation");
                        cols.add("Salary");

                        //do not add column names to data of table

                        //create the table
                        JTable tab = new JTable(data,cols);

                        //set green line border to the table
                        tab.setBorder(BorderFactory.createLineBorder(Color.green, 2));

                        //set some font to the table
                        tab.setFont(new Font("Arial", Font.BOLD, 20));

                        //set row height to 30px
                        tab.setRowHeight(30);

                        //set grid color to red
                        tab.setGridColor(Color.red);

                        //get the table header into head
                        JTableHeader head = tab.getTableHeader();

                        //create content pane
                        Container c = getContentPane();

                        //set border layout to content pane
                        c.setLayout(new BorderLayout());

                        //add head of the table at top and remaining table below the top
                        c.add("North",head);
                        c.add("Center",tab);
                }

        public static void main(String args[])
        {
                        //create the frame
                        JTableDemo demo = new JTableDemo();
                        demo.setSize(500,400);
                        demo.setVisible(true);

                        //close the frame
                        demo.setDefaultCloseOperation(JFrame.EXIT_ON_CLOSE);
                }
        }
```

Output:

```
C:\> javac JTableDemo.java
C:\> java JTableDemo
```

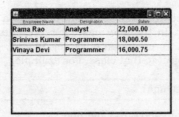

In this program, to create rows of the table, we are using Vector class objects. These objects are stored again in another Vector class object which forms the data for the table.

In Program 11, we used `BorderLayout` to arrange the table header and its body in the content pane. `BorderLayout` is useful to arrange the components in the four borders of the screen identified as North, East, South and West and also in the center of the screen which is identified as Center. This is shown in Figure 28.5. In this program, the table header is added in the North and the table in the Center of the content pane. Also note that in the output, the columns can be dragged and moved from one place to another place in the table. For example, the first column 'Employee Name' can be swapped with the second column 'Designation' by dragging and dropping it on the second column.

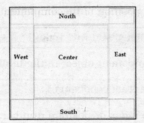

Figure 28.5 BorderLayout

JTabbedPane Class

A pane represents a frame area. A tabbed pane represents a frame with tabs attached to it. `JTabbedPane` is useful to create a tabbed pane, such that on each tab sheet a group of components can be added. The user can choose any component from the tab sheet.

To create a tabbed pane, we can simply create an object to `JTabbedPane`, as:

```
JTabbedPane jtp = new JTabbedPane();
```

The following statement creates an empty tabbed pane with the specified tab placement of any of these—JTabbedPane.TOP, JTabbedPane.BOTTOM, JTabbedPane.LEFT, or JTabbedPane.RIGHT.

```
JTabbedPane jtp = new JTabbedPane(int tabplacement);
```

The following methods can be used to work with JTabbedPane:

❑ To add tab sheets to the tabbed pane:

```
jtp.add("title", object);
jtp.addTab("title", object);
jtp.addTab("title", ImageIcon ii, object);
```

Here, title represents tab sheet title and object represents a component or it may represent a group of components collectively. In the later case, it represents an object of JPanel class which contains a group of components. To create an object of JPanel, we should first create a class that extends JPanel and create an object to that class. For example,

```
class MyPanel extends JPanel
```

Now, pass MyPanel class's object to addTab() method.

❏ To remove a tab and its components from the tabbed pane:

```
jtp.removeTabAt(int index);
```

❏ To remove a specified component from the tabbed pane:

```
jtp.remove(Component c);
```

❏ To remove all the tabs and their corresponding components:

```
jtp.removeAll();
```

❏ To get the component when the position of the component is given:

```
Component c = jtp.getComponentAt(int index);
```

❏ To get the currently selected component object in the tabbed pane:

```
Component c = jtp.getSelectedComponent();
```

❏ To get the selected component's index or position number:

```
int x = jtp.getSelectedIndex();
```

❏ To know the number of tab sheets present in the tabbed pane:

```
int x = jtp.getTabCount();
```

❏ To set a component at a particular position in the tabbed pane:

```
jtp.setComponentAt(int index, Component c);
```

Program 12: Write a program to create a tabbed pane with two tab sheets. In the first tab sheet, we display some push buttons with names of capital cities. In the second tab sheet, we display some checkboxes with names of countries.

```
//Tabbed Pane
import java.awt.*;
import javax.swing.*;

class JTabbedPaneDemo extends JFrame
{
        JTabbedPaneDemo()
        {
                //create content pane
                Container c = getContentPane();

                //create tabbed pane
```

```
                    JTabbedPane jtp = new JTabbedPane();

                    //add two sheets, CapitalsPanel and CountriesPanel are classes
                    //which extend JPanel and contain a group of components.
                    jtp.addTab("Capitals", new CapitalsPanel());
                    jtp.addTab("Countries", new CountriesPanel());

                    //add the tabbed pane to content pane
                    c.add(jtp);
            }

            public static void main(String args[])
            {
                    //create the frame
                    JTabbedPaneDemo demo = new JTabbedPaneDemo();
                    demo.setTitle("JTabbed pane");
                    demo.setSize(300,400);
                    demo.setVisible(true);

                    //close frame
                    demo.setDefaultCloseOperation(JFrame.EXIT_ON_CLOSE);
            }
    }

    //the components of this class go into Capitals tab sheet
    class CapitalsPanel extends JPanel
    {
            CapitalsPanel()
            {
                    //create 3 push buttons and add to panel
                    JButton b1 = new JButton("Washington");
                    JButton b2 = new JButton("London");
                    JButton b3 = new JButton("Tokyo");

                    add(b1);
                    add(b2);
                    add(b3);

            }
    }
    //the components of this class appear in Countries tab sheet
    class CountriesPanel extends JPanel
    {
            CountriesPanel()
            {
                    //create 3 check boxes and add to panel
                    JCheckBox c1 = new JCheckBox("UnitedStates");
                    JCheckBox c2 = new JCheckBox("Britain");
                    JCheckBox c3 = new JCheckBox("Japan");

                    add(c1);
                    add(c2);
                    add(c3);
            }
    }
```

Output:

```
C:\> javac JTabbedPaneDemo.java
C:\> java JTabbedPaneDemo
```

JSplitPane Class

JSplitPane is used to create a split pane which divides two (and only two) components.

To create a split pane:

```
JSplitPane sp = new JSplitPane(orientation, component1, component2);
```

Here, orientation is:

JSplitPane.HORIZONTAL_SPLIT to align the components from left to right.

JSplitPane.VERTICAL_SPLIT to align the components from top to bottom.

The following methods are useful to work with JSplitPane:

❑ Setting the divider location between the components:

```
sp.setDividerLocation(int pixels);
```

❑ Getting the divider location:

```
int n = sp.getDividerLocation();
```

❑ To get the top or left side component:

```
Component obj = sp.getTopComponent();
```

❑ To get the bottom or right side component:

```
Component obj = sp.getBottomComponent();
```

❑ To remove a component from the split pane:

```
sp.remove(Component obj);
```

❑ To remove a component at a specified location:

```
sp.remove(int index);
```

❑ To set a component as top component in the split pane:

```
sp.setTopComponent(Component obj);
```

❑   To set a component as bottom component:

```
sp.setBottomComponent(Component obj);
```

❑   To set left component in the split pane:

```
sp.setLeftComponent(Component obj);
```

❑   To set right component in the split pane:

```
sp.setRightComponent(Component obj);
```

Program 13: Write a program that creates a split pane, which divides the frame into two parts horizontally. In the left part, we create a button and in the right part, we create a text area. When the button is clicked, the text is displayed inside the text area.

```
//Split pane  with text area and button.
import java.awt.*;
import java.awt.event.*;
import javax.swing.*;
class JSplitPaneDemo extends JFrame implements ActionListener
{
     //vars
     String str="This is my text being displayed in the text area" + " and
      this text will be wrapped accordingly";
     JButton b;
     JTextArea ta;
     JSplitPane sp;

     JSplitPaneDemo()
     {
             //create content pane
             Container c = getContentPane();

             //set border layout to content pane
             c.setLayout(new BorderLayout());

             //create a push button and text area
             b= new JButton("My button");
             ta= new JTextArea();

             //set wrapping of the line for text area
             ta.setLineWrap(true);

             //create horizontal split pane that contains b,ta
             sp = new JSplitPane(JSplitPane.HORIZONTAL_SPLIT, b,ta);

             //set the divider location at 300 pixels in split pane
             sp.setDividerLocation(300);

             //add split pane in the center of container
             c.add("Center",sp);

             //add action listener to the button
             b.addActionListener(this);

             //close frame
             setDefaultCloseOperation(JFrame.EXIT_ON_CLOSE);
     }
     public void actionPerformed(ActionEvent ae)
     {
             //when button clicked, set the string to the text area
             ta.setText(str);
```

```
        }
        public static void main(String args[])
        {
                //create the frame
                JSplitPaneDemo spd = new JSplitPaneDemo();
                spd.setSize(400,400);
                spd.setTitle("My split pane");
                spd.setVisible(true);
        }
}
```

Output:

```
C:\> javac JSplitPaneDemo.java
C:\> java JSplitPaneDemo
```

JTree Class

JTree class is useful to create a tree structure where a set of nodes can be displayed in a hierarchical manner. Each node may represent an item or some text.

To create a tree, we can create an object to JTree, as:

```
JTree tree = new JTree(root);
```

Here, root represents root node of the tree from where other nodes will span. This root node and other nodes can be created using DefaultMutableTreeNode class, as:

```
DefaultMutableTreeNode node = new DefaultMutableTreeNode("Item");
```

We can also create a tree by passing a Hashtable object that contains key and value pairs to the JTree object, as:

```
JTree tree = new JTree(Hashtable obj);
```

Similarly, a tree can be created by passing a Vector object that contains other objects, to the JTree object, as:

```
JTree tree = new JTree(Vector obj);
```

The following methods can be used to work with JTree:

❑ To add the nodes to root node, we can use add() method:

```
root.add(node);
```

❑ To find the path of selected item in the tree, getNewLeadSelectionPath() method of TreeSelectionEvent class is useful. This method returns TreePath object.

```
TreePath tp = tse.getNewLeadSelectionPath();
```

❑ To find the selected item in the tree, we can use getLastPathComponent() method of TreePath class.

```
Object comp = tp.getLastPathComponent();
```

Here, comp represents the component or node selected by the user.

❑ To know the path number (this represents the level):

```
int n = tp.getPathCount();
```

Program 14: Write a program to create a JTree with a root node and other nodes spanning from root node.

```java
//JTree demo
import java.awt.*;
import javax.swing.*;
import javax.swing.event.*; //TreeSelectionListener
import javax.swing.tree.*; //TreePath

class JTreeDemo extends JFrame implements TreeSelectionListener
{
        //vars
        DefaultMutableTreeNode root,dir1,dir2,file1,file2,file3;
        JTree tree;
        Container c;
        String msg="";
        JTextArea ta;

        JTreeDemo()
        {
                //create content pane c
                c = getContentPane();

                //set border layout to c
                c.setLayout(new BorderLayout());

                //create root node
                root = new DefaultMutableTreeNode("C:\\");

                //create other nodes
                dir1 = new DefaultMutableTreeNode("JavaPrograms");
                dir2 = new DefaultMutableTreeNode("Other Programs");
                file1 = new DefaultMutableTreeNode("JButtonDemo.java");
                file2 = new DefaultMutableTreeNode("JCheckBoxDemo.java");
                file3 = new DefaultMutableTreeNode("xyz.c");

                //add dir1 to root node
                root.add(dir1);

                //add other nodes to dir1
```

```
                        dir1.add(file1);
                        dir1.add(file2);
                        dir1.add(dir2);

                        //add file3 as a node in dir2
                        dir2.add(file3);

                        //create the tree from root node
                        tree = new JTree(root);

                        //add the tree to container
                        c.add("North", tree);

                        //create 3 empty labels and add to container
                        ta = new JTextArea();
                        c.add("South", ta);

                        //add tree selection listener to the tree
                        tree.addTreeSelectionListener(this);

                        //close the frame
                        setDefaultCloseOperation(JFrame.EXIT_ON_CLOSE);
                }

        //this method belongs to tree selection listener
        public void valueChanged(TreeSelectionEvent tse)
        {
                        //let us find out the newly selected item path
                        TreePath tp = tse.getNewLeadSelectionPath();
                        msg += "\nPath of selected component = "+ tp;

                        Object comp = tp.getLastPathComponent();
                        msg += "\nComponent selected = " + comp;

                        int n = tp.getPathCount();
                        msg += "\nLevel of component = "+ n;

                        //send the user selection to the label
                        ta.setText(msg);
                        msg = "";
        }

        public static void main(String args[])
        {
                        //create the frame
                        JTreeDemo td = new JTreeDemo();
                        td.setSize(400,300);
                        td.setTitle("JAVA TREE");
                        td.setVisible(true);
        }
}
```

Output:

```
C:\> javac JTreeDemo.java
C:\> java JTreeDemo
```

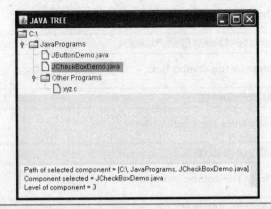

In this program, we create a tree with a root node C:\. The child node is JavaPrograms and other nodes are JButtonDemo.java, JCheckBoxDemo.java, and Other Programs. This Other Programs has another node xyz.c. When the user clicks on any node, the selected node's information is displayed in the text area.

JComboBox Class

JComboBox allows us to create a combo box, with a group of items which are displayed as a drop-down list. The user can select a single item only.

To create a combo box, we can simply create an object to JComboBox, as:

```
JComboBox box = new JComboBox();
```

This preceding statement creates an empty combo box

```
JComboBox box = new JComboBox(Object arr[]);
```

This preceding statement creates a JComboBox that contains the elements in the specified array arr[].

```
JComboBox box = new JComboBox(Vector v);
```

This statement creates a JComboBox that contains the elements in the specified Vector v.

Using JComboBox becomes easy with the following methods:

❑ To add the items to the combo box, we can use addItem() method:

```
box.addItem("India");
```

❑ To retrieve the selected item from the combo box:

```
Object obj = box.getSelecedItem();
```

❑ To retrieve the selected item's index:

```
int i = box.getSelectedIndex();
```

- ❏ To get the item of the combo box upon giving its index:

```
Object obj = box.getItemAt(int index);
```

- ❏ To get number of items in the combo box:

```
int n = box.getItemCount();
```

- ❏ To remove an item obj from the combo box:

```
box.removeItem(Object obj);
```

- ❏ To remove an item from the combo box when index is given:

```
box.removeItemAt(int index);
```

- ❏ To remove all items from the combo box:

```
box.removeAllItems();
```

Program 15: Write a program to create a combo box with names of some countries. The user can select any one name from the list and the selected country name is displayed again in the frame.

```java
//JComboBox demo
import java.awt.*;
import javax.swing.*;
import java.awt.event.*;

class JComboBoxDemo extends JFrame implements ItemListener
{
        //vars
        JComboBox box;
        JLabel lbl;

        JComboBoxDemo()
        {
                //create content pane
                Container c = getContentPane();

                //do not set any layout to c
                c.setLayout(null);

                //create an empty combobox
                box = new JComboBox();

                //add items to it
                box.addItem("India");
                box.addItem("America");
                box.addItem("Germany");
                box.addItem("Japan");
                box.addItem("France");

                //set the location of combo box
                box.setBounds(100,50,100,40);

                //add combo box to the container
                c.add(box);

                //create an empty label
                lbl = new JLabel();
```

```
                    //set the location of label
                    lbl.setBounds(100,200,200,40);

                    //add the label to content pane
                    c.add(lbl);

                    //attach item listener to combo box
                    box.addItemListener(this);

                    //close the frame
                    setDefaultCloseOperation(JFrame.EXIT_ON_CLOSE);
            }
            public void itemStateChanged(ItemEvent ie)
            {
                    //know which item is selected
                    String str = (String)box.getSelectedItem();

                    //display the selected item in the label
                    lbl.setText("You selected: "+str);
            }
            public static void main(String args[])
            {
                    //create the frame
                    JComboBoxDemo demo = new JComboBoxDemo();
                    demo.setTitle("My combo box");
                    demo.setSize(500,400);
                    demo.setVisible(true);
            }
    }
```

Output:

```
C:\> javac JComboBoxDemo.java
C:\> java JComboBoxDemo
```

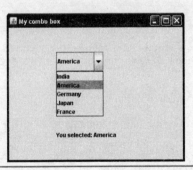

JList Class

JList class is useful to create a list which displays a list of items and allows the user to select one or more items.

To create a list, we can simply create an object to JList, as:

```
JList lst = new JList();
```

This creates an empty list.

```
JList lst = new JList(Object arr[]);
```

This creates a list with the elements of the array arr[].

```
JList lst = new JList(Vector v);
```

This constructs a JList that displays the elements in the specified Vector.

The following methods are useful to work with JList:

❑ To know which item is selected in the list, when only a single item is selected:

```
Object item = lst.getSelectedValue();
```

❑ To know the selected item's index whne only a single item is selected:

```
int index = lst.getSelectedIndex();
```

❑ To get all the selected items into an array arr[]:

```
Object arr[] = lst.getSelectedValues();
```

❑ To get the indexes of all the selected items into an array arr[]:

```
int  arr[] = lst.getSelectedIndices();
```

Program 16: Write a program to create a list box with names of some countries such that the user can select any one or more items from the list and the selected country names are displayed again in the frame.

```java
//JComboBox demo
import java.awt.*;
import javax.swing.*;
import javax.swing.event.*;

class JListDemo extends JFrame implements ListSelectionListener
{
    //vars
    JList lst;
    JLabel lbl;
    Object arr[];
    String msg="";

    JListDemo()
    {
        //create content pane
        Container c = getContentPane();

        //do not set any layout to c
        c.setLayout(null);

        //create an array with items list
        String items[] = {"India", "America", "Germany", "Japan",
            "France"};

        //create a list box with the items
        lst = new JList(items);

        //set the location of list box
        lst.setBounds(100,50,100,100);
```

```
                //add list to the container
                c.add(lst);

                //create an empty label
                lbl = new JLabel();

                //set the location of label
                lbl.setBounds(50,200,400,40);

                //add the label to content pane
                c.add(lbl);

                //attach item listener to list box
                lst.addListSelectionListener(this);

                //close the frame
                setDefaultCloseOperation(JFrame.EXIT_ON_CLOSE);
        }
        public void valueChanged(ListSelectionEvent le)
        {
                //know which items are selected
                arr = lst.getSelectedValues();

                //retrieve selected items and add to string msg
                for(int i=0; i<arr.length; i++)
                msg += (String)arr[i];
                //display the selected items in the label
                lbl.setText("selected: "+msg);
                //reset the string
                msg="";
        }
        public static void main(String args[])
        {
                //create the frame
                JListDemo demo = new JListDemo();
                demo.setTitle("My combo lst");
                demo.setSize(500,400);
                demo.setVisible(true);
        }
}
```

Output:

```
C:\> javac JListDemo.java
C:\> java JListDemo
```

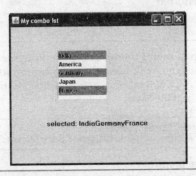

As you can see, the list box is displayed in the output. To select the items sequentially, we can use Shift+clicking on the items. To select randomly, we can use Control+clicking on the items.

JMenu Class

A menu represents a group of items or options for the user to select from. JMenu is used to create a menu with some options. After creating the menu, it should be added to the menu bar. See Figure 28.6 to get an idea of the menu bar, menu, and menu items.

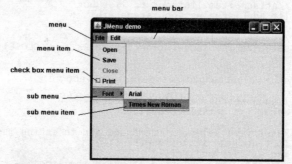

Figure 28.6 File and Edit are menus attached to menu bar

To create a menu, the following steps should be used:

❑ Create a menu bar using JMenuBar class object.

```
JMenuBar mb = new JMenuBar();
```

❑ Attach this menu bar to the container.

```
c.add(mb);
```

❑ Create separate menus to attach to the menu bar. For example, we want to create file menu with the name "File".

```
JMenu file= new JMenu("File");
```

❑ Attach this menu to the menu bar.

```
mb.add(file);
```

❑ A menu consists of a group of menu items. These menu items can be created using JMenuItem class. Sometimes, we can use a check box or a radio button as a menu item. For creating such check box, we should use JCheckBoxMenuItem and for creating radio button as a menu item we should use JRadioButtonMenuItem.

```
JMenuItem op = new JMenuItem("Open");
JCheckBoxMenuItem pr = new JCheckBoxMenuItem("Print");
```

❑ Attach the menu item to the menu.

```
file.add(op);
```

This completes creation of a menu. It is possible to create a menu inside another menu. It is called submenu. To create a submenu, one can follow the steps:

❏ Create a menu.

```
JMenu font= new JMenu("Font");
```

Here, font represents a submenu to be attached as an item in a menu.

❏ Now attach it to a menu.

```
file.add(font);
```

❏ Create menu items using JMenuItem, JCheckBoxMenuItem, or JRadioButtonMenuItem.

```
JMenuItem f1 = new JMenuItem("Arial");
```

❏ Attach menu items to the submenu.

```
font.add(f1);
```

To disable an item in the menu, we can use setEnabled(false) method and to enable it, we can use setEnabled(true);

To display a horizontal line which separates a group of items from another group in the menu, we can use addSeparator() method.

It is the duty of the programmer to know which item has been selected by the user. It helps him to write the code representing the further action depending on the user selection. In case of menu items, the selected item can be known, by using isArmed() method. This method returns true if the item is selected, otherwise false. In case of check box menu items or radio button menu items, we can use getModel() method first on the item so that it gets the Model object which contains the state of the item. Then isSelected() method can tell whether the item is selected or not by referring to the data inside the Model object. These things can be observed in Program 17.

Program 17: Write a program to create a menu with several menu items.

```
//Menu creation
import java.awt.*;
import java.awt.event.*;
import javax.swing.*;
class MyMenu extends JFrame implements ActionListener
{
        //vars
        JMenuBar mb;
        JMenu file,edit,font;
        JMenuItem op,sa,cl,cp,pt,f1,f2;
        JCheckBoxMenuItem pr;

        MyMenu()
        {
                //create container
                Container c = getContentPane();
                c.setLayout(new BorderLayout());

                //create a menubar
                mb = new JMenuBar();

                //add menubar to container
                c.add("North",mb);

                //create the File,Edit menus
```

```
                        //and attach them to menubar
                        file= new JMenu("File");
                        edit= new JMenu("Edit");
                        mb.add(file);
                        mb.add(edit);

                        //create menu items
                        op= new JMenuItem("Open");
                        sa= new JMenuItem("Save");
                        cl= new JMenuItem("Close");
                        cp= new JMenuItem("Copy");
                        pt= new JMenuItem("Paste");

                        //add Open,Save,Close to File menu
                        //and Copy,Paste to Edit menu
                        file.add(op);
                        file.add(sa);
                        file.add(cl);
                        edit.add(cp);
                        edit.add(pt);

                        //Make close disabled
                        cl.setEnabled(false);

                        //create Print checkbox and add it to File menu
                        pr= new JCheckBoxMenuItem("Print");
                        file.add(pr);

                        //add a separator (horizontal line) to File menu
                        file.addSeparator();

                        //Create a Font submenu and add it to File menu
                        font = new JMenu("Font");
                        file.add(font);

                        //create menu items
                        f1 = new JMenuItem("Arial");
                        f2 = new JMenuItem("Times New Roman");

                        //add menu items to sub menu
                        font.add(f1);
                        font.add(f2);

                        //attach action listeners to all menu items
                        op.addActionListener(this);
                        sa.addActionListener(this);
                        cl.addActionListener(this);
                        cp.addActionListener(this);
                        pt.addActionListener(this);
                        pr.addActionListener(this);
                        f1.addActionListener(this);
                        f2.addActionListener(this);

                        //close frame
                        setDefaultCloseOperation(JFrame.EXIT_ON_CLOSE);
        }

        //this method is executed when a menu item is clicked
        public void actionPerformed(ActionEvent ae)
        {
                        //know which menu item is clicked
                        if(op.isArmed()) System.out.println("Open is selected");
                        if(sa.isArmed()) System.out.println("Save is selected");
                        if(cl.isArmed()) System.out.println("Close is selected");
                        if(cp.isArmed()) System.out.println("Copy is selected");
                        if(pt.isArmed()) System.out.println("Paste is selected");

                        if(pr.getModel().isSelected()) System.out.println("Printing
```

```
        on...");
        else System.out.println("Printing off...");

        if(f1.isArmed()) System.out.println("Arial Font is selected");
        if(f2.isArmed()) System.out.println("Times New Roman is selected");
    }

    public static void main(String args[])
    {
        //create the frame
        MyMenu mm = new MyMenu();
        mm.setTitle("JMenu demo");
        mm.setSize(500,400);
        mm.setVisible(true);
    }
}
```

Output:

```
C:\> javac MyMenu.java
C:\> java MyMenu
```

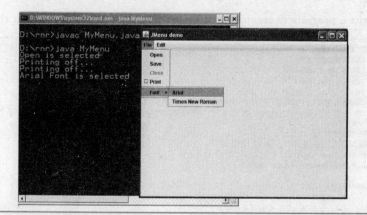

In this program, we create two menus—file and edit and add them to the menu bar. There is a submenu Font which is added in the file menu. When the user clicks on any menu items, at DOS prompt, we displayed the clicked items.

In Program 17, we are merely catching which item is selected by the user and displaying that item's name at DOS prompt. We should go further depending on the user selection. For example, if the user has clicked on 'open' item in File menu, then the file should be actually opened and displayed in a separate window. How to achieve this? We can write a method like openFile() where we display a file dialog box which displays all the files available in the system. Then the user can select any file he wants to open. That filename and the path should be found and its contents should be read using some input stream like FileReader and then the contents should be sent to a text area in another frame. Thus the user can view the contents in another frame.

For this purpose, we need JFileChooser class. JFileChooser class has method to display a file open dialog box, as:

```
    int i =fc.showOpenDialog(this);   //fc is JFileChooser object
```

Similarly, we can also display a file save dialog box where the user can select a file name and attempt to save data in the file, as:

```
int i =fc.showSaveDialog(this);   //to handle File -> Save item
```

When the user approves a file in the dialog box, then the getSelectedFile() method will help to get the filename into File object as:

```
File f = fc.getSelectedFile();
```

Now, the selected file name can be obtained by using f.getName() and its path from f.getPath(). This method gives the path and the filename. So, that full path and filename can be sent to a FileReader, as:

```
BufferedReader br = new BufferedReader(new FileReader(fname));
```

Here, the FileReader is again connected to the BufferedReader. Using br.readLine() method, we can read the contents of the file string by string and can display them in a text area. This text area can be displayed along with the content in another frame for the user to view. This is done in the next program

Program 18: Write a program to create a menu and handle the file open event for the user.

```
//Menu creation
import java.awt.*;
import java.awt.event.*;
import javax.swing.*;
import java.io.*;
class MyMenu extends JFrame implements ActionListener
{
        //vars
        JMenuBar mb;
        JMenu file,edit,font;
        JMenuItem op,sa,cl,cp,pt,f1,f2;
        JCheckBoxMenuItem pr;

        MyMenu()
        {
                //create container
                Container c = getContentPane();
                c.setLayout(new BorderLayout());

                //create a menubar
                mb = new JMenuBar();

                //add menubar to container
                c.add("North",mb);

                //create the File,Edit menus
                //and attach them to menubar
                file= new JMenu("File");
                edit= new JMenu("Edit");
                mb.add(file);
                mb.add(edit);

                //create menu items
                op= new JMenuItem("Open");
                sa= new JMenuItem("Save");
                cl= new JMenuItem("Close");
                cp= new JMenuItem("Copy");
                pt= new JMenuItem("Paste");
```

```
                       //add Open,Save,Close to File menu
                       //and Copy,Paste to Edit menu
                       file.add(op);
                       file.add(sa);
                       file.add(cl);
                       edit.add(cp);
                       edit.add(pt);

                       //Make close disabled
                       cl.setEnabled(false);

                       //create Print checkbox and add it to File menu
                       pr= new JCheckBoxMenuItem("Print");
                       file.add(pr);

                       //add a separator (horizontal line) to File menu
                       file.addSeparator();

                       //Create a Font submenu and add it to File menu
                       font = new JMenu("Font");
                       file.add(font);

                       //create menu items
                       f1 = new JMenuItem("Arial");
                       f2 = new JMenuItem("Times New Roman");

                       //add menu items to sub menu
                       font.add(f1);
                       font.add(f2);

                       //attach listeners to all menu items
                       op.addActionListener(this);
                       sa.addActionListener(this);
                       cl.addActionListener(this);
                       cp.addActionListener(this);
                       pt.addActionListener(this);
                       pr.addActionListener(this);
                       f1.addActionListener(this);
                       f2.addActionListener(this);

                       //close frame
                       setDefaultCloseOperation(JFrame.EXIT_ON_CLOSE);
            }

//this method is executed when a menu item is clicked
public void actionPerformed(ActionEvent ae)
{
                       //know which menu item is clicked
                       if(op.isArmed()) this.openFile();
                       if(sa.isArmed()) //this.saveFile();

                       if(cl.isArmed()) System.out.println("Close is selected");
                       if(cp.isArmed()) System.out.println("Copy is selected");
                       if(pt.isArmed()) System.out.println("Paste is selected");

                       if(pr.getModel().isSelected()) System.out.println("Printing
                        on...");
                       else System.out.println("Printing off...");

                       if(f1.isArmed()) System.out.println("Arial Font is selected");
                       if(f2.isArmed()) System.out.println("Times New Roman is selected");

}
//this method is called when File->Open is selected
void openFile()
{
                       //create an object to JFileChooser class
                       JFileChooser fc = new JFileChooser();
```

```
                          //display file open dialog box
                          int i =fc.showOpenDialog(this);

                          //if the user selected a file name then
                          if(i == JFileChooser.APPROVE_OPTION) {
                          //get the selected file into File object
                          File f = fc.getSelectedFile();

                          //The file name is given by f.getName();
                          //File name with path is given by f.getPath();
                          String fname = f.getPath();

                          //open another frame and pass the fname to it
                          OpenFrame of = new OpenFrame(fname);

                          of.setSize(500,400);
                          of.setVisible(true);
                }
        }

        public static void main(String args[])
        {
                //create the frame
                MyMenu mm = new MyMenu();
                mm.setTitle("JMenu demo");
                mm.setSize(500,400);
                mm.setVisible(true);
        }
}

//this is another class which creates another frame
//to display file contents
class OpenFrame extends JFrame
{
        //catch the file name
        OpenFrame(String fname)
        {
                //create content pane
                Container c = getContentPane();
                c.setLayout(new FlowLayout());

                //create a text area and add to content pane
                TextArea ta = new TextArea(22,60);
                c.add(ta);

                //vars
                String str="";
                String str1="";

                try{
                //create reader to read from file
                BufferedReader br = new BufferedReader(new FileReader(fname));

                //read string by string and add to str1
                while((str = br.readLine()) != null)
                str1+= str+"\n";

                //display the file content in text area
                ta.setText(str1);

                //close the file
                br.close();
                }catch(Exception e){}

        }
}
```

Output:

```
C:\> javac MyMenu.java
C:\> java MyMenu
```

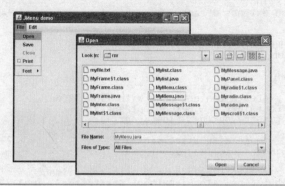

When the File -> Open option is selected by the user, the Open dialog box appears as shown in the output. In this dialog box, if the user selects a file with the name MyMenu.java, then the contents of the file will appear in a separate frame as shown in the next figure:

JToggleButton Class

A toggle button looks like a push button, but has two states—pushed and released. When the user clicks on the button, it goes into pushed state and some task can be performed. When the user clicks the same button once again, it goes into released state and another task may be performed. JToggleButton class is useful to create a toggle button, as:

```
JToggleButton but = new JToggleButton("label");
```

This creates a toggle button with a label on it.

```
JToggleButton but = new JToggleButton("label", ImageIcon obj);
```

This creates a toggle button with label and image.

isSelected() method is useful to determine the state of the toggle button. If this method returns true, the button is selected, otherwise it is not selected.

Program 19: Write a program to show the functioning of a toggle button.

```java
//A toggle button with start and stop images
import java.awt.*;
import java.awt.event.*;
import javax.swing.*;
class JTButton extends JFrame implements ActionListener
{
        //vars
        JToggleButton but;
        ImageIcon img1;

        JTButton()
        {
                //create content pane with flow layout
                Container c = getContentPane();
                c.setLayout(new FlowLayout());

                //image with start signal
                img1 = new ImageIcon("start.gif");

                //create toggle button with start image
                but = new JToggleButton("Start/Stop", img1);

                //add button to content pane
                c.add(but);

                //add action listener to button
                but.addActionListener(this);
        }

        public void actionPerformed(ActionEvent ae)
        {
                //image with stop signal
                ImageIcon img2 = new ImageIcon("stop.gif");

                //if toggle button is selected display stop signal image
                //else display start signal image
                if(but.isSelected())
                but.setIcon(img2);
                else but.setIcon(img1);

        }

        public static void main(String args[])
        {
                //create the frame
                JTButton demo = new JTButton();
                demo.setSize(400,400);
                demo.setVisible(true);
                demo.setDefaultCloseOperation(JFrame.EXIT_ON_CLOSE);
        }
}
```

Output:

```
C:\> javac JTButton.java
C:\> java JTButton
```

In this program, we create a toggle button with an image 'start.gif'. When the button is clicked again, it displays the image 'stop.gif'. Again when the button is clicked, it displays 'start.gif'. Like this, it toggles between the two images.

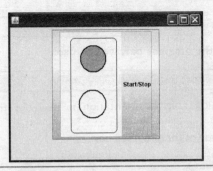

When the button is clicked, it displays the image as shown here:

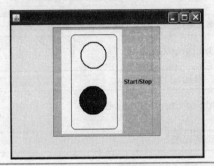

JProgressBar Class

A progress bar visually displays the progress of some task. As the task progresses towards completion, the progress bar displays the task's percentage of completion. This percentage is represented visually by a rectangle which starts out empty and gradually gets filled as the task progresses. Progress bar can be displayed horizontally or vertically. JProgressBar is used to create the progress bar, as:

```
JProgressBar bar = new JProgressBar();
```

This creates a horizontal progress bar.

```
JProgressBar bar = new JProgressBar(orientation);
```

Where the orientation can be SwingConstants.HORIZONTAL (0) for displaying horizontal progress bar or SwingConstants.VERTICAL (1) for displaying vertical progress bar.

```
JProgressBar bar = new JProgressBar(alignment, int min, int max);
```

Here, the min and max represent the starting and ending values of the progress bar.

❑ To know the minimum value of progress bar, we can use:

```
int n = bar.getMinimum();
```

❑ To know the maximum value of progress bar, we can write:

```
      int n = bar.getMaximum();
```

❑   To get the alignment of the progress bar, we can use:

```
      int n = bar.getOrientation();
```

This method returns 0 if HORIZONTAL orientation is used for the progress bar. It returns 1 if VERTICAL alignment is there.

❑   To know the current value of the progress bar:

```
      int n = bar.getValue();
```

❑   To set the value of the progress bar to a particular value:

```
      bar.setValue(int value);
```

❑   To set the minimum of the progress bar:

```
      bar.setMinimum(int value);
```

❑   To set the maximum value of the progress bar:

```
      bar.setMaximum(int value);
```

❑   To set the alignment, we can use:

```
      bar.setOrientation(int orientation);
```

Here, if the orientation given is 0, it is set to HORIZONTAL, if it is 1 then it is set to VERTICAL.

❑   To display the percentage of progress, we can use setStringPainted() method, as:

```
      bar.setStringPainted(true);
```

When true is passed to this method, progress percentage will be displayed as a string, otherwise not.

Program 20: Write a program to create a push button and a progress bar, such that everytime, the button is clicked by the user the progress bar progresses by 5 units.

```
//JToggleButton
import java.awt.*;
import javax.swing.*;
import java.awt.event.*;
class ProgressDemo extends JFrame implements ActionListener
{
    //vars
    JButton b;
    JProgressBar bar;

    ProgressDemo()
    {
        //create content pane with flow layout
        Container  c = getContentPane();
        c.setLayout(new FlowLayout());
```

```
                    //create a button
                    b = new JButton("Click repeatedly");

                    //create a progress bar
                    bar = new JProgressBar();

                    //set gray as foreground color
                    bar.setForeground(Color.gray);

                    //display the percentage string
                    bar.setStringPainted(true);

                    //add button and progress bar to c
                    c.add(b);
                    c.add(bar);

                    //add action listener to button
                    b.addActionListener(this);
            }

            public void actionPerformed(ActionEvent ae)
            {
                    //every time the button is clicked,
                    //increment the progress bar value by 5
                    bar.setValue(bar.getValue()+5);

            }

            public static void main(String args[])
            {
                    //create the frame
                    ProgressDemo d = new ProgressDemo();
                    d.setSize(400,400);
                    d.setVisible(true);
                    d.setDefaultCloseOperation(JFrame.EXIT_ON_CLOSE);
            }
    }
```

Output:

```
C:\> javac ProgressDemo.java
C:\> java ProgressDemo
```

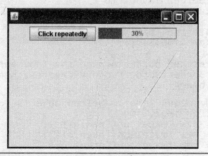

JToolBar Class

JToolBar class is useful to create a tool bar. A tool bar is a bar to which some components can be attached. It is possible to attach push buttons, radio buttons, check boxes, list boxes, etc. to the tool bar. To create a tool bar:

```
        JToolBar tb = new JToolBar();
```

This creates a tool bar with HORIZONTAL orientation.

```
        JToolBar tb = new JToolBar(int orientation);
```

Here, orientation is 0 for HORIZONTAL orientation and 1 for VERTICAL orientation.

```
        JToolBar tb = new JToolBar(String str, int orientation);
```

This creates a tool bar with the name str and the specified orientation.

After creating the tool bar, we can add components to it, using add() method, as:

```
        tb.add(component);
```

Program 21: Write a program to create a tool bar with 3 push buttons added to it. The push buttons are created with images to denote new, open, and print options. When the user clicks on any button, the selected button is displayed in the label.

```
        //JToolBar
        import java.awt.*;
        import javax.swing.*;
        import java.awt.event.*;
        class JToolBarDemo extends JFrame implements ActionListener
        {
                //vars
                String str;
                Container c;
                JToolBar tb;
                JButton b1,b2,b3;
                JLabel lbl;

                JToolBarDemo()
                {
                        //create content pane
                        c = getContentPane();

                        //set border layout to c
                        c.setLayout(new BorderLayout());

                        //create tool bar
                        tb = new JToolBar();

                        //set etched border around the tool bar
                        tb.setBorder(BorderFactory.createEtchedBorder(Color.green,
                        Color.black));

                        //load images into ImageIcon objects
                        ImageIcon img1, img2, img3;
                        img1 = new ImageIcon("new.gif");
                        img2 = new ImageIcon("open.gif");
                        img3 = new ImageIcon("print.gif");

                        //create 3 push buttons with images
                        b1 = new JButton(img1);
                        b2 = new JButton(img2);
                        b3 = new JButton(img3);

                        //add the push buttons to the tool bar
                        tb.add(b1);
                        tb.add(b2);
```

```
                tb.add(b3);

                //add the tool bar in c at top
                c.add("North", tb);

                //create a label and add to c at center
                lbl = new JLabel();
                lbl.setFont(new Font("SansSerif", Font.PLAIN, 30));
                c.add("Center", lbl);

                //add action listener to buttons in tool bar
                b1.addActionListener(this);
                b2.addActionListener(this);
                b3.addActionListener(this);
        }

        public void actionPerformed(ActionEvent ae)
        {
                //know which button is clicked
                if(ae.getSource() == b1) str = "New clicked";
                if(ae.getSource() == b2) str = "Open clicked";
                if(ae.getSource() == b3) str = "Print clicked";

                //display the string in the label
                lbl.setText(str);

        }

        public static void main(String args[])
        {
                //create the frame
                JToolBarDemo tbd = new JToolBarDemo();
                tbd.setSize(400,400);
                tbd.setVisible(true);
                tbd.setDefaultCloseOperation(JFrame.EXIT_ON_CLOSE);
        }
}
```

Output:

```
C:\> javac JToolBarDemo.java
C:\> java JToolBarDemo
```

JColorChooser Class

This class is useful to create a color chooser dialog box with several colors so that the user can select any color. To create a color chooser dialog box, we can use showDialog() method of JColorChooser class, as:

```
Color color = JColorChooser.showDialog(this, "Select a color", selectedcolor);
```

showDialog() method takes 3 arguments—the parent component of the dialog, the title for the dialog, and the initial color set when the color dialog is shown. In the color dialog, if the user selects a color and then press OK button, then the selected color is returned by the showDialog() method. This selected color can be used for any purpose by the user.

Program 22: Write a program to create a color chooser dialog box for the user to select a color from and the selected color is displayed as background color for the frame.

```java
//JColorChooser demo
import java.awt.*;
import java.awt.event.*;
import javax.swing.*;
class JColorChooserDemo extends JFrame implements ActionListener
{
    //vars
    JButton b;
    Container c;

    JColorChooserDemo()
    {
        //create the content pane
        c = getContentPane();
        c.setLayout(new FlowLayout());

        //creat a push button
        b = new JButton("Select a Color");

        //add button to content pane
        c.add(b);

        //add action listener to button
        b.addActionListener(this);
    }

    public void actionPerformed(ActionEvent ae)
    {
        //take the initial color as null
        Color selectedcolor= null;

        //create the color chooser with dialog box to select a color
        Color color = JColorChooser.showDialog(this, "Select a color",
         selectedcolor);

        //if color is not null then some color is selected
        if(color != null)
        {
            //get the selected color
            selectedcolor = color;
        }

        //show back ground color of frame with the selected color
        c.setBackground(color);
    }

    public static void main(String args[])
    {
```

```
            //create the frame
            JColorChooserDemo demo = new JColorChooserDemo();
            demo.setSize(400,400);
            demo.setVisible(true);
            demo.setDefaultCloseOperation(JFrame.EXIT_ON_CLOSE);
        }
    }
```

Output:

```
C:\> javac JColorChooserDemo.java
C:\> java JColorChooserDemo
```

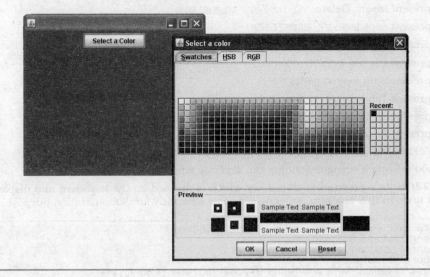

Handling Keyboard Events

A user interacts with the application by pressing keys either on the keyboard or by using mouse. A programmer should know which key the user has pressed on the keyboard or whether the mouse is moved, pressed, or released. These are also called 'events'. Knowing these events will enable the programmer to write his code according to the key pressed or mouse event.

KeyListener interface of java.awt.event package helps to know which key is pressed or released by the user. It has 3 methods:

❏ public void keyPressed(KeyEvent ke): This method is called when a key is pressed on the keyboard. This include any key on the keyboard along with special keys like function keys, shift, alter, caps lock, home, end, etc.

❏ public void keyTyped(KeyEvent ke): This method is called when a key is typed on the keyboard. This is same as keyPressed() method but this method is called when general keys like A to Z or 1 to 9, etc. are typed. It cannot work with special keys.

❏ public void keyReleased(KeyEvent ke): This method is called when a key is released.

KeyEvent class has the following methods to know which key is typed by the user:

❏ char getKeyChar(): This method returns the key name (or character) related to the key pressed or released.

❑ `int getKeyCode()`: This method returns an integer number which is the value of the key pressed by the user.

The following are the key codes for the keys on the keyboard. They are defined as constants in KeyEvent class. Remember VK represents Virtual Key.

❑ To represent keys from a to z: `VK_A  to VK_Z`

❑ To represent keys from 1 to 9: `VK_0 to VK_9`

❑ To represent keys from F1 to F12: `VK_F1 to VK_F12`

❑ To represent Home, End: `VK_HOME, VK_END`

❑ To represent PageUp, PageDown: `VK_PAGE_UP, VK_PAGE_DOWN`

❑ To represent Insert, Delete: `VK_INSERT, VK_DELETE`

❑ To represent caps lock: `VK_CAPS_LOCK`

❑ To represent alter key: `VK_ALT`

❑ To represent Control key: `VK_CONTROL`

❑ To represent Shift key: `VK_SHIFT`

❑ To represent Tab key: `VK_TAB`

❑ To represent arrow keys: VK_LEFT, VK_RIGHT, VK_UP, VK_DOWN

❑ To represent Escape key: VK_ESCAPE

❑ `static String getKeyText(int keyCode)`

This method returns a string describing the keyCode such as HOME, F1, or A.

Program 23: Write a program to trap a key which is pressed on the keyboard and display its name in the text area. In this program, we consider some keys only for demonstration purpose.

```java
//To catch some of the keys of the keyboard
import java.awt.*;
import java.awt.event.*;
import javax.swing.*;
class KeyBoardEvents extends JFrame implements KeyListener
{
        //vars
        Container c;
        JTextArea ta;
        String str="";

        KeyBoardEvents()
        {
                //create content pane
                c = getContentPane();

                //create a text area and set some font to it
                ta = new JTextArea("Press a key");
                ta.setFont(new Font("Arial", Font.BOLD, 30));

                //add text area to content pane
                c.add(ta);

                //add key listener to text area
                ta.addKeyListener(this);
        }

        public void keyPressed(KeyEvent ke)
        {
                //get the key code of the key pressed on keyboard
                int keycode = ke.getKeyCode();

                //find which key is pressed
```

```
            if(keycode == KeyEvent.VK_F1) str += "F1 key";
            if(keycode == KeyEvent.VK_F2) str += "F2 key";
            if(keycode == KeyEvent.VK_F3) str += "F3 key";
            if(keycode == KeyEvent.VK_PAGE_UP) str += "Page Up";
            if(keycode == KeyEvent.VK_PAGE_DOWN) str += "Page Down";
            if(keycode == KeyEvent.VK_ALT) str += "Alter";
            if(keycode == KeyEvent.VK_HOME) str += "Home";
            if(keycode == KeyEvent.VK_END) str += "End";
            ta.setText(str);
            str="";
        }

        public void keyReleased(KeyEvent ke)
        {}

        public void keyTyped(KeyEvent ke)
        {}

        public static void main(String args[])
        {
            //create the frame
            KeyBoardEvents kbe = new KeyBoardEvents();

            kbe.setSize(400,400);
            kbe.setVisible(true);
            kbe.setDefaultCloseOperation(JFrame.EXIT_ON_CLOSE);
        }
    }
```

Output:

```
C:\> javac KeyBoardEvents.java
C:\> java KeyBoardEvents
```

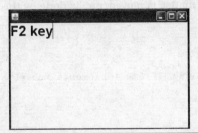

Handling Mouse Events

The user may click, release, drag, or move a mouse while interacting with the application. If the programmer knows what the user has done, he can write the code according to the mouse event. To trap the mouse events, `MouseListener` and `MouseMotionListener` interfaces of `java.awt.event` package are used.

MouseListener interface has the following methods:

❑ `void mouseClicked(MouseEvent e)`: Void MouseClickedThis method is invoked when the mouse button has been clicked (pressed and released) on a component.

❑ `void mouseEntered(MouseEvent e)`: This method is invoked when the mouse enters a component.

❑ void mouseExited(MouseEvent e): This method is invoked when the mouse exits a component.

❑ void mousePressed(MouseEvent e): This method is invoked when a mouse button has been pressed on a component.

❑ void mouseReleased(MouseEvent e): This method is invoked when a mouse button has been released on a component.

MouseMotionListener interface has the following methods:

❑ void mouseDragged(MouseEvent e): This method is invoked when a mouse button is pressed on a component and then dragged.

❑ void mouseMoved(MouseEvent e): This method is invoked when the mouse cursor has been moved onto a component but no buttons have been pushed.

The MouseEvent class has the following methods:

❑ int getButton(): This method returns a value representing a mouse button, when it is clicked It returns 1 if left button is clicked, 2 if middle button, and 3 if right button is clicked.

❑ int getClickCount(): This method returns the number of mouse clicks associated with this event.

❑ int getX(): This method returns the horizontal x position of the event relative to the source component.

❑ int getY(): This method returns the vertical y position of the event relative to the source component.

Program 24: Write a program to create a text area and display the mouse event when the button on the mouse is clicked, when the mouse is moved, etc. is done by the user.

```
//Mouse events
import java.awt.*;
import java.awt.event.*;
import javax.swing.*;
class MouseEvents extends JFrame implements MouseListener,

MouseMotionListener
{
        //vars
        String str="";
        JTextArea ta;
        Container c;
        int x,y;

        MouseEvents()
        {
                //create content pane
                c = getContentPane();
                c.setLayout(new FlowLayout());

                //create a text area and set some font to it
                ta = new JTextArea("Click the mouse or move it",5,20);
                ta.setFont(new Font("Arial", Font.BOLD, 30));

                //add text area to content pane
                c.add(ta);

                //add mouse listener, mouse motion listener to text area
                ta.addMouseListener(this);
                ta.addMouseMotionListener(this);
```

```
        }
        public void mouseClicked(MouseEvent me)
        {
                //know which button of mouse is clicked
                int i = me.getButton();
                if(i==1)
                str += "Clicked Button: Left";
                else if(i==2)
                str += "Clicked Button: Middle";
                else if(i==3)
                str += "Clicked Button: Right";

                this.display();
        }

        public void mouseEntered(MouseEvent me)
        {
                str += "Mouse entered";
                this.display();
        }

        public void mouseExited(MouseEvent me)
        {
                str += "MouseExited";
                this.display();
        }

        Public void mousePressed(MouseEvent me)
        {
                x = me.getX();
                y = me.getY();
                str += "Mouse Pressed at: "+x+"\t"+y;
                this.display();
        }

        public void mouseReleased(MouseEvent me)
        {
                x = me.getX();
                y = me.getY();
                str += "Mouse Released at: "+x+"\t"+y;
                this.display();
        }

        public void mouseDragged(MouseEvent me)
        {
                x = me.getX();
                y = me.getY();
                str += "Mouse Dragged at: "+x+"\t"+y;
                this.display();
        }

        public void mouseMoved(MouseEvent me)
        {
                x = me.getX();
                y = me.getY();
                str += "Mouse Moved at: "+x+"\t"+y;
                this.display();
        }

        public void display()
        {
                ta.setText(str);
                str="";
        }

        public static void main(String args[])
        {
```

```
                        //create the frame
                        MouseEvents mes = new MouseEvents();
                        mes.setSize(400,400);
                        mes.setVisible(true);
                        mes.setDefaultCloseOperation(JFrame.EXIT_ON_CLOSE);
                }
        }
```

Output:

```
C:\> javac MouseEvents.java
C:\> java MouseEvents
```

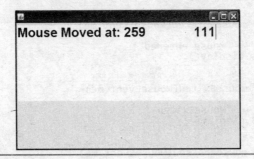

Conclusion

Since AWT components are heavy-weight and dependent internally on native methods, swing has been invented. Swing components are light weight and take very less resources of the system. The screens designed in swing look same on all operating systems. But, if the programmer wishes to provide a different look and feel depending on the operating system, he can do so. This is the flexibility in swing. Also, swing has more and more number of features which made it to be programmers' favorite package. This is the reason that today almost all software development companies look for swing programmers for their projects.

GRAPHICS PROGRAMMING — LAYOUT MANAGERS

W e create several components like push buttons, checkboxes, radio buttons etc., in GUI. After creating these components, they should be placed in the frame (in AWT) or container (in swing). While arranging them in the frame or container, they can be arranged in a particular manner by using layout managers. JavaSoft people have created a `LayoutManager` interface in `java.awt` package which is implemented in various classes which provide various types of layouts to arrange the components.

Important Interview Question

What is a layout manager?

A layout manager is a class that is useful to arrange components in a particular manner in a frame or container.

The following classes represent the layout managers in Java:

- ❑ FlowLayout
- ❑ BorderLayout
- ❑ CardLayout
- ❑ GridLayout
- ❑ GridBagLayout
- ❑ BoxLayout

To set a particular layout, we should first create an object to the layout class and pass the object to `setLayout()` method. For example, to set `FlowLayout` to the container that holds the components, we can write:

```
FlowLayout obj = new FlowLayout();
c.setLayout(obj);  //c is container
```

FlowLayout

FlowLayout is useful to arrange the components in a line one after the other. When a line is filled with components, they are automatically placed in the next line. This is the default layout in applets and panels.

To create FlowLayout, we can use the following ways:

❏   `FlowLayout  obj = new FlowLayout();`

This creates flow layout. By default, the gap between components will be 5 pixels and the components are centered in the first line.

❏   `FlowLayout obj = new FlowLayout(int alignment);`

Here, the alignment of components can be specified. To arrange the components starting from left to right, we can use `FlowLayout.LEFT`. To adjust the components towards right, we can use `FlowLayout.RIGHT` and for center alignment, we can use `FlowLayout.CENTER`.

❏   `FlowLayout obj = new FlowLayout(int alignment, int hgap, int vgap);`

Here, the hgap and vgap specify the space between components. hgap represents horizontal gap and vgap represents vertical gap in pixels.

Program 1: Write a program to create a group of push buttons and arrange them in the container using flow layout manager. The buttons are right justified.

```
//FlowLayout demo
import java.awt.*;
import javax.swing.*;
class FlowLayoutDemo extends JFrame
{
        FlowLayoutDemo()
        {
                //create content pane
                Container c = getContentPane();

                //create FlowLayout object with alignment: right
                //and 10px horizontal and vertical gap
        FlowLayout obj = new FlowLayout(FlowLayout.RIGHT,10,10);

                //set the layout to content pane
                c.setLayout(obj);

                //create 4 push buttons
                JButton b1,b2,b3,b4;
                b1 = new JButton("Button1");
                b2 = new JButton("Button2");
                b3 = new JButton("Button3");
                b4 = new JButton("Button4");

                //when we add the buttons to c, they are added as per flow layout
                c.add(b1);
                c.add(b2);
                c.add(b3);
                c.add(b4);
        }
        public static void main(String args[])
        {
                //create the frame
                FlowLayoutDemo demo = new FlowLayoutDemo();
                demo.setSize(400,400);
                demo.setTitle("Flow layout");
                demo.setVisible(true);
                demo.setDefaultCloseOperation(JFrame.EXIT_ON_CLOSE);
        }
}
```

Output:

```
C:\> javac FlowLayoutDemo.java
C:\> java FlowLayoutDemo
```

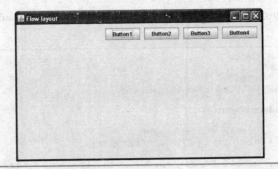

BorderLayout

BorderLayout is useful to arrange the components in the 4 borders of the frame as well as in the center. The borders are identified with the names of directions. The top border is specified as 'North', the right side border 'East', the bottom one as 'South' and the left one as 'West'. The center is represented as 'Center'. See Figure 29.1.

To create a BorderLayout, we can use the following ways:

❑ `BorderLayout obj = new BorderLayout();`

This creates a BorderLayout object without any gaps between the components.

❑ `BorderLayout obj = new BorderLayout(int hgap, int vgap);`

Here, hgap represents horizontal gap and vgap represents vertical gap between components in pixels.

While adding the components to the container the direction should be specified, as:

```
c.add("North", component);  //c is container
```

Here, the component is added in the container in North direction.

We can also add the component in North direction, as shown here:

```
c.add(component, BorderLayout.NORTH);
```

In the preceding statement, we are specifying the direction with the constant, `BorderLayout.NORTH`. Similarly, other constants EAST, WEST, SOUTH, CENTER can be used.

	North	
West	Center	East
	South	

Figure 29.1 Direction of components in BorderLayout

Program 2: Write a program to create a group of push buttons and add them to the container by using BorderLayout.

```
//BorderLayout demo
import java.awt.*;
import javax.swing.*;
class BorderLayoutDemo extends JFrame
{
        BorderLayoutDemo()
        {
                //create content pane
                Container c = getContentPane();

                //create border layout with 10px horizontal and vertical
                //gap between components
                BorderLayout obj = new BorderLayout(10,10);

                //set border layout to c
                c.setLayout(obj);

                //create 4 push buttons
                JButton b1,b2,b3,b4;
                b1 = new JButton("Button1");
                b2 = new JButton("Button2");
                b3 = new JButton("Button3");
                b4 = new JButton("Button4");

                //add buttons to c
                c.add("North",b1);
                c.add("East", b2);
                c.add("South",b3);
                c.add("Center",b4);
        /*
                the above statements can be re-written as:
                c.add(b1, BorderLayout.NORTH);
                c.add(b2, BorderLayout.EAST);
                c.add(b3, BorderLayout.SOUTH);
                c.add(b4, BorderLayout.CENTER);
        */

        }
        public static void main(String args[])
        {
                //create the frame
                BorderLayoutDemo demo = new BorderLayoutDemo();
                demo.setSize(400,400);
                demo.setVisible(true);
                demo.setDefaultCloseOperation(JFrame.EXIT_ON_CLOSE);

        }
}
```

Output:

```
C:\> javac BorderLayoutDemo.java
C:\> java BorderLayoutDemo
```

In preceding program, the components are arranged in the four borders as well as in the center of the container.

CardLayout

A CardLayout object is a layout manager which treats each component as a card. Only one card is visible at a time, and the container acts as a stack of cards. The first component added to a CardLayout object is the visible component when the container is first displayed.

To create CardLayout object, we can use the following ways:

❑   `CardLayout obj = new CardLayout();`

Here, the card layout object is created without any gaps between the components.

❑   `CardLayout obj = new CardLayout(int hgap, int vgap);`

The preceding statement creates a card layout with the specified horizontal and vertical gaps between the components.

❑   While adding components to the container, we can use add() method as:

```
c.add("cardname", component);
```

❑   To retrieve the cards one by one, the following methods can be used:

   • `void first(container)` : to retrieve the first card.

   • `void last(container)` : to retrieve the last card.

   • `void next(container)` : to go to the next card.

   • `void previous(container)` : to go back to previous card.

   • `void show(container, "cardname")` : to see a particular card with the name specified.

Program 3: Write a program to create a group of push buttons and add them to the container using CardLayout.

```
//Card layout demo
import java.awt.*;
import java.awt.event.*;
import javax.swing.*;
class CardLayoutDemo extends JFrame implements ActionListener
{
    //vars
    Container c;
```

```
        CardLayout card;
        JButton b1,b2,b3,b4;

        CardLayoutDemo()
        {
                //create container
                c = getContentPane();

                //create CardLayout object with 50 px horizontal space
                //and 10 px vertical space
                card = new CardLayout(50,10);

                //set the layout to card layout
                c.setLayout(card);

                //create 4 push buttons
                b1 = new JButton("Button1");
                b2 = new JButton("Button2");
                b3 = new JButton("Button3");
                b4 = new JButton("Button4");

                //add each button to c on a separate card
                c.add("First card",b1);
                c.add("Second card",b2);
                c.add("Third card",b3);
                c.add("Fourth card", b4);

                //add action listeners to buttons
                b1.addActionListener(this);
                b2.addActionListener(this);
                b3.addActionListener(this);
                b4.addActionListener(this);

        }
        public void actionPerformed(ActionEvent ae)
        {
                //when a button is clicked show the next card
                card.next(c);

                /* To show a particular card, e.g. Third card, we can use as:
                card.show(c, "Third card");
                */
        }

        public static void main(String args[])
        {
                //create frame
                CardLayoutDemo demo = new CardLayoutDemo();
                demo.setSize(400,400);
                demo.setTitle("Card layout");
                demo.setVisible(true);
                demo.setDefaultCloseOperation(JFrame.EXIT_ON_CLOSE);
        }
}
```

Output:

```
C:\> javac CardLayoutDemo.java
C:\> java CardLayoutDemo
```

In preceding program, the components are arranged on 4 cards whose names are First card, Second card, Third card and Fourth card. When a button on a card is clicked, the next card is displayed.

Observe the preceding output. If the Button1 is clicked there, the next card with Button2 will be displayed as shown here.

Using a Layout Inside Another Layout

It is possible to use a layout inside another layout. For example, we can set a particular layout to a group of components and that group can be added to a frame or container by using another layout. In the previous program, we used card layout to display push buttons on each card. Suppose we want to display a group of components on the second card. How can we do this? First, we should write a class which extends JPanel class. JPanel class is useful to create a panel to which a group of components can be attached, as see here:

```
class MyPanel extends JPanel
```

The default layout used by a panel is flow layout. If we want any other layout, we can set it using setLayout() method.

In MyPanel class, we should create the components and attach them to panel, as:

```
this.add(component1);
this.add(component2);
```

Now, create an object to MyPanel and pass that object as a component to the container by using card layout, as:

```
c.add("Second card", new MyPanel());
```

Since, we are creating MyPanel object, and it contains a group of components, all those components are attached to the Second card.

In Program 4, we create a container with the card layout manager. Then, a push button is added to the first card. In case of second card, we want to add a group of components, a text field, a check box and a push button. We want to add these components to the second card by using border layout. For this purpose, we create a panel and add the components by using border layout manager. Then, we add the panel object to the second card.

Program 4: Write a program to add a group of components: a text field, a check box and a push button, using border layout to a panel. Then the panel object is added in the container which uses card layout.

```java
//Using border layout inside card layout.
import java.awt.*;
import java.awt.event.*;
import javax.swing.*;

class LayoutsDemo extends JFrame implements ActionListener
{
        //vars
        Container c;
        CardLayout card;
        JButton b1;

        LayoutsDemo()
        {
                //create container
                c = getContentPane();

                //create CardLayout object w
                card = new CardLayout();

                //set the layout to card layout
                c.setLayout(card);

                //create a push buttons
                b1 = new JButton("Button1");

                //add button to c on first card
                c.add("First card",b1);

                //add panel object to c on second card
                //MyPanel is the sub class of Panel class
                c.add("Second card",new MyPanel());

                //add action listeners to buttons
                b1.addActionListener(this);
        }
        public void actionPerformed(ActionEvent ae)
        {
                //when a button is clicked show the second card
        card.next(c);
        }

        public static void main(String args[])
        {
                //create frame
                LayoutsDemo demo = new LayoutsDemo();
                demo.setSize(400,400);
                demo.setTitle("Card layout");
                demo.setVisible(true);
                demo.setDefaultCloseOperation(JFrame.EXIT_ON_CLOSE);
        }
}
```

```
class MyPanel extends JPanel
{
        //vars
        JTextField tf;
        JCheckBox cb;
        JButton b;

        MyPanel()
        {
                //set border layout to panel
                this.setLayout(new BorderLayout());

                //create components
                tf = new JTextField("Text Field", 15);
                b = new JButton("OK");
                cb = new JCheckBox("Check box");

                //add them to panel
                this.add("North", tf);
                this.add("South", b);
                this.add("East", cb);
        }
}
```

Output:

```
C:\> javac LayoutsDemo.java
C:\> java LayoutsDemo
```

When the preceding button on first card is clicked, the user is led to second card where three components are displayed by using border layout, as shown here.

GridLayout

GridLayout is useful to divide the container into a two-dimensional grid form that contains several rows and columns. The container is divided into equal-sized rectangles, and one component is placed in each rectangle.

To create GridLayout object, we can write as:

❑   GridLayout obj = new GridLayout();

This creates a grid layout with a default of one column per component, in a single row.

❑   GridLayout obj = new GridLayout(int rows, int cols);

This creates a grid layout with specified number of rows and columns.

❑   GridLayout obj = new GridLayout(int rows, int cols, int hgap, int vgap);

Here, hgap represents horizontal gap between components and vgap represents vertical gap between components.

Program 5: Write a program to create five push buttons and add them to the content pane using border layout manager.

```
//GridLayout demo
import java.awt.*;
import javax.swing.*;
class GridLayoutDemo extends JFrame
{
        GridLayoutDemo()
        {
                //create container
                Container c = getContentPane();

                //create grid layout with 2 rows, 3 cols and 50 px
                //gap between components
                GridLayout grid = new GridLayout(2,3,50,50);
                c.setLayout(grid);

                //create 5 push buttons
                JButton b1 = new JButton("Button1");
                JButton b2 = new JButton("Button2");
                JButton b3 = new JButton("Button3");
                JButton b4 = new JButton("Button4");
                JButton b5 = new JButton("Button5");

                //add buttons to c
                c.add(b1);
                c.add(b2);
                c.add(b3);
                c.add(b4);
                c.add(b5);
        }
        public static void main(String args[])
        {
                //create a frame
                GridLayoutDemo demo = new GridLayoutDemo();
                demo.setSize(500,400);
                demo.setTitle("Grid layout");
                demo.setVisible(true);
                demo.setDefaultCloseOperation(JFrame.EXIT_ON_CLOSE);
        }
}
```

Output:

```
C:\> javac GridLayoutDemo.java
C:\> java GridLayoutDemo
```

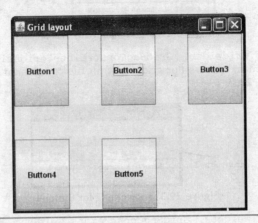

GridBagLayout

GridBagLayout class represents grid bag layout manager where the components are arranged in rows and columns. This layout is more flexible as compared to other layouts since in this layout, the components can span more than one row or column and the size of the components can be adjusted to fit the display area. The intersection of rows and columns where a component can be placed is called a 'grid' or 'display area'.

When positioning the components by using grid bag layout, it is necessary to apply some constraints or conditions on the components regarding their position, size and space in or around the components etc. Such constraints are specified using GridBagConstraints class.

To create grid bag layout, we can create an object to GridBagLayout class, as:

```
GridBagLayout obj = new GridBagLayout();
```

To apply some constraints on the components, we should first create an object to GridBagConstraints class, as:

```
GridBagConstraints cons = new GridBagConstraints();
```

This will create constraints for the components with default values. The other way to specify the constraints is by directly passing their values while creating the GridBagConstraints object, as:

GridBagConstraints cons = new GridBagConstraints(int gridx, int gridy, int gridwidth, int gridheight, double weightx, double weighty, int anchor, int fill, Insets insets, int ipadx, int ipady);

Let us now understand each of the constraints.

❑ GridBagConstraints.gridx, GridBagConstraints.gridy: They represent the row and column positions of the component at upper left corner of the component. See Figure 29.2.

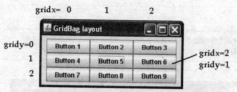

Figure 29.2 gridx and gridy values

❑ `GridBagConstraints.gridwidth`, `GridBagConstraints.gridheight`: Specify the number of columns (for gridwidth) or rows (for gridheight) in the component's display area. The default value is 1. See Figure 29.3.

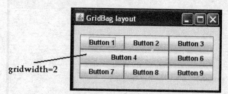

Figure 29.3 gridwidth=2 for Button4

❑ `GridBagConstraints.weightx`, `GridBagConstraints.weighty`: When the frame is resized, the components inside the container should also be resized or not – is determined by the weightx and weighty constraints. When these values are not set, by default, they take 0.0. This means the components size will not change when the frame is resized. The components will have their original size. If the weightx and weighty values are set to a value from 0.0 to 1.0, then the components size will also change along with the size of the frame. weightx is for resizing the component horizontally and weighty is for resizing the component vertically. Generally, weights are specified with 0.0 and 1.0 as the extremes, the numbers in between are used as necessary. Larger numbers indicate that the component's row or column should get more space. Figure 29.4 depicts components when resized and not resized.

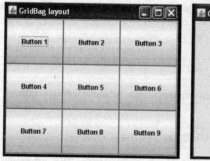 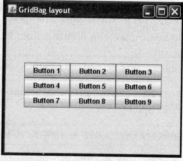

weightx= 0.7 weighty= 0.7   weightx= 0.0 weighty= 0.0

Figure 29.4 components resized and not resized

❑ `GridBagConstraints.anchor`: When the display area is larger than the component, anchor constraint will determine where to place the component in the display area. The positions of the component in the display area are shown in the Figure 29.5 here. The default value is `GridBagConstraints.CENTER`.

FIRST_LINE_START	PAGE_START	FIRST_LINE_END
LINE_START	CENTER	LINE_END
LAST_LINE_START	PAGE_END	LAST_LINE_END

Figure 29.5 The anchor values of a component

❑ `GridBagConstraints.fill:` While the weightx and weighty constraints are useful to resize the component according to the frame's size, 'fill' is useful to resize the component according to the space available in its display area. If the display area is larger than the component, then the component should stretch and occupy the display area horizontally or vertically and it is decided by the fill constraint. Possible values are as follows:

`GridBagConstraints.NONE` (the default) `GridBagConstraints.HORIZONTAL` (make the component wide enough to fill its display area horizontally, but don't change its height) `GridBagConstraints.VERTICAL` (make the component tall enough to fill its display area vertically, but don't change its width) `GridBagConstraints.BOTH` (make the component fill its display area entirely). The effect of fill constraint is shown in Figures 29.6(a), (b) and (c).

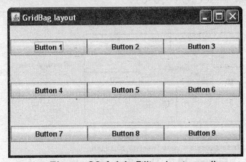

Figure 29.6 (a) Filling horizontally

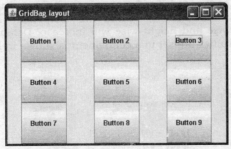

Figure 29.6 (b) Filling vertically

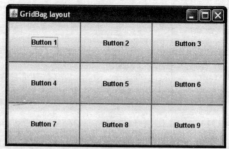

Figure 29.6 (c) Filling in both directions

❑ `GridBagConstraints.insets`: This constraint is useful to leave some space around the component at the four edges of component. This space is left around the component and the boundary of its display area. insets is the object of Insets class, so it is created as:

```
Insets insets = new Insets(5,10,15,20);
```

Here, we are leaving 5px at top of the component, 10px at left, 15px at bottom and 20px at the right of the component. See Figure 29.7.

By default, it is given as:

```
Insets insets = new Insets(0,0,0,0);
```

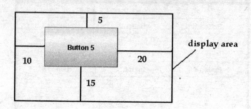

Insets insets = new Insets(5,10,15,20);

Figure 29.7 The effect of insets constraint

❑ `GridBagConstraints.ipadx`, `GridBagConstraints.ipady`: ipadx and ipady are useful to leave space horizontally and vertically within the component. After adding the space, the components size width-wise and height-wise will increase. Default value is 0. What happens when ipadx and ipady values are set to a component is shown in Figure 29.8.

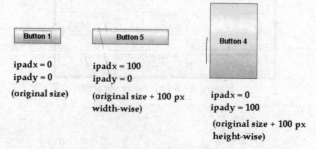

Figure 29.8 The effect of ipadx and ipady constraints

Program 6: This program is designed to display 5 push buttons using grid bag layout manager at certain positions. Please observe the output of the program first and then observe one by one the constraints set to the buttons.

```java
//GridBagLayout demo
import java.awt.*;
import javax.swing.*;
class GridBagLayoutDemo extends JFrame
{
        //vars
        GridBagLayout gbag;
        GridBagConstraints cons;

        GridBagLayoutDemo()
        {
                //get the content pane
                Container c = getContentPane();

                //create GridBagLayout object
                gbag = new GridBagLayout();

                //set gridbag layout to content pane
                c.setLayout(gbag);

                //create GridBagConstraints object
                cons = new GridBagConstraints();

                //create 5 push buttons
                JButton b1 = new JButton("Button 1");
                JButton b2 = new JButton("Button 2");
                JButton b3 = new JButton("Button 3");
                JButton b4 = new JButton("Button 4");
                JButton b5 = new JButton("Button 5");

                //for all buttons, use horinzontal filling
                cons.fill = GridBagConstraints.HORIZONTAL;

                //display button1 at x,y coordinates 0,0
                cons.gridx = 0;
                cons.gridy = 0;

                //resize all the components when the frame is resized
                cons.weightx = 0.7;
                //cons.weighty = 0.7;

                //set the above constraints to button1
                gbag.setConstraints(b1,cons);

                //add button1 to content pane
                c.add(b1);

                //display button2 at x,y coordinates 1,0
                cons.gridx = 1;
                cons.gridy = 0;

                //remaining constraints applicable as set for previous button
                //set constraints to button2
                gbag.setConstraints(b2,cons);
                c.add(b2);

                //display button3 at x,y coordinates 2,0
                cons.gridx = 2;
                cons.gridy = 0;

                //remaining constraints applicable as set for previous button
                //set constraints to button3
                gbag.setConstraints(b3,cons);
```

```
                c.add(b3);

                //display button4 at x,y coordinates 0,1
                cons.gridx = 0;
                cons.gridy = 1;

                //add 100 px height-wise
                cons.ipady = 100;

                //let button4 occupy 3 columns width-wise
                cons.gridwidth = 3;

                //remaining constraints applicable as set for previous button
                //set constraints to button4
                gbag.setConstraints(b4,cons);
                c.add(b4);

                //display button5 at x,y coordinates 1,2
                cons.gridx = 1;
                cons.gridy = 2;

                //reset the ipady value to 0
                cons.ipady = 0;

                //leave space above the button for resizing vertically
                cons.weighty = 0.8;

                //position the button starting from center of bottom line
                cons.anchor = GridBagConstraints.PAGE_END ;

                //leave 50px space at bottom of button5
                cons.insets = new Insets(0,0,50,0);

                //let the button occupy 2 columns width
                cons.gridwidth = 2;

                //set constraints to button5
                gbag.setConstraints(b5,cons);
                c.add(b5);

        }

        public static void main(String args[])
        {
                //create the frame
                GridBagLayoutDemo demo = new GridBagLayoutDemo();
                demo.setSize(400,400);
                demo.setTitle("GridBag layout");
                demo.setVisible(true);
                demo.setDefaultCloseOperation(JFrame.EXIT_ON_CLOSE);
        }
}
```

Output:

```
C:\> javac GridBagLayoutDemo.java
C:\> java GridBagLayoutDemo
```

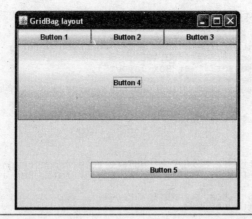

BoxLayout

BoxLayout of `javax.swing` package allows multiple components to be laid out either vertically or horizontally. The components will not wrap so, for example, a vertical arrangement of components will stay vertically arranged when the frame is resized. We can create BoxLayout class object with the combinations shown below:

❑ `BoxLayout box = new BoxLayout(JPanel object, axis-orientation);`

Here, all the components which are inside a JPanel object are arranged by using axis-orientation. This 'axis-orientation' can be:

❑ `BoxLayout.X_AXIS`: Here, components are arranged along x-axis.

❑ `BoxLayout.Y_AXIS`: Here, components are arranged along y-axis.

❑ `BoxLayout.LINE_AXIS`: Here, components are arranged like lines in text.

❑ `BoxLayout.PAGE_AXIS`: Here, components are arranged like lines in several pages.

Program 7: Write a program to understand the usage of BoxLayout.

```
//BoxLayout Demo
import java.awt.*;
import javax.swing.*;
class BoxLayoutDemo extends JFrame
{
    BoxLayoutDemo()
    {
        //create container and set flow layout
        Container c = getContentPane();
        c.setLayout(new FlowLayout());

        //create a JPanel object which holds components
        MyPanel1 mp1 = new MyPanel1();

        //add the panel to content pane
        c.add(mp1);

        //create another JPanel object which holds another set
        //of components
        MyPanel2 mp2 = new MyPanel2();

        //add the panel to content pane
        c.add(mp2);
    }
```

```
            public static void main(String args[])
            {
                    //create the frame
                    BoxLayoutDemo demo = new BoxLayoutDemo();
                    demo.setSize(400,400);
                    demo.setTitle("Box layout");
                    demo.setVisible(true);
                    demo.setDefaultCloseOperation(JFrame.EXIT_ON_CLOSE);
            }
    }
    class MyPanel1 extends JPanel
    {
            MyPanel1()
            {
                    //create BoxLayout object to arrange components along x-axis
                    BoxLayout box1 = new BoxLayout(this, BoxLayout.X_AXIS);

                    //set box layout to JPanel
                    setLayout(box1);

                    //create 3 push buttons and add them to panel using box layout
                    JButton b1, b2, b3;
                    b1 = new JButton("Button1");
                    b2 = new JButton("Button2");
                    b3 = new JButton("Button3");

                    add(b1);
                    add(b2);
                    add(b3);
            }
    }

    class MyPanel2 extends JPanel
    {
            MyPanel2()
            {
                    //create BoxLayout object to arrange components along y-axis
                    BoxLayout box2 = new BoxLayout(this, BoxLayout.Y_AXIS);

                    //set box layout to JPanel
                    setLayout(box2);

                    //create 3 push buttons and add them to panel using box layout
                    JButton b1, b2, b3;
                    b1 = new JButton("Button1");
                    b2 = new JButton("Button2");
                    b3 = new JButton("Button3");

                    add(b1);
                    add(b2);
                    add(b3);
            }
    }
```

Output:

```
C:\> javac BoxLayoutDemo.java
C:\> java BoxLayoutDemo
```

This program uses box layout to arrange some components along x-axis and some more components along y-axis. The components which are arranged along x-axis are added inside a JPanel object where box layout is used and that object is added to content pane. Similarly, the components which are arranged along y-axis are added inside another JPanel object where box layout is used and that object is also added to content pane. The two JPanel objects are created which are added to the content pane by using flow layout.

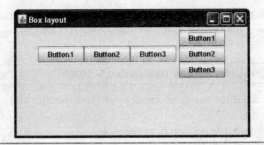

Box Class

BoxLayout is implemented with the help of Box class defined in `javax.swing` package. We can imagine the Box class object as an invisible area where the components can be placed by using box layout. Box class provides basically two types of boxes, horizontal box and vertical box.

The following methods help us to work with box layout:

❑ To create a box where the components are arranged from left to right, we can use `createHorizontalBox()` method, as:

```
Box b = Box.createHorizontalBox();
```

❑ In case, we want to arrange the components vertically from top to bottom, we can use `createVeriticalBox()` method.

```
Box b = Box.createVerticalBox();
```

❑ Now, the components can be added to Box object using `add()` method.

```
b.add(component);
```

❑ The size of components can be set by using `setPreferredSize()`, `setMinimumSize()` and `setMaximumSize()` methods of `JComponent` class.

- `setPreferredSize()`: This method tells the container to use some preferred size for the component so that the component fits nicely in the container.
- `setMinimumSize()`: This method sets some minimum size of the component.
- `setMaximumSize()`: This method sets the maximum size of the component.

Similarly, to retrieve the size of components, we can use `getPreferredSize()`, `getMinimumSize()` and `getMaximumSize()` methods.

❑ By default, there will be no space left between the components in a box layout. To add space we need fillers. There are three types of fillers defined in Box class.

- **Struts:** to leave some space between components.

```
b.add(Box.createHorizontalStrut(20));
```

This strut leaves horizontal space of 20px between the components in the box.

```
b.add(Box.createVerticalStrut(20));
```

This method adds a vertical space of 20px between the components in the box.

❑ **Rigid areas:** to leave some space between components and also to set the vertical size of the box.

```
b.add(Box.createRigidArea(new Dimension(5,20));
```

This method leaves a fixed rectangular space of 5px width and 20px height between the components.

❑ **Glue:** to separate components as much as possible.

```
b.add(Box.createHorizontalGlue())
```

This method throws the components maximum distance that is possible horizontally.

```
b.add(Box.createVerticalGlue())
```

This method adds vertical glue in the box so that the components are kept at a maximum distance that is possible vertically.

Let us design a program to understand how to use Box class:

❑ First, we create a horizontal box to place components, for example, a label and a text field. For this purpose, we create the components, i.e., a label and text field, as:

```
JLabel l1= new JLabel("Enter Name:");
JTextField t1= new JTextField(20);
```

Then, we set the maximum size of the text field to the preferred size, as:

```
t1.setMaximumSize(t1.getPreferredSize());
```

Then, we create a horizontal box and add the components in the box, as:

```
Box horiz1 = Box.createHorizontalBox();
horiz1.add(l1);
horiz1.add(t1);
```

Suppose, we wish to leave some horizontal space between the label and text field, we can use a strut as:

```
horiz1.add(Box.createHorizontalStrut(20));  //gap 20 px
```

❑ In the same way, we create a second horizontal box to place another label and a text field. The same steps described earlier can be used in this case also.

❑ Finally, We create a third horizontal box where we want to place two push buttons.

❑ Now, we create a vertical box and add the preceding three horizontal boxes inside it, as:

```
Box vert = Box.createVerticalBox();
vert.add(horiz1);
vert.add(horiz2);
vert.add(horiz3);
```

❑ To leave some vertical space between the three horizontal boxes, we can add a vertical strut between the boxes as:

```
vert.add(Box.createVerticalStrut(100));   //gap of 100 px
```

The preceding steps are shown in Figure 29.9 and are implemented in Program 8.

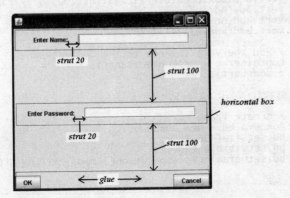

Figure 20.9 Components arranged using Box class

Program 8: Write a program to create three horizontal boxes with components and finally add them inside another vertical box.

```
//Box layout manager
import java.awt.*;
import javax.swing.*;

class BoxDemo extends JFrame
{
    BoxDemo()
    {
        //create a label and a text field
        JLabel l1= new JLabel("Enter Name:");
        JTextField t1= new JTextField(20);
        t1.setMaximumSize(t1.getPreferredSize());

        //create top horizontal box and add above components to it
        Box horiz1 = Box.createHorizontalBox();
        horiz1.add(l1);
        horiz1.add(Box.createHorizontalStrut(20));   //gap 20 pxl
        horiz1.add(t1);

        //create a label and a text field
        JLabel l2= new JLabel("Enter Password:");
        JTextField t2= new JTextField(20);
        t2.setMaximumSize(t2.getPreferredSize());

        //create a middel horizontal box and add above components to it
        Box horiz2 = Box.createHorizontalBox();
        horiz2.add(l2);
        horiz2.add(Box.createHorizontalStrut(20)); //gap 20 px
        horiz2.add(t2);

        //create two push buttons
        JButton b1= new JButton("OK");
        JButton b2= new JButton("Cancel");

        //construct the bottom horizontal box and add components in it
        Box horiz3 = Box.createHorizontalBox();
        horiz3.add(b1);
        horiz3.add(Box.createHorizontalGlue()); //throw buttons apart
```

```
                    horiz3.add(b2);

                    //add the three horizontal boxes inside a vertical box
                    Box vert = Box.createVerticalBox();
                    vert.add(horiz1);
                    vert.add(Box.createVerticalStrut(100));   //gap of 100 px
                    vert.add(horiz2);
                    vert.add(Box.createVerticalStrut(100));
                    vert.add(horiz3);

                    //add the vertical box to the content pane
                    Container c = getContentPane();
                    c.add(vert);
            }
        public static void main(String args[])
            {
                    //create frame
                    BoxDemo bd = new BoxDemo();
                    bd.setSize(400,350);
                    bd.setVisible(true);
                    bd.setDefaultCloseOperation(JFrame.EXIT_ON_CLOSE);

            }
        }
```

Output:

```
C:\> javac BoxDemo.java
C:\> java BoxDemo
```

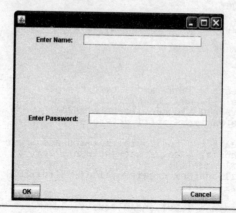

Conclusion

Layout managers are useful to arrange a group of components in a particular manner in a container as wished by the programmer. FlowLayout is the simplest layout manager and GridBagLayout is the most flexible and complex layout manager among all other layouts. While working with a group of components, the programmer should first plan his output and accordingly decide which layout should be used in a particular application. Then only he can start writing his program.

APPLETS

W|hen a HTML (Hyper Text Markup Language) page wants to communicate with the user on Internet, it can use a special Java program, called 'applet' to communicate and respond to the user. The user can interact by typing some details or by clicking the components available in the applet program. The program then processes and displays the results.

We can understand an applet as a Java byte code embedded in a HTML page, generally for the purpose of achieving communication with the user. We can think of an applet as:

```
Applet = Java byte code + HTML page.
```

Important Interview Question

What is an applet?

  An applet represents Java byte code embedded in a web page.

Creating an Applet

To create an applet, we need to write a Java program and compile it to get byte code. Then we should embed (include) it into a HTML page on a particular location wherever we want it to be displayed. This page is then stored in the web server. A client machine communicates with the web server, the server then sends the HTML page that contains the applet. The page is then transmitted to the client where the applet is executed on the client's web browser. Thus applets are executed at client side by the web browser. Thus applets travel thousands of kilometers of distance on Internet and reach the client machines before their execution on the client.

To create an applet, we have Applet class of java.applet package and JApplet class of javax.swing package. These classes use the following methods, which are automatically run by any applet program. So, these methods should be overridden in an applet program.

❑ public void init(): This method is the first method to be called by the browser and it is executed only once. So, the programmer can use this method to initialize any variables, creating components and creating threads, etc. When this method execution is completed, browser looks for the next method: start().

❑ public void start(): This method is called after init() method and each time the applet is revisited by the user. For example, the user has minimized the web page that contains the applet and moved to another page then this method's execution is stopped. When the user comes back to view the web page again, start() method execution will resume. Any calculations and processing of data should be done in this method and the results are also displayed.

❏ `public void stop()`: This method is called by the browser when the applet is to be stopped. If the user minimizes the web page, then this method is called and when the user again comes back to this page, then start() method is called. In this way, start() and stop() methods can be called repeatedly. For example, an applet with some animation might want to use the `start()` method to resume animation, and the `stop()` method to suspend the animation.

❏ `public void destroy()`: This method is called when the applet is being terminated from memory. The `stop()` method will always be called before `destroy()`. The code related to releasing the memory allocated to the applet and stopping any running threads should be written in this method.

Executing init(), start(), stop() and destroy() methods in that sequence is called 'life cycle of an applet'. Note that none of these methods are compulsory while writing an applet.

Important Interview Question

What is applet life cycle?

An applet is born with init() method and starts functioning with start() method. To stop the applet, the stop() method is called and to terminate the applet completely from memory, the destroy() method is called. Once the applet is terminated, we should reload the HTML page again to get the applet start once again from init() method. This cyclic way of executing the methods is called applet life cycle.

Please note that the 'public static void main(String args[]) ' method is not available in case of applets. This means, we can compile the applet code but we can not run it using a JVM. Now the question is, where are the applets run?

Once the applet is created, we compile and obtain its byte code. This byte code is embedded in HTML page and the page is sent to the client computer. The client machine contains a browser like Internet explorer, Netscape Navigator or Mozilla Firefox where the HTML page is viewed by the user. The same browser will execute the applet of the HTML page. The browser contains a small virtual machine called 'applet engine' which understands and runs the applet code.

Important Interview Question

Where are the applets executed?

Applets are executed by a program called applet engine which is similar to virtual machine that exists inside the web browser at client side.

Applets can show images and animation, play sounds, take user input and send it to the server ,etc. Applets cannot interact and spoil the resources of the client system and hence they are harmless. This restricted environment where the applets are executed is called 'sandbox'. The sandbox provides an applet with some amount of memory to get executed and does not allow the applet to do any illegal operations on the client system. For example:

❏ An applet cannot run any executable program in the client system.

❏ An applet cannot communicate with any server other than the server from which it was downloaded.

❏ An applet cannot read from a file or write into a file that belongs to the client computer.

❏ An applet cannot find sensitive data like user's login name, email-address, etc.

Uses of Applets

`Applets` can be used for multiple purposes. Some of the uses of applets are:

❏ Applets are used on Internet for creating dynamic web pages. There are two types of web pages: Static and Dynamic. Static web pages provide some information to the user but the user cannot interact with the web page other than viewing the information. Dynamic web pages interact with the user at the runtime. For example, a student can type his hall ticket number in a text field and click the retrieve button to get back his results from his University server. Applets are useful to provide such interaction with the user at runtime.

❑ Another use of applets is for creating animation and games where the images can be displayed or moved giving a visual impression that they are alive.

In fact, applets are one of the main reasons for the popularity of Java on Internet. In 1995, when JavaSoft people demonstrated some animation using an applet on HotJava browser, developers started believing that it is possible to perform animation in the browsers.

Important Interview Question

What is HotJava?

HotJava is the first applet-enabled browser developed in Java to support running of applets.

Now-a-days most of the websites on Internet are dependent on other softwares like PhotoShop, Flash, DreamWeaver, etc. for creating, editing, and providing animation to the images. But for validating the form data, scripting languages like JavaScript and PHP are better. Hence the use of applets is diminishing rapidly.

<APPLET> tag

<APPLET> tag is useful to embed an applet into an HTML page. It has the following form:

```
<APPLET  CODE= "name of the applet class file"
              CODEBASE= "path of the applet class file"
              HEIGHT= maximum height of applet in pixels
        WIDTH= maximum width of applet in pixels
        ALIGN= alignment (LEFT,RIGHT,TOP,BOTTOM,MIDDLE)
        ALT= alternate text to be displayed>

              <PARAM NAME = parameter name VALUE= its value>
     </APPLET>
```

The <PARAM> tag is useful to define a variable (parameter) and its value inside the HTML page which can be passed to the applet. The applet can access the parameter value using getParameter() method, as:

```
String value = getParameter("pname");
```

Here, pname is the parameter name and its value is retrieved by the above method into String type variable: value.

Important Interview Question

Which tag is used to embed an applet into a HTML page?

<APPLET> tag is used to insert an applet into HTML page.

A Simple Applet

Let us create an applet that displays 'Hello applet' in the applet frame. To display a message, we can take the help of paint() method of Component class of java.awt package. Remember all the methods of the applet and the applet class itself should be declared 'public', otherwise they are not available to the browser to execute.

Program 1: This is Java program that creates an applet with yellow background color and a message "Hello Applets!".

```java
//A simple applet
import java.awt.*;
import java.applet.*;
public class MyApp extends Applet
{
        //set a background color for the frame
        public void init()
        {
                setBackground(Color.yellow);
        }
        //display message in applet window
        public void paint(Graphics g)
        {
                g.drawString("Hello Applets!", 50, 100);
        }
}
```

Output:

```
C:\> javac MyApp.java
```

Now, MyApp.class is created. This byte code should be embedded into a HTML page using <APPLET> tag, as shown below:

```html
<! MyApp.html that embeds MyApp applet>
<html>
<applet code="MyApp.class" height=300 width=400>
</applet>
</html>
```

Save the above code with the name: MyApp.html. This HTML page contains the applet which can be opened in the browser, or an applet viewer supplied by the Sun Microsystems Inc., can be used to test the applet. For this purpose, open any browser and in the browser's address bar, type .html file name along with the directory path. The applet opens in the browser. Or, give the command at system prompt as:

```
C:\> appletviewer MyApp.html
```

to open the applet in the applet viewer.

Opening of the applet in the browser also in the applet viewer is shown here.

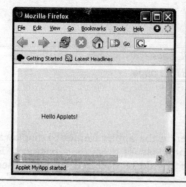

Let us write another applet using the methods: init(), start(), stop() and destroy() along with paint() method to track and display the execution sequence of these methods. Remember, none of these methods are compulsory for creating an applet.

Program 2: This Java program creates an applet with some background color and foreground color with a message. The message string is stored in msg and is displayed in paint() method.

```
//applet creation
import java.awt.*;
import java.applet.*;

public class App1 extends Applet
{
    //vars
    String msg="";

    //this method is executed when an applet is loaded
    public void init()
    {
        //set backround color for applet frame
        setBackground(Color.yellow);

        //set foreground for text in frame
        setForeground(Color.red);

        //set font for text in applet
        Font f = new Font("Arial", Font.BOLD, 20);
        setFont(f);

        //store method name in msg
        msg+=" init ";
    }

    //this method is executed after init()
    public void start()
    {
        //add this method name to msg
        msg+=" start ";
    }

    //to stop the applet
    public void stop()
    {
        //add this method name to msg
        msg+= " stop ";
    }

    //to remove applet from memory
    public void destroy()
    {
        //add this metho name to msg
        msg+= " destroy ";
    }
```

Output:

```
C:\> javac App1.java
C:\>

Now, create a HTML page to embed the App1 applet into it, as shown below:

<! MyApp.html that embeds App1 applet>
<html>
<applet code="App1.class" height=200 width=300>
</applet>
```

```
    </html>

    Open the above MyApp.html file in the applet viewer, as:
    C:\> appletviewer MyApp.html
```

See the output of Program 2. Minimize the applet frame and you will see stop() method executed, then maximize it to see if the start() method is executed. When ever the applet frame is resized paint() method is again executed, thus showing the updated contents of the applet frame.

An applet with Swing Components

Let us see how to use swing components in an applet. We know how to create components using javax.swing package. In Program 3, we create a text field for receiving the name of the user, a text area to receive the address and a list box to receive the user selected items. Two push buttons OK and Cancel are created additionally at the bottom of the form. When the user enters his data and clicks the OK button, the data is retrieved from the form and again displayed in the text area. In actual application, the same data is sent to a server on the network where it is stored, processed and a reply to the customer is sent. When the Cancel button in the form is clicked, the data typed in the form will be cleared.

Program 3: In this program, we create a form where the user can type his details and select items according to his requirement.

```
//Online shopping form
import java.awt.*;
import java.awt.event.*;
import javax.swing.*;
public class MyForm extends JApplet implements ActionListener
{
    //vars
    String str="", str1="", str2="";
    Object x[];
    JLabel n,a,i,lbl;
    JTextField name;
    JTextArea addr;
    JList lst;
    JButton b1,b2;
    Container c;
    public void init()
    {
        //create JFrame and container
        JFrame jf = new JFrame();
        c = jf.getContentPane();
        //display yellow background color in container
        c.setBackground(Color.yellow);
        //do not set any layout to c
```

```
                c.setLayout(null);
                //set the size and title for frame
                jf.setSize(500,400);
                jf.setTitle("My Form");
                //display the frame
                jf.setVisible(true);
                //Display heading in the frame using a label
                Font f = new Font("Dialog",Font.BOLD,26);
                lbl = new JLabel();
                lbl.setFont(f);
                lbl.setForeground(Color.red);
                lbl.setText("Z-ELECTRONICS ONLINE SHOP");
                lbl.setBounds(200,10,500,50);
                c.add(lbl);
                //TextField and a label for entering name
                n = new JLabel("Name: ", JLabel.LEFT);
                name = new JTextField(30);
                n.setBounds(50,100,100,30);
                name.setBounds(200,100,200,30);
                c.add(n);
                c.add(name);
                //TextArea and a label for entering address
                a = new JLabel("Address: ", JLabel.LEFT);
                addr = new JTextArea(5,50);
                a.setBounds(50,150,100,30);
                addr.setBounds(200,150,200,100);
                c.add(a);
                c.add(addr);
                //List box for multiple selection
                i = new JLabel("Select items: ", JLabel.LEFT);
                String[] data = {"TVs", "Washing machines", "DVD players",
                "Refrigerators"};
                lst = new JList(data);
                i.setBounds(50,270,100,30);
                lst.setBounds(200,270,200,100);
                c.add(i);
                c.add(lst);
                //add Two push buttons: OK and Cancel
                b1 = new JButton("OK");
                b2 = new JButton("Cancel");
                b1.setBounds(200,400,100,30);
                b2.setBounds(350,400,100,30);
                c.add(b1);
                c.add(b2);
                //add listeners to buttons
                b1.addActionListener(this);
                b2.addActionListener(this);
        }
        //this method is executed when the buttons are clicked
        public void actionPerformed(ActionEvent ae)
        {
                //know which button is clicked
                str = ae.getActionCommand();
                //if the button label is OK then
                if(str.equals("OK"))
                {
                        //retrieve data from text field, text area and list boxes
                        str1= name.getText()+"\n";
                        str1+= addr.getText()+"\n";
                        x = lst.getSelectedValues();
                        for(int i=0;i<x.length; i++)
                        str2 +=(String)x[i]+"\n";
                        //display the data in text area
                        addr.setText(str1+str2);

                        //make the strings empty
                        str1="";
                        str2="";
                }
```

```
                        else{
                                //if Cancel button is clicked, clear the data in the form
                                name.setText("");
                                addr.setText("");
                                lst.clearSelection();
                        }
                }
        }
```

Output:

```
C:\> javac MyForm.java
C:\>
Now embed the byte code MyForm.class generated above in a HTML page, as shown
below:

 <! This MyForm.html contains MyForm applet>
<html>
<applet code="MyForm.class" width=400 height=400>
</applet>
</html>

 Open the above MyForm.html in an appletviewer as:
C:\> appletviewer MyForm.html
```

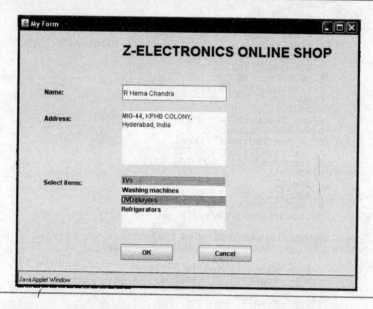

In the above output, the user can select any one item or several items from the list box. To select a group of items which are in sequence, the user can use SHIFT+CLICK on the items. To select the items randomly, the user can use CONTROL+CLICK on the items.

Animation in Applets

One of the uses of applets is in performing animation and developing games. Animation represents moving the objects from one place to another so that the objects look alive. To animate an object, we should first load it into Image class object, as:

```
Image img = getImage(getDocumentBase(),"plane.gif");
```

Image class belongs to java.awt package and getImage() method belongs to Applet class. getDocumentBase() is a method of Applet class that gives the directory path where the image is located. This directory path may change because, after creating an applet the applet is loaded into a specific directory of a web server software. If the images are also loaded along with the applet in the same directory, getDocumentBase() method returns that directory path. If the image is available in some other directory, its path should replace the method. Here we have used an image by the name of 'plane.gif' that we want to load into img object.

To display the image in the applet frame, we can use drawImage() method of Graphics class, as:

```
g.drawImage(img,x,y, obj);
```

Here, img represents the Image class object where the image is found. X and y represent the coordinates starting from where the image should be displayed. obj represents the ImageObserver object which stores the history of how the Image is loaded into memory. Since this is not needed by us, we can pass null in its place.

In program 4, we create an applet to load an image 'plane.gif' into Image object and display it in the applet frame using drawImage(). For this purpose, we can draw an image with an aero plane in blue background using paint software and save it as 'plane.gif' using the option:

❑   File -> Save As...

And typing the filename as "plane.gif" as shown here:

❑   Filename: plane

❑   Save as type: GIF.

The image that is shown in Figure 30.1. using GIF file can be created in various ways. You can use any of the .gif files available on Internet or create your own .gif file using softwares like Flash or Dreamweaver, etc.

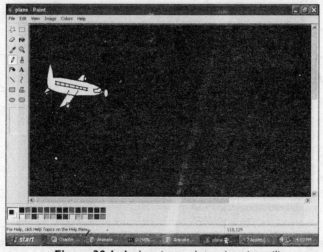

Figure 30.1 A plane image drawn in paint utility

The location of the image is changed by changing the x coordinate from 0 to 800px. So the image looks as if it is moving from left to right. Between each move, we insert a time delay of 20 milliseconds using Thread.sleep() method. If this time is increased, the speed of the movement will be reduced. If the time is decreased, the speed can be increased.

Program 4: Moving an aero plane picture from left to right.

```
//Animation in applets
import java.awt.*;
import java.applet.*;
public class Animate extends Applet
{
      public void paint(Graphics g)
      {
            //load the image into Image object img
            Image img = getImage(getDocumentBase(),"plane.gif");

            //move the image from left to right by changing
            //x coordinates from 0 to 800px and take y coordinate as 0
            for(int x=0; x<800; x++)
            {
                  g.drawImage(img,x,0,null);
                  try{
                        Thread.sleep(20);//delay for 20 milliseconds
                  }catch(InterruptedException ie){}
            }
      }
}
```

Output:

```
C:\> javac Animate.java
C:\>
<!Animate.html>
<html>
<applet code= "Animate.class", height=600 width=800>
</applet>
</html>
C:\> appletviewer Animate.html
```

Here is another program which animates a group of images. First, we create four images fig1.gif, fig2.gif, fig3.gif, fig4.gif in 'Paint' that are almost similar, except the hand positions as shown in Figure 30.2. The hands of these images are drawn slightly different. Of course, the second image is repeated as fourth image. These images can be displayed one by one with some time gap between each one, so that the image appears waving its hands from bottom to top and again from top to bottom.

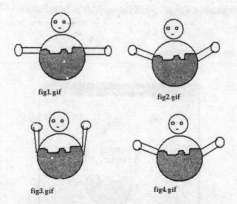

fig1.gif

fig2.gif

fig3.gif

fig4.gif

Figure 30.2 Four images for animation

Program 5: This program demonstrates animation using several images. By displaying all the images continuously one by one we get an illusion that the same image is moving. Press Control+C at System prompt to terminate the applet.

```
//Continuous animation
import java.awt.*;
import java.applet.*;
public class Animate extends Applet
{
      public void paint(Graphics g)
      {
            //load the images into Image objects
            Image img1 = getImage(getDocumentBase(), "fig1.gif");
            Image img2 = getImage(getDocumentBase(), "fig2.gif");
            Image img3 = getImage(getDocumentBase(), "fig3.gif");

            //continuous animation
            for(;;)
            {
                  //display images one by one with time gap of 200milli
                  seconds
                  try{
                        g.drawImage(img1,50,50,null);
                        Thread.sleep(200);

                        g.drawImage(img2,50,50,null);
                        Thread.sleep(200);

                        g.drawImage(img3,50,50,null);
                        Thread.sleep(200);

                        g.drawImage(img2,50,50,null);
                        Thread.sleep(200);

                  }catch(InterruptedException ie){}
            }
      }
}
```

Output:

```
C:\> javac Animate.java

<!Animate.html>
<html>
```

```
<applet code= "Animate.class", height=300 width=400>
</applet>
</html>

C:\> appletviwer Animate.html
```

A simple Game with an Applet

One of the important uses of applets is for developing games. Let us write a simple game where we display a push button and ask the user to click it. When the user tries to place the mouse pointer on the button, the button will jump to a new location. This new location will be decided using a random() method so that no one can guess to what location the button will jump.

In this game, we create a push button with an image that uses a smiling face. When the user clicks the button, the image is changed to a crying face. For this purpose, two images (fig.gif and fig1.gif) can be drawn in paint as shown in Figure 30.3.

fig.gif   fig1.gif

Figure 30.3 Figures useful in our game

To prevent the user from placing the mouse on the button, we should receive mouse events so that we can understand what the user is doing. For this purpose, we should attach two listeners to the button: MouseMotionListener and MouseListener. They got methods to catch any mouse event. In any case, the button location is changed as:

```
int x = (int)(600*Math.random());
int y = (int)(500*Math.random());
b.setBounds(x,y,250,75);
```

The setBounds() method positions the button at a random location specified by x and y coordinates. It is almost impossible to click the button and get some score in this game.

Program 6: In this program, we create a push button. When the user tries to place the mouse on the button, the button jumps to a new location randomly. When the user clicks on the button, the score is increased by 100.

```
//An applet where a button is displayed for the user to click.
import java.awt.*;
```

```
import java.awt.event.*;
import javax.swing.*;
public class ButtonGame extends JApplet implements MouseMotionListener,

MouseListener
{
        //vars
        JButton b;
        JLabel lbl;
        static int score=0;
        public void init()
        {
                //goto content pane
                Container c = getContentPane();
                c.setLayout(null);

                //create the button with laughing image
                ImageIcon ii = new ImageIcon("fig.gif");
                b = new JButton("Click Me", ii);
                b.setFont(new Font("Helvetica", Font.BOLD, 30));
                b.setBounds(400,300,250,75);
                c.add(b);

                //create a lable to display score
                lbl= new JLabel();
                lbl.setFont(new Font("Impact", Font.PLAIN, 30));
                lbl.setText("Score: "+score);
                lbl.setBounds(550,20,150,50);
                c.add(lbl);

                //add listeners to button
                b.addMouseMotionListener(this);
                b.addMouseListener(this);
        }

        public void mouseDragged(MouseEvent me)
        {
                //change the button coordinates randomly when the mouse is dragged
                int x = (int)(600*Math.random());
                int y = (int)(500*Math.random());
                b.setBounds(x,y,250,75);
        }

        public void mouseMoved(MouseEvent me)
        {
                //change the button coordinates randomly when mouse on it
                int x = (int)(600*Math.random());
                int y = (int)(500*Math.random());
                b.setBounds(x,y,250,75);
        }

        public void mouseClicked(MouseEvent e)
        {
                //when user clicks on the button change the image
                //as crying image and and add 100 to score
                ImageIcon ii = new ImageIcon("fig1.gif");
                b.setIcon(ii);
                lbl.setForeground(Color.red);

                score+=100;
                lbl.setText("Score: "+score);

        }

        public void mouseEntered(MouseEvent e)
        {
                //change the button coordinates randomly when mouse entered it
                int x = (int)(600*Math.random());
```

```
            int y = (int)(500*Math.random());
            b.setBounds(x,y,250,75);
    }

    public void mouseExited(MouseEvent e)
    {
            //when mouse is exited from the button, display laughing image
            ImageIcon ii = new ImageIcon("fig.gif");
            b.setIcon(ii);

    }

    public void mousePressed(MouseEvent e){}

    public void mouseReleased(MouseEvent e){}

}
```

Output:

```
C:\> javac ButtonGame.java
C:\>

<! ButtonGame.html that embeds ButtonGame applet>
<html>
<applet code="ButtonGame.class" width=800 height= 600>
</applet>
</html>

C:\> appletviewer ButtonGame.html
```

Applet Parameters

Along with applet tag, we can use <param> tag to pass information to applets. For example, to pass name and salary of an employee to an applet from HTML page, we can write the applet and param tags as:

```
<applet code="Tax.class" width=300 height=300>
<param name="t1" value= "Nag">
<param name="t2" value= "150000.50">
</applet>
```

<param> tag has two attributes 'name' and 'value'. 'name' represents the name of the parameter and 'value' indicates its value. For example, in the above code, we have two parameters: t1 and t2 and their values are "Nag" and "150000.50" respectively.

To receive the values of the parameters, an applet uses getParameter() method. This method takes the parameter name and returns its value as a string.

```
name = getParameter("t1");
str = getParameter("t2");
```

where name and str and String type variables. getParameter() method should be used inside the init() method of the applet.

<param> tag is useful for passing information to the applets. This eliminates the need for modifying the applet even if we want to pass different data. The following program demonstrates how to use <param> tag to pass name and salary of an employee to an applet called 'Tax.class' and how the applet receives the data using getParameter() method and processes the data.

Program 7: Program to pass name and salary to an applet and get the tax calculated.

```
//Calculating tax by taking name and salary from param tags
import java.awt.*;
import java.applet.*;
public class Tax extends Applet
{
      //vars
      String name,str;
      float sal;
      float tax;

      public void init()
      {
            //accept name from t1 parameter
            name = getParameter("t1");

            //accept salary into str from t2 parameter
            //and convert str into float type sal
            str = getParameter("t2");
            sal = Float.parseFloat(str);

            //call calculateTax() method and pass sal to it.
            calculateTax(sal);
      }

      public void calculateTax(float sal)
      {
            //calculate tax value based on salary.
            if(sal<=100000)
            tax = 0.0f;
            else if(sal <= 200000)
            tax = sal*0.1f;
            else tax = sal*0.2f;
      }
      public void paint(Graphics g)
      {
            //display the tax details
            g.drawString("Hello"+ name, 20, 100);
            g.drawString("Your Salary: "+sal, 20,120);
            g.drawString("Pay the Tax: "+ tax, 20, 140);
```

```
            }
         }
```

Output:

```
    C:\> javac Tax.java
    C:\>

    <!Accept.html - this page sends name and salary to the applet >
    <html>
    <h1> INCOME TAX CALCULATOR </h1>

    <! param tag takes name and its value as strings>
    <applet code="Tax.class" width=300 height=300>
    <param name="t1" value= "Nag">
    <param name="t2" value= "150000.50">
    </applet>

    </html>

    C:\> appletviewer Accept.html
```

Playing Audio in Applets

It is possible to play audio files such as .au and .wav files in applets. These files are generally useful to play sound in background while a game is being run on the screen or they can be useful to play a song or some music.

AudioClip is an interface that is provided in java.applet package. It contains three methods: loop(), play() and stop(). The method loop() is useful to play an audio file repeatedly. play() method is for playing the audio file only once and stop() method stops playing the audio in the middle.

We can use getAudioClip() method of Applet class to create an object that can be referenced by AudioClip interface, as shown in the following statement:

```
    AudioClip clip = getAudioClip(getDocumentBase(), str);
```

Here, the reference 'clip' refers to the object that contains the audio filename as a string 'str'. The method getDocumentBase() refers to the current directory where the audio file can be found. Now, we can call loop(), play() and stop() methods using the reference as,

```
clip.loop();
clip.play();
clip.stop();
```

The following applet depicts how to play the audio files (.au or .wav) using the AudioClip interface.

Program 8: Program to create an applet to play the audio files.

```
//an applet to play sound files
import java.applet.*;
import java.awt.*;
import java.awt.event.*;

public class Audio extends Applet implements ActionListener
{
    //Declare reference variables
    Label lbl;
    TextField tf;
    Button b1, b2;
    AudioClip clip;

    public void init()
    {
        //create a label
        lbl = new Label("Enter .au or .wav filename: ", Label.RIGHT);

        //a text field to receive the filename
        tf = new TextField(15);

        //two buttons to play and stop
        b1 = new Button("Play");
        b2 = new Button("Stop");

        //add the components to applet frame
        add(lbl);
        add(tf);
        add(b1);
        add(b2);

        //add action listener to buttons
        b1.addActionListener(this);
        b2.addActionListener(this);

    }

    //this method is called when a button is clicked
    public void actionPerformed(ActionEvent ae)
    {
        //get the filename from text field
        String str = tf.getText();

        //remove any extra spaces from filename
        str = str.trim();

        //pass the filename to AudioClip object
        clip = getAudioClip(getDocumentBase(), str);

        //know which button is clicked
        Button b = (Button)ae.getSource();

        //if b1 is clicked then play, else stop
        if (b == b1)
            clip.play();
        else clip.stop();

    }
```

```
        }
```

Output:

```
C:\> javac Audio.java
C:\>
```

Embed the applet in a webpage as shown in the following code.

```
<! sound.html - this page contains Audio applet>
<html>
<applet code= "Audio.class" width = 450 height = 350>
</applet>
</html>

C:\> appletviewer sound.html
```

Conclusion

An applet represents Java byte code that is embedded in an HTML page, so that when the page is sent to the client, the applet is executed in the client-side browser and the results are displayed. Applets are useful to provide dynamic nature to the web pages by communicating with the user at runtime and also by providing animation.

GENERIC TYPES

When we create a class with an instance variable to store an Integer object, it can be used to store Integer type data only. We cannot use that instance variable to store a Float class object or a String type object. This becomes a limitation. Let us take a class:

```
class A
{
    Integer x;
}
```

Now, it is not possible to store a String in this class A, since the instance variable x is of type Integer and it can store only an Integer object. To store String type value in class A, we can rewrite the class, as:

```
class A
{
    String x;
}
```

Now, can we store a Float class object into the instance variable x ? No, it is not possible. To do so, we can write another copy of class A, as:

```
class A
{
    Float x;
}
```

Like this, to store different types of data into a class, we have to write the same class again and again by changing the data type of the variables. This can be avoided if we use a 'generic class'.

Generic Class

A generic class represents a class that is type-safe. This means a generic class can act upon any data type. Similarly, a generic interface is also type-safe and hence it can use any data type. Generic classes and generic interfaces are also called 'parameterized types' because they use a parameter that determines which data type they should work upon.

When a generic class or generic interface is written, the programmer need not rewrite the same class or interface whenever he wants to use the class or the interface with a new data type. The same class or interface can work with any data type. This becomes the greatest advantage for the programmers.

What is a generic type?

A generic type represents a class or an interface that is type-safe. It can act on any data type.

Generic types are designed to act upon objects. Hence they cannot work with primitive data types.

Since, generic class acts on any data type, we cannot specify a particular data type when designing the class. In the place of the data type, we use a generic parameter like <T>, or <GT> and write the class as:

```
class Myclass<T>
{
      class code;
}
```

Here, <T> is called 'generic parameter' and it determines at the time of compilation, which data type actually the programmer wants to use with this class. In the remaining places where a data type is to be used, the programmer can use T, as shown below:

```
class Myclass<T>
{
      T obj;
}
```

Here, the programmer's intention is to store T type object where T represents any data type. The data type is specified by the programmer at the time of creating the object to Myclass, as:

```
Myclass<String> obj = new Myclass<String>();
```

Here, we are specifying <String> data type after Myclass name. This means, T assumes String data type and hence Java compiler creates the following class internally :

```
class Myclass
{
      String obj;
}
```

The above code is compiled by the compiler and is executed by JVM. The point is whenever a generic class or interface is written, Java compiler internally creates non-generic version of the class or interface by substituting the specified data type in place of generic parameter T. This is called 'erasure'.

What is erasure?

Creating non-generic version of a generic type by the Java compiler is called erasure.

Program 1: To understand how to create a generic class, let us write a program in which we will take a class by the name of 'Myclass'. In Myclass, we want to store an object of any data type.

```
//A generic class - to store any type of object
//here, T is generic parameter which determines the datatype
class Myclass<T>
```

```
{
        //declare T type object
        T obj;

        //a constructor to initialize T type object
        Myclass(T obj)
        {
                this.obj = obj;
        }

        //a method which returns T type object
        T getobj()
        {
                return obj;
        }
}
class Gen1
{
        public static void main(String args[])
        {

                //create Integer class object
                Integer i = 12; //This is same as: Integer i = new Integer(12);

                //create Myclass object and store Integer object in it
                Myclass<Integer> obj = new Myclass<Integer>(i);

                //retrieve Integer object by calling getobj()
                System.out.println("U stored: "+ obj.getobj());

                //In the same way, use Myclass for storing
                //Float object and retrieve it
                Float f = 12.123f;   //Same as:Float f = new Float(12.123f);
                Myclass<Float> obj1 = new Myclass<Float>(f);
                System.out.println("U stored: " +obj1.getobj());

                //we can use Myclass to store String type data also
                Myclass<String> obj2 = new Myclass<String>("Ravi Kumar");
                System.out.println("U stored: " +obj2.getobj());
        }
}
```

Output:

```
C:\> javac Gen1.java
C:\> java Gen1
U stored: 12
U stored: 12.123
U stored: Ravi Kumar
```

In Program 1, we created Myclass object 3 times and stored 3 different objects: Integer object, Float object and String objects into it.

To create an Integer object in this program, we have written:

```
Integer i = 12;
```

Observe that Integer is a wrapper class and we are storing directly 12 into its variable i. In this case, Java compiler creates Integer class object internally and stores a value 12 as shown below:

```
Integer i= new Integer(12);
```

This is called 'auto boxing'.

Generic Method

We can make a method alone as generic method, by writing the generic parameter before the method return type as:

```
<T> void display()
{
     method code;
}
```

In this case, the method becomes a generic method and can act on any data type. To represent the data type, we should use T inside the method.

Program 2: In this program, let us write a generic method that receives an array and displays the elements of the array. The array elements may be of any data type.

```
//A generic method - to read and display any type of array elements
class Myclass
{
     //This method accepts T type array
     static <T>void display(T[] arr)
     {
          //use for-each loop and read elements of array
          for(T i: arr)
               System.out.println(i);
     }
}
class Gen2
{
     public static void main(String args[])
     {
          //read elements from Integer type array using display()
          Integer arr1[] = {1,2,3,4,5,6};
          System.out.println("Reading Integer objects: ");
          Myclass.display(arr1);

          //read elements from Double type array using display()
          Double arr2[] = {1.1, 2.2, 3.3, 4.5};
          System.out.println("Reading Double objects: ");
          Myclass.display(arr2);

          //read elements from String type array using display()
          String arr3[] = {"Raju", "Rani", "Ravi", "Kiran"};
          System.out.println("Reading String objects: ");
          Myclass.display(arr3);

     }
}
```

Output:

```
C:\> javac Gen2.java
C:\> java Gen2
Reading Integer objects:
1
2
```

```
3
4
5
6
Reading Double objects:
1.1
2.2
3.3
4.5
Reading String objects:
Raju
Rani
Ravi
Kiran
```

Generic Interface

It is possible to develop an interface using generic type concept. An generic interface looks something like this:

```
interface Fruit<T>
{
        //method that accepts any object
        void tellTaste(T fruit);   //public abstract
}
```

Here, T represents any data type which is used in the interface. We know already that whenever there is an interface, we should also have implementation classes that implement all the methods of the interface. We can write an implementation class for the above interface, as:

```
class AnyFruit<T> implements Fruit<T>
{
        public void tellTaste(T fruit)
        {
                //write body for this method as needed
        }
}
```

Here, T represents generic parameter that shows any data type.

Program 3: In this program, let us see how to create a generic interface Fruit and a generic implementation class AnyFruit. Then the implementation class is used to decide the taste of the fruits: a Banana and an Orange.

```
//A generic interface
interface Fruit<T>
{
        //method that accepts any object
        void tellTaste(T fruit);   //public abstract

}
//this class implements Fruit interface
class AnyFruit<T> implements Fruit<T>
{
        public void tellTaste(T fruit)
        {
                //know the class name of the object passed to this method
                String fruitname = fruit.getClass().getName();

                //then decide the taste and display
                if(fruitname.equals("Banana"))
```

```
                        System.out.println("Banana is sweet");
                        else if(fruitname.equals("Orange"))
                        System.out.println("Orange is sour");
            }
        }
        class Banana
        {

        }
        class Orange
        {
        /
        }
        class Gen3
        {
            public static void main(String args[])
            {
                //create Banana object and pass it to AnyFruit class
                Banana b = new Banana();
                AnyFruit<Banana> fruit1 = new AnyFruit<Banana>();
                fruit1.tellTaste(b);

                //create Orange object and pass it to AnyFruit class
                Orange o = new Orange();
                AnyFruit<Orange> fruit2 = new AnyFruit<Orange>();
                fruit2.tellTaste(o);

            }
        }
```

Output:

```
    C:\> javac Gen3.java
    C:\> java Gen3
    Banana is sweet
    Orange is sour
```

Effect of generics on collections

After developing the concept of generic types in JDK1.5, JavaSoft people used the concept to re-write all the collection classes of java.util package. The classes are re-defined as:

```
    HashSet<T>
    LinkedHashSet<T>
    Stack<T>
    LinkedList<T>
    ArrayList<T>
    Vector<T>
    HashMap<K,V>
    Hashtable<K,V>
```

Where, T represents the type of the element. K and V represent types of elements marked as Key and Value pair.

To understand how the collection classes are re-written, let us write a program using Hashtable. We will begin by writing the code using versions prior to JDK1.5 version. Then we will rewrite the code using generic type concept added since JDK1.5 version.

Program 4: In this program, we have created a Hashtable with cricket players' names and their scores in a match. Here, we do not use generic type concept.

```
    //Hashtable before jdk1.5 - no generic type concept
    import java.util.*;
    class HT1
    {
```

```
public static void main(String args[])
{
        //create Hashtable object
        Hashtable ht = new Hashtable();   //generic types not used

        //store String type key and Integer type value
        ht.put("Ajay", new Integer(50));   //auto boxing is not used .
        ht.put("Sachin", new Integer(90));
        ht.put("Dhoni", new Integer(75));

        //retrieve Sachin's score
        String s = "Sachin";
        Integer score =(Integer)ht.get(s);  //casting is required here
        System.out.println("Score= "+ score);
}
}
```

C:\>javac HT1.java

HT1.java uses unchecked or unsafe operations.

Recompile with –Xlint:unchecked for details.

Please observe the messages given by the Java compiler above. It is saying unchecked operations are being performed. When creating Hashtable object we wrote:

```
Hashtable ht = new Hashtable();
```

Here, we did not mention what type of data being stored into ht. So the compiler was unaware of which type of data might be stored in the Hashtable. Hence it gives a message that says 'it is an unchecked operation'. If Hashtable is used as a generic type, then the programmer specifies the data type clearly, as:

```
Hashtable<String, Integer> ht = new Hashtable<String,Integer>();
```

This represents the Hashtable will be used to store a String as key and an Integer object as its value. In this case, the compiler would not make any complaint.

```
C:\>java HT1
Score= 90
```

The same program can be rewritten using generic type concept. In this case, the programmer informs the compiler which data types he is going to store in the Hashtable, at the time of creating the object, as:

```
Hashtable<String, Integer> ht = new Hashtable<String,Integer>();
```

Once, the compiler knows that the programmer wishes to store String type key and Integer type value, it will check the Hashtable object. This is done to verify if the programmer is actually storing the same data types or not. This is shown in Program 5.

Program 5: Here, we create a Hashtable with generic type concept so that it can be used to store any data type.

```
//Hashtable is rewritten using generic types in jdk1.5
//as Hashtable<K,V>
import java.util.*;
class HT2
{
     public static void main(String args[])
     {
```

```
                    //create Hashtable object using String and Integer types
                    Hashtable<String,Integer> ht = new Hashtable<String,Integer>();

                    //store string type key and Integer type value
                    ht.put("Ajay", 50);   //auto boxing is done
                    ht.put("Sachin", 90);
                    ht.put("Dhoni", 75);

                    //retrieve Sachin's score
                    String s = "Sachin";
                    Integer score = ht.get(s);  //casting is not required
                    System.out.println("Score= "+ score);

            }
    }
```

Output:

```
    C:\> javac HT2.java
    C:\> java HT2
    Score= 90
```

Please observe the differences between Program 4 and Program 5 where Hashtable is written using and without using generics.

After discussing generics, we can conclude the following points:

❑   A generic class or a generic interface represents a class or an interface which is type-safe.

❑   A generic class, generic interface or a generic method can handle any type of data.

❑   Generic types are defined as sub types of the class 'Object'.

❑   So, they act on objects of any class.

❑   They cannot act on primitive data types.

❑   Java compiler creates a non-generic version of the class by substituting the specified data type in a generic class. This is called erasure.

❑   By using generic types, it is possible to eliminate type casting in many cases.

❑   All the classes of java.util package have been rewritten using generic types.

❑   We cannot create an object to a generic parameter. For example,

```
    class Myclass<T>  //T is generic parameter
    T obj = new T(); //invalid
```

Conclusion

Generic classes in Java are similar to templates in C++ but there is considerable difference between them. The main aim of generic types is to provide type-safety for the classes and interfaces. A generic class, generic interface or a generic method eliminates the need of being re-written every time there is a change in a data type. The programmer can use same generic type on any data type and hence generics are very flexible and useful in writing the programs.

JAVA DATABASE CONNECTIVITY

Interconnection between two or more computers is called a 'network'. A network might consist of just two computers or two thousand computers. The advantage of a network is to send and receive information from one computer to another computer. A computer that receives information or some service through the network is called 'client' and the other computer which provides the required service is called 'server'. A network consists of many clients and servers.

Database Servers

A database is a repository of data. We can store data permanently in a database and retrieve it later whenever needed by using some query commands. Databases like Oracle, Sybase, MySQL and SqlServer are in use nowadays. Data is stored generally in the form of tables in these databases. To retrieve data from the tables and give it to the users, we need some program. This program is called 'database client' program. To understand the database client, let us take an example. If oracle10g is installed in your computer, go to 'Start' menu and click:

```
Start -> Programs -> Oracle Database 10g Express Edition -> Run SQL command
```

It opens a window at DOS prompt where SQL> prompt appears. Type connect and, it asks to enter user-name and password. Type 'scott' and 'tiger' as default values. Then you would be connected to the oracle database. Please see the Figure 32.1. This application is called SQL*Plus which is a client program to connect to the oracle server at any moment.

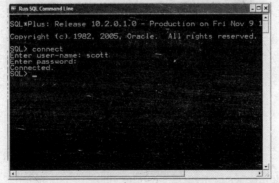

Figure 32.1 SQL*Plus client to connect to Oracle database

Database Clients

Using SQL*Plus application, it is possible to store data into oracle database. Also retrieving the data as well as updating it is also possible. Since, SQL*Plus is retrieving data from the oracle server in your system, SQL*Plus is called database client and oracle database is called database server. Now type a query as:

```
SQL> select * from tab;
```

It displays all the tables available in oracle database. Press Cntrol+Alt+Del to see Task Manager Dialog box as shown in Figure 32.2 below, where you can spot out Oracle.exe file running in your system. This is nothing but the oracle database. It is possible to load SQL*Plus client software in a system and the oracle database server program in another system connected on a network. The client will be able to connect to the database server and retrieve the data on the network. See Figure 32.5.

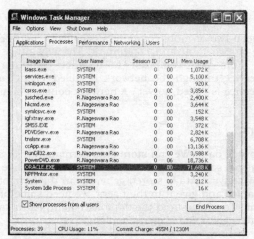

Figure 32.2 Oracle.exe running in the system

Similarly, MySQL is a database. To connect to this database, go to Start-> MySQL -> MySQL Server 5.0 -> MySQL Command line client. It asks for password, where you type: 'root' at DOS prompt Now you can see the screen shown in Figure 32.3.

Figure 32.3 MySQL client

To see the names of databases in MySQL, give the following command:

```
mysql> show databases;
```

To come out of MySQL, we can type quit at `mysql>` prompt. We can understand that MySQL program is client program and the server program `mysqld-nt.exe` which runs internally is called MySQL database server. To see the MySQL server in your system, press Control+Alt+Del to display Task Manager Dialog as shown in Figure 32.4.

Figure 32.4 MySQL server running in the system

`SQL*Plus` or MySQL client programs connect to database servers and retrieve the data from them. The same thing can be done through a Java program which connects to a database and retrieves data from it. This technology is called Java Database Connectivity (JDBC).

JDBC (Java Database Connectivity)

JDBC is an API (Application Programming Interface) that helps a programmer to write Java programs to connect to a database, retrieve the data from the database and perform various operations on the data in the Java program.

Important Interview Question

What is JDBC?

JDBC (Java Database Connectivity) is an API that is useful to write Java programs to connect to any database, retrieve the data from the database and utilize the data in a Java program.

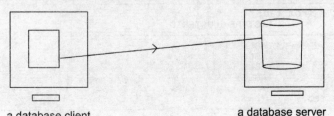

a database client   a database server

Figure 32.5 A database client and server

Every database vendor will provide a document representing all the commands to connect and utilize the database features. This document is called 'API (Application Programming Interface) document'. API document is a file that contains description of all the features of a software, a product or a technology. For example, the vendor of oracle database has given the following information for the programmers who use his product, in his API document:

❑ To connect to oracle database, use oLog() function.

❑ To execute a command, use oexec() function.

❑ To disconnect from oracle, use oLogoff() function.

The syntax and usage of these functions are also explained by the vendor in his API document. Any programmer wishing to use oracle database should learn these functions. This is not enough. If the same programmer wants to work with MySQL database, he should learn the syntax and usage of functions provided by MySQL vendor in his API document. For example,

❑ To connect to MySQL database, use mysql_connect() function.

❑ To execute a command, use mysql_execute() function.

❑ To disconnect from MySQL, use mysql_disconnect() function.

In the above manner these functions are provided, a separate set of functions are provided in API documents of different databases and the programmers have to learn them every time they want to use a different database. This is cumbersome as there are hundreds of functions to learn. This is the reason, software scientists have thought of creating a common API document. By using the functions of this common API document, programmers can communicate with any database in the world. Such a document is called ODBC (Open Database Connectivity) API.

ODBC is a document that contains common functions to communicate with any database. It is created by Microsoft Corporation. If any organization creates a software depending on this ODBC document, it is called ODBC driver.

In the same way, Sun Microsystems Inc. has also created an API document named JDBC (Java Database Connectivity) API and the actual software which is created according to JDBC API, is called JDBC driver. JDBC API is defined in java.sql package. This package contains interfaces like Connection, Statement, ResultSet, ResultSetMetaData, PreparedStatement, Driver, CallableStatement and classes like Date, Time, DriverManager etc. Several companies have started developing software containing these interfaces and classes. These softwares are called JDBC drivers. For example, classes12.jar is a driver developed by Oracle corporation using which we can connect to oracle database and communicate with it. Similarly gate.jar is a JDBC driver from inet to connect to oracle. Similarly, Mysql-connector-java-3.0.11-stable-bin.jar is a driver to connect to MySQL database. Also, we have jdbc-odbc driver provided by Sun Microsystems.

Working with Oracle Database

Oracle is the most popular database all over the world. After connecting to oracle database, SQL> prompt appears where you should enter SQL (Structured Query Language) commands. Let us see how to use SQL commands to do certain useful tasks on the Oracle database.

```
SQL> select * from tab;
TNAME                    TABTYPE CLUSTERID
-------------------------------------------------------------
ACCOUNT                  TABLE
DEPT                     TABLE
EMP                      TABLE
SALGRADE                 TABLE

4 rows selected.
```

Suppose, we want to create a table with the name 'emptab' with 3 columns: eno (int type), ename (String type) and sal(float type), we can type SQL command as:

```
SQL> create table emptab(eno int, ename varchar2(20), sal float);
```

Table created.

It is seen that using the above SQL command we have created a table by the name of 'emptab', in which varchar2(20) represents that we can store a maximum of 20 characters in ename column. To see the information about the table created by us, we can use description command, as:

```
SQL> desc emptab;
Name            Null?          Type
------------------------------------------------
ENO                            NUMBER(38);
ENAME                          VARCHAR2(20);
SAL                            FLOAT(126);
```

Let us store data into the table 'emptab' created by us. For this purpose, we should use 'insert' command as:

```
SQL> insert into emptab values(&eno, '&ename', &sal);
Enter value for eno: 1001
Enter value for ename: Venkat Rao
Enter value for sal: 8900.95
old 1: insert into emptab values(&eno, '&ename', &sal)
new 1: insert into emptab values(1001, 'Venkat Rao', 8900.95)
1 row created.
```

In this way, we inserted a row into oracle database. To enter another row, the above command can be repeated by typing '/' at SQL> prompt as:

```
SQL>/
Enter value fro eno: 1002
Enter value for ename: Gopal
Enter value for sal: 5600.55
```

To save all entered rows into the table, we can use 'commit' command, as:

```
SQL> commit;
```

To see all the rows of our emptab, we should use 'select' command in the following way:

```
SQL> select * from emptab;
ENO             ENAME                    SAL
-----------------------------------------------------
1001            Venkat Rao               8900.95
1002            Gopal                    5600.55
1003            Laxmi                    5000
1004            Nitin Prakash  12000
```

In the above command, '*' represents all the columns of the rows. If we want only eno and ename columns, we can give select command, as:

```
SQL> select eno,ename from emptab;
ENO             ENAME
-------------------------------------------------
1001            Venkat Rao
1002            Gopal
```

```
1003          Laxmi
1004          Nitin Prakash
```

In case, we want to retrieve the names of employees whose salary is more than Rs. 6000.00, we can give the following command:

```
SQL> select ename from emptab where sal>6000;

ENAME
-------------
Venkat Rao
Nitin Prakash
```

Let us now update the salary of an employee in emptab. Let us increase the salary by Rs. 1000 to the employee whose eno is 1002.

```
SQL> update emptab set sal= sal+1000 where eno=1002;
```

1 row updated.

If we want to delete an employee row whose eno is 1001:

```
SQL> delete from emptab where eno= 1001;
```

1 row deleted.

Now, we want to insert one row related to a new employee 'Mahendra' as:

```
SQL> insert into emptab values(9999, 'Mahendra', 13000);
```

1 row created.

To save all the changes into the database, we can use 'commit' command. Similarly, to un-save the changes, 'rollback' can be used.

```
SQL> rollback;
Rollback completed.
```

Now we will close the SQL client giving 'exit':

```
SQL> exit;
```

The commands we used are called SQL commands. The same commands can be used on any other database with slight modifications.

Working with MySQL Database

MySQL is a free database software provided by mysql.com. We can create only one database in oracle, but in MySQL, it is possible to create multiple databases. After going into MySQL, we can see mysql> prompt where we should enter commands. To see what databases are existing in MySQL, give the following command:

```
mysql> show databases;
```

Database
mysql
test

The above output means that there are 2 databases currently available in MySQL and they are: mysql and test. Let us see which tables are available in the database 'test'. We should first enter test database, as:

```
mysql> use test;
Database changed
```

Now, to see the tables in test database,

```
mysql> show tables;
```

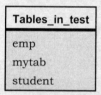

Tables_in_test
emp
mytab
student

Now let us create a table with the name 'emptab' in test database. eno, ename and sal are the columns in emptab.

```
mysql> create table emptab(eno int, ename char(20), sal float);
```

Query OK, 0 rows affected

Let us see the description of emptab by giving 'desc' command.

```
mysql> desc emptab;
```

Field	Type	Null	Key	Default	Extra
eno	int(11)	YES		Null	
ename	char(20)	YES		Null	
sal	float	YES		Null	

3 rows in set

We did not store any data so far into the emptab. Let us now store some rows into emptab.

```
mysql> insert into emptab values(1001, "Nagesh", 7800);
```

Query OK, 1 row affected

```
mysql> insert into emptab values(1002, "Ganesh", 10000.00);
```

Query OK, 1 row affected

In this way, we can store some rows into emptab. To see all the rows of the table, we can use select query as:

```
mysql> select * from emptab;
```

eno	ename	sal
1001	Nagesh	7800
1002	Ganesh	10000
1003	Vinaya	5000.55
1004	Rahul	7800

4 rows in set

Suppose we want to retrieve employees names whose salary is Rs. 7800.

```
mysql> select ename from emptab where sal = 7800;
```

ename
Nagesh
Rahul

2 rows in set

Suppose we want to delete the row of an employee whose employee number is 1001.

```
mysql> delete from emptab where eno = 1001;
```

Query OK, 1 row affected

To update the salary to Rs. 15000 of an employee whose name is "Rahul",

```
mysql> update emptab set sal= 15000 where name= "Rahul";
```

Query OK, 1 row affected

Rows matched: 1 changed: 1 warnings: 0

Finally, to close MySQL, we can give 'quit' command to see the system prompt, as:

```
mysql> quit;
```

Bye

In the similar manner, we can work with Sybase, SQL Server or MSAccess databases. We can give commands to create tables, store data in the tables as well as retrieve data from the tables and process data.

Without the help of database clients, it is possible to connect to a database server by using a Java program as its client. This is where JDBC API plays significant role.

Stages in a JDBC Program

The following stages are used by Java programmers while using JDBC in their programs:

❑ **Registering the driver:** A database driver is a software containing classes and interfaces written according to JDBC API. Since there are several drivers available in the market, we should first declare a driver which is going to be used for communication with the data base server in a Java program.

❏ **Connecting to a database:** In this stage, we establish a connection with a specific database through the driver which is already registered in the previous step.

❏ **Preparing SQL statements in Java:** We should create SQL statements in our Java program using any of the interfaces like Statement, PreparedStatement, CallableStatement, etc., which are available in `java.sql` package.

❏ **Executing the SQL statements on the database:** For this purpose, we can use `execute()`, `executeQuery()` and `executeUpdate()` methods of Statement interface.

❏ **Retrieving the results:** The results obtained by executing the SQL statements can be stored in an object with the help of interfaces like ResultSet, ResultSetMetaData and DatabaseMetaData.

❏ **Closing the connection:** We should close the connection between the Java program and the database by using `close()` method of Connection interface.

Registering the Driver

This is the first step to connect to a database. A programmer should specify which database driver he is going to use to connect to the database. There are 4 ways to register a driver.

❏ By creating an object to driver class of the driver software, we can register the driver. For example, to register JdbcOdbcDriver of the Sun Microsystems, we can create an object to the driver class: JdbcOdbcDriver, as shown below:

```
sun.jdbc.odbc.JdbcOdbcDriver obj = new sun.jdbc.odbc.JdbcOdbcDriver();
```

❏ The second way to register a driver is by sending the driver class object to `registerDriver()` method of DriverManager class. For example, the object of JdbcOdbcDriver class can be passed to `registerDriver()` method, as:

```
DriverManager.registerDriver( new sun.jdbc.odbc.JdbcOdbcDriver());
```

❏ The third way to register the driver is to send the driver class name directly to `forName()` method, as:

```
Class.forName("sun.jdbc.odbc.JdbcOdbcDriver");
```

❏ In case, the user should specify the driver name at the time of running the program, we can use `getProperty()` method of System class to receive the driver name, as:

```
String dname = System.getProperty("driver");
Class.forName(dname);
```

Here, `getPropert()` method accepts the driver name from the user and stores it in dname. Then `forName()` method creates an object to the class whose name is in dname. The question is how to provide the driver name while running the program? The following syntax will make it clear:

```
C:\> java –Ddriver = driverclassname Programname
```

For example, to send the driver class name: JdbcOdbcDriver to Myprog, we can type at system prompt, as:

```
C:\> java –Ddriver = sun.jdbc.odbc.JdbcOdbcDriver  Myprog
```

In this case, the name: `sun.jdbc.odbc.JdbcOdbcDriver` is sent to `System.getProperty()` method and then `Class.forName()` method will create an object to it.

Important Interview Question

What is a database driver?

A database driver is a set of classes and interfaces, written according to JDBC API to communicate with a database.

How can you register a driver?

To register a database driver, we can follow one of the 4 options:

- By creating an object to driver class

- By sending driver class object to DriverManager.registerDriver() method.

- By sending the driver class name to Class.forName() method.

- By using System class getProperty() method.

Connecting to a Database

To connect to a database, we should know 3 things:

❑ **URL of the database:** Here, URL(Uniform Resource Locator) represents a protocol to connect to the database. Simply speaking it locates the database on the network.

❑ **Username:** To connect to a database, every user will be given a username which is generally allotted by the database administrator.

❑ **Password:** This is the password allotted to the user by the database administrator to connect to the database.

Let us take an example. To connect to oracle database using Sun Microsystems' jdbc-odbc driver, we can write the following statement:

```
DriverManager.getConnection("jdbc:odbc:oradsn", "scott", "tiger");
```

Here, "`jdbc:odbc:oradsn`" is the URL. oradsn represents the DSN (data source name), a name given to the database for the reference in the Java program. "scott" is the username and "tiger" is password.

Let us take another example. To connect to oracle database using the thin driver provided by Oracle corp, we can write the following statement:

```
DriverManager.getConnection("jdbc:oracle:thin:@localhost:1521:oracle", "scott",
"tiger");
```

We advise you to go through the user manuals supplied by the database vendors where they explain clearly the ways to connect to the database with examples.

Important Interview Question

What is DSN?

Data Source Name (DSN) is a name given to the database to identify it in the Java program. The DSN is linked with the actual location of the database.

Preparing SQL Statements

We need SQL(Structured Query Language) statements which are useful to make different operations like adding data to the database, updating the data of the database and deleting un-useful data from the database and also retrieving the data from the database. SQL statements can be classified into two types: select and non-select statements.

❏ **select statements:** These statements help to retrieve the data from the database in the form of rows. For example, to retrieve all the rows and with all columns, we can write:

```
select * from emptab;
```

To pass this type of statements to the database, first of all we should create Statement object as:

```
Statement stmt = con.createStatement();
```

We should pass the SQL statement to `executeQuery()` method so that it executes the query on the database and gets back the resultant rows.

```
ResultSet rs = stmt.executeQuery("select * from emptab");
```

Now the results are available in ResultSet object rs. We can retrieve the results from rs using the methods of ResultSet interface. See table 32.1.

Table 32.1

ResultSet method	Its function
1. boolean next()	This method moves the cursor to the next row in the ResultSet object.
2. int getRow()	Returns the current row number.
3. String getString()	Retrieves a string from the row of the ResultSet.
4. int getInt()	Retrives an integer value from the row of the ResultSet.
5. float getFloat()	Retrieves a float value from the row of the ResultSet.
6. double getDouble()	Retrives a double value from the row of the ResultSet.
7. long getLong()	Retrives a long value from the row of the ResultSet.
8. Date getDate()	Retrives an object from the ResultSet row as java.sql.Date class object.

Important Interview Question

What is ResultSet?

ResultSet is an object that contains the results (rows) of executing a SQL statement on a database.

❏ **non-select statements:** These statements represent all other statements except select statements. create, update, insert, delete, etc., statements come under this category.

For example, to create the table mytab, we can use create statement as:

```
create table mytab(col1 number, col2 number);
```

To execute the above statement, we should first create Statement object, as:

```
Statement stmt = con.createStatement();
```

And then, we should pass the SQL statement to executeUpdate() method, as:

```
int n = stmt.executeUpdate("create table mytab(col1 number, col2 number)");
```

In the above statement, n represents the number of rows updated in the table. Let us take another example.

```
int n = stmt.executeUpdate("update emptab set sal= 15000 where eno = 1005");
```

Here, we are updating the salary of an employee whose eno is 1005. There is only 1 row in emptab with eno value 1005. So, only 1 row is updated by the above query. So, n value becomes 1.

```
int n = stmt.executeUpdate("delete emptab where eno > 1005");
```

Here, all the rows with eno values greater than 1005 from emptab will be deleted. Now n value represents how many such rows are deleted.

Let us write a Java program to connect to oracle database and retrieve the rows from emptab. In this program, we are using Oracle 10g xe version to create the database table. If you refer to Oracle 10g documentation (user manual), you can find the following URL to be used to connect to the database:

```
jdbc:oracle:thin:@localhost:1521:xe
```

Let us take a table emptab with 3 columns which can be created with the SQL command:

```
create table emptab(eno int, ename varchar2(20), sal float);
```

Insert some rows into the table emptab. Now let us think about retrieving the rows of the table.

Program 1: This is a program to retrieve all the rows from emptab of oracle database.

```java
//To retrieve data from Oracle database
import java.sql.*;
class OracleData
{
    public static void main(String args[]) throws Exception
    {
        //Register the driver
        DriverManager.registerDriver(new
        oracle.jdbc.driver.OracleDriver());

        //Establish connection with the database
        Connection con=DriverManager.getConnection(
        "jdbc:oracle:thin:@localhost:1521:xe","scott","tiger");

        //Create a SQL statement
        Statement stmt = con.createStatement();

        //Execute the stmt
        ResultSet rs = stmt.executeQuery("select * from emptab");
```

```
                    //all rows of emptab are in rs. Now retrieve column data
                    //from rs and display
                    while(rs.next()){
                    System.out.println(rs.getInt(1));
                    System.out.println(rs.getString(2));
                    System.out.println(rs.getFloat(3));
                    System.out.println("=====================");
                    }

                    //close the connection
                    con.close();
            }
    }
```

Output:

```
C:\> set classpath=C:\jars\ojdbc14.jar;.;
C:\> javac OracleData.java
C:\> java OracleData
1001
Nageswara Rao
7800.55
=====================
1002
Vijay Kumar
6000.0
=====================
1003
Durga
5000.75
=====================
1004
Ganesh
12000.77
=====================
```

Observe the following statement in the above program:

```
ResultSet rs = stmt.executeQuery("select * from emptab");
```

When this statement is executed, all the rows of the emptab will be retrieved and stored into the ResultSet object rs. Here, 'rs' works like a reference which is positioned initially just before the first row, as shown in Figure 32.6.

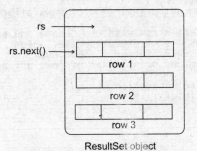

ResultSet object

Figure 32.6

To position rs at first row, we can use rs.next() method. This method puts the reference rs at first row and returns true. If row is not available in the ResultSet object, then it returns false. By using rs.next() method in a loop, we can visit every row of the ResultSet object.

Again, we know that each row contains 3 columns:

- eno is int type
- ename is String type
- sal is float type

To retrieve the data from these columns, we can use getXXX() methods, as:

- rs.getInt(1); //here, 1 represents 1st column data to retrieved as int type
- rs.getString(2); //retrieve 2nd column data as String type
- rs.getFloat(3); //retrive 3rd column data as float type

Observe that, before compilation of the program, we set the classpath to C:\jars\ojdbc14.jar. This file represents the driver software supplied by Oracle corp. When we install Oracle 10g xe version, this ojdbc14.jar file can be found in the directory: C:\oraclexe\app\oracle\product\10.2.0\server\jdbc\lib. The driver .jar file is copied into a separate directory C:\jars, and hence we set the classpath as shown above.

Program 2: In this program, we insert two rows into emptab. The first row is inserted with only one column: eno value 777, as:

```
    insert into emptab(eno) values(777);
    In this case, a row with eno value 777, ename value null and sal value 0.0 will
    be inserted into emptab. We insert another row with all column values, as:
    insert into emptab values(779, 'Satyaraj', 5000.00);
    //This program demonstrates how to insert rows into a table
    import java.sql.*;
    class Insertion
    {
        public static void main(String args[])throws Exception
        {

            //register oracle driver
            DriverManager.registerDriver(new
            oracle.jdbc.driver.OracleDriver());

            //get a connection with the database
            Connection con;
            con = DriverManager.getConnection(
            "jdbc:oracle:thin:@localhost:1521:xe","scott","tiger");

            //create a statement to insert a row with only eno value as 777
            Statement stmt = con.createStatement();
            int norows = stmt.executeUpdate("insert into emptab(eno)
            values(777)");
            System.out.println("no of rows affected = "+ norows);

            //insert a row with eno, ename and sal values
            norows = stmt.executeUpdate("insert into emptab
            values(779,'Satyaraj',5000.00)");
            System.out.println("no of rows affected = "+ norows);

            //close connection
            con.close();
        }
    }
```

Output:

```
    C:\> set classpath=C:\jars\ojdbc14.jar;.;

    C:\> javac Insertion.java
    C:\> java Insertion
    no rows affected: 1
```

```
no rows affected: 1
```

Program 3: This is a program to understand how to update and delete rows from emptab in oracle database. We use the SQL statements in the following way:

```
update emptab set sal=30000 where eno>1001;
```

Here, we are storing 30000 into the salary of all the employees whose employee numbers are greater than 1001. Similarly, we use:

```
delete emptab where eno>1001;
```

This will deleted all the rows from the table whose employee numbers are greater than 1001.

```java
// This program demonstrates how to update/delete rows
import java.sql.*;
class Updation
{
    public static void main(String args[])throws Exception
    {
        //accept the driver class name from system prompt into dname
        String dname = System.getProperty("driver");

        //create an object to the driver class whose name is in dname
        Class.forName(dname);

        //connect to oracle database
        Connection con =
DriverManager.getConnection("jdbc:oracle:thin:@localhost:1521:xe","scott",
"tiger");

        //create SQL statement
        Statement stmt = con.createStatement();

        //executed SQL statement to update salary
        int norows = stmt.executeUpdate("update emptab set sal=30000 where
eno>1001");
        System.out.println("no of rows updated = "+ norows);

        System.out.println("Press a key to continue...");
        System.in.read();

        //execute SQL statement to delete a row
        norows = stmt.executeUpdate("delete emptab where eno>1001");
        System.out.println("no of rows deleted = "+ norows);

        //close connection
        con.close();
    }
}
C:\> set classpath=C:\jars\ojdbc14.jar;.;
C:\> javac Updation.java
C:\> java -Ddriver=orcle.jdbc.driver.OracleDriver Updation
no rows updated: 1
Press a key to continue…

no rows deleted: 2
```

Observe that in the above program, we are passing the driver name from system prompt. And the System class's getProperty() method is used to access it.

Using jdbc-odbc Bridge Driver to Connect to Oracle Database

Sun Microsystems Inc. provides a default driver called jdbc-odbc bridge driver along with Java software that is useful to connect to any database. Let us see how to use this driver with oracle database.

Step 1. First of all, we should create a DSN (Data Source Name) that represents the name for the database, by clicking on the Start button and following the path:

```
         Start -> Settings -> Control Panel -> Administrative Tools -> Data Sources
(ODBC).
```

We can find ODBC Data Source Administrator dialog box as shown in Figure 32.7.

Step 2. In this dialog box, select User DSN tab and click the Add button at right side. Now the list of drivers available will be displayed in a separate dialog box. Select Microsoft ODBC for Oracle driver in the list and click the Finish button. See Figure 32.8.

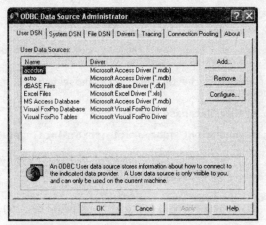

Figure 32.7 Creating DSN for oracle database

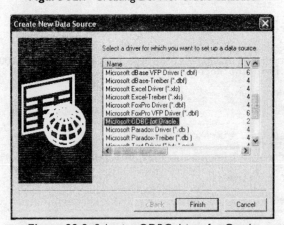

Figure 32.8 Selecting ODBC driver for Oracle

Step 3. Now, you can see Microsoft ODBC for Oracle Setup dialog box appears. Type the DSN name and user name and then click the OK button, as shown in Figure 32.9.

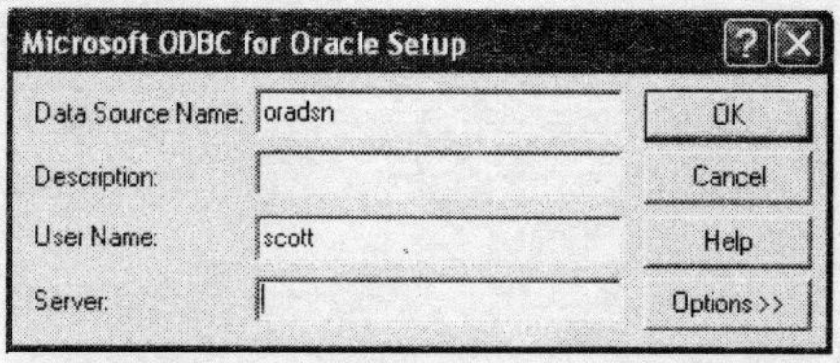

Figure 32.9 DSN and User Name

Now, we can verify that a new DSN with the name 'oradsn' has been created in UserDSN tab. Click the OK button to close the ODBC Data Source Administrator.

After creating the DSN name as shown above, the next thing we should do is to register the driver. To register Sun's jdbc-odbc bridge driver, we can use the following statement in our program:

```
DriverManager.registerDriver(new sun.jdbc.odbc.JdbcOdbcDriver());
```

To connect to the database, using this driver, we can write:

```
Connection con=DriverManager.getConnection(
"jdbc:odbc:oradsn","scott","tiger");
```

Here, oradsn is the DSN name that we have just created. scott is the username and tiger is the password.

Program 4: Let us see how to use Sun's jdbc-odbc bridge driver to connect to oracle database and retrieve all the rows from emptab. Now we need not use ojdbc14.jar since it is another driver called by the name 'thin driver'.

```
//To retrieve data from Oracle database using jdbc-odbc bridge driver
import java.sql.*;
class OracleData
{
        public static void main(String args[]) throws Exception
        {
                //Register the driver
                DriverManager.registerDriver(new sun.jdbc.odbc.JdbcOdbcDriver());

                //Establish connection with the database
                Connection con=DriverManager.getConnection(
                "jdbc:odbc:oradsn","scott","tiger");

                //Create a SQL statement
                Statement stmt = con.createStatement();

                //Execute the stmt
                ResultSet rs = stmt.executeQuery("select * from emptab");

                //all rows of emptab are in rs. Now retrieve column data
                //from rs and display
                while(rs.next()){
                System.out.println(rs.getInt(1));
                System.out.println(rs.getString(2));
                System.out.println(rs.getFloat(3));
                System.out.println("=====================");
                }

                //close the connection
                con.close();
        }
}
```

Output:

```
C:\> javac OracleData.java
C:\> java OracleData

1001
Nageswara Rao
7800.55
========================
1002
Vijay Kumar
6000.0
========================
1003
Durga
5000.75
========================
1004
Ganesh
12000.77
========================
```

Retrieving Data from MySQL Database

Let us open MySQL database and see which databases are there, by typing 'show databases' command, as:

```
mysql> show databases;
```

Database
mysql
test

The above output means that there are 2 databases currently available in MySQL and they are: mysql and test. Let us first move into test database, as:

```
mysql> use test;
```

Database changed

Create a table emp now using create statement in the database 'test', as:

```
mysql> create table emp(eno int, ename char(20), sal float);
```

Then enter some rows into the emp using insert statement as:

```
mysql> insert into emp values(100, "Sirisha", 5000.55);
```

Create and store some rows into the database as shown in preceding steps, and finally give commit command to save all these transactions.

```
mysql> commit;
```

Now, let us write a Java program to see how to retrieve all the rows from the emp of test database that is available in MySQL database. mysql.com company provides a driver mysql.jar along with a user manual where they provide help regarding how to register their driver. Register the mysql driver in the following manner:

```
DriverManager.registerDriver(new com.mysql.jdbc.Driver());
```

To connect to the database, we should use:

```
Connection con=DriverManager.getConnection(
"jdbc:mysql://localhost:3306/test?user=root&password=student");
```

Here, user name is 'root' and password is 'student'.

Program 5: In this program, we retrieve the data from the table emp of test database.

```java
//To retrieve data from MySQL database
import java.sql.*;
class MysqlData
{
        public static void main(String args[])throws Exception
        {
                //Register the driver
                DriverManager.registerDriver(new com.mysql.jdbc.Driver());

                //Establish connection
                Connection con=DriverManager.getConnection(
                "jdbc:mysql://localhost:3306/test?user=root&password=student");

                //Create a SQL statement
                Statement stmt = con.createStatement();

                //Execute the stmt
                ResultSet rs = stmt.executeQuery("select * from emp");

                //retrieve from ResultSet and display column data
                while(rs.next()){
                System.out.println(rs.getInt(1));
                System.out.println(rs.getString(2));
                System.out.println(rs.getFloat(3));
                System.out.println("=====================");
                }

                //close connection
                con.close();
        }
}
```

Output:

```
C:\> set classpath=c:\jars\mysql.jar;.;
C:\> javac MysqlData.java
C:\> java MysqlData
100
Sirisha
5000.55
=====================
101
Nataraj
9000.90
=====================
```

Retrieving Data from MS Access Database

Microsoft Access is also one of the databases used by many organizations. We can create a database in MS Access and create tables in the database. For this, select the options:

```
Start -> Programs -> Microsoft Office -> Microsoft Access -> Create a new file -
> Blank database
```

File New Database dialog box will be displayed as shown in Figure 32. 10. Type the database name as 'Mydb' in a directory, for example, D:\rnr. Then click the Create button.

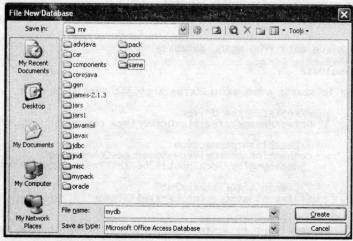

Figure 32.10 Creating a database in MS Access

When we enter the MS Access, a dialog box is displayed where double click 'Create table by entering data' option. This is shown in Figure 32.11.

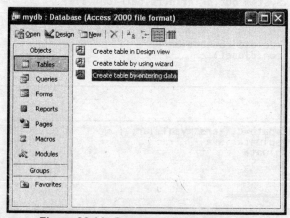

Figure 32.11 Creating a table in MS Access

Then, we will see a spread sheet with several rows and columns where we can enter column names in the table and column data as shown in Figure 32.12. Rename Field1 as eno, Field2 as ename and Field3 as sal. Then enter data.

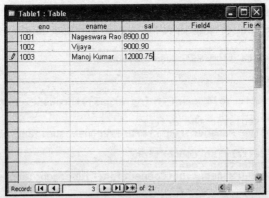

Figure 32.12 Entering data into the table in MS Access

Then select File -> Save option and Enter Filename as 'emptab' and then click OK button.

MS Access prompts us to enter a primary key. Click on 'NO' button. And close the table. Come out of MS Access now.

To connect to MS Access, we can use Sun Microsystems' jdbc-odbc bridge driver. To use this driver, it is necessary to create a DSN (Data Source Name) by going to Start -> Settings -> Control Panel -> Administrative Tools -> Data Sources (ODBC).

We can find ODBC Data Source Administrator dialog box where select User DSN tab and click the Add button at right side. Now the list of drivers available will be displayed in a separate dialog box. Select Microsoft Access (*.mdb) driver in the list and click Finish button. It displays ODBC Microsoft Access Setup dialog box as shown in Figure 32.13. In this box, enter:

```
Data Source Name: accdsn
```

Then click the Select button to select the database. Then select the directory with the name: D:\rnr where mydb.mdb will appear. Click on that directory. Then click the OK button and you will come back to ODBC Microsoft Access Setup dialog box where you click OK button and close it.

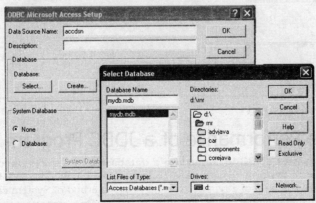

Figure 32.13 Typing DSN and selecting a database for the driver

Now DSN is created, we can mention it while connecting it to MS Access database, as:

```
Connection con= DriverManager.getConnection("jdbc:odbc:accdsn","","");
```

Here, no need to give username and password. So, we just used "" and "" in these places.

Program 6: In this program, we connect to MS Access database and retrieve the data from emptab.

```
//To retrieve data from MSAccess database
import java.sql.*;
class AccessData
{
    public static void main(String args[])throws Exception
    {
        //Register the driver
        DriverManager.registerDriver(new sun.jdbc.odbc.JdbcOdbcDriver());

        //Establish connection
        Connection con=
        DriverManager.getConnection("jdbc:odbc:accdsn","","");

        //Create a SQL statement
        Statement stmt = con.createStatement();

        //Execute the stmt
        ResultSet rs = stmt.executeQuery("select * from emptab");

        //retrieve from ResultSet and display column data
        while(rs.next()){
        System.out.println(rs.getInt(1));
        System.out.println(rs.getString(2));
        System.out.println(rs.getFloat(3));
        System.out.println("=====================");
        }
    }
}
```

Output:

```
C:\> javac AccessData.java
C:\> java AccessData
1001
Nageswara Rao
8900.0

=====================
1002
Vijaya
9000.9

=====================
1003
Manoj Kumar
12000.75
=====================
```

Improving the Performance of a JDBC Program

A Java program that uses JDBC to connect to a database and retrieve the data from the database may take some time to perform these tasks. To know how much time has been taken by a JDBC program, we can take the help of currentTimeMillis() method of System class. This method gives the current time in milliseconds since January 1st 1970. By using currentTimeMillis() in the beginning of a program and again at the end the program, we can measure the time at the beginning and end of the program. The difference in these times gives the execution time of the program in milliseconds.

By reducing the execution time of a JDBC program, we can improve its performance. The execution time of a JDBC program depends on the following factors:

- ❑ The driver used to connect to the database will influence the execution time. Each driver will exhibit different performance and hence, selecting a good driver that gives optimum performance will improve the performance of a JDBC program.

- ❑ `setFetchSize()` method of Statement interface is useful to tell the driver how many rows at a time to be fetched from the database. By increasing the number of rows to be retrieved at a time, it is possible to improve the performance of a JDBC program.

- ❑ Sometimes, PreparedStatement interface can be used in place of Statement interface for improving the performance.

(a) Affect of Driver

Different vendors provide different drivers to be used in a JDBC program. The performance of these drivers will be different and hence the programmer should first test each driver and adopt a driver which gives better performance for his database.

Let us create a table in oracle database with the name mytab, with 2 columns as:

```
create table mytab(a int, b int);
```

The following program will help us to insert a total of 999 rows into mytab. This program uses oracle driver which is called 'thin' driver supplied by Oracle corp.

Program 7: In this program, we use 'thin' driver to connect to oracle database. We insert a total of 999 rows into the database and find the time for this insertion operation.

```java
//To store 999 rows into Oracle database - Oracle driver
import java.sql.*;
class Performance
{
    public static void main(String args[]) throws Exception
    {
        //Register the driver
        DriverManager.registerDriver(new
        oracle.jdbc.driver.OracleDriver());

        //Establish connection with the database
        Connection con=DriverManager.getConnection(
        "jdbc:oracle:thin:@localhost:1521:xe","scott","tiger");

        //Create a SQL statement
        Statement stmt = con.createStatement();

        //count the time before insertion
        long t1 = System.currentTimeMillis();

        //insert 999 rows into mytab
        for(int i=1; i<1000; i++)
        stmt.executeUpdate("insert into mytab values("+i+","+i+")");

        //count the time after insertion
        long t2 = System.currentTimeMillis();

        //display the time taken
        System.out.println("Time = "+ (t2-t1));

        //close the connection
        con.close();
    }
}
```

Output:

```
C:\> set classpath=C:\jars\ojdbc14.jar;.;
C:\> javac Performance.java
C:\> java Performance
Time = 6203
```

This means, 'thin' driver has taken 6203 milliseconds of time to insert 999 rows into mytab. This time may vary from system to system. Please observe the following looping statement to insert the rows in the above program:

```
for(int i=1; i<1000; i++)
        stmt.executeUpdate("insert into mytab values("+i+","+i+")");
```

Here, we have taken

```
        insert into mytab values(
```

as a string. Then we attach i value as a string to it. So, we wrote +i. Then we attach a comma using +",". Then we attach again another i value as +i. Then a simple brace is attached by writing +")". So the total statement would yield a form like:

```
        insert into mytab values(1,1);    //when i is 1.
```

Now, let us write the same program using Sun's jdbc-odbc bridge driver. For this purpose, we should create DSN as oradsn.

Program 8: In this program, we use 'jdbc-odbc' driver to connect to oracle database and find the time for inserting 999 rows.

```
//To store 999 rows into Oracle database - jdbc-odbc driver
import java.sql.*;
class Performance
{
        public static void main(String args[]) throws Exception
        {
                //Register the driver
                DriverManager.registerDriver(new sun.jdbc.odbc.JdbcOdbcDriver());
                //Establish connection with the database
                Connection con=DriverManager.getConnection(
                "jdbc:odbc:oradsn","scott","tiger");
                //Create a SQL statement
                Statement stmt = con.createStatement();
                //count the time before insertion
                long t1 = System.currentTimeMillis();
                //insert 999 rows into mytab
                for(int i=1; i<1000; i++)
                stmt.executeUpdate("insert into mytab values("+i+","+i+")");
                //count the time after insertion
                long t2 = System.currentTimeMillis();
                //display the time taken
                System.out.println("Time = "+ (t2-t1));
                //close the connection
                con.close();
        }
}
```

Output:

```
C:\> javac Performance.java
C:\> java Performance
```

```
Time = 7125
```

Please observe the time taken by jdbc-odbc driver. It is taking more time than the thin driver. So, thin driver is faster and hence offering better performance than jdbc-odbc driver.

Important Interview Question

Will the performance of a JDBC program depend on the driver?

Yes, each driver offers a different performance.

(b) Affect of setFetchSize()

setFetchSize() method of Statement interface is useful to fetch a number of rows at a time from the database. setFetchSize(1) will make the driver fetch only one row at a time from the database. If we specify setFetchSize(100) then the driver will be able to fetch 100 rows at a time from the database and hence the time of execution will be less.

Program 9: In this program, we use setFetchSize() method to retrieve only one row at a time from the database. We calculate the time taken to retrieve all the 999 rows from mytab.

```
//To retrieve 999 rows from Oracle database one at a time.
import java.sql.*;
class Performance1
{
        public static void main(String args[]) throws Exception
        {
                //Register the driver
                DriverManager.registerDriver(new
                oracle.jdbc.driver.OracleDriver());
                //Establish connection with the database
                Connection con=DriverManager.getConnection(
                "jdbc:oracle:thin:@localhost:1521:xe","scott","tiger");
                //Create a SQL statement
                Statement stmt = con.createStatement();
                //retrieve at a time 1 row only
                stmt.setFetchSize(1);
                //count the time before retrieval
                long t1 = System.currentTimeMillis();
                //retrieve all rows from mytab
                ResultSet rs = stmt.executeQuery("select * from mytab");
                //display all the rows
                while(rs.next())
                System.out.println(rs.getInt(1)+"\t"+rs.getInt(2));
                //count the time after retrieval
                long t2 = System.currentTimeMillis();
                //display the time taken
                System.out.println("Time = "+ (t2-t1));
                //close the connection
                con.close();
        }
}
```

Output:

```
C:\> set classpath=C:\jars\ojdbc14.jar;.;
C:\> javac Performance1.java
C:\> java Performance1
Time = 5547
```

This means `setFetchSize(1)` has taken 5547 milliseconds of time to retrieve all the rows of mytab. In the above program, change the `setFetchSize()` method to retrieve 100 rows at a time, as shown below:

```
        stmt.setFetchSize(100);
```

Then re-run the program, to see the

```
    Time = 2032
```

This means when we retrieve 100 rows at a time from the database, the time taken by the program is considerably reduced and we are able to achieve better performance.

Do not be under the impression that the more the number of rows are fetched the less the time of execution it takes. No. Please observe the Table 32.2 to understand how the number of rows in `setFetchSize()` will affect the execution time. The execution time may vary on different systems.

Table 32.2

setFetchSize()	Time taken in milliseconds
setFetchSize(1);	5547
setFetchSize(100);	2032
setFetchSize(150);	2016
setFetchSize(200);	2008
setFetchSize(250);	1984
setFetchSize(300);	2047
setFetchSize(350);	2068

From the above table, one can understand that the time taken is minimum when `setFetchSize()` has retrieved between 200 and 250 rows at a time. This value should be used by the programmer in his JDBC program to get maximum performance. When `setFetchSize()` is retrieving more than 300 rows, why the time is more again? The reason is: to retrieve those many rows, the driver has to allocate a lot of memory and fill the memory every time it retrieves the rows. This would take more time. So, `setFetchSize()` with too higher values may reduce the performance.

(c) Affect of PreparedStatement

Using PreparedStatement in place of Statement interface will improve the performance of a JDBC program. Let us first write a program using Statement interface to insert 999 rows into mytab and find how much time it is taking.

Program 10: In this program, we use Statement object to insert 999 rows into mytab.

```
//Using Statement
import java.sql.*;
public class Performance2
{
    public static void main(String args[]) throws Exception
    {

    //register the driver
    DriverManager.registerDriver(new
```

```
        oracle.jdbc.driver.OracleDriver());

        //establish the connection
        Connection con =

        DriverManager.getConnection("jdbc:oracle:thin:@localhost:1521:xe","scott",
        "tiger");

        //create Statement object
        Statement stmt = con.createStatement();

        //calculate time before insertion
        long t1 = System.currentTimeMillis();

        //insert 999 rows into mytab
        for(int i=1; i<1000; i++)
        {
                stmt.executeUpdate("insert into mytab values("+i+","+i+")");
        }

        //calculate time after insertion
        long t2 = System.currentTimeMillis();

        System.out.println("Time= "+ (t2-t1));

        //close connection
        con.close();
        }
}
```

Output:

```
C:\> set classpath=C:\jars\ojdbc14.jar;.;
C:\> javac Performance2.java
C:\> java Performance2
Time = 6312
```

When a SQL statement is sent to database, the following tasks are performed:

❑ The SQL statement's syntax should be verified to know whether it is correct or not. The SQL statement is divided into small pieces called 'tokens'. These tokens are also verified to know whether they are in SQL format or not.

❑ Then another verification is done to know whether the table or view mentioned in the statement exists or not.

The above two stages are called 'parsing' and takes some time. When a SQL statement is executed, Statement interface does parsing every time the statement is executed. In the above program, the for loop is executed 999 times and a total of 999 rows are inserted into the table. So, Statement interface will conduct parsing for 999 times. This takes more time.

On the other hand, if we use PreparedStatement, it does parsing only once. Since the same statement is repeated 999 times, parsing is enough if one only once. This saves time and hence PreparedStatement offers better performance.

Let us see how to use PreparedStatement. First of all, we should create PreparedStatement object using prepareStatement() method of Connection interface.

```
PreparedStatement stmt = con.prepareStatement("insert into mytab values(?, ?)");
```

Here, ? represents the value to be passed to the columns of the row. The first ? represents the value to be passed to first column and the second ? represents the value for second column. These values can be passed usig setXXX() methods, as:

```
stmt.setInt(1, i); //replace first ? with i value
stmt.setFloat(2, 15.5f);  //replace second ? with 15.5
```

Program 11: Let us now re-write the previous program using PreparedStatement and insert 999 rows into mytab.

```java
// Demonstrates how to use a PreparedStatement
import java.sql.*;
public class Performance3
{
        public static void main(String args[]) throws Exception
        {

        //register the driver
        DriverManager.registerDriver(new oracle.jdbc.driver.OracleDriver());

        //establish the connection
        Connection con =
        DriverManager.getConnection("jdbc:oracle:thin:@localhost:1521:xe","scott",
        "tiger");

        //create PreparedStatement object
        PreparedStatement stmt = con.prepareStatement("insert into mytab
        values(?,?)");

        //calculate time before insertion
        long t1 = System.currentTimeMillis();

        //insert 999 rows into mytab
        for(int i=1; i<1000; i++)
        {
                //set values for ?,?
                stmt.setInt(1,i);
                stmt.setInt(2,i);

                //execute the statement
                stmt.executeUpdate();
        }
        //calculate time after insertion
        long t2 = System.currentTimeMillis();

        System.out.println("Time= "+ (t2-t1));

        //close connection
        con.close();
        }
}
```

Output:

```
C:\> set classpath=C:\jars\ojdbc14.jar;.;
C:\> javac Performace3.java
C:\> java Performance3
Time = 2828
```

Please observe the execution time when PreparedStatement is used. You will find that the time is less as compared to that of Statement. Remember, using PreparedStatement improves performance when we want to execute the same statement repeatedly.

What is parsing?

Parsing represents checking the syntax and grammar of a statement as a whole and also word by word.

What is the difference between Statement and PreparedStatement?

Statement parses a statement before its execution on the database. This parsing is done every time the statement is executed, and hence it may take more time when the same statement gets executed repeatedly. PreparedStatement conducts parsing only once when the same statement is executed repeatedly and hence it gives better performance.

Here, two more examples of using PreparedStatement is furnished:

```
1. PreparedStatement stmt = con.prepareStatement("update emptab set sal = ?
where eno= ? ");
stmt.setFloat(1, 10000.55f); //set 10000.55 to first ?
stmt.setInt(2,1002);  //set 1002 to second ?
int n = stmt.executeUpdate();  //n gives no. of rows affected
```

```
2. PreparedStatement stmt = con.prepareStatement("select * from emptab");
ResultSet rs = stmt.executeQuery();  //rs contains rows of emptab
```

Stored Procedures and CallableStatement

Stored procedure is a set of statements written using PL/SQL (Procedural language/ Structured Query language). To perform some calculations on the tables of a database, we can use stored procedures. Stored procedures are written and stored at database server. When a client contacts the server, the stored procedure is executed, and the results are sent to the client. Let us see why stored procedures are written in Oracle, at server side.

When a client/server software is created, we observe two main parts of the software:

❑ The first part represents the screens which accepts the input from the user and also display results to the user. The program code that helps to create such screens is called 'Presentation logic'.

❑ The second part represents the logic that converts the input into the output. It contains some business procedures and calculations related to the activities of an organization. This is called 'Business logic'.

It is advisable to create presentation logic and business logic separately without mixing them together. When they are developed separately, their maintenance becomes easy. For example, to modify presentation logic, the programmer need not think about business logic. He can modify any one without affecting the other. Similarly, it is possible to develop presentation logic and business logic using separate technologies. For example, the screens representing the presentation logic can be created using Java or VisualBasic whereas it is possible to create the business logic in Oracle in the form of 'stored procedures'.

What are stored procedures?

A stored procedure represents a set of statements that is stored and executed at database server, sending the results to the client.

To understand a stored procedure concept, let us write a stored procedure 'myproc.sql' to increase the salary by Rs. 500 of an employee whose eno is 1003 in emptab. Here we assuming that emptab already exists in the database.

```
-- myproc.sql
-- to increase the salary of employee whose eno=1003
create or replace procedure myproc(no in int, isal out float) as
salary float;
begin
  select sal into salary from emptab where eno=no;
  isal := salary+500;
end;
```

In the above code, we use created or replace key word to create the procedure. The procedure name is 'myproc'. It has two parameters: 'no' which is called in parameter and 'isal' which is called out parameter. When a client calls this procedure, it supplies the value for in parameter. The result is calculated and stored in out parameter, which is sent back to the client.

When 'no' is sent by the client, the corresponding row is retrieved by the following statement:

```
select sal into salary from emptab where eno=no;
```

This will store the salary of the employee into 'salary' variable. This salary is then incremented by Rs.500 and then stored into the out parameter 'isal'. The value in isal is only available to the client.

Type this stored procedure at SQL> prompt in oracle. Or, you can type the stored procedure in a Notepad file then copy and paste it at SQL> prompt. Then type '/' and press <Enter> to execute it. It displays a message: 'Procedure created'.

The next step is calling this stored procedure from our JDBC program. To do so, we need CallableStatement interface. For example, we can write:

```
CallableStatement stmt = con.prepareCall("{ call  myproc(?,?)}");
```

In the above statement, prepareCall() is used to call the stored procedure: 'myproc'. After procedure's name, we got two '?' marks which represent the in parameter and out parameter. Let us now provide some value to in parameter, as:

```
stmt.setInt(1,1004); //pass 1004 to in parameter
```

To retrieve the data from the out parameter, first we should register the type of the parameter as:

```
stmt.registerOutParameter(2,Types.FLOAT);
```

Here, the out parameter is registered as FLOAT type. All types are defined in Types class of java.sql package. Some types are:

```
Types.INTEGER
Types.FLOAT
Types.CHAR
Types.BOOLEAN
Types.DOUBLE
Types.DATE
```

Once the 2nd parameter (i.e., out parameter) is registered, the CallableStatement should be executed, as:

```
stmt.execute();
```

Now the result comes from the stored procedure into 2nd parameter, which should be collected into incsal variable, as:

```
float incsal= stmt.getFloat(2);
```

These steps are shown in Program 12.

Program 12: In this program, we create CallableStatement to call the stored procedure and retrieve the result from oracle server.

```
/* Demonstrates how to call a stored procedure. Already the procedure is stored
at server. Aim of the procedure is to increment the salary of employee whose
eno=1003.
*/

import java.sql.*;
class CallProc
{
    public static void main(String args[])throws Exception
    {

    //register the driver
    DriverManager.registerDriver(new oracle.jdbc.driver.OracleDriver());

    //establish a connection with database
    Connection con;
    con = DriverManager.
    getConnection("jdbc:oracle:thin:@localhost:1521:xe","scott","tiger");

    //create CallableStatement to call myproc
    CallableStatement stmt = con.prepareCall("{ call  myproc(?,?)}");

    //set 1003 as employee number to in parameter
    stmt.setInt(1,1003);

    //register the out parameter as of float type
    stmt.registerOutParameter(2,Types.FLOAT);

    //execute CallableStatement
    stmt.execute();

    //get the result into incsal variable
    float incsal= stmt.getFloat(2);
    System.out.println("Incremented salary= "+ incsal);

    //close connection
    con.close();
    }
}
```

Output:

```
C:\> javac CallProc.java
C:\> java CallProc
Incremented salary= 15500.00
```

When we executed the stored procedure 'myproc', notice that it will not modify the actual salary in the emptab. To modify the actual salary, we should use 'update' statement also in the stored procedure.

CallableStatement is useful to call not only stored procedures, but also functions written in PL/SQL. To understand this, let us first write a function that takes a number from us and returns its square value.

```
-- myfun.sql
-- function that returns square of a number
```

create or replace function myfun(i number) return number as:

```
BEGIN
    return i*i;
END myfun;
```

Here, we use create or replace key word to create function. Our function name is 'myfun' that accepts a number through in parameter 'i'. Then square value is calculated by the expression i*i and returned by this function.

Type this function code at SQL> prompt. At the end type '/' and press <Enter>. It displays a message: Function created.

Let us write a Java program to call this myfun function.

Program 13: This program uses CallableStatement to call a function and gets the returned value from the function.

```
/* Demonstrates how to call a function
   To increment salary of employee whose eno=1003
*/
import java.sql.*;
class CallFun{
    public static void main(String args[])throws Exception
    {
        //register a driver
        DriverManager.registerDriver(new oracle.jdbc.driver.OracleDriver());
        //establish a connection with database
        Connection con;
        con =
DriverManager.getConnection("jdbc:oracle:thin:@localhost:1521:oracle","scott"
,"tiger");

        //create CallableStatement and call myfun. Here, first ? is out parameter
        //and second ? is in parameter.
        CallableStatement stmt =  con.prepareCall("{?= call  myfun(?)}");

        //register the out parameter as integer type
        stmt.registerOutParameter(1,Types.INTEGER);
        //set the in parameter to 50
        stmt.setInt(2,50);
        //execute the CallableStatement
        stmt.execute();
        //get the result from out parameter into value
        int value= stmt.getInt(1);
        System.out.println("Square value= "+value );

    }
}
```

Output:

```
C:\> javac CallFun.java
C:\> java CallFun
Square value= 2500
```

What is the use of CallableStatement?

CallableStatement is useful to call stored procedures and functions which run at a database server and get the results into the client.

Types of Result Sets

There are two types of Result sets, namely, Forward ResultSet and Scrollable ResultSet. So far, in our programs, we retrieved the results into a ResultSet object rs, as shown:

```
Statement stmt = con.createStatement();
ResultSet rs = stmt.executeQuery("select * from emptab");
```

Since the results are available in 'rs', we can retrieve the rows one by one in forward direction using rs.next() method. Suppose we want to retrieve the rows in reverse direction, is there any method like rs.previous()? Fortunately this method is available, but it is not supported by the ResutlSet object 'rs'. This means using ResultSet, it is possible to move in forward direction only. This is called 'forward result set'.

There is another type of result set, where we can move in both forward and backward directions. This is called 'scrollable result set'. This type of result set is created by passing two constants to createStatement() method, as:

```
Statement stmt = con.createStatement(CONST1, CONST2);
```

Here, CONST1 may take any one of the following:

```
ResultSet.TYPE_SCROLL_SENSITIVE
ResultSet.TYPE_SCROLL_INSENSITIVE
```

And CONST2 may be one of the following:

```
ResultSet.CONCUR_READ_ONLY
ResultSet.CONCUR_UPDATABLE
```

The constant ResultSet.TYPE_SCROLL_SENSITIVE represents that any changes done to the ResultSet will also affect the database. Where as, the constant ResultSet.TYPE_SCROLL_INSENSITIVE indicates that any changes done to the ResultSet will not reflect in the database. Most of the driver vendors provide this type of result set only (TYPE_SCROLL_INSENSITIVE), since they feel that there will be more load on the driver if they provide TYPE_SCROLL_SENSITIVE nature to the driver.

ResultSet.CONCUR_READ_ONLY represents that we can read the data from the ResultSet object, it cannot be modified. When ResultSet.CONCUR_UPDATABLE is used, it allows insertion, updating and deletion activities on the rows of the result set.

The following are the important methods that act on scrollable result set:

Table 32.3

Method	Its use
rs.next()	Moves the result set reference to the next row.
rs.previous()	Moves the result set reference to the previous row.

Method	Its use
rs.first()	Moves to the first row.
rs.last()	Moves to the last row.
rs.absolute(int n)	Moves to the nth row in the result set.
rs.updateRow()	Updates the data in a row.
rs.insertRow()	Inserts a row into the result set.
rs.deleteRow()	Deletes a row from result set and also from the database.
rs.getRow()	Returns the number of the current row.

Important Interview Question

What is scrollable result set?

Scrollable result set represents a result set object where moving in forward and backward direction is possible. It also provides methods to update the rows in the result set.

Let us write a JDBC program using scrollable result set where we want to do some modifications to the rows in the result set, which should also be applied to the database. For this purpose, the Statement object should be created as:

```
Statement stmt = con.createStatement(ResultSet.TYPE_SCROLL_SENSITIVE,
        ResultSet.CONCUR_UPDATABLE);
```

In this program, we can update a row following the steps:

❑ First, go to the row to be updated. For example, to update 3rd row:

```
rs.absolute(3);
```

❑ Set new data in the columns of the row.

```
rs.updateInt(1, 1006);
rs.updateString(2, "aaaaa");
rs.updateFloat(3, 4500.50f);
```

❑ Re-write the row with new data.

```
rs.updateRow();
```

The same way, if we want to insert a new row into the table:

❑ Allot memory for storing one row's data.

```
rs.moveToInsertRow();
```

❑ Store new data into the row.

```
rs.updateInt(1, 1000);
rs.updateString(2, "xxxxxx");
rs.updateFloat(3, 9999.90f);
```

❑ Now insert the new row into the table, as:

```
rs.insertRow();
```

The way to delete a row follows as:

❑ Go to the row to be deleted. To delete 4th row:

```
rs.absolute(4);
```

❑ Now, delete the row from the table.

```
rs.deleteRow();
```

Oracle 10g xe is made scroll sensitive. So we should use this database in our program. Earlier versions like Oracle 8 and Oracle 8i do not support scrollable result sets.

Program 14: This program uses scrollable result set to retrieve the data from the database and also perform operations like inserting new row, deletion and updation of rows.

```java
// Demonstrates how to use scrollable result sets
import java.sql.*;
class RS
{
    public static void main(String args[])throws Exception
    {
    //register the driver
    DriverManager.registerDriver(new oracle.jdbc.driver.OracleDriver());
    //connet to Oracle 10g xe database
    Connection con =
    DriverManager.getConnection("jdbc:oracle:thin:@localhost:1521:xe","scott",
    "tiger");
    //create scroll sensitive, scrollable result set
    Statement stmt = con.createStatement(ResultSet.TYPE_SCROLL_SENSITIVE,
    ResultSet.CONCUR_UPDATABLE);
    //execute the query
    ResultSet rs = stmt.executeQuery("select * from emptab");
    //display all the rows from result set
    while(rs.next()){
            System.out.println(rs.getString(1));
            System.out.println(rs.getString(2));
            System.out.println(rs.getString(3));
            System.out.println("=========================");

    }
    //display only first row
    rs.first();
    System.out.println("=======first()==========");
    System.out.println(rs.getInt(1));
    System.out.println(rs.getString(2));
    System.out.println(rs.getFloat(3));
    System.out.println("=========================");
    //display 3rd row
    rs.absolute(3);
    System.out.println("=======absolute(3)======");
    System.out.println(rs.getInt(1));
    System.out.println(rs.getString(2));
    System.out.println(rs.getFloat(3));
    System.out.println("=========================");
    //wait till Enter pressed
    System.in.read();
    //find how many rows are there in this resultset
    rs.last();
    System.out.println("No of Rows= "+rs.getRow());
```

```
                    //wait till Enter pressed
                    System.in.read();
                    //make the query again
                    rs = stmt.executeQuery("select eno,ename,sal from emptab");
                    //update 3rd row in result set and store it into the database
                    rs.absolute(3);
                    rs.updateInt(1,1006);
                    rs.updateString(2,"Laxman Kumar");
                    rs.updateFloat(3,4500f);
                    rs.updateRow();
                    //wait till Enter pressed
                    System.in.read();
                    //insert a new row
                    rs.moveToInsertRow();
                    rs.updateInt(1,1000);
                    rs.updateString(2,"Mahesh");
                    rs.updateFloat(3,3990f);
                    rs.insertRow();
                    //wait till Enter pressed
                    System.in.read();
                    //delete 4th row
                    rs.absolute(4);
                    rs.deleteRow();
                    //close the result set
                    rs.close();
                    //close connection with the database
                    con.close();
                    }
        }
```

Output:

```
C:\> set classpath=C:\jars\ojdbc14.jar;.;
C:\> javac RS.java
C:\> java RS
777
Vijaya
5600.75
====================
779
Satyaraj
5000
====================
1001
Nagesh
12000.5
====================
1002
Venkat
2000
====================
======first()==========
777
Vijaya
5600.75
====================
======absolute(3)======
1001
Nagesh
12000.5
====================
<Enter>
No of Rows= 4
<Enter>
<Enter>
C:\>
```

Now check the database to find out if the above changes are also reflected in the database table.

Storing Images into Database

SQL offers BLOB (Binary Large Object) data type to store image files like .gif or .jpg into the database table. At the time of creating table, the data type of the column where we plan to store the image should be declared as 'blob' type. Suppose we want to store an image in the first column 'photo'. The number is the next column 'no'. The table can be created as:

```
create table bigtab(photo blob, no int);
```

To store an image into photo column of the 'bigtab' table, we should follow the steps:

❑ Load the image into a File object.

```
File f = new File("x.gif");
```

❑ Attach the File object to FileInputStream for reading the image.

```
FileInputStream fis = new FileInputStream(f);
```

❑ Read the image using FileInputStream and store it into the table using setBinaryStream() method of Statement interface.

```
stmt.setBinaryStream(1, fis, (int)f.length());
```

Here, 1 represents the first column of the table where the image should be stored. fis represents the FileInputStream object that reads the image and f.length() gives the image size in bytes.

❑ Execute the statement using executeUpdate(). Then the image is stored into the table.

```
stmt.executeUpdate();
```

Program 15: In this program, we store an image x.gif into the first column of the bigtab table. In this program, we use PreparedStatement.

```
/* This program demonstrates how to store binary data(image) */
import java.io.*;
import java.sql.*;
public class StoreImage
{
    public static void main(String args[])throws Exception
    {

    //register the driver
    DriverManager.registerDriver(new oracle.jdbc.driver.OracleDriver());

    //establish connection
    Connection con;
    con =
DriverManager.getConnection("jdbc:oracle:thin:@localhost:1521:xe","scott",
    "tiger");

    //use PreparedStatement to update the table: bigtab
    PreparedStatement stmt = con.prepareStatement("update bigtab set photo
=? where no = 10");
    //Load the photo or image into a File object.
```

```
        File f = new File("plane.GIF");

        //Attach the file to FileInputStream for reading the image
        FileInputStream fis = new FileInputStream(f);

        //Write the file contents into the table
        stmt.setBinaryStream(1,fis,(int)f.length());
        System.out.println("Image length = " + f.length());

        //Execute the statement
        System.out.println("No of rows affected = "+stmt.executeUpdate());
    }
}
```

Output:

```
C:\> set classpath=C:\jars\ojdbc14.jar;.;
C:\> javac StoreImage.java
C:\> java StoreImage

Image length = 34040
No of rows affected = 1
```

Retrieving Images from Database

❑   Get the image from the table into Blob class object.

```
Blob b = rs.getBlob(1);
```

Here, 1 represents the 1st column from where the image is retrieved and stored into b.

❑   Create a byte array and store the image from b into the byte array.

```
byte arr[] = new byte[size of image];
arr = b.getBytes(1, (int)b.length());
```

Here, getBytes() method is retrieving the image from b, starting from 1st byte and the entire length of the image is retrieved(all bytes).

❑   Write this byte array arr into a file.

```
FileOutputStream fos = new FileOutputStream("x1.gif");
fos.write(arr);
```

It means that the image is stored into the file as x1.gif file.

Program 16: This program retrieves the image from 1st column of bigtab and stores it in the current directory with the name x1.gif.

```
/* Demonstrates how to retrieve binary data(image) */
import java.sql.*;
import java.io.*;

public class GetImage
{
    public static void main(String args[])throws Exception
    {
        //register the driver
        DriverManager.registerDriver(new oracle.jdbc.driver.OracleDriver());
```

```
                        //establish connection
                        Connection con =
                        DriverManager.getConnection("jdbc:oracle:thin:@localhost:1521:xe","scott",
                        "tiger");

                        //create a statement
                        Statement stmt = con.createStatement();

                        //execute the statement
                        ResultSet rs = stmt.executeQuery("select * from bigtab");

                        //go to first row
                        rs.next();

                        //Get the image from the table into Blob object.
                        Blob b = rs.getBlob(1);

                        //Create a byte array having the size of image
                        byte b1[] = new byte[(int)b.length()];

                        //store the Blob object into the byte array.
                        b1 = b.getBytes(1,(int)b.length());

                        System.out.println("Image length = "+ b.length());

                        //Write this byte array into a file: x1.gif
                        FileOutputStream fos = new FileOutputStream("x1.gif");
                        fos.write(b1);

                        //close the file
                        fos.close();

                        //close connection
                        con.close();
                        }
        }
```

Output:

```
        C:\> set classpath=C:\jars\ojdbc14.jar;.;
        C:\> javac GetImage.java
        C:\> java GetImage
        Image length = 34040
```

Open x1.gif file to see the image that is stored into the bigtab of the database.

Storing a file into database

To store a large volume of data as well as text files into a table, we can take the help of CLOB (Character Large Object) datatype of SQL. Using CLOB, it is possible to store an entire file, a text book or a resume etc., into a column of the table.

First, create a table with the name myclob to store a text file.

```
        create table myclob(col1 clob, col2 int);
```

Here the first column is declared as 'clob' type where we can store a text file. Now insert a row into myclob as:

```
        insert into myclob(col2) values(100);
```

Here, we are not inserting any thing into col1, but inserting 100 into col2.

Now, following the steps to insert a text file into col1 of myclob table.

❏ Load myfile.txt into File object as:

```
File f = new File("myfile.txt");
```

❏ To read data from File object f, connect it to a FileReader.

```
FileReader fr = new FileReader(f);
```

❏ Now, read data from the FileReader and send it to 1st column of the table using `setCharacterStream()` method.

```
Stmt.setCharacterStream(1, fr, (int)f.length());
```

Here, 1 represents that the data should be set to 1st column. The data is read from 'fr' and the length of the file is given by `f.length()`.

Program 17: In this program, we store `myfile.txt` file into myclob table. See that the file `myfile.txt` already exists in the present directory.

```java
//To store a file content into a table
import java.io.*;
import java.sql.*;
class ClobDemo
{
      public static void main(String args[]) throws Exception
      {
      //register the driver
      DriverManager.registerDriver(new oracle.jdbc.driver.OracleDriver());

      //establish connection
      Connection con =
      DriverManager.getConnection("jdbc:oracle:thin:@localhost:1521:xe","scott",
      "tiger");

      //create SQL statement
      PreparedStatement stmt = con.prepareStatement("update myclob set col1= ?
      where col2 = 100");

      //load the file into File object
      File f = new File("myfile.txt");

      //connect the File to FileReader for reading
      FileReader fr = new FileReader(f);

      //store the file into col1 as character stream
      stmt.setCharacterStream(1, fr, (int)f.length());

      //disply file size
      System.out.println("File size= "+ f.length());

      //execute the statement
      System.out.println("No. of rows affected= "+ stmt.executeUpdate());

      //close connection
      con.close();
      }
}
```

Output:

```
C:\> set classpath=C:\jars\ojdbc14.jar;.;
C:\> javac ClobDemo.java
C:\> java ClobDemo
```

```
File size= 1881
No. of rows affected= 1
```

Retrieving a File from the Database

To retrieve the file from the column of a table, we can follow the steps:

❑ First, we should retrieve the file from the result set using getClob() method.

```
Clob c = rs.getClob(1);
```

Here, getClob() method is retrieving data from 1st column and storing it into Clob class object c.

❑ Use getCharacterStream() method to get the file data from the Clob object into a reader object.

```
Reader r = c.getCharacterStream();
```

❑ Store the data from Reader into a new file with the name newfile.txt.

```
FileWriter fw = new FileWriter("newfile.txt");
while((ch = r.read()) != -1)
    fw.write((char)ch);
```

Here, we are reading data from Reader object r and writing it into FileWriter which stores it into newfile.txt.

Program 18: In this program, we read the contents of myfile.txt file from myclob table and store the same into newfile.txt.

```
//To retrieve text file content from a table
import java.io.*;
import java.sql.*;
class ClobDemo1
{
    public static void main(String args[]) throws Exception
    {
    //register the driver
    DriverManager.registerDriver(new oracle.jdbc.driver.OracleDriver());

    //establish connection
    Connection con =
    DriverManager.getConnection("jdbc:oracle:thin:@localhost:1521:xe","scott",
    "tiger");

    //create SQL statement
    Statement stmt = con.createStatement();

    //read table rows into ResultSet
    ResultSet rs = stmt.executeQuery("select * from myclob");

    //go to first row
    rs.next();

    //read data from col1
    Clob c = rs.getClob(1);

    //display file length
    System.out.println("File size= "+ c.length());

    //read file data from c and store into Reader object
```

```
            Reader r = c.getCharacterStream();

            //read data from Reader and write into newfile.txt
            int ch;
            FileWriter fw = new FileWriter("newfile.txt");
            while((ch = r.read()) != -1)
            fw.write((char)ch);

            //close the file
            fw.close();

            //close the connection
            con.close();
            }
    }
```

Output:

```
    C:\> set classpath=C:\jars\ojdbc14.jar;.;
    C:\> javac ClobDemo1.java
    C:\> java ClobDemo1
    File size= 1881
```

Important Interview Question

What is BLOB?

   Binary Large Object (BLOB) is a SQL datatype that represents binary data to be stored into a database. BLOB helps us to store images into a database.

What is CLOB?

   Character Large Object (CLOB) is a SQL datatype that represents larger volumes of text data. CLOB helps to store text files into a database.

ResultSetMetaData

ResultSetMetaData is an interface which contains methods to get information about the types and properties of the columns in a ResultSet object. The following program demonstrates how to use retrieve the information about the ResultSet.

ResultSet has a method getMetaData() which returns the information about the result set into ResultSetMetaData object. It can be called as:

```
    ResultSetMetaData rsmd =rs.getMetaData();
```

Program 19: Let us find out the information of the columns of the table: emptab This information is available in ResultSet object which can be again retrieved into ResultSetMetaData.

```
    /* Demonstrates how to find out ResultSet information
        using ResultSetMetaData
    */

    import java.sql.*;
    class RSInfo
    {
        public static void main(String args[])throws Exception
        {

        //register the driver
        Class.forName("oracle.jdbc.driver.OracleDriver");
```

```
                    //establish a connection
                    Connection con =
                    DriverManager.getConnection("jdbc:oracle:thin:@localhost:1521:xe","scott",
                    "tiger");

                    //create the statement
                    Statement stmt = con.createStatement();

                    //get rows into ResultSet object
                    ResultSet rs = stmt.executeQuery("select * from emptab");

                    //get information about result into ResultSetMetaData
                    ResultSetMetaData rsmd =rs.getMetaData();

                    //count no. of columns in resultset
                    int n= rsmd.getColumnCount();
                    System.out.println("No. of columns= "+n);

                    //display information about each column
                    for(int i=1; i<=n; i++)
                    {
                    System.out.println("Column Number: "+i);
                    System.out.println("=====================");
                    System.out.println("Column name= "+rsmd.getColumnName(i));
                    System.out.println("Column type= "+rsmd.getColumnTypeName(i));
                    System.out.println("Column width= "+rsmd.getColumnDisplaySize(i));
                    System.out.println("Column Precision= "+rsmd.getPrecision(i));
                    System.out.println("Is currency= "+rsmd.isCurrency(i));
                    System.out.println("Is Read Only= "+rsmd.isReadOnly(i));
                    System.out.println("Is Writable= "+rsmd.isWritable(i));
                    System.out.println("Is Searchable= "+rsmd.isSearchable(i));
                    System.out.println("Is Signed= "+rsmd.isSigned(i));
                    }

                    //close connection
                    con.close();
                    }
            }
```

Output:

```
C:\> set classpath=c:\jars\ojdbc14.jar;.;
C:\> javac RSInfo.java
C:\> java RSInfo

No. of columns= 3
Column Number: 1
=====================
Column name= ENO
Column type= NUMBER
Column width= 22
Column Precision= 38
Is currency= true
Is Read Only= false
Is Writable= true
Is Searchable= true
Is Signed= true
Column Number: 2
=====================
Column name= ENAME
Column type= VARCHAR2
Column width= 20
Column Precision= 20
Is currency= false
Is Read Only= false
Is Writable= true
Is Searchable= true
```

```
Is Signed= true
Column Number: 3
=====================
Column name= SAL
Column type= NUMBER
Column width= 22
Column Precision= 126
Is currency= true
Is Read Only= false
Is Writable= true
Is Searchable= true
Is Signed= true
```

DatabaseMetaData

DatabaseMetaData is an interface to get comprehensive information about the database as a whole. This interface is implemented by driver vendors to let users know the capabilities of a Database Management System (DBMS) in combination with the JDBC driver that is used with it.

To know which tables and views are available in a database, we can use getTables() method, which is in the form shown below:

```
ResultSet  rs = dbmd.getTables(String catalog, String schemaPattern, String
tableNamePattern, String[] types);
```

Here, we can pass null objects to catalog, schemaPattern and tableNamePattern. For the 4th parameter, we can pass a String type array that contains the type: table or view, as:

```
String x[] = {"TABLE"};  //if this is passed, information of all tables is
retrieved
String x[] = {"VIEW"};   //if this is passed, information of all views is
retrieved
```

Program 20: In this program, let us connect to oracle database with thin driver and let us know which features are offered by the database and driver vendors.

```
//Demonstrates how to find out Database Capabilities  using DatabaseMetaData
import java.sql.*;
class DBCap
{
      public static void main(String args[])throws Exception
      {

      //register driver
      Class.forName("oracle.jdbc.driver.OracleDriver");

      //establish connection with database
      Connection con =
      DriverManager.getConnection("jdbc:oracle:thin:@localhost:1521:xe","scott",
      "tiger");

      //get the information about the database into DatabaseMetaData
      DatabaseMetaData dbmd =con.getMetaData();

      //display information about the database
      System.out.println("DB Name= "+dbmd.getDatabaseProductName());
      System.out.println("DB Version= "+dbmd.getDatabaseProductVersion());
      System.out.println("DB Driver Name= "+dbmd.getDriverName());
      System.out.println("Driver Major Version= "+
      dbmd.getDriverMajorVersion());
      System.out.println("Driver Minor Version= "+
```

```
            dbmd.getDriverMinorVersion());
            System.out.println("URL of DB= "+dbmd.getURL());
            System.out.println("Current UserName= "+dbmd.getUserName());

            System.out.println("==========TABLES==============");
            String t[] = {"TABLE"};
            ResultSet rs= dbmd.getTables(null,null,null,t);
            while(rs.next())
            {
                    System.out.println(rs.getString("TABLE_NAME"));
            }
            //wait till Enter pressed
            System.in.read();
            System.out.println("==========VIEWS==============");
            String v[] = {"VIEW"};
            rs= dbmd.getTables(null,null,null,v);
            while(rs.next())
            {
                    System.out.println(rs.getString("TABLE_NAME"));
            }
            //close connection
            con.close();
            }
    }
```

Output:

```
C:\> set classpath=c:\jars\ojdbc14.jar;.;
C:\> javac DBCap.java
C:\> java DBCap

DB Name= Oracle
DB Version= Oracle Database 10g Express Edition Release 10.2.0.1.0 - Production
DB Driver Name= Oracle JDBC driver
Driver Major Version= 10
Driver Minor Version= 2
URL of DB= jdbc:oracle:thin:@localhost:1521:xe
Current UserName= SCOTT
==========TABLES==============
DR$CLASS
DR$DBO
DR$DELETE
DR$INDEX
:
:
COUNTRIES
DEPARTMENTS
EMPLOYEES
JOBS
JOB_HISTORY
LOCATIONS
REGIONS
:
:
<Enter>
==========VIEWS==============
CTX_CLASSES
CTX_INDEXES
CTX_INDEX_ERRORS
CTX_INDEX_OBJECTS
CTX_INDEX_PARTITIONS
CTX_INDEX_SETS
CTX_INDEX_SET_INDEXES
CTX_INDEX_SUB_LEXERS
CTX_INDEX_SUB_LEXER_VALUES
CTX_INDEX_VALUES
CTX_OBJECTS
```

```
CTX_OBJECT_ATTRIBUTES
CTX_OBJECT_ATTRIBUTE_LOV
CTX_PARAMETERS
CTX_PENDING
CTX_PREFERENCES
        :
        :
```

Types of JDBC Drivers

There are 4 types of JDBC drivers. Each driver will have its own advantages and disadvantages, as well. Let us have a look at these drivers one by one.

Type 1

❑ **JDBC-ODBC Bridge driver:** This driver receives any JDBC calls and sends them to ODBC (Open DataBase Connectivity) driver. ODBC driver understands these calls and communicates with the database library provided by the vendor. So, the ODBC driver, and the vendor database library must be present on the client machine. See Figure 32.14.

❑ **Advantages:** The JDBC-ODBC Bridge allows access to almost any database, since the database's ODBC drivers are already available on the client machine.

❑ **Disadvantages:** The performance of this driver is less, since the JDBC call goes through the bridge to the ODBC driver, then to the native database connectivity library. The result comes back through the reverse process.

Another requirement is that the ODBC driver and the native database connectivity library must already be installed on the client machine.

TYPE 1: JDBC- ODBC BRIDGE DRIVER

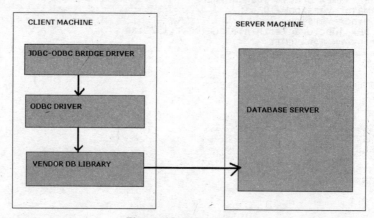

Figure 32.14 Type I driver

Type 2

❑ **Native API-partly Java driver:** It converts JDBC calls into database-specific calls with the help of vendor database library. The type 2 driver communicates directly with the database server; therefore it requires that some binary code be present on the client machine. See Figure 32.15.

❑ **Advantages:** Type 2 drivers typically offer better performance than the JDBC-ODBC Bridge.

❑ **Disadvantages:** The vendor database library needs to be loaded on each client machine. This is the reason; type 2 drivers cannot be used for the Internet. Type 2 drivers show lower performance than type 3 and type 4 drivers.

TYPE 2: NATIVE API - PARTLY JAVA DRIVER

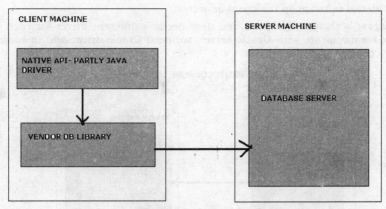

Figure 32.15 Type 2 driver

Type 3

❑ **Net protocol-pure Java driver:** It follows a three-tiered approach whereby the JDBC database requests are passed through the network to a middle-tier server (Ex: Net Server). The middle-tier server translates the request to the database-specific library and then sends it to the database server. The database server then executes the request and gives back the results. See Figure 32.16.

❑ **Advantages:** This driver is server-based, so there is no need for any vendor database library to be present on the client machines.

❑ **Disadvantages:** Type 3 drivers require database-specific coding to be done in the middle tier (in NetServer). Maintenance of the middle-tier server becomes costly.

TYPE 3: NET PROTOCOL PURE JAVA DRIVER

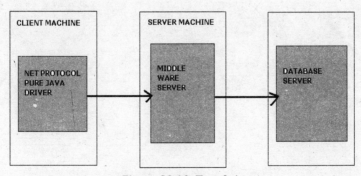

Figure 32.16 Type 3 driver

Type 4

❑ **Native protocol-pure Java driver:** This driver converts JDBC calls into the vendor-specific database management system (DBMS) protocol so that client applications can communicate directly with the database server. Level 4 drivers are completely implemented in Java to achieve platform independence and eliminate deployment administration issues. See Figure 32.17. Generally type 4 drivers are used on Internet.

❏ **Advantages:** This driver has better performance than types 1 and 2. Also, there's no need to install any special software on the client or server.

❏ **Disadvantages:** With type 4 drivers, the user needs a different driver for each database. For example, to communicate with Oracle server, we need Oracle driver and to communicate with Sybase server, we need Sybase driver.

TYPE 4: NATIVE PROTOCOL PURE JAVA DRIVER

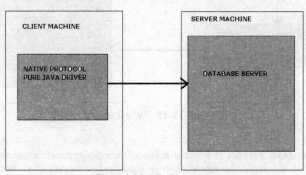

Figure 32.17 Type 4 driver

Conclusion

JDBC helps to communicate with any database through a Java program which is an essential feature for any project development environment, since each software requires data representing different transactions to be stored and retrieved later on demand. JDBC eliminates the need of mastering the commands to communicate with different databases by providing a common mechanism to communicate with any database in the world. Each time the database is changed, the Java program need not be changed and hence this provides better maintenance of code across different platforms.

ENUMERATIONS AND ANNOTATIONS

I n this chapter, you learn about some special elements of Java language called enumerations and annotations. Similar to classes and interfaces, enumerations and annotations are also a type in Java that can be implemented in several Java elements. As an enumeration is similar to a class, you can create instance variables, methods, and constructors inside it. You can also find the concept of enumerations in other programming languages, such as C, C++. In Java, annotations are also used to add metadata information to the Java elements.

Enumerations

An enumeration is similar to a class that contains only constant values. Remember a constant represents a fixed value and it does not change. For example, as there are fixed number of days in a week, namely Sunday, Monday, Tuesday, Wednesday, Thursday, Friday and Saturday, you can . take these days as constants and construct the following enumeration called Days:

```
enum Days{
     SUNDAY, MONDAY, TUESDAY, WEDNESDAY, THURSDAY, FRIDAY, SATURDAY
}
```

An enumeration is always represented by the word enum, followed by the name of the enumeration, which in this case is Days. After this, you need to write the constants within a pair of {}. In the preceding code snippet, the constants are written in capital letters; however, you can also use small letters to represent constants. Each of these constant can be referred by its individual name, such as Days.SUNDAY, Days. MONDAY.

The following code snippet shows another enumeration, Color, with some color names as constants:

```
enum Color{
    RED, GREEN, BLUE, WHITE, BLACK
}
```

The position of constants inside an enumeration will be counted from 0 onwards. For example, in the preceding code snippet, the 0 position is given to RED, 1 to GREEN, and 2 to BLUE.

You can also retrieve all the constants from an enumeration by using the values() method. It is a static method, which returns all the constants into an array of enumeration-type.

The syntax to use the values() method is given in the following code snippet:

```
Days alldays[ ] = Days.values();
```

In the preceding code snippet, the values() method is used on Days enumeration which returns all the constants into alldays[ ] array, so that alldays[0] represents SUNDAY, alldays[1] represents MONDAY, and so on. These values can be retrieved separately again from alldays[ ] using a for each loop, as shown in the following code snippet:

```
for(Days d: alldays)
System.out.println(d);
```

Now, let's write some programs to learn how to work with enumerations in Java:

Program 1: Write a Java program to declare an enumeration, Days,and retrieve all days from it using the values() method.

```
//create an enumeration with day names
enum Days
{
    Sunday, Monday, Tuesday, Wednesday, Thursday, Friday, Saturday
}
class DisplayEnum
{
    public static void main(String args[ ])
    {
        //using values() method retrieve all enum constants into
        //alldays[ ] array
        Days alldays[ ] = Days.values();
        //using for each loop, retrieve the enum constants from
        //alldays[ ] and display them
        for(Days d: alldays)
            System.out.println(d);
    }
}
```

The output of Program 1 is as follows:

```
C:\>javac DisplayEnum.java
C:\>java DisplayEnum
Sunday
Monday
Tuesday
Wednesday
Thursday
Friday
Saturday
```

Since enumeration has constants, they can be used to perform various tasks inside a switch statement depending upon the choice of the user. For example, the form of the Color enumeration can be represented by the following code snippet:

```
enum Color{
    RED, GREEN, BLUE, WHITE, BLACK
}
```

The constants of the preceding code snippet can be used with the case option in the switch statement, as shown in the following code snippet:

```
switch(c) //here c represents the Color constant
{
    case RED: System.out.println("Red color");
    case GREEN: System.out.println("Green color");
    .....
}
```

Program 2: Write a program to create an enumeration with color names and then display the name of a particular color depending on a specific choice.

```
//create a Color enumeration with color names as constants
enum Color{
    RED, GREEN, BLUE, WHITE, BLACK
}

//we want to use the Color enumeration in this class
class ColorTest
{
    //enumeration constant is declared as instance variable
    Color c;

    //initialize the variable
    ColorTest(Color c)
    {
        this.c = c;
    }
    /*this method displays the color name depending on the constant.
    if BLACK color is given, it will display 'Not a good color'*/
    void display()
    {
        switch(c)
        {
            case RED: System.out.println("Red color"); break;
            case GREEN: System.out.println("Green color"); break;
            case BLUE: System.out.println("Blue color"); break;
            case WHITE: System.out.println("White color"); break;
            default: System.out.println("Not a good color");
        }
    }
    public static void main(String args[ ])
    {
        //create ColorTest object and pass a color as choice
        ColorTest ct = new ColorTest(Color.GREEN);
        //call display() method to display the color name
        ct.display();
    }
}
```

The output of Program 2 is as follows:

```
C:\> javac ColorTest.java
C:\> java ColorTest
Green color
```

Important Interview Question

What are enumerations?

Enumerations are similar to classes in Java that contain a fixed set of constants. Enumerations are useful when dealing with a sequence of fixed values.

Now, let's declare another enumeration with the name, Icecream,, with the varieties of ice creams along with their prices, as shown in the following code snippet:

```
enum Icecream {
        Vanilla(20.00), Chocolate(22.50), Strawberry(23.00), Raspberry(25.00);
}
```

In the preceding code snippet, Vanilla(20.00) represents the constant, Vanilla, and its price Rs. 20.00. All enumerations in Java are considered as class types. In fact, they are all subclasses of the Enum class of the java.lang package. Since all enumerations inherit the Enum class, they cannot inherit any other class. This is because Java does not support multiple inheritance. Since enumerations are class types, it is possible to write instance variables, constructors and methods inside an enumeration, as shown in the following code snippet:

```
enum Icecream {
    //constants in the enumeration
    Vanilla(20.00), Chocolate(22.50), Strawberry(23.00), Raspberry(25.00);

    //an instance variable
    private double price;

    //a parameterized constructor which initializes price with p
    Icecream(double p)
    {
        price = p;
    }
} //end of enumeration
```

It is also possible to include the getPrice() method to retrieve the price of any constant, as shown in the following code snippet:

```
static void getPrice(int i)
{
    Icecream allicecreams[ ] = Icecream.values();
    System.out.println("Pay Rs. "+allicecreams[i].price);

}
```

For example, if you call the method as getPrice(0), the 0th constant, that is Vanilla is referred and the allicecreams[0].price attribute of the Icecream enumeration represents the price of Vanilla, that is 20.00.

There is a method called ordinal() that is available in the Enum class. This method retrieves the position of constants in the enumeration. The ordinal()method starts counting from 0 onwards. For example, the ice.ordinal() method will retrieve 0 for Vanilla and 2 for Strawberry, where ice is the reference of the Icecream enumeration.

Program 3: Write a program to know how to create an enumeration with constants, instance variable, constructor, and a method.

```
import java.io.*;
//create enumeration with the name Icecream
enum Icecream
{
    //constants with values
    Vanilla(20.00), Chocolate(22.50), Strawberry(23.00), Raspberry(25.00);

//an instance variable
private double price;

//a parameterized constructor which initializes price with p
```

```
Icecream(double p)
{
  price = p;
}

//a static method to display the price upon taking the sequence number
static void getPrice(int i)
{
    Icecream allicecreams[ ] = Icecream.values();
    System.out.println("Pay Rs. "+allicecreams[i].price);
}
} //end of enumeration
class GetEnum
{
  public static void main(String args[ ]) throws IOException
  {
    //Display all the icecreams available from the enumeration.
    System.out.println("AVAILABLE ICECREAMS");
    for(Icecream ice: Icecream.values())
    {
      //ordinal() method starts counting from 0
      int no = ice.ordinal();
      System.out.println(no+"  "+ ice);
    }
    //Get the user choice as a number
    BufferedReader br = new BufferedReader(new InputStreamReader(System.in));
    System.out.print("Your choice: ");
    int choice = Integer.parseInt(br.readLine());
    Icecream.getPrice(choice);

  }
}
```

The output of Program 3 is as follows:

```
C:\> javac GetEnum.java
C:\> java GetEnum
AVAILABLE  ICECREAMS
0 Vanilla
1 Chocolate
2 Strawberry
3 Raspberry
Your choice: 1
Pay Rs. 22.5
```

After discussing enumerations, let's proceed to learn about annotations in Java.

To comprehend the total subject on enumerations, let us write another program. In this program, we are taking planets data as an enumeration. We want to use two values along with each constant as shown in the following code:

```
enum Planets
{
    Mercury(57910, 3.30e23), Venus(108200, 4.87e24), Earth(149600, 5.98e24);
}
```

Here, 'Mercury' is the constant which is nothing but a planet's name. It is associated with 2 values. The first one is 57910 which represents the distance of the planet in kilo meters from Sun and the second value is 3.30e23 which is the mass of the planet in kilograms. Since two values are there, we should take two variables in the enumeration, as:

```
private long distance;
private double mass;
```

The next step is to initialize the two variables, using a constructor, as:

```
Planets(long x, double y)
{
    distance = x;
    mass = y;
}
```

Since, we have two variables, it is advisable to write two accessor methods in the form of getDistance() and getMass() which return the distance and mass respectively.

```
long getDistance()
{
    return distance;
}

double getMass()
{
    return mass;
}
```

Now, to display the constants and the associated values, we should use values() method, as:

```
Planets p[] = Planets.values();
```

Here, p[0] represents the first planet's name, i.e. 'Mercury' and p[1] represents second planet's name, i.e. 'Venus', etc.

We should call the getDistance() method to retrieve the distance of the planet. So, p[0].getDistance() represents 57910 and p[1].getDistance() represents 108200, etc. Similarly, we can call getMass() method to retrieve corresponding mass of the planet, as: p[0].getMass(), p[1].getMass(), etc. This code can be implemented using for each loop, as:

```
for(Planets p: Planets.values())
{
    System.out.print(p);  //display planet name
    System.out.print(p.getDistance());  //display its distance
    System.out.print(p.getMass());  //display its mass
}
```

Program 4: Write a Java program to create an enumeration with planets names and their distances and mass. Then retrieve all the data and display in tabular form.

```
//retrieving enumeration constants and values.
enum Planets
{
    /*constants in the enumeration, each with 2 values.
      planets name, distance and mass. */
    Mercury(57910, 3.30e23), Venus(108200, 4.87e24),
    Earth(149600, 5.98e24), Mars(227940, 6.42e23), Jupiter(778330, 1.90e27);

    //take 2 variables to represent the 2 values
    private long distance;
    private double mass;

    //initialize the two variables
    Planets(long x, double y)
    {
        distance = x;
        mass = y;
    }
```

```
        //to retrieve distance values from enum
        long getDistance()
        {
            return distance;
        }

        //to retrieve mass values from enum
        double getMass()
        {
            return mass;
        }
}
class DisplayEnum1
{
        public static void main(String args[])
        {
            //this is for heading
            System.out.println("PLANET"+"\t\t"+"DISTANCE(Km)"+"\t"+"MASS(Kg)");

            //display all constants names and values
            for(Planets p: Planets.values())
            {
                System.out.print(p + "\t\t");
                System.out.print(p.getDistance() + "\t\t");
                System.out.print(p.getMass() + "\n");
            }
        }
}
```

The output of Program 4 is as follows:

```
C:\> javac DisplayEnum1.java
C:\> java DisplayEnum1

PLANET              DISTANCE(Km)              MASS(Kg)
Mercury             57910                     3.3E23
Venus               108200                    4.87E24
Earth               149600                    5.98E24
Mars                227940                    6.42E23
Jupiter             778330                    1.9E27
```

Annotations

Sometimes, while creating a program, you need to provide additional information regarding various programming elements, such as classes, interfaces, fields, or methods. Consider the following code snippet where the method1() method is defined in the A class by a particular programmer:

```
class A
{
    void method1()
    {

    }
}
```

Now, suppose that some other programmer needs to create a sub class, B, to the A class and wants to override the method1() in the B class. Once, he has created the B class with a method, he may want to check that his method is really overriding the method of the A class or not, since it is possible that the method name in the B class might be misspelled. To check this, he needs to attach additional information to the method in the B class, as shown in the following code snippet:

```
class B extends A
{
@Override
void method1()
{

}
}
```

In the preceding code snippet, the @Override tag is used to tell the Java compiler that the method of the B class should override the method of the A class. Now, the compiler checks whether or not the method1() method is available in the A class. If the method1() method is not available in the A class, then the compiler displays an error saying that "This method is not overriding the method of super class". Therefore, the @Override tag makes the Java compiler check whether or not the method in B is really overriding the method of A. This @Override tag is called an annotation.

So, what are annotations? Annotations are tags that provide additional information to the Java compiler or Java Virtual machine (JVM) regarding the declaration of a method, a field, a class, or an interface. You can also consider annotations as metadata since metadata represents data about data. In this case, annotations represent data about classes, methods, fields, and interfaces.

Important Interview Question

Define annotation.

An annotation is a tag attached to a programming element, such as a class, interface, field, or a method to indicate some additional information about that element, which can be verified and used by Java compiler or JVM.

While using an annotation, the @ symbol is used before it, such as @Override, @Deprecated, or @SuppressWarnings. All annotations are declared as the subtypes of the Annotation interface, which is available in the java.lang.annotation package. The purpose of annotations is to provide additional information about the programming elements that can be used to control the behavior of the compiler or configuring the application at runtime by the JVM.

Let's now discuss some of the common built-in annotations available in Java.

The @Override Annotation

The @Override annotation represents that a method in the sub class should override a method in its super class. If the sub class method does not actually overrides the super class method, then the Java compiler displays an error message. This annotation should be used only on methods.

To understand the @Override annotation, let's write a program. In this program, we create a class, named One with the doSomething() method. Another class, Two, is written as a subclass to the One class. In the Two class, we write another method, called doSomething(), which overrides the method of the One class. If, by mistake, the sub class method name is typed in lower case as dosomething(), then this method cannot override the super class method. To check if the sub class method actually overrides the super class method, you can use the @Override annotation above the sub class method.

Let's try to understand this concept better with the help of a program.

Program 5: Write a program to use the @Override annotation to check whether the sub class method really overrides the super class method or not.

```
// Let us write a super class with a method inside it.
class One
{
    void doSomething()
    {
```

```
                System.out.println("Hai");
        }
}
//The sub class method should override the super class method.
class Two extends One
{
    @Override
    void dosomething()
    {
        System.out.println("Hello");
    }
}
public class Test
{
    public static void main(String args[])
    {
        Two t = new Two();
        t.doSomething();
    }
}
```

The output of Program 5 is as follows:

```
C:\> javac Test.java
Test.java:11: method does not override or implement a method from a supertype
@Override
^
1 error
```

Observe that the method in the sub class is written as void dosomething(), whose name is not matching with the method in the super class; and therefore, it does not override the super class method. This is checked by Java compiler and it displays an error message in the output. On the other hand, if you write the method name in sub class as doSomething(), then no error is displayed.

The @SuppressWarnings Annotation

The @SuppressWarnings Annotation is used to suppress warnings issued by the compiler. This annotation can be applied to a class, method, or interface.

To understand the workings of the @SuppressWarnings annotation, let's take a program to create a Hashtable and store two pairs of key values.

Program 6: Write a program to create a Hashtable that stores roll number and name of two students as key-value pairs using the put() method.

```
//Compile this program using jdk1.6 compiler or later version of it.
import java.util.*;
class Sample
{
    public static void main(String args[])
    {
        Hashtable ht = new Hashtable();
        ht.put(10, "Lakshmi");
        ht.put(11, "Gopi Krishna");
    }
}
```

The output of Program 6 is as follows:

```
C:\> javac Sample.java
Note: Sample.java uses unchecked or unsafe operations.
Note: Recompile with -Xlint:unchecked for details.
```

The output of this program displays a message that this program uses unchecked or unsafe operations. Actually, there is no error in the program; however, the Java compiler (of jdk1.6 or above) has a much stronger type checking and expects us to create Hashtable object, as shown in the following code snippet:

```
Hashtable<Integer, String> ht = new Hashtable<Integer, String>();
```

The preceding code snippet tells the compiler that the key and value types are Integer and String. Since these types are not given, compiler is showing a warning message. Now, you can ask the compiler to suppress this message using the @SuppressWarnings tag above the main() method, as shown in the following code snippet:

```
/*The message given by java compiler is suppressed with the help of
        @SuppressWarnings annotation. */
import java.util.*;
class Sample
{
    @SuppressWarnings("unchecked")
    public static void main(String args[])
    {
        Hashtable ht = new Hashtable();
        ht.put(10, "Lakshmi");
        ht.put(11, "Gopi Krishna");
    }
}
```

In this case, there will not be any warning message given by Java compiler as @SupressWarnings annotation suppresses the unchecked warning messages.

The @Deprecated Annotation

The @Deprecated Annotation indicates to the compiler that the method is deprecated and hence its use should be avoided. It is not recommended to use deprecated methods, as they can be modified or removed from the future versions of Java. When a programmer wants to mark a method as deprecated, he can use the @Deprecated tag before that method. When this tag is used, the Java compiler displays a message that the method is deprecated. Let's try to understand the @Deprecated annotation with the help of a program.

Program 7: Write a program that uses a deprecated method in the Myclass class. When the user calls this method, the Java compiler should show a warning message saying that the method is deprecated.

```
/* Example to understand deprecated annotation */
class Myclass
{
    @Deprecated
    void myMethod()
    {
        System.out.println("This method is deprecated");
    }
}
class DeprecatedTest
{
    public static void main(String args[])
    {
        Myclass obj = new Myclass();
        obj.myMethod();
    }
}
```

The output of Program 7 is as follows:

```
C:\> javac DeprecatedTest.java
Note: DeprecatedTest.java uses or overrides a deprecated API.
Note: Recompile with -Xlint:deprecation for details.
```

Note that the myMethod() method in the Myclass class has been annotated using the @Deprecated annotation. Therefore, when the user calls this method from the DeprecatedTest class, the Java compiler shows a warning message as seen in the output of the preceding program.

Apart from the @Deprecated annotation, various other annotations, such as @Inherited and @Documented are also used in Java. For example, the @Inherited annotation, allows you to declare any annotation in a super class that can be inherited into its sub class. It implies that once an annotation is declared using the @Inherited annotation in the super class, the same annotation also applies to its sub class automatically.

Normally annotations are not documented by the javadoc compiler; however, if the @Documented tag is attached with an annotation, then that annotation appears in the Application Programming Interface (API) document created by the javadoc compiler, which then compiles the annotation.

Custom Annotations

Java contains several built-in annotations, such as @Override, @Deprecated, @SuppressWarnings, @Inherited, and @Documented. You can also create your own custom annotations in Java by using the @interface keyword, as shown in the following code snippet.

```
@interface MyAnno
```

In this case, MyAnno is the name of the annotation that you created. Defining an annotation is similar to defining a general interface in Java. Since an interface contains only abstract methods, you can also write the values (or members) of the annotation in the form of abstract methods, as shown in the following code snippet:

```
@interface MyAnno
{
        int value1();
        String value2();
}
```

In the preceding code snippet, the value1() and value2() methods represent members of the MyAnno annotation. These members provide additional information to the compiler or JVM about a class, method, or interface. To assign default values to the value1() and value2() members, you can write the same annotation as:

```
@interface MyAnno
{
        int value1() default 0;
        String value2() default  "";
}
```

In this case, 0 and a blank string are used as default values for value1() and value2() members. The following code snippet shows how to use this annotation:

```
@MyAnno()   //here default values are used for members
@MyAnno(value1=10, value2="Hello")   //here we assign 10 and Hello for members
```

The allotted data for value1 is 10 and for value2 is Hello, which can be retrieved later by the Java compiler or JVM.

While writing values (abstract methods) of annotations, you should keep the following rules in your mind:

❑ Methods should not have any parameters

❑ Methods should not have any throws clauses

❑ Methods should return one of the following: primitive datatypes, String, Class, enum or an array of these types

Types of Annotations

There are 3 types of annotations: Marker annotation, Single-value annotation, and Multi-value annotation. Let's discuss each one of them in detail.

The Marker Annotation

A marker annotation is an annotation that only has a name. It does not have any values or members associated with it. Marker annotation generally specifies some information about a class, interface, field, or method. The following code snippet shows an example for marker annotation:

```
@interface MyMarker
{ }
```

The @MyMarker tag is used to write the marker annotation.

The Built-in annotations, such as @Override and @Deprecated are some examples of marker annotations.

The Single-Value Annotation

A single-value annotation is an annotation that contains only one value or member. This member can be passed as a single value to a class, interface, or a method. To create a single-value annotation, you should use the @interface tag and the annotation name, as shown in the following code snippet:

```
@interface MySingle
{
    int value();
}
```

In the preceding code snippet, no default value is allotted for the member value() of the MySingle annotation. You can allot some default value for the member, as shown in the following code snippet:

```
@interface MySingle
{
    int value() default 1;
}
```

Note that the member name should be value() only. In the MySingle annotation, the member is declared with a default value of 1. If no other value is assigned for the member, then the default value of 1 is used.

To use this annotation by providing 100 value, we can write @MySingle(100)

In this case, you are providing 100 as value for the value() member. Another way to provide the value for the member is as follows:

```
@MySingle(value=100)
```

The Built-in annotation @SuppressWarnings is an example for single-value annotation.

The Multi-Value Annotation

A multi-value annotation contains more than one member. The following code snippet shows an example for multi-value annotation:

```
@interface MyMulti
{
    int value1();
    String value2();
    String value3();
}
```

In this case, MyMulti is the name of the annotation. It has 3 members: value1(), value2(), and value3(). No default values are assigned to these members. You can also assign default values to the members, as shown in the following code snippet:

```
@interface MyMulti
{
    int value1() default 1;
    String value2() default "";
    String value3() default "abc";
}
```

In this case, 1 is assigned as the default value for value1(), an empty string as default value for value2(), and the abc string as the default value for value3().

The following code snippet shows how to use this multi-value annotation:

```
@MyMulti(value2="Srinu", value3="Ameerpet, Hyderabad")
```

The preceding code snippet defines the data for value2 and value3 but not for value1.

```
@MyMulti(value1=10, value2="Srinu", value3="Ameerpet, Hyderabad")
```

In the preceding code snippet, data for all the three members of MyMulti annotation is specified.

Using the Annotations

You can use annotations for various types in a Java program, such as class, interface, field, or method. The Built-in annotation @Target tag is used to specify at which type the annotation is used. This annotation takes one or more constants to specify the type at which the annotation is used. These constants are specified as the element types of the java.lang.annotation package.

Table 33.1 lists the element types that can be used with annotations:

Table 33.1: Element Types to be used with Annotations

Element Types	Where the Annotations can be applied
ElementType.PACKAGE	Package
ElementType.TYPE	Class, interface or enumeration
ElementType.FIELD	Fields
ElementType.METHOD	Methods
ElementType.CONSTRUCTOR	Constructors
ElementType.LOCAL_VARIABLE	Local variables

For example, if you want to create the MyMulti annotation for a class, you can write the code for it as:

```
@Target(ElementType.TYPE)
@interface MyMulti
{
    int value1();
    String value2();
    String value3();
}
```

Suppose, you want to create the MyMulti annotation for a class, field, or a method, then you should write these constants inside {} after @Target, as shown in the following code snippet:

```
@Target( {ElementType.TYPE, ElementType.FIELD, ElementType.METHOD} )
@interface MyMulti
{
    int value1();
    String value2();
    String value3();
}
```

When using annotations, you can also specify at what level an annotation should be available. There are 3 levels: source code level, class level, and runtime level. These levels are indicated by the constants specified in the RetentionPolicy enumeration of the java.lang.annotation package.

Table 33.2 lists the retention types that can be used at different levels of a program:

Table 33.2: Retention Types to be used at Different Levels of a Program

Retention Type	Where the Annotation is Retained
RetentionPolicy.SOURCE	Refers to the source code. This retention type is discarded during compilation.
RetentionPolicy.CLASS	Refers to the .class file. This retention type is accessible to Java compiler, but not available to JVM.
RetentionPolicy.RUNTIME	Refers to the runtime file, which is a .class file. This retention type is accessible to Java compiler at compilation time and JVM at runtime.

The following code snippet shows how to create the MyMulti annotation that is available to the JVM at runtime and can also be used at the class level:

```
@Retention(RetentionPolicy.RUNTIME)
@Target(ElementType.TYPE)
@interface MyMulti
{
    int value1();
    String value2();
    String value3();
}
```

Now, let's write a program to see how to create a single-value annotation on our own and how to retrieve it at runtime by the JVM. We know that the single-value annotation stores only one value. This annotation can be applied to a class, an interface, field, or method.

Program 8: Write a program to create a single-value annotation that stores only one value and retrieve it during runtime by the JVM.

```java
import java.lang.annotation.*;
import java.lang.reflect.*;
/*create a single value annotation which can be applied to a method.
 Make it available to the JVM at runtime */
@Retention(RetentionPolicy.RUNTIME)
@Target(ElementType.METHOD)
@interface MySingle
{
    int value();    //this variable name must be value only
}
/*We will apply MySingle annotation to a method in the following class */
class Myclass
{
    /*annotate a method using MySingle annotation. Store value 100 into
  MySingle annotation */
    @MySingle(value=100)
    public void myMethod()
    {
        System.out.println("Hello");
    }
}
//access the MySingle annotation value using another program
public class Demo
{
    public static void main(String args[]) throws Exception
    {
        //create Myclass object
        Myclass obj = new Myclass();

        //getClass() method returns Class object and
        //getMethod() returns the Method class object
        Method m =  obj.getClass().getMethod("myMethod");

        //now retrieve the single annotation associated with the method
        MySingle anno = m.getAnnotation(MySingle.class);

        //retrieve and display the value in the annotation
        System.out.println("Value= "+anno.value());
    }
}
```

The output of Program 8 is as follows:

```
C:\> javac Demo.java
C:\> java Demo
Value= 100
```

Now, let's write another program to see how to create a multi-value annotation and how to retrieve it at runtime by the JVM. We know that the multi-value annotation can store several values. This annotation can be applied to a class, an interface, field, or method.

Program 9: Write a program to create a multi-value annotation that stores only 3 values: one integer number and two strings. The annotation can also be retrieved during runtime by JVM.

```java
import java.lang.annotation.*;
/*create a multi value annotation and apply it to a class. Make it available
to the JVM at runtime */
@Retention(RetentionPolicy.RUNTIME)
@Target(ElementType.TYPE)
@interface MyMulti
{
```

```
      int value1();
      String value2();
      String value3();
}
/*annotate a class using MyMulti annotation. Store values into
MyMulti annotation */
  @MyMulti(value1=10, value2="Srinu", value3="Ameerpet, Hyderabad")
class Myclass
{
   void myMethod()
   {
       System.out.println("Hello");
   }
}
/*access the MyMulti annotation values using another program */
class Demo1
{
    public static void main(String args[]) throws Exception
    {
        //store the class name in an object c
        Class obj = Class.forName("Myclass");
        /*now retrieve all annotations associated with the class into
     Annotation[] array */
        Annotation[] annot = obj.getAnnotations();

        //use a for each loop to repeat with each annotation
        for(Annotation x : annot){
         /*if the specific annotation (x) belongs to MyMulti then store it into
          MyMulti object */
         if(x instanceof MyMulti)
        {
          MyMulti a = (MyMulti)x;
          //retrieve the values associated with that MyMulti object
          System.out.println("Value1= "+a.value1());
          System.out.println("Value2= "+a.value2());
          System.out.println("Value3= "+a.value3());
        }
        }
     }
  }
}
```

The output of Program 9 is as follows:

```
    C:\> javac Demo1.java
    C:\> java Demo1
    Value1= 10
    Value2= Srinu
    Value3= Ameerpet, Hyderabad
```

Conclusion

Enumerations in Java represent certain fixed values or constants that assist to process a sequence of tasks easily. As compared to the enumerations of other languages, Java enumerations are also used as class types.

Annotations provide additional information about the programming elements, such as classes, interfaces, fields, or methods. Development and deployment tools, such as Java compiler or javadoc compiler can read this additional information and process it. These tools are used to check whether the programming elements are according to the information obtained. This helps in minimizing the chances of compile-time and runtime errors, which means that the program can be utilized on different platforms or applications in a more effective manner.

NEW FEATURES OF JAVA 7

J avaSoft people wanted to add some new features as part of Java 7.0 version. To know which features to be added, they reviewed the feed back from software developers who suggested a list of features to be added into Java. This project of reviewing and adding new features is called 'Project Coin'.

We will discuss these latest features along with programming examples in this chapter. Please note that you should have jdk1.7 or higher version to compile and run the programs shown in this chapter.

Using strings in switch statement

Up to Java 7.0, there is no way of using strings in switch statement. We can use only byte, short, int or char types in the switch statement. But starting from Java 7.0 onwards, it is permitted to use string inside a switch statement to decide the course of action inside the switch block.

```
/* this code is invalid up to Java 7.0
but valid from Java 7.0 onwards. */
String day = "Tue";
switch(day)
{
    case "Mon": System.out.println("Monday"); break;
    case "Tue": System.out.println("Tuesday"); break;
    …
}
```

Program 1: Write a Java program to understand how to use string in a switch statement.

```
//switch supporting String type
class Switch7
{
    public static void main(String args[])
    {
        String day = "Tue";

        switch(day)
        {
            case "Sun" : System.out.println("Sunday"); break;
            case "Mon" : System.out.println("Monday"); break;
```

```
                case "Tue" : System.out.println("Tuesday"); break;
                case "Wed" : System.out.println("Wednesday"); break;
                case "Thu" : System.out.println("Thursday"); break;
                case "Fri" : System.out.println("Friday"); break;
                case "Sat" : System.out.println("Saturday"); break;
                default    : System.out.println("Wrong day");
            }
        }
    }
```

Output:

```
C:\> javac Switch7.java
C:\> java Switch7
Tuesday
```

Binary literals with prefix 0B

A literal represents a value which is stored into a variable in a program. For example,

```
int num = 56;
```

Here, 56 is called an integer type literal since it is stored into int type variable num. Suppose, we want to store octal values, we can write that literal with a prefix '0' and hexadecimal values with a prefix '0x', as shown in the following code:

```
int num = 012;  //this is octal value
int num = 0x12; //this is hexadecimal value
```

From Java 7.0 onwards, it is possible to create binary literals which can be represented with a prefix 0b or 0B, as:

```
int num = 0b1101;  //this is binary value

short num = (short)0b1101;  //binary value is converted into short
```

By default literal values are considered as integers. This is the reason, in the previous example, the binary value is converted into short type using cast operator before it is stored into short type varaible.

Program 2: Write a program to display a binary number in other number systems.

```
//display a binary number in other number systems
class Binary7
{
    public static void main(String args[])
    {
        int num = 0b1010; //binary

        System.out.printf("\nIn Decimal = %d", num);
        System.out.printf("\nIn Octal = %o", num);
        System.out.printf("\nIn Hexadecimal = %x", num);
        System.out.printf("\nIn Binary = %s", Integer.toBinaryString(num));
    }
}
```

Output:

```
C:\> javac Binary7.java
C:\> java Binary7

In Decimal = 10
In Octal = 12
In Hexadecimal = a
In Binary = 1010
```

Introduction of Underscore in Numeric Literals

To improve readability, underscore (_) is introduced in the numeric literals. It is possible to use several underscores in a binary number, integers, float or double numbers.

```
byte b = (byte)0b01011_10;
int x = 0B1010_1100_0110;
int num = 10_00_000;
float y = 13.14_15_92f;
```

Catching Multiple Exceptions

Before Java 7.0, we should write multiple catch blocks to catch several exceptions. For example, the following program catches two exceptions using two catch blocks.

Program 3: Write a program to show how to catch two different exceptions using two catch blocks.

```
//Catching multiple exceptions using multiple catch blocks - before Java 7.0
class Catch7
{
    public static void main(String args[])
    {
        try{

            /* Since array size is negative, it rises
            NegativeArraySizeException. */
            int arr[] = new int[-5];

            /* Since str does not contain integer, it rises
            NumberFormatException. */
            String str = "Hello";
            int num = Integer.parseInt(str);
        }
        //NegativeArraySizeException rises if array size is -ve
        catch(NegativeArraySizeException obj)
        {
            System.out.println(obj);
        }
        //NumberFormatException rises if array size is +ve
        catch(NumberFormatException obj)
        {
            System.out.println(obj);
        }

    }
}
```

Output:

```
C:\> javac Catch7.java
C:\> java Catch7
java.lang.NegativeArraySizeException
```

In the previous program, the array size is taken as -5, so the output shows NegativeArraySizeException. If the array size is changed to 5, then NegativeArraySizeException will not occur, but the next exception, i.e. NumberFormatException will occur. To handle these two exceptions, we have written two separate catch blocks.

In Java 7.0, we can catch more than one exception in the same catch block using or symbol (|). For example, instead of writing two catch blocks, we can write a single catch block in the above program, as:

```
catch(NegativeArraySizeException | NumberFormatException  obj)
{
        System.out.println(obj);
}
```

Type Inference for Generic Instance Creation

While creating objects (instances) for a generic class, we should mention the datatype of element to be stored into the class. For example, we can create an ArrayList object to store string type elements, as:

```
ArrayList<String> obj = new ArrayList<String>();
```

In the preceding statement, we are creating ArrayList class object. Since this object will be used to store strings, we should mention the String datatype in the sharp brackets as <String> after the class name. Observe that the datatype <String> is mentioned two times in the statement. This is the way the object is created to generic class. But, in Java 7.0, it is reduced to one time, as:

```
ArrayList<String> obj = new ArrayList<>();
```

The <String> is not mentioned at right hand side expression. Only, <> are mentioned at right side. Since it is mentioned once after the class name at left side, Java compiler can understand (infer) that the ArrayList is used for storing strings.

Program 4: Write a program to understand the differences of creating generic class objects before and after Java 7.0

```
//Reducing type inference for generic class object creation
import java.util.*;
class Generic7
{
    public static void main(String args[])
    {
        //before Java 7.0
        ArrayList<String> lst1 = new ArrayList<String>();
        lst1.add("Hai");
        lst1.add("Hello");

        System.out.println("List1= "+ lst1);

        //from Java 7.0 onwards
        ArrayList<String> lst2 = new ArrayList<>();
        lst2.add("Apple");
```

```
        lst2.add("Grapes");

        System.out.println("List2= "+ lst2);
    }
}
```

Output:

```
C:\> javac Generic7.java
C:\> java Generic7
List1= [Hai, Hello]
List2= [Apple, Grapes]
```

Try-with-resource Statement

We use try, catch and finally blocks to handle exceptions. In the versions earlier to Java 7.0, we should close all the resources using a finally block. For example, if a file is opened for storing data, it should be closed in a finally block, else the file data will be corrupted.

Program 5: The following program demonstrates the code to copy the content of in.txt file into another file out.txt, character by character.

```
//Copying a file content to another file - Before Java 7.0
import java.io.*;
class TryDemo
{
   public static void main(String args[])
   {
        int ch;
        FileInputStream fin = null;
        FileOutputStream fout = null;

        try{
          //in.txt file is the input file
          fin = new FileInputStream("in.txt");
          //out.txt file is the output file
          fout = new FileOutputStream("out.txt");

          //copy character by character
          while((ch = fin.read()) != -1)
            fout.write(ch);
        }
        catch(IOException ie)
        {
            //read() and write() rise IOException, so catch it
            ie.printStackTrace();
        }
        finally{
            try{
            fin.close();
            fout.close();
            }
            catch(IOException ie)
            {
                //close() method rises IOException, so catch it
                ie.printStackTrace();
            }
        }
    }
}
```

From Java 7.0 onwards, the try block is so designed that we can open the resources within the try block, as:

```
try( FileInputStream fin = new FileInputStream("in.txt");
        FileOutputStream fout = new FileOutputStream("out.txt"))
{
        statements;
}
```

Observe the try block in the form of try( ){ }. Now, we need not write the finally block to close these files, as the resources which are opened in the try block will be automatically closed. Java 7.0 ensures this.

Program 6: Rewrite the previous program in the version Java 7.0.

```
//Copying a file content to another file - Java 7.0
import java.io.*;
class Try7
{
    public static void main(String args[])
    {
        int ch;

        try( FileInputStream fin = new FileInputStream("in.txt");
            FileOutputStream fout = new FileOutputStream("out.txt")){

          while((ch = fin.read()) != -1)
            fout.write(ch);
        }
        catch(IOException ie)
        {
            ie.printStackTrace();
        }
    }
}
```

Conclusion

In this Appendix, we have covered the new language features which were introduced into Java 7.0. The examples make these features understandable easily. These features make Java programming more convenient for a programmer.

QUESTION INDEX

I

PROGRAM INDEX

II